Rabad of Posquières

Rabad of Posquières

A Twelfth-Century Talmudist

Revised Edition

ISADORE TWERSKY

THE JEWISH PUBLICATION SOCIETY OF AMERICA
Philadelphia, Pennsylvania
5740/1980

Library of Congress catalog card number 79-88696
ISBN 0-8276-0123-9
Manufactured in the United States of America

First published in 1962 by Harvard University Press

TO

My Father and Mother

The dedication is now a memorial. My father (d. 26 Sivan, 5732) and my mother (d. 1 Tevet, 5737) of blessed memory, the beloved and revered Rebbe and Rebbitzen of Talne, left a legacy of goodness and kindness, piety, probity and wisdom. ת. נ. צ. ב. ה.

PREFACE

Jewish intellectual history to the dawn of the nineteenth century is comparable to a fast-moving stream coursing through a complex network of tributaries and offshoots. The waters of the rivulets which poured into or eddied alongside the mainstream of Judaism were colored by a dazzling variety of cultural disciplines: philosophy and mysticism, rationalism and pietism, exegesis and commentary, poetry and belles-lettres, linguistics and grammar. They did not always flow evenly or simultaneously. At various times, the philosophic tributary swelled in certain areas while the mystical waters raged elsewhere; or the philosophic tributary changed its course, only to have its former bed occupied by mystical currents. Poetry and belles-lettres were like wadies: their waters might reach inundating proportions and they might dry up completely. The courses of these streams deserve to be—and, to a great extent, have been—charted, their ebbs and peaks registered, their force and calm measured; each of them left an imprint on the evolving Jewish intellect and spirit. The mainstream, however, was the *halakah* (Jewish Law)—its ever-expanding corpus of literature and its cumulative body of practice.

Yet, this position of undisputed centrality in history notwithstanding, it has not received a commensurate position in historiography. The following book on an outstanding medieval Talmudist, Rabad of Posquières, who lavishly enriched the major genres of halakic literature and perceptibly accelerated the development of a critico-conceptual method of halakic study, is offered as a modest contribution to this field of historical research. Rabad was a thoroughgoing Talmudist; his prolific literary output was characterized by a striking unity of form and content. In this study, I have attempted to treat Rabad primarily as an halakic scholar, relating other attributes and interests to this central characteristic. I hope that it will be found worthy of acceptance.

In presenting highly specialized halakic materials in English, I have tried to keep the book from becoming cumbersome and overtechnical without indulging in loose generalizations. Therefore, though I have only sometimes provided detailed illustrations and analyses of halakic problems, I have always aimed at giving full documentation of every general statement so that the interested reader will be able to check all the references. (Attention should be called to the list of abbreviations and the note on references printed at the end of the book.)

My appraisal of Rabad is clearly appreciative, perhaps excessively sympathetic. I trust that this is the result not of overexposure to medieval hyperbole but of an objective examination of the sources themselves. Rabad emerges from such an examination as an individual whose influence surpasses local bounds and temporal barriers.

I was fortunate to have enjoyed good will and encouragement from many quarters. Teachers, colleagues, and friends have been very helpful and I am grateful to all of them. I am especially indebted to Professor Harry A. Wolfson whose scholarship has excited me and friendship has warmed me over a period of many years. He supervised the progress of my work with his customary kindness and perceptive criticism and offered many suggestions concerning style, structure, and substance. He has done more for me than I can acknowledge. I am profoundly grateful to Professor Saul Lieberman for the sustained cordial interest which he has shown in my work and for letting me benefit so liberally from his vast knowledge. His careful reading of my manuscript led to some important additions and necessary modifications and enriched me greatly. It is a unique privilege to discuss problems of Jewish learning with him. My father-in-law, Rabbi Dr. Joseph Soloveitchik, combining keen professorial interest with great paternal devotion, placed his immense Talmudic erudition and penetrating observations at my disposal and I drew freely from them. His impact on my work—and life—is incalculable.

The friendship and intellectual companionship of Professor Frank M. Cross, chairman of the department of Near Eastern Languages and Literatures at Harvard, have been very dear to me. If not for his friendly prodding and genuine interest, the manuscript might still be awaiting that elusive final touch.

My wife helped immeasurably and contributed in many ways to the completion of this work. I appreciate the devoted assistance of Miss Carol Cross, who did a remarkable job in preparing the typescript. Her patience with a difficult manuscript was inexhaustible. The editorial staff of the Harvard University Press has been most cooperative; special thanks are due to Miss Ann Louise Coffin for her kind help in many technical and editorial matters. Publication of this book was made possible by the Lucius N. Littauer Foundation at Harvard, aided by a subvention from the Alexander Kohut Memorial Foundation. Parts of Chapter VI appeared in the *Proceedings* of the American Academy of Jewish Research, 1957 and are used here with permission of the editors.

I would not attempt to depict my feelings of love and gratitude toward my parents. The dedication is merely a token expression.

ISADORE TWERSKY

Harvard University
July 1961

CONTENTS

Rabad of Posquières

INTRODUCTION TO REVISED EDITION

A retrospective-reflective approach to my book on Rabad evokes many strong impressions and varying assessments which vie for primacy in determining the contents of these present remarks. It seemed to me that if I were permitted to take a cue from the general medieval literary tradition which often accentuated the role of direct address or personal "appeal to the reader," the following reminiscence would be the most appropriate point of departure for a succinct statement which ex hypotheso should be not only retrospective but also partially prospective. My study of Rabad developed out of a short-lived burst of youthful scholarly exuberance: I decided (more than twenty years ago) with great enthusiasm and a heightened sense of expectation to write an intellectual history of the Jews in southern France during the Middle Ages. I was convinced then—and still am—that such an investigation would be significant, suggestive, and repercussive, that it could be paradigmatic for the study and understanding of the development and atrophy of Jewish culture in specific foreign environments. Many years later, in a piece that turned out to be a combined review article and programmatic essay, I articulated the rationale which prompted my initial decision and which still sustains an abiding hope, God willing, to implement it.

Jewish history in southern France, often seen merely as an epicycle of the Spanish or northern French spheres of influence, invites scholarly attention both because of its intrinsic, substantive value as well as its self-transcending methodological relevance. On one hand, the chronological span of the period is rather clearly delimited and therefore sustains one's hopes for a meaningful overview of or synoptic approach to the entire period and, on the other, the cultural productivity is sufficiently impressive and comprehensive so as to present a colorful microcosm of medieval Jewish intellectual history. Independent literary and intellectual activity makes its appearance toward the middle of the eleventh century—with the works of R. Moses ha-Darshan of Narbonne—and continues uninterruptedly, with vigor and intensity, until the beginning of the fourteenth century—with the works of R. Menaḥem ha-Me'iri of Perpignan. In the intervening centuries, there is a remarkable efflorescence of Jewish culture in Provence: rabbinics, philosophy, mysticism, ethics, exegesis, grammar and lexicography, poetry, and belles lettres are cultivated. Certain clearly defined indigenous trends reach maturation while there is an appropriation of new intellectual motifs and tendencies. There is hardly a facet of the total Jewish religious and intellectual experience that is not reflected—and all in a compact period of time. There are legists who enriched all the major genres of halakic literature and accelerated the development of a new, critico-comparative method of Talmudic study which was to become a mainstay of halakic thinking and writing. There are students of philosophy and philosophers and devotees of philosophy, as well as patrons and protagonists, who are responsible for preserving and transmitting the accumulated philosophic and scientific learning of Arabic-speaking Jewry as well as for interpreting it, disseminating it, and extending its frontiers. There are kabbalists who—at first haltingly and reservedly, then boldly and confidently—move mystical speculation and experience to the center of the stage: some of the oldest known kabbalistic texts were redacted or first circulated here and the earliest devotees of the new doctrines organized themselves in Provence at this time. Poets energetically ply their humanistic trade and enthusiastically vindicate it—producing rationales of the poetic art, articulating the consciousness of the artist, and defining his place in society. Exegetes make durable contributions to the field of Scriptural commentary and enlarge its scope by combining midrashic interpretation with philosophical allegory and philological insight. Polemicists and apologists marshall erudition and ingenuity in their defense of Judaism against persistent theological arraignments and social-economic attacks. ("Aspects of the Social and Cultural History of Provençal Jewry," *Journal of World History,* XI (1968), 11–12.)

In any event, at the time, I turned to Rabad, my old "friend" from years of Talmud study, assuming that this pivotal personality would provide one sure, sturdy fulcrum: I thought that a quick review of the scholarly literature would round out my spotty acquaintance with his life and works and produce a micro-view of the state of research. This procedure, repeated a number of times with regard to other key figures, would thus set the stage for preparation of the desired synthesis while also revealing the few glaring lacunae and prime desiderata. The chasm between my jaunty innocent expectation and the austere literary reality was immense; my enthusiasm was displaced by a sobriety which manifested itself in an overpowering awareness of the need for abundant monographic study and also the systematic publication of vast amounts of manuscript material in many areas. Rabad himself, a creative, colorful, controversial writer of astounding force and originality as well as versatility whose impact on Talmud study and the development of rabbinic literature was formative as well as formidable, had yet to be analyzed comprehensively; moreover, all his works had not even been published, and available printed works were often defective or incomplete. The fragmented scholarly reality was simultaneously a disappointment and a catalyst. I ended up substituting a full-length study of Rabad—perhaps the first such monograph on one of the leading *rishonim,* as pointed out to me by a colleague—for the projected polychromatic cultural history.

Since then, we have seen a full-scale explosion of Provençal studies, particularly the publication of scores of rabbinic works—commentaries on the Talmud, *Hilkot ha-Rif* or *Mishneh Torah,* volumes of responses and mini-codes—or new, refined editions of works which, although in print, had been marred by errors or omissions and certainly lacked any apparatus of references, annotations or variant readings. R. Jonathan ha-Kohen of Lunel, R. Meshullam and his five sons, especially R. Aaron and R. Asher, R. Moses ha-Kohen, R. Abraham b. Nathan ha-Yarḥi, R. David b. Levi, R. Judah Lattes, R. Meshullam b. Moses, R. Meïr ha-Kohen, R. Manoaḥ, R. David b. Samuel ha-Kokabi (d'Estella), and we should probably include also R. Menahem ha-Me'iri, have been resuscitated, escorted into the full light of history, and may now be confronted as real "live" authors. Moreover, many of Rabad's own works have been edited or reissued and his responsa collected. These publications often come in rapid, almost dizzying, succession and have yet to be carefully digested. In sum, *toratam shel ḥakme Provence,* hitherto known from random publications or stray citations in florilegia (*shiṭot*) and the works of later authors, has been opened up, inviting serious study and comparative evaluation: literary tendencies, genres, ideological commitment and methodological orientation, personal likes and dislikes, tradition and innovation (that is, halakic novelties in theory or practice), presence of extra-halakic components, reflection of social realities and historical contingencies, and cognate themes. So many diverse materials embedded in the spacious, sprawling edifice known as rabbinic literature need to be identified and analyzed. All this brings us so much closer to the possibility of producing the synthesis and, more immediately, of a complete, finely honed characterization and assessment of Rabad.

Similar work, from the vantage point of Rabad and Provençal studies, in the "Spanish background," in the contemporary developments among French and German "neighbors" as well as the post-Rabad continuation and consolidation or qualification and variation of concerns and orientations is clearly of inestimable importance for our topic. New responsa collections of R. Isaac Alfasi or R. Joseph ibn Migas, volumes of additional Tosafot or commentaries from the school of Rashi and writings of R. Meir of Rothenburg, editions of the works of Naḥmanides and Rashba, codes and commentaries which relate to the *Mishneh Torah,* inevitably rivet attention upon themselves. They are indispensable for a balanced appreciation of Rabad. Sources concerning aggadah, Bible exegesis, liturgy, Kabbalah, philosophy, and polemics have also been printed. The conceptual matrix in which such central, often elusive phenomena as rationalism, moderate rationalism, antirationalism, and literalism are discussed is thus wider and firmer. The relation of halakah to these other areas may be investigated more fully while divergent schools of exegesis of the Bible and aggadah may be better understood. The complexities involved in the confrontation between Kabbalah and philosophy may be fathomed. To this cornucopia of unpublished sources should be added the scholarly studies that provide new facts, emphasize hitherto-unperceived connections, and indicate new perspectives emerging from shifts in thought and sensibility, augmented information, or refined methods of interpretation.

Students of Rabad must make a special effort to keep up with the ever-growing corpus of Maimonidean literature which, ex hypotheso, deals with Rabad who, as the first major (even though not thoroughly systematic) critic of the *Mishneh Torah,* could never be dissociated from Maimonides and his extraordinary code of law. (A clear statement to this effect was penned by Rabbi S. Zevin in his introduction to A. Hilbitz, *Li-leshonot ha-Rambam,* page 3.) From this point of view practically all rabbinic literature—commentaries, responsa, novellae, minor codes—is a potential contributor to a fuller understanding of Rabad's historical impact and sometimes of his original intent.

As a final note in this regard, we should underscore that all this tremendous progress notwithstanding, the agenda of unfinished, scholarly business with regard to Rabad himself is long and demanding. Systematic, annotated editions of Rabad's own major works (for example, all his hassagot, but especially on the *Mishneh Torah,* or his trail-blazing *Sifra* commentary) are still not available and remain scholarly desiderata. Here, too, incidentally, the literary fate of Rabad is often interwoven with Maimonides; the magnificent S. Frankel edition of Book III (*Zemanim*) of the *Mishneh Torah* includes the hassagot, with variants collected from the seven manuscripts. In addition, collection of the copious citations from his commentaries—for example, on *Berakot, ᶜErubin,* or *Baba Meẓiᶜa*—strewn throughout rabbinic literature would contribute decisively to the restoration and reconstruction of his oeuvre. I have dealt to some extent with Rabad as a commentator of the Talmud, directly, and of the Bible indirectly, but the abundant philological-exegetical material ensconced in his writing needs to be assembled and appraised. Exhaustive study of his works for evidence of change and continuity, the impact of Spanish and French developments (particularly the latter), systematic thematic analysis, comparison of his methods, interpretations, attitudes, and conclusions with those of other towering halakists of the high Middle Ages (the golden age of halakic creativity in western Europe)—these tasks still await completion.

Nevertheless, the terrain is less forbidding as a result of what has been accomplished in the last few decades, the directional signals are clear, and the hope is great. While I feel no need to succumb to any kind of historical revisionism, quite rampant these days, were I to rewrite this book now I would undertake to add some new dimensions to the analysis of Rabad's great oeuvre and to integrate new facts.

A few additional comments concerning the emphatic characterization of Rabad as a halakic scholar, a thoroughgoing Talmudist (see page vii), a "man of halakah," seem to be in order. This emphasis, the axis of the entire study, was not intended to gloss over his involvement and interest in related fields, which were amply discussed, nor was this intended to suggest that he be ensconced in a rigid, unchanging mold fashioned to suit every halakist; I was not dealing with archetypes but with the literary oeuvre and intellectual profile of one great, influential sage. The purpose was to focus sharply on his major interests and preoccupations, achievements and impact, and to guard against "assimilatory" or imperialistic tendencies of modern scholarship which relate major figures to the presumptively more "important" or more "universal" disciplines, whether philosophy, mysticism, exegesis, or even belles lettres—areas which lend themselves more easily to comparison with general tendencies and attainments. There is no doubt whatsoever that my conviction about the centrality of halakah and halakic literature in Jewish history as well as Jewish historiography needs to be firmly and boldly underscored; its centrality in Judaism, which is halakocentric, and hence in any religious phenomenology is obvious and need not be belabored. Until recently, most scholars still operated under the eighteenth-century aversion to Talmud study as a whole, viewing it as a *geistestoetendes Geschaeft* (the phrase of Solomon Maimon) that yields neither spiritual satisfaction nor intellectual benefit. S. Dubnow's treatment of R. Moses Naḥmanides is a notorious example of scholarly imbalance and ideologically motivated historiographical parochialism. The need for sustained, meticulous scholarship in this field is clear and compelling, and its agenda is long and demanding—editions of sources, biographical studies, sociohistorical investigations, jurisprudential-thematic analyses, methodological inquiries, and comprehensive literary histories. Progress is clearly discernible as conventional, but wobbly distinctions and flagrant distortions are gradually eliminated and replaced by careful judgments and reasoned analysis. I intended my study of Rabad to be viewed from this perspective.

In reviewing and reassessing the ramified importance of halakah, certain salient, intertwined themes in the work of Rabad and his contemporaries may be briefly noted. The most significant is probably the role of intellectual freedom, a clear sense of conceptual-ideational progress in which the crucial, invigorating dialectic of authority and innovation unfolds. These halakists, critics all, articulate a sturdy rationale outlining the importance, permissibility—indeed indispensability—of intellectual freedom and criticism. Various epigrams or slogans expressing this concept were to become current. Many rabbinic authors, Rabad included, speak of *meleket shamayim* ("labor for the sake of heaven"), which says that the responsible Talmudist, by definition committed to the weightiness of tradition and precedent, will eschew misplaced dogmatism. He must be simultaneously cautious and creative, conservative and innovative. On the one hand, he will not consider himself free to desist from recording a novel interpretation or original conclusion just because no previous writer mentioned it. Inasmuch as his view *may* be the correct one, he is morally obligated to advance it, for he is engaged not in a private and optional academic enterprise but in *meleket shamayim.* On the other hand, the significance and solemnity of halakic study will so sensitize and humble him that he will cite views of predecessors even if opposed to his own position. Inasmuch as these opposing views *may* be correct, he is morally obligated to deflate his own authoritativeness and keep the realm of the possible and conjectural open. *Meleket shamayim,* in short, is concomitantly a stimulant and a depressant: a spur to originality and inventiveness but also a motive for conservatism and restraint. It embodies in part the idea articulated by Naḥmanides concerning an inevitable measure of "relativism," of the recognition of multiple views in halakic interpretation. (See my "Beginnings of Mishneh Torah Criticism" and "ᶜal Hassagot ha-Rabad.") Hence, Rabad motivates his selective criticism of R. Isaac Alfasi in terms of *meleket shamayim.* Alfasi's greatness notwithstanding—and all concurred concerning the seminal value of the *Halakot*—his work invited critical commentary. There is no inconsistency or insincerity in the fact that Rabad records his deep-seated humility in the face of this Talmudic giant and then produces some serious and substantive criticisms. This situation, which is typical for the halakist, must elicit a finely calibrated response, honest and courageous, resourceful and respectful, combining diffident acceptance with deft augmentation. The complex dialectic of rigidity and resilience, receptivity and sensitivity is thus clearly silhouetted although its complexity and tension are not camouflaged or reduced.

Razah vindicates his sustained criticism of Alfasi by suggesting a mandate for intellectual freedom based on the metaphysical concept of *kabod,* glory of God in man, whose chief trait is reason and unbridled pursuit of truth. His exposition culminates in his quotation of a version of the adage: "love Plato, love Aristotle, but above all love the truth"—cited by Jonah ibn Ganah and found even earlier in Dunash ibn Labrat. It is interesting to note that this definition of *kabod* aroused the wrath of Naḥmanides (see G. Vajda, *Recherches*).

R. Meshullam b. Moses insists in the introduction to his *Sefer Hashlamah* that a measure of egalitarianism and freedom in Torah study is an unquestionable legacy of the Sinaitic Revelation when "great and small were equal." He then buttresses this position with some crucial, very effective quotations from Talmudic literature which help explain and illustrate the persistence of originality—or, more importantly, the tenacious striving for originality.

In the next generation, R. Menahem ha-Me'iri tries to clinch his explanation of why Maimonides' *Mishneh Torah* was inadequate to the needs of halakists, all its novelty and excellence notwithstanding. He claims that the very nature of study demands independent understanding, dynamic review of the process of interpretation and adjudication, and not merely passive knowledge of the conclusions. We may hear echoes of Rabad's rejection of the *Mishneh Torah* (see below, page 131) for "why should I rely upon his choice when it is not acceptable to me and I do not know whether the contending authority is competent to differ or not." There is an innate passion for total comprehension which alone yields gratification and repose or, to change the metaphor, a compulsion to disentangle and identify the strands that compose the neat, harmonious texture. The cognitive process is both compelling and indispensable.

Furthermore, Rabad, Razah, Ramak, and others refine the hassagot as a special, expressive, and repercussive genre of pointed, precise, and persuasive critique directed against monumental works in the field of rabbinic literature. The role and art of criticism, in carefully structured literary terms, should thus be underscored. Brief, delphic strictures or glosses, while illustrating that special "intermixture of self-expression and self-control" (Peter Gay, *Style in History*), provide here an appropriate, pliant vehicle. The hassagot constitute a wide-ranging form of writing based on broad information and a firm self-assured erudition, on a sharp style and polemical skill. They combine criticism and commentary while implicitly formulating methodological rules and generalizations (for example, Razah on the nature of Alfasi's *Halakot*).

Of special interest is the fact that teachers often encouraged their students to undertake clearly defined exercises in criticism, offering their own works as targets or subjects for criticism. Needless to say, no recklessness is intended, no levity or disrespect is fostered; the goal is a commitment to unrelenting examination of the sources and their varying interpretations. While patronage of scholars and translators was established in Spain, we may discern here a different form of intellectual patronage of young scholars, geared to develop their independence and sustain their creative impulses. Masters expose themselves and their work in order to inculcate the notion that one should be temperate and thoughtful in criticism but also resourceful, vigilant, and courageous in interpretation. Of course, as the polemical style of this period indicates, restraint was often overlooked; the hassagot literature, anything but an anemic, stylized genre, abounds in personal invective and vitriolic rebuttal. Incisive analysis and ad hominem gibes are interwoven.

Going a step further, we may call attention to the creative interaction not only between masters and disciples but between colleagues and also between revered predecessors and emerging luminaries (for example, see addendum for page 230); we discern a pattern of ongoing criticism concerning major themes and central problems in the halakah (as distinct from the aforementioned critique of massive, monumental halakic oeuvres). Halakah is an exoteric discipline and its literature is intended to be available and intelligible to all interested or qualified readers. Except for an occasional case of a legal directive that should not be publicly promulgated (*halakah ve'en morin ken*), Talmudists did not "conceal their meaning behind veils of indirection, difficulty and ambiguity" (P. Gay, *Style in History*). Hence, the persistent, open-ended discussion of key themes, axial problems or authoritative formulations—and Maimonides and Rabad are central by all standards—is noteworthy. There is no premeditated ambiguity, and yet there is ongoing deliberation and debate. Talmud study is effervescent. There is a great dialogue spanning the generations. Alfasi, ibn Migas, R. Meshullam, Razah, Rabad, R. Jonathan, R. Meïr ha-Kohen, Naḥmanides, ha-Me'iri, and Rashba are engaged in a common, collective enterprise of commentary and criticism, with later authorities identifying with or dissociating themselves from earlier ones. If, to a great extent, later, post-Maimonidean Hebrew philosophic literature is a sort of dialogue between philosophers—by virtue of quotations, discussions, endorsement, or refutation of classic views—rabbinic literature is even more markedly intrinsically dialogic.

To return to Rabad himself, we must underscore the dominant dynamism and openness of his writing. This is all the more striking for it seems paradoxical: an authoritarian scholar who is susceptible to revisionism, refinement, and reformulation. While in his responsa he exudes a sense of authority-authoritativeness and reveals a hypersensitivity to criticism, emphatically demanding respectful attention and unquestioned acceptance of his views, he was constantly revising his own works. To be sure, the unrelenting criticism of Razah was a major factor—a stimulant as well as an irritant—and, as we now know (see especially I. Ta-Shema), led to substantive reworking of his *Baᶜale ha-Nefesh* or the Commentary on *Kinnim,* but it is clear that the intellectual dynamism discernible in Rabad's writing is not merely a consequence of the familiar literary syndrome: criticism and defense coupled with counter-criticism. Indeed, such dynamism is a salient feature of medieval rabbinic literature as a whole. Maimonides, for example, constantly revised his major works as a result of increasingly critical re-examination of Geonic interpretations or progressive precision in the final formulation of his own views. In the case of Maimonides, the massive intellectual effort connected with the preparation of the *Mishneh Torah,* as well as its defense and dissemination, served as a gadfly for critical self-examination and continuous correction, refinement, or retraction. In some instances, thanks to a few extant holographs or corrected copies of the *Mishneh Torah,* we actually see Maimonides, the author-artist at work, erasing, adding, deleting, rectifying, and rearranging. Rabad also kept rethinking interpretations, reassessing inferences, introducing stylistic and substantive changes which reflect subtly varying nuances or genuinely divergent emphases—partly in response to the penetrating, often persuasive criticism of Razah and partly as a manifestation of the nature of halakic study, which favored intellectual growth and necessitated unflagging alertness and scholarly dynamism.

Note in conclusion that this dynamism and criticism are perceived by later writers as a precedent encouraging authors not to be passive or docile. R. Menahem Tamar (fifteenth-century Spain, author of the still unpublished *Tanḥumot ᶜEl*), for example, derives a double lesson from the fact of Rabad's criticism of Maimonides: the fallibility of all sages, their acknowledged greatness and authoritativeness notwithstanding, and the permissibility of criticism. Hence, the *innate* dynamism of rabbinic literature is bolstered and sustained by the example of the *rishonim* and their intellectual autonomy. Rabad and his contemporaries are prominent in this respect.

ISADORE TWERSKY

Harvard University
November 1979

Rabad of Posquières

A Twelfth-Century Talmudist

I. LIFE

Incidental references in documentary and literary sources indicate that there were individual Jews and Jewish settlements in southern France as early as the third and fourth centuries. There is, however, no historical evidence of Jewish cultural achievement in this region until much later. The only literary remnant of the entire period of Roman, Visigothic, and early Frankish domination—and even this is not established beyond all doubt—is a long liturgical hymn which has been incorporated into the prayerbook and is still recited. Otherwise, although comfortable from the economic point of view and relatively free from the political point of view, from the cultural point of view the Jews were not productive. There is one big lacuna in the intellectual history of the period.

The first great historical figure in the annals of Jewish literary and intellectual history in southern France is R. Moses ha-Darshan of Narbonne, who flourished at the beginning of the eleventh century. From then on, there was an uninterrupted, although not too sturdy, chain of scholars, with emphasis on oral instruction and a very minimal literary output. In the twelfth century, Provence was the scene of a remarkable efflorescence of Jewish learning—in many respects a Jewish counterpart, or even an element perhaps, of the "renaissance of the twelfth century." Infusion of new blood and new intellectual motifs into such thriving communities as Narbonne, Lunel, Béziers, Marseilles, Carcassonne, and Montpellier together with the maturation of certain clearly defined trends in Provençal life coincided to create one of the most colorful chapters of Jewish history. During this period, Provence —*Provincia Narbonensis* or *Provincia Romana*, in the widest territorial limits to which this term is applied—emerged as a pivotal center of contemporary Jewish life, and its achievements left their imprint on the evolution of Jewish culture in general and the development of Jewish law in particular.

Rabbi Abraham ben David (Rabad) of Posquières was one of the most creative Talmudic scholars of that twelfth-century galaxy whose members are designated in later chronicles and rabbinic texts as the "sages of Provence," "elders of Narbonne," or "wise men of Lunel." He is by no means an obscure or unknown figure who has to be "excavated" by antiquarians, for his searching criticism of Maimonides' *Mishneh Torah* earned him widespread attention and established his fame as an authoritative Talmudist. Yet, although his niche in the gallery of Talmudic celebrities is reserved, the nature and significance of his *halakic* work have not been clarified nor have his ramified achievements been fully assessed. His personality, moreover, has often been encrusted with stereotypes. This study attempts to reconstruct his biography as precisely as possible, to chronicle his role in the intellectual history of the Jews in southern France during the twelfth century, and to chart the course of his influence on subsequent generations. Characterization of his works, description of his halakic methodology, and analysis of the literary sources used by him expand the scope of this study by focusing attention on some basic problems of medieval Jewish intellectual history. Discussion of his disciples and followers reads almost like an embryonic biographical dictionary of the cultural and communal leaders of southern French Jewry at the turn of the twelfth century. Rabad's reaction to the introduction of the philosophic literature of Spanish Judaism into Provence and his relation to the emergent medieval Kabbalah introduce the student to two far-reaching developments of Jewish history. The major emphasis, however, must remain on Rabad's contribution to halakic literature and methodology, for, although he was conversant with cognate areas of nonhalakic learning, he was first and foremost a Talmudist.

1. Family and Teachers

As is the case with practically all medieval Jewish historical figures except Maimonides,[1] the sources are completely uncommunicative as

1. Maimonides constitutes a notable exception to the general paucity of information concerning the place and date of birth of most medieval historical figures. For an example of the precise data concerning Maimonides, see B. Dinaburg, *Yisra'el ba-Golah* (Tel-Aviv, 1946), II, 290. The lack of biographical details in the Middle Ages is well known; see S. Munk, *Mélanges de Philosophie Juive et Arabe* (Paris, 1859), 154; H. Malter, *Saadia Gaon* (Philadelphia, 1942), 16 ff.

to the date of Rabad's birth. Inference and supposition hold reign. Zunz,[2] followed by Graetz,[3] Gross,[4] and others, conjectured 1125 as the year of his birth. Auerbach,[5] whose reasoning was accepted by Atlas,[6] was inclined to change this date to 1115 because of a statement quoted by Simeon b. Ẓemaḥ Duran in the name of Rabad. Speaking of himself and his contemporaries, Rabad says in the idiom of Job: "He [Maimonides] is youthful while we are aged."[7] The connotation of the term "aged" (*yeshishim*),[8] as well as the traditional view prevalent in most chronicles about Rabad's advanced age at the time he composed his critique of Maimonides,[9] warranted in Auerbach's opinion the assumption of an age gap of at least twenty years. Reifmann, with scholarly caution, was careful not to commit himself.[10] Recent writers, especially those contributing general articles to encyclopedias, evidently merely as a compromise and with no decisive evidence, tend to respect both major hypotheses by suggesting 1120 as the year of Rabad's birth.[11] Pending the discovery of some new data, it will be impossible to resolve this academic controversy. Definite knowledge of Rabad's birth date would, of course, be helpful in ascertaining the chronology of his writings and also in appraising their worth.[12]

2. L. Zunz, "Abraham b. Isaak und Abraham b. David," *Wissenschaftliche Zeitschrift fur jüdische Theologie*, II (1839), 309.

3. Graetz, IV, 265, n. 4.

4. Gross, 341; *GJ*, 447. See also Salomon Kahn, "Les Juifs de Posquières . . . au moyen-âge," *Memoires de l'Académie de Nîmes*, 7th ser., XXXV (1912), part 3, 6.

5. Abraham b. Isaac of Narbonne, *Ha-Eshkol*, ed. B. H. Auerbach (Halberstadt, 1868), XX, n. 13.

6. Atlas, Hebrew introduction to Rabad, *BK*, 16. See also H. L. Gordon, *The Maggid of Caro* (New York, 1949), 67.

7. Simeon b. Ẓemaḥ Duran, *Sefer ha-Tashbeẓ* (Amsterdam, 1738), 72: בתשובה להראב״ד ז״ל מצאנו שאמר על רבי משה ״הוא נער ואנחנו ישישים״; also quoted by J. Sambary, see note 9.

8. *Yashish* clearly implies a very old, also venerable, person; see *Moʿed Ḳaṭan*, 25b. At the end of his commentary on *Ḳinnim*, Rabad defines "Yashish": ולא נקרא ישיש אלא זקן וחכם. The German Tosafist Mordecai b. Hillel also describes Rabad as "yashish"; Samuel Kohn, *Mardochai ben Hillel: Sein Leben und seine Schriften* (Breslau, 1879), 99. On the same term applied to Rashi's son-in-law, R. Meïr b. Samuel, who lived to a very old age, see E. Urbach, *Baʿale ha-Tosafot* (Jerusalem, 1955), 39.

9. Auerbach, *Ha-Eshkol*, XX. See also Ḳonforte, *Ḳore ha-Dorot* (Pietrekov, 1895), 20: הראב״ד גדול בשנים יותר מהרמב״ם; J. Sambary, *Liḳḳutim Midibre Yosef*, in A. Neubauer, *Medieval Jewish Chronicles and Chronological Notices* (Oxford, 1887–1895), I, 124. In the first, anonymous supplement to the *Sefer ha-Kabbalah* (*ibid.*, 84), it is reported that Rabad הפליג בישיבה ובשנים.

10. J. Reifmann, "Toledot ha-Rabad Ba'al ha-Hassagot," *ha-Maggid*, VI (1862), 382.

11. *Sinai*, XXXVI (1955), 320; *Encyclopedia Hebraica* (Jerusalem, 1949), I, 294; *Encyclopedia of Great Men in Israel* (Jerusalem, 1946), I, 32; B. Bergmann, ed., *Katuv Sham: Hassagot ha-Rabad ʿal Baʿal ha-Ma'or* (Jerusalem, 1957), 22.

12. See Chapter II for a discussion of the date of the *Baʿale ha-Nefesh*.

His birthplace was equally uncertain in early biographical notices about him. While some assumed it to be Posquières,[13] the city in which he later flourished and whose name he lifted from comparative obscurity to historical fame at least in Jewish history,[14] others suggested Narbonne,[15] the cultural metropolis of Jewish life in Provence, or even Lunel.[16] This uncertainty was finally eliminated by the publication in 1909 of a very important manuscript of Menaḥem ha-Me'iri entitled *Magen Abot*. Ha-Me'iri, prominent Provençal scholar in the thirteenth century, mentions Narbonne as the city of Rabad's birth.[17]

Knowledge of his family background is defective. It would be of considerable interest to know some details about the antecedents of such an original and keen scholar. Incidental literary allusions indicate strains of greatness and learning in his family. That his grandfather was possessed of substantial halakic knowledge is attested by the fact that he is quoted by Rabad, though with disapproval, as having dissented from a ruling of R. Judah b. Barzilai of Barcelona on some aspect of

13. *Oẓar Yisrael* (New York, 1907), I, 192; S. M. Ḥones, *Toledot ha-Posḳim* (Warsaw, 1922), 116; M. Schlesinger, ed., *Orḥot Ḥayyim* (Berlin, 1902), II, 7; B. Drachman, ed., *Dibre ha-Ribot* (New York, 1907), XI.

14. The fact that Rabad's name is invariably linked with Posquières need not have misled anyone into assuming that this was his birthplace, for it is common practice in medieval writing to associate scholars with the site of their school or major literary activity rather than with their birthplace. For example, Yeḥiel b. Joseph of Paris was born at Meaux; Meïr of Rothenburg was born at Worms; Samson of Sens was probably not born in Sens. See H. Gross, "Etude sur Simeon b. Abraham de Sens," *REJ*, VI (1883), 175, n. 1. Also, Meïr b. Isaac of Trinquetaille was born in Carcassonne; see *GJ*, 246. Abraham b. Nathan ha-Yarḥi was born at Avignon, not Lunel; see M. Higger, "Yarḥi's Commentary on Kallah Rabbati," *JQR*, XXIV (1933), 331. Meshullam b. Nathan of Melun was born in Narbonne; see the discussion by Z. H. Jaffe in Guedemann, *Ha-Torah weha-Ḥayyim* (Warsaw, 1896), I, 234. Dunash b. Labrat, usually identified as "from Fez," was probably born in Bagdad; see *Dunash b. Labrat: Shirim*, ed. N. Aloni (Jerusalem, 1947), 5.

15. See §1, note 13; also Bergmann, *Katuv Sham*, 22.

16. E. Carmoly, *La France Israelite* (Francfort S/M, 1858), 120. Reifmann suggested Beaucaire; see *Ha-Maggid*, VI, 382.

17. Menaḥem ha-Me'iri, *Magen Abot*, ed. I. Last (London, 1909), 103: והלך לו הרב משם לנרבונא עיר מולדתו. Actually this is already noted, though less explicitly, in the supplement to the *Sefer ha-Kabbalah* of Abraham ibn Daud: ומגדולי התלמידים היו הרב אברהם בר׳ דוד ... ורוב מכל אלו חכמים נולדים בנרבונה ולמדו מרבניה אבל מפני החירום יצאו משם ובכל מקום שהיו הולכים היו מרביצים תורה עד שהאירו עיני כל הגולה כשמש בחצי השמים. See Neubauer, *Medieval Jewish Chronicles*, I, 84. In view of this, D. Kaufmann's emendation of the sixteenth-century chronicle of Azriel Trabotto seems gratuitous. There is no need to substitute Posquières for Narbonne in the passage describing Rabad (הראב״ד זהו הרב רבינו אברהם בר׳ דוד מנרבונה היה), since the author is most likely indicating Rabad's birthplace. The very sequence of the brief description given there suggests that Trabotto is referring to Rabad's birthplace and not a later center of activity. See D. Kaufmann, "Liste de Rabbins Dressee par Azriel Trabotto," *REJ*, IV (1882), 212, 223, n. 86.

ritual law concerning the dietary laws (*terefa*).[18] The fact that he disagreed with the eminent and authoritative Judah b. Barzilai—in the words of ha-Me'iri "the great and illustrious scholar in all Catalonia"[19] —and the fact also that the dissent dealt with a decision on practical ritualistic questions which are reserved exclusively for experts who are proficient in the Tractate *Ḥullin* indicate that he was a self-reliant Talmudic authority. This independence of mind, moreover, seems to have been transmitted to his grandson.

Next to nothing is known about Rabad's father. There is a significant reference to him, when he was already dead, in a letter of Maimonides, where the latter appends to his name the encomiastic phrase "may the memory of the righteous be for a blessing."[20] If this phrase, which is used also by Benjamin of Tudela and Judah ibn Tibbon with reference to Rabad's father,[21] is genuine and not a later gloss introduced by a pious copyist, it is very meaningful. First of all, this term, as far as I could observe, was not too widespread in medieval writings; it is only among moderns that it has been bandied about loosely. Secondly, Maimonides was sparing in his use of panegyrics, even of departed persons.[22] Consequently, such an attribution of piety and sanctity—which usually implies also a measure of scholarship—cannot be dismissed lightly. The fact that Rabad never cites his father or refers to him in his writings need not be construed negatively to imply, *ex silentio*, that he was not worth quoting or that he transmitted nothing quotable, for, in similar instances, the absence of quotation by a son of the teachings of a father does not necessarily mean that the latter was not

18. *TD*, 12. Although Rabad carefully reproduces his grandfather's reasoning, he concurs theoretically with the more lenient view of Judah b. Barzilai. Nevertheless, with regard to actual practice, he counsels the adoption of his grandfather's more rigid opinion, which is an efficacious preventive against error. In his hassagot on Maimonides, he also quotes his grandfather's view. See *MT*, *Sheḥiṭah*, XI, 13.

19. *Magen Abot*, 26. On Judah b. Barzilai, see S. Albeck, "Meḥoḳeḳe Judah," *Festschrift zur Israel Lewy*, ed. M. Brann and J. Elbogen (Breslau, 1911), 104–131; B. Z. Benedict, 101, and the literature quoted there: S. Assaf, *Misifrut ha-Geonim* (Jerusalem, 1933), 2.

20. *Ḳobeẓ Teshubot ha-Rambam we-Iggerotaw*, ed. A. L. Lichtenberg (Leipzig, 1859), 27a: רבי אברהם בן דוד זצ״ל הרב הגדול שבפישקירא י״א. Compare discussion of this passage in *ha-Maggid*, XXII (1868), 390, 397; *REJ*, IV (1882), 224. J. Heilprin, *Seder ha-Dorot* (Warsaw, 1876), 154 disputes this identification.

21. *Itinerary*, 4; *Ḥobot ha-Lebabot*, ed. A. Zifroni (Jerusalem, 1928), 55 (introduction to ch. 2).

22. A. Marx, "The Correspondence between the Rabbis of Southern France and Maimonides about Astrology," *HUCA*, III (1926), 327, 329. Reprinted in Marx, *Studies in Jewish History and Booklore* (New York, 1944).

a scholar.[23] Even Maimon, known independently as a scholar, judge, and author, is quoted only once by his son, Moses Maimonides, in the *Mishneh Torah* and once in the introduction to the *Mishnah Commentary*.[24]

Another conjecture that one may make about Rabad's father is that he was wealthy and left his son a substantial material heritage; this would account for at least one of the sources of Rabad's great wealth which contemporaries mention.[25] This assumption may perhaps be corroborated by the phrase "aristocrats of the land" used by Rabad's son, Isaac of Posquières, to describe his ancestors.[26]

With regard to Rabad's wife, we know that she was the daughter of the famous Rabi (R. Abraham b. Isaac).[27] There is a eulogy of her in a poem written by her father in honor of his son-in-law.[28] In this poem, Rabi compares his daughter to the matriarch Sarah. She bore Rabad two sons, David and Isaac, both of whom became leading exponents of the emergent Kabbalah.[29] Otherwise she remained the silent partner in his life. Without directly attributing this either to his wife or mother —if to either of them—in all his writings Rabad displays great sensitiveness and tenderness toward women.[30]

23. An analogous situation is the question of the father of R. Isaac b. Sheshet Perfet (Ribash). Since the son never refers to his father, E. Atlas ("Ha-Ribash u-bene doro," *ha-Kerem*, I [1887], 10) assumed that he was not a great Talmudist. Hershman, the most recent biographer of Isaac b. Sheshet, shows on the basis of other contemporary references that he must have been a prominent personality; Abraham M. Hershman, *Rabbi Isaac ben Sheshet Perfet and his Times* (New York, 1943), 9. For similar cases, see Benedict, "R. Moses b. Joseph of Narbonne," *Tarbiẓ*, XIX (1948), 19: Malter, *Saadia Gaon*, 28; S. K. Mirsky, "R. Jonathan of Lunel," *Sura*, II (Jerusalem, 1956), 248.

24. *MT*, *Sheḥiṭah*, XI, 10; see A. Freimann, "Teshubot R. Maimon Abi ha-Rambam," *Tarbiẓ*, VI (1935), 164–176, and literature cited there.

25. *Itinerary*, 5 והוא עשיר גדול. Also, the German Tosafist Mordecai b. Hillel refers to him as "ha-Nagid," which connotes great wealth. See Samuel Kohn, *Mardochai ben Hillel*, 99.

26. G. Scholem, "Teʿudah Ḥadashah le-Toledot Reshit ha-Kabbalah," *Sefer Bialik* (Tel-Aviv, 1934), 143: כי אבותי היו אצילי הארץ ומרביצי תורה ברבים. See §1, note 73.

27. This relation is explicit in the descriptions of ha-Me'iri and de Lattes; see Auerbach, *Ha-Eshkol*, XIII.

28. The poem is printed in all standard editions of the Talmud at the end of Tractate *Ḳinnim*. Z. Frankel (*Darke ha-Mishnah* [Warsaw, 1923], 356, n. 3), Gross (342), and Atlas Rabad, *BK*, (17) quote the poem. Reifmann, "Rabad Baʿal ha-Hassagot," *Bet Talmud*, IV (1885), 381, emends the text and shows that Sarah was not the name of Rabad's wife, that she was compared to Sarah.

29. See Chapter V, §3.

30. See, for example, *MT*, *Ishut*, XXI,10; *Gerushin*, X, 23; *Nedarim*, XIII, 7. *BH*, 4 and the explanation of the midrashic notion of *diu-parẓufin*, quoted by Scholem, *Reshit ha-Kabbalah*, 79 (see the allusion in Meïr ibn Sahula, *Be'ur le-Perush ha-Ramban* [Warsaw, 1875], 46).

There is a relative abundance of knowledge concerning Rabad's father-in-law Rabi (1110–1179) who held the office of Ab-Bet-Din of Narbonne, the presiding judge of the celebrated rabbinical court—a most prestigious and dignified position.[31] Though to subsequent generations Rabi is not as well-known as his son-in-law and some other contemporaries, and his importance is in the long run transitory and restricted, in his lifetime his influence was widespread. Rabi's essential literary activity, like that of so many of the other rabbis of his time, consisted of commentaries, responsa, and codification. Of his commentaries, which were well-known and are occasionally quoted by Razah, Rabad, Naḥmanides, ha-Me'iri, and others,[32] the original texts had been unknown and considered lost until S. Assaf salvaged one fragment on *Baba Batra* from a Munich manuscript.[33] His responsa had no better fate. Some were printed in the following collections: *Temim Deᶜim*, *Sefer ha-Terumot*, and *Orḥot Ḥayyim*; some were quoted by Isaac b. Abba Mari (in the *Sefer ha-ᶜIṭṭur*), Meshullam b. Moses (in the *Sefer ha-Hashlamah*), Naḥmanides and Aaron ha-Kohen of Lunel; but the bulk were consigned to dusty archives.[34] Again, it was the indefatigable Assaf who edited a sizable collection of Rabi's responsa.[35] His codificatory work called *ha-Eshkol* was the subject of a heated scholarly controversy during the latter half of the nineteenth and the beginning of the twentieth century when it was printed for the first time (in two different versions).[36] This marks the first serious attempt at a comprehensive legal code made by French Jews.[37] Modeled on Alfasi's *Halakot*, or, as Albeck maintains, on Judah b. Barzilai's *Sefer ha-ᶜIttim*,[38] *ha-Eshkol* was an important advance for Provençal Talmudic scholarship, but no original innovation. Its immediate

31. On Abraham b. Isaac of Narbonne, see Gross, "R. Abraham b. Isaak, ab-bet-din aus Narbonne," *MGWJ*, XVII (1868), 241–255, 281–294; *JE*, I, 111; J. H. Michael, *Or ha-Ḥayyim* (Frankfurt a.M., 1891), 133 ff.; also the editions of the *ha-Eshkol* by Auerbach (Halberstadt, 1868) and Albeck (Jerusalem, 1935) and their introductions. Concerning the famous court of Narbonne, see Benedict, 107 (appendix A), and the responsum published by Assaf, *Sinai*, XI (1947), 158.

32. Albeck, *Ha-Eshkol*, 15.

33. S. Assaf, "Ḳeṭa miperusho shel Rabi lemasseket Baba Batra," *Oẓar ha-Ḥayyim*, XII (1936), 52–64.

34. Albeck, *Ha-Eshkol*, 18–21; Auerbach, *Ha-Eshkol*, XVI.

35. *Sifran*, 1–50; also Assaf, "Teshubot min . . . baᶜal ha-Eshkol," *Sinai*, XI (1947), 157–165.

36. By Auerbach and Albeck; see §1, note 31.

37. L. Ginzberg, "Abraham b. David," *JE*, I, 112.

38. Albeck, *Ha-Eshkol*, 51 ff.; see also Judah b. Barzilai, *Sefer ha-ᶜIttim*, ed. J. Shore (Berlin, 1903); J. L. Zlotnik, "Shene Ḳeṭᶜaim le-hashlamat Sefer ha-ᶜIttim," *Sinai*, VIII (1945), 116–138.

influence on the codification of law, especially by French authors, is discernible in such collections as *Sefer Miẓwot Gadol*, *Orḥot Ḥayyim*, *Kol Bo*, *Toledot Adam*, and *Shibbale ha-Leḳeṭ*, but it was ultimately eclipsed by other codificatory works such as the *Mishneh Torah* of Maimonides, the *Torat ha-Bayit* of Rashbah (R. Solomon b. Adret) and the *Ṭurim* of Jacob b. Asher.[39] In all these fields and genres of literary activity, Rabi is of historical value only, having been overshadowed in every enterprise in which he engaged; but in his day he was respected and acknowledged as a weighty authority. He was one of the pioneers of Provençal-Jewish learning.

Very cordial relations seem to have existed between father-in-law and son-in-law. Rabi, an essentially modest man always seeking reconciliation and harmonization of divergent views and trends,[40] took great pride in his keen, caustic son-in-law. He probably realized the latter's superior talents. Mindful no doubt of the Talmudic dictum that one is never jealous of his son or disciple, Rabi did not hesitate to compare himself to Jethro, Moses' father-in-law, and Rabad, to Moses.[41] The poem which he composed in honor of his son-in-law is one long panegyric, sincere and moving. It is somewhat puzzling that Rabi never mentions Rabad by name, neither in *ha-Eshkol* nor in his responsa. Auerbach submits that it was Rabi's literary policy to veil all references to living authorities. Rabad must have been concealed behind this camouflage of anonymity.[42]

Rabi, in all probability, deserves to be considered as one of Rabad's teachers, although the latter nowhere explicitly speaks of him as such. The standard reference is "my master, my father-in-law,"[43] in which phrase the term "master" is a conventional encomium without necessarily implying that he was his teacher. Rabad cites him frequently and is often eager either to vindicate his father-in-law's opinions which have been impugned or to authenticate his own views by identifying them with those of his father-in-law. In one of his responsa touching upon the question of the order and arrangement of the fringes upon the prayer shawl, he concludes his complicated exposition with the follow-

39. Gross, "R. Abraham b. Isaak," XVII, 250.
40. *Ibid.*; Auerbach, *Ha-Eshkol*, XV.
41. See §1, note 27.
42. Auerbach, *Ha-Eshkol*, XIV; see also Gross, "R. Abraham b. Isaak," XVII, 342, who refers to two such places; my remarks in *Kiryath Sefer*, XXII (1957), 443.
43. הרב אדוני חמי ז"ל. See Albeck, *Ha-Eshkol*, 14, for a partial list of references. Rabad's hassagot on Razah contain many more examples: *KS*, I, 20, 40, 41, 44, 50; II, 2, 18, and *passim*.

ing words: "I illustrated this method [of knotting the fringes] before my father-in-law, and he was very happy with me."[44] Similarly, in his critical annotations on Razah, he braces a novel interpretation of his by saying: "I showed it to my master, my father-in-law, and he rejoiced over it."[45] He resents it very strongly when on one occasion Razah sought "to separate" him from his father-in-law by contriving a discrepancy between their theories.[46] The significance of this appeal to his father-in-law's authority and prestige is noteworthy, for, apart from his two eminent teachers and a few *Geonim*, Rabad rarely turns to earlier or contemporary scholars for support or corroboration.[47] It would appear that some of Rabad's novel theories were alluded to or indirectly inspired by Rabi.[48]

Rabad's attitude toward Rabi, however, is not one of absolute deference. He is no servile student or unquestioning son-in-law. He freely disassociates himself from his father-in-law's teachings. Thus, when in the course of their epistolary duel Razah censures Rabad for dissenting from an interpretation of Rabi, Rabad retorts that he is not bound to concur with his father-in-law on every point.[49] Similarly, when Razah leans on Rabi for support, Rabad expresses amazement at his father-in-law's theory.[50] On one occasion Rabad rejects a conclusion of Alfasi, for "even though my master the Rabbi endeavored to defend his teachings, they are indefensible."[51] Sometimes he concurs with his father-in-law's inference, but rejects his interpretative procedure.[52] There are instances, moreover, when he completely demolishes his father-in-law's opinions and, in the heat of halakic disputation, does not even hesitate to use derisive epithets against him.[53]

Two responsa in *Temim Deᶜim* illuminate Rabad's occasional critical attitude to his father-in-law. In response to a query concerning water poured into *tamad* (an inferior wine) by a non-Jew, Rabad first cites his

44. *TD*, 36.
45. *KS*, I, 39.
46. *Dibre ha-Ribot* (Matters of Controversy. A rabbinical disputation between Zerahiah ha-Levi and Abraham ben David), ed. B. Drachman (New York, 1907), 15.
47. Benedict, *Kiryath Sefer*, XXIV (1947), 9, suggests that Rabad's agreement with his father-in-law is often a consequence of his customary defense of Alfasi, for in almost all instances where he agrees with his father-in-law, the latter agrees with Alfasi.
48. See §5, notes 108, 109, and others.
49. *Dibre ha-Ribot*, 15.
50. *KS*, I, 29: תמה אני על אדוני הרב ז״ל.
51. *Ibid.*, I, 50: ואע״פ שטרח אדוני הרב ז״ל לקיים דבריו, לא נתקיימו.
52. *Ibid.*, I, 58: הדקדוק שדקדק אדוני הרב חמי ז״ל יפה דקדק, אבל הפרוש שפירש לא טוב בעיני.
53. Benedict, *Kiryath Sefer*, XXIV, 9.

father-in-law's opinion and presents his textual proof for this view. He immediately qualifies this exposition by commenting: "I agreed with him on this score, but I also added to and modified his views." Rabad then states his objection on principle, for "my soul rebounds from such excesses." The explicit corollary of Rabi's explanation was that a non-Jew may even handle wine and remove grape shells from the wine cask. If such proximity would be permitted, Rabad protests, one of the main social barriers between Jew and non-Jew would be destroyed. He, in turn, presents his own textual analysis and infers that whereas the tamad in such a case is ritually fit, the latter actions are definitely prohibited. This consultation was issued during the lifetime of his father-in-law, and yet Rabad did not feel restrained in the expression of his views or constrained to concur.[54]

A second responsum dealing with a case in civil jurisprudence records a debate between father-in-law and son-in-law. Rabi mustered a series of formalistic arguments which were logically and legalistically unassailable. Rabad was, however, annoyed by his father-in-law's excessive emphasis on abstract legal theory which completely ignored the immediate, concrete conditions of the case. He argued incessantly that the court should not be guided by abstract legalistic formulas, but should seek an equitable verdict by actually analyzing the motives of the defendant in this case. Rabad emphasizes his persistence in the matter and his unremitting arguments which finally convinced his father-in-law.[55]

In addition to Rabi (d. 1179), who was his teacher perhaps only in an informal way, Rambi (R. Moses b. Joseph) of Narbonne (d. 1165) and R. Meshullam b. Jacob of Lunel (d. 1170) were Rabad's direct teachers. They were two of the most respected and influential scholars of the time, residing in cities which were the cultural focuses of Jewish life in Provence and Languedoc. Endowed with creative talents as Rabad was, and independent as his writings were to be, he was very fortunate to have enjoyed the instruction of the greatest Provençal scholars.

54. *TD*, 83: והשויתי עמו לטעם זה והריני מוסיף וגורע מדבריו. His father-in-law was probably still living when this was issued, for Rabad does not append to his name the usual term of reference for the dead. For a similar view on this question by ha-Me'iri, who was undoubtedly conversant with Rabad's view, see *Bet ha-Beḥirah* on ᶜ*Abodah Zarah* (Jerusalem, 1944), 132, and J. Katz, "Sublanut Datit be-Shiṭato shel R. Menaḥem ha-Meiri," *Zion*, XVIII (1953), 27. Concerning Rabad's position on social separations, see also the view quoted by ha-Me'iri, *Magen Abot*, 37, and the interpretation of Katz, "Sublanut Datit," 28.

55. *TD*, 56: הרבה נשאתי ונתתי עם הרב חמי ז"ל על זה ונתעצמתי עמו ... ולא יכלי ליה עד דאמרי ליה שאין לנו לילך אחר טענותיה אלא להוציא דין אמת לאמתו.

The first of these, Rambi, is mentioned reverently by Rabad in his responsa and commentaries, and is described by him as "my principal teacher."[56] Besides Rabad, many other great scholars are to be counted among his distinguished disciples, notably Razah and Jonathan ha-Kohen. Even mature scholars of repute like Rabi who were not his direct students regarded him as an authoritative master of Talmudic knowledge and constantly turned to him for scholarly advice and learned support. Rambi's literary activity was fecund and keen; his status in Provençal life as teacher and judge was lofty. Of particular significance is the fact that his scholarly career marks the early stages in the evolution of a distinct Provençal tradition and native halakic literature. In short, he fostered a Provençal "school." An illustration of this local color in Rambi's writings is his consistently critical attitude toward the Spanish school, represented by Alfasi and Judah b. Barzilai, which was then infiltrating and coming to dominate southern France. Somewhat like Menaḥem ha-Me'iri one hundred and fifty years later,[57] Rambi aimed to preserve Provençal traditions in the face of foreign cultural imports. He was truly one of the pillars of Talmudic learning in Provence during the first half of the twelfth century. The fact that he was one of the early post-Geonic medieval scholars to be called "Gaon" is eloquent testimony to his status.[58]

The attitude of Rabad toward this towering teacher is one of devotion tempered with independence. He quotes his master often and relies upon his teachings.[59] When he did not grasp some theory expounded by Rambi, he suspended judgment on the matter rather than reject it. At the end of one selection printed in *Temim Deᶜim*, Rabad refers to an opinion which "he heard in the name of Rambi"[60] concerning the topic he has just treated at length. "For many years I did not fully comprehend his opinion."[61] Now, it seems, his own exposition and analysis corroborate Rambi's hitherto unfathomed view. This meeting of minds obviously makes Rabad very happy. Finally, he consulted freely with

56. "My teacher par excellence" רבי המובהק. See *Ḳiddushin*, 33a. See the excellent study by Benedict, "R. Moses b. Joseph of Narbonne," *Tarbiẓ*, XIX (1948), 19–34.

57. See ha-Me'iri's introduction to his *Magen Abot*, 1–11, esp. 5.

58. Benedict, *Kiryath Sefer*, XXIV, 20, n. 15; see S. Poznanski, *Babylonische Geonim im Nachgaonäischen zeitalter* (Berlin, 1914), 105. It is interesting to note the general reference of the thirteenth-century kabbalist R. Isaac b. Jacob ha-Kohen to גאונים קדומים רבני פרובינציא. See Scholem, *Reshit ha-Kabbalah* (Jerusalem, 1948), 18.

59. *TD*, 106; see also Benedict, *Kiryath Sefer*, XXIV, 22.

60. The fact that he heard this opinion "in the name of Rambi" indicates that he was au courant with his master's teachings even after he left his classroom.

61. *TD*, 111.

Rambi and sought enlightenment from him on any moot problems that he encountered.[62]

There are instances, however, where Rabad exerts his independence and dissents from his preceptor's opinions. Thus, he observes concerning a statement of Razah against Alfasi: "The reason that he [Razah] wrote stems from Rambi and is very weak in my eyes."[63] On another occasion when he is forced to reject an opinion of Rambi he comments that "the honor of the old man [Rambi] will be unimpaired" but he cannot accept this view.[64] However, even in such instances of dissent, his critique is moderate. When taking exception to certain views of Rambi, Rabad still cites and explains these views at great length. As is the case with his father-in-law, this is at once an assertion of sovereignty and expression of respect. Moreover, even when Rabad unqualifiedly rejects the view of Razah who is usually following in Rambi's footsteps, Rabad is respectful toward Rambi. He often attempts to disassociate Razah's view from the original thesis of their joint teacher. "I testify," he asserts, "that R. Moses b. Joseph of blessed memory never adjudged the problem in such a manner."[65]

The uniqueness of the critical overtones in Rabad's attitude is best illustrated by comparison with the attitude of another famous student of Rambi—Razah. In the case of this classmate of Rabad, Rambi commanded his unswerving allegiance. Razah's *Sefer ha-Ma'or* is infused with Rambi's spirit and is guided by his principles. In general Rambi had the good fortune to be universally respected and followed. His teachings often became precedents and his customs were consequential for the establishment of the law.[66]

Rabad's second teacher was Meshullam b. Jacob of Lunel, whom he mentions in his glosses and responsa and whom he describes as "our Rabbi, the light of Israel."[67] When speaking of his own views in relation to those of Meshullam, he says modestly: "this is the opinion of his pupil."[68] Meshullam, whom Rabi,[69] Benjamin of Tudela,[70] Judah ibn

62. Benedict, *Kiryath Sefer*, XXIV, 22, n. 35, and *passim*.
63. *KS*, I, 47.
64. *Ibid.*, II, 36. See *Bekorot*, 30b.
65. *Sefer ha-Terumot*, XLIX, 4, 6. This is quoted by Benedict, *Kiryath Sefer*, XXIV, 22.
66. *Ibid.*; *Sefer ha-Ma'or* on Alfasi, *Giṭṭin*, 6b.
67. *Sifran*, 195; see *Berakot*, 28b.
68. *Sifran*, 198.
69. *Orḥot Ḥayyim*, I, 102a: כתב הראב״י ז״ל: פי׳ לנו הנדיב ר׳ משולם בר׳ יעקב. Rabi also refers to him as his teacher, *Sifran*, 49.
70. *Itinerary*, 3: ··· ושם רבינו משולם הרב הגדול ז״ל וחמשה בניו חכמים גדולים ועשירים.

Tibbon,[71] and Berechiah ha-Naḳdan,[72] all contemporaries, have described as a many-sided savant and munificent Maecenas of Jewish culture, encouraged and helped the methodical transmission of the philosophic and scientific learning of Spanish Jewry to French Jewry.[73] His home and school were dynamos of religious and secular learning. He is, in the glowing metaphors of Judah ibn Tibbon, "the pure candelabra, lamp of the commandment and the Torah, the great rabbi, a saintly pious person . . . The oil of his understanding is pure and beaten [for the light], to cause the lamp of wisdom to burn continually. He craved for books of wisdom and according to his ability assembled, disseminated and had them translated." Under his aegis a decisive change in the character of Provençal Jewish learning took place: a Torah-centered community completely devoid of secular learning[74] turned, with remarkable zest and gusto, to the cultivation of philosophy and other extra-Talmudic disciplines.[75] Provençal counterpart of Samuel

71. In his introduction to the Hebrew translation of *Ḥobot ha-Lebabot*, ed. A. Zifroni, 2: המנורה הטהורה, נר מצוה ותורה, הרב הגדול החסיד הקדוש רבנא משולם נר״י . . . אשר שמן תבונתו זך כתית להעלות נר החכמה תמיד . . . ויכסף לספרי החכמות . . . וכפי יכלתו קבץ ורבץ והעתיק בין מחכמת התורה וחכמת הל׳ וחכמת האמונה . . .

72. Berechiah ha-Naḳdan, *Ethical Treatises*, ed. with English trans. Hermann Gollancz (London, 1902), Hebrew text, 1: . . . אדוני הנדיב ר׳ משלם נר עולם אשר לבש צדק כמדו·

73. Later scholars attributed great significance to this; see the letter of Jacob b. Makir to Rashbah, *Minḥat Ḳena'ot* (Pressburg, 1838), 85: זקנינו הרב הגדול ר׳ משולם ובניו וחתניו היו אצילי הארץ ועמודי עולם, והיה החכם אדוני זקני מתגדל עמהם והעתיקו הרבה מספרי החכמה על פיהם . . . ואחר אשר הם התירוה לבא בקהל, מי יאסר אותה לעינהם·

74. This is attested by such scholarly observers as Abraham bar Ḥiyya, *Ḥibbur ha-Meshiḥah weha-Tishboret*, ed. J. Guttmann (Berlin, 1913), 2; Abraham ibn Daud, *Sefer ha-Kabbalah*, ed. Neubauer, *Chronicles*, I, 78; Judah ibn Tibbon, introduction to *Ḥobot ha-Lebabot*, 2; also *Will* of Judah ibn Tibbon, ed. I. Abrahams, *Hebrew Ethical Wills* (Philadelphia, 1948), 57. All focus attention on the exclusively rabbinic nature of Jewish learning in the "lands of Edom." "There were among them scholars proficient in the knowledge of Torah and Talmud, but they did not occupy themselves with other sciences because their Torah study was their [sole] profession and because books about other sciences were not available in their regions" (Judah ibn Tibbon).

75. Abraham bar Ḥiyya who condemns the indifference and ignorance of French scholars with regard to very practical aspects of geometry and algebra, in the same breath mitigatingly notes that there were absolutely no Hebrew books available on these subjects and that his Provençal hosts repeatedly urged him to provide them with Hebrew texts, either translated or original. See his revealing introductions to the *Ẓurat ha 'Areẓ* (Offenbach, 1720), and *Sefer ha-ᶜIbbur* (London, 1851); also the introduction to his encyclopedia *Yesode ha-Emunah u-Migdal ha-Tebunah*, published by M. Steinschneider, "Die Encycklopädie des Abraham bar Chijja," *Gesammelte Schriften* (Berlin, 1925), 390. See the annotated Spanish translation by José M. Millas-Vallicrosa, *HUCA*, XXIII (1950–1951), 645–669. The first two were composed at the request and for the sake of the Provençal sages; see Zunz (*Zur Geschichte und Literatur* [Berlin, 1845], 483), Graetz (IV, 128), and Renan (*Les Rabbins Français*, Paris [1877], 523) who maintain that Abraham bar Ḥiyya was in Provence. Gross (*GJ*, 369) doubts it. See J. Guttmann, introduction, *Ḥibbur ha-Meshiḥah*, IX, nn. 2–3.

ha-Nagid, he was an independent author under whose tutelage many other scholars began to develop their potentialities. His five sons and one son-in-law, each one of them achieving prominence in a different field, symbolize the diversity and virility of Provençal Jewish culture.[76]

Teacher-student relations between Meshullam and Rabad must have been excellent. On the part of the teacher, Meshullam was selfless. With unbounded interest, he stimulated his promising young disciple to literary creativity. He was probably impressed with Rabad's vast accumulation of knowledge and sound critical insights—for Rabad came to Lunel as a maturing scholar. Meshullam therefore urged Rabad to cultivate his powers of self-expression and to sharpen his critical faculties. He even suggested one of his own books as the target of Rabad's criticism. Under Meshullam's tutelage Rabad composed his pioneer work *Issur Ma-Shehu*, which is, in substance, a critique of a similar work by his teacher.[77] On the part of the student, Rabad was appreciative, always cognizant of the fact that Meshullam sponsored his literary debut. With considerable pride and joy, he repeatedly refers back to Meshullam and especially to this early work.[78] Rabad maintained close contact with Meshullam's family in Lunel and had a steady correspondence with many of them.[79] He seems never to have forgotten his debt to Meshullam.

In recapitulating the essential characteristics of each of the three teachers—Rabi, Rambi, and Meshullam—one can single out those aspects which presumably exerted a formative influence on Rabad. First of all, there is the question of the relation of Provençal and Spanish traditions. Rambi was very conscious of his Provençal heritage and imposed upon himself the task of defending and preserving all oral

---

The same discrepancy—or stimulating tension—between their restricted knowledge and their intense desire for supplementary learning is indicated by many others: Samuel ibn Tibbon, introduction to Hebrew translation of *Moreh Nebukim*: אבל כמו שהביאה תשוקת חכמי הארץ הזאת ונבוניה אותם ... לשלוח אחרי הספר הנזכר אל מצרים בשמעם את שמעו ... והשתדלו בזה השתדלות גדולה ... ועוד כי הוסיפו כוסף על תאותם בעמדם על קצת מעניני הספר ... . Judah al-Ḥarizi, introductions to *Musre ha-Pilosofim*, ed. A. Loewenthal (Frankfurt a.M., 1896), 1; and to *Moreh Nebukim*, ed. L. Schlosberg (London, 1851), 2; Jonathan ha-Kohen, letter to Maimonides *Teshubot ha-Rambam*, ed. A. Freimann (Jerusalem, 1934), LVI; Judah ibn Tibbon, introduction to *Ḥobot ha-Lebabot*, 2, and introduction to *Sefer ha-Riḳma*, ed. M. Wilensky (Berlin, 1929), 5: אנשים החלו לדרשה וטעמו טעם דרשה, וכאשר ראו כי אורו עיניהם, ונפקחו אזניהם, נמשכו אחריה׳ ונכספו לעמוד על ספריה ...

76. *Itinerary*, 3; see *GJ*, 279–280 and J. Lubozky, introduction to *Sefer ha-Hashlamah* (Paris, 1885), 4–12.

77. See Chapter II, §1.

78. *TD*, 9, 14, 245, and others.

79. *TD*, 7, 8, 9; see also Chapter V, §2.

traditions, tendencies, and customs of Provence over and against the Spanish innovations of Alfasi introduced into southern France by Judah b. Barzilai. In order to control and, if necessary, discountenance their Talmudic interpretations and halakic conclusions, he limited his scope and focused his sights primarily on those orders of the Talmud which occupied the Spanish scholars (the trilogy of *Moᶜed, Nashim, Neziḳin*)—even though Provençal scholars were accustomed also to study less practical orders such as *Ḳodashim.*[80] Rabi, on the contrary, was a disciple of Judah b. Barzilai and an ardent follower of the Spanish school.[81] It will be necessary in the course of an analysis of Rabad's halakic writings to determine his attitude toward these antithetical tendencies. His innate independence naturally would modify both extremes. We shall see how he reconciled these divergent theses by creating a dialectical synthesis. His devotion to Alfasi will appear to be very great—but restrained, discriminating, and selective. He will essay to defend, amplify, and vindicate Alfasi's views whenever feasible—and even in some apparently hopeless, far-fetched situations—but he will also, with conviction and honesty, modify, question, and reject other views. Custom and practice—the emergent tradition of the Provençal "school"—will condition many of his views and will tend to turn the scale against Alfasi. "Our custom," "in our region," "I never saw such a practice" will be key phrases in halakic discussion.[82]

One feature which was common to both Rabi and Rambi was their preoccupation with codification. Rabi composed a special work designed as a comprehensive code, while Rambi laid great stress on the codificatory nature of his commentaries. Prior to every discussion or analysis,

80. Benedict, *Kiryath Sefer*, XXIV, 33; also Benedict, 99 (especially n. 130) who mentions that the first communication between Spain and Provence is a request by ibn Migas, written by Judah ha-Levi, for a commentary on *Ḳodashim*; see *Diwan* of Judah ha-Levi, ed. H. Brody (Berlin, 1894), I, 217–218. See also *Megillah*, 28b; *Baba Meẓiᶜa*, 114b; and *Tosafot, ad. loc.* Maimonides wrote commentaries only on these three orders, plus tractate *Ḥullin*; see introduction to *Mishnah Commentary*. Jacob Aksai, translator of the commentary on *Nashim* says: פירש ג׳ סדרי גמרא כדין כל מפרש. Alfasi limited his *Halakot* to practically the same subject matter. This apparently represents the traditional scope of Talmudic studies in Spain. It is only in his all-inclusive *Mishneh Torah* that Maimonides breaks with the Spanish tradition. See also *Teshubot ha-Rosh* (n.d.), XXXI, 9, and ha-Me'iri, *Bet ha-Beḥirah* on Abot, 66. This is also the emphasis of ha-Me'iri, *Bet ha-Beḥirah* on *Nedarim, Nazir, Sotah* (Halberstadt, 1860), 5b: והוסיף אומץ לכתוב בחבוריו כל עניני התלמוד, הן בענינים הצריכים לנו בזה הזמן, הן בשאר הענינים. For Geonic study of *Neziḳin* only, see S. Schechter, *Saadyana* (Cambridge, 1903), 64, n. 3.

81. *Sifran*, 2; see also Benedict, 109, appendix 3.

82. *MT*, *Tefillah*, XIII, 6; *Berakot*, XI, 16; *Milah*, III, 1; ᶜ*Erubin*, I, 16; *Sukkah*, VI, 12; *Ishut*, III, 23; *TD*, 7; and others.

he formulated the practical halakic conclusion. In common with his masters, Rabad's interest in codification was consideration and his literary contributions were significant. Moreover, their literary approach was identical. Unlike those codifiers who separated code from commentary, limiting their codes only to the actual, operative law, Rabi and Rambi unified the two aspects, presenting the final, normative conclusion together with its textual basis. This method was used and greatly refined by Rabad.[83]

Meshullam's influence on Rabad's career in Talmudic scholarship has already been noted. It seems safe to assume that the enlightened atmosphere of his circle was not entirely dissipated with regard to the young Talmudist and that Rabad was favorably disposed toward extra-Talmudic learning. One gets the impression that the general scope of his own learning was wide and that he was reasonably well-versed in most extra-Talmudic writings. When necessary or apposite, he introduced scraps of this learning modestly and allusively. Disciplined halakist that he was, he refrained from ostentatious references and avoided all digressions. His moderate use of philosophic material is strikingly accurate.[84] The few anonymous references to "philologists" (*ba^cale ha-lashon*) or grammarians are equally exact and reveal a tone of authority and confidence. He cites the philologists for corroboration or takes issue with their principles.[85] Many exegetical comments, strewn generously through his writings, show his linguistic deftness.[86] He is able to discuss the poetry of Kalir and Saadia, while Judah ibn Tibbon relied on his literary taste in translating from Arabic to Hebrew.[87] He appears, in short—and he is not isolated in this respect—as a resourceful halakist who, although fully preoccupied with his own

83. See Chapter II.
84. See Chapter VI; also *BH*, 80.
85. E.g., *MT*, *Ishut*, I, 4 (see Jonah ibn Ganah, *Sefer ha-Shorashim*, 498); *BH*, 80; Commentary on ᶜ*Abodah Zarah*, 45a (concerning אני אובין ואדון): ואין בעלי הלשון מודים לי . . . אך כמדומה לי שאני יכול להעמידה ומפני אריכות הלשון לא אכתוב הנה . . . See S. Lieberman, *Tosefet Rishonim* (Jerusalem, 1937), I, 100; J. N. Epstein *Mabo le-Nusaḥ ha-Mishnah* (Jerusalem, 1948), I, 89.
86. Gross, 164, already had observed: "Er besass allenfalls auch exegetische Kenntnisse, die er sich in Verkehre mit der Jüngern von Joseph b. Isaac Kimchi und wahrscheinlich mit den Letztern selbst angeeignet hatte, aber schriftstellerisch trat er in der Bibelexegese nicht auf." See E. Urbach's conjecture in *Ḳiryath Sefer*, XXXIV (1959), 108. I have collected much material illustrating the wide range of Rabad's interests and creative attainments in exegesis. See, for example, Commentary on ᶜ*Eduyot*, V, 2; *BH*, 3; Rabad, *BK*, 33; *MT*, *Sheḳalim*, II, 10; *Kil'ayim*, X, 15; *Kelim*, X, 19.
87. *Shibbale ha-Leḳeṭ ha-Shalem*, ed. S. Buber, 18; KS, III, 38; *Ḥobot ha-Lebabot*, 55 (introduction to ch. 2). See also his poem (epilogue to the *Ḳinnim Commentary*) published by Marx, *REJ*, LXI (1911), 133-135.

expertise, keeps abreast of developments in related fields and is able, when the occasion demands, to use or pass judgment upon them.

Yet another contemporary scholar, Joseph ibn Plat,[88] figures prominently in Rabad's writings. Rabad was in close contact with ibn Plat and discussed with him a number of controversial issues. He reports that he was aided by ibn Plat in solving a complicated question concerning some aspect of dietary law, and he records the reason which ibn Plat adduced in favor of their conclusion—one that he himself had not considered.[89] Ibn Plat, who was a traveling scholar, of Spanish origin perhaps, spent some time in Narbonne and Lunel, where he instructed many other Provençal Talmudists, notably Rabi, Razah, and Asher b. Meshullam. The latter availed themselves of this opportunity and consulted with him orally or in writing. Rabi, for instance, wrote to him: "I have come to draw water out of your wells of salvation; blessed is the Creator who privileged you to teach statutes and ordinances in Israel."[90]

As can be anticipated by now, Rabad was not a passive consultant of ibn Plat. The latter's fame notwithstanding, Rabad remained true to his standards of independence. He wrote a series of refutations against ibn Plat's opinion concerning problems of ritual slaughtering.[91] He critically annotated a famous, oft-quoted responsum which ibn Plat sent to Rabi on the question of which ritualistic performances should be preceded by the pronouncement of a benediction.[92] It seems further that Rabad composed a polemical tract (*ḥibbur ha-maḥloḳet*) against ibn Plat concerning the course of action in case of conflicting claims of *ḥazaḳah* (literally, possession, that is, claim of ownership based on undisturbed possession during a legally fixed period).[93] This critique in itself would not militate against Zunz's assumption that ibn Plat was Rabad's teacher, for the same situation existed with regard to Meshullam. In

88. On Joseph ibn Plat, see Albeck, *ha-Eshkol*, 11; *GJ*, 284; A. Epstein, *Glossen zu Gross' Gallia Judaica* (Berlin, 1897), 12; Epstein, "Joseph ibn Plat und der Pardes," *MGWJ*, XLIV (1900), 289–296; Marx, 206; Assaf, 3; S. Abramson, *Kiryath Sefer*, XXVI (1950), 92, n. 143; Benedict, *Kiryath Sefer*, XXVIII (1952), 213, n. 41. It is possible that ibn Plat was a Spaniard, as his name suggests, and that he emigrated to Provence together with many other Spanish scholars. He shows acquaintance with the religious customs of Spain and mentions Lucena specifically; see *Sifran*, 3, 200.

89. *TD*, 7; see also *Shibbale ha-Leḳet*, II, 47: כך הורה (הראב״ד) הלכה למעשה ונעזר··· מן הר״ר יוסף אבן פלאט ז״ל·

90. *Sifran*, 200: אני אברהם בר׳ יצחק זלה״ה באתי לשאוב מים ממעיני הישועה שלך· ברוך היוצר שזכה אותך ללמד חוק ומשפט בישראל·

91. *TD*, 23.

92. This responsum was critically edited by Assaf, *Sifran*, 200–206. It is found in David b. Joseph's *Sefer Abudarham* (Warsaw, 1878), 15–17, together with Rabad's annotations.

93. *KS*, II, 14.

fact, the tone of both critiques is very similar. Yet, Zunz bases his view on certain literary evidence—a number of references to ibn Plat in Rabad's writings—which is far from definite or conclusive.[94] It would seem rather that Joseph ibn Plat was only an erudite senior colleague of Rabad and does not merit a place alongside Rambi and Meshullam as one of his teachers.

As is the case with so many other biographical and chronological details, it is difficult to draw a clear line of demarcation between the formative, preparatory period of Rabad's career and the period of his teaching and writing. One cannot even establish the chronology of his student years with any exactitude. Though his birthplace, Narbonne, was a comparatively populous city and intellectual center, well-qualified to offer all the instruction he craved—"a place . . . whence the study of the law spreads over all countries"—it is understandable why Rabad should desire sooner or later to spend some time in Lunel, which was the emergent hub of southern France. The cultural center of gravity was gradually shifting from Narbonne to Lunel.[95] Meshullam's fame as Talmudic authority and patron of culture, around whom there had nucleated a galaxy of scholars, was widespread, and Rabad must have been attracted toward this circle. Having already been a student of Rambi at his famous school in Narbonne, Rabad must have made great strides in his learning before leaving for Lunel. He came to Lunel as a proficient student, far advanced in his Talmudic studies. There Rabad was welcomed and encouraged by Meshullam, who considered him ready to produce his first written piece. The brief yet meaningful sketch by David of Estella, in which the description of Rabad as an independent scholar is connected with Lunel,[96] may also be interpreted to mean that Rabad's earliest fame as scholar is associated with Lunel. Furthermore, he flaunted his independence of mind by adhering steadfastly to a bold decision in ritual law which was apparently opposed by all the Lunel scholars at that time.[97] Other references singling out Rabad as a

94. Zunz, "Abraham b. Isaak und Abraham b. David," *Wissenschaftliche Zeitschrift*, II, 308. None of the references that Zunz collected—from *TD*, *Sefer Adam we-Ḥawah*, *Sefer he-Terumot*—mention Joseph ibn Plat as a teacher of Rabad. In them, Rabad merely cites the views of ibn Plat. Zunz's view is repeated by Reifmann, *ha-Maggid*, VI, 382 and Drachman, *Dibre ha-Ribot*, XI.

95. *Itinerary*, 3-4; see Benedict, 96.

96. David of Estella, *Kiryat Sefer*, in Neubauer, *Medieval Jewish Chronicles*, II, 231: ובימים ההם הופיע בגבול לוניל אור בהיר הוא הרב הגדול רבינו אברהם בן דוד מפושייקיירש.

97. *Orḥot Ḥayyim*, II, 407. This was a very bold judgment. I find no other Talmudic authority who dared permit such a case. See *Ḥullin* 46b and commentaries *ad. loc.*; also *Bet Joseph on Ṭur Yoreh Deᶜah*, 39.

special, noteworthy personality within the celebrated group of Lunel scholars also apply most likely to this period.[98] To complete the picture one may conjecture that he then returned to Narbonne, studied under Rabi, and became his son-in-law. A mature scholar, Rabad was ready to begin disseminating his knowledge throughout Provence.

2. *Provence in the Twelfth Century*

The twelfth-century Jewish community in Provence to which Rabad turned—and on which he was destined to leave an indelible imprint—was a dynamic, animated place, pulsating with intellectual activity and characterized by a high degree of originality. Traditional, highly ramified Talmudic studies, stimulated by contact with the sustained rabbinic scholarship of Spain and northern France, flourished.[1] Midrash, in particular, both compilation and independent composition, was a widespread and favorite subject; it constituted one of the areas of greatest creativity. Philological and philosophical studies, recently introduced by Spanish émigrés, notably the Tibbonites and Kimḥis, began to be cultivated and were destined to attain a reasonably high level of creativity, synthesis, and definitive summation. The natural sciences, and most prominently medicine, were developed by Jews and Christians alike. Belletristic literature—religious and secular poetry with a sprinkling of rhymed prose—was making its appearance in Provence. The appearance of a corpus of mystical literature—systematic tracts, commentaries on early classics of mysticism, cryptic manuals, and mystical allusions in otherwise conventional literary forms—was yet another facet of this pervasive cultural dynamism.

This mental restlessness was not confined to the Jewish community; all Provence was bustling with activity. One need mention only the lyric poetry of the Midi Troubadours and their elaborate doctrines of chivalry and courtly love.[2] It is particularly significant that this activity

98. Assaf, "Yaḥaso shel ha-Rabad el ha-Rambam," *Ḳobeẓ Rabbenu Moses b. Maimon*, ed. J. L. Fishman (Jerusalem, 1935), 277, n. 14. R. Meïr of Rothenberg also refers to "Rabad of Lunel"; see Gross, 343, n. 35.

1. The simultaneous revival of Roman law at such centers as Montpellier and Toulouse is noteworthy; see Paul Vinogradoff, *Roman Law in Medieval Europe* (New York, 1909).

2. For a later Hebrew troubadour, see J. Schirmann, "Isaac Gorni, poète hébreux de Provence," *Lettres romanes*, III (1949) 175–200. See also I. Davidson, *Tarbiẓ*, II (1930), 90–100.

was most pronounced on the theological-spiritual plane. Speculation was rife and heresies of all sorts were rampant. On one hand, religious liberalism entrenched itself, especially among the counts and nobles, and this engendered intermittent friction between the temporal and sacerdotal powers. Fulminating popes and defiant counts became common spectacles. On the other hand, extreme dualistic and ascetic doctrines—of ancient Gnostic, especially Manichean, provenance—gained adherents who, in turn, became vociferous critics of the Catholic Church, its dogmatic foundation as well as its institutional superstructure. An assortment of mystical tenets also caught the fancy of imaginative Provençal thinkers. In other words, religious thought and practice were in flux throughout the twelfth century; the inhabitants of Albi, Toulouse, Béziers, Narbonne, and Lyons were cultivating old ideas while blazing new paths. The religious tension was so noticeable and the theological debates so ubiquitous that Jews must have sat up and taken notice.[3] In short, the stirring, receptive Jewish community was itself encased in a flourishing, fast-moving country.

Although they were not exempt from humiliation and discrimination, the socio-political status of the Jews in southern France was comparatively favorable. They were befriended by most of the Languedocian counts with sustained benevolence. They enjoyed a measure of social prominence; some were appointed to important administrative and notarial offices, much to the displeasure of the popes.[4] A wider range of economic activities was accessible to them in the ports, metropolises, and villas of this region; some were captains of commerce[5] while others

3. In addition to J. Guiraud, *Histoire de l'Inquisition au Moyen Age* (Paris, 1935) cited by Scholem, *Reshit ha-Kabbalah*, 15, see H. C. Lea, *A History of the Inquisition of the Middle Ages* (New York, 1922), I, esp. chs. 2–4; Steven Runciman, *The Medieval Manichee; A Study of the Christian Dualist Heresy* (Cambridge, 1947), 116–171. Richard Emery, *Heresy and Inquisition in Narbonne* (New York, 1941).

4. E.g., Abba Mari b. Jacob in Bourg de St. Giles—*Itinerary*, 4; Kalonymus ha Nasi in Beaucaire—Judah al-Ḥarizi, *Taḥkemoni*, ch. 46. See G. Saige, *Les Juifs du Languedoc anterieurement au XIVe siècle* (Paris, 1881), 15–16; L. I. Newman, *Jewish Influence on Christian Reform Movements* (New York, 1925), 133–150; S. Grayzel, *The Church and the Jews in the Thirteenth Century* (Philadelphia, 1933), 125 (Innocent III to the Count of Toulouse). Pope Alexander III (1159–1181), however, had Jewish officials in his own court; see H. Vogelstein and P. Rieger, *Geschichte der Juden in Rom* (Berlin, 1895), I, 225.

5. See I. Loeb, "Les Negotiants juifs à Marseille au milieu du XIIIe siècle," *REJ*, XVI (1888), 73–83; and the reservations of R. Emery, *The Jews of Perpignan in the Thirteenth Century* (New York, 1959), 5–6; also, S. Kahn, "Documents inédits sur les Juifs de Montpellier au Moyen Age," *REJ*, XIX (1889), 259–281 and *Itinerary*, 4:
הוא מקום יפה לסחורה, קרוב מן הים שתי פרסאות, ובאים אליו מכל מקום לסחורה אדום וישמעאל מארץ אל-ערוה ולונברדייא, ומלכות רומא רבתא ומכל ארץ מצרים וארץ ישראל וארץ יון וארץ ספרד ואינגלטירה.

occupied key positions in the textile industry.[6] Some managed to retain their ancient property rights (note especially the famous *villa judaica* of Narbonne or the *burgus judaicus* of Nîmes) and continued as independent *allodeurs* or even as seigneurs of "domaine utile."[7] Yet, this greater diversification (trade, crafts, professions, and realty) notwithstanding, the pervasive process of compulsory restriction and progressive shrinkage of the spheres of economic activity was at work here too and moneylending was to remain the major economic enterprise.[8]

The basic precariousness of the Jewish position and its haunting insecurity were most pointedly brought to mind by the physical manifestations of religious humiliation and oppression which lingered on in these regions. In Béziers, for instance, Palm Sunday was the occasion for street brawls during which the bishop urged the Christian populace to stone the Jews. In Arles, where the bishops had jurisdiction over the Jewish residents, they had to transport stones for public works on communal-owned donkeys. Toulouse had its ceremony of *calafus judeorum:* on the eve of all Christian holidays, the seigneur slapped the Jewish community leaders on the face. In time—during the twelfth century for the most part—these vestigial forms of religious harassment were commuted to special taxes and extraordinary fines, but even these poignantly emphasized the alien status of Jews.[9] This was reenforced

6. G. Saige, *Juifs du Languedoc*, 5; in light of this, see Rabad's statement in *Sifra Commentary*, 89a: אבל לבישת שעטנז וכיוצא בו שאין הגוים מוזהרין עליהם אין ישראל נמנע מלעשות לגוים ומזמיני' אותם להם; also Rabad, *BK*, 339; *MT*, *Kele ha-Mikdash*, VIII, 2, 13; *Shabbat*, IX, 15. Jews undoubtedly participated in the newly established fairs of southern France; for the fairs at Nîmes (established 1151) and Carcassone (established 1158), see A. Dupont, *Les Cités de la Narbonnaise Première* (Nîmes, 1942), 611–614; A. Gouron, *La Reglementation des Métiers en Languedoc au Moyen Age* (Paris, 1958), 40–42. Such fairs which often lasted for eight days, may have been in Rabad's mind when he wrote: ירוד שהוא תופס ח׳ ימים או י׳ והיום איד הוא בסוף הירוד כעין אותן של מגרש. *Commentary on ᶜAbodah Zarah*, 13a. For מגרש as Perpignan, see *GJ*, 457.

7. G. Saige, *Juifs du Languedoc*, 5; J. Regné, *Étude sur la Condition des Juifs de Narbonne* (Narbonne, 1912), 171 ff. H. Pirenne, *Economic and Social History of Medieval Europe* (New York, n.d.), 133.

8. This is the thesis of R. Emery, *Jews of Perpignan*, 5–6; see my review notes in *American Historical Review*, LXV (1959), 160; also, *TD*, 43, 44, 46; J. Kimḥi, *Sefer ha-Berit*; the *Milḥemet Miẓwah* of Meïr b. Simon of Narbonne is a defense of usury; see H. Gross, "R. Meir b. Simeon's Milḥemeth Miṣwah," *MGWJ*, XXX (1881), 295–305, 442–452, 554–569; and now S. Stein, "Me'ir b. Simeon's *Milḥemeth Miswah*," *Journal of Jewish Studies*, X (1960), 45–63; also S. Grayzel, *Church and Jews*, 86, 105, and others.

9. Devic and Vaissette, *Histoire Generale de Lanquedoc*, II, 486, II, 813; G. Saige, *Juifs du Languedoc*, 10–12; A. Dupont, *Les Cités*, 525–530, 673–678; H. Gross, "Zur Geschichte der Juden in Arles," *MGWJ*, XXVII (1878), 61–71, 130–137, 145–160, 193–201, 248–256, 377–382, 470–477 and further installments, esp. 150; J. Mann, *Texts and Studies in Jewish History* (Cincinnati, 1931), I, 16 ff.; A. Granget, *Histoire du*

by the humiliating oath *more Judaico.*[10] It is small wonder, therefore, that, together with pleas for amicable relations and upright business dealings, bitterly resentful and contemptuous attitudes toward Christianity are found even in Provençal Jewish writings.[11]

As for the "inner," spiritual life of the community—the entire complex of its religious and cultural mores—one can, on the basis of assorted references, reconstruct the picture of a land of intense religiosity, sincere pietism, scrupulous ceremonialism, ethical altruism, and rigorous moralism—to the extent of asceticism and self-abnegation. Its Torah-centered educational system was geared to the cultivation and intensification of these spiritual qualities. Such a picture might in fact be reconstructed as follows.

There are certain general testimonies concerning the religious habits and social consciousness of Provençal Jews, all of which underscore the same qualities and traits. The informative traveler Benjamin of Tudela says about the people of Provence: "They would support and instruct every student who came from a distant land to study Torah. They would supply the students with food and clothing at public expense for the duration of their stay in the school. Ritually observant people, they habitually perform meritorious acts, standing in the breach to assist all their brethren, near and far." Elsewhere he observes that "there is there a holy community of Israelites who are engaged in the study of the Torah day and night."[12] Precisely the same qualities of magnanimous philanthropy and pure devotion to Torah scholarship which Benjamin found in Provence as a whole are singled out by him with reference to Rabad in particular.

Diocese d'Avignon (Avignon, 1862), I, 352–353. Also, C. Roth, "The Eastertide Stoning of the Jews," *JQR*, XXV (1945), 361–371. Rabad's lengthy explanation of the famous passage in ᶜ*Abodah Zarah*, 11b (סך קירי פלסתר) becomes more meaningful in light of these conditions: ועכשו מי שהוא רואה בשפלותו בשעה זו רואה ומי שאינו רואה בשפלותו בשעה זו שאנו בכאן שמא לא יראה עוד כל ימיו לפי שאין המעשה הזה נעשה אלא אחת לע׳ שנה. לפי׳ כל מי שרוצה בנקמתו של עשו יבוא עכשו ויראה דלא אהני ליה רמאה ליעקב ברמאותיה שעשה לעשו שהרי הוא תחת עשו. אע״ג שבעונותינו בכל יום היו יכולין לראות הענין הזה שהרי ישראל תחת ידם. His severe judgment on the popes should perhaps be correlated with the Provençal situation, where the popes constantly remonstrated against local officials for their leniency toward Jews: פי׳ נשיאיה הם האפיפיורים שלהם פפא בלע״ז, ואין באותם האפיפיורים שיהא לו חלק לעולם הבא. *Commentary on* ᶜ*Abodah Zarah*, 10b.

10. See, for example, Gross, "Juden in Arles," *MGWJ*, XXVII, 147–149. All this notwithstanding, Bernard of Clairvaux still found reason to decry the rampant "Judaizing" tendencies in southern France: see his letter to the Count of Toulouse in *Life and Works of St. Bernard*, ed. J. Mabillon and S. Eales (London, 1889) II, 707 (letter ccxli).

11. S. Stein, "Milḥemeth Miṣwah," *Journal of Jewish Studies*, X, 58–59; see Rabad's statements quoted supra, nn. 8–9. Also, Rabad, *BK*, 313.

12. *Itinerary*, 3, 4.

A similar evaluation is offered by David Kimḥi in a letter to the Spanish physician Judah Alfakar: "Our house is wide open to every wayfarer and person seeking rest. We weary ourselves in the study of the Torah day and night, support the poor unostentatiously, do righteousness at all times, furnish books for needy children of the poor, and provide teachers' salaries for study of Scripture and Talmud." Probably setting himself up as a representative of Provençal rabbis, he adds the following personal note: "There is no rabbi in Spain or France who is more observant of Talmudic laws, severe or lenient, than I." [13] Though this letter is apologetic and, therefore, somewhat hyperbolic perhaps—written in the heat of the Maimonidean controversy in an effort to dispel Alfakar's suspicions concerning the noxious effects of philosophic study (which found a home in Provence) [14]—the details of the description are unassailable. The pervasive emphasis on piety and ceremonial conformity is accurate. Furthermore, although written at the beginning of the thirteenth century, the letter undoubtedly reflects earlier conditions as well. Interestingly enough, it reflects the spirit of some of the remarks of his father, Joseph Kimḥi. Although general and abstract, uttered in the course of an imaginary disputation between a Jew and a Christian, the remarks have historic value in their specific context: "Jews observe their Sabbath and festivals punctiliously"; "we have not forgotten our sacred Law, for even the women know the commandments and statutes and are intimately acquainted with the minute details of rabbinical enactments." Kimḥi also speaks of the exemplary philanthropic spirit and practice of the Jews.[15]

While the comments on charity and generosity speak for themselves,[16] the picture of religious orthodoxy may perhaps be substantiated by the following argument *ex silentio*: there are no complaints about religious laxity, about material prosperity bringing in its wake religious indifference or liberal thought causing a decline in ritual observance. Even the few plaintive notes heard in contemporary writing—especially in the introductions to codes, where they come as justification for the composition of these works—are clearly qualified: laxity or improper observance stem not from contemptuous indifference or rationalized liberalism but from inadvertence and ignorance. Asher b. Saul, citing

13. *Ḳobeẓ Teshubot ha-Rambam*, III, 3d.

14. Sarachek, *Faith and Reason* (Williamsport, 1935), 101–102.

15. J. Kimhi, *Milḥemet Ḥobah* (Constantinople, 1700), reprinted in J. Eisenstein, *Oẓar ha-Wikkuḥim* (New York, 1928), 67–77.

16. See, for example, J. Bergmann, *Ha-Ẓedaḳah be-Yisra'el* (Jerusalem, 1944), 65 ff.

the need for his *Sefer ha-Minhagot*, says: "I saw people treating the customs lightly," but adds, "because they do not know the reasons."[17] Rabad likewise notes that some people err in ritual matters but blames this on lack of knowledge.[18] This is a far cry from some of the heated statements found later in the very same areas—or even earlier elsewhere[19]—concerning both the causes and consequences of religious laxity; the corrupting influence of extreme allegorization, for instance, becomes a recurrent theme. It can be contrasted, for example, with the exhortatory statements made by such an itinerant preacher and scholar as Moses of Coucy, who reprimanded his listeners for flouting rabbinic customs.[20] There is no such articulateness concerning religious laxity in Provence of our period.

It may be assumed, furthermore, that the repeated references to intensive study were not mere homiletical hyperbole, for Provence was covered at this time with a network of flourishing schools and academies. Narbonne, Lunel, Posquières, Béziers, Montpellier, Marseilles, Arles, Trinquetaille, Toulouse, and others were citadels of learning. From distant Cairo, Maimonides singled out Provence as one of the greatest centers of Talmudic study in a period of general eclipse.[21] Sheshet b. Isaac of Spain depicts Narbonne—often a metonymy for all of Provence—as the source from which rivers of learning flow in all directions.[22] Earlier Benjamin of Tudela had characterized Narbonne as "a place of eminence in consequence of the studies carried on there; from there the study of the law spreads over all countries";[23] while later, Yedayah

17. *Sifran*, 129: כי ראיתי אנשים מזלזלים בהם מפני שאין יודעים טעמם.

18. *BH*, 4: אשר רובם מתנהגים עליהם בשגגה; see also *TD*, 1.

19. As in the commentaries of the northern French exegete Joseph Bekor Shor; see M. H. Segal, *Parshanut ha-Miḳra* (Jerusalem, 1944), 72. See Reuben b. Ḥayyim, *Sefer ha-Tamid*, ed. B. Toledano *Oẓar ha-Ḥayyim*, VII (1931), 10: שאין באחת מן המצות שום דבר רע לפי שאינם משלים, כמו שחשבו התועים.

20. *Sefer Miẓwot Gadol* (Venice, 1522), 3, Positive commandment 3 (concerning phylacteries); see Urbach, *Ba^cale ha-Tosafot*, 71, and my remarks in *Tarbiẓ*, XVI (1957), 225. In general, see L. Ginzberg, *Ginze Schechter* (New York, 1929), II, 536–538; Grünspan, "Le-Korot Miẓwat Tefillin we-Haznaḥatah," *Oẓar ha-Ḥayyim*, IV (1928), 159–164.

21. His letter to the sages of Provence, *Oẓar Neḥmad*, II (1857), 3–4 (also *Ḳobeẓ Teshubot ha-Rambam*, II, 44): הרי אני מודיע לכם שלא נשאר בזמן הזה הקשה אנשים להרים דגל משה ולדקדק בדברי רב אשי אלא אתם וכל הערים אשר סביבותיכם ... אבל בכל המקומות האלה אבדה תורה מבינם ... ולא נשאר לנו עזרה אלא אתם אחינו אנשי גאולתנו. See also Abraham Maimonides, *Milḥamot ha-Shem*, ed. R. Margaliyot (Jerusalem, 1953), 52. For Maimonides' entire correspondence with Provence, see S. M. Stern, "Ḥalifat ha-Miktabim ben ha-Rambam we-Ḥakme Provence," *Zion*, XVI (1951), 18–29.

22. D. Kaufmann, "Lettres de Scheschet b. Isaac," *REJ*, XXIX (1899), 67: עד הנה ממקור מים חיים אשר בה יצאו כל נהרות להשקות את הארץ.

23. *Itinerary*, 4.

Bedersi described the Narbonne school of R. Meshullam b. Moses as conducive both to scholarship and saintliness.[24]

Moreover, if, as is now generally assumed, the *Ḥuḳḳe ha-Torah*—a unique syllabus, rich in pedagogic insights, outlining the various stages of education up to the equivalent of a seven-year institute for advanced study—is of Provençal provenance,[25] there must have been some measure of educational theory behind this activity and these institutions. The *Ḥuḳḳe ha-Torah* insisted upon the absolute primacy and indispensability of education; a sense of urgency and commitment pervades the entire document. It strives, by a variety of stipulations and suggestions, to achieve maximum learning on the part of the student and maximum dedication on the part of the teacher. It operates with such "progressive" notions as determining the occupational aptitude of students, arranging small groups in order to enable individual attention, grading the classes in order not to stifle individual progress. The teacher is urged to encourage free debate and discussion among students, arrange periodic reviews—both short-range and long-range—utilize the vernacular in order to facilitate accurate comprehension. Above all, he is warned against insincerity and is exhorted to be totally committed to his noble profession. The question whether these statutes are an *œuvre d'imagination*, never realized in practice—as maintained by Isidore Loeb[26]—or actually constitute an historic document—as believed by most scholars[27]—is not really too crucial. Such imaginativeness—if this is the case—must have been conceived only in a country where rabbinic scholarship was well established in practice and of paramount importance in theory. The least that can be said—with maximum concession to Loeb's skepticism—is that the very existence of the *Ḥuḳḳe ha-Torah* and its educational scheme are themselves meaningful.

The *Ḥuḳḳe ha-Torah*, fostering, as it does, traditional rabbinic learning, also focuses attention on another facet of Jewish life in Provence: the prevalence of intensely pietistic, partially ascetic tendencies. This is

24. Neubauer, "Yedaya de Beziers," *REJ*, XX (1890), 245–248; reprinted by S. Assaf, *Meḳorot le-Toledot ha-Ḥinnuk* (Tel-Aviv, 1925–36), II, 33–35: כי שם נמצאו חכמים מחוכמים, אנשי השם בכל חכמה ומדע.

25. Published for the first time by M. Guedemann, *Ha-Torah weha-Ḥayyim*, I, 73–80, and reprinted by S. Assaf, *Meḳorot le-Toledot ha-Ḥinnuk*, I, 6–16; see B. Dinaburg, *Kiryath Sefer*, I (1924), 107; Benedict, 98; Scholem, *Reshit ha-Kabbalah*, 85; also, Assaf, *Misifrut ha-Geonim*, 4, n. 10.

26. In his review of Guedemann, *REJ*, II (1881), 158–164.

27. See n. 123; also S. Baron, *Social and Religious History of the Jews* (Philadelphia, 1958), VI, 395, n. 163.

most clearly reflected in the passage which describes *perushim*, an elite group of advanced students who isolate themselves almost hermetically in a special building for seven years, eating and sleeping there and refraining from idle chatter. They must study uninterruptedly, for only "one who kills himself for it" can become truly wise and proficient in Torah. These students, we are informed in a preceding article, are to be recruited from the ranks of the firstborn, for every father, and especially a descendant of the tribe of Levi, is urged to "consecrate" his oldest son to study.[28] Instead of saying that this paragraph merely describes the institution of perushim, it would be more accurate to say that it fervently recommends this institution as necessary for the spiritual well-being of the community. Here is the core of the article:

> Just as we institute readers who officiate at public services in order to serve as the medium through which the community at large may fulfill its obligation of prayer, so we should institute professional students to study the Torah uninterruptedly in order to serve as the medium through which the community at large may fulfill its obligation of study and in this way the divine kingdom will not be turned backward. Perushim are students consecrated to the study of the Torah. In Mishnaic Hebrew they are called *perushim* and in Scriptural Hebrew, *nezirim* (nazirites) . . . Such isolation (and abstemiousness) leads to purity.[29]

The subsequent article specifies that the perushim "should not leave the house until the end of seven years. They should eat and drink there and sleep there . . . If the perushim should leave the house of study before the seven years have passed, they will be liable to pay a predetermined fine."

Now, while these quasi-monkish scholars, whose sole mandatory function was study, were not full-fledged ascetic pietists, this possibility is latent just below the surface. Voluntary segregation for purposes of intense, uninterrupted study of the Torah—especially when accompanied by a devout sense of mission, of symbolic representation of the entire community—was the natural prelude to more intense forms of abstention and mortification aimed at attaining saintliness and purity:

28. This statement apparently had interesting repercussions. It is reported (*Orḥot Ḥayyim*, II, 562) in the name of Asher b. Saul—his authorship is noteworthy—that in Provence one did not mourn the death of the firstborn because "the firstborn was [consecrated] to God." Assaf ingeniously explains this odd custom, which puzzled many commentators, in light of the *Ḥuḳḳe ha-Torah*; see *Misifrut ha-Geonim*, 4, n. 10.

29. Assaf, *Meḳorot le-Toledot ha-Ḥinnuk*, I, 10: כי כאשר מעמידין חזנים להוציא רבים ידי חובתם מן התפלה כך מעמידים תלמידים קבועים להגות בתורה בלי הפסק, להוציא רבים ידי חובתם מתלמוד תורה, ולא תהיה מלכות שמים נסוגה אהורנית. פרושים—הם תלמידים המקודשים ללמוד תורה, ונקראין בלשון משנה פרושים ובלשון מקרא נזירים. והפרישות מביאה לידי טהרה.

"isolation leads to purity." The use of such terms would inevitably channel people's thinking in the direction of the famous string of aphorisms attributed to the saintly Pineḥas b. Yaïr[30]—a popular figure in Provençal midrashim. Or they might be reminded of other Talmudic idioms which associate isolation with sanctification.[31]

Such a development seems to have taken place. These terms and concepts, in abeyance for the most part since Talmudic times, began to be freely associated and juxtaposed. Asher b. Meshullam, known as Asher the "Parush," is described not only as "poring over books day and night" but also as "separated from mundate matters, fasting, and not eating meat."[32] Terms such as *nazir*, *ḥasid* (pious),[33] *ḳadosh* (holy),[34] not found hitherto in any significant measure, become common designations. There is R. Jacob ha-Nazir who was engaged in mystical studies and is credited by kabbalistic tradition with having swayed Maimonides to Kabbalah.[35] Professor Scholem has observed that this R. Jacob ha-Nazir was also called ḥasid by R. Ezra of Gerona at the beginning of the thirteenth century.[36] It should be added that Rabad's father-in-law was already referred to as ḥasid and ḳadosh by Isaac b. Abba Mari of Marseille,[37] while Rabad himself, whose exemplary piety and self-imposed, mild ascetism were usually noted, was called both ḥasid and ḳadosh.[38] Judah ibn Tibbon describes Meshullam of Lunel

30. *Sotah*, 49b; *ᶜAbodah Zarah*, 20b; see A. Büchler, *Types of Jewish-Palestinian Piety* (London, 1922), 42 ff.; R. Mach, *Der Zaddik in Talmud und Midrasch* (Leiden, 1957); G. Scholem, "Die Lehre vom Gerechten . . .," *Eranos Jahrbuch*, XXVII (1958), 237–299.

31. E.g., *Yomah*, 8b; *Sanhedrin*, 106b; *Berakot*, 5b; *Genesis Rabbah*, 44.

32. *Itinerary*, 3.

33. On the usage of this term, see S. Schecter, *Studies in Judaism: Second Series* (Philadelphia, 1908), 148–181; Scholem, *Major Trends in Jewish Mysticism*, 92 ff., 371, n. 35, and bibliography on 428. Add to his references, Büchler, *Jewish-Palestinian Piety*, 43, and the new edition of the *Sefer Ḥasidim* by R. Margaliyot (Jerusalem, 1957). It is significant that the term ḥasidut emerges almost contemporaneously as the designation of a mystical-pietistic movement in Germany.

34. That "ḳadosh" designates any saintly person, not necessarily a martyr (as maintained by S. Rappaport) was already observed in *Oẓar Neḥmad*, IV (1864), 38 in connection with Rabad. See also *GJ*, 562. Actually, this usage may be traced back to *Midrash Shoḥer Ṭob*, XVI, 2: אלו בקשו אבות העולם שתהא דירתן למעלה היו יכולין, ואע״פ לא נקראו קדושים עד שמתו ונסתם הגולל בפניהם, לכך נאמר לקדושים אשר בארץ. Also, *Bereshit Rabbati*, 159. Death, not martyrdom, was the prerequisite for this title. See also *Teshubot ha-Rambam*, ed. Freimann, LVII: "רבינו יהונתן ··· בן כבוד גבירנו וקדושנו מרינו ורבינו דוד זצ״ל".

35. *Sifran*, 124, n. 6; Scholem, "Miḥoḳer Limeḳubbal," *Tarbiẓ* VI (1935), 96.

36. Scholem, *Reshit ha-Kabbalah*, 86.

37. *Sefer ha-ᶜIṭṭur* (*Lemberg*, 1860), I, 29a, 34b. See Assaf, *Sifran*, 2, n. 1.

38. Naḥmanides, *Sefer ha-Zekut*, introduction; Rashbah, *Torat ha-Bayit*, *Bet ha-Nashim*, introduction; Aaron ha-Kohen of Lunel, *Orḥot Ḥayyim*, I, 102b, and others; see Gross, XXIII, 170–171, who refers to Moses de Leon, *Sefer ha-Nefesh ha-Ḥakamah* (I have not found this reference).

as "he-ḥasid ha-ḳadosh."[39] R. Jonathan ha-Kohen of Lunel—also designated by the term ḥasid[40]—is described as leading an ascetic life, despising luxuries and rejecting pleasures, dedicating himself unqualifiedly to learning;[41] he is the same type of saintly scholar represented by Rabad. It is almost as if the insightful description of Jonathan is a practical application of the ideal abstractly depicted in the *Ḥuḳḳe ha-Torah*. Asher b. Saul, whose *Sefer ha-Minhagot* already has decidedly pietistic and mystical strains, designates Joseph ibn Plat as ḥasid.[42] Rabad himself describes the father of a certain Judah, whom he sincerely admires, as ḥasid.[43] It is noteworthy that R. Meshullam, the antagonist of R. Tam who went from Provence to settle in Melun, is described as *parush*,[44] just as Pineḥas b. Meshullam, the judge who went from Provence to Egypt where he was cordially received by Maimonides, is described as ḥasid.[45] On the other hand, R. Sheshet ben Isaac of Barcelona, who sojourned in Narbonne for many years is eulogized as the "foundation of all the ḥasidim."[46] Other individual perushim of this time are known by name.[47] Interesting is Abraham ibn Ezra's laudatory acknowledgment of two ḥasidim in Béziers who graciously befriended him: Abraham b. Ḥayyim and Isaac b. Judah.[48] Razah designated Lunel as "a place of learning and *ḥasidut*," and referred to "its sages and ḥasidim."[49] Outstanding is Rabad's son Isaac the Blind who was to become the ḥasid par excellence in kabbalistic literature[50]—just as Rabad himself was to become the critic par excellence in halakic literature. R. Isaac is also called ḳadosh[51] and parush,[52] so that practically

39. Judah ibn Tibbon, introduction to *Ḥobot ha-Lebabot*.

40. Samuel ibn Tibbon, introduction to *Moreh Nebukim*: החסיד הכהן ר׳ יהונתן. Assaf, "Kinot," *Minḥah li-Yehudah* (Jerusalem, 1950), 164: אוי על חסיד בהודו, הנאה במקראו ובתלמודו.

41. N. Wider, "Sifro ha-Nisraf shel Judah ibn Shabetai," *Meẓudah*, II (1944), 124 ff.

42. *Sifran*, 142.

43. *TD*, 11: החכם החסיד ר׳ אברהם; see Benedict, *Sinai*, XIV (1951), 193 ff.

44. *Sefer Mordecai* on *Shabbat*, section 452; Urbach, *Baᶜale ha-Tosafot*, 125, n. 1.

45. *Teshubot ha-Rambam*, ed. Freimann, LVIII.

46. Judah al-Ḥarizi, *Taḥkemoni*, ch. 46.

47. *Sefer Ma'or wa-Shemesh* (Livorno, 1839), 9; see *REJ*, XV (1887), 88; Assaf, *Misifrut ha-Geonim*, 4.

48. Abraham ibn Ezra, *Sefer ha-Shem* (Fiorda, 1834), 1 (the rhymed dedication).

49. Quoted by Marx, 222, n. 3: ואני יראתי לומר דבר זה עד שבאתי למקום התורה והחסידות מגדל לוניל ... ומתוך כך הרציתי דברי אלה לפני אחד מיוחד מגדולי הארץ וחכמיה וחסידיה. See also Samuel ibn Tibbon, introduction to *Moreh Nebukim* and al-Ḥarizi, introduction to his translation of Maimonides' Mishnah Commentary (about Marseille).

50. Gross, XXIII, 181; Scholem, *Reshit ha-Kabbalah*, 102.

51. *Oẓar Neḥmad*, IV (1864), 37.

52. D. Sassoon, *Ohel David*, II, 1014.

all the current titles and their implied attributes are united in him; he is truly symbolic in this respect. In sum, the Provençal atmosphere seems to have been charged with such traits of piety and inclinations to mystical thought and practice; *perishut* was becoming fashionable and Provence was one of its best agents.

3. *Teaching and Writing*

The first station in Rabad's itinerary was at Montpellier, a citadel of Talmudic learning and a bastion of general culture. Moses b. Judah, Meshullam's son-in-law and correspondent of Rabad, lists Montpellier as the seat of one of the three foremost rabbinical courts in southern France.[1] Most manuscripts indicate that Maimonides addressed his celebrated epistle on astrology to the Jewish community of Montpellier, where Jonathan ha-Kohen was probably residing at that time (1194).[2] Benjamin of Tudela mentions with fervent admiration many famous scholars of Montpellier,[3] while Judah al-Ḥarizi lavishes several lines of glowing metaphors on the city and its sages.[4] Moreover, in addition to cultivating specifically Jewish learning, the Jews of Montpellier were interested in the advance of general culture. They were among the first teachers at the European-wide famous medical school of this city.[5] Rabad established himself in this city and presumably achieved prominence there.

There is no direct information on his stay here or about his official status in the community. One reference in later code books relates that it was his custom to buy an *etrog* (a kind of citron used with the festive wreath on the Feast of Booths of *Sukkot*) for the entire community of Montpellier for the holiday of Sukkot.[6] This casual report may suggest more than a manifestation of his sociability or an illustration of the use of his wealth for communal needs. It might imply a position of recognized

1. *TD*, 7.
2. *GJ*, 322, and Marx, "The Correspondence between the Rabbis of Southern France and Maimonides," *HUCA*, III, 324.
3. *Itinerary*, 2–3.
4. Judah al-Ḥarizi, introduction to his translation of Maimonides' Mishnah Commentary; see also Samuel ibn Tibbon, introduction to *Moreh Nebukim*.
5. Cl. Devic and Dom Vaissette, *Histoire Générale de Languedoc* (Toulouse, 1872), II, 806; A. Germain, *L'Ecole de Médecine de Montpellier* (Montpellier, 1880), 6; the bibliographical review in S. Baron, *Social and Religious History of the Jews*, VIII, 398.
6. *Orḥot Ḥayyim* (Florence, 1750), I, 116b; *Kol Bo* (Lemberg, 1860), 71.

leadership, for the joint use of one etrog by an entire community—a practice originating most likely in the financial inability of many individuals to purchase an etrog as well as the scarcity of this fruit—was a controversial halakic issue. On purely formal grounds and upon the basis of the letter of the Scriptural commandment traditionally interpreted, authorities frowned upon the practice of the common use of one eṭrog.[7] However, by certain legal arrangements which required the sanction of recognized legal authority, ways could be found by which this sharing was permissible. Presumably such sanction was officially given by Rabad in Montpellier. That this was common procedure is indicated by the fact that the compiler of the *Kol Bo* mentions other Talmudic authorities who, *ex officio*, encountered the same problem in their domain.[8]

To infer purely from this bit of legalistic subtlety that Rabad had an official position in the community of Montpellier would not be very certain. The aforementioned letter of Moses b. Judah, however, suggests that Rabad conducted a school in Montpellier or was a member of the local court (*bet-din*). For, in closing this letter, he mentions the three celebrated courts of Montpellier, Lunel, and Nîmes, whose aid he invokes and whose opinion he seeks. He believes their view vital, in all matters of Jewish law—"from *alef* to *tav*," that is from *alpha* to *omega*, or from "a" to "z." In a personal letter addressed to Rabad, such a reference appears irrelevant or incongruous, unless some connection can be established between Rabad and these centers. He studied and wrote in Lunel and was associated by contemporaries with the city's scholars. At Nîmes, he later headed a flourishing school, where this letter seems to have been sent. If teaching activities or other official duties on Rabad's part at Montpellier may be assumed, all the references in Moses b. Judah's letter will be apropos. Moses is recalling the centers where Rabad flourished previously, all of which remained prominent thanks to the seeds which Rabad planted. Nîmes is the greatest of all—

7. Levit. 23:40; *Sukkah* 29b, ff.; *Oraḥ Ḥayyim*, 649, 658; Commentary of Rashbam on *Baba Batra*, 137b. The problem was already widespread in the Geonic period: see B. M. Lewin, ed., *Oẓar ha-Geonim* (Jerusalem, 1934), *Sukkah*, 56.

8. *Kol Bo*, 71. That Rabad acted in an official rabbinic capacity is more easily inferred from the full-length description given by the Provençal R. David b. Levi in the *Sefer ha-Miktam*, ed. A. Sofer (New York, 1959), 96: אך הראב״ד ז״ל היה נוהג לקנות משלו אתרוג אחד לכל הקהל מונשפלייר, והיו יוצאין בו כל הקהל, שהיה נותנו לכל אחד ואחד על מנת להחזיר, וביומא דערבה היה מבקש לכל אחד ואחד עד כדי שיפרע דמי האתרוג, וכל זה היה עושה מפני שיש מפקפקין לצאת בשל צבור לפי שהוא משותף לכולם. והיה מקנה אותה לכל אחד ואחד בהקנאה גמור׳ על מנת להחזירו לו. All the sources—*Orḥot Ḥayyim, Kol Bo, Sefer ha-Miktam*—for this fact are Provençal.

"from there," as he says, "Torah radiates to all neighboring communities"—for that is where Rabad was at the time and his presence eclipses all residues of previous influence.[9]

Nîmes, where Jewish émigrés from Spain were cordially received as early as the seventh century, was Rabad's next residence in his Provençal travels.[10] He refers to his stay there in one of his responsa. The query directed to him in a certain letter had already been brought up by his "colleagues" at Nîmes, and there he adduced lucid, convincing demonstrations for his answer which he summarily reproduced in this reply.[11] This is a clear-cut reference to his school, for the term "colleague" usually applies to Rabad's senior students, whom he treated most cordially.[12] It is this school or court of Nîmes which Moses b. Judah, in a very allusive hyperbole, describes as being situated in the cell of *Gazit* (or "Chamber of Hewn Stones"), an interior chamber of the Temple which served as the meeting place of the great *Sanhedrin*.[13] This laudatory comparison was made presumably in the early sixties, before Rabad settled at Posquières and established there the most famous of his schools. At the time, he was still heading a school in Nîmes, from which learning was being disseminated to many parts of Provence.[14]

Posquières,[15] the city with which Rabad is historically associated, was, in the middle decades of the twelfth century, a small, sparsely populated Jewish community, shrouded in insignificance when compared to the

9. *TD*, 7: ג׳ בתי דינים · · · והג׳ יושב בלשכת הגזית שמשם יוצאה תורה לכל סביבותיו· והוא בנמשי. Another reference by David b. Levi to a presumably official act of Rabad in Montpellier is found in *Sefer ha-Miktam* (Lemberg, 1904), 13: ושמענו שהרב ר׳ אברהם ברבי דוד ז״ל היה מוחה ביד בני ההר כשהיו אוכלין פירות מן האילנות שהיו שם בבית הקברות · · ·

10. On Nîmes, see the brief sketch by S. Kahn, *Notice sur les Israelites de Nîmes* (Nîmes, 1901), and its bibliography on p. 5, n. 1; see especially Menard, *Histoire de la Ville de Nîmes* (Nîmes, 1871), I, 200–201.

11. *TD*, 19.

12. See page 39.

13. M. *Middot*, V, 4.

14. Much confusion among historians concerning Rabad's activities at Nîmes and Posquières was created by the term "Ḳiryat Yeᶜarim," "city of forests" (see Jos. 9:17)—one of the many nicknames which Provençal Jews applied to French cities. Some (Gross, Zunz, Reifmann, and Kahn) identified it with Nîmes: see Gross, 344; Zunz, *Wissenschaftliche Zeitschrift*, II, 310; Reifmann, *ha-Maggid*, VI (1862), 382; Kahn, *Juifs de Posquières*, 7. Carmoly (*La France Israelite*, 119) believes it to be Carcassonne. Atlas (English introduction, Rabad, *BK*, 12, n. 5) and Marx (204), relying on the same text of ha-Me'iri, show that Posquières was called "Ḳiryat Yeᶜarim."

15. For a few background facts and a list of the various Hebrew spellings of this name, see *GJ*, 446. The following variations should be added to Gross's list: פישקירה in *Dibre ha-Yamim le-Joseph ha-Kohen*, ed. D. Gross (Jerusalem, 1955), 35; פיסקיירה in Azariah dei Rossi, *Maẓref la-Kesef* (Vilna, 1865), 18; פושקראש in Vatican ms. 202, quoted by Scholem, "Te'udah Ḥadashah," *Sefer Bialik*, 143.

greater southern centers. It could boast of only a few scholars, foremost among whom, perhaps, was Menaḥem b. Simeon the exegete and grammarian.[16] Not far from Nîmes and about two miles from Lunel, such a community would understandably suggest itself as the perfect site for a rabbinic school. Here a respected scholar, provided with the necessary funds, could maintain a thriving school for advanced students in Talmud. Peaceful, secluded, surrounded by forests, it was conducive to study, reflection, and research. Thoughts such as these must have appealed to Rabad, for whom pedagogic and scholarly interests had always been paramount, for, by 1165 approximately,[17] he was located in Posquières at the head of an already famous school.

Benjamin of Tudela, that observant traveler with the penetrating eye and facile pen who visited Posquières during Rabad's lifetime, left an invaluable description of Rabad's school, which mirrors the sincerity and nobility of Rabad's personality.[18] Benjamin portrays Rabad as being generous not only with his immense erudition but also with his great wealth. His house was practically converted into a dormitory for the

16. Benjamin of Tudela (*Itinerary*, 4) mentions Joseph b. Menaḥem Benveniste, Benjamin, Abraham b. Moses, and Isaac b. Moses; see *GJ*, 398, 450; M. Barul, *Menachem ben Simon aus Posquieres und sein Kommentar zu Jeremia und Ezechiel* (Berlin, 1907); E. Urbach, "Hassagot ha-Rabad ʿal Perush Rashi," *Kiryath Sefer*, XXXIV (1959), 107–108; also the references in M. Steinschneider, *Jewish Literature* (London, 1857), 331, n. 20.

17. For a discussion of the date of Benjamin's journeys, see Israel Davidson, ed., *Sepher Shasshuim* of Joseph ibn Zabara (New York, 1914), Appendix A; see the references in S. Baron, *Social and Religious History of the Jews*, VI, 435, n. 88.

18. *Itinerary*, 4: ושם ישיבה גדולה על יד הרב הגדול רבי אברהם בר רבי דוד זצ״ל, רב פעלים, חכם גדול בתלמוד ובפסוק. ובאים מארץ מרחק אליו ללמוד תורה, ומוצאים מקום מנוחה בביתו והוא מלמדם. ומי שאין לו להוציא הוא מוציא להם משלו וממונו לכל צרכיהם. והוא עשיר גדול. This fact, objectively reported by Benjamin of Tudela, has an interesting history of its own. It is one of the few facts about Rabad repeated with differing emphases by practically every student of this period—for the *Itinerary* was available in many translations. Some writers mention it with ostensible pride, some report it with scholarly detachment, while others are caught unawares by the historicity of this fact and repeat it begrudgingly. A distant echo—to mention one curious case—is heard from the pages of Jean François de Maucomble's *Histoire abregée de la Ville de Nîmes* (Amsterdam, 1767), 24. This son of the Enlightenment, who took to history and poetry after interrupting a military career for reasons of poor health, apparently lost no sympathy on the Jews. However, because of Benjamin's *Itinerary*, which he must have read in French or Latin translation, he was compelled to admit that even Jews could be generous. Note the half-heartedness of the admission: "Si nous n'avions des monumens certains sur cette partie de l'histoire de l'esprit humain, on auroit aujourd'hui bien de la peine à se persuader qu'un Juif ait en cette générosité." (!) Maimonides was also reputed to have been extraordinarily philanthropic and successors were very impressed with his generosity as they were by Rabad's; see Naḥmanides' letter in *Ḳobeẓ Teshubot ha-Rambam*, III, 9 (בנדבת כיסו במעשיו הנפלאים); Menaḥem b. Zeraḥ, *Ẓedah la-Derek* (Warsaw, 1880), 6 (חסיד גדול נוסף על חכמתו ונדיב בעל אכסניא); *REJ*, IV (1882), 179.

students, and he provided for all the other needs of the indigent students out of his own pocket.[19] His students were many and came from afar, for even then it was common for students to leave their homes and travel in order to attend a well-known school or study under a recognized authority in his field.[20] In northern France, at a somewhat earlier date, Rashi, who traveled great distances in search of instruction, left a picturesque description of itinerant students: "Like doves that wander from one dovecot to the second to seek their food, so they go from the school of one scholar to the school of another scholar to seek explanations (reasons) for the Torah."[21] In the celebrated Babylonian schools of Sura and Pumbeditha there were students from Palestine, Egypt, Africa, Spain, Italy, and Byzantium,[22] while "there resided in Egypt Israelites who came from all the lands to R. Moses [Maimonides]."[23] Similarly, students poured in to Rabad's school from all sides.[24] A thirteenth-century kabbalistic tract mentions eminent students from Spain, Germany, and Damascus who converged on Rabad's school at Posquières.[25] One famous student was brought by his father from Carcassonne to study under Rabad. Benjamin of Tudela comments, probably on the basis of personal interviews, that "they come from distant lands to him to study Torah."

The school's success and reputation were direct consequences of Rabad's limitless attention and devotion. His intense love for learning and his total intellectual commitment to Talmudic studies motivated the establishment and maintenance of the school. He referred to his

19. The medieval "college" originated as an "endowed hospice or hall of residence." See C. H. Haskins, *The Rise of Universities* (New York, 1923), 26.

20. Medieval institutions of higher learning—Jewish or Christian—came into existence, subsequently to be institutionalized, as a result of the fame and authority of regional scholars, whether R. Isaac of Dampierre and Rabad of Posquières or Peter Abelard of Paris and Irnerius of Bologna. Planned establishment of universities was a thirteenth-century development; see, for example, Cyril E. Smith, *The University of Toulouse in the Middle Ages* (Milwaukee, 1958), 32–34.

21. Rashi, Cant. 5:16.

22. Assaf, *Teḳufat ha-Geonim we-Sifrutah* (Jerusalem, 1955), 43.

23. Neubauer, *REJ*, IV (1882), 179. On traveling students, see also ha-Me'iri, *Magen Abot*, 11, 14; A. Neuman, *The Jews in Spain* (Philadelphia, 1948), II, 91; Assaf, *Meḳorot le-Toledot ha-Ḥinnuk* (Tel Aviv, 1954), I, 33; A. Aptowitzer, *Mabo le-Sefer Rabi'ah* (Jerusalem, 1932), 346; I. Davidson, introduction to *Sepher Shaashuim* (New York, 1914), XV. On the perils which traveling students faced, see P. Kibre, "Scholarly Privileges: Their Roman Origins and Medieval Expression," *American Historical Review*, LIX (1954), 548-550.

24. Menaḥem ha-Me'iri, *Bet ha-Beḥirah* on *Abot*, ed. S. Waxman (New York, 1944), 67.

25. Scholem, *Reshit ha-Kabbalah*, 124.

disciples as colleagues and friends (*ḥaverim*).[26] Even if this term suggests that they were well-advanced students, such modesty and spirit of comradeship is noteworthy. This personal relationship with students and colleagues presents a sharp contrast to the emotionally detached, often combative attitude displayed in his critical writings. Although the *Yeshivah* was first-rate, Rabad constantly desired to improve it in quality and quantity by attracting promising young scholars. In answer to the letter of Judah b. Abraham, he expressed the wish that the latter might join the Yeshivah circle in order to share in and contribute to the joy of learning.[27] He constantly referred to the school. Many of his favorite theories were elaborated in its classrooms. He shared the results of his investigations with his students and often employed "modern" methods of visual aid to illustrate his lectures. For instance, Rabad encouraged the empirical study of animal anatomy, knowledge of which was basic for many aspects of the dietary law, by actually bringing to class parts of the animal, such as the bunch of converging sinews in the thigh (*ẓomet ha-gidin*).[28] Classroom discussion on many occasions provided the stimulus for his novellae and theoretical innovations. Many of his famous *hassagot* were obviously intended for school use. Some were suggestions for further study, while others were challenging invitations to more speculation.[29] It is also possible that some of the pieces preserved in *Temim De'im* were initially composed for the benefit of the school.[30]

Rabad's life was spent in various cities of southern France such as Narbonne, Lunel, Montpellier, Nîmes, Posquières, and, for a while, Carcassonne, which served as his successive places of residence.[31] He

26. *TD*, 19: כבר שאלוני חברי; 50 מעזרת המקום ומעזרת חברי ישמרם הא—ל; 113 וחברינו הסכימו בידינו. See also *MT*, *Zekiyah U-Matanah*, VIII, 12; hassagot on Alfasi, *Giṭṭin*, 33b; Assaf, "Yaḥaso shel ha-Rabad," *Kobez ha-Rambam*, 278: כל זה הסכמנו ונעשה על פינו ועל פי חבירנו. The use of the term "Talmid-Ḥaver" by ha-Me'iri (*ibid.*) has the same connotation. Also Crescas, *Or Adonai* (Vienna, 1860), 2a ובהסכמת החברים ובעזרתם. See *Taᶜanit*, 7b; *Baba Batra*, 158b.

27. *TD*, 11.

28. *Ibid.*, 3: ואמר תחלה מה שראו עיני ומשמשו ידי והראיתי לתלמידי. See *MT*, *Sheḥitah*, VIII, 14: ומעולם לא בדקתי צומת הגידין אלא מן הארכובה ולמעלה. That these very modest beginnings were relatively advanced, in the perspective of general history, see now C. O'Malley, "The Inception of Anatomical Studies in the University of Paris," *Bulletin of the History of Medicine*, XXXIII (1959), 436–445.

29. For example, *MT*, *Shabbat*, XXV, 13; *Lulab*, VIII, 5; *Miḳwa'ot*, III. The first part of ᶜ*Edut*, XXII, 2 is probably a student's remark.

30. See my discussion of *TD*, 61, page 74 ff.

31. A fourteenth-century Provençal writer, Jacob b. Moses of Bagnols—who compiled a long roster of Provençal authorities—apparently places Rabad in the city of Arles also: וכן התיר הראב"ד ז"ל בעיר ארלדי. See Neubauer, *REJ*, IX (1884), 53. There are,

was not much of a traveler. Though there were definite literary connections between the scholars of northern and southern France,[32] he never visited Paris, Sens, Vitry, Ramerupt, or other centers of Jewish learning in northern France. It is therefore doubly significant that he did visit Spain. Rabad himself states that he was in Barcelona.[33] Provence and Catalonia were bound at this time not only by geographical proximity, but also by some sort of feudal-institutional unity. The counts of Barcelona had achieved suzerainty over most of Provence at the beginning of the twelfth century, and communication between the two regions must have been frequent.[34] Some assume that Rabad's father-in-law also visited Barcelona.[35] Shortly after Rabad's visit Jonathan ha-Kohen of Lunel went to Toledo to study,[36] while yet another Provençal scholar, Meïr ha-Kohen of Narbonne, later settled there.[37]

One tangible result of Rabad's trip to Barcelona was the broadening of his horizon. He must have observed the folkways and traditions of Spanish Jewish life carefully, for he later cited the customs of Barcelona in matters of civil law.[38] Rabad's literary acquaintance with Spain was, thus, supplemented by personal contact and firsthand experience. The influence of Spanish-Jewish learning in Provence was growing, as was personal contact between the countries. Rabad's trip is another link in the chain which drew Spain and southern France closer together.

The date of Rabad's spanish excursion is unknown; it may have preceded his removal to Posquières or provided an interlude during this period. In any event, his halcyonic existence in Posquières was violently disturbed in 1172 by some hostility on the part of Elzear, the local seigneur of Posquières. The exact sequence of this event—its feudal

however, no other reference to Arles as one of Rabad's places of residence. Moreover, the phrase may be interpreted to mean that he issued a decision—through the medium of a responsum—in connection with a case from Arles. Kahn, "Juifs de Posquières," 7 without any documentation, speaks parenthetically of a "momentary sojourn in Arles"; also *JE*, II, 116.

32. See Chapter IV, §2. Note also that R. Samuel ben Meïr already quotes Narbonne sages collectively; see his *Perush ha-Torah* on Ex. 25:33 (ושוב שמעתי שכן מפרשים בנרבונא), ed. D. Rosin (Breslau, 1881), 126. Legend, however, made Rabad pay a visit to Rameru, the home of R. Tam; see D. Kaufmann, "Liste de rabbins dressée par Azriel Trabotto," *REJ*, IV, 212, 215, 223, n. 87.

33. Marx, 206, n. 3; see Benedict, 109. Marx reads "דין ברצלונא" which implies merely that he answered questions sent to him from Barcelona, while the version in *KS*, I, 25 is "בברצלונא".

34. Devic and Vaissette, *Histoire de Languedoc*, III, 852.

35. Assaf, 1; Benedict, 109, analyzes this issue thoroughly.

36. See Chapter V, §1.

37. *GJ*, 422; see *Yesod ʿOlam*, ed. Cassel (Berlin, 1848), II, 35.

38. *TD*, 51

antecedents and implications—is not clearly established, and its details have to be reconstructed from the reticent sources which mention it. If not for the extreme brevity, bordering on concealment, of the sources, we might have found here interesting material on the dynamics of feudalism.

Until the publication of ha-Me'iri's *Magen Abot*, the only reference to these sudden tribulations of Rabad was in the sixteenth-century chronicle, *Shebet Yehudah*, of Solomon ibn Virga. There are two entries which read: (1) "1172—the oppressor Elzear seized the Rabbi, Abraham son of Rabbi David"; (2) "and in the year 1173, the lord was seized and exiled to Carcassonne before the Master."[39] This meager report can now be supplemented by the following parenthetical observation recorded by ha-Me'iri in connection with the composition of Rabad's *Hilkot Lulab:* ". . . which the Master composed upon leaving Posquières because of the wars of one of the lords who fought with his lord."[40]

A few brief, prefatory comments on the feudal situation and dynastic rivalries in this area at the time will help illumine the sketchy and vague allusions of our texts. The two most powerful suzerains, approximating and in some respects exceeding, the status and hegemony of the king were the counts of Toulouse and of Barcelona. There was practically unremitting strife and friction between them for suzerainty over southern France—a fact which underlies most of the feudal history of the twelfth century. The most important local dynasty, whose homage was a precious prize, was the house of Trencavel, which held such important viscounties as Béziers, Carcassonne, and Nîmes. Alliances and counter-alliances among lords were legion. Yet feudal vicissitudes during the twelfth century did not substantially affect the comfortable position, relatively free of restrictions, enjoyed by Provençal Jewry, for most rulers looked favorably upon their traditional prerogatives. Most consistently sympathetic was the house of Trencavel. Under Raymond Trencavel the Jews of Béziers were allowed to pay a special Easter fine in lieu of the humiliation, affront, and actual beating to which they had always been subject on this holiday. As a result and in appreciation of this seigneurial benevolence, the Jews took no part in the bourgeois plot of 1167 which cost Raymond his life. This chain reaction of favor and gratitude was carried further when, in 1169, Raymond's son, Roger

39. Solomon ibn Virga, *Shebet Yehudah*, ed. Shoḥet-Baer (Jerusalem, 1947), 146, 221.
40. *Magen Abot*, 103.

II, recaptured the city of Béziers, mercilessly punished the inhabitants, and excepted the Jews from the vengeful massacre. Roger's friendship was manifest further not only in his liberal tax policy, but also in his elevation of Jews to influential administrative and notarial positions: the bailiff of Carcassonne was Moses Caravita, while another Jew, Nathan, was one of Roger's chief stewards. Moreover, Roger seems to have taken important Jewish figures under his personal protection. Placing chosen individuals under personal protection (*sauvegarde*) was one of the means by which powerful suzerains or even the king extended their direct influence and encroached upon the domain of lesser vassals. Jews, who protruded roughly from all ends of the feudal hierarchy, were especially prone to such protection. It was during the ascendancy of this Roger that Rabad became involved with the local seigneur and it was Roger's amicability that offset the seigneur's animosity.[41]

In light of these facts, the statements of ha-Me'iri and ibn Virga can be interpreted as follows: "One of the lords" referred to by ha-Me'iri is probably Elzear, seigneur of Posquières and Uzes, explicitly mentioned by the later chronicle.[42] There was general feudal unrest at the time and, in particular, ha-Me'iri speaks of "wars" between a vassal ("one of the lords"), Elzear, and his suzerain ("his lord"), or Roger of Carcassonne. Rabad, whose wealth must have aroused the envy of neighboring vassals, was a victim of the unrest and was "seized," most likely imprisoned, by Elzear. Ha-Me'iri comments only on a feudal war between vassal and suzerain which compelled Rabad to leave Posquières, without mentioning Rabad's "seizure," while ibn Virga reports the seizure independently of the feudal clash and its consequences, but the two are undoubtedly intertwined. Rabad's seizure was a breach of feudal discipline by Elzear, for Rabad seems to have been under the personal protection of Roger II, Elzear's suzerain. Therefore, Roger intervened in favor of Rabad, and in the following year Elzear was "exiled to Carcassonne before the master." This last phrase, which troubled Graetz and for which he found no meaning,[43] might indicate that he was exiled to Carcassonne where, according to ha-Me'iri, Rabad was temporarily residing. It connotes, in other words, the presence of

41. Devic and Vaissette, *Histoire de Languedoc*, III, 813, 852; V, 27 ff., 38–39. Also, G. Saige, *Les Juifs de Languedoc*, 17, 133; Graetz, IV, 266, 415; *GJ*, 477.

42. While an Elzear was seigneur of Posquières both before and after 1172, there is none in 1172; see Vaissette, *Histoire de Languedoc*, IV, 228 for a genealogy of the seigneurs of Posquières. Perhaps the date in the *Shebet Yehudah* is inexact.

43. Graetz, IV, 415.

Rabad. Or it might mean that Elzear was exiled to Carcassonne "before the Master," in order to clear the way for Rabad's peaceful return to Posquières. Exile (usually accompanied by confiscation of territory) was common punishment for a feudal felony. So, while implementing justice, Roger again asserted his friendship to the Jews of Provence.

The exact sequence of Rabad's moves again was clarified by ha-Me'iri. Upon leaving Posquières, as an aftermath of his clash with Elzear, Rabad went to his birthplace, Narbonne. It was only after a delegation of notables from Carcassonne "entreated him" to honor their community with his presence that he moved there. He spent some time in Carcassonne, at the home of Menaḥem b. Isaac, where he composed the *Hilkot Lulab*; he then returned to Posquières.[44]

Details about the rest of his life are scanty. It must have been a peaceful period, for it was certainly a prolific one. He was plucking the ripe and full-grown fruits of his relentless industry and mature scholarship. The bulk of his hassagot on Alfasi, Razah, and Maimonides were composed during this period. Many of his responsa were issued. His reputation was widespread and his prestige was immense. A chronicle designates him rather laconically as the "greatest of all" the eminent Provençal sages,[45] while the salutation of a legal question addressed to him aptly invokes the Biblical metaphor designating Abraham as "the father of a multitude."[46] Even in distant Cairo, Maimonides describes Rabad as "the great rabbi of Posquières." One of the praiseworthy characteristics of R. Meïr, a Provençal scholar who had migrated to Egypt and whom Maimonides mentions with obvious approval to Samuel ibn Tibbon, is that he had been a student of Rabad.[47] The incident of the Carcassonne dignitaries who so earnestly and cordially invited him to their city also attests to his fame and popularity. Finally, Rabad himself asserts that his word is law in all Provence, and with a flourish of righteous indignation, he rebukes the sages of Béziers for questioning and rejecting his decisions. He writes to them as follows:

44. Graetz (IV, 266) is uncertain whether Rabad spent the time in Nîmes or Carcassonne.

45. Supplement to *Sefer ha-Kabbalah*, Neubauer, *Medieval Jewish Chronicles* I, 84: כל אלה עמודיהם גדולים בתורה שבכתב ושבעל פה אבל הרב ר׳ אברהם ב״ר דוד הגדול על כלם. The order in which the names are listed, Rabad's being first, also seems significant; see Benedict, "Le-Miklol le-Ḥakme Provence," *Kiryath Sefer*, XXVII (1951), 239.

46. *TD*, 113 (see Gen. 71:5).

47. *Ḳobeẓ Teshubot ha-Rambam*, 27a. Simeon b. Ẓemaḥ Duran, *Sefer ha-Tashbeẓ*, 72, also quotes the phrase הרב הגדול אשר בפושקירוש. This is the only extant Maimonidean reference to Rabad.

"Such is the custom in all Provence, in accord with what we have said; moreover, our colleagues have concurred with us and have not rebuffed our teaching as, we have been told, you have done."[48] If excess arbitrariness and self-esteem appear in this passage, as in the entire letter, there are also an illuminating reflection of Rabad's true position in Provence and a realistic appraisal of his influence.

The image of the trajectory, frequently used by biographers to depict the careers of their subjects, is not very appropriate for Rabad. Having made an early literary start, his teaching and scholarship continued unabated. He went "from strength to strength," from codes to commentaries to hassagot. There was no literary decline or cultural atrophy. His old age crowned his youthful and middle-age activities. The final mishnah of *Ḳinnim*, which he so aptly interpreted, is justly applicable to Rabad:

> R. Simeon b. Akashieh says: Uninstructed persons, the older they become, the more their intellect gets distracted, as it is said: "He removeth the speech of men of trust and taketh away the sense of the elders" (Job 12:20); whereas of aged scholars it is not so. On the contrary, the older they get, the more their mind becomes composed, as it is said: "With aged men there is wisdom and understanding in length of days" (Job 12:12).

4. *Personality*

The querulous incident concerning the sages of Béziers focuses attention on Rabad's personality. Having already described certain aspects, perhaps capturing some of its sensitivity and intensity, it may be helpful to delineate more fully a few general character traits and in this way obtain a picture of Rabad the man—the man behind the scholar—his strengths and weaknesses, passions and convictions, virtues and qualities. Such a sketch must be subject to rigid discipline if it is not to pass from the carefully lined notebook of the historian to the supple and suggestive canvas of the artist. Enthusiastic devotion or unreasonable antipathy must not be allowed to substitute for realistic evaluation. If one claims that Rabad was vitriolic, fair, opinionated, moderate, amiable, withdrawn, generous, forthright—whatever the

48. *TD*, 113. Note the interesting apologetic use made of this letter by David Ganz, *Ẓemaḥ David* (Warsaw, 1871), 4.

claim, be it flattering or damning—it must be empirically substantiated. If one encounters, and is compelled to combat, preconceived judgments in the course of literary and conceptual analysis, how much more must one be wary of distortions in the delicate, often evasive task of characterization.

There is no doubt that Rabad was an independent, outspoken, and aggressive individual, possessed of great self-esteem and confidence. Vigorously and candidly, in theory and in practice, he focused attention on his traits of autonomous judgment and self-reliant, logical reasoning. He chose to depict himself—and others did the same[1]—as an unflinching individualist and critic, engaged in an unrelenting quest for the true and the accurate. (This quest was oriented almost exclusively toward halakic objectives, in keeping with his character as a "man of halakah," although he did not rigidly limit his vision so as to exclude cognate areas of nonhalakic learning.) He assured his correspondents that "he does not traverse strange roads in pursuit of remote possibilities but keeps to the paved roads with theories that good taste accepts and reason dictates," adding that "excluding nonsensical matters, I can adjudicate all legal cases."[2] In the conclusion of a consultation which he forwarded to an eager correspondent he notes: "Continue to inquire, my son, about all matters which are doubtful to you, for interpretations belong to God and to the children [intellectual faculties] which He has graciously given to his servant Abraham."[3] He advises another scholar: "Open your eyes and observe that the truth is in keeping with my explanation."[4] Elsewhere, he declares forcefully, with only a weak, perfunctory qualification, that all predecessors and contemporaries, including his teachers, groped in the dark like blind men in the absence of his novel and accurate interpretation.[5] "This is the proper and correct interpretation" recurs in his writings almost with the rhythmic regularity of a refrain.[6] Very expressive is the resounding declaration at the beginning of his commentary on *ᶜEduyot:* ". . . in all these matters I have nothing to fall back upon, neither from a rabbi or a teacher, but only upon [that which

1. His father-in-law writes (in the poem at the end of *Ḳinnim*): וזכני להיות חותן לרבן הקשה אדם קשה כברזל. והוא מלמד ומרדע ודרבן. See Naḥmanides, *Milḥamot*, *Yebamot*, 20b:
2. *TD*, 50; see also 61.
3. *Ibid.*, 59 (see Gen. 33:5, 40:8); see also 3, 19, 21, and others.
4. *Ibid.*, 114; see *MT*, *ᶜErubin*, V, 15, *Nezirut*, II, 5; *KS*, I, 33, 35. *Hassagot* on Alfasi, *Ketubot*, 45a, 48a (השכל והראיה מורים על דברי כאשר פירשתי, והמשכיל יבין) 51a, 59b.
5. *Dibre ha-Ribot*, 35: ולולא כבוד רבותי הייתי אומר בו כי במקל של סומים היו בו כל ימינו, אך עת לכל חפץ תחת השמים וכמה מקומות הניחו לי אבותינו להתגדר בהם . . .
6. E.g., *KS*, I, 15; *TD*, 16; *BH*, 23; see *Hassagot* on Alfasi, *Ketubot*, 21b.

I have received] with the help of God alone who teaches man to understand."[7]

To offset these ostentatious flourishes of vigorous self-reliance, one might point to a few casual expressions of humility and diffidence scattered through his writings. He modestly informs one of his cherished friends that he undertakes to answer his queries "not by virtue of my wisdom, for I am unworthy," and implores him to supplement and correct his statements whenever necessary.[8] To yet another admirer he retorts: "I have seen the letter with your questions and I am unworthy to answer."[9] In one instance he avoids making a practical decision concerning a question of prayer because of his unworthiness.[10] He deftly manipulates Biblical metaphor: "I, Abraham, am but dust and ashes."[11] But these occasional concessions to the literary conventions of humility are not too significant in the total picture. There are those cases where Rabad lavishes praise upon a correspondent, and a measure of calculated diffidence definitely tends to make the praise more effective. In general, instances of Rabad's humility, whether real or feigned, are rare in comparison with their abundance in the writings of his contemporaries, while such uncamouflaged assertions of greatness as appear in the writings of Rabad are scarce in others.[12]

In view of the high premium which Rabad placed on his ability and acumen, it is not fortuitous that he appears as a strident polemicist and so much of his halakic activity is centered in a polemical context. To be sure, the eristic element always played a prominent role in Jewish intellectual development. Polemics have stimulated, immediately or remotely, many important creations in all branches of Jewish literature. In the field of rabbinics, for example, one thinks immediately of the massive critical literature inspired by such writers as Alfasi and Maimonides, or the prolonged literary debate between such rivals as Rashbah

7. אין עמי בכל אלה לא מפי רב ולא מפי מורה כי מעזרת הא־ל לבדו המלמד לאדם דעת. See a similar statement by Rashi, Ezek. 42:3: ואני לא היה לי לא רב ולא עוזר בכל הבנין הזה אלא כמו שהראוני מן השמים. A. J. Levy, Rashi's *Commentary on Ezechiel* (Philadelphia, 1931) omits this phrase. Most manuscripts and early editions, however, have it, as shown by Heschel, "ᶜAl Ruaḥ ha-Ḳodesh," *Alexander Marx Jubilee Volume* (New York, 1949), 193, n. 105.

8. *TD*, 11.

9. *Ibid.*, 51.

10. *MT*, *Tefillah*, III, 10.

11. *KS*, I, 30; see *Hassagot* on Alfasi, *Ketubot*, 38b, 51a.

12. E.g., R. Samuel b. Meïr, *Perush ha-Torah*, Ex. 3:11: מי שרוצה לעמוד על עיקר פשוטו של מקראות הללו ישכיל בפירושי זה, כי הראשונים ממני לא הבינו. Compare on Rashi, I. Repha'el, "Rashi bi-Teshubotaw," *Sefer Rashi*, ed. J. Maimon (Jerusalem, 1956), 573–574.

and R. Aaron ha-Levi of Barcelona. Dissension—in varying degrees of moderation or violence—was always and still remains to a great extent an inextricable element of halakic research and writing. Yet, the constancy of the eristic element notwithstanding, Rabad seems to have set an all-time record in this respect. From his *Issur we-Heter* through his critical annotations on Joseph ibn Plat's famous responsum, his reverent yet forthright critique of Alfasi and his animadversions against Razah and Maimonides, Rabad moved constantly in an arena of controversy and debate. Regardless of whether there were pressing practical implications to the debate or whether the only issue at stake was academic truth and logical exactitude, Rabad saw and stressed the necessity for incessant discussion, qualification, and reevaluation. Only such interminable refinement of views would yield a measure of truth.

Rabad was not only committed to debate in practice but seems to have cultivated a certain theoretical conception of what might be called amicable disagreement, by means of which he justifies his predilection for polemics. In his early epistolary dispute with Razah, Rabad defends his occasional lapse into harshness by presuming to follow a Spanish precedent. He disclaims any intent of personal degradation or *ad hominem* argumentation. Spanish scholars, he avers, "love each other exceedingly but when they debate an halakic issue they appear to be implacable enemies."[13] He assures Razah that he desires their intellectual relationship to be guided by the custom of the Spaniards. It is interesting to note that, although Razah refused to acknowledge the prevalence of such a custom among Spanish scholars,[14] in the introduction to his commentary on *Ḳinnim*, whose sole purpose was to subject Rabad's parallel commentary to a relentless scrutiny, he echoes a similar apology. His objective was to refute those assertions which were logically inadmissible, for "this is the measure of the Torah—love of kindness and paths of peace. The ultimate end of its battles is love and peace."[15] Personal prejudice, he avows, is totally absent. He merely pleads for an objective hearing and evaluation of his views.

This theme is further developed by Rabad in the prefatory remarks

13. *Dibre ha-Ribot*, 30: שהם אוהבים זה לזה ובהוכחם על דבר תורה נראים כאויבים זה לזה. See *Ḳiddushin*, 30b: *Abot de R. Nathan*, ch. 1.

14. *Dibre ha-Ribot*, 47: ומנהגי ספרד שאמרת לא ראיתים ולא שמעתים מעולם שיש בו רעה תחת טובה וקלון תחת כבוד, והמנהג הזה לא לספרדים כי אם לסר פריד הם ש״נ בהם ואיש כי יגע בהם.

15. *Ḳinnim Commentary*, introduction: אכן מה שקשה עלינו בהגיוננו אנחנו משיבין לפניו ואל ישר בעיניו להסתיר פניו ולאטום אזניו ... וכן מדת התורה באהבת חסד ונתיבות שלום וסוף מלחמותיה אהבה ושלום.

to his critique of Alfasi. In a reverent tone, similar to that of Razah toward him, Rabad underscores the ubiquitous need for disagreement. Only for the sake of objectivity and veracity did he vanquish his natural reluctance to cross swords with such an intellectual giant as Alfasi. There were many points on which he could not possibly concur with Alfasi and their mutual cause of "making the Torah great and glorious" would be best served by a frank avowal of their differences.[16] It was the same solicitousness for the cause of independent investigation and reasoning that motivated Rabad's indictment of the *Mishneh Torah* as an arbitrary codification of law which presented the reader with a definitive, monolithic interpretation and implicitly demanded that others relinquish their scholarly prerogative of weighing the cogency of divergent conclusions, assessing the reasoning behind them, and reaching a decision on the basis of independent judgment. Rabad naturally refused to acquiesce in such a scheme and it was this refusal which gave rise to the hassagot.

If Rabad believed this eristic conception to be generally valid and beneficial—witness his approbatory reference to Spanish precedent—it was particularly appropriate for a person of his temperament and intellect. His innate creative faculties, of which he was fully cognizant were supplemented and further nourished by an exemplary assiduousness and total devotion to study. He felt consequently that he was intellectually superior and his tireless efforts in study deserved recognition. In a supposedly sincere tone which nevertheless appears supercilious, he consoles Razah for not being able to compete with him scholastically and for not penetrating into the depth of his statements:

> How much sleep have I kept from my eyes and how much food have I spoiled by not eating it in time as a result of my engagement in the study of Torah. My fat and blood, intestines and heart—I devoted all to it. Consequently, be not angry if you do not overtake me in attention and understanding.[17]

Such unabashed self-commendation and its concomitant spirit of independence understandably made for frequent disagreement—often couched in harsh terms.

One gets the impression, moreover, that this sense of independence and self-esteem was occasionally so extreme that it warped his view of

16. *Hassagot* on Alfasi, *Ketubot*, 14b.
17. *Dibre ha-Ribot*, 31.

the role of polemics and resulted in onesidedness. Being so sure of himself, so confident in his talents and proud of his achievements, he was not inclined to accept criticism supinely. It almost appears as if the polemics were restricted to a one-way route, leading from him to others. He must have been sustained in this feeling by the deferential attitude generally shown him. Consequently, his view on the role of polemics notwithstanding, when some colleagues or disciples differed with him —as, for example, Meïr b. Isaac of Trinquetaille,[18] Razah, or the sages of Béziers[19]—he denounced them forcefully. Such blunt disparagement of colleagues and correspondents did not in the least diminish their reverence and deference to Rabad. They accepted his criticism in stride.[20]

Yet, while he was undoubtedly a proud and powerful person, he was not hard or cantankerous. Much of his apparently excessive stridency of expression must be assigned to conventional stylistic usage. Unreserved criticism, even to the extent of satire and defamation of character, was a commonplace in medieval literature not only among avowed antagonists but also among friends, even relatives.[21]

In addition to this external qualification, the immediate effect of this harshness is offset by the presence of some internal, alleviating factors. Despite the halakic polemics and stylistic belligerency, which usually went hand in hand, Rabad seems to have been eminently fair, "acknowledging the truth and seeking the truth in his heart." Just as his admiration and acceptance are invariably tempered by dissent, so is his criticism flavored with praise and acclamation. He saved many a kind word for Razah and Maimonides. It is almost as if he were allocating what seemed to him to be just proportions of praise and criticism.

Moreover, Rabad possessed that sterling quality of fairness which, according to the Talmud, was responsible for the ultimate acceptance and authoritativeness of the opinions propounded by the school of Hillel against those of the school of Shammai: "what was it that entitled Beth Hillel to have the halakah fixed in agreement with their rulings? Because they . . . studied their own rulings and those of Beth Shammai and even presented those of Beth Shammai before their

18. Ha-Me'iri, *Bet ha-Beḥirah* on *Abot,* 67; see ch. V.
19. *TD*, 113.
20. At first Razah resented this very much. See *Dibre ha-Ribot*, 29: ואני בראשית דברי עשיתי עצמי כאחד מקטני תלמידיך ואתה לקחת הדברים כפשוטן וחרשת על גבי והארכת למעניתך. Later, the stridency is almost assumed; see introduction to his hassagot on *BH*.
21. See Chapter III, §4, and my remarks in *Tarbiz*, XXVI (1956), 220.

own."[22] Rabad did the same. Instead of launching a frontal assault on the position of his adversary, he first fortifies this position by analyzing its foundations. Rather than dismiss the discredited view—whose original formulation might sometimes be inaccessible to the interested student—with a curt reference, Rabad brings a sufficiently lengthy exposition to enable the reader immediately to judge the validity of the conflicting views. In his disagreement with Judah b. Barzilai, Rabad quotes him accurately and impartially.[23] When he sides with Barzilai against his grandfather, he meticulously reproduces the view and supporting arguments of his grandfather.[24] The heart of his essay on the "power of attorney" is prefaced by a neat, objective presentation of the four views already promulgated in this connection.[25] Many hassagot on the *Mishneh Torah* are introduced by a clarification of Maimonides' intention and only subsequently does he register his reservations or dissensions.

He goes one step further. When a writer based his argument on an earlier source which he refers to parenthetically or paraphrases only partially, Rabad fills in all the gaps in the reproduction of this view. Then he attacks it with his usual argumentative skill and demolishes it. For instance, Razah in one place quotes Hai Gaon and with the strength of this reference refutes Alfasi's statement. Rabad, who prefers Alfasi's view and wishes to vindicate it, first amplifies Hai Gaon's statement, which Razah described only cursorily, then demonstrates the superiority of Alfasi's view and does away with Razah's critique.[26] Rabad's attitude toward his halakic opponents, in short, is analogous to that of Ḥasdai Crescas toward his philosophic opponents: "not wishing to appear as if he were arguing in the absence of his opponent, he felt it was necessary for him to present Aristotle's case before trying to demolish it."[27]

This clarification, a gracious gesture of intellectual generosity, is not offered exclusively as a prelude to criticism. Rabad also elaborates and elucidates statements with which he concurs but which he feels are too brief or obscure. For instance, he commends an explanation which Razah adduced for a vague theory of Alfasi, but his own didactic and analytic sense—as well as his sense of fairness—was not satisfied by

22. *ᶜErubin*, 13b.
23. *TD*, 62.
24. *Ibid.*, 12.
25. *Ibid.*, 61.
26. *KS*, I, 51; *Hassagot, Berakot*, 24a.
27. Wolfson, *Crescas' Critique of Aristotle* (Cambridge, Mass., 1929), 3.

Razah's presentation: "He did not illuminate it adequately and one who is not an expert will not benefit from his words."[28] Rabad then supplied the necessary "illumination." He frequently admits that Razah is heading in the right direction but his gropings have to be extended and Rabad extends them.[29] Many more examples are found in his *Mishneh Torah hassagot*.

Another trait, while not contributing directly to the extenuation of harshness in Rabad's writings, acts as a general antidote to his apparent aggressiveness and overconfidence. Though a person of rigid independence and certitude, Rabad took to heart the Talmudic maxim "teach your tongue to admit 'I do not know.'" He was not reluctant, if necessary, to suspend judgment on a problem, ponder over its contents time and again, and display doubt. He admits that he frequently left a subject unsolved for "many days" until new light was shed on it. Sometimes he submitted a tentative explanation which was subsequently revised in the light of further study.[30] He states a well-known difficulty and then adds: "This matter annoyed me for many years until I reflected and observed that the Mishnah nowhere says."[31] In this case it was the sudden abandonment of the stereotype approach to the text which allowed him to resolve the question. In the hassagah on a Maimonidean decision, identical with a similar decision of Alfasi which Rabad had previously refuted, he repeats the grounds of his rejection but continues: "this was our opinion for many years until I noticed again the beginning of the Baraita."[32] This new text led him to reconsider. Finally—and this was the next logical step—he consented to leave a problem in abeyance if no satisfactory solution was forthcoming. In his *Baba Ḳamma* commentary he notes, in passing, that a certain view of Alfasi struck him as problematic, but he does not reveal the nature of the difficulty. Approximately two decades later, in his *Mishneh Torah hassagot*, he indicates what aspects of the view disturbed him—and he candidly admits that he still had found no way to resolve the difficulty.[33] He simply does not know.

There is also in Rabad—as he reveals himself in his theoretical con-

28. *KS*, I, 10: טוב הוא הפירוש אבל הוא לא האיר אותו כל צורך ומי שאינו בקי לא יועיל מדבריו.
29. *Ibid.*, I, 19, 20, and others; also *Hassagot*, *Sukkah*, 12a.
30. *KS*, II, 25; Rabad, *BK*, 61.
31. *Ibid.*, 110.
32. *MT*, *Shabbat*, XXV, 13; see also *Hassagot*, *Pesaḥim*, 10a.
33. Rabad, *BK*, 68; *MT*, *Ḥobel u-Mazik̦*, VII, 11. See also *Sifra Commentary*, 87b: ונפלאה דעת ממני נשגבה לא אוכל לה עד יבא ויורה צדק לנו.

ceptions and attitudes—a sustained, therefore significant, tendency to moderation. This dynamic person, outspoken and uncompromising, confident and determined, adopted a moderate stand as often as he did an extremist position. It is whimsical to dismiss Rabad as a Spartan halakist, rigidly exacting and doctrinaire. He was often a liberalizing influence, advocating greater latitude in observance or more lenient interpretation of the law.

The same is true in the realm of thought and *anschauung*; in the regrettably scarce comments on or allusions to philosophical and ethical problems, there is marked, even preponderating moderation. For example, when seen in perspective, his polemical comments on the question of anthropomorphism espouse an intermediate, conciliatory view. There were three possibilities. The uncompromising rationalists insisted upon the unequivocal propagation of the abstract God-idea, free of all corporeal allusions. They contended that none of the anthropomorphic or anthropopathic expressions in Scripture were to be interpreted literally. Anyone who is misled by the literal sense of certain Scriptural verses into accepting divine corporeality has fallen into notorious error, bordering on outright heresy. On the other hand, a small group of simple-minded traditionalists and extreme literalists maintained that belief in the corporeality of God was a perfectly sound doctrine. Scriptural passages and rabbinic homilies abound in descriptions of God in terms of qualities, affections, and emotions characteristic of human beings and under no circumstances is such a belief to be considered reprehensible. The majority of medieval thinkers held an intermediate view. Anthropomorphic attributes were used metaphorically, to vivify the subject matter and facilitate its comprehension. Belief in the corporeality of God was certainly absurd. However, any person who accepts such anthropomorphic statements literally as a result of his inability to think in abstract terms or professes a belief in the corporeality of God because he cannot extricate himself from materialistic conceptions should not be condemned. To each according to his intellectual comprehension and rational faculties. This moderate view was shared by Rabad.[34]

Rabad's ethical views, as sketched in the *Shaᶜar ha-Ḳedushah* of the *Baᶜale ha-Nefesh*, are also realistic and moderate.[35] There is no extreme

34. *Ibid.*, *Teshubah*, III, 7; see Chapter VI, §2.

35. *BH*, 81, 87, and others. Note especially the three-fold classification of motives or intentions which elevate and legitimatize sexual intercourse; see page 92, n. 157.

pietism nor are demands made for any form of asceticism. He tacitly assents to Maimonides' repeated formulations of the golden mean theory.[36] In depicting the interminable conflict which goes on in man between good and evil as a conflict between the irrational soul and the rational soul or between the evil imagination and the good imagination, Rabad employs the conventional terminology found in medieval philosophy.[37] Carnal appetites—the discussion centers for the most part on sexual indulgences—are to be satisfied within a framework of "eudaemonistic prudence." Lust is to be regulated, not extirpated; virtue means control, not extinction. Even in the nonascetic school, Rabad's attitude must be considered quite latitudinarian.

A very sententious animadversion against Maimonides affirms the same general moderation and earthly realism in matters of psychology and human conduct. In his enumeration of negative commandments, Maimonides includes the following: "That soldiers be not afraid nor fear their enemies in time of war, for it is said 'Be ye not affrighted at them.'" Rabad adds: "This is a promise, not an admonition."[38] It seems that Maimonides demands from man full and unconditional control of his emotions. Man must put a distance between himself and his emotions; he must be able, if necessary, to overcome his innermost drives. This is better understood in light of Maimonides' view concerning transgressions committed under compulsion or duress.[39] If man sins because of external compulsion—physical pressure, for instance—then not only is the deed not punishable but the doer is fully exonerated; if, however, man sins because of inner emotional fears or psychological weakness, the deed is not actually punishable but is considered theoretically culpable. Emotional pressures, which should be subject to control, are not as extenuating as physical pressures. Rabad obviously feels that such totalitarian control and self-discipline are unrealistic and unattainable. Man is not an automaton. Consequently, it seems improbable that Scripture should simply admonish man not to be afraid in battle and even couch this admonition in terms of a negative commandment, similar to such injunctions as not to desecrate God's name or not to forget the evil doings of Amalek. Rabad submits that "thou shalt

36. *MT*, *Deᶜot*, *passim*.
37. *BH*, 3, 80; see *Ḥobot ha-Lebabot*, ed. A. Zifroni, 245; Abraham ibn Ezra, *Commentary* on Ex. 23:25 and, generally, Wolfson, *Philo*, II, 268 ff.
38. *MT*, *Miẓwot Lo Taᶜaseh*, 58; see also *Melakim*, VII, 15; Naḥmanides repeats Rabad's comment: Bible Commentary, *Deut.*, 20:4.
39. *MT*, *Yesode ha-Torah*, V.

not be affrighted at them" must be understood as a benevolent promise and divine commitment.

More illustrations of this sort, lifted from exegetical or halakic contexts,[40] are readily forthcoming but should not be cited loosely, for they may not always reflect cherished personal views. They frequently stem from compelling interpretative reasons rather than personal bias or conviction. One must proceed cautiously in the correlation of personal character traits with opinions expressed in the course of halakic discussion. What can presumably be asserted is that the presence of so many instances of moderation, especially in nonhalakic contexts, modifies further the picture of a perpetually frowning scholar, possessed of a harsh temperament and extremist tendencies.

In conclusion, Rabad's harshness was essentially a literary mannerism and did not too seriously affect personal relations. He can be envisaged as a poignant personality, caustic and witty, an individual of astounding force and energy, totally committed to rabbinic scholarship, confident in his erudition, firm in his convictions, weighty in his influence, but this did not isolate him or prevent his "disposition from being pleasant with people."

5. *Influence*

The one indisputable, self-evident generalization to be inferred from a study of Rabad's life and activities is his importance for his generation; the forthcoming description and evaluation of Rabad's works will, in turn, underscore the importance of his legacy for successive generations. It almost seems gratuitous to proclaim that in terms of Jewish learning, he was a seminal personality.

His influence on contemporaries was profound. I have specified various forms of Rabad's influence on his disciples, as well as the general stimulus which he provided for colleagues, correspondents, and casual acquaintances who eagerly awaited his decisions and opinions.[1] This was true, moreover, not only of devoted admirers but of antagonists and dissenters as well. It is all too natural that a former pupil, finding himself on one occasion at academic loggerheads with Rabad, should still retain a reverential attitude while pressing his own view.[2] It is more

40. E.g., *MT*, *Ḳeri'at Shema*, IV, 7 (see *Tosafot*, *Berakot*, 16b); *Zekiyah u-Matanah*, III, 8; *TD*, 56.

1. See Chapter V.

2. Ha-Me'iri, *Bet ha-Beḥirah* on *Abot*, 67.

revealing that a former classmate, finding himself almost always on the other side of the fence from Rabad, should consistently respect him and designate him as his master and mentor. In one place he refers to him as "a just and righteous teacher of the Oral and Written Law . . . whose wisdom I crave." [3] In another place, after invoking the Biblical metaphor "blessed be Abraham of God most high" and reiterating the epithet of "just and righteous teacher," he requests that Rabad lend an ear to "the words of his children and disciples." [4] All this is comprehensible only in light of the pervasive esteem in which Rabad was held and the widespread influence which his learning achieved.

The final and all-inclusive testimony of reverence—a most symbolic act of appreciation—which his contemporaries rendered him was upon his death. Solomon ibn Virga reports that in 1198 "the great luminary Abraham b. David was summoned before the divine court" and *kohanim*, who were enjoined against all impurity stemming from contact with the dead, dug his grave.[5] Now, the Talmud relates that kohanim dug the grave of R. Judah *ha-Nasi* (the prince or Patriarch), about whom it was said that "on the day of Rabbi's death sanctity ceased to exist." [6] In connection with this Talmudic statement, R. Ḥayyim ha-Kohen, a prominent thirteenth-century Tosafist, expressed his boundless reverence for his great master R. Tam by proclaiming that "were I present when R. Tam passed away, I would have made myself ritually impure (by contact with his corpse)." [7] Maimonides formulated the following law: "If a *nasi* [prince, i.e. the acknowledged head of the Jewish people] dies, all, even the kohanim, must make themselves ritually impure for him . . . because it is the bounden duty of all to pay him respect." [8] The interment of Rabad by kohanim is therefore an extraordinary symbol of esteem and approbation for a beloved leader who led a life of inspirational sanctity and exemplary morality and an outstanding scholar who dominated the field of halakic learning in his day.

3. Razah, *Hassagot* on *BH*, 7; note the longer form of this statement as quoted by J. Sambary in Neubauer, *Medieval Jewish Chronicles*, I, 125.

4. Introduction to *Ḳinnim Commentary*; see Gen. 14:20.

5. *Shebet Yehudah*, 146–147. Note also ha-Me'iri's report that the *kohanim* of Narbonne insisted on yielding their prerogative to Rabad, urging him to precede them in the public reading of the Torah; see *Giṭṭin*, 59b, *Bet ha-Beḥirah* on *Giṭṭin* (Jerusalem, 1943), 248.

6. *Ketubot*, 103b.

7. *Tosafot*, *ibid.*; see Urbach, *Baᶜale ha-Tosafot*, 96, n. 40. Perhaps the kohanim in question here are also disciples of Rabad, for he counted among his disciples such scholars as Jonathan ha-Kohen, Isaac ha-Kohen, and perhaps also Samuel ha-Kohen.

8. *MT*, *Abel*, III, 10.

That this influence continued posthumously can be ascertained both directly—by collecting overt references—and indirectly—by buoying up latent influences and unexpressed indebtedness. An historiographical register compiled from the annals of chroniclers, the statements of Talmudists, and even the evaluations of modern historians would provide a clear indication of the extent, nature, and durability of his influence. The number, importance, and representativeness of the names to be entered on this register as well as the quality of their comments would speak volumes. The documentation of this register could be elaborated and its purview extended by tracing the less tangible, unacknowledged influences of Rabad's works—that is, by projecting into relief the prototypal quality of some of his works which hovered over so much of subsequent halakic study. To determine the full measure of Rabad's influence in general or his impact on an individual scholar or a particular school, both methods of investigation must be applied. Naḥmanides, for instance, states his admiration quite eloquently and unambiguously, but the genuine nature and full extent of his indebtedness to Rabad transcend these explicit references. Similarities in opinion, especially in halakic reasoning and exegetical method, must be studied and appraised. Similarly, Rabad's impact on the subsequent codification of Jewish law was substantial and is readily discernible, but there is more than immediately meets the eye. Not all the components of his legacy in this field are overtly identified or explicitly attributed to him. The accurate gauge will depend on a correlation of the latent as well as the visible elements.

Starting with the eyewitness report of Benjamin of Tudela[9] and the passage contained in the first, anonymous, supplement to Abraham ibn Daud's *Sefer ha-Kabbalah*,[10] there is hardly a chronicler—professional or incidental, i.e. one who prefaced a rabbinic or philosophic work with an historical survey—who does not take note of Rabad and underscore his greatness. The list practically exhausts Jewish historiography through the ages: Menaḥem ha-Me'iri,[11] David of Estella,[12] Isaac de Lattes,[13] Isaac b. Joseph Israeli,[14] Ḥasdai Crescas,[15] Joseph b. Ẓaddik of Arevalo,[16] Abraham b. Solomon of Torrutiel,[17] Abraham b. Samuel

9. *Itinerary*, 4.
10. Neubauer, *REJ*, X (1885), 102; reprinted in *Medieval Jewish Chronicles*, I, 84.
11. *Bet ha-Beḥirah* on *Abot*, 66 ff.; *Magen Abot*, 135.
12. *Ḳiryath Sefer* in Neubauer, *Chronicles*, II, 231.
13. *Shaᶜare Zion*, ed. S. Buber (Jaroslau, 1885), 39; also Neubauer, *Chronicles*, II, 236.
14. *Yesod ᶜOlam*, 2, V (Berlin, 1878), II, 35.
15. *Or Adonai*, 21.
16. *Zeker Ẓaddiḳ* in Neubauer, *Chronicles*, I, 94.
17. *Supplement to Sefer ha-Kabbalah, ibid.*, 102.

Zacuto,[18] Solomon ibn Virga,[19] Azariah dei Rossi,[20] Azriel Trabotto,[21] Gedalyah ibn Yaḥya,[22] Joseph Solomon del Medigo,[23] David Ganz,[24] Joseph Sambary,[25] David Ḳonforte,[26] Jeḥiel Heilprin,[27] and Ḥayyim Azulai.[28] Such an assortment of references to the "greatest rabbi," "the shining light," "great sage," "one whose wisdom filled the entire land," "the abundance of his wisdom," "one who is singled out as unique among the rabbis," "the greatest commentator," "the rock whence we were hewn and the hole of the pit whence we were digged," "the great rabbi . . . all of whose words are sweet and very reasonable" underscores the cumulative reverence and appreciation which permeate this list. Some merely echo their predecessors' comments or paraphrase them with slight variations, but all felt compelled to mention him regardless of the extensiveness or restrictiveness of their survey. Sometimes just the amount of space devoted to Rabad in a cursory or compressed account, such as the *Ḳiryat Sefer* of David of Estella, is itself an indication of the importance attached to him.

Another section of our register must be allocated to rabbinic scholars who praised Rabad, borrowed from him, or were stimulated by him. That Provençal sages, practically without exception, remained in the orbit of his influence was to be expected; even during his own lifetime he could assert accurately if immodestly: "this is the custom in all Provence, in accord with what we have said."[29] The writings of his disciples and intimate contemporaries—people like Jonathan ha-Kohen and Asher b. Saul, who were the outstanding personalities in Provence at the turn of the century and embodied the learning of their time—amply testify to this fame. He was designated as "the sage of our generation" by Isaac b. Abba Mari of Marseilles[30] and as "the greatest among the judges" by an unidentified Provençal writer.[31] The *Sefer ha-*

18. *Yuḥasin ha-Shalem*, ed. Filipowski (London, 1857), 120.
19. *Shebet Yehudah*, 146, 221.
20. *Me'or ᶜEnayim* (Vilna, 1863); *Imre Binah*, 114; *Yeme ᶜOlam*, 110; *Maẓref le-Kesef*, 13, 25, 62.
21. Kaufmann, "Liste de Rabbins," *REJ*, IV, 212.
22. *Shalshelet ha-Kabbalah* (Warsaw, 1877), 57–58.
23. *Maẓref le-Ḥokmah* (Warsaw, 1890), 42, 66, 79, 90, 121; *Nobelot Ḥokmah*, p. 5 of unnumbered introduction, 195b.
24. *Ẓemaḥ David* (Frankfurt, 1692), 39b.
25. *Liḳḳuṭim Midibre Yosef* in Neubauer, *Chronicles*, I, 124–125.
26. *Ḳore ha-Dorot* (Pietrekov, 1895), 20.
27. *Seder ha-Dorot* (Warsaw, 1876), 149.
28. *Shem ha-Gedolim* (Warsaw, 1878), 4.
29. *TD*, 113.
30. *Sefer ha-ᶜIṭṭur*, II, 21.
31. *TD*, 206; see Gross, 403, n. 2.

Hashlamah of Meshullam b. Moses,[32] the hassagot of R. Moses ha-Kohen,[33] the *Sefer ha-Menuḥah* of R. Manoah,[34] the *Sefer ha-Miktam* of R. David b. Levi,[35] the *Sefer ha-Tamid* of Reuben b. Ḥayyim,[36] the *Sefer ha-Shalman* of R. Meshullam b. Gershom,[37] the *Orḥot Ḥayyim* of R. Aaron ha-Kohen,[38] the anonymous *Kol-Bo,*[39] the *Bet ha-Beḥirah* of ha-Me'iri,[40] the *Toledot Adam we-Ḥawah* of R. Jeruḥam b. Meshullam,[41]—all the major rabbinic works of Provençal provenance down to the fourteenth-century expulsions, which terminated the physical as well as the spiritual life of the Franco-Jewish communities, bear Rabad's imprint in such matters as method, purpose, or bulk of quotations.

In this respect Provence serves as a microcosm for all rabbinic literature. Scholars of Franco-Germany, Spain, North Africa, Italy, Palestine, Slavic countries—scholars from literally all corners of the Jewish pale of settlement—knew, studied, and esteemed Rabad. His name or teachings come to the fore in the *Tosafot,*[42] in the works of R. Meïr of Rothenburg,[43] the *Hagahot Maimuniyot,*[44] the Sens commentaries,[45] the pseudepigraphic commentary on *Nedarim* attributed to R. Eleazar of Metz[46] and that on the *Sifra* attributed to R. Samson

32. On *Berakot*, ed. H. Brody (Berlin, 1893), 6, 7, 11, 13, 16, 17, 18, 19, 24, 25; *Seder Neziḳin*, ed. Lubozky (Paris, 1885), introduction, XVII, and *passim*; *Taᶜanit and Megillah*, ed. J. Grossberg (Mayenne, 1888), 238, 239, 245, 248, 250.

33. On *MT*, *Sefer ha-Madda*, *Sefer Ahabah*, and *Hilkot Shabbat*, ed. S. Atlas, *HUCA*, XXVII (1956), 1–98, esp. 2, 14, 23, 36, 39, 47, 59, 75.

34. *Sefer ha-Menuḥah* (Pressburg, 1879), 4a, 6a, 8b, 9b, 13a, 13b, 17b, 19b, 22a, 22b, 24b, 25b, 28a, 28b, 29b, 30a, 30b, and innumerable others.

35. *Sefer ha-Miktam* (on *Sukkah*, *Beẓah*, *Moᶜed Ḳaṭan*, *Pesaḥim*), introduction, VIII. Also the copious quotations ר׳ דוד בשם הראב״ד in the *Orḥot Ḥayyim*; see *Sefer ha-Miktam* on *Megillah*, ed. M. Grossberg (Lemberg, 1904), VI ff.

36. See ha-Me'iri, *Bet ha-Beḥirah* on *Abot*, 69; fragments from *Sefer ha-Tamid*, ed. J. M. Toledano, supplement to *Oẓar ha-Ḥayyim*, VII (1931).

37. See *ha-Me'iri*, *Bet ha-Behirah* on *Abot*, 69; *Sefer ha-Menuḥah*, 17b, and *Sefer ha-Miktam* on *Beẓah*, 223.

38. *Sefer Toledot Adam we-Ḥawah* (Kapust, 1808), 18, 26a, 28b, 29a, 29b, 30a, 31a, 32a, 37a, and others.

39. See Index, *Orḥot Ḥayyim* (Berlin, 1902), II.

40. E.g., *Kol Bo* (Lemberg, 1860), 11, 23, 48 (eighteen times); see also Tchernowitz, *Toledot ha-Posḳim*, II, 253. On the relation between the *Kol Bo* and the *Orḥot Ḥayyim*, see Schlesinger, Introduction to *Orḥot Ḥayyim*, II, 24.

41. Under the title גדולי המפרשים, גדולי המגיהים, *passim.*

42. *Taᶜanit*, 25a; *Yomah* 18b; *Temurah* 12b; *Yebamot* 5a; *ᶜAbodah Zarah* 38a.

43. *Hilkot Semaḥot* (Livorno, 1789); see, for example, sec. 73; also 32, 35, 80, 81, 84; *Responsa* (Prague), 947; (Cremona), 81; (Lemberg), 228; see Tchernowitz, *Toledot ha-Posḳim*, III, 367.

44. E.g., *MT*, *Issure Bi'ah*, XXI, 9, and *passim.*

45. On *ᶜEduyot*, II, 9; III, 1, 3, 9; see Gross, *REJ*, VII (1883), 61, n. 2; Zunz, *Zur Geschichte und Literatur* (Berlin, 1845), 565; Gross, 540.

46. *MGWJ*, XXXIV (1875), 506; *GJ*, 349.

of Sens[47] as well as that on *Tamid* attributed to Rabad himself,[48] the massive compendium of R. Mordecai b. Hillel[49]—the outstanding rabbinic works produced in France and Germany during their most creative period.[50] Naḥmanides,[51] the latter's anonymous disciples,[52] Samuel b. Isaac ha-Sardi,[53] Rashbah,[54] Baḥya b. Asher,[55] Asher b. Yeḥiel,[56] his son Jacob b. Asher,[57] Menaḥem Recanati,[58] Nissim Gerondi,[59] Isaac b. Sheshet Perfet,[60] David b. Joseph Abudarham,[61] Ẓedekiah b. Abraham ᶜAnaw,[62] David b. Zimra,[63] Moses Alashkar,[64] David b. Judah Meser Leon,[65] Joseph Kolon,[66] Beẓalel Ashkenazi,[67] Joseph Karo,[68] Menaḥem Azariah Fano[69]—these are only some of the more illustrious, representative members of the rabbinic constellation during the later Middle Ages—especially of the Spanish and Italian schools—who occupy prominent places in our register. The list might be augmented by including such names as Solomon Luria[70] and Moses Isserles[71] as representatives of an entire generation of east-European

47. Urbach, *Baᶜale ha-Tosafot*, 260 ff.

48. Z. Frankel, *Darke ha-Mishnah*, 333; Urbach, *Baᶜale ha-Tosafot*, 294 ff.

49. S. Kohn, *Mardochai ben Hillel*, 99.

50. See Reifmann, *Arbaᶜah Ḥarashim* (Prague, 1860), 8, for one (Cracow) version of the *Sefer Ḥasidim* which contains a substantial interpolation from the *BH*. Many later works could also be cited; e.g., R. Jacob Landau, *Sefer ha-Agur* (Venice, 1546), 95, 836, 886, 991; R. Israel Isserlein, *Terumat ha-Deshen* (Venice, 1519).

51. Introduction to *Sefer ha-Zekut*; *Hilkot Niddah*; and throughout his writings.

52. E.g., *Perush Talmid ha-Ramban le-Masseket Taᶜanit*, ed. J. Hoffman (New York, 1941). Rabad is the most oft-quoted source. See the extensive review and discussion of sources by Benedict, *Ḳiryath Sefer*, XXIX (1954), 391–429.

53. *Sefer ha-Terumot, passim*; see the list compiled by Gross, 403, n. 2; also Tchernovitz, *Toledot ha-Poskim*, II, 135–137.

54. *Torat ha-Bayit, passim*, especially introduction to *Bet ha-Nashim*; *Ḥiddushe ha-Rashbah ᶜal Masseket Niddah* (Jerusalem, 1938), *passim* under "piske hilkot ha-Rabad." *Responsa* of Rashbah, 53, 344, 669; see also Tchernovitz, *Toledot ha-Poskim*, II, 119–120.

55. *Perush ᶜal ha-Torah* (Pisaro, 1507), sections *Ki Tisa*, *Shemini*, *Aḥare Mot*, *Re'eh*.

56. *Halakot, passim*; *Responsa* (Venice, 1552), *Kelal* 94, 5.

57. *Ṭur, passim.*

58. *Sefer Recanati*: *Piske Halakot* (Sedilkow, 1836), 8a, 10b, 24a, 25b, 32b.

59. Commentary on Alfasi, *passim*. *Responsa* (Königsberg, 1840), 7, 49, 57, 64.

60. Hershman, *Rabbi Isaac b. Sheshet Perfet*, 83.

61. *Sefer Abudarham* (Warsaw, 1877), 8, 10, 42, 48, 58, 77, and others.

62. *Shibbale ha-Leḳeṭ ha-Shalem*, ed. Buber (Vilna, 1886), introduction, 8.

63. *Responsa*, 267; Commentary on *MT*, *passim*; *Yeḳar Tiferet*, ed. S. B. Werner (Jerusalem, 1945).

64. E.g., *Responsa* (Sabbionetta, 1554), 29, 50, 58.

65. *Kebod Ḥakamim*, ed. S. Bernfeld (Berlin, 1899), 114, 120.

66. *Responsa* (Lemberg, 1798), 100.

67. *Responsa* (Venice, 1595), 1 (p. 12); *Shiṭṭah Meḳubbeẓet, passim.*

68. *Bet Joseph, passim;* e.g., *Ṭur Yoreh Deᶜah*, 29 f.; *Kesef Mishneh*, introduction.

69. *Responsa*, 108.

70. *Yam shel Shelomoh*, *Ḥullin*, introduction.

71. *Darke Mosheh* and *Mappah*, *passim.*

codifiers and commentators. One might easily add scores of names from the subsequent generations of *Aḥaronim* whose prime task was to comprehend and interpret the writings of their predecessors (*Rishonim*), among whom Rabad was preeminent.

The vestiges of this influence are not uniform; they vary in quantity and intensity. The Tosafists, for instance, simply quote Rabad and discuss his views, the nature of the *Tosafot* excluding any personal remarks or eulogistic digressions. The same is true for the *Sefer ha-Ḥinnuk* of R. Aaron ha-Levi of Barcelona, which has only a number of casual references to Rabad's views without any honorific comments.[72] There are cases, however, where the bulk of quotations and references —minus eulogistic digressions—is itself more expressive than explicit evaluations and acknowledgments. The Sens Tosafot, for instance, nowhere elaborate Rabad's praises, but his influence permeates their contents. As a matter of fact, he is mentioned so frequently in these Tosafot on *ᶜEduyot* that Zunz was led to believe, erroneously, that these must have been composed in thirteenth-century Provence. Similarly, he is the most oft-quoted scholar in the *Orḥot Ḥayyim* of R. Aaron ha-Kohen, and is "foremost among Provençal authorities" consulted by Isaac b. Sheshet Perfet. These are cases where statistics speak clearer than words.

Most of those listed, however, found occasion actually to record their esteem, not only to illustrate it. For example, Naḥmanides, in addition to the many objective references similar to those found in the Tosafot and the other works just mentioned, speaks more elaborately of Rabad as "the saintly scholar" and "the most illustrious rabbi" and describes his erudition and piety with awe. Rashbah, explaining the omission of certain laws from his *Torat ha-Bayit*—which often reads like an elaboration of the *Baᶜale ha-Nefesh*—observes that "there previously arose a saintly person, the great rabbi Rabad and amply explained these laws. And who will come after the king to attempt that which he has already done. He has refined and purified, revealed unfathomed depths of the law as if from the mouth of Moses, and explained that which is difficult."[73] R. David b. Zimra, author of a commentary on the *Mishneh Torah* designed to refute Rabad's hassagot, depicts Rabad as "a mighty

72. *Sefer ha-Ḥinnuk* (Jerusalem, 1952), 241, 263, 496.

73. *Torat ha-Bayit, Bet ha-Nashim*, introduction: שכבר עמד אחד קדוש הרב הגדול ר׳ אברהם ברבי דוד ז״ל וביאר עניניהם ביאור רב, ומי יבא אחרי המלך את אשר כבר עשה וזקק וטהר כמפי משה גולה עמוקות ופירש את הקשה. Later, however, Rashbah changed his mind and decided to include these laws by adding another section (בית המים) to the *Torat ha-Bayit*. See Bet Joseph on *Ṭur Yoreh Deᶜah*, 201[3]: והרשב״א . . . כתב שלא רצה לשלוח יד בדיני מקואות

elm who needs no support, for he is an expert in the entire Talmud, both Babylonian and Palestinian, *Sifra*, *Sifre*, *Tosefta*." He charges many Maimonidean followers with inadequate comprehension of Rabad's hassagot and flighty dismissal of his intended criticisms.[74] This indicates incidentally that defense and explication of the *Mishneh Torah* are not to be equated with a negative, downgrading attitude to Rabad. It was rather their high regard for Rabad which prompted such scholars as David b. Zimra and Vidal of Tolosa to rehabilitate Maimonides and bolster his code. There is not a Maimonidean commentator who is not by the same token a close student of Rabad.

A third part of our register might consist of entries from modern historians who have come into contact with Rabad. It would start with names like Graetz, Geiger, Luzzato, Jost, Zunz, Frankel, Weiss, Gross, Reifmann, Guedeman, Auerbach, Renan-Neubauer, Michael, Yavetz, Dubnow, Tchernowitz, Drachmann, and end with Albeck, Assaf, Atlas, Baron, Benedict, Bergmann, Freimann, Marx and Scholem—some of whom have yet to say their final word.[75] The nearly consensual verdict of all these critical scholars—regardless of various shades of criticism and personal bias—underscores Rabad's importance. Some may criticize or condemn him but all start and end with a Talmudist of towering stature.

Such references are only part of a record which is much more extensive. This may be illustrated in a number of ways: first, by selecting one prominent Talmudist, Naḥmanides—similar pictures could be painted with regard to many others—and trying to sketch a complete picture of influence and indebtedness.

Naḥmanides eulogizes Rabad in considerable detail on two occasions. In the introduction to his *Hilkot Niddah* he reports that he advised some "God-fearing" colleagues who petitioned him to compose a certain book as follows: "Seek from the book of the Lord and read it attentively, for not one of the laws is missing therein. There has already preceded me a saintly scholar for whom it is fitting to expound the law and

---

לפי שסמך על מ״ש הראב״ד זל, ומ״מ מצינו בקצת ספרי ת״ה אחר גמר הבית הז׳ כתובים דיני מקואות ונקובים בשם שער המים. This was discovered and edited—in the short and long versions—by D. S. Löwinger, "Bet ha-Mayim la-Rashbah," *ha-Ẓofeh le-Ḥokmat Yisrael*, XIV (1930), 363–374, and "Shaʿar ha-Mayim," *ha-Soḳer*, I (1933), 7–37.

74. See his commentary on *MT*, ʿ*Abadim*, IX, 3. Even against the *Kesef Mishneh*, he says: ראיתי מי שכתב על השגת הראב״ד ··· וגם את זה אני חושד שלא הבין כונת השגת הראב״ד. See *Yeḳar Tif'eret*, 20. Similarly, R. Moses Alashkar described Maimonides as the greatest of all codifiers but fully appreciated the value of the hassagot: ומה שאמרתם שהראבד ז״ל לא השיג על הרמב״ם ז״ל בזה, ודאי, דאין דרך הראבד ז״ל להשיג האמת. See his *Responsa*, 23, 26.

75. See the bibliography for complete references.

he composed a noteworthy book on this subject." He prefaces his *Sefer ha-Zekut* with a resounding declaration of homage to Rabad: "In truth, oh Lord, my loins are filled with convulsion and my pen and paper shake in my hands as a reed shakes in water, for I know the excellence of that man in wisdom and his greatness in fear of God." Once struck, this keynote continues to reverberate; throughout this work, with consistent reverence, he separates himself from Rabad as a disciple from a master.

Such praise is not empty hyperbole. Naḥmanides must have been a close student of Rabad's writings, for his own works are saturated with halakic concepts and methods familiar from Rabad. First of all, Naḥmanides was a member of that school of critico-conceptual study which Rabad in southern France and the Tosafists in northern France simultaneously initiated;[76] it might be noted that Naḥmanides not only lauds Rabad but often extols "our French masters," thus being one of the very first Spanish sages unreservedly to place himself in the French orbit.[77] Like Rabad, Naḥmanides was a keen analyst and Talmudic logician, dissecting problems, posing questions, defining concepts, integrating and differentiating topics. Furthermore, many halakic theories and exegetical comments submitted by Rabad appear in Naḥmanides' writings. Many are quoted expressly; Rabad's name is practically ubiquitous in Naḥmanides' commentaries and novellae. In fact, some of his smaller, independent works even seem to be patterned after Rabad's writings. The *Hilkot Niddah* is avowedly indebted to Rabad. Study of his more important *Torat ha-Adam*, a compendium on laws of mourning, reveals that this also, to a great extent, is built around quotations from Rabad and their discussion. The core of practically every section consists of an analysis of Rabad's view.[78] Whether these quoted passages were extracted from a separate work of Rabad—similar to the *Baᶜale ha-Nefesh*—or were collected by Naḥmanides from scattered sources in commentaries and response cannot be ascertained. In light of the fact that most Rishonim refer to Rabad quite frequently in this area—the analogous, almost contemporaneous compendium (*Hilkot Semaḥot*) of R. Meïr of Rothenburg also revolves around a minute analysis of Rabad's teachings[79]—one might conjecturally posit the

76. See pages 62 ff.

77. *Ḥiddushim, Baba Batra*, end: הם המורים הם המלמדים הם המגלים לנו כל נטמן. See also *Ḥiddushim* to *Berakot* 50a; *Ḥullin*, 94a.

78. *Torat ha-Adam* (Venice, 1598), *passim.*

79. See §5, note 43. Note also, e.g., the bulk of references to and quotations from Rabad in the four commentaries on *Moᶜed Ḳaṭan*, Harry Fischel Institute Publications,

existence of a lost work on *Hilkot Abelut*. In any case, Rabad's influence on Naḥmanides' *Torat ha-Adam* is extensive enough to warrant the assumption of its conscious dependence on him.

While many citations are provided with proper references, others remain anonymous or unacknowledged. Rabad's tentative formulation of a definition for the concept of "indirect damage" (gerama), for instance, underlies Naḥmanides' more definitive elaboration;[80] Rabad's theories on the various ways of retracting vows,[81] degrees of impurity stemming from corpse uncleanness,[82] degrees of sanctity in the high priesthood[83]—these and many others are repeated by Naḥmanides. In the realm of exegesis, Rabad's original explanations of terms like *biḳḳoret*[84] and *pilegesh*,[85] objects such as "myrrh,"[86] phrases like "thou

---

Section III (Rishonim), I (Jerusalem, 1937). Also, *Ḥiddushe ha-Ritba ᶜal Moᶜed Ḳaṭan*, ed. Ch. Bloch (New York, 1935), and now the *Sefer ha-Miktam*, ed. A. Sofer, 265–350, copiously annotated. Also, Ha-Me'iri, *Bet ha-Beḥirah* on *Moᶜed Ḳaṭan* ch. III, and *Orḥot Ḥayyim*, II, 561–602, cite many new views in the name of Rabad.

80. *MT*, *Ḥobel u-Maziḳ*, VII, 7; *Baba Batra*, 22b, and *Tosafot*; Naḥmanides, *Ḥiddushim*, *Baba Batra* (*Dina de-garme*).

81. *MT*, *Shebuᶜot*, VI, 12; see *Kesef Mishneh*, *ad. loc.*

82. *MT*, *Tume'at Met*. XII, 6 (see also *ibid.*, III, 3, and *Nezirut* VII, 1); Naḥmanides Bible Commentary, Numbers 19:16; see *Sefer ha-Hashlamah* on *Berakot*, ed. H. Brody, 11.

83. *MT*, *Bi'at Miḳdash*, II, 5; Naḥmanides Bible Commentary, Levit. 10:6.

84. *ᶜEduyot* Commentary, IV, 3; Naḥmanides Bible Commentary, Levit. 19:20. For the traditional explanation, see *Keritot*, 11a; *Targum Onkelos* and Jonathan b. Uziel, Levit. 19:20; Abraham ibn Ezra, Bible Commentary, *ad. loc.* Naḥmanides points out that this explanation has been repeated by "all the commentators." In his *Sifra Commentary*, 89b, Rabad also adopts this explanation. Rabad arrived at his novel interpretation by identifying "biḳḳoret" with "piḳḳoret." The interchangeability of "pe" and "bet" is a basic lexicographical principle for Rabad; cf. *MT*, *Ṭume'at Met*, XIV, 7; *Shabbat*, IX, 20, where he equates "boẓeᶜa" with "poẓeᶜa." On "pe" and "bet" as interchangeable consonants in Hebrew and Aramaic, see N. Torczyner, *Ha Lashon weha-Sefer* (Jerusalem, 1948), I, 367–371. Rabad also knows of the interchangeability of "ᶜayin" and "ḥet" (*Sifra Commentary*, 88b; see *Mekilta*, I, 571), "dalet" and "taw" (*Sifra Commentary*, 76b), "zayin" and "samek" (*BH*, 75); see Joseph Kimḥi, *Sefer ha-Zikkaron*, ed. W. Bacher (Berlin, 1888), 2. Naḥmanides reproduces precisely this explanation without even alluding to Rabad. Even though his first proof text for the identity of biḳḳoret and piḳḳoret is the passage in *ᶜEduyot* concerning which Rabad initially advanced his suggestion, Naḥmanides introduces the entire matter by "I am of the opinion . . ." This has led many to overlook the original source and to credit Naḥmanides with the discovery of this explanation; see, for example, *ha-Maggid*, XII (1868), 373, *Oẓar Neḥmad*, IV (1864), 541.

85. *MT*, *Ishut*, I, 4, and *Naᶜarah Betulah*, II, 17; Naḥmanides, Gen. 25.6, and *Teshubot Rashbah ha-Meyuḥasot la-Ramban*, 284 (quoted also by Menaḥem b. Zeraḥ, *Ẓedah la-Derek* [Warsaw, 1880], 136 [*Ma'amar* III, *kelal*, I); see L. M. Epstein, *Marriage Laws in the Bible and the Talmud* (Cambridge, Mass., 1942), 71.

86. *MT*, *Kele ha-Miḳdash*, I, 3 (see also *Berakot*, IX, 1 [where Rabad is silent] and *Sifra Commentary* 28a); Naḥmanides, Ex. 20:23. This explanation runs counter to the prevalent view, originating with Saadia, which sees in the Talmudic "myrrh" the blood of an animal found in India. See, in general, I. Markon, "*Mor Deror* explained

shalt not go up and down as a talebearer among thy people,"[87] the first two verses of Exodus 22,[88] and episodes like the "seven days of consecration,"[89] are adopted by Naḥmanides. There are also similarities between them in more comprehensive interpretations which border on actual exposition of theories and values. Both see the creation of women not merely for the sake of propagation but in order to form a more perfect social unit, illustrating complete collaboration.[90] Both interpreted the verse "Be ye not affrighted at them" as "a promise, not an admonition."[91] The discrepancies in the theory of free will arising from the fate of Pharoah and the Egyptians are harmonized by them in the same way, with reference to the same corroborative verses; both explicitly reject the Maimonidean formulation in *Hilkot Teshubah.*[92]

Identity of attitudes toward people and problems further reveals basic affinities between them. Their common reverence for Alfasi, which resulted in concerted refutations of Razah's critique—and, in the case of Naḥmanides, even in a respectful refutation of Rabad's own mild critique—is a case in point. Their attitude to Maimonides in halakah and philosophy is strikingly similar; Naḥmanides explicitly invokes Rabad in support of his position.[93] They shared a common interest in arriving at the precise textual meaning, even if this differed from the accepted midrashic exegesis.[94] Both, finally, believed that codes should be predicated on commentary and exposition, and both practiced this in their respective contributions to the codification of Jewish law. So, while chronology rules out any personal relation between Rabad (d. 1198) and Naḥmanides (b. 1194), the remarkable identity of doctrines and interpretations, methods and attitudes, affirms a sustained literary-ideational relation.

Similarly pervasive influence may be discovered on other people or,

---

by Saadya and His Successors," *Saadya Studies,* ed. E. I. Rosenthal (Manchester, 1943), 97–102.

87. *Sifra Commentary,* 89a; Naḥmanides, Levit. 19:16.

88. *MT, Genebah,* IX, 8; Naḥmanides, Ex. 22:1. See *Mekilta* (*ad. loc.*), III, 102, *Sanhedrin,* 72a. The first to suggest this novel, literal explanation seems to have been R. Ḥananel.

89. *Sifra Commentary,* 42a; Naḥmanides, Levit. 8:22.

90. *BH,* 4; Naḥmanides, Gen. 2:18, 24.

91. *MT, Miẓwot Lo Taᶜaseh,* 58; Naḥmanides, Deut. 20:4.

92. *MT, Teshubah,* VI, 5; Naḥmanides, Gen. 15:14. See Shem Tob ibn Shem Tob, *Derashot* (Padua, 1567), 10a.

93. *Ḳobeẓ Teshubot ha-Rambam,* III, 9b.

94. *Sifra Commentary,* 6a; *MT, Genebah,* IX, 8; Naḥmanides, *Mishpaṭ ha-Ḥerem,* as emended by S. Lieberman, *L. Ginzberg Jubilee Volume,* 330; see Chapter II, §4, note 41.

as will be seen in tracing the destiny and influence of his major works, on entire areas of study. Instead of extending the personalistic approach by further augmenting the acknowledged indebtedness of specific individuals to Rabad—Rashbah would be another excellent test case—a more general phase of Rabad's influence, his impact on the method of study, may be indicated. Undoubtedly Rabad's most influential, if least tangible, achievement was his contribution to the development of halakic methodology, especially to what may be designated as the critico-conceptual approach to Talmudic study. This analytic method was never fully formulated or described in abstract terms; it is implicit in his writings and has to be derived from them. In order to view this in its proper perspective and to appreciate Rabad's place in the history of halakic learning, the main stages of its development must be reconsidered schematically.

After the final redaction of the Babylonian Talmud at the end of the fifth or the beginning of the sixth century, the religious authorities of the period were faced with a very pressing task: they had to make the contents of the Talmud as intelligible and manageable as possible and in this way to assure its absolute supremacy and hegemony in Jewish life. As a result, the Geonim and their contemporaries devoted themselves to a thorough, often rudimentary, explanation of the text. They did not shy away from apparently prosaic tasks; they commented on phrases and words, they interpreted difficult passages; they spelled out allusions and references. They forged, in short, the tools necessary for simple comprehension of the text and, subsequently, for deeper study This phase of activity is exemplified by the purely lexical commentaries of pseudo-Hai on *Tohorot* and of Saadia on *Berakot*, the *Alpha Beta* of R. Makir (brother of R. Gershom), and by various manuals, compendia, and handbooks such as Nissim b. Jacob's *Sefer ha-Mafteaḥ*.[95] The number as well as popularity of these assorted handbooks, which obviously filled a real need, are indirectly revealed by the apprehensiveness of some Geonim who feared that excessive reliance on these auxiliary handbooks might replace the study of the Talmud itself.[96]

95. See especially the introduction to the *Sefer ha-Mafte'aḥ*: אבל זה הקיצור דבר מיוחד בתלמוד ולפי שראיתי מן התלמידים בזמננו זה לא עמדו על זה ויטרחו בבקשת אותה הראיה ולא ימצאו אותה ויתקשה עליהם ההלכה ותסתתם. On early lexica, see also *Teshubot ha-Geonim*, ed. S. Assaf (Jerusalem, 1927), 172–179: פירוש מלים על זרעים וטהרות, and *Teshubot Geonim Ḳadmonim*, ed. D. Cassel (Berlin, 1848), 39b–42b.

96. Responsum of R. Paltoi Gaon, *Ḥemdah Genuzah* (Jerusalem, 1863), 110; see the variant in *ha-Eshkol*, II, 50, cited by L. Ginzberg, *Geonica*, I, 118, n. 1.

Geonic responsa, also, to a great extent, are concerned with text elucidation; there are numerous brief responsa doing exactly the same thing that the bulkier commentaries are doing—explaining words and phrases and providing rather unsophisticated expositions of the text.[97] Indeed, such explicative responsa sometimes ended up as commentaries. This brief, lexical nature of Geonic commentaries explains the following remark of R. Samuel b. Ḥofni: "If any of you desire to have one of the prophetic writings interpreted for you or to have a tractate of the Mishnah or Talmud explained, let him kindly inform us and we shall hurry to fulfill his will."[98]

The main burden of these responsa reflect the second, complementary phase of Geonic activity: universal application of the Talmudic law and maximum standardization of its practice. Scholars answered detailed inquiries concerning religious practice and ritual law sent to them from all corners of the globe: France, Spain, Africa, and India. Unlike medieval responsa which often took the form of long halakic essays dealing with theoretical issues, Geonic responsa were usually brief, undocumented, primarily concerned with daily problems.[99]

Greater sweep and vision are displayed in the various methodological investigations into the form and nature of the Talmud. These more ambitious literary projects formulated a systematic approach to the Talmud, fixed rules for determining the normative conclusions, and in the course of their discussions and illustrations sometimes elucidated basic issues and concepts. This was accompanied by partial reorganization and codification of the contents of the Talmud, abbreviation of its discussions, and incipient schemes of classification. Representative of

97. See Maimonides' description of the literary activities of the Geonim in his introduction to the MT: גם חיברו הגאונים שבכל דור ודור חיבורים לבאר הגמרא· מהם מי שפירש הלכות יחידות ומהם שפירש פרקים יחידים שנתקשו בימיו ומהם מי שפירש מסכתות וסדרים, ועוד חיברו הלכות פסוקות בענין איסור והיתר וחיוב ופטור בדברים שהשעה צריכה להם כדי שיהיו קרובים למדע מי שאינו יכול לירד לעומקה של גמרא. Also, ha-Me'iri, *Bet ha-Beḥirah* on *Abot*, 65: מהם שלא ראינו כתוב ממעשה ידיהם כלום, ומהם שלא ראינו מהם רק תשובות שאלות, למדנו מהם הרבה לענין פסק והוראה, ומהם שראינו מהם פירושין בקצת מסכיות או לפעמים בקצת פרקים או לפעמים בקצת שמועות והלכות מפוזרות, מהם שראינו קצת חיבורים בעניינים פרטים בלתי כוללים כל התלמוד או רבו מהם בפי׳ התלמוד אבל ברמזים ודרכים קצרים אין בהם שבר רעבון המתלמדים כלל. This evaluation is implicit also in R. Isaac b. Sheshet's encomium on R. Tam: והמאור השני ר׳ יעקב איש תם אשר כמוהו בפלפול לאנהיה מאחר שהתלמוד נחתם . . . כי בימיו עדין לא נעשו חבורין על התלמוד כי אם מעט מזער, כגון שאלתות והלכות גדולות ופרוש ר״ח ורש״י ז״ל, וגם באלה אין בהם דבר חדש על הכתוב בתלמוד כי אם באור ומעט תוספות. See Urbach, *Baᶜale ha-Tosafot*, 19. Jacob Aksai, translator of Maimonides' Mishnah Commentary on *Nashim* repeats: הגאונים . . . כולם נתכוונו בחיבוריהם ובפירושיהם לבאר השס כדי להקל . . . מעל התלמידים·

98. S. Assaf, "Miktabim mi-Geone Babel," *Tarbiẓ*, XI (1940), 152.

99. Assaf, *Teḳufat ha-Geonim*, 215–216.

this activity are such works as the *She'eltot*, *Halakot Gedolot*, *Halakot Pesuḳot*, *Shaᶜare Shebuᶜot*, *Meḳah u-Memkar*, *Mebo ha-Talmud* (of Samuel b. Ḥofni and Samuel ha-Nagid), culminating in the *Halakot* of Alfasi. These mark the first step toward encompassing the totality of the Talmud, paying attention to the complete text and freely manipulating its many parts.

A deeper, more integrated attempt at the unification and systematization of the discursive text of the Talmud was made by the Franco-German school. Rashi's commentary did more than define, in isolation, technical words and obscure phrases; it envisaged the Talmud as a literary unit, introduced a sense of contiguousness, and began to correlate diverse passages. The Tosafot already roam freely throughout the Talmud, recognize its contradictions and disharmonies, and undertake to unify it. They are concerned with the "harmonization of apparent contradictions and the inter-linking of apparent irrelevancies."[100] They probe into the inner strata of Talmudic logic, define fundamental Talmudic concepts, and formulate the disparities as well as similarities between various passages in the light of conceptual analysis.[101]

This approach, which may be described as the critico-conceptual approach or the method of halakic criticism, emerged simultaneously in northern and southern France and really revolutionized Talmudic study. Rabad was one of its most skillful practitioners and contributed much to its perfection. It does not seem that this method of analysis, differentiation, deductive elaboration, and conceptual reconstruction emerged full-blown, with all its dialectical insight, analytic acumen, and acuity. Its earliest exponents often resorted to arbitrary solutions and technical differentiations. Having expertly collated a docket of related passages and convincingly illustrated their inconsistencies, it was possible to fall back on such stock answers as "this is of rabbinic origin while the other is Scriptural." It is, therefore, important to stress that Rabad was rarely "technical" and only infrequently resorted to ready-tailored solutions. By seeking conceptually grounded explanations, he helped refine the comparative method of legal study. He displayed special concern with abstract problems rather than textual questions,

100. Wolfson, *Crescas*, 26.

101. R. Solomon Luria, *Yam Shel Shelomah*, *Ḥullin*, introduction: לולי חכמי הצרפתים בעלי התוספות שעשאוהו בכדור אחד . . . והפכוהו וגלגלוהו ממקום למקום שנראה לנו כחלום מבלי פותר . . . אלא סוגיא זו אומרת בכה וסוגיא זו אומרת בכה ולא קרב זה אל זה, ונמצא מיושר התלמוד ומקושר וכל (החתימות) (הסתומות) יתפשרו ותוכן פסקיו יאושרו. See Urbach, *Baᶜale ha-Tosafot*, 538.

concepts rather than terms. By their critico-comparative method Rabad and his colleagues, in sum, performed for halakic study something similar to what Aristotle accomplished for philosophic thought by the method of abstraction. They were not only expositors of the text but also investigators. They were "constantly looking for new problems, discovering difficulties, raising objections, setting up alternative hypotheses and solutions, testing them, and pitting them against each other."[102] As a result, abstract, complex concepts, discussed fragmentarily in numerous, unrelated sections of the Talmud, are for the first time defined with great rigor and precision. Talmudic analysis is precipitated into a new and higher phase.

Rabad was so given over to conceptual analysis and classification that, although he usually kept his logic down to earth and grounded it upon solid textual foundations,[103] occasionally he would force the text to conform to his analysis. After presenting an original explanation of a text, for example, Rabad concludes with a final word of persuasion: "The matter should be thus explained, even though the language of the text is not clear in light of this explanation." Similarly, cognizant that his interpretation of a seemingly erroneous statement in the *Mishneh Torah* does not dovetail with the obvious sense of Maimonides' statement, Rabad comments that "even though his language does not indicate this, reason points to it." Again, Rabad vigorously rejects a Maimonidean theory—which he considered a logical vagary—with the pretext that there is no textual support for it. However, even though he subsequently chanced upon a Tosefta which apparently corroborates Maimonides' theory, Rabad prefers to manipulate this passage rather than abandon his logical distinctions.[104]

Yet, although primarily concerned with conceptual analysis, Rabad brought to bear upon his Talmudic methodology a painstaking quest for textual impeccability. Various forms of textual criticism are discernible in his writings: establishment of the most authentic text, discovery of later interpolations, discussion of the relative value of equally acceptable *variae lectiones*, questions on the reliability of transmission, manuscript

102. Wolfson, *Crescas*, 26.

103. For example, *BH*, 13: מסתברא ... ורמיזא הא מילתא; *MT*, *Berakot*, XI, 15; *Lulab*, VIII, 1; *Sheḥiṭah*, X, 11.

104. Rabad, *BK*, 57: כך ראוי לפרש אע"פ שהלשון אינו מחוור לזה הפירוש. *MT*, *Sukkah*, VI, 11: אעפ"י שאין לשונו מראה אבל השכל מורה על זה. *MT*, *Maᶜaser Sheni*, III, 9; see also *Mekirah*, XXVII, 3.

corruption in the process of transcription, genuine or pseudepigraphic authorship of texts. There is here, as in the writings of other great medieval rabbis, an embryonic science of diplomatics.[105]

Rabad's jurisprudence, moreover, was not a completely abstract, self-contained discipline, divorced from the realities of life and contingencies of history, the facts of nature and the inclinations of the individual. Experience, observation, sensitivity, the restraining force of custom, contemporary pressures were sometimes key factors in the formulation of interpretive subtleties and halakic profundities. Rabad introduces empirical proofs, sociological reasons, psychological insights, physiological explanations, principles of equity, realistic appraisals, and historical considerations. Such common sense, supra-legal considerations often supplement or refine his theories and expositions, so that the immanent development of halakic concepts is fruitfully related to and integrated with other less formal factors.[106]

Rabad's influence in this respect is not only general—in the sense that the method reached advanced stages in his hands—but also particular: many of his theories and insights were endorsed and transmitted by subsequent generations of Talmudists. Many doctrines and concepts were incorporated root and branch into standard works of Jewish law: a preponderant amount in the realm of ritual, a considerable number in civil and criminal law, and an uneven number in the vast juridical expanses covered by the *Shulḥan ᶜAruk* as a whole. Persuasively, with analytic verve and skill,[107] Rabad propounded new theories which were striking and many imperceptibly became common property of all Talmudists. Theories on the concept of indirect damage,[108]

105. For example, Rabad, *BK*, 122, 137, 202; *Sifra* Commentary, 21b, 47a, 71b, 94b; *Hassagot*, on Alfasi, *Berakot*, 6b, *Pesaḥim*, 13a; *TD*, 61, 62 (see *Responsa* [Warsaw, 1870] of ibn Megas, 114); *MT*, *Tefillah*, V, 15; *Ẓiẓit*, II, 7; *Nezirut*, V, 8; *Temurah*, [II, 3; *Ṭume'at Oklin*, 1, 4; *Ṭume'at Ẓaraᶜat*, XII, 8; *Parah Adumah*, V, 5. See ha-Me'iri, *Bet ha-Beḥirah* on *Beẓah*, 46; *REJ*, XXXVIII (1899), 119.

106. Rabad, *BK*, 137, 243, 244, *TD*, 3, 31, 43, 44, 46, 56; *Hassagot* on Alfasi, *Berakot*, 34a; *BH*, ch. II; MT, *Ḳeri'at Shema*, IV, 7; *Yom Ṭob*, VIII, 16; *Issure Bi'ah*, XIV, 8; *Nezirut*, IX, 16; *Miḳwa'ot*, III, 8; *Zekiyah u-Matanah*, III, 8; *Ṭoᶜen we-Niṭᶜan*, III, 7.

107. It should also be noted that Rabad's expository style was usually concrete and imaginative. Intricate principles were illustrated by creating all sorts of novel situations and hypothetical possibilities to which a law is relevant. See, for example, *BH*, *passim*; *TD*, 63, where he works out a variety of situations relevant to the law in *Shebu'ot* 45a (חנוני על פנקסו).

108. *MT*, *Ḥobel u-Maziḳ*, VII, 7, 11; *Tosafot*, *Baba Batra*, 22b; Naḥmanides, *Dina de-Garme* (end of *Ḥiddushim*, *Baba Batra*); *Sefer ha-Terumot*, LI, 6 (וכן כתב הראב״י): *Ḥoshen ha Misphaṭ*, 386, and *Sifte Kohen*, *ad. loc.*

power of attorney,[109] washing of hands before the meal and after the meal,[110] prohibition against deriving benefit or pleasure from implements used for idolatrous rites,[111] partial or complete nullification of testimony because of various disqualifications,[112] different components of prayer,[113] nature of legal doubt,[114] retraction of vows,[115] majority rule in cases of *terefah*,[116] patterns of menstrual uncleanness,[117] nature of the sanctity of the land of Israel,[118] liabilities concerning the

109. *TD*, 61, *Ḥoshen ha-Mishpaṭ*, 122–123; see Chapter II, pages 74 ff.

110. *TD*, 66–67; *MT*, *Berakot*, VI, 2; *Oraḥ Ḥayyim*, 158 ff., 181; see Chapter II, pages 76 ff.

111. *Hassagot*, *Pesaḥim*, 6b; see *Yoreh De'ah*, 10, 1; 142, 4.

112. *Sanhedrin*, 9b; *Makkot* 7a, and Rosh, *ad. loc.* who quotes Rabad. *Baba Batra*, 43a, and Naḥmanides, *ad. loc.*; *MT*, *ᶜEdut*, XII, 1. Since this is one of Rabad's most famous halakic principles, it may be worthwhile to analyze it here. Sometimes the Talmud has a case where the testimony of disqualified witnesses is totally discarded, while sometimes part is retained as valid and part is rejected. Talmudic commentators were hard put to reconcile these various cases. Rabad elaborated an abstract principle which determines and explains this juristic distinction. When a witness testifies, among other things, about some matter pertaining directly to himself, where he is directly involved and the testimony concerns his own person, then the court may split his testimony. That part concerning his person is rejected, while the rest remains valid. On the other hand, a relative or any technically disqualified witness who offers testimony is invalidated. This distinction is imbedded in the divergent character of the disqualifying traits. In the first case, there are no reservations concerning the very truthfulness and reliability of the witness, except that what he states about himself is not valid. Therefore the court dismisses this part of the testimony as irrelevant, or simply deletes it from the record as if it had never been presented; the rest is retained independently. In the second case, the witness is initially disqualified because of an a priori reluctance on the part of the court to accept his testimony. There is some question concerning his reliability and trustworthiness as an individual. Consequently, there is no reason to discriminate between various portions of his testimony: if part is nullified, all of it is nullified, for his very trustworthiness is doubted.

Related to this was the question of the status of a husband's testimony concerning his wife: is this comparable to testimony about any relative, or are the personalities of husband and wife so intimately associated that this is tantamount to testimony about his person? Rabad classifies a husband's testimony about his wife in the first category—as if he were testifying about his own person. Unlike Maimonides who states that a wife is merely the closest relative of a husband (and consequently the testimony is completely discarded, as in the case of all relatives), Rabad reaffirms his principle—articulated elsewhere in the context of ethical discussions—that one's wife is like his body (and therefore only the part of the testimony concerning the wife would be cancelled, while the veracity and validity of other statements are left intact).

113. *MT*, *Tefillah*, I, 10.

114. *Pesaḥim*, 9b; Razah and Rabad, *ad. loc.*; see *MT*, *Ḥameẓ u-Maẓah*, II, 10, and commentaries, *ad. loc.*

115. *MT*, *Shebuᶜot*, VI, 12; see *Kesef Mishneh*, *ad. loc.*

116. *TD*, 12; *Yoreh Deᶜah*, 37:2 and *Bet Joseph* on *Ṭur*, *Yoreh Deᶜah* (מצאתי כתוב בשם הראב״ד).

117. *BH*, 38–39; see *Niddah* 63a, and *Tosafot*, *ad. loc.*; *MT*, *Issure Bi'ah*, VIII, 1; *Yoreh Deᶜah*, 189.

118. *MT*, *Bet ha-Beḥirah*, VI, 14.

kidnapping of slaves,[119] impurity[120]—these are but some of his original theories, resulting from his critico-conceptual method of study, which spread far and wide in rabbinic literature.

As a concluding historical epitaph, mention may be made of an out-of-the-way episode which obliquely points up the essence of Rabad's fame and the main contours of his historical image as a creatively independent scholar. The official protocol of the religious disputation of 1413–1414,[121] which took place in Tortosa under the aegis of anti-Pope Benedict XIII, reports that the discussions were hopelessly deadlocked when the Christians presented the Jews with a list of scurrilous, blasphemous, anti-Christian statements found in the Talmud. The Christian spokesman—Joshua ha-Lorki, an apostate physician known as Hieronymus de Sancta Fide—claimed that the overwhelmed Jewish representatives were incapable of refuting his charges and declined further debate. Only the well-known philosopher Joseph Albo and one other scholar submitted detailed memoranda attempting to vindicate the integrity of the Talmud and these attempts were fully discredited by a professor of Bible named Andreas Bertrandi. At this point, the protocol continues, an otherwise unknown Jew suggested a fresh approach to the entire problem. He contended that the method of Talmudic study should be analogous to the accepted method of Scriptural study, since both are divine. Difficulties should be obviated by explaining all details in keeping with the general spirit of the work. He claims that, in fact, various scholars always interpreted difficult passages in the Talmud differently, each in light of his own over-all approach. As a specific illustration he mentions the fact that one of the opinions taken over from the *Mishneh Torah* into Hieronymus' list was refuted by Rabad who submitted an explanation of his own.[122] This suggestion could not be expected to alter the course of the disputation—Hieronymus, incidentally, was ignorant of Rabad's explanation and asked to be enlightened—but it is significant for our study that this unknown Jew was able to employ Rabad's dissenting opinions skillfully and appropriately, in a manner which Rabad would surely endorse. He

119. *MT*, *Gezelah*, VIII, 14; IX, 1; see *Sukkah*, 30a, *Baba Batra*, 44a, and *Tosafot*, *ad. loc.* Also, *MT*, *Ṭoʿen we-Niṭʿan*, V, 4; *Baba Ḳamma*, 59b; *Ketubot*, 51a, and *Tosafot*, *ad. loc.*

120. *MT*, *Ṭume'at Met*, VII; 4, XI, 1; XII, 6; see *Berakot*, 19b and *Tosafot*, *ad. loc.*; *Sefer ha-Hashlamah* on *Berakot*, 11.

121. Baer, *Toledot ha-Yehudim bi-Sefarad ha-Noẓrit* (Tel Aviv, 1945), 442, 569.

122. *MT*, *Issure Bi'ah*, XXI, 9, and *Hagahot Maimuniyot*, ad. loc.; BH, 84.

intimates actually that Rabad was a vigorous exponent of the independent, critical method of study which embraced the Talmud as one harmoniously integrated unit and interpreted its parts accordingly.

II. WORKS

Rabad's literary activity, whose nature and scope is here described on a more or less chronological basis, was not only original but also many-sided. He made substantial contributions to every category included in Steinschneider's classification of the various accretions to and interpretations of the original corpus of Jewish law: (a) commentaries (*perushim*); (b) additions (*tosafot*) and discontinuous critical investigations or novellae (*ḥiddushim*); (c) compilations and compendia for practical use (*likkuṭim*, *ḳobeẓim*, *ḳiẓẓurim*); (d) decisions on actual cases (*pesaḳim*) and responsa (*teshubot*); (e) independent, systematic works on the law or various aspects of it.[1] The generic affinities of Rabad's works will reveal themselves in the process of description, while an attempted chronological survey promises to shed some light on Rabad's interests and methods, on development and continuity in his work.[2]

1. Early Writings

Disregarding the elaborate lecture notes of his student years—presumably never collected in book form but sometimes referred to in other writings[3]—Rabad's first known and partially extant work is a

1. Steinschneider, *Jewish Literature from the Eighth to the Eighteenth Century*, Eng. trans. (London, 1857), 73.

2. Marx (207) made an important contribution to the clarification of the chronology of Rabad's works. Many of his conjectures, however, need to be modified, while there are a number of problems which he did not touch upon at all.

3. *Hassagot* on Alfasi, *Beẓah*, 1: כבר נמצאו בבלואי סחבות הזכרונות אשר כתבנו בנעורנו מפי מלמדנו. See Marx, 206, n. 4; Assaf in *Sifran*, 185, n. 1. Razah apparently did the same; see introduction to *Sefer ha-Ma'or*, ... פירושי מקצת הלכות חמורות וראשי דברים שכתבתי לי בילדותי לזכרון ... On the widespread custom of students writing notes in the presence of their teachers, see E. Urbach, *Baʿale ha-Tosafot* (Jerusalem, 1955), 20; also, for an earlier period, S. Lieberman, *Hellenism in Jewish Palestine* (New York, 1950), 87.

small treatise entitled *Issur Mashehu.* The interesting history of this book's identification provides a neat illustration of scholarly conjecture—or progress by hypothesis. Rabad refers to it on several occasions as *Sefer Issur we-Heter,*[4] while it is usually cited by others as *Issur Mashehu* because of its opening sentence.[5] This has led some historians—Carmoly, for instance—to list it under two separate titles in the enumeration of Rabad's works.[6] The identity of *Issur we-Heter* with *Issur Mashehu* was, however, correctly conjectured by Reifmann[7] and Michael,[8] and convincingly demonstrated by Gross.[9] Drachman persisted in citing these titles as two distinct works.[10] Marx had already pointed out, on the basis of a quotation from Rashbah, that this work was written as a critique of a similar book by Rabad's teacher, R. Meshullam[11]—a fact which Gross had denied.[12] A fragment of this work was finally published by Assaf who conclusively established the identity of these two titles and also unassailably demonstrated its relation to an antecedent work of the same kind by R. Meshullam.[13]

In this work Rabad, the animadversionist and controversialist of the future, already displayed his inclinations to intellectual independence. He did not merely annotate his master's work discursively, but organized the material and gave it an original, independent mold, producing not a stack of disjointed observations and scholia but a well-integrated work.

This methodological variation between his early work and his later hassagot may be attributed to his age, status, and the nature of the undertaking. It seems that R. Meshullam commissioned his promising young disciple to study and review his latest work. Disagreement would be encouraged and nonconformity welcomed. It was a challenging assignment which an imaginative teacher designated for a worthy pupil. Rabad mentions repeatedly that he wrote this "before" or "in the

4. Assaf, *Sifran,* 185, lists five places in the hassagot and responsa where Rabad mentions this work. Marx, 205, n. 1, adds two more references from *KS.*

5. Assaf, *Sifran,* 185, for the numerous places where it is so cited, especially in the responsa and novellae of Rashbah.

6. E. Carmoly, *La France Israelite* (Francfort a/M, 1858), 125.

7. J. Reifmann, "Toledot ha-Rabad Baᶜal ha-Hassagot," *ha-Maggid,* VI (1862), 389.

8. J. H. Michael, *Or ha-Ḥayyim* (Frankfurt a.M., 1891), 25.

9. Gross, 537. Kahn, "Les Juifs de Posquières," 6, following Gross in practically all details, still says rather hesitantly that they are "probably identical."

10. *Dibre ha-Ribot,* ed. B. Drachman (New York, 1907), XII.

11. Marx, 205, and n. 1.

12. Gross, 537, n. 8.

13. *Sifran,* 185–198. Gedalyah ibn Yaḥyah's explicit identification of the two titles (*Shalshelet ha-Ḳabbalah* [Warsaw, 1877], 57), mentioned by Assaf, is based on Azriel Trabotto's chronicle (published by D. Kaufmann, *REJ,* IV [1882], 212).

presence of" his master R. Meshullam. Wherever he differs, he adds by way of introduction or conclusion: "this is your pupil's view"; "your pupil dissents from your view."[14]

The most effective and pedagogically valid way to execute such an undertaking was to recast all the primary source material and relevant Geonic opinions in the form of an independent work. Issues between himself and his master could be indicated and clarified in the framework of a general, comprehensive discussion. Moreover, such a method of organization and presentation offered an opportunity for originality in style and composition, and what is even more important, in classification and selection of data. Rabad's propensity for classification and his quest for generalizations, for basic halakic categories, are already discernible in this work, which opens with a sweeping statement concerning the eight ways in which any amount of a forbidden particle (*issur mashehu*) can disqualify the entire mixture in which it happens to be present. This list, which he culled from various Talmudic sources, "some of which are well-known, others are known only to the wise," was intended to be exhaustive.[15] It collates all cases subsumed under one basic halakic principle concerned with the laws of mixture (*ta ᶜarubet*).

This line of reconstruction also explains why the criticisms in this book are so moderate, restrained, and decorous in tone compared to some of the acrimonious observations of Rabad's old age. One would normally expect a hot-headed, capable youth to be more reckless and bold than a mellowed scholar, as was the case with Rabad's classmate, Razah, who, at a very unripe age, antagonized many contemporaries by hurling his sharp shafts at the venerable Alfasi. When one considers, however, that Rabad wrote his *Issur we-Heter* on a commission from his master who gave him a carte blanche to register his reservations, queries, and differences without restraint or deference, one is not surprised that Rabad refrains from personal, extratextual comments. His divergent views are clearly recorded, minus the peppery epithets and satirical embellishments so common in his later works.

In addition to its manifestation of independence and fondness for systematization and classification,[16] this pioneer work is a significant

14. *Sifran*, 195, 198. Such an introduction to creative writing was a common phenomenon; see Urbach, *Baᶜale ha-Tosafot*, 20.

15. *Sifran*, 189.

16. See *BH*, *passim*, e.g., end of ch. 1 (*Shaᶜar ha-Perishah*), 14; or end of ch. 3 (*Shaᶜar ha-Ketamim*), 46–47; Rabad, *BK*, 353 ff.; *ᶜEduyot Commentary*, IV, 12; *TD*,

precursor of Rabad's later literary activities in many other ways. Several traits, clearly defined in subsequent writings, are present here in embryo. He displays a rather leisurely style, abounding in proofs and illustrations of his contentions. He pauses periodically for a résumé of the important points established in the preceding section and prerequisite for the following section—a literary mannerism carried to an enervating extreme in the *Ba^cale ha-Nefesh*.[17] Even at this early age he takes issue with Alfasi and rejects all of the proofs by means of which Alfasi attempted to corroborate a certain decision: "I do not grasp these reasons at all nor are they clear in our mind."[18] Rabad is already preoccupied with textual emendations and the establishment of a critical text; in one place he suggests a major emendation in the text of Alfasi. His concluding remarks read like a mandate for critical text revision:

> It is possible that the Rabbi ordered to correct [this passage] in his *Halakot* and it was not corrected, for I heard that he changed his mind [in a few places] and ordered to correct them. I say that these passages were among those, and if they were not among them, he left passages for his successors [to correct].[19]

On the negative side, there is reason to believe that *Issur we-Heter* (a clearly delimited topic) was encumbered with digressions and included material not directly relevant to the subject. In later works, also, his schemes of classification are occasionally vitiated by inclusion of extraneous material. Thus, Simeon b. Ẓemaḥ Duran refers to a parenthetic remark from this book in connection with his discussion of the custom of holding scholarly discourses on halakic and *aggadic* themes during the course of the meal at wedding celebrations.[20] Rabad also, in the extant fragment of this work, on one occasion adopts the Talmudic device of "digression by association": "Since we have come across this dictum of R. Ashi, let us say a few words concerning it."[21]

66–67 (*Perush Yadayim*). Many hassagot apparently relate to problems and methods of classification; e.g., *MT*, *Miẓwat* *ᶜaseh*, 239; *Shabbat* IX, 15. Rabad's method is generally deductive. He usually opens with a definition or key sentence, presents rules and principles, and then proceeds to cite all the illustrative material and to discuss the pertinent details.

17. E.g., *BH*, 25, 29.

18. *Sifran* 191: ואנן לא חזינן להני טעמי כלל ולא מחוורי גבן. The critical nature of *Issur we-Heter* is also indicated in later works, e.g., *Hassagot*, *Pesaḥim*, 18a: וכבר דקדקתי אני אחריו בחבור האסור והיתר . . . והם דברים של טעם. 19a.

19. *Ibid.*, 195: ואפשר שצוה הרב לתקן בהלכותיו ולא נתקן כי שמעתי שחזר בו וצוה לתקן אותם. Note a similar statement by Rabi, *ha-Eshkol*, ed. Auerbach (Halberstadt, 1868), II, 100. See also *Hassagot* on Alfasi, *Ketubot*, 42a.

20. S. Duran, *Magen Abot*, ed. A. Jellinek (Leipzig, 1855), 42a. This is apparently not a quotation, as in *Sifran*, 187.

21. *Sifran*, 193; see, for example, *Hassagot* on Alfasi, *Giṭṭin*, 6a; also *TD*, 7, 63.

Although it was a youthful production, Rabad did not retrospectively see in it traces of immaturity or amateurishness. He never repudiated its conclusions or retracted its statements. As a matter of fact, he cites it in later works and responsa. When, on one occasion, Razah writes that "some of the sages of this generation maintain . . .," Rabad calmly adds: "I am the one who wrote this in my treatise, in the presence of R. Meshullam."[22] Other Rishonim also refer back to it as an authoritative tract.[23]

A treatise on those commandments which were currently valid in Palestine (*Ḥibbur ha-Miẓwot ha-Nohagot ᶜAtah ba'Areẓ*) seems to be a second work of his early period. Rabad himself mentions that he composed this work in Narbonne at the request of R. Asher b. Saul and R. Abraham b. Joseph who were about to emigrate to the Holy Land.[24] His reference to Narbonne suggests two possible dates for the composition of this work: either his early Narbonne-Lunel period or his second sojourn in Narbonne in 1172.[25] The latter seems untenable, for, if he had composed it in 1172, one would surmise that ha-Me'iri, who describes Rabad's activities of this year in considerable detail,[26] would have alluded to it. Moreover, his 1172 stay in Narbonne seems to have been of short duration—a temporary station on the way from Posquières to Carcassonne—and hardly suitable for writing.

This lost treatise and the circumstances surrounding its genesis are interesting historically as another parenthetic illustration of the centrality of Palestine in medieval Jewish life and thought. It dovetails nicely with the general "Palestinian orientation" of medieval Jewish history and the many Provençal sentiments and actions directed toward Palestine. We shall comment presently on Rabad's concern with such subjects as special laws which were not in practice outside of Palestine. *Zeraᶜim* and *Ḳodashim*, laws relating to the soil of Palestine and to the Temple in Jerusalem, had always been popular subjects for study among French scholars.[27] While the study of subjects relating to Palestine was

22. *Hassagot*, *Pesaḥim*, 19a.
23. See §1, note 5.
24. *KS*, I, 1. וכבר פירשתי בספר המצות שחברתי זה כמה שנים; 39: כתבתי בחבור המצות הנוהגות עתה בארץ . . . כאשר הייתי בנרבונא.
25. Reifmann, "Rabad Baᶜal ha-Hassagot," *Bet ha-Talmud*, IV (1862), 381, found the following variation on the above quote: כאשר הייתי אצלו כתבתיהו and Asher b. Saul resided in Lunel. Even if one accepts this reading, it is not very significant. It still refers presumably to the same Narbonne-Lunel period. It is also possible that Asher was then living in Narbonne.
26. *Magen Abot*, 103; see Chapter I, §3, note 44.
27. See Chapter I, §1, note 80.

never abandoned by Jews anywhere—extensive selections from texts dealing with these subjects were even incorporated into the liturgy—the persistent emphasis laid on them by Provençal scholars not only reflects their inconsumable passion for Palestine but is probably connected with the incipient rise of a movement for a return to the Holy Land.[28] Provençal scholars, headed by R. Jonathan ha-Kohen of Lunel who was one of Rabad's most distinguished disciples, were among the vanguard going to Palestine in the famous rabbinic emigration of 1211.[29] One of Rabad's colleagues, R. Jacob ha-Nazir, a key figure in early Provençal mysticism, was in Palestine in 1187.[30] This is, interestingly, the year of Saladin the Great's conquest of Palestine, which was greeted enthusiastically in Provence.[31] Rabad's other writings sometimes echo these sentiments.[32] The fact that this manual was composed as a *livre de circonstance* at the request of two pious individuals adds to our estimate of Rabad's reputation as a Talmudic authority, his willingness to be helpful to all those who were in search of knowledge, and his devotion to the Land of Israel and its laws.

While the *Issur we-Heter* and the *Ḥibbur ha-Mizwot* can be assigned to Rabad's early sojourn in Narbonne, all his other works, which may be classified compositely under the headings of codes, commentaries, responsa, sermons (*derashot*), and hassagot, were written more or less simultaneously during long and protracted periods. Rabad did not dedicate a specific number of years to the composition of codes nor did he spend an uninterrupted period of time producing commentaries,

28. Of course, "realistic" motives, in the form of political adversity and religio-social humiliation, were not lacking; see Chapter I, §2, note 9. Also, the epilogue to the commentary on Jeremiah by Menaḥem b. Simeon of Posquières: ... והש״י שהוציאו מבית האסורים ... יוציאנו מהרה מיד הצרים ואכזרים אשר היינו בתוכם נאסרים וירוממנו לרשת ארצנו וישיב לנו כבודינו, ושונאינו ירדו למטה תחתינו ... Quoted from Paris ms. 192b by E. Urbach, "Hassagot ha-Rabad ᶜal perush Rashi la-Torah," *Kiryath Sefer*, XXXIV (1959), 107.

29. This is according to ibn Virga, *Shebet Yehudah*, 147. Joseph ibn Ẓaddik, however, has 1205 as the year of his death; Neubauer, *Medieval Jewish Chronicles*, I, 94; see *Encyclopedia Judaica*, IX, 287. For some bibliographical references, see Gross, *REJ*, VI (1883), 177. S. Krauss, "L'Emigration de 300 rabbins en Palestine en l'an 1211," *REJ*, LXXXII (1926), 333–352; J. Mann, "Ha-Tenuᶜot ha-Meshiḥiyot bime Masᶜe ha-Zelab ha-Rishonim," *Ha-Teḳufah*, XXIII (1925), 243–261, XXIV (1926), 335–358; in general, H. J. Zimmels, "Erez Israel in der Responsenliteratur des späteren Mittelalters," *MGWJ*, LXXIV (1930), 44–64; I. Baer, "Ereẓ Israel we-Galut be-ᶜene ... Yeme ha-benayim," *Me'assef Zion*, VI, 149–171.

30. Scholem, "Mi-Ḥoḳer Limeḳubbal," *Tarbiẓ*, VI (1935), 96; *Sifran*, 124.

31. Judah al-Ḥarizi, *Taḥkemoni*, ch. 29. David Ḳimḥi, *Commentary on Psalms*, 146:3. See E. Ashtor-Strauss, "Saladin and the Jews," *HUCA*, XXVII (1956), 305–327, esp. 325–326.

32. E.g., *Commentary on ᶜEduyot*, VIII, 7; *BH*, 89 (end).

but experimented recurrently with different literary forms. While some of the works may be dated more or less precisely, most cannot be definitely dated.

The *Ḥibbur Harsha'ot* (also referred to as the *Piske Harsha'ot* or *Din Harsha'ah*),[33] a small brochure on the power of attorney or laws of agency, seems to be one of Rabad's early codificatory writings, cited in his later works. This comprehensive treatise consists of a systematic arrangement and classification of the relevant laws, interspersed with interpretations propounded by Alfasi and the Geonim. It begins with a quotation of the fundamental Talmudic text on the subject, and this is followed by a discussion of four different interpretations offered by his predecessors. Rabad points out the deficiencies of these interpretations and the many problems left unsolved by them.[34] He takes up the question of readings and textual variations, and then expounds his own view. He resumes the discussion of Alfasi's view on a few particular points which did not fit in previously. Transition from section to section is smooth and natural, the development of the theme is logical, the polemics are pertinent, and the work as a whole is well-integrated.

33. *TD*, 61; see Rabad, *BK*, 174, 274; *KS*, I, 17.

34. Noteworthy is his critique (*TD*, 62, end) of R. Judah b. Barzilai's interpretation of one of the underlying texts (*Shebuᶜot*, 31a), on grounds of fallacious reasoning. Rab and Samuel differ concerning the homiletical connotation of the verse "he did that which is not good among his people" (Ezek. 18:18). Rab applied it to the case of one who accepted delegated authority or power of attorney. Since Samuel was of the opinion that *harsha'ah* is permissible he construed the verse as referring to "one who acquires a field the title of which is disputed." Inasmuch as Rab connected this verse with one accepting power of attorney, Barzilai inferred that he must totally dissent from the view of Samuel and maintain that writing of *harsha'ah* is forbidden and invalid. Now Rabad terms this line of reasoning a "gross error," for the inference is inconclusive. If such delegation of authority is completely invalid, and does not empower the bearer to collect debts from the creditor, then the verse from Ezekiel is meaningless; the agent did not do a thing. It was this illogical deduction which led Rabad to refute Barzilai at great length. Rabad, in turn, qualified Rab's interpretation of the verse as referring solely to a case where both debtor and creditor reside in the same locality. Then, one who accepts delegated powers is considered a meddler in the private affairs of other; he had no reason to initiate a quarrel with the debtor. However, if the two principals are distant from each other, the agent is certainly performing a good deed by collecting the debt, for otherwise the money would be irretrievable. This distinction was almost universally accepted; see *MT*, *Sheluḥin we-Shutafin*, III, 5; commentary of R. David b. Zimra, *ad. loc.*, *Yeḳar Tif'eret*, 17; *Ḥoshen ha-Mishpaṭ*, 123:15; R. Moses Isserles, *ad. loc.*, expands the principle. It is interesting that, in his explanation of the impropriety of accepting delegated powers, Rabad asserts that the agent thereby acts the part of a lawyer (מקנה ליה לאידך כי היכי דנטעין ליה טפי). Lawyers, of course, have no place in Jewish law where the judge, in the course of his searching and comprehensive investigation, is both prosecutor and attorney for the defense. Special pleading by counsellors of law is discountenanced. See *Abot* I, 8 (and commentaries *ad. loc.*, especially of Maimonides and Duran).

While this work presents a digest of the various laws and recapitulates a number of different views, Rabad's own views and insights on the matter constitute a most original and durable contribution. For, among students of the subject of power of attorney, the following problem was raised: does the delegation of power of attorney mean merely the designation of an agent or deputy to fulfill a commission, or does it entail the acquisition of certain proprietary rights on the part of the deputy who is thus in a more authoritative position to compel the defendant to negotiate directly with him? Rabad is the first to have analyzed the issue thoroughly. His interpretation of the knotty text in *Baba Ḳamma* and his practical conclusion that power of attorney involves both of the above-mentioned aspects were adopted with minor variations by such Rishonim as Naḥmanides and Rashbah and later by Joseph Karo (in the *Shulḥan ʿAruk*) and Sabbatai Kohen (in the *Sifte Kohen*).[35] Nevertheless, even though Rabad's analysis determined the course of subsequent investigation, he is not credited with the solution.[36]

This widespread neglect in referring to the source results, it is to be conjectured, from the circumstances of its promulgation. Rabad must have publicized these views originally in a school lecture or outline which spread rapidly and became public property before the work was written in final form. Having become public property, the view was repeatedly used without mention being made of its source. This little pamphlet is the only written source in which Rabad's view is expounded, even though he had occasion to discuss it in his commentary on *Baba Ḳamma* and his hassagot on Razah. In these latter works, when the occasion for discussing the subject of the power of attorney arose, Rabad did not repeat his conclusions nor reproduce his argumentations but merely indicated that he already "explained it and elaborated upon it" in a special treatise to which he refers the reader.[37] The Talmudic maxim "since [the book] is so small it might be lost [if copied

35. *Baba Ḳamma*, 70a, *Shebuʿot*, 33b, and commentaries *ad. loc.*; *Ḥoshen ha-Mishpaṭ*, 122–123; see *MT*, *Sheluḥin*, III, 5. It is clear that Rabad's text in *Baba Ḳamma* did not conclude והלכתא שליח שויא; see *Diḳduḳe Soferim* on *Baba Ḳamma* (Munich, 1882), 157; and *Oẓar ha-Geonim*, 52.

36. The sole acknowledgment is to be found possibly in a reference of Razah to "R. Abraham," which may mean either Rabi or Rabad. See on this Auerbach, *Ha-Eshkol*, XV; Atlas, Rabad, *BK*, 38, n. 50; and *TD*, 217. It does not seem likely that Rabad would gloss over this reference without special comment if it were aimed at himself; see *KS*, I, 18.

37. Rabad, *BK*, 174: כבר פרשתיה והרחבתי בה בפסקי הרשאות בדברים נכוחים. See the parallel statement in *KS*, I, 17; also, *Hassagot* on Alfasi, *Ketubot*, 45a.

separately]" was fully realized in this case. Had he incorporated this work into his full-length commentary, its fate might have been different.

Rabad's work on *Tractate Yadayim*, which, in common with the *Ḥibbur Harsha'ah*, cannot be precisely dated, is printed in *Temim Deᶜim* under the title of "Commentary" (*Perush*).[38] Weiss, accepting this description unqualifiedly, considers this work to be a commentary and classifies it as such.[39] Gross, however, includes this treatise among Rabad's codificatory collections.[40] It is, in truth, difficult to describe this as a commentary. In form and objective it is primarily a code which, as usual for Rabad, is coupled with textual commentary. In some respects it recalls the sixth chapter of *Baᶜale ha-Nefesh*, which is a combination of both.[41]

This work again displays Rabad's predilection for and skill in classification of laws. It opens with an exhaustive catalogue of all the differences between the washing of the hands before the meal and after the meal. Moreover, the description of their few common aspects as contrasted with their numerous underlying divergencies actually provides a definition of the two rites. The contrasting method is effectively used for purposes of classification and definition. The richness of this analysis, which prevails practically root and branch in the *Shulḥan ᶜAruk*,[42] is brought into sharp relief by a glance at *Hilkot Berakot* of the *Mishneh Torah* which devotes only one entry to these differences.[43] This work also abounds with significant instances of Rabad's critical inclinations and his desire for a thorough understanding of laws; he is not content merely to record their existence but seeks

38. *TD*, 66–67. It is reproduced, slightly abbreviated and with a few variations, in *Kol Bo* (Lemberg, 1860), 23; see also *Orḥot Ḥayyim*, I, 2b (הלכות ידים). It was also printed (on the basis of an independent manuscript) by S. Schönblum, *Shelosha Sefarim Niftaḥim* (Lemberg, 1877), 48a–49b, where it is designated as "masseket yadayim la-Rabad."

39. I. H. Weiss, *Dor Dor we-Doreshaw* (Berlin, 1924), IV, 285, n. 16.

40. *GJ*, 449. Rashbah, *Torat ha-Bayit*, VI (New York, 1954), 69a, calls it הל' נטילת ידים.

41. The same form characterizes the work of his younger colleague R. Asher b. Meshullam; see *TD*, 120; ha-Me'iri refers to it as קונדריס החילוקין שבין יו"ט ראשון לשני *Magen Abot*, 36; *Bet ha-Beḥirah* on *Bezah* (Jerusalem, 1957), 37.

42. *Oraḥ Ḥayyim*, 158 ff., 181. Ha-Me'iri's little treatise on the same subject—an important intermediary in the transmission of Rabad's views—is also dominated by the *Perush Yadayim*; see *Bet Yad* (*dine neṭilat yadayim*) at end of *Bet ha-Beḥirah* on *Berakot* (Warsaw, 1911), 204–216, esp. ch. 14, p. 216; also, Rashbah, *Torat ha-Bayit*, VI.

43. *MT*, *Berakot*, VI, 15.

to fathom their rationale.[44] He refers to this work with considerable pride.[45]

2. *Talmud Commentaries*

Rabad's commentaries on the Talmud are not as significant as his other works. Their influence in the long run was not widespread, even though immediate successors like Rashbah and ha-Me'iri quote the commentaries extensively. The reason for their restricted influence is to be sought in the prerogatives of the earlier commentaries of R. Ḥananel, representative of the North African-Spanish school, and of Rashi, representative of the Franco-German school, which were perfectly adequate and satisfactorily fulfilled the needs of most students. These commentaries became classic, standard companions of the Talmud, and it was difficult for others to impinge on their prerogative. This explains in part why so few of Rabad's commentaries were preserved and, incidentally, why Maimonides' venture into the field of Talmudic commentary met a similar fate.[1] Their commentaries did not respond to any contemporary challenge nor did they fill a glaring gap and were, therefore, allowed to fall into oblivion.

In the introduction to his *Or Adonai*, Crescas asserts that Rabad wrote a complete commentary on the entire Talmud.[2] David of Estella

44. See *TD*, 67, where he analyzes (in a quest for *ṭaᶜame halakot*) a number of basic problems concerning the water, utensils, and other requirements. See, in this connection, *MT*, *Abot ha-Ṭume'ot*, VIII, 8; *Miḳwa'ot*, XI, 3, and *Oraḥ Ḥayyim*, 162:2. His explanation here of the first mishnah in *Yadayim* (מוסיפים על השניים) differs from that in the hassagah on *MT*, *Miḳwa'ot*, XI, 7–8.

45. *MT*, *Berakot*, VI, 2, and hassagot of R. Moses ha-Kohen *ad. loc.*, ed. S. Atlas, *HUCA*, XXVI (1956), 41. A longer version of Rabad's hassagah is quoted from Paris ms. 181 by E. Urbach, "Hassagot ha-Rabad le-Mishneh Torah . . .," *Kiryath Sefer* XXXIII (1958), 365.

1. In the introduction to the Mishnah commentary, Maimonides mentions that he composed commentaries on *Ḥullin* and nearly all of the three orders, *Moᶜed*, *Nashim*, *Neziḳin*. Practically nothing is extant. The commentary on *Rosh ha-Shanah*, of doubtful authenticity, was edited by Brill (Paris, 1865), and again by S. Shulman (New York, 1958). See Freimann, *Ḳuntres ha-Mefaresh ha-Shalem* (New York, 1945), 338. Fragments on *Shabbat* have been identified by Assaf, Sachs, and Freimann; see *Sinai*, III (1940), 103–134; XIII (1950), 66–68, 248; *Responsa* of Abraham Maimonides, ed. A. Freimann and S. Goitein, 8, n. 4. See also S. Lieberman, *Hilkot Jerushalmi la-Rambam* (New York, 1947), 5, and article cited there. Interesting—but not very convincing—is R. Menaḥem b. Zeraḥ's explanation of the luckless role of Maimonides' commentaries: פירושי הרמב״ם לא התפשטו, ממיעוט עסק הבאים אחריו בתלמוד בבלי; *Ẓedah la-Derek* (Warsaw, 1880), 6.

2. Ḥasdai Crescas, *Or Adonai* (Vienna, 1860), 2a: חבר פרושים בכל התלמוד.

mentions very imprecisely that Rabad "explained most of the Talmud."[3] Ha-Me'iri, who devised a system of literary sobriquets—each very allusive and revealing—for all authorities quoted in his *Bet ha-Beḥirah*, deemed it fit to describe Rabad as "one of the greatest of the commentators."[4] Whatever the case may be—whether he explained all or most of the Talmud—his commentaries are numerous. Gross[5] and Michael[6] have compiled a list of twenty-three tractates in connection with which Rabad's commentaries are mentioned. Marx[7] has added a twenty-fourth. Rabad's commentary on *ᶜAbodah Zarah* (60a) provides another: *Demai*. They are: *Berakot, Shabbat, ᶜErubin, Pesaḥim, Beẓah, Moᶜed Ḳaṭan, Taᶜanit, Rosh ha-Shanah, Sukkah, Yebamot, Ketubot, Ḳiddushin, Giṭṭin, Nedarim, Baba Ḳamma, Baba Meẓiᶜa, Baba Batra, Makkot, Sanhedrin, ᶜAbodah Zarah, Shebuᶜot, ᶜEduyot, Ḥullin, Ḳinnim.*[8] There is no real need to assume, however, that he commented on these tractates in their given order. He probably did much on the spur of the moment, in response to an inner urge or external demand, for there is evidence indicating that he skipped from tractate to tractate. In his commentary on *Baba Ḳamma*, for instance, he refers to previous commentaries on *Ketubot* and *Baba Meẓiᶜa*.[9] It is possible that he inaugurated the entire commentatorial project with a selection of tractates from *Nashim*, because the commentaries on *Ketubot* and *Yebamot* seem to be among the earliest.

The time span of this commentatorial activity, like that of his codificatory writings, is a long one. In his critique of Razah (c. 1187), Rabad mentions that he wrote the same thing as Razah forty years ago in his commentary on *Ketubot*.[10] This supplies an approximate *terminus a quo*. On the other hand, it seems that in the 1170's he was still engaged

3. David of Estella, *Ḳiryath Sefer*, ed. A. Neubauer, in *Medieval Jewish Chronicles*, II, 231.

4. Menaḥem ha-Me'iri, *Bet ha-Beḥirah*, *passim*: גדולי המפרשים, מגדולי המפרשים, מומחין שבמפרשים.

5. Gross, 456.

6. Michael, *Or ha-Ḥayyim*, 27–28.

7. Marx, 205, n. 8.

8. The commentary on *Tamid*, ascribed to Rabad in all standard editions, is pseudepigraphic; see the most recent discussion in Urbach, *Baᶜale ha-Tosafot*, 294 ff.; also, Z. Frankel, *Darke ha-Mishnah* (Warsaw, 1923), 333. The reasons for this attribution, however, deserve further study in light of the connections between Provence and Franco-Germany and the parallels between this and Rabad's genuine writings. The reference in *Shiṭṭah Meḳubbeẓet* on *Baba Batra*, 75b (כמו שאמרנו במשנת מדות) may perhaps imply a commentary on *Middot* also; see A. S. ha-Levi, introduction to *Derashat ha-Rabad* (London, 1955), 9, n. 2.

9. Rabad, *BK*, 17.

10. *KS*, II, 12: אף אני כך כתבתי בפירוש כתובות זה ארבעים שנה.

in writing his commentaries, for in the work on *Baba Ḳamma* he mentions "R. Jacob, may his soul rest in Eden." If we follow Atlas in identifying this Jacob with the famous R. Jacob Tam, who died in 1171, this is clear proof that he wrote after the latter date.[11] The reference here to his *Baᶜale ha-Nefesh* also contends for a later date, for it does not seem that this masterpiece was a product of his very early period.[12]

Of this imposing undertaking only shreds have remained. Many sizable extracts are preserved in the *Shiṭṭah Meḳubbeẓet* of R. Beẓalel Ashkenazi. Stray citations are strewn throughout the writings of the Rishonim. Significant portions of his commentaries on *Berakot* and *ᶜErubin*, for instance, can be reconstructed from the liberal quotations or paraphrases found in the writings of Rashbah and ha-Me'iri on these tractates. Part of the commentary on *Shebuᶜot* is known to exist.[13] J. M. Toledano once handled the commentary on *Berakot*.[14] Also extant is a manuscript copy of the commentary on *ᶜAbodah Zarah*.[15] The only complete manuscript to be printed is the commentary on

11. Rabad, *BK*, 346, n. 6; see Freimann, *Kiryath Sefer*, XX (1943), 26. Atlas' identification may be bolstered by noting that the use of "R. Jacob" to designate R. Tam was very widespread in southern France. E.g., Rabi *TD*, 217; Razah, *passim*. See Reifmann, *Toledot R. Zeraḥyah ha-Levi* (Prague, 1853), 42; R. Asher b. Saul, *Sefer ha-Minhagot*; *Sifran*, 166; R. Asher b. Meshullam, *TD*, 120, and see parallel quotation in ha-Me'iri, *Bet ha-Beḥirah*, *Beẓah*, 146 and n. 55; R. Moses ha-Kohen, *Hassagot*, ed. Atlas, *HUCA*, XXVII (1956), 36; R. Isaac b. Abraham of Narbonne, *REJ*, LVIII (1909), 301–303; R. Abraham b. Nathan ha-Yarḥi, "Tashlum ha-ᶜIṭṭur weha-Manhig," *Emet le-Yaᶜakob* (Berlin, 1937), 115, n. 72; R. Meshullam b. Moses, *Sefer ha-Hashlamah*, ed. J. Lubozky (Paris, 1885), XIX; R. David ben Levi, *Sefer ha-Miktam*, ed. A. Sofer, 208, 332. A group of R. Tam's responsa is included in *TD* (147–149) under the name of R. Jacob.

12. Rabad, *BK*, 100. The date of the *Baᶜale ha-Nefesh* is discussed further in this chapter. Most assume it was a mature work; see, for example, the writer in *Encyclopedia Judaica* (I, 450), who speaks of its composition "in hohen alter."

13. Marx, 205, n. 5. The Bodleian Library has a fragment entitled תוספ׳ הראב״ד על שבועות; see A. Neubauer, *Catalogue of Hebrew Manuscripts in the Bodleian Library* (Oxford, 1886), 4565.

14. J. M. Toledano, *Sarid U-Falit* (Tel-Aviv, n.d.), 63.

15. Marx, "A New Collection of Manuscripts," *Proceedings of the American Academy for Jewish Research*, IV (1932–1933), 147. I learned recently that Rabbi A. Sofer, the indefatigable editor of medieval rabbinic texts, is preparing this difficult manuscript for publication. This will be a great achievement, for, judging from the great number of references to it both in his own writings (e.g., *TD*, 84, 107, 113) and those of contemporaries and successors, it is one of Rabad's most valuable works. It will, also, most likely provide an index to his views on urgent problems of twelfth-century Jewish life, especially Jewish-Christian social and commercial—even ideological—contacts. The publication of ha-Me'iri's commentary on *ᶜAbodah Zarah*, for example, led to a very illuminating study of his views on religious tolerance and social intercourse with non-Jews; see J. Katz, "Sublanut Datit be-Shiṭato shel R. Menaḥem ha-Me'iri," *Zion*, XVIII (1953), 15–30. In the meantime, paging rapidly through the transcription which Rabbi Sofer kindly lent me, I was able to note some hitherto

Baba Ḳamma,[16] which provides a representative sample of his Talmudic commentaries and on the basis of which some general judgments may be formulated.

Using *Baba Ḳamma* as a prototype—the same seems to be true of ᶜ*Abodah Zarah* also—it may be posited that the Talmudic commentaries have greater affinity with the Tosafistic method of textual elucidation and analysis than with the method of complete, terse textual annotation associated with Rashi. Rabad's commentary is a discursive succession of brief definitions and elaborate expositions, pointed explanations of difficult and rare words accompanied by logical analysis of fundamental halakic concepts. That he was not concerned exclusively with juridical issues is manifestly clear from an abundance of minute notes dealing with etymological, historical, or practical matters.[17] Furthermore, although his interests were primarily halakic, he often stops to explain and imaginatively reconstruct aggadic exegesis also.[18]

---

unknown sources used by Rabad and some novel explanations of puzzling texts as well as a reference to his commentary on *Demai*. While allusions to contemporary life are not as abundant as in the commentary of ha-Me'iri, there are significant statements. (While my book was in press, this text appeared; it was too late for me to expand my treatment of it.)

16. There is no doubt that this manuscript is rightly attributed to Rabad. Atlas has presented a number of convincing proofs in the introduction to his edition of the text. Freimann (*Kiryath Sefer*, XX [1943], 26) and Higger (*Jewish Social Studies*, V [1943], 398) unqualifiedly endorse the proofs. Weinberg's qualms about accepting Rabad as the author because of one contradiction between this work and his hassagot on the *Mishneh Torah* are not very disturbing; see Atlas, introduction to Rabad, *BK*, 9–14.

17. Rabad, *BK*, 54, 61, 200, 230, 342, and others.

18. Note, for example, his approach to the Talmudic interpretation of II Sam. 23:15: "And David longed and said: 'Oh that one would give me water to drink of the well of Beth-lehem, which is by the gate.'" The entire historic narrative of David in the cave of Adullam after the battle with the Philistines is interpreted symbolically by the Talmud (*Baba Ḳamma*, 60b) as referring to a legal discourse in which David was engaged concerning some intricate problems of damage liability. "And David longed" symbolizes his intellectual thirst for the correct solution of a problem resulting from the action of some of his soldiers. The impetus to this whole allegory was undoubtedly given by the well-known midrashic identification of "water" and "Torah" (*ibid.*, 17a and parallels; on a list of places where "water" is used for Torah, see R. Margaliyot, "Ḳinnuye Ḥibah la-Torah," *Sinai*, XVII [1953], 150–151), based on the verse in Isaiah (55:1): "Ho, every one that thirsteth, come ye for water." Rabad makes an ingenious attempt to explain how the derash is logically derived from the context, how "water" actually connotes "learning" in this instance. Inasmuch as "water" is qualified in this verse as coming exclusively from "the well of Beth-lehem," it cannot mean actual drinking water; for if David really thirsted for water, any water would be suitable to quench his thirst. It follows that the only possible conclusion is that the verse refers to "words of the Torah"; Rabad, *BK*, 153.

It is interesting to note the tone and emphasis of R. David Kimḥi's explanation of these verses in his Bible Commentary on II Sam. He introduces the original Talmudic allegorization of this passage with the warning that "the words of our sages are puzzling" and, after discussing it in considerable detail and exposing its weaknesses and

With equal ease and skill, Rabad weaves select lines of the Talmudic text into a detailed explanation which reads like an independent little essay, the explanatory remarks often indistinguishable from the text. It is in reality a mosaic of text interspersed with his comments and notes. His style in the commentaries, in keeping with what we have seen elsewhere, is lengthy, fluent, and easy—a fact immediately sensed in the first few pages. On many occasions, he stops to illustrate the logical sequence of the text and its arrangement. Finally, in common with his method in other commentaries, he cites a number of various explanations, discusses and clarifies them, salvages the tenable aspects, and offers his own.[19]

Rabad preserved a sense of proportion and continuity by not incorporating into his commentary any lengthy digressions or excursuses which transcend his immediate concerns or the immediate needs of the reader. He resisted and yet satisfied such temptations by adding a number of appendixes which constitute minor essays on particular topics. The extant text of the *Baba Ḳamma* commentary contains an appendix concerning the question of the culpability of informers—a problem on which Alfasi and the Geonim were at loggerheads. He considered this as more than an explanatory note; it was rather an independent little exercise, "a handy treatise," to which he refers his readers.[20] Other places in the text refer the reader to the end of the book for further elaboration on the subject—but these are no longer extant.[21] Perhaps Rabad had in mind the literary precedent of Alfasi who appended a number of short halakic monographs at the

---

inconsistencies, he concludes with a final disavowal: "this explanation is very remote from the literal meaning." Such forceful rejection of an imaginative midrash, which clearly cannot pass as the literal interpretation of the text, must have been stimulated by some peculiar circumstances. Kimḥi, Rabad's compatriot, was undoubtedly acquainted with Rabad's commentaries and probably recognized Rabad's attempt to justify the Talmudic exegesis from the context. The stress and determination in this part of the commentary seem to be Kimḥi's reaction to Rabad's tour de force. He wants to make it unmistakably clear that this is not the literal meaning.

Another example is Rabad's explanation of the passage where the Talmud quotes Job 27:8 and cites two opposite interpretations of the pronominal suffix in the last word Rabad, *BK*, 338. See also his explanation of the first few pages in ʿ*Abodah Zarah*.

19. Rabad, *BK*, 15, 22, 45, 107, 112, and many others. Attention to the sequence and arrangement, even style, of the text is characteristic of all his commentaries; see ʿ*Eduyot Commentary*, I, 14; *Sifra Commentary*, 1a; ʿ*Abodah Zarah Commentary*, 2a.

20. Rabad, *BK*, 353; see *KS*, I, 23: סוף דבר הרוצה לעמוד על העיקר יראה חבור יפה שחברנו בדין מסור. Also *MT*, *Ḥobel u-Maziḳ*, VIII, 4.

21. Rabad, *BK*, 303, 332. For a similar case elsewhere, see ʿ*Eduyot Commentary*, VII, 2; also, *Sifra Commentary*, 102b: ובסוף זה הסדר פירשתי בו פירוש יפה לפי שמצאתי בסוכה ירושלמי.

end of his compendium for more detailed treatment of specific problems.[22]

Atlas entitled his excellent edition of this work *Novellae on Tractate Baba Ḳamma* (*Sefer Ḥiddushe ha-Rabad ᶜal Masseket Baba Ḳamma*). Justification for this title is sought in the innumerable works of Rishonim described as ḥiddushim (novellae). Also, Abraham Zacutto wrote in *Yuḥasin ha-Shalem:* "he [Rabad] composed novellae to tractates of the Talmud."[23] Freimann, in a very learned review of Atlas' edition, remarks that "commentary" (perush) would be a more appropriate and accurate title.[24] The nature of this work corroborates Freimann's contention; it is clearly a commentary and not a series of novellae like those of Naḥmanides, Rashbah, or R. Yomṭob b. Abraham (Riṭba). Certainly the use of the term "ḥiddushim" by a sixteenth-century chronicler is insufficient reason to label such a work "novellae." On the contrary, if terms used in descriptions of his writings are to be a guide, the use of the word "commentary" in this case by ha-Me'iri, David of Estella, and Crescas should be weighed.[25] Above all—and this fact is noted by Atlas, also—Rabad himself cites this work as a commentary on *Baba Ḳamma*.[26]

3. *Codes*

Before taking up the *Hilkot Lulab*, which seems to come next chronologically, it is best to comment on the general nature of Rabad's codes. Some are minor collections of laws, like the treatise on ritualistic cleanliness of the hands, already discussed. Others, like the *Baᶜale ha-Nefesh*, constitute important contributions to the development of jurisprudence and the codification of Jewish law. The common denominator of all is their preoccupation with practical matters, some of compelling urgency, some so common that they are repeatedly treated by the leading scholars of every generation.[1]

22. B. Cohen, "Three Arabic Halakic Discussions of Alfasi," *JQR*, XIX (1929), 355–410.

23. *Yuḥasin ha-Shalem*, 120; see Atlas, Hebrew introduction to Rabad, *BK*, 14.

24. Freimann, *Kiryath Sefer*, XX (1943), 26.

25. See §2, notes 2, 3, 4.

26 *MT*, *Ḥobel u-Maziḳ*, VIII, 4. He also cites his ᶜ*Abodah Zarah* commentary as "perush"; see *TD*, 16, 84.

1. See the revealing remarks of Naḥmanides, *Hilkot Niddah*, printed at end of *BH*, 89: שאלו ממני . . . לחבר אליהם הלכות נדה כי הם מן הצורך הנה נהגו חכמי הדורות לתרגם הלכות שחיטה איש ואיש ככתבו וכלשונו . . .

Are these codificatory treatises portions or installments of a planned magnum opus or are they independent productions? It has been assumed by Konforte,[2] followed by a number of modern historians—Jost and Carmoly, for instance[3]—that Rabad wrote a comprehensive code similar in scope and detail to Maimonides' *Mishneh Torah* and that the isolated, variegated works we possess are the extant fragments of this larger composition. This view is inferentially sustained by the late medieval chronicle of Sambary.[4] Gross has been an articulate antagonist of this theory.[5] Nevertheless, Marx, spurred on by Rabad's repeated references to his "halakot" and mindful of the above-mentioned fragments, reaffirms the possibility of such an inclusive code.[6]

One passage is of considerable importance for a final verdict on this matter. In a critical annotation on Razah concerning the eligibility of a youngster to be counted as a full-fledged participant in a quorum (*minyan*), Rabad remarks, "I have already written in the halakot what appears to me to be the actual law in this case."[7] This reference to "halakot" is ascertainable, for the identical conclusions stated summarily in the hassagah are expounded at greater length in section one of *Temim Deᶜim* entitled: "The laws (halakot) of summoning to participation in grace (*zimmun*) and grace and benedictions."[8] From this it can be deduced that "halakot" actually refers to legal compendia. This same extract in *Temim Deᶜim* affirms that only fractions of these codes are extant. Its title suggests a table of contents similar to that of the eleven chapters in Maimonides' *Mishneh Torah* devoted to *Hilkoṭ Berakot*. Yet we have merely one selection dealing with a small problem relevant to one section.

One fact emerges clearly. In his well-developed style which combines commentary and code, Rabad wrote a greater number of codificatory works than are now known. Some, if not all, of the frequent cross references to his "halakot," are directed to these works. It would, however, be premature or injudicious to translate Marx's hypothesis into a

2. Konforte, *Ḳore ha-Dorot* (Pietrekov, 1895), 19: חבר ספר גדול כמו ספר הרמב״ם מדינין
3. J. M. Jost, *Geschichte des Judenthums und Seiner Sekten* (Leipzig, 1858), II, 446. E. Carmoly, *La France Israelite* (Francfort s/M., 1858), 125.
4. Neubauer, *Medieval Jewish Chronicles*, I, 124.
5. Gross, 538; *GJ*, 448.
6. Marx, 203; see also R. Isaac b. Sheshet, *Responsa*, 82: שהראב״ד ז״ל כתב בהלכותיו.
7. *Hassagot, Berakot*, 35b: וכבר כתבתי בהלכות מה שנראה לי מפסק הלכה.
8. *TD*, 1: הלכות זמון וברכת המזון וברכות. Cf., however, *Orḥot Ḥayyim*, I, 34b, where this is quoted as תשובת שאלה.

verity or to unqualifiedly endorse Konforte's theory. The fact that Rabad never alludes to such a comprehensive code, not even in his animadversions against Maimonides, militates most cogently against this assumption. Indeed, he refers to these as individual, unrelated works. This is true especially of *Ba^cale ha-Nefesh*. In addition, the terse description of Rabad's literary and scholarly achievements by Isaac de Lattes, in the fourteenth century, implies a discrete series of separate codes and explanatory compilations.[9]

In general, clear cognizance of Rabad's codificatory writings—as a unit or as individual works—completely confounds the opinion of those students who depict Rabad as an uncompromising opponent of codes and an ideological foe of codification.[10] He is said to align himself with the camp of "expansionists"—to use Tchernowitz' metaphor—those who aspired to leave the "sea of the Talmud" uncharted so they might rise and fall on the crests of intricate analysis and the troughs of complicated argumentation. A simple existential judgment, based on factual detail, controverts this view, for Rabad has clearly revealed himself as a master codifier and legist.

Setting up a barrier between codificatory writings and commentaries is generally a rash act. Such a dichotomy is in large measure unfounded, for the two often went hand in hand, either as parallel projects or in the form—cultivated most consistently by the Franco-German school—of commentaries which paid special attention to the codificatory upshot of a general discussion.[11] Naḥmanides, for instance, is said to have changed the course of Talmudic learning in Spain by steering it away from excessive preoccupation with codes. Whereas before Naḥmanides there was an almost uninterrupted series of codes—e.g. those produced by Samuel ha-Nagid, Isaac ibn Ghayyat, Reuben Albargeloni, Judah b. Barzilai, Maimonides—after him there were only two codes by Asher b.

9. Isaac de Lattes, *Sha^care Zion*, ed. S. Buber (Jaroslau, 1885), 39; also Neubauer, *Medieval Jewish Chronicles*, II, 236: אשר חבר חבורים גדולים, דרך חבור ופסק . . . ומהם ספר בעל הנפש.

10. Ch. Tchernowitz, *Toledot ha-Poskim* (New York, 1946), I, 11; G. Sarton, *Introduction to the History of Science* (Washington, 1931), II, 365, 375.

11. This is expressed clearly in a postscript to the *Sefer ha-Terumah*: וגם שם סוף כל הלכה והלכה חוזר ומפרש בקוצר הפסק עם ראיות למען ירוץ קורא בו. See also Radad's hassagah on *MT*, introduction: סבר לתקן ולא תיקן כי הוא עזב דרך כל המחברים אשר היו לפניו כי הם הביאו ראיה לדבריהם . . . Ha-Me'iri writes as follows: וזה שעל דרך ערב לאיש לפי טבעו להשיג ידיעת הדברים מצד החקירה והחפוש . . . מהשיג ידיעתם דרך קבלה לבד ולזה לא נתקררה דעת כל משכיל עד שיראה מחקר הדברים במקום יסודם ובצור מחצבם . . . ואחרי ראותו מקור הדברים ושרשם ועניני חקירתם יערב להם . . . לדעת מה שיעלה מהם דרך פסק . . . *Bet ha-Beḥirah* on *Nedarim*, *Nazir*, *Sotah* (Halberstadt, 1860), 5b.

Yeḥiel and his son Jacob, both of whom were German émigrés to Spain. The pendulum supposedly swung under the impact of Naḥmanides' commentaries, novellae, criticisms—"expansive" writings in short. Yet, these same writers will have to acknowledge that Naḥmanides himself advantageously engaged in codification. His *Torat ha-Adam*, a compendium on the laws of mourning and burial ceremonies, is outstanding by virtue of its neat arrangement, imposing array of sources, original exposition, and felicitous style. *Hilkot Niddah* is a handy summation of the laws of purity, written in brief, concise strokes. He also composed a collection of laws concerning excommunication (*Mishpaṭ ha-Ḥerem*) and one concerning the examination of slaughtered animals (*Hilkot Bediḳah*). Naḥmanides obviously was not conscious of any discrepancy between the two modes of writing and their underlying objectives.

The same is true for Rabad. He engaged in both kinds of activity simultaneously and did not feel or appear ambivalent. Not only did he write, successively, both codes and commentaries, but his commentaries constantly specify the practical, normative conclusion while his codes shed light on innumerable problems of textual interpretation.[12] They were the obverse and reverse of the same coin.[13]

Rabad's lost code entitled *Hilkot Lulab*, concerning which there is the precise testimony of ha-Me'iri,[14] illustrates the general nature of his codes, underscores the essential unity within the apparent duality of codes and commentaries, and also indicates their time span. As a result of a contemporary debate concerning the ritualistic aspects of *Lulab* and *Etrog*, in which ha-Me'iri found himself at loggerheads with the Naḥmanidean school whose protagonists were bidding for halakic hegemony in Provence, ha-Me'iri composed a defensive tract into which he incorporated extensive quotations and paraphrases from Rabad's original work. This work reflected for the most part genuine Provençal tradition. Since ha-Me'iri's objective was to vindicate these customs

12. Note the following characterization of his writings in the supplement to the *Sefer ha-Kabbalah*: והוא עשה ספרים הרבה לבאר כל ספיקא בפירוש ובפסק הלכה. Neubauer, *Chronicles*, I, 84. Ha-Me'iri's description is probably to be interpreted along the same lines: וראש לכל החיבורים שנעשה דרך הרכבת פירוש הם פירושי הרב הגדול הראב״ד ז״ל ופירושי הרב אבן מיגאש ז״ל. Later he adds concerning ibn Megas: הפליג בפי׳ התלמוד בפי׳ מלא ובפסקים אמתיים. Introduction to *Bet ha-Beḥirah* on *Abot*, 68–69.

13. This fact about Naḥmanides' writings seems to me to have been mentioned parenthetically in an article which I am unable to recall. It suggested to me the above comparison of Rabad and Naḥmanides.

14. *Magen Abot*, 103 ff.

and precedents, he leaned heavily on Rabad. On the basis of ha-Me'iri's stenographic account and extensive discussion, the nature of Rabad's *Hilkot Lulab* can be reconstructed.

The code was written at Carcassonne in the home of "the honored scholar Menaḥem b. Isaac" in 1172, the year of Rabad's flight from Posquières. It apparently analyzed systematically all the topics treated in the third chapter of Tractate *Sukkah*—a description of the four species (used to make the festive wreath for the holiday: branch of the palm tree, citron, myrtle branch, and willow) and their disqualifications. The differences between the more stringent specifications for observance on the first day, on which the Scriptural law is fulfilled, and the lenient requirements for the remaining days, on which only a legislated rabbinic ordinance is carried out, are discussed in detail. As ha-Me'iri informs us, one part was devoted to public clarification of his doubts: "Rabad wrote that his intention was to explain next the doubts which occurred to him about Lulab."[15] He presents a series of problems and their proposed solutions. Thinking aloud, he indulges in self-refutation, refinement of these theories, and elaboration of new hypotheses. The whole work was rife with original explanations and unique solutions.[16] Parts of it were, consequently, attributed to special inspiration, to the "appearance of the holy spirit" (*ruaḥ ha-ḳodesh*) in his academy.[17] Both in his hassagot on Razah and on Maimonides, he quotes this work with unabashed pride.[18] He vehemently indicts Razah for plagiarizing it.[19]

The *Ba^cale ha-Nefesh*, a code on the laws of uncleanness and purity, is the most important of Rabad's codes and one of the choice flowers of medieval Jewish codification in general. It was written before his commentaries on the *Sifra* or on *ᶜEduyot*, for in the former he mentions the *Baᶜale ha-Nefesh*[20] while there is a reference to the *Sifra* commentary in his work on *ᶜEduyot*.[21] It was written a considerable time before 1186, the year of Razah's death, for Razah managed to study it and compose a

15. *Magen Abot*, 131.
16. His explanation concerning the ritual fitness of myrtle branches broken on the top (ḳeṭumim), with the concomitant reconciliation of two passages in *Sukkah*, 32b and 34a, is a classic example. See the following two notes.
17. *MT*, *Lulab*, VIII, 5: כבר הופיע רוח הקודש בבית מדרשנו.
18. *Ibid.*; *Hassagot*, *Sukkah*, 15b: וכבר הכל מחובר יפה יפה בחיבור הלכות לולב שחברתי.
19. *Ibid.*: בחושך שמו יכוסה· ולמה כסה מי הוא המפרש וכבר נודע מכמה שנים כי אני הוא המפרש (also, *KS*, II, 28). Yet, in his *Sifra Commentary*, 102b, he introduces the same view as "some say." See Benedict, *Ḳiryath Sefer*, XXVII (1950–1951), 247, and n. 97.
20. *Sifra Commentary*, 56a.
21. *ᶜEduyot Commentary*, III, end.

set of critical annotations on it.[22] If the *Selᶜa ha-Maḥleḳot*[23] which Razah mentions in his *Sefer ha-Ma'or* is identical with these annotations on *Baᶜale ha-Nefesh* (as assumed by Sambary,[24] Gross,[25] and Weiss[26]) or even if it is a larger work of which these form only one part (as assumed by Reifmann[27]), this also points back to a date around 1180. For even if one rejects Reifmann's date on the completion of the *Sefer ha-Ma'or* and accepts, with Marx and others, a later date for its final redaction—which seems to be the correct assumption[28]—its publication still must have been considerably before his death in 1186. Consequently, his critical notes on the *Baᶜale ha-Nefesh* and, ipso facto, the *Baᶜale ha-Nefesh* itself, were completed even before that time. Finally, Rabad himself cites the *Baᶜale ha-Nefesh* as "a handy treatise" (*ḥibbur yafeh*) in his hassagot on Razah, which are to be dated at about the same period (1185–1187),[29] and there is a cross reference to it in his commentary on *Baba Ḳamma*, which dates from sometime after 1171.[30]

An exact *terminus ad quem* for the *Baᶜale ha-Nefesh* would be forthcoming if the second ethical treatise of Berechiah ha-Naḳdan, entitled *Maẓref*, could be dated with precision, for this work apparently contains the earliest quotation from the *Baᶜale ha-Nefesh.*[31] Gollancz, editor and translator of Berechiah ha-Naḳdan's philosophic writings, places this work approximately in the 1180's[32]—which tallies nicely with the preceding data. Guttmann, however, conjectures that Berechiah, a professional eclectic who drew freely from previous philosophic and ethical writings, wrote before 1170, for he very conspicuously makes no use of ha-Levi's *Cuzari* which was just at this time gaining currency in the Hebrew translation of Judah ibn Tibbon.[33] If this argument from silence is valid, the *Baᶜale ha-Nefesh* would emerge as one of Rabad's early codificatory writings, preceding his treatise on

22. These notes are printed together with the *Baᶜale ha-Nefesh* in many later editions.

23. For the correct form of this title, see Marx, 200, n. 1.

24. Sambary, ed. Neubauer, *Chronicles,* I, 124.

25. Gross, 545, n. 4.

26. Weiss, *Dor Dor we-Doreshaw,* IV, 285, n. 15.

27. Reifmann, *Toledot R. Zeraḥyah ha-Levi,* 6, 56, n. 59.

28. Marx, 230; see also Urbach, *Baᶜale ha-Tosafot,* 86.

29. *KS,* II, 11.

30. Rabad, *BK,* 100.

31. Berechiah ha-Naḳdan, *Ethical Treatises,* ed. H. Gollancz, 125, 127; see J. Guttmann, "Zwei Jungst edirte Schriften des Berachja ha-Naḳdan," *MGWJ,* XLVI (1902), 536–547.

32. Gollancz, *Ethical Treatises,* introduction.

33. Guttmann, "Schriften des Berachja ha-Naḳdan," *MGWJ,* XLVI, 538.

Hilkot Lulab. The references to *Baᶜale ha-Nefesh* in Rabad's commentary on *Baba Ḳamma* and in Razah's *Sefer ha-Ma'or*—both of which *might* have been written any time after 1171—could be marshaled in support of the earlier date as well.

The subject matter of the *Baᶜale ha-Nefesh*—laws of uncleanness and purity, with special reference to menstrual conditions—was a constant motif of literary creativity, expressing itself in the form of practical compendia or theoretical novellae. Thus, at about the same time that Rabad produced this work, Maimonides was promulgating a lengthy decree of great literary value concerning the rigid enforcement and application of all laws pertaining to uncleanness and purity.[34] A short time after the *Baᶜale ha-Nefesh*, Naḥmanides complied with the request of some scholars and produced a similar, though more abbreviated, work.[35] One section of Rashbah's *Torat ha-Bayit* is devoted to this topic.[36] It is little wonder then that Rabad focused his scholarship and literary talent on this problem, and it is a fitting accolade that his work came to dominate this area of writing. In seven close-knit chapters Rabad magisterially collected and organized the labyrinthine "laws of women": (1) symptoms, laws, and effects of menstruation; (2) states of impurity and abstinence; (3) ritual cleansing and purification; (4) laws of the ritual bath—qualifications and disqualifications. This is capped by an ethical-homiletical discussion of "holiness." The scope of this undertaking is obviously wide; its textual raw material is knotty and challenging.[37] Moreover, Rabad had few precedents to guide him.[38] A sampling of earlier collections of this material—four discourses in the *She'eltot*,[39] a terse, discursive section of the *Halakot Gedolot*,[40] a few pages of the *ha-Eshkol*[41]—reveals at a glance the great advance

34. *Teshubot ha-Rambam*, ed. A. Freimann (Jerusalem, 1934), 97. Note the common use by Rabad and Maimonides of סלו סלו פנו דרך הרימו מכשול מדרך עמי.

35. Naḥmanides, *Hilkot Niddah*, printed at the end of the *BH*, 89.

36. Rashbah, *Torat ha-Bayit*, VII (*Bet ha-Nashim*).

37. *Niddah*; *Mikwa'ot*; stray references throughout the Talmud; *Kallah* and *Kallah Rabbati* (ed. M. Higger [New York, 1936]; see S. A. Wertheimer, "Mishnat Masseket Kallah," *Bate Midrashot* [Jerusalem, 1950], I, 221, 227 ff.); see also *Baraita de-Niddah* with the lengthy introduction by C. M. Horowitz, *Tosefta ᶜAtiḳata* (Frankfurt a.M., 1890), IV.

38. See the observation in *ha-Eshkol*, ed. Auerbach, I, 70: הגאון ר׳ יצחק ז״ל קצר מאד בדיני נדה, ורוב הלכות בדיני וסתות לא הביא. לכן אסדר מה דחזי לן עקר בדינים אלו עפ״י סדר הגמרא. גם מדיני כתמים לא הביא הרב ועיינת בכל מילי דרבואתא ולא אשכח בהון...

39. *She'eltot*, nn. 85, 86, 89, 96.

40. Ed. E. Hildesheimer (Berlin, 1892), 625–630.

41. *Ha-Eshkol*, ed. Albeck, I, 3–7. Auerbach's edition has much more (I, 70–158), but still discursively arranged.

made by the *Baᶜale ha-Nefesh*. Unfettered by these previous presentations, Rabad completely refashioned the material, and molded it—differentiated and expanded (especially chapter two)[42]—into distinct blocs.

Rabad's aim in composing the *Baᶜale ha-Nefesh* and its relationship to his other codificatory writings should be clarified in light of the divergent approaches to the compilation of codes. They might be written from a theoretical point of view, as Maimonides did with his code. The present time during which part of the law was in abeyance was, in his opinion, an historical anomaly, a fleeting moment in the pattern of eternity. The real historical dimensions were those in which the Torah and its precepts were fully realized, that is, the time after the restoration of the Davidic dynasty, when "all the ancient laws will be reinstituted . . . sacrifices will again be offered, the Sabbatical and Jubilee years will again be observed in accordance with the commandments set forth in the Law."[43] Maimonides' all-embracing theoretical approach and scale of religious-intellectual values necessitated the inclusion of all laws and ideas, even those momentarily devoid of practical value. Oral Law was to be studied exhaustively; hence the scope and nature of the *Mishneh Torah*, which has been aptly labeled a *Corpus Juris Mosaici*.[44]

Rabad did not share this theoretical approach in his codes. As a codifier he belongs to that observance-oriented, practical school—the school of instruction (*hora'ah*)—represented by such major works as the *She'eltot*, the various Geonic *Halakot*, Alfasi and, later, the *Shulḥan ᶜAruk*, which is concerned with concrete problems and issues whose validity and applicability are not confined either temporally or geographically. His other writings, to be sure, display a remarkably comprehensive grasp and all-embracing view of Oral Law. They manifest a total dedication to its study in all aspects—remotely abstract phases of the otherwise relevant civil law as well as problems of Palestinian agriculture and the sacrificial cult in the Temple which were completely divorced from practical application.[45] It is only that in the codes Rabad's chief principle was observance. Codes, he believed, should facilitate the

42. *Niddah* 63b; *MT*, *Issure Bi'ah*, VIII, 1; *Yoreh Deᶜah*, 189; and *BH*, 38–39.

43. *MT*, *Melakim*, XI, 1.

44. B. Cohen, "Classification of Law in the Mishneh Torah," *JQR*, XXV (1935), 521.

45. This fact is amply demonstrated by the *Dibre ha-Ribot*, *Sifra Commentary*, *Ḳinnim Commentary*, and numerous hassagot. See also page 72. The following statement by R. Moses of Coucy is typical: *Sefer Miẓwot Gadol*, introduction: ויש מהמון עם

understanding of the operative laws—hence the presence in them of textual commentary—and guide the people in translating concepts into rules of conduct. Note the following statement:

> Because I have seen that wrongdoings concerning these matters have multiplied and their inner meaning is beyond the grasp of many people, that these matters are prone to lead to error and most people do actually err inadvertently with respect to them, I applied my heart to search, seek, and investigate their inner meaning and to arrive at their true character. As a result, I have composed this book.[46]

Keeping faith with such a preamble, his codes—*Issur we-Heter*, *Hilkot Lulab*, *Perush Yadayim*—are concerned with routine practice and observance, as are extensive sections of his responsa in *Temim De*ᶜ*im* dealing with such subjects as forbidden wine or ritually inedible meat. The section on grace and benedictions was evoked by a prevalent errant practice which annoyed Rabad because it had no textual foundation nor could it point to a Geonic precedent. Rabad saw fit to "review the question of zimmun for I have noticed many who allow themselves to be unjustly lenient" in this matter.[47] Many hassagot, fall in line with this analysis by reiterating the necessity for practical conclusions. Some statements of Maimonides are rejected because they fail to formulate the actual practice.[48]

By the same token, the *Ba*ᶜ*ale ha-Nefesh* was intended to serve as a practical guide or manual of instruction. The need for such a work was especially pressing, for the raw, unrefined subject matter was foreign or incomprehensible to many.[49] The resultant pitfalls in the path of observance were perilous. Rabad sifted the bulky material and codified only those laws which were practical and operative. After a pietistic introduction which injects the motive of fear and inculcates restraint, he starts the halakic part by describing those restrictions designed to

---

שאומרין מה לנו ולמצות סדר קדשים, קל והומר למצות סדר זרעים ולמצות סדר טהרות, לדברים שאין נוהגין בזמן הזה· אל יאמר אדם כן כי המצות אשר צוה אדון העולם יש לידע יסודותיהם אף על פי שאינ׳ צריכין עתה· כי על כל המצות נצטוינו ולמדתם אתם . . . It is interesting that his code, like that of Rabad, is limited to practical laws. See also ha-Me'iri, *Bet ha-Beḥirah* on *Nedarim*, *Nazir*, *Sotah*, 5b: אבל שידעו גרסת ההלכה, כל העולה ממנה דרך פסק, בכל הדברים שבאו בהלכה ההיא, הן מן הדברים הרגילים הן מן הדברים שאין לעניניהם מקום בזמן הזה . . .

46. *BH*, 4.

47. *TD*, 1: הרי אני חוזר על ענין זימון כי ראיתי רבים מקילים. His father-in-law was presumably among the "unjustly lenient"; see *Sefer ha-Hashlamah* on *Berakot*, 39–40.

48. See, for example, *MT*, *Issure Bi'ah* V, 12, 13, 24; also *KS*, II, 20: וזה הקרחי מה שצריך הלכה למעשה לא דבר·

49. See §3, note 46.

eliminate all "occasions leading to sin."[50] True to the nature of a practical work, the minor matters of actual conduct take precedence over the abstract theory. It is interesting to note the difference between Maimonides and Rabad in this respect. Maimonides also formulated those laws governing prohibited acts which offer the occasion for sin (*hergel ᶜaberah*), but he did so much later in the book, in a less conspicuous position.[51] Consonant with his comprehensive view of study and knowledge, even in a code, Maimonides starts with the basic theories and major premises, definitions and concepts, and then develops the minor premises and minute details. Rabad reversed the procedure. For the same reason, Rabad omits the special theories concerning persons who have a running issue (*zabin*), for the enactment of R. Zeira rendered them obsolete.[52] Maimonides retained them. At the beginning of the sixth chapter of the *Baᶜale ha-Nefesh*, Rabad reminds us again that he will include "only those matters which are of present-day importance."[53] An expository summation of all the laws would require a complete commentary and that is beyond the scope of a practical guide for "matters which we need and are ready at hand."[54] Even the *Shaᶜar ha-Ḳedushah*, the one truly theoretical section of the whole book devoted, as it is, to ethical norms and attitudes, is justified by Rabad in the same utilitarian terms.[55]

It is necessary for purposes of a balanced bibliographical survey to stress the originality of the *Baᶜale ha-Nefesh* and its creative systematization of law. Whereas the majority of his works, especially the critical ones, may be characterized as learned reactions coming in the wake of external stimuli—in other words, his enormous erudition, once activated and galvanized by others, proved most fruitful—his codes are thoroughly original, in conception, form, and content. Even his commentaries, all their original explanations notwithstanding, follow a prepared text. His systematic works, especially the *Baᶜale ha-Nefesh*,

50. *BH*, 5; see *Shabbat*, 13a; *Abot de R. Nathan*, II, 2; *Seder Eliyahu Rabbah* (Vienna, 1902), 76 (ch. 16). The *Sefer ha-Eshkol* also starts on a pietistic note: ונשמרת מכל דבר רע׳ . . . מצינו עשרה מילי דחסידותא. See also *Sefer ha-Oreh*, ed. S. Buber (Lemberg, 1903), 27: ומצינו עשרה מילי דחסידותא דהוה נהוג בהון רב. This is apparently characteristic of many Franco-German halakic works; see E. Urbach, "Liḳḳutim misifre debe Rashi," *Sefer Rashi*, ed. J. L. Maimon (Jerusalem, 1956), 323.

51. *MT*, *Issure Bi'ah*, XI; *BH*, 5.

52. Levit., XV; *Niddah*, 66a; *MT*, *Issure Bi'ah*, VI.

53. *BH*, 61: לא אכתוב כאן כ״א הענינים המצויין והמזדמנין תמיד.

54. *Ibid.*, 76: בענין הצריכין לנו והמזומנין לידינו. See also *Sifra Commentary*, 56a: ספר בעלי הנפש שחברנו . . . על פי ההלכה, הלכה למעשה.

55. *BH*, 78: ואני רוצה להאריך ולהרחיב בשער הזה מפני שיש תועלת באריכותו והוא מהעניינים שרוב בני האדם נכשלים בהם ונלכדים בפח מוקשיהם ועל זה ראיתי להציע בהם עד שיהיו פשוטים ומובנים לכל דורשיהם.

add another dimension which may pass unnoticed if Rabad is considered exclusively as a critic or even as a commentator.

The *Baᶜale ha-Nefesh* epitomizes, in many ways, Rabad's general impact on codification. It was influential in two realms: the theoretical and the halakic. Ethicists and moral philosophers from Jonah Gerondi to Israel ibn Al-Nakawa and Elijah di Vidas found especially in the last chapter of the *Baᶜale ha-Nefesh* a source of inspiration and moral guidance.[56] This chapter—in many respects a "first" in Jewish literature—discusses, on an abstract-theoretical level which nevertheless has practical-moral implications, the ethical norms and dispositions which enable one to attain purity of heart and action. It evolves a philosophy of sublime, religiously impeccable living. It outlines principles whereby plain, instinctual *hedoné* can be elevated, endowed with purposiveness, and combined with spiritually motivated elements.[57] Along with Maimonides, even though totally independent of him, Rabad may be considered one of the initiators of that literary tradition in which "rabbis and philosophers . . . quite freely discussed the intimate relationships between men and women in so far as they had legal or ethical bearing."[58] It is small wonder, therefore, that so many writers mentioned this work and quoted from it rather copiously, while others absorbed and reproduced so much of its essence without explicitly citing it. It is possible to trace its lineage in subsequent literature in the writings of the following authors: Berechiah ha-Naḳdan,[59] R. Abraham b. Nathan ha-Yarḥi,[60] R. Jonah Gerondi,[61] R. Meïr of Rothenburg,[62]

56. The *Shaᶜar ha-Ḳedushah* was apparently copied separately and circulated as an independent treatise; see *GJ*, 447; E. Carmoly, *La France Israelite*, 125. The Bodleian has a manuscript of the *Shaᶜar ha-Ḳedushah*; see Neubauer, *Catalogue*, 904.

57. *BH*, 81: הנה דרשתי וחקרתי במעט שכלי ומצאתי תוכן המעשה הזה על ארבע כוונות לבדי, ועל החמישית לא מצאתיו. Actually, he lists three basic motives or intentions which sublimate carnal joy: (a) procreation; (b) fulfillment of one's marital responsibilities to one's wife; (c) preventive against sin or a barrier against illicit extramarital relations. These offer much greater latitude than the halakic and hygienic formulas of Maimonides; see *MT*, *Ishut*, XIV, 1–7; *Deᶜot*, IV, 19. There are interesting parallels between this classification, which Rabad considered to be both original and exhaustive, and that found in the *Mozene Ẓedeḳ*, ed. J. Goldenthal (Paris, 1839), 137 ff.; see also, *BH*, 3, 86; and *Mozene Ẓedeḳ*, 68–69. It is most unlikely, however, that Rabad was acquainted with this work of Algazali, even if one assumes, with Haberman and Gutstein, that its translation into Hebrew by Abraham ben Ḥisdai was one of his earliest undertakings; see M. Gutstein, "Midarke ha-Targum," *Gotthold Weil Jubilee Volume* (Jerusalem, 1952), 75, n. 6.

58. S. Baron, *Social and Religious History of the Jews* (New York, 1937), II, 113.

59. Gollancz, *Ethical Treatises*, 125–127.

60. *Perush Masseket Kallah Rabbati*, ed. J. Toledano (Tiberias, 1906), 32 ff.

61. *Yesod ha-Teshubah* (Jerusalem, n.d.), 5.

62. *GJ*, 448.

R. Baḥya b. Asher,[63] R. Aaron ha-Kohen of Lunel,[64] R. Jacob b. Asher,[65] the anonymous author of *Orḥot Ẓaddiḳim*,[66] R. Israel ibn Al-Nakawa,[67] R. Eleazar Azkari,[68] and R. Elijah di Vidas.[69] This descent may be extended directly into later kabbalistic and ḥasidic literature. In practically all these cases one gets not merely meager references but very substantial excerpts which often set the tone for extensive sections of these works. The quotations by R. Jacob b. Asher in the *Ṭur Eben ha-ᶜEzer*, for instance, serve almost as slogans embodying the quintessence of its spirit.

In the realm of halakah, one may say without overemphasis, the *Baᶜale ha-Nefesh* dominated all systematic discussion of its subject matter, starting with Naḥmanides' *Hilkot Niddah* through Rashbah's *Torat ha-Bayit* down to the *Shulḥan ᶜAruk* and its standard commentaries. A comparative study of the *Baᶜale ha-Nefesh* and the *Shulḥan ᶜAruk* reveals that in cases of controversy Rabad's view almost always became authoritative even when he controverted regnant Geonic opinion;[70] one can practically count on one's fingers those instances where Rabad's view was explicitly rejected in deference to a conflicting opinion.[71] Nor can the long-range authoritativeness of his views be attributed to their acceptance and restatement by other medieval codifiers—even though this is intrinsically significant. For even in those rare instances when later authorities like Rashbah and R. Asher b. Yeḥiel disagree with him, his view reigns supreme in the *Shulḥan ᶜAruk*.[72] Or, on the contrary, when a conflicting view seems inherently superior, Rabad's view is rejected even if bolstered by these authorities.[73] It was not merely the consensus of opinion which turned the scales in Rabad's favor, but his own authority and the cogency of his views, which happened in most cases to be supported also by succeeding

63. *Perush ᶜal-ha-Torah* (Pisaro, 1507), 178.
64. *Orḥot Ḥayyim*, II, 72.
65. *Ṭur Eben ha-ᶜEzer*, introduction, 25; also *Ṭur Oraḥ Ḥayyim*, 240.
66. *Orḥot Ẓaddiḳim* (Frankfort, 1687), 26a, b (ch. 26: Teshubah). There is an interesting correlation there between the *Baᶜale ha-Nefesh* and the *Sefer ha-Roḳeaḥ*.
67. *Menorat ha-Ma'or*, ed. H. Enelow (New York, 1931), III, 110; IV, 72.
68. *Sefer Ḥaredim* (Lublin, 1924), 82–83; also, 23, 21, 66.
69. *Reshit Ḥokmah* (Vilna, 1900), 317.
70. E.g., *BH*, 7 (against the *She'eltot*, supported by Razah); *Yoreh Deᶜah*, 194, 23; see *MT*, *Issure Bi'ah*, V, 13.
71. E.g., *BH*, 11, 14 (see *Ketubot*, 4a); *Hassagot* Razah on *BH*, 11; *MT*, *Issure Bi'ah*, XXII, 1; *Eben ha-ᶜEzer*, 22, 11; and *Yoreh Deᶜah*, 192, 4. Also, *BH*, 15, and hassagot Razah, *ad. loc.*; *Yoreh Deᶜah*, 193, 1; and see *Sifte Kohen*, *ad. loc.*
72. E.g., *BH*, 8; *Yoreh Deᶜah*, 188, 3–4; see *MT*, *Issure Bi'ah*, V, 13–14.
73. *BH*, 16; *Yoreh Deᶜah*, 184, 9; see *Tosafot*, *Niddah*, 16a; *MT*, *Issure Bi'ah*, IV, 13.

authorities. Finally, his views were not only accepted and restated, but often the very phraseology used by Rabad and the specific illustrations or practical applications which he mentions—everything was reproduced.[74]

The standard guides to medieval rabbinic literature are not totally reliable in tracing views to their origin, for Rabad is not always duly credited or mentioned as the ultimate authority of a given statement. Sometimes intermediate authorities like R. Jonathan ha-Kohen or Rashbah, who were under his indirect literary tutelage, are cited as the underlying source.[75] This is common procedure, resulting from the nature of the transmission and preservation of juridical, especially codificatory material. The process of transmission seems to have been something like this. Authoritative codifiers like Karo and Isserles never worked in a vacuum nor did they produce comprehensive codes ex nihilo. They were guided by existing, already classical works from the pen of Rishonim who had scrutinized the writings of immediate and remote predecessors, selected relevant views and decisions, and then formulated certain parts of the law systematically and comprehensively. While there were not many codes as universal in scope as the *Mishneh Torah*, there were a number of smaller codes, restricted in scope, but exhaustively authoritative within their self-imposed limitations. The long-range influence of Rishonim, no matter how prolific or creative they were, depended on whether they themselves produced such codes or whether their writings were incorporated into similar works of later Rishonim which, in turn, became the basis of entire sections of the *Shulḥan ᶜAruk*. Thus, while views were often perpetuated only as a result of their incorporation in later works, their authorship was just as often eclipsed in the process. Rabad bears out this procedural routine. In those sections of *Yoreh Deᶜah* dealing with the laws of menstrual uncleanness and marital relations in general, Rabad exerted tremendous weight through his *Baᶜale ha-Nefesh* but even more via Rashbah's *Torat ha-Bayit*, a comprehensive code upon which Karo and all the contemporary codifiers drew unrestrictedly. It is, therefore, under-

74. E.g., 7, and *Yoreh Deᶜah*, 195, 7 (see *Nedarim*, 20a, and *MT*, *Issure Bi'ah*, XXI, 4); *BH*, 13, and *Oraḥ Ḥayyim*, 240, 6, 11, 13 (see *Tosafot*, *Niddah*, 17a, and *Berakot*, 26a; *Bet Joseph* on *Ṭur Oraḥ Ḥayyim*, 240) *BH*, 15, and *Yoreh Deᶜah*, 193. (See *Hagahot Maimuniyot* on *MT*, *Issure Bi'ah*, XI, 18).

75. *BH*, 17 and *Yoreh Deᶜah*, 184, 4; *BH*, 22, and *Yoreh Deᶜah*, 189, 33–34; *BH*, 56, and *Yoreh Deᶜah*, 188, 40; *TD*, 4, and *Yoreh Deᶜah*, 99, 6; *TD*, 6, and *Yoreh Deᶜah*, 110 (*Sifte Kohen*, 35, and *Pitḥe Teshubah*, *ad. loc.*).

standable why views are often traced back only to Rashbah rather than to their ultimate source in Rabad.

This truncated genealogy of halakic views is more pronounced in other areas of law in which Rabad composed no systematic treatise of his own. His imprint on subsequent codification in these areas is accountable for only in terms of the above-outlined process: synthesizing intermediaries who embedded his scattered remarks in formal manuals which subsequently became influential. For instance, Rabad's influence on many sections of the *Ḥoshen ha-Mishpaṭ* is considerable, as evidenced by quotations in the text, lengthy discussions in commentaries such as the *Sifte Kohen*, and final determination of the normative view. This influence is for the most part indirect, having been mediated or channeled by the *Sefer ha-Terumot* of R. Samuel b. Isaac ha-Sardi which directly dominates extensive sections of the *Ḥoshen ha-Mishpaṭ* just as the *Torat ha-Bayit* does in *Yoreh Deᶜah*. Unlike Rashbah, however, R. Samuel ha-Sardi did not draw from any organized work of Rabad on criminal and civil law but from fragmentary responsa, hassagot, and incidental glosses which he judiciously used and interpreted. In this case he really helped perpetuate Rabad's views, the original form of which would undoubtedly have diminished their influence. Consequently, views are frequently referred back to ha-Sardi, whereas further investigation actually projects the source back to Rabad.[76]

In order to gauge the full extent of Rabad's influence on the codification of Jewish law, it would be necessary not only to trace the destiny of his self-contained treatises—*Baᶜale ha-Nefesh*, as indicated above, or *Perush Yadayim* which can be shown to have been completely swallowed up in the relevant sections of the *Shulḥan ᶜAruk*[77]—and to evaluate the importance of those aggregates of views preserved by others—views on civil law as found in the *Sefer ha-Terumot*—but also to identify fragmentary views scattered throughout the *Shulḥan ᶜAruk* and its cognate literature. Many of the opinions expounded in *Temim Deᶜim* and accepted later as authoritative are not attributed to Rabad but to those derivative sources which were closer to the *Shulḥan ᶜAruk*. An interesting explanation, attributed to R. Jonah Gerondi, is found for the first time in Rabad's *Sifra* commentary. At the beginning of that section of

76. E.g., *TD*, 50, and *Ḥoshen ha-Mishpaṭ*, 73, 12, and *Sifte Kohen, ad. loc.*; *TD*, 54, and *Ḥoshen ha-Mishpaṭ*, 81, 29; *TD*, 55, and *Ḥoshen ha-Mishpaṭ*, 39, 3 (note *Sifte Kohen*), and 70, 1.

77. *TD*, 66–67; *Oraḥ Ḥayyim*, 162.

the *Shulḥan* ᶜ*Aruk* devoted to repentance and the Day of Atonement, R. Moses Isserles comments: "Every person should search and investigate into his actions and repent. A doubtful transgression requires more repentance than an undoubted transgression, for one regrets it more when he knows certainly that he has committed a sin than when he does not know." This notion is expressed, to be sure, in R. Jonah Gerondi's commentary on *Berakot*, as indicated parenthetically in the text of Isserles, but its antecedent is surely Rabad's explanation as to why a guilt-offering brought when one is in doubt if he committed a sinful act is more expensive than a guilt-offering brought for a definite commission of sin: when the nature of the sin is not definitely known, the feeling of culpability is less acute, repentance is more difficult, and a greater fine is appropriate.[78]

No one would contend that Rabad be added to the triumvirate—Alfasi, Maimonides, and R. Asher b. Yeḥiel—which guided Karo in his codification. Karo's explicit proclamation specified his reliance on these three scholars.[79] They were professional codifiers who produced massive Talmudic codes in one form or another, while Rabad was essentially an analyst and commentator who did not stop to produce a comprehensive systematization of law. All this notwithstanding, Rabad's influence on Karo, as on that entire century of codifiers and synthesizers, was appreciable; it is simply the measure of this indebtedness which must be recognized and evaluated.

There is one more point to be made concerning the *Ba*ᶜ*ale ha-Nefesh* and Rabad's share in codification—a small point of general precedent rather than directly ascertainable influence. Practically all projects of codification antecedent to the *Shulḥan* ᶜ*Aruk* adhered to the form of the *Ba*ᶜ*ale ha-Nefesh*, which proceeded logically from textual interpretation and discussion to the formulation of the codificatory upshot.[80] As a matter of fact, most contemporary opposition to the *Shulḥan* ᶜ*Aruk*—articulated by such people as R. Mordecai Jaffe,[81] R. Meïr of Lublin,[82]

78. *Oraḥ Ḥayyim*, 603; *Sifra Commentary*, 26.

79. Introduction to *Bet Joseph*; see Tchernowitz, *Toledot ha-Posḳim*, III, 29. Karo's statement follows that of R. David b. Zimra, *Responsa* II, 626: כל הגלילות האלו קבלו עליהם את הריאף ואת הרמבם ואת הרא״ש להיות הכרעותם הכרעה . . .

80. See §3, note 11; also the characteristic statement of ha-Me'iri, *Bet ha-Beḥirah* on *Nedarim*, *Nazir*, *Sotah*, 5b: רצון רוב המתלמדים אשר ראו עינינו בדורנו זה . . . הוא לשנות את ההלכה עם המחקר הנמצא שם בתלמוד. Rashbah, introduction to *Torat ha-Bayit*: ואכתוב בע״ה דרך משא ומתן מאיזה צד באו העניינים כדי שימצא המעיין מקום מוצא המים ויהיו מימיו נאמנים.

81. In his multivolume code, *Lebush*; see Tchernowitz, *Toledot ha-Posḳim* III, 103.

82. *Responsa* (Venice, 1618), 135.

and R. Solomon Luria[83] in terms reminiscent of Rabad's statements[84] —revolved around its abandonment of this conventional-integrative form. Rabad's works are not the only influential precedent for this; analogous Geonic treatises and works of French and German rabbis are available in abundance. But Rabad's works certainly constitute one of the precedents. It should be added that, while the *Shulḥan ᶜAruk* implicitly adopted the Maimonidean form of presentation, sans phrase and sans explication, it remained in the orbit of the observance-oriented, practical school. Like Rabad and unlike Maimonides, the author limited his subject matter to practical laws.

4. *Commentaries on Halakic Midrashim*

Rabad's commentatorial activity extended not only to the Talmud and to the Mishnah, but also to the Halakic or Tannaitic Midrashim.[1] These commentaries should be recognized as a pioneer effort on his part. The Tannaitic Midrashim, though invaluable as an important source of Oral Law and indispensable for any integrated investigation of the development of Jewish jurisprudence, were not exploited fully before the twelfth century nor was their systematic study cultivated in European schools. Maimonides, modern scholars posit, was one of the first to utilize the Tannaitic Midrashim substantially. Recent studies endeavor to reveal Maimonides' use of these Midrashim and to find in them the original source of many of his controversial or otherwise inexplicable decisions.[2] However, neither Maimonides nor any other scholar ventured an independent study of these legal corpora in

83. *Yam shel Shelomah*, *Ḥullin*, introduction.

84. Note Karo's own statement in the introduction to the *Bet Joseph*: ואם יאמר אדם לבחור בספרי הקצורים . . . באמת שזו דרך קצרה וארוכה כי מעולם לא יוכל לדעת שום דין כהלכתו . . . על כן . . . נערתי חצני לסקל המסילה והסכמתי לחבר ספר כולל כל הדינים הנוהגים בביאור שרשיהם ומוצאיהם מהגמרא עם כל חילוקי סברות הפוסקים . . .

1. See, in general, D. Hoffman, *Zur Einleitung in die halakischen Midrashim* (Berlin, 1887); *JE*, "Midrash"; Ch. Albeck, *Untersuchungen ueber die halakischen Midrashim* (Berlin, 1929); J. N. Epstein, *Mebo'ot Le-Sifrut ha-Tannaim* (Jerusalem, 1957), pt. III.

2. L. Finkelstein, "Maimonides and the Tannaitic Midrashim," *JQR*, XXV (1935), 472: "Maimonides was the first Jewish codifier to realize the value of the tannaitic Midrashim for Jewish tradition and law. Before his time, they had hardly been utilized." See also J. N. Epstein, "Mekilta we-Sifre be-Sifre ha-Rambam," *Tarbiẓ*, VI (1935), 343–382, and the literature cited on 343, n. 1; B. M. Lewin, "Midreshe Halakah u-Fiske ha-Rambam," *Ḳobeẓ R. Moses b. Maimon*, ed. J. L. Fishman, 101–145; M. Kasher, *Mekore ha-Rambam weha-Mekilta, Me'ah Halakot be-Mishneh Torah* (New York, 1943).

comparison with the Mishnah and Talmud. As rare and novel as were independent, self-contained commentaries on the Mishnah, commentaries on these Midrashim were nonexistent. Rabad was the first to undertake this commentatorial task.

This last assertion of absolute priority requires some elaboration and, perhaps, modification, for it is possible that the commentary on the *Sifra* by R. Hillel b. Eliakim of Greece,[3] preceded that of Rabad. Establishment of priority between these two is a moot question. Geiger places Hillel about a generation after Rabad, and consequently assumes direct literary influence of the latter on Hillel.[4] Gross assumes them to be contemporaries and cautiously allows for a mutual "give and take."[5] Michael, without proper documentation, dates Hillel very early, presenting him as a disciple of Rashi.[6] As for the possibility of Hillel's influence in Provence, the works of Jewish scholars living in Italy and Byzantium were generally well-known in Provence and used by Rabad himself.[7] That the writings of Hillel in particular had infiltrated southern France is ascertained by the fact that R. Isaac b. Abba Mari of Marseilles mentions Hillel in his *Sefer ha-ᶜIṭṭur* (c. 1190).[8] As for Rabad's possible influence on Hillel, Sassoon lists a manuscript commentary on the *Sifre* which was attributed to Rabad but actually came from the pen of Hillel who utilized Rabad's writings to a great extent.[9] Until new evidence is forthcoming, one must suspend judgment on the question of priority between the commentaries of Hillel of Greece and Rabad of Provence.

Some time after the composition of Rabad's commentary on the *Sifra*, there was attributed to R. Samson b. Abraham of Sens, prominent French tosafist who excelled primarily in Mishnah commentaries, a

3. Excerpts were published by A. Jellinek, *Ḳuntres ha-Rambam* (Vienna, 1878), 29–32; A. Freimann, "Perush R. Hillel ᶜal Baraita de-R. Ishmael," *Sefer Zikkaron Likbod S. A. Poznanski* (Warsaw, 1927), 170–180. The entire manuscript was described by R. N. Rabinowitz, *Diḳduḳe Soferim* (Munich, 1873), V, *'Erubin*, introduction. See Aptowitzer, *Mabo le-Sefer Rabiah* (Jerusalem, 1932), 337; Starr, *History of the Jews in the Byzantine Empire*, 227. With regard to the question of priority, reference should be made to the unknown commentaries on the *Sifra* by R. Abraham מתיבץ; see *JQR* (Old Series) IV (1892), 94.

4. Geiger, "Mechilta und Sifre," *Jüdische Zeitschrift für Wissenschaft und Leben*, IX (1871), 22–23.

5. Gross, *REJ*, VII (1883), 63, and literature cited there; see also A. Aptowitzer, *Mabo*, 337.

6. Michael, *Or ha-Ḥayyim*, 790; also *JE*, VI, 401.

7. See Chapter V.

8. Gross, "Jesaja b. Mali da Trani," *ZfhB*, XIII (1909), 121.

9. D. Sassoon, *Ohel David* (London, 1932), I, 106–108. This was edited by S. Koleditzky (Jerusalem, 1948).

commentary on this text.[10] The similarities between these two works are staggering. One is tempted to assert instantaneously that Rabad's commentary served as the basis of the other work, which incorporated outright about 50 per cent of it and then embroidered this literary core with supplementary and alternate interpretations.[11] Although the author never mentions Rabad by name, he does refer frequently to the "sages of Lunel," "the sages of Provence," and the "books of Lunel."[12] All these references can be traced back to and verified in Rabad's commentary. Besides, there are innumerable passages that were taken over and not acknowledged by the author.

Urbach has most recently defended the hypothesis, repeatedly suggested by S. Lieberman, that this commentary was not written by R. Samson of Sens, but is a later production attributed to him.[13] According to this, there is no question whatsoever about the clear-cut temporal priority of Rabad's commentary. Indirect support for this view is offered by the following curious fact. In his brief sketch of the history of rabbinic literature, ha-Me'iri does not mention a commentary on the *Sifra* as one of R. Samson's achievements. Isaac de Lattes, however, who is slavishly faithful, almost plagiaristic, in his reproduction of ha-Me'iri's description, inserts the following observation in his outline of R. Samson's career: "also a commentary on *Torat Kohanim.*"[14] The immediate inference is that by the time Isaac de Lattes was writing —the end of the fourteenth century—this pseudepigraphic attribution had already gained currency. At any rate, it is clear that this commentary, even if by R. Samson or a member of his school, is posterior to and influenced by Rabad's work.

Rabad's commentary on the *Sifra* was published by I. H. Weiss[15] and its identity, which had been doubted by the author of *Ḥawwot*

10. Warsaw, 1826.

11. For this conclusion, reached independently after a discursive comparison of both works, I later found corroboration in H. Gross's article "Etude sur Simson b. Abraham de Sens," *REJ*, VI (1883), 167–186; VII, 40–77, and in the relevant chapter of E. Urbach's important study, *Baʿale ha-Tosafot*, 219 ff.

12. Gross, "Simson b. Abraham," 61; Urbach *Baʿale ha-Tosafot*, 260.

13. *Ibid.*; see S. Lieberman, *Tosefet Rishonim* (Jerusalem, 1937), I, 62; II, 295; III, 168; also, J. L. Maimon, "Rashi," *Deyuḳna'ot shel Maʿalah* (Jerusalem, 1946), 131.

14. *Shaʿare Zion*, 37; *Bet ha-Beḥirah* on *Abot*, 69.

15. Vienna, 1862 (reprinted New York, 1947). There is also a different manuscript copy of this commentary, which supplements the hitherto unique manuscript used by Weiss for his edition; see Marx, "A New Collection of Manuscripts," *Proceedings*, 146. On the fragmentary Constantinople edition of 1523, see *ZfhB*, XI (1907), 47. See also Freimann, "Die hebraischen Kommentare zu den 13 Middot des Rabbi Ismael," *Festschrift Adolf Schwarz* (Berlin, 1917), 109–118.

Ya'ir, was definitely established by the editor.[16] Rabad himself mentions this commentary in some of his later works, in his hassagot on Maimonides[17] and his commentary on *ᶜEduyot*.[18] Marx reminds us that this commentary was not Rabad's sole work on the Tannaitic Midrashim. He also composed commentaries on the *Mekilta* and the *Sifre* which are quoted by Rashbah and R. David Pardo.[19] Yet David of Estella, writing in the fourteenth century, mentions only the *Sifra* commentary.[20] The other two were presumably no longer extant, escaped his attention, or else were not very important in his opinion. The *Sifra*, it should be mentioned, was first in the Codex which reached Europe, preceding even the *Mekilta*, and was valued by Maimonides above all the other Midrashim.[21] Rashi, too, used the *Sifra* more than all the other Halakic Midrashim, especially in his Talmud commentary.[22] Its preeminence is further attested to by the fact that, following Rabad, there was a rash of commentaries on it. Leviticus had a special place in Jewish education; children, because of a reason given in the Midrash,[23] began their study of the Pentateuch by reciting the first verses of Leviticus. Probably for the same reason its Tannaitic commentary *Sifra* was popular among advanced students.[24] It is possible that Rabad's two other commentaries were rather brief or fragmentary and only the *Sifra* commentary, which we possess and which the fourteenth-century chronicler notes, was a full-dress work.

Unlike Rabad's codificatory works, which were predominantly practical in purpose, the purpose of this work on the *Sifra* seems to be primarily theoretical. Apparently, the challenge to which this commentary responded was the widespread Karaite heresy, for while no Karaite community is known to have flourished in southern France at this time, there were Karaites in neighboring Spain. Rabad's introductory paragraph is marked by an unmistakable tone of urgency. His exhortation to the faithful and admonition to the unbelievers convey a

16. *Ḥawwot Ya'ir* (Frankfort a/M., 1699), 108. Weiss, *Sifra*, VIII.
17. *MT, Kelim*, II, 5.
18. *ᶜEduyot*, III, end.
19. Marx, 203, n. 1; see H. Azulai, *Petaḥ ᶜEnayim* (Livorno, 1790), on *Nazir*, ch. IV.
20. Neubauer, *Chronicles*, II, 231.
21. Finkelstein, "Maimonides and the Tannaitic Midrashim," *JQR*, XXV, 472.
22. J. Maimon, *Deyuḳna'ot shel Maᶜalah*, 206, 211.
23. *Leviticus Rabbah*, *Ẓaw*, VII, 4.
24. L. Finkelstein, *Mabo le-Massektot Abot ve-Abot d'Rabbi Natan* (New York, 1950), 108.

sense of immediacy and personal involvement. In general, Jews everywhere looked upon Karaism as a serious challenge and a sustained threat.[25] While the Karaites mustered arguments against the Oral Law and its traditional prescriptions—to be replaced in time by their own "burden of inheritance"[26]—the protagonists of rabbinic Judaism turned to a study of the Bible and the Oral Law and indicated their proximity, harmony, and historical interrelations. The well-known Spanish-Jewish philosopher Abraham ibn Daud, alarmed by a short-lived flourish of Karaism in Castile, hastened to compose an important historical chronicle (1161) illustrating the unbroken continuity of Judaism, which bolstered the normative value and regulatory authority of traditionalist teachings.[27] It is not surprising either that many halakic works, including the *Mishneh Torah* of Maimonides, started with an historical introduction which depicted the "chain of tradition" and sketched the uninterrupted transmission of the Oral Law. Rabad's commentary on the *Sifra* should be viewed in this context. At about the same time that the philosopher Abraham ibn Daud (also known as Rabad) penned his chronicle in defense of the historicity of rabbinic Judaism, our Rabad selected the *Sifra* for detailed study because of its essential importance for the methodology of the Oral Law.[28] Inasmuch as the bulk of the *Sifra* is derived from Scripture by an application of the "thirteen hermeneutical rules" which form an introduction to

25. For a good general introduction see now L. Nemoy, *Karaite Anthology* (New Haven, 1952) (Yale Judaica Series, VII); Z. Ankori, *Karaites in Byzantium* (New York, 1959). A pertinent example for our purposes is the attitude of R. Samson of Sens; see Gross, *REJ*, VII, 40. On Karaites in Spain, see I. Loeb, *REJ*, XIX (1889), 206 ff.; J. Rosenthal, *JQR*, XVIII (1956), 206 ff. On Abraham ibn Ezra and the Karaites, see D. Rosin, "Die Religionsphilosophie Abraham Ibn Esra's," *MGWJ*, XLIII (1899), 76–77, and P. R. Weis, "Abraham ibn Ezra weha-Ḳara'im," *Melilah*, I (1944), 35–53; II (1946), 121–134; III–IV (1950), 188–203. On Karaites in Franco-Germany, see A. Marmorstein, "Spuren karäischen Einflusses in der gaonäischen Halachah," *Festschrift Adolf Schwarz*, ed. Aptowitzer-Krauss (Berlin, 1917), 459, n. 5. Also, A. Freimann, "Meschullam b. Kalonymos' Polemik gegen die Karäer," *Judaica: Festschrift zu Hermann Cohen* (Berlin, 1912), 569–578. It is most significant that these polemical notes of Meshullam, who corresponded with scholars from southern France, are quoted in *ha-Eshkol*, ed. Auerbach, III, 71 (כתב ... להשיב את המינין). See Mann, *Tarbiẓ*, VI (1935), 241, n. 12. See also *Sefer ha-ʿIttim*, 267: לא נמצאת מינות ... אלא במקצת כפרים הסמוכים לארץ אדום.

26. See now, N. Wieder, "Three Terms for 'Tradition,'" *JQR*, XLIX (1958), 112, who translates the Hebrew *sebel ha-yerushah* as "the inherited tradition."

27. Abraham ibn Daud, *Sefer ha-Ḳabbalah*, ed. Neubauer, *Chronicles*, I, 47.

28. *Genesis Rabbah*, III, 5: ויקרא ... שהוא מלא הלכות רבות. Also, Rabad's comments at beginning of *Sifra Commentary*, 1a: מפני כי הספר הזה ויקרא מלא מצות וחוקים והמדרש שדרשו בו נמשכין עליו כמה קלין וחמורין וכמה כללות ופרטות וכמה גזירות שוות, לפיכך קבע בתחלתו המדרש הזה שהוא פתח לכל ויסוד לכל המצוות. Also, *ibid.*, 112b: ... המדרשות, פי׳ שהם כמו חוקים לפי שאינן מפורשים בתורה והם קבלה.

it[29] and inasmuch, also, as traditionalism stands on the validity, juristic efficacy, and authority of these rules, Rabad undertook to elucidate and vindicate this exegetical method.

These thirteen rules were always an object of strife between Rabbinites and Karaites. They were combated by the latter and esteemed by the former. Judah Hadassi, a contemporary of Rabad living in Constantinople, who was an articulate protagonist of Karaite doctrine, vents his wrath on this *Baraita of R. Ishmael* (which expounds the thirteen rules) in his learned *Eshkol ha-Kofer*, and this antagonism must have existed long before him.[30] Anan, the founder of Karaism, was sharply assailed by later Karaite authorities for not having emancipated himself completely from rabbinite exegetical and juridical methods.[31] It must have been to counteract this opposition to traditional hermeneutics on the part of the Karaite schismatics—in the words of Rab Amram Gaon "heretics and scoffers who hold in contempt the words of scholars"—that as early in the history of the conflict between Rabbinites and Karaites as the ninth century the thirteen rules were incorporated into the *Siddur* (prayer book) of Amram Gaon.[32] Inclusion in the daily prayer book was clearly a token of esteem and a sign of popularity. Undoubtedly, it was for the same reason that in the tenth century Saadia, the arch nemesis of the Karaites, also composed a commentary in Arabic on these rules. This commentary was certainly unknown to Rabad for it was not translated from the Arabic until the thirteenth century by Naḥum ha-Maᶜarabi.[33]

Rabad begins his commentary on the *Sifra* with a short, pointed prologue on the necessity of tradition in all realms of action and reflection, especially religion. Here is the core of his contention:

Tradition is the source of them all and the underlying principle of all commandments of the Lord our God. If not for tradition, whence could we

29. A brief description and useful bibliography can be found in H. Strack, *Introduction to the Talmud and Midrash* (Philadelphia, 1945), 95 ff.

30. Judah ha-Dassi, *Eshkol ha-Kofer*, 162. See Freimann, "Die hebraischen Kommentare," 109, who discusses this point.

31. Nemoy, *Karaite Anthology*, 8; *idem*, *HUCA*, VII (1930), 319–321; H. Ben-Sasson, "Rishone ha- Ḳara'im," *Zion*, XV (1950), 43.

32. *Siddur Rab Amram*, ed. A. L. Frumkin (Jerusalem, 1912), II, 206. See also the similar phrase of R. Natronai Gaon quoted by Rabad's disciple Abraham b. Nathan ha-Yarḥi, *Sefer ha-Manhig*, 82: וכופר בדברי חכמים ומבזה דברי משנה ותלמוד; *Oẓar ha-Geonim*, ed. B. M. Lewin, *Pesaḥim*, *Teshubot*, 120.

33. It was printed for the first time by S. Schechter in *Bet Talmud*, IV (1885), 235 ff. and reprinted by J. Müller in *Oeuvres Complets de Saadia*, IV, 73 ff. See Steinschneider, *Die hebraieschen Uebersetzungen des Mittelalters* (Berlin, 1893), 395, 935.

know how to explain the meaning of the commandments? How would we know, in explaining the verse "In the beginning God created" that it (*Bereshit*) means "in the beginning" and how would we know that "*Elohim*" is the name of the Creator? Even the language with which we speak and request all our needs, in detail, from the Creator—if not for tradition, how would we beseech [God]?[34]

Consequently, Rabad submits, the traditions which have been transmitted from generation to generation are indispensable. "We must, therefore, believe firmly in and rely upon the teachings of our ancients, the early scholars who received [the tradition] from their forefathers and the latter from their forefathers, concerning all the details of the commandments and the midrashim, even if the midrash deviates from the literal approach."[35] If not for the fact that the immediate task of textual commentary was pressing and also exacting, he would expatiate more on the philosophical-ideological aspects of tradition "in order to harass the opinions of the heretics who refuse to obey and believe."[36] He yields, however, to the inexorable demands of exegesis and exposition which, by demonstrating the inherent consistency and intelligibility of the text and its methods, indirectly serve as a bulwark for the faithful. The actual commentary, illustrating and vindicating the exegetical and juridical methods of the Rabbinites, is more forceful than abstract theorizing about the indispensability of tradition. From this perspective then—besides its fundamental halakic value—Rabad's commentary on the *Sifra* merits a place in Jewish apologetic literature as one of the twelfth-century anti-Karaite polemics.

The commentary itself is fluid and lucid. As is his custom, Rabad brings many explanations, considers their merit, explains why a certain one is preferable, or offers a new interpretation. He pays considerable attention to the nature and method of the *Sifra* and frequently points out similarities between various passages and the exegetical rules that govern them. Philological details—or peculiarities—of the text are scrutinized. Instead of repeating the explanation of those selections that are quoted and discussed in the Talmud—a pedestrian, unimaginative

34. *Sifra Commentary*, 1a: והקבלה אב לכולן ועקר לכל מצוות הא־ל אדוננו; see *Shabbat*, 31a; Judah ha-Levi, *Cuzari*, III, 35; Abraham ibn Ezra, *Yesod Mora*, VI (Prague, 1833), p. 25b.

35. *Sifra Commentary*, 1a. See Abraham ibn Ezra, introduction to Bible Commentary, fifth method of exegesis.

36. *Sifra Commentary*, 1a: לשבר דברי המינין הממאנים לשמוע ולהאמין. See the harsher statement of R. Amram Gaon (Siddur, II, 207): מינין מלעיגין ובוזין דברי חכמים. For use of "minim," see W. Bacher, *Ha-Rambam Parshan ha-Miḳra* (Tel-Aviv, 1932), 141.

task which merely provides added convenience for the student without revealing any originality of the author—he simply refers the reader to the Talmudic source. If there is a special problem or some inconsistency between the two sources, however, he explains both in detail. In this he uses extensively, for purpose of comparative study, the Tosefta and the Palestinian Talmud. As usual, textual criticism is important for him. Some very bold suggestions and emendations are proposed.[37] Vernacular glosses—even an occasional Arabic one—are common.[38] Finally, it would seem, as Weiss noted, that Rabad produced a revised edition of this commentary.[39] The fact also that there are cross references from this commentary to the ᶜ*Eduyot* commentary and from the latter to the *Sifra* commentary, indicates either that both works were prepared simultaneously in manuscript or that they both underwent revision.[40]

Better than any other work, this commentary illustrates Rabad's attitude to derash and his sustained efforts to reconcile rabbinic exegesis with the literal meaning of the text. For, unlike the quasi-codificatory Mishnah which states the abstract law without indicating its Scriptural source, the halakic Midrashim are actually extended legal commentaries on the text. Consequently, a commentary on one of these Midrashim presupposes not only a modicum of exegetical skill, but a definite commitment to and a clear grasp of Talmudic canons of hermeneutics. Rabad was devoted to the literal approach and his initial quest was always for the precise textual meaning;[41] but he took great pains to

37. *Sifra Commentary*, 4a, 12b, 14a, 19a, 19b, 25b, 76b, 78b for illustrations of all points mentioned in this paragraph—and *passim*.

38. E.g., *Ibid.*, 98b.

39. *Ibid.*, introduction, VIII, 80a.

40. *Ibid.*; ᶜ*Eduyot Commentary*, III, end.

41. See, for example, *Sifra Commentary*, 6a: וא״ת · · · תשובתך לפי שאין מקרא יוצא מידי פשוטו, ואע״פ שאנו דורשין. Note also *MT*, *Genebah*, IX, 8: שאע״פ שדרשו חכמים · · · אעפ״כ אינו יוצא מידי פשוטו. Naḥmanides echoes this attitude: ואני אומר בשמא, לאחר בקשת המחילה, שזהו פשט הכתוב בתורה · · · ואל תהיה חוסם עינך בזה מפני שדרשו חז״ל המקרה הזה לענין אחר · · · שאעפ״כ אין מקרא יוצא מידי פשוטו. *Mishpaṭ ha-Ḥerem* (*Teshubot ha-Meyuḥasot*, 288) as emended S. Lieberman, *L. Ginzberg Jubilee Volume*, 320. Karl's conclusion that Maimonides always sought the literal sense of the text except when the actual halakah is based upon the rabbinic derash, in which case he habitually cites and explains the derash, is thus applicable also to Rabad as to most medieval rabbis; see Z. Karl, "ha-Rambam kefarshan ha-Torah," *Tarbiẓ* VI (1935), 152–163. This supplements W. Bacher's basic monograph, *Die Bibelexegese Moses Maimunis* (Strassburg, 1897) (Hebrew: *Ha-Rambam Parshan ha-Mikra* [Tel Aviv, 1932]). See also M. Roth, "Shiṭat ha-Rambam bi-Derashot Ḥazal," *Ha-Rambam: Kobez Torani Madaᶜi*, ed. J. L. Maimon (Jerusalem, 1955), 187–191. Another alternative was to retain the halakic conclusion while rejecting its hermeneutical derivation; see Karl, "ha-Rambam," *Tarbiz*, VI, 152–153; M. Segal, *Parshanut ha-Mikra* (Jerusalem, 1944), 62.

justify derash, to demonstrate the reasonability and, if possible, even the linguistic probability of halakic exegesis.[42] While there is, for the most part, no attempt to blur the demarcation line between the two meanings,[43]

42. For example, the *Sifra* (88b) has the following homily on the verse "Thou shalt not oppress thy neighbor" (Levit. 19:13,: "I might think that even if a person said 'so and so is strong' and he himself is not strong, 'so and so is wise' and he himself is not wise, 'so and so is rich' and he himself is not rich [he would be violating the rule of 'thou shalt not oppress thy neighbor'], Scripture, therefore, teaches us [in the adjacent clause] 'thou shalt not rob him.' [From this we deduce that] just as robbery is meant only with reference to money, similarly oppression concerns money. In what manner? One who withholds the wages of a hired servant." This explanation is very challenging and nebulous, for there is no apparent connection between the verse and the homiletical deduction; in the words of I. H. Weiss (*Massoret ha-Talmud, ad. loc.*), this passage "is one of the most obscure." Rabad produces here a superb piece of exegesis and commentary, impressively documented, and with what is a remarkable tour de force renders the hermeneutics of this passage intelligible. "It seems to me," Rabad suggests, "that he [the Tannaitic commentator] renders 'thou shalt not oppress (*taᶜashoḳ*)' as if it were 'thou shalt not covet (*taḥashoḳ*).' For there are many similar examples in Scripture where the '*ᶜayin*' and the '*ḥet*' interchange, for instance, '*ᶜushu*' is like '*ḥushu*,'" and Rabad marshalls a cogent array of Scriptural and aggadic illustrations. One is swayed by the rapid pace, the wide range, and the deft exegesis, on the basis of which he concludes: "So, in our case, were it not that this verse was written adjacent to 'thou shalt not rob,' I would be inclined to interpret *lo taᶜashoḳ* in the sense of *ḥesheḳ*, i.e., be not desirous through envy to covet your neighbor['s qualities] if he is wise, strong and rich and you are not like him—and if one did covet his neighbor's qualities, he would violate a prohibitive injunction. Therefore, Scripture adds in the next phrase, 'thou shalt not rob.'" For a Tannaitic example of the interchange of *ᶜayin* and *ḥet*, see *Mekilta*, I, 57.

43. Sometimes Rabad openly admits his inability to relate the *derash* to the original verse; see, for example, *MT*, *Parah Adumah*, III, 2. There is in this case an initial rejection of a passage in the *Sifre* (compared to M., *Parah*, IV) a questioning of the midrashic method used to reach this deduction (the same language elsewhere is interpreted differently—see *Sifra*, 21a), and, finally, a reserved attempt to reinterpret its meaning. Sometimes, he merely indicates the apparent superfluousness of the derash (in this case, the *Mekilta*); see, for example, *MT*, *Genebah*, IX, 8. The reaction of the *Maggid Mishneh* (*ad. loc.*) to this critique of Rabad is interesting. He assumes that this implies that Rabad approached midrashic exegesis with reservations and he, therefore, triumphantly confronts Rabad with a number of other midrashic deductions which are indispensable for the halakah. The fact is, however, that Rabad merely allowed himself in this case to substitute his exegesis for the Tannaitic one, but he never thought of questioning midrashic deductions in general; such an attitude would have been impossible for any great Talmudist.

Rabad's hassagah on *MT*, *Issure Bi'ah*, XVII, 13 (see *Kele ha- Miḳdash*, V, 10) is not a case of literal exegesis versus free midrashic exposition—as Gross, XXIII, 26, has construed it—for the Talmud (see *Yebamot*, 59a; *Yoma*, 13a) is not at all cognizant of the relevance of the verse cited (II Chron. 24:3) to the problem. It seems that nobody was bothered by this verse from an halakic point of view before Rabad called attention to it; see L. Ginzberg, *Legends of the Jews*, VI, 354, n. 11. However, after Rabad focused attention on the verse, many subsequent commentators—starting with R. Samson of Sens—raise the question with regard to the Talmud itself; see *Ḥiddushe Ritba* on *Yoma*, 10b; *Tosafot Yeshanim*, *Yoma*, 13b. The verse might mean, as the commentators (e.g., *Maggid Mishneh*) suggest, that Jehoiada took the women successively rather than simultaneously. See also *Oẓar ha-Geonim* on *Yoma*, 77, and *Yebamot*, 138; *Sefer Toledot ᶜAdam* (Vilna, 1928), 21.

there is an effort to invest the midrashic one with cogency and validity.[44]

5. *Mishnah Commentaries*

Rabad's commentaries on the Mishnah should be related to the process by means of which the Mishnah became a subject of independent study. Though prior to the Talmud in point of time, the Mishnah, owing to the fact that it was incorporated into the Talmud, gradually became subservient to and assimilated in the Talmud as a unit of study. Thus, even though the writing of commentaries on the Mishnah and the Talmud began at about the same time (the tenth century), the Talmud had several practically complete commentaries by the end of the eleventh century (e.g. those of R. Ḥananel and Rashi) while commentaries on the Mishnah were rare and fragmentary. The Geonic period produced a commentary on *Ṭohorot* which was confined to textual difficulties and lexical questions but did not embrace halakic discussion, casuistic debate, or conceptual analysis.[1] Reference is also made to other commentary fragments from the pen of such Geonim as Paltoi, Sherira, and Saadia.[2] There was, in addition, the commentary of R. Nathan b. Abraham, head of the school (*ab Yeshibah*), who wrote in Palestine at the end of the eleventh century.[3] It remained for Maimonides to compose a commentary on the entire Mishnah, which was not immediately as influential as it should have been, for only fragments were translated from the Arabic original to the Hebrew: the introduction by Judah al-Ḥarizi and *Abot* plus the tenth chapter of *Sanhedrin* by Samuel ibn Tibbon. Since the bulk was not translated

44. *Sifra Commentary*, 1a: ולסמוך על דברי קדמונינו החכמים הראשונים . . . בכל דקדוקי המצות והדרשים ואם יצא המדרש מדרך הפשט. Also, *ibid.*, 37a, 78b; Rabad, *BK*, 160: צריכים אנו ליישב המקראות לפי הדרש.

1. J. N. Epstein, *Der gaonaische Kommentar zur Mischnaordnung Teharoth*, Berlin, 1921; and *Tarbiẓ*, XVI (1945), 71–134.

2. Assaf, *Teḳufat ha-Geonim we-Sifrutah*, 137 ff.

3. A manuscript of this commentary was described by Assaf, *Kiryath Sefer*, X (1933–1934), 381–388; 525–544; reprinted in *Teḳufat ha-Geonim*, 294–322. Excerpts were published by J. Sachs in the *Memorial Volume of Rabbi Kook*, ed. J. L. Fishman (Jerusalem, 1945), 171–179. The complete text is now available in the new (*el ha-Meḳorot* edition of the Mishnah. For the Mishnah and Talmud commentary of R. Isaac ibn Giat, see S. Assaf, "Sefer ha-Ner le R. Isaac ibn Giat," *Tarbiẓ*, III (1932), 213–214. Attention was first called to this by Bamberger and Geiger as noted by Lieberman, *Tosefet Rishonim*, III, 107.

until the fourteenth century—and then only imperfectly—its contemporary impact was considerably cushioned.[4]

Rabad's contributions to Mishnah study—at about the same time perhaps as Maimonides'[5]—although not so ramified, were important and influential, for they were written in Hebrew. The fact that Maimonides' Arabic commentary did not penetrate the major intellectual strata until much later clearly augments the historic significance of Rabad's and other contemporary Hebrew commentaries.[6] Furthermore, the Mishnah treatises that Rabad selected—*ʿEduyot* and *Ḳinnim*—were abstruse and not at all popular or appealing, both requiring expert, specialized knowledge. *Ḳinnim* is a remote, unpractical treatise concerned with the offering of sacrificial birds.[7] *ʿEduyot*, a treatise containing the testimony of later teachers regarding various halakic statements of earlier authorities, is a compact, discursive work, almost encyclopedic in range by virtue of its allusions to topics scattered throughout the entire Talmud. Of the twelve tractates comprising Tohorot, which Maimonides described as "bristling with fundamental difficulties, even in early times . . . and which even the greatest masters find hard to comprehend, let alone the students,"[8] three were expounded by Rabad: *Niddah* (which has Talmud), throughout the *Baʿale ha-Nefesh*; *Miḳwa'ot*, in the sixth chapter of the same work; *Yadayim* (especially the part on the ritual uncleanness of unwashed hands) in a separate little treatise. Many sections of *Ṭohorot*, as well as *Zeraʿim*, were

4. On the original text and translations, see A. Yaari, "Perush ha-Mishnah leha-Tambam Bimeḳoro," *Kiryath Sefer*, IX (1932), 101–109, 228–235; also, *ibid.*, XII (1935), 132. The selections that were translated were not chosen exclusively for their commentatorial value. The general introduction, besides depicting the chain of tradition, defines the various constituents of the Oral Law. *Abot* contains an exposition of his ethical theory—in the famous *Shemonah Peraḳim*—while chapter ten of *Sanhedrin* contains the initial formulation of the Maimonidean creed, the thirteen articles of belief.

5. Maimonides started his commentary in Spain at the age of twenty-three and completed it ten years later in Egypt (i.e., c. 1168); see end of his commentary on *ʿUḳzin*.

6. Contemporaneously, there are several other scholars dedicating themselves to Mishnah study—almost as if there had been a prearranged plan to "redeem" the Mishnah: Shemaya, Rashi's disciple; Moses b. Abraham of Pontoise, R. Tam's disciple; Isaac b. Melkizedek, the well-known scholar from Siponto; Samson of Sens, the noted Tosafist; see, in general, Frankel, *Darke ha-Mishnah*, 339–358; H. Albeck, *Mabo la-Mishnah* (Jerusalem, 1959), 237–257.

7. Rabad himself writes in the rhymed introduction to his commentary: להאיר את שתי עיני במראות, בקנין גוף הלכות התלויות, ופתרונם כמו במות טלואות, אשר חלפו ועברו הזמנים, ולא ירד אנוש בם לפלאות.

8. Mishnah commentary, introduction to *Ṭohorot*; see Judah b. Barzilai, *Perush Sefer Yeẓirah*, ed. S. J. Halberstamm (Berlin, 1885), 50–51: טהרות היום בעונותינו היא מאד יקרות ואין ידוע לן עקר. Quoted by S. Lieberman, *Tosefet Rishonim*, IV, introduction, 11.

explained in the course of his annotations of these sections in the *Mishneh Torah*—explanations which have proved invaluable for the comprehension of these passages and the establishment of a correct text.

Rabad's commentaries display the exhaustive knowledge necessary for such an undertaking. He is both methodical and comprehensive. He cites alternative explanations, weighs them, and decides between them. He occasionally reverts to a passage in order to add yet another interpretation. Passages explained elsewhere in Talmudic literature are dismissed with a cross reference, for his is not an elementary commentary but an advanced work for competent students who can find their way in the Talmud. His desire for generalizations is indulged in these works by synthetic summaries and formulaic descriptions.[9] Finally, whenever possible, he uses the Tosefta, the Palestinian Talmud, and even the Midrash.[10]

ᶜEduyot is one of the last works prior to his hassagot, for in it he quotes the *Sifra* commentary (which in turn refers to the *Baᶜale ha-Nefesh*).[11] The *Ḳinnim* commentary is much earlier.[12] Like the *Baᶜale ha-Nefesh* it was certainly many years before 1186, for Razah managed to compose a countercommentary on *Ḳinnim*, the underlying aim of which is a critique of Rabad. A more specific, perhaps earlier *terminus ad quem* is suggested by the poem of his father-in-law (who died in 1179), which singles out Rabad's prowess in this commentary for special praise.[13]

One major difference between the approach and aim of Maimonides and Rabad must be indicated in order to preserve a proper historical perspective. Rabad and most of his contemporary commentators endeavored to shed light upon and interpret only those sections of the Mishnah which had no further explanation in the Talmud. They concentrated first and foremost upon *Zeraᶜim* and *Ṭohorot*. Those sections of these two orders—*Berakot* and *Niddah*—which were graced with Amoraic commentary, that is Talmud, remained for the most part untouched by these commentators, as seen in their exclusion from R.

9. *ᶜEduyot*, end of ch. 1, and ch. 4.
10. Frankel, *Darke ha-Mishnah*, 355–356.
11. *ᶜEduyot*, III, end.
12. It is quoted in the *Sifra Commentary*, 24b.
13. The poem, printed at the end of the *Ḳinnim Commentary* and possibly motivated by this commentary (see Chapter I) mentions: ודורש טוב במשניות סדורות כמו קנין ופתחי האסורות.

Samson of Sens' commentary on *Zera*ᶜ*im* and *Ṭohorot*.[14] Rabad omitted those passages of the Mishnah which were satisfactorily explained in the Talmud, just as he omitted those passages of the *Sifra* quoted in the Talmud. He merely gave cross reference to these places.[15] Maimonides, on the other hand, desired to condense the rambling Talmudic explanations and distill the quintessence from the lengthy discussions. He would manipulate, refashion, and recast these conclusions and insights in the form of a self-contained commentary on a self-contained literary unit. His expressed aim was to render the Mishnah an independent cadre, which would provide a worthwhile subject of study.[16] Rabad was intrigued by Mishnah study because it was baffling and difficult; he wanted to supplement what the Amoraim had omitted, to elucidate the uninterpreted sections of the Mishnah, but not to detach it completely from the Talmud. His commentaries gave the Mishnah a modicum of literary independence, but the cross references to the Talmud caused the two to remain substantially interwoven.

Why was Mishnah study such a specialty, such a priceless commodity? The answer lies in the challenging nature of the Mishnah alluded to above. It was precisely its inherent difficulty, the defiant challenge which a laconic Mishnah not elucidated by Amoraic explanation hurled at its prospective students, that accounted for the scarcity of commentators. Scholars shied away from the Mishnah. The following testimony by the generally fearless Razah, expressing his reluctance to deal separately with Mishnah, is very telling. As a preface to his critical annotations on the sixth chapter of the *Ba*ᶜ*ale ha-Nefesh*, which contains a concise commentary on *Miḳwa'ot* (a treatise concerned with ritual baths—hence the following play upon the word "water"), Razah writes: "Upon entering the gate of water, my heart melted and turned to water. For the waters rose high, a stream which I am unable to cross *because we have no Talmud* for most of the *Mishnayot* in it."[17] For a man of Razah's temperament, such diffidence is unusual. At the same

14. Jacob Aksai, translator of Maimonides' Mishnah Commentary on *Nashim*, mentions that R. Samson of Sens also explained other Mishnah treatises (*Sheḳalim*, ᶜ*Eduyot, Middot, Ḳinnim*) which lack Talmud.

15. ᶜ*Eduyot*, I, 1: ואיני מקבל על עצמי לפרש כאן כל המשנה שהיא שקועה בגמרתנו . . . רק המשניות שאינם משוקעות בגמרא, בהן אני מפרש מה שיראוני מן השמים.

16. Maimonides, introduction to Mishnah Commentary: ד׳ תועלות גדולות, האחת, שאנו מלמדים פירוש המשנה על נכון ובאור מליה . . . והתועלת השנית הפסקים . . . והשלישית להיות כמבוא לכל המתחיל בעיון החכמה . . .

17. *Hassagot* on *BH*, 62: בבאי בשער המים, נמס לבי ויהי למים, כי גאו המים, נחל אשר לא אוכל לעבור מפני שאין לנו גמרא לרוב המשניות שבו.

time Maimonides accused "a great man, a man of great speculative power in the West" of not knowing Mishnah and hence falling into many pitfalls.[18] Mishnah commentary required assiduous labor, academic daring, and powers of abstraction and generalization. In the introduction to his commentary on the Mishnah, Maimonides remarks:

> One is able to explain this order [Zeraᶜim] after much wearisome labor and great toil. Tosefta and *Baraitot* must aid him. He must glean those halakot concerning its subject matter from the entire Talmud and must with his intellect deduce the principles and problems of these tractates from those halakot.[19]

Maimonides obviously possessed this scholastic courageousness and Rabad shared it with him. With confidence and knowledge, or confident in his knowledge, Rabad approached those parts of the Mishnah lacking Talmudic elaboration in order to elucidate minute textual questions as well as to formulate broad conceptual descriptions. In light of the many difficulties and the widespread reluctance of twelfth-century scholars to grapple with the Mishnah, Rabi's praise of his son-in-law becomes more meaningful. He extols Rabad as one "who investigates and accurately grasps the meaning of the books" and as aptly interpreting *mishnah* treatises like *Ḳinnim* or those concerned with tithing and other abstruse subjects.[20] The knowledge and expository ability that Rabad displayed were truly a rare combination. Rabad's own introduction to *ᶜEduyot* transcends the realm of rhetoric when read with these facts in mind. "In all these [matters] I have nothing to fall back upon, neither from a Rabbi or a teacher," for there were actually no traditional patterns or precedents. Rabad was breaking new ground and he was aware of it: "I beseech the Creator Blessed be He to guide me in this matter in a straight path." He proclaims at the end that he is prepared to undertake the commentatorial task—"and I take it upon myself to explain."[21] Since few ventured into the area of Mishnah commentary, such a task did indeed call for special resolution.

6. *Sermons and Responsa*

Rabad cultivated yet another literary genre—derashot, or sermons—whose products cannot be consigned to any definite year. One of these

18. Mishnah Commentary, *Miḳwa'ot*, IV, 4.
19. *Ibid.*, introduction: יכול אדם לפרש הסדר ההוא אחר יגיעה רבה ועמל גדול . . .
20. See Chapter I, §1, note 28.
21. *ᶜEduyot Commeutary*, introduction: אין עמי בכל אלה לא מפי רב ולא מפי מורה . . .

derashot, though, is already mentioned in the scholia on Razah (c. 1185–1187), while another is referred to in sections of *Temim De^cim.*[1] This type of literary production also had social overtones, for some of them were presumably delivered orally. The term *derashah* may denote either a full-dress pulpit oration delivered on some special occasion—usually one of the major holidays—or a comprehensive written manual for a similar occasion. Simeon b. Zemaḥ Duran quotes Rabad as saying that it was his custom to speak at the festive meal of wedding celebrations.[2] Naḥmanides refers to him as a "saintly person, a preacher for whom it is fitting to preach."[3] The derashah was a common form of writing and technique of exposition in Provence, a country devoted to midrashic study and compilation. Many homiletical collections, such as the *Midrash Tadshe* or the *Midrash ^cAseret ha-Dibrot* were apparently written or redacted in Provence.[4] Others made their debut into northern European Jewish literature via Provence; many lost midrashim are known only by means of quotations in Provençal writings. The derashah used so extensively by later Spanish scholars such as Naḥmanides, R. Nissim, and ibn Shu^caib was first popularized in Provence. The derashot of another Provençal scholar—Samuel b. David, Rabad's disciple or colleague—supply a further illustration of this.[5]

We know of derashot for Rosh ha-Shanah (New Year), Day of Atonement, and Passover. These derashot seem to be detailed elucidations of select subjects, short discourses on various facets of holiday observance. They embrace both the halakic aspects as well as the aggadic motifs of these holidays. Rabad himself refers to his derashah

1. *TD.* 31; *KS,* II, 40.
2. Duran, *Magen Abot,* 42a (on III, 3); see Assaf, in *Sifran,* 187.
3. Naḥmanides, introduction to *Hilkot Niddah* (printed with the *BH*), 89. Among the moderns, J. Reifmann (*Bet Talmud,* IV [1885], 382), undoubtedly basing himself upon Duran, describes Rabad as a preacher, while A. Shulman ("le-Ḳorot ha-Darshanut," *ha-Goren,* IV [1903], 102 ff.) ranks Rabad among the all-time greats in the history of preaching.
4. Reifmann, *Toledot R. Zeraḥyah,* 48, n. 18; A. Epstein, *Ḳadmoniyot ha-Yehudim* (Vienna, 1887), I. The prevalence of midrashic exegesis in Provence, even in the independent mold of Scriptural commentaries, is attested to by a statement of R. David Kimḥi in the introduction to his commentary on *Chronicles.* Justifying the need for his own undertaking, with its marked orientation to literalist exegesis, Kimḥi notes: "I found here in Narbonne commentaries on this book . . . but I observed that they follow the midrashic approach." One would expect Kimḥi, a philologian and grammarian by training, to be especially sensitive toward homiletical interpretations. See V. Aptowitzer, "Deux Problèmes d'Historie Littéraire," *REJ,* LV (1908), 84–92.
5. Benedict, "R. Samuel b. David," *Kiryath Sefer,* XXVII (1950–1951), 243, 247.

on Passover,[6] as do his pupil R. Abraham ibn Yarḥi,[7] and the Provençal authors of the *Kol Bo*, the *Sefer ha-Miktam*, and the *Sefer ha-Menuḥah.*[8] Their references, which are mostly on halakic matters, can be supplemented by a description of a manuscript in the Sassoon collection on the *Order for the Nights of Passover according to the Sefardi Rite*. This manuscript contains numerous references to Rabad, especially to his derashah on Passover, and includes both halakic and aggadic insights.[9]

The derashah for the Day of Atonement is cited in the Bible commentary of R. Isaac b. Ḥayyim in connection with his analysis of the various components of "confession" (*widduy*). In order to arrange and substantiate his presentation, he drew upon "what Maimonides wrote in *Hilkot Teshubah* and Rabad, in the derashah on the Day of Atonement."[10] Halakic norms and aggadic embellishment are inextricably connected in the delineation of such a complex, vital theme as "repentance" (*teshubah*).

The derashah on Rosh ha-Shanah which Rabad mentions in his annotations on Razah,[11] and to which R. Nissim Gerondi[12] and ha-Me'iri[13] also refer, was recently published on the basis of the unique Bodleian manuscript which Neubauer discovered.[14] The fusion of halakah and aggadah in this work, the only extant derashah, is evident. True to classical form, it opens with homiletical considerations and passes on to solid halakic analysis. Aside from shedding more light on his method in halakah and enabling a comparison of the views expressed here with those in his commentaries and hassagot, this work gives us an insight into Rabad's approach to aggadah and illustrates how he combined new philosophical with traditional homiletical material. In his other writings, there are hardly any clues to this question. His commentaries gloss over aggadic digressions, for their aim is purely halakic. Codes, and critical annotations on codes, certainly are not the medium

6. *TD*, 31; see *Orḥot Ḥayyim*, II, 176b, where this is cited as a responsum.

7. *Ha-Manhig* (Berlin, 1855), 73. This is a substantive excerpt from the aggadic portion.

8. *Kol Bo*, 48; *Sefer ha-Miktam*, ed. A. Sofer (New York, 1959), 404 (דרשא [!] של פסח), 406, 417; *Sefer ha-Menuḥah* (Pressburg, 1879), 24b.

9. Sassoon, *Ohel David*, I, 303–304.

10. This quotation is cited in *Letterbode* II, 177: וממה שכתבו הר"ם בהלכות תשובה והרב ר' אברהם בר דוד בדרשת יום הכפורים.

11. *KS*, II, 40.

12. Commentary of R. Nissim, *Rosh ha-Shanah*, ch. II.

13. Ha-Me'iri, *Ḥibbur ha-Teshubah*, ed. A. Sofer, with introduction by S. Mirsky (New York, 1950), 354.

14. *Derashat ha-Rabad le-Rosh ha-Shanah*, ed. A. S. ha-Levi (London, 1955). See my review of this in *Kiryath Sefer*, XXXII (1957), 440–443.

for aggadic exposition. An occasional responsum contains a bit of aggadic homily but there is nothing substantial.[15] This derashah, consequently, is a welcome addition to the bibliography of Rabad's printed works.

Temim Deᶜim, considered as a collection primarily of Rabad's responsa, obviously defies any precise dating. His responsa were written, by definition, at various times and on various occasions. Some can be dated by the manner of reference to certain people—for instance, whether he mentions his father-in-law as living or dead. Numbers thirty-five and thirty-six were obviously written soon after the death of R. Abraham b. Meir, but the date of his death is still unascertainable.[16] Even the collection as a whole cannot be dated, for it does not appear that the "collected responsa of Rabad" were published in his lifetime. An explicit reference of Razah informs us, for example, that the responsa of Rabad's father-in-law were edited in the latter's lifetime.[17] No such collection is known or mentioned concerning Rabad. The heterogeneous character of *Temim Deᶜim* implies, in fact, that it is a later compilation.[18]

This fact illuminates some other features of the book known as *Temim Deᶜim*. It is conventionally referred to as a collection of Rabad's responsa, although only sections came from Rabad's pen.[19] A study of the *Temim Deᶜim* demonstrates unequivocally that, besides complete responsa, the text contains random glosses, marginal annotations, and assorted literary fragments.[20] Responsa of other French writers, as well as selections from Rabi's *ha-Eshkol* and R. Tam's *Sefer ha-Yashar*, and a few important Geonic pieces also made their way into this collection. The following description of responsa collections fits *Temim Deᶜim* perfectly: "Responsa collections included novellae to isolated Talmudic passages, collections of laws for certain occasions, *taḳḳanot* of communities, responsa, contemporary decisions."[21]

15. See, for example, *Shibbale ha-Leḳeṭ*, 4; *Sefer ha-Miktam* on *Megillah*, 22. There are also few mystical explanations in his writings, as is noted (at the end of Ch. VI).

16. *Ha-Maggid*, XII (1868), 397.

17. *Sefer ha-Terumot*, XLV: להר״ר אברהם בר׳ יצחק יש טעמים על דרך אחרת, הנם כתובים על ספר תשובותיו. Quoted by Assaf, in *Sifran*, 3.

18. It is possible, however, that sections 1–67, all from Rabad, formed an early nucleus for this collection.

19. *TD*, 1–67, 83, 84, 112, 113, 202, 206; Gross, 402, has an incomplete list.

20. E.g., *TD*, 3, is found, with minor variations, in a Bodleian ms. as a self-contained "note on bedikah"; see Neubauer, *Catalogue*, 654, 1. I have examined a photostat of it. Noteworthy is the fact that it starts with a refutation of Rashi.

21. Irving Agus, *Rabbi Meir of Rothenburg* (Philadelphia, 1947), I, XXIV.

That the present text is fragmentary and that medieval writers such as the author of the *Kol Bo* did not possess a complete text of responsa identical with the extant edition is indicated by a comparison of *Temim Deᶜim* with certain citations in the *Kol Bo*. Three illustrations will establish this point:

1. In number twenty-five—a gloss or fragment of a code, not a responsum—Rabad concurs with a theory expressed by the Tosafist and commentator R. Samuel b. Meïr (Rashbam) that in the cleansing of impure vessels by submersion in boiling water the vessel should always be removed before the boiling or bubbling subsides.[22] The *Kol Bo* quotes an exactly antithetical opinion in the name of Rabad.[23]

2. Number twenty-seven concerns the use of salt in unleavened bread (*maẓah*) on the first day of Passover and expresses the view that its use on the first day is forbidden because it renders the mazah too rich (*maẓah ᶜashirah*); but its use is permissible on the remaining days of Passover. The *Kol Bo* reproduces a lengthy extract from Rabad's responsum, missing in the extant edition, which presents the problem in a completely different light.[24]

3. The author of the *Kol Bo*, who ordinarily names his sources with considerable precision, cites a certain legal opinion anonymously while it is explicitly propounded in *Temim Deᶜim* in Rabad's name.[25]

Rabad's responsa are usually detailed and lengthy, exhausting the subject under discussion. They constitute short halakic essays, a fact which is in direct contrast to the terse, pointed answers issued by the Geonim and occasionally by some later authorities such as Maimonides.[26] In explanation of this development from the plain to the elaborate, Agus submits that the length of responsa is inversely proportionate to the authority of the writer—and hence the responsa of the early Geonim are brief while those of later scholars are elaborate.[27] Freehof's suggestion on this matter is more tenable. Early inquiries,

22. *TD*, 25; see *Tosafot, Ḥullin*, 108b ("shenafal"); *Oraḥ Ḥayyim*, 452, 1, and *Yoreh Deᶜah*, 121, 2.

23. *Kol Bo*, 48.

24. *Ibid.* According to the *Kol Bo*, the use of a great quantity of salt is forbidden throughout all eight days of Passover because salt (according to the Talmudic rule of "whatever is salted is ritually considered as if boiled or roasted"—*meliaḥ keroteaḥ*) like heat, ferments and causes leavening. See Rashbah, *Responsa* (Vienna, 1812), 445.

25. *Ibid.*; *TD*, 35. *TD*, 25–36, seem to be fragments of a code on Passover; the numbering in our editions is artificial and arbitrary.

26. I. H. Weiss, *Bet Talmud*, I (1881), 357; IV, 194; Solomon Freehof, *The Responsa Literature* (Philadelphia, 1955), 31; Assaf, *Tekufat ha-Geonim we-Sifrutah*, 216.

27. Agus, *Rabbi Meir of Rothenburg*, XVIII.

he suggests, were concerned in large measure with simple *explication de texte* or else they requested a clear decision in a specific dispute. The inquirers were usually not scholarly, for knowledge of the Talmud was not too widespread outside of Babylonia. Direct answers, devoid of elaboration or expository comment—"a mere 'yes' or 'no,' or 'permitted' or 'prohibited'"—were adequate. No *pieces justificatives* had to be appended. Later inquirers, however, were well-versed in Talmudic law and lore and could read a responsum with discrimination and understanding. Hence the respondent had to justify his view and cite the relevant Talmudic passages and codificatory opinion; the responsa were no longer mere judicial decisions but halakic discussions. The scholarly status of the inquirer, in short, determined to a great extent the length or brevity of the responsum. Freehof points to the responsa of R. Tam and Rashbah as ripe specimens of the full-length responsum.[28] Rabad's responsa are of such a nature. They have the character of a learned correspondence, an epistolary exchange of views and opinions. They exhaust a subject, explain all pertinent Talmudic passages, and usually digress into various ramifications of the subject as well. Not mere decisions or arbitrations, they were meant to be exercises in the Oral Law.

The value of these responsa in *Temim Deᶜim*—as well as those cited in *Sefer ha-Terumot*, *Orḥot Ḥayyim*, and others[29]—cannot be overestimated. They illumine certain, often paradoxical, aspects of his character: his self-esteem and the resulting arbitrariness and condescension, his tenderness, humility, passion for study.[30] He is seen rising to heights of rhetoric and emotion and moving on a plateau of restraint and objectivity. The correspondence with Razah in *Dibre ha-Ribot*, for instance, demonstrates irony, satire, disdain, feigned reverence, confidence and triumph, hesitation and retreat.[31] His style—the mixed Hebrew-Aramaic idiom which was the *lingua franca* of Talmudic scholars—reveals his mastery of Hebrew and the flexibility which the

28. Freehof, *Responsa Literature*, 32. A. Freimann, introduction to *Teshubot ha-Rambam*, XL, notes that Maimonides' responsa to his scholarly peers are long and documented while those to untutored inquirers sometimes consist of only one word. However, Abraham Maimonides, *Birkat Abraham* (Lyck, 1859), 43, explains contrariwise that since his father usually wrote to great scholars, he did not have to elaborate.

29. Gross, 403, has compiled a list. Not all of Rabad's responsa have been correctly identified, especially because of the widespread confusion resulting from the identical means of anagrammatic reference to himself and to his father-in-law; see Benedict, *Sinai*, XX (1957), 235.

30. *TD*, 6, 9, 11, 113, and others.

31. *Dibre ha-Ribot*, 7, 15, 17, 20, 30, 31, 37, 48.

language attained in his hands. Biblical metaphors are expanded, invested with new connotations, recast into new molds; Talmudic idioms and maxims are applied in novel circumstances and thus endowed with different nuances. In short, "the writer stands revealed in his thoughts, impulses and actions and not merely as the name of a person going about by a time-honored title."[32]

Like most other responsa, these contain some information on contemporary personalities and conditions. Those questions addressed to Rabad reflect the deferential and reverential attitude of contemporaries toward him—even if one allows for the usual dose of rhetoric and meaningless hyperbole.[33] His detailed answers, furthermore, reflect local customs, native traditions, and social climate; they reveal the nature and actuality of economic problems in Provence. Thus, one observes, for instance, Provençal variants in the liturgy, customs of prayer for such special days of semi-festive character as *Purim* and the intermediate days of the major holidays, or different traditions concerning the details of the marriage ceremony.[34] From the economic-social sphere, the usual problems of usury and other business connections between Jews and non-Jews are encountered.[35]

Most important, however, responsa present an x-ray picture of a creative mind at work. One observes Rabad leisurely drawing upon his vast reservoirs of knowledge, relating new situations and problems to old concepts and categories, responding alertly and vigorously to ever-changing stimuli. A conceptual-halakic analysis of responsa—an operation rarely performed by modern historians—reveals more lucidly than any routine textual study the writer's attitudes on various general issues. Such broad problems of Jewish intellectual history as attitudes toward the Palestinian Talmud or the Geonic writings are best defined and comprehended on the basis of an investigation of responsa and similar

32. J. Mann, *Texts and Studies in Jewish History and Literature* (Cincinnati, 1931), I, 63.

33. *TD*, 7, 8.

34. *Ibid.*, 38 (see *MT*, *Ishut*, III, 21); 40, 41; see *Sifran*, 32; Albeck, *ha-Eshkol*, 183.

35. *TD*, 43, 44, 46, 47 (see *Yoreh Deᶜah*, 170, 2). The closeness of these relations is presumably reflected in the extent to which Rabad is willing to transform local custom into legal precedent: וכן אני אומר בכל דבר שאין דינו מפורש אצלנו ואין לנו בו מנהג ידוע, שהולכים בו אחר מנהגות שלהם וקרוב דבר זה לדינא דמלכותא דינא. *TD*, 50; see also Rabad, *BK*, 311. This is a rather sweeping extension of the Talmudic principle. Ha-Me'iri, for example, applies it only to such matters as taxation; see *Bet ha-Beḥirah* on ᶜ*Abodah Zarah* (Jerusalem, 1944), 41; also *Bet Joseph* on *Ṭur Ḥoshen ha-Mishpaṭ*, 369. See generally, E. Urbach, *Baᶜale ha-Tosafot*, 59, n. 40, and I. Agus, *Teshubot Baᶜale ha-Tosafot* (New York, 1954), 54.

spontaneous utterances. Conformity or innovation, leniency or rigidity in legal decisions, formalistic reasoning or logical-empirical deduction—the most reliable criteria for gauging these individual approaches are actual, extemporaneous performances and "applied rabbinics" as mirrored in the responsa literature.

7. *Hassagot on Alfasi, Razah, and Maimonides*

We turn finally to that distinctive body of literature known as hassagot—critical glosses, scholia, or animadversions—with which the name Rabad is inextricably linked. Chronologically, the hassagot were his last works—a triumphant finale to a gloriously prolific career. He composed copious hassagot on the *Halakot* of Alfasi, the *Sefer ha-Ma'or* of Razah, and the *Mishneh Torah* of Maimonides—three comprehensive works whose subject matter was the Talmud at large. As the Hebrew term hassagah—a term introduced into medieval Hebrew by Judah ibn Tibbon via his translation of a critical study in grammar by Jonah ibn Janaḥ[1]—denotes, these glosses are both criticism and commentary, dissent and elaboration, stricture and supplement. They are not exclusively polemical, although the polemical emphasis varies in intensity and acuity from one to the other. The critique on Alfasi is mild and objective; that on Maimonides may be described as moderate, marred by occasional outbursts of intemperate invective; while that on Razah is most caustic and degradingly *ad hominem*. Their common denominator is a quest for independent comprehension and a sense of intellectual freedom expressed either in pointed criticism or reasoned corroboration.

As for the dates of their composition, the hassagot on Alfasi are clearly the earliest, for he cites them frequently in the later writings.[2] The question is how early. Were they an immediate antecedent to those on Razah or did they antedate the latter by many years, perhaps decades? Gross remarks that they were begun after 1172, but he is not very concerned with dating them.[3] Marx is of the opinion that they were written about 1185, two or three years before those on Razah.[4] By implication it seems that Tchernowitz—who pays no attention whatsoever to the

1. Jonah ibn Janaḥ, *Sefer ha-Riḳma*, ed. M. Wilensky (Berlin, 1929), 19, n. 17.
2. See §7, note 7; Benedict, *Kiryath Sefer*, XXV (1948–1949), 171, n. 9.
3. Gross, 544.
4. Marx, 206.

problem of dating—would also subscribe to this temporal relation between the two sets of hassagot. He assumes that the hassagot on Alfasi were a mere pretext on the part of Rabad and were produced as a prelude to the hassagot on Razah. Having decided to subject his erstwhile colleague to an academic drubbing, he produced some makeshift criticisms of Alfasi in order to conceal the bitterness of his critique on Razah under a mask of objectivity and impartiality. The two consequently followed each other in quick succession.[5]

A more plausible assumption which eliminates some of the loopholes opened by the alternative dating would be that, like the commentaries and codes, these hassagot on Alfasi were inaugurated considerably before those on Razah, but were continued over a protracted period of time. For if Rabad wrote his hassagot on Alfasi's *Halakot* as late as 1185, then his numerous statements to the effect that he anticipated so many of Razah's contentions and conclusions in this matter are rather meaningless. Whatever the date of its composition, Razah's *Sefer ha-Ma'or* was certainly completed before 1185.[6] In such a case, Razah would be the anticipator and not vice versa. Consequently, such allegations as "we already wrote all this" or "I also said this in my hassagot" make no sense.[7] Furthermore, the latent implication of these assertions borders on a charge of plagiarism, which Rabad frequently and freely leveled at Razah.[8] Rabad seems not only to be establishing priority, for the historical record, but to be suggesting that Razah might have availed himself of these notes. Finally, there appear to be references to these hassagot on Alfasi which imply a temporal gap of as much as two or more decades between his work and that of Razah.[9]

To reconstruct the process, it would seem that Rabad began his hassagot on Alfasi before Razah's glosses were even circulated. As was the case with his commentaries, he probably began with the order of *Nashim*. This explains why what is certainly an introductory passage—in which he lauds Alfasi unreservedly and records his own deep-seated

5. Tchernowitz, *Toledot ha-Poskim*, I, 161.
6. See §3, note 28.
7. *KS*, II, 10, 11, 16, and others.
8. See *Hassagot*, *Pesaḥim*, 14b, 17a. That this charge extends to oral communications as well, see *KS*, I, 47, quoted below n. 25 and *Dibre ha-Ribot*, 47: נראה מדבריך שאינך מסכים . . . לתירוצנו שעלה בלבנו בימים ההם . . . וכן העידות בעצמך שהוא לך כחומץ לשינים וכעשן לעינים. While he is generally averse to the conventional anonymity of medieval writing, he is excessively keen to label his views which Razah referred to or reproduced anonymously.
9. *KS*, I, 7, 11, 62; II, 8, 9.

humility in the face of this Talmudic giant—is found at the beginning of his annotations on *Ketubot*.[10] Otherwise, this passage appears hopelessly misplaced. Furthermore, the first references to his own "hassagot," "a treatise of hassagot," or just "our treatise" all relate to *Ketubot*.[11] They obviously formed the nucleus of his "treatise of hassagot," which was continuously expanded and amplified. One might conjecture that he continued adding even after Razah's *Sefer ha-Ma'or* appeared, for there are a few hassagot which already refer to Razah's criticism.[12]

It seems that he did not get much beyond *Nashim*. In his hassagot on Razah, there are practically no references to any other glosses on Alfasi besides those on *Nashim*. Naḥmanides' *Sefer ha-Zekut*—a mature defense of Alfasi against Rabad's strictures—which is in print, embraces only *Seder Nashim*. Also, just as Rabad's introduction is found at the beginning of *Ketubot*, so Naḥmanides' apology for his undertaking a defense of Alfasi against Rabad—two authorities highly revered by him—is found at the beginning of *Yebamot*. *Giṭṭin* concludes with the customary epitaph: "*Sefer ha-Zekut* is finished and completed."[13] It is true that there are stray references in later works to other sections of *Sefer ha-Zekut*[14] and isolated hassagot by Rabad on other tractates,[15] but these appear to be peripheral, added incidentally and irregularly to the main core of *Nashim*. The fact that the *Sefer ha-Zekut* has the character of an unabridged work dedicated to a systematic and exhaustive refutation of the bulk of Rabad's criticisms indicates that the latter were devoted primarily to *Nashim*.

The earlier dating suggested sheds more light on the relation between Rabad's two sets of hassagot on Alfasi and Razah and on the nature of each independently. Rabad started at first to criticize Alfasi and take exception to some of his halakic interpretations or normative conclusions.

10. *Hassagot* on Alfasi, *Ḳetubot*, 14a; see also *ibid.*, beginning of *Giṭṭin*: עתה אומר מעט מן הדברים שצריכין עיון. Actually, the introductory passage belongs at the beginning of *Yebamot*, for that is where his hassagot on Alfasi apparently began, as evidenced by the *Sefer ha-Zekut* on *Yebamot*, 2a ff. The early printers' whims or calculations are responsible for the fragmentary character of all the printed hassagot on Alfasi or Razah.

11. *KS*, II, 11, 15.

12. *Hassagot* on Alfasi, *Giṭṭin*, 46b; also, *ibid.*, *Ketubot*, 38a–b.

13. See the *Sefer ha-Zekut* printed in *Shibeᶜah ᶜEnayim* (Livorno, 1745), 18–53.

14. On *Yomah* and *Pesaḥim*; see Azulai, *Shem ha-Gedolim* (Warsaw, 1876), 30.

15. Gross, 544, n. 3. *Tumat Yesharim* (Venice, 1622), 234–237, contains some isolated hassagot on *Baba Ḳamma*, *Baba Batra*, *Makkot*, and *Shebuᶜot*. These are introduced by the editor as אלו השגות מצאתי בהלכות הרב הגדול ראב״ד while the next section, a separate unit, begins: הגהות שכתב הרב המובהק ראב״ד ז״ל בכתובות ובגיטין.

That these were substantive criticisms penetrating to the heart of the matter is indicated by the fact that they merited a detailed rebuttal by Naḥmanides, the most vigilant guardian and comprehensive interpreter of Alfasi's *Halakot*.[16] On some occasions Naḥmanides honestly confesses his inability to reinstate Alfasi's views in the face of Rabad's questioning.[17] Nevertheless, true to the dual connotation of the term "hassagah"—both criticism and commentary—these notes also contain interpretative amplification of Alfasi's statements and defense of his opinions against other critics.[18] Some hassagot start with a detailed explanation of Alfasi's statement and only then explore various interpretative alternatives. Occasionally an hassagah consists merely of a Talmudic note, not directly related to Alfasi and certainly not directed against him.[19] The bulk, however, is a direct critique—not in the least disrespectful but decidedly independent[20]—of the *Halakot*.

When Razah's *Sefer ha-Ma'or* appeared, it was but natural for Rabad to "review" it. Here was the work of a noted professional colleague which covered territory very familiar to him, territory that he had only recently traversed. He felt that Razah had carried the criticism of Alfasi to unjustified and unpardonable extents and that often Razah was captious and carping for no good reason—critique for critique's sake.[21] Anticipating the more comprehensive refutation of Razah's strictures to be undertaken by Naḥmanides about half a century later, Rabad penned a sharp answer to Razah, the avowed purpose of which was

16. Naḥmanides first refuted Razah's critique—far more severe than that of Rabad—in his *Milḥamot* and later turned to Rabad in his *Sefer ha-Zekut*. See *Sefer ha-Zekut*, *Yebamot*, 18b.

17. *Ibid.*, *Yebamot*, 9a, 11b, 38a. באמת שדברי ה״ר אברהם הן הן דברים של עיקר, נכונים וברורים ועולים כהוגן. An indication of the complexity or dialectical involvement of this defense-criticism, is Naḥmanides' statement, in one place (*Milḥamot*, *Shabbat*, 7b) that Rabad's attempted defense of Alfasi is futile, for his position is really indefensible, as asserted by Razah. Rabad said the same about Rabi; *KS*, I, 50.

18. E.g., *Hassagot* on Alfasi, *Ḳetubot*, 38b, 43a. Naḥmanides apparently had such passages in mind when he wrote about Rabad (*Sefer ha-Zekut*, *Ḳetubot*, 22a): שהוא מן המזכין בדברי רבינו היה.

19. *Hassagot* on Alfasi, *Giṭṭin*, 33b.

20. Sometimes Rabad becomes rather nettling, as, e.g., *Hassagot* on Alfasi, *Ketubot*, 56b: והיכי מעלינן פילא בקופא דמחטא ... ורמינן דיקלי וזקפינן להו ומדחקינן טובא ללא צורך. See Naḥmanides, *Milḥamot*, Yebamot, 25a: ואין הפיל הגדול הזה יכול ליכנס בנקב של מחט סדקית הזאת. See *Baba Mezi*ᶜ*a*, 38b.

21. *KS*, I, 15, 52, and *passim*, esp. II, 8: זה דרכו לחפש אחר המומין והשבושין. Also, *Hassagot*, *Pesaḥim*, 18b; 26b; *Beẓah*, 19a, and others: כי חבב בעיניו להיות מחדש חדוש גדול וחשב ג״כ להיות חולק על הרב במקצת, ועל כן מסבב פני הדברים להיותם מסכימים לפירושו. See Naḥmanides, *Milḥamot*, *Pesaḥim*, 10a.

defense of Alfasi.[22] The hassagot on Razah are not therefore in themselves a valid criterion by which to gauge Rabad's attitude to Alfasi nor should they lead to the conclusion that he was a blind follower of Alfasi. He was in these notes overtly pro-Alfasi and, like Naḥmanides, did not attempt to conceal this highly positive axiological frame of reference. Nevertheless, the double meaning of "hassagah" is not belied here either. Even in these hassagot, he frequently records his dissent from the *Halakot* and refers to his own criticisms of Alfasi. He often supports Razah, expands his statements or elaborates his theories. He points out correlations and coincidences between their views and even has an occasional word of praise for Razah.[23] An attempt to preserve his independence while defending Alfasi against Razah is discernible throughout the work.

Yet, the sharpness of Rabad's critique should not be underestimated. This is undoubtedly the most vituperative of his polemical writings,[24] climaxing a lifetime process of mutual criticism and attack between the two scholars. Following the acrimonious exchange in the youthful *Dibre ha-Ribot* and, apparently, considerable oral disputation as well,[25] Razah had criticized several of Rabad's works (*Ḳinnim* commentary, *Baᶜale ha-Nefesh*). The fact that they were fellow townsmen and former classmates undoubtedly aggravated their rivalry. Many points of academic controversy could become live halakic issues.[26] The accusations of plagiarism, amateurishness, and general incompetence[27] which Rabad periodically hurled at Razah become more pointed in light of their personal connections and prolonged feuding.

What is the date of these hassagot on Razah? Marx, with great ingenuity which carries the power of conviction, dates them about

22. Naḥmanides, for instance, explicitly announced that his *Milḥamot* was intended to defend Alfasi—even if the defense was strained sometimes; see introduction to *Milḥamot*; also *Sefer ha-Zekut*, *Ketubot*, 61b, and others. For Rabad, see *Hassagot* on Alfasi, *Bezah*, 21a.

23. *KS*, I, 2, 10, 21, 50, 67; II, 30. Also, *Hassagot*, *Berakot* 8b; 13a; *Pesaḥim*, 25b; *Sukkah*, 12a; *Bezah*, 19b and others.

24. See, for example, *KS* on *Rosh ha-Shanah*, ed. Bergmann, 72: הנה שם השם רוח שקר בפיו וזאת עדות על כל שקריו ופחיזותיו אשר אסף רוח בחפניו להנבא שקרים ולהתעות הפתיים והסכלים בעדיי אחרים אשר נתעטר בהם ספר הסירוס אשר חבר. Ḥasidah's manuscript (*KS*, II, 41) concealed much of this vituperation in code.

25. *KS*, I, 47: אני מעיד עלי עדות שמים וארץ כי מכמה שנים ספר לי התירוץ הראשון שהיה משתבח בו . . . ואני זכור שקראתי עליו כחומץ לשנים וכעשן לעינים והקשיתי עליו כל מה שהקשה עתה על עצמו.

26. E.g., concerning liturgical practices, *KS* on *Rosh ha-Shanah*, ed. Bergmann, 72. See also ha-Me'iri, *Magen Abot*; *Hassagot*, *Bezah*, 8a.

27. E.g., *KS* on *Rosh ha-Shanah*, 47, 64 (אין בזה חדוש והתינוקות יודעין כן) *Hassagot Sukkah*, 5a; *Taᶜanit*, 1b.

1186–1187. He assumes that Razah's *ha-Ma'or ha-Ḳaṭan*, on the order of *Mo^ced*, was criticized by Rabad during the last year of Razah's life and the *ha-Ma'or ha-Gadol*, on the orders of *Nashim* and *Neziḳin*, soon after Razah's death. On the basis of this assumption Marx seeks to explain the striking difference in temper between the criticisms of these two parts. While the first is bitter and relentless, the second is disarmingly moderate and unassuming, with personally derogatory comments few and far between. This discrepancy is accounted for by the change in Razah's "status": at first he was a living adversary and could be treated uninhibitedly, but when he passed away Rabad realized that he must blunt the edge of his critique.[28] He remembered the Talmudic maxim: "You must not argue against a lion (scholar) after his death."

Against this suggestion, which is acceptable as a working hypothesis, Benedict submits that the hassagot on Razah followed those on Maimonides (after 1193).[29] His reasoning is that the latter, which refer back to a great number of Rabad's previous works, including the hassagot on Alfasi, make no mention whatsoever of the hassagot on Razah. That this noteworthy curiosity provides no proof is clear from that fact that other earlier works, like the *Ba^cale ha-Nefesh*, are also not alluded to in the hassagot on *Mishneh Torah*. It would be impossible to contend that the *Ba^cale ha-Nefesh* is also later than these hassagot, for it is mentioned in the *Sifra* commentary which in turn is mentioned in the *^cEduyot* commentary, and both these commentaries are referred to in the hassagot. Finally, if the hassagot on *Mishneh Torah* were begun after 1193—and this is not disputed—it is unlikely that Rabad could have accomplished much more than this in the last years of his life. The composition of these hassagot was a herculean task and there is no need, nor is it remotely possible, to assign another extensive project to the last few years of an old man—possibly an octogenarian.

Neither Marx nor Benedict posit the question whether the hassagot on Razah were all written at one time (c. 1186–1187) and then circulated or whether the text was subject to revision and addition. Here there seems to be some internal evidence that a number of Rabad's hassagot on the *Sefer ha-Ma'or* were added much later, perhaps even later than those on the *Mishneh Torah*. While this does not allow one to assume

28. Marx, 207. Naḥmanides' critique is most harsh against the *Ma'or ha-Gadol* and remarkably restrained when dealing with the *Ma'or ha-Ḳaṭan*. See his introduction to the *Milḥamot*.

29. Benedict, *Kiryath Sefer*, XXV (1948–1949), 171, n. 9.

that the hassagot on Razah, considered as a complete, integrated work, were not terminated or "published" until this very late date, one can assert that Rabad was constantly revising and expanding them. As with the *Sifra* commentary and the hassagot on Alfasi, it appears that these hassagot also contain later additions.

For instance, there is widespread debate among medieval scholars over a text in tractate *Beẓah* concerning the setting aside of *ḥallah* (the priest's share of the dough) on holidays. Both the interpretation of the text and the final conclusions as to actual practice are controversial issues. Alfasi concludes that the setting aside of ḥallah on holidays is forbidden. Razah takes issue with his textual interpretation (which revolves around the correlation of two different Talmudic passages) and also with his practical conclusion. According to Razah, it is prohibited only in Palestine (where the strict laws of ḥallah are still operative and the failure to set aside the priest's portion renders all the dough ritually unfit [*ṭebel*]), but elsewhere it is permitted. Now, Maimonides reproduces Alfasi's unqualified view: "One who kneads dough the day before a holiday may not separate the ḥallah from it on the holiday." In his hassagah on this passage, Rabad concurs with Razah, and explains with careful precision why "we make a distinction between dough kneaded in Palestine (*ḥallat Ereẓ Israel*) and dough kneaded outside of Palestine (*ḥallat ḥuẓ la'areẓ*)." This is, naturally, also a criticism of Alfasi. Yet, in the hassagah on that annotation of Razah which dissents from Alfasi and introduces the above-mentioned distinction, Rabad states: "I also submitted the same criticism of the Master's words, but after a long time I retracted because. . . ." He then retracts the view presented in the *hassagah* on Maimonides—presumably the criticism here referred to, for I can find no other mention of this view—and throws his weight behind Alfasi's conclusion. It would be strange to say that a few years after this retraction he resurrected the defunct view and opposed it to Maimonides' statement. Rather, the critique of Maimonides—and *ipso facto* of Alfasi—came first and it was this opinion which he rescinded in the note on Razah. The sequence of the hassagot seems clear.[30]

Another illustration contains no implicit cross reference from one set

30. *Beẓah*, 9b; Alfasi, Razah, and Rabad, *ad. loc.*; *MT*, *Yom Ṭob*, III, i, and Rabad: אף אני כך תפסתי על דברי הרב ז״ל ולאחר ימים רבים חזרתי בי . . . ; see *Sefer ha-Miktam*, *Beẓah*, 189. An analogous bit of evidence is to be found in *Pesaḥim*, 36a, concerning dough kneaded with wine, oil, or honey. Rabad's comment in his critique of Razah, *ad. loc.*, refers most likely to *MT*, *Ḥameẓ u-Maẓah*, V, 20.

of hassagot to the other, but the logical progression of Rabad's thought supports our assumption. The critical annotation on Razah, which presents a new theory concerning a staple halakic problem, must have been written after a parallel hassagah on the *Mishneh Torah* which repeats the regnant theory.[31]

The title of the hassagot on the *Sefer ha-Ma'or*, *Katub Sham* (which means "it is written there"), is derived from the formulaic introduction of the criticized passages. Rabad prefaces his critique by a quotation from Razah's statement which is always introduced by the words "*Katub Sham.*" The identity of this title with the hassagot was conjectured by Edelmann and Berliner and affirmed, independently, by Marx and Ḥasidah.[32]

Those hassagot printed in the standard folio editions are extremely

31. The rabbis ordained that on the day before Passover one must conduct a search (*bediḳah*) for unleavened bread (*ḥameẓ*). Subsequently—and this is a Scriptural requirement—one must renounce (by declaration) the ownership of anything leavened that may have remained undiscovered in one's possession. What is to be done in a doubtful case, when the presence of anything leavened is not precisely known? The stock answer is that after the act of renunciation and relinquishment (*biṭṭul*) the uncertainty may be resolved by choosing the more lenient possibility and the person may be spared the additional search, since the uncertainty itself hinges on a later rabbinic enactment. If, however, the uncertainty arises before the renunciation, the more stringent alternative must be applied and the search must be repeated, for then the uncertainty entails the possible transgression of a Scriptural commandment. This view is maintained by the Tosafot, by Razah, and, as the *Maggid Mishneh* points out, is the view of Rashi and the Geonim. Now, in the hassagot on the *Mishneh Torah*, Rabad reproduces this view, which was the rampant, practically consensual scholastic tradition. But in the hassagot on Razah, who also expressed this view, Rabad broaches an entirely new theory, a novel insight into the nature of uncertainty as it relates itself to the particular question of the search for leaven. Rabad submits that the very search, the act of *bediḳah* itself, was instituted for precisely such dubious situations: if one knows definitely that there is anything leavened present, he must naturally remove it and if, on the other hand, it is absolutely certain that no leavened object is present, then nothing further need be said or done. Uncertainty necessitates the search and is of its essence. Now, if the hassagah on the *Mishneh Torah* followed the parallel note on the *Sefer ha-Ma'or* and was the last time Rabad dealt with this question, he would certainly have incorporated in it his new theory, which was not only original but obviated many more questions than the conventional scholastic theory. The critical annotation on Razah which presents Rabad's new theory must have been written last and was the only occasion he had to formulate it. Again, the sequence of the hassagot seems clear. *Pesaḥim*, 9b; *Tosafot, ad. loc.* (*Tesha*); Razah and Rabad, *ad. loc.*; *MT*, *Ḥameẓ u-Maẓah*, II, 10. The view projected by R. Aaron ha-Levi against Rabad—quoted in the *Maggid Mishneh, ad. loc.*—is actually Rabad's own theory which he expounded in the hassagah on Razah.

32. Marx, 202, and references to Edelmann and Berliner; Ḥasidah, introduction to *KS*. It should be observed that, while Reifmann speculated about the meaning of the title in one place, failing to relate it to the hassagot, and Marx takes him to task for this, he concurred with Edelmann, Berliner, and Marx in a second learned note—and this Marx overlooked; see *Bet Talmud*, IV, 381—which Marx noted; *ha-Maggid*, VI, 382—which he neglected.

fragmentary and hardly representative of the whole. They were selected rather capriciously by the author of a certain *collectaneum* (*Tumat Yesharim*) from an initially jumbled and incomplete manuscript. Not only were the contents reduced but the style was often mollified and its acerbity eliminated.[33] This is clearly revealed by a comparison of the printed fragments with the two available manuscripts as well as with quotations in later works. Naḥmanides, for example, repeatedly refers to hassagot which are not found in our editions.[34]

As for the hassagot on the *Mishneh Torah*, it is generally accepted that they were not begun until after 1193, for the *Mishneh Torah* does not seem to have reached Provence before that date.[35] They are thus chronologically last, but qualitatively and historically first. Rabad's towering stature and, to a great extent, the durability of his fame as an halakic authority derive primarily from this set of animadversions against Maimonides, written in an epitaphic, often recondite style and paying such extraordinary attention to minute details. In attempting to delineate the main features of Rabad as an author, it becomes clear that he is different from such personalities as Rashi or Maimonides. Each of the latter produced a comprehensive work, a literal magnum opus, which was preserved in its entirety. Even though they aimed for self-effacement by drawing all their material from ancient sources without pretending to present their own views, their distinctive personality was recognized, revealed, and revered. Maimonides' magisterial re-arrangement and systematization of Talmudic law—for all its overtures to anonymity—was original and novel; it was stamped with his personality and was therefore associated with his genius. It was minutely analyzed and scrupulously interpreted. The choice of a term and the turn of a phrase were invested with significance and taken to reflect

33. *Tumat Yesharim* (Venice, 1622). The editor depicts the confusion as follows: גם הם היו בתכלית הבלבול, השגות בתוך הפסוקים, ובתוך ההשגות פסקים, ודברי פוסק אחד בתוך דברי פוסק אחר. See B. Bergmann's introduction to his edition of *Katub Sham* (Jerusalem, 1957), 10 ff. The Bodleian Hebrew ms. 2357, of which I have a microfilm, contains Rabad's hassagot on Razah for *Giṭṭin*, *Yebamot*, *Ketubot*, *Baba Ḳamma*, *Baba Meẓiᶜa*, *Baba Batra*, *Sanhedrin*, *Makkot*. See also, Marx, 201–202, for the scope of these hassagot.

34. *Milḥamot*, *Shabbat*, 1a, 6b, 18a, 54a, 67a; *ᶜErubin*, 11b, 30b, 31b, 34a; *Pesaḥim*, 3b, 5a, 7a, 19b, *passim*.

35. Gross (XXIII), 19, n. 1; A. Geiger, "Moses ben Maimon," *Nachgelassene Schriften* (Berlin, 1876), III, 90–91. See, however, Maimonides' letter to Joseph b. Judah, from which it would appear that the *Mishneh Torah* (as was later to be the case with the *Moreh Nebukim*) was circulated in installments; *Iggerot ha-Rambam*, ed. Baneth, I, 52.

peculiar Maimonidean opinions. Rashi, too, achieved historical immortality by virtue of his unparalleled Scriptural and Talmudic commentary. Professedly eclectic and theoretically bound by traditional sources, Rashi's contributions were keenly sensed and appreciated by all. Rashi and his sources became inseparable; "Rashi says" is often used colloquially to cite a Talmudic statement or Midrashic maxim, for all his sources were imperceptibly fused with his commentary. Both these Talmudists appropriated all the stores of Jewish learning, made it their own, and produced monumental works with which they were historically associated.

Rabad is not identified historically with any such encompassing works. Even if one assumes with Crescas that he composed a complete Talmudic commentary like that of Rashi or, with Konforte, that he produced a comprehensive code of law similar to that of Maimonides, they were not preserved. He may be quoted frequently, even profusely, in the *Shiṭṭah Meḳubbeẓet* and in the works of other medieval scholars, but neither as commentator nor codifier has he achieved uniqueness or distinction. In the collective historical consciousness of Jewish scholarship, he has earned the reverent and expressive sobriquet *Baᶜal Hassagot* (animadversionist or controversialist) par excellence, and it is the hassagot which obligated every serious student of Jewish law to give sustained, often preferential, consideration to his views. Even though his responsa, minor codificatory works, commentaries and the highly influential *Baᶜale ha-Nefesh* were all well-known and circulated widely, and would certainly have influenced the course of halakah, he lives historically as "the Critic," the keen analyst who applied his incisive reasoning, textual expertness, and conceptual lucidity to all and everything. Just as Rashi has become the *Parshandata*, "the Interpreter"—so Rabad has become the *Baᶜal Hassagot*, the relentless critic and master of Talmudic analysis.

If the study of Jewish law, especially its codification, is inconceivable without Maimonides' *Mishneh Torah*, so the study of the *Mishneh Torah* is inconceivable without Rabad's strictures. As a matter of fact, ever since the Constantinople edition in 1509 (the third printed edition) of the *Mishneh Torah*,[36] Rabad's hassagot have in all subsequent

36. Ch. Friedberg, *Bet ᶜEḳed Sefarim* (Tel Aviv, 1952), 699. Also, M. Luzki, *Ha-Hoẓa'ot ha-Shelemot shel Sefer Mishneh Torah*, at the end of the new *MT* edition (New York, 1947); J. Avida, "Le-Toledot ha-Hoẓa'ot ha-Rishonot shel Mishneh Torah," *Sinai*, XV (1951), 138–143, and supplement 247–248. Note also the interesting bibliographical comments on the early editions of the *Mishneh Torah* by Isaiah Sonne,

standard editions accompanied Maimonides' text, just as the commentary of Rashi and the accumulated interpretations of the Tosafists accompany the Talmud or as the supplementary notes of R. Moses Isserles accompany the *Shulḥan ᶜAruk* of R. Joseph Karo. In this capacity they have served as a powerful stimulant both to concentrated Maimonidean research and perceptive reexamination of the sources.

As far as Rabad himself is concerned, the hassagot also represent the near-perfection or epitome of his entire halakic endeavor. External or formal relation between them can be found in the fact that the hassagot refer to a great number of his works: commentaries on the *Sifra*, *ᶜEduyot*, *Baba Ḳamma*, hassagot on Alfasi, responsa, codes on *Hilkot Lulab*, *Yadayim*, and possibly *Ḳiddushin.*[37] A representative bibliography of his writings is thus provided. A more essential relation is shown by the fact that the hassagot incorporate many early views and established customs and, above all, employ his analytic, critico-comparative method of study. They practically serve as a microcosm of Rabad's life and work; operating with them alone, one could reconstruct a fairly accurate image of Rabad. These annotations and animadversions—the hassagot par excellence—must, therefore, be examined in greater detail: their nature, scope, function, style, underlying motives, relation to his other writings, and their significance as a substantive epitome of Rabad's halakic creativity, reflecting his methods, values, and, contributions.

"Ṭiyyulim be-hisṭoriyah ubibliografiyah," *Alexander Marx Jubilee Volume* (New York, 1950), 209–235. It seems that commercial competition among early Jewish printers led the Constantinople publishers to add as many features as possible to the text of the *Mishneh Torah*. As a result, the standard folio as we know it today—text and *hassagot* flanked by commentaries—came into being. This is one instance of how the early printers left their mark on literature.

37. *Berakot*, VI, 2; *Lulab*, VIII, 5; *Ishut*, XVI, 26; *Gerushin*, XV, *Kil'ayim*, VIII, 7; *Kelim*, II, 5; *Ḥobel u-Maziḳ*, VIII, 4; *Malweh we-Loweh*, VI, 7; XVI, 7.

III. WORKS II: CRITICISM OF THE *MISHNEH TORAH*

The beginning of *Mishneh Torah* research is coterminous with the composition of the hassagot just as its most durable characteristics are already underscored in them. Allowing for varying emphases and stresses, two major trends are discernible in all subsequent Maimonidean studies: (1) criticism of Maimonides for omitting what may loosely be called the apparatus criticus from his *Mishneh Torah* and, concomitantly, partial disqualification of this work as an ultimate guide in codification; (2) conversely, concerted efforts to supply the necessary sources and explanations for his statements and thus rehabilitate the *Mishneh Torah* as an authoritative code. These two approaches, apparently antithetical yet in many respects mutually complementary, are the axes around which all commentaries, supercommentaries, and critical supplements revolve. Both were suggested by Rabad.

1. *Literature on the* Mishneh Torah

The argument concerning the lack of sources, which led to a systematic exposé of other weaknesses and errors, was fully articulated by Rabad in one of the early hassagot. Rabad's immediate successors in the field of Maimonidean critique, such as R. Moses ha-Kohen, shared this concern.[1] R. Moses of Coucy, author of the *Sefer Miẓwot Gadol* which

1. See, for example, D. Kaufmann, "The Etz Chayim of Jacob b. Jehudah of London," *JQR* (Old Series), V (1893), 368: ועל כי הגאון [רמב״ם] לא הביא בספרו ראיה לדבריו, גם לקצת דבריו חלוקין גאוני עול׳ האחרו׳ ... אשר על פיהם אנו חיים ... ועמד הרב ר׳ משה מקוצי ... וחבר חבור מכל התורה על פי ספר הגאון ... והביא ראיות לרוב דבריו ומה שפסקו הגאונים

is actually based on the *Mishneh Torah* and organized in accord with Maimonidean principles of classification, mentions the lack of sources as a serious deficiency impairing the value and restricting the usefulness of the *Mishneh Torah.*[2] R. Asher b. Yeḥiel correlates the ability—even the possibility—to use the *Mishneh Torah* with knowledge of the sources: "One should not rely upon his reading in this book to judge and issue decisions unless he finds proof in the Talmud."[3] Ha-Me'iri also stresses this deficiency, even though he does not explicitly condemn it.[4] Ḥasdai Crescas practically reproduces Rabad's objections.[5] R. Isaac b. Sheshet Perfet endorses R. Asher b. Yeḥiel's view concerning the need to trace all decisions back to original sources; people who rely exclusively on the code are denigrated as "rendering decisions in haughtiness."[6] Faint echoes of this refrain may be heard even from R. Joseph Karo who admits that he would have liked to pattern his book on that of Maimonides but was compelled to alter his plans "because he brings only one opinion while I had to elaborate and write the opinions of other codifiers and their reasons."[7] What more need be said than to call attention to the fact that Maimonides himself was conscious of this shortcoming, discussed it a number of times in his correspondence, and anticipated the criticism it would provoke.[8]

The second trend in Maimonidean study—corroborating and elucidating the *Mishneh Torah* by unearthing its Talmudic sources and

---

אחרונים הביא מפסקיהם בספרו ··· . The letter of R. Sheshet, published by A. Marx, "Texts by and about Maimonides," *JQR*, XXV (1935), 414–420: ואחרי אשר איננו מביא ראיות מדברי חכמי התלמוד לדבריו, מי ישמע אליו. The *Will* of Joseph ibn Kaspi, in *Hebrew Ethical Wills*, ed. I. Abrahams, I, 153: כי לא יספיק לכם הקבלה מספר משנה תורה, שחבר רבינו משה ואעפ"י שאמר הוא ז"ל ואינו צריך לספר אחר ביניהם.

2. *Sefer Mizwot Gadol*, introduction: אמנם לא הביא הגאון שום ראיה בספריו וכל אדם שיורה מתוך ספריו ויבקשו ממנו כתב ראייה מניין, אם לא למד הראיה או אפי' למדה ואינו זוכר יהא לו הדבר ההוא כחלום בלא פתרון ···

3. *Responsa*, XXXI, 9: וכן כל המורים הוראות מתוך דברי הרמב"ם ז"ל ואינן בקיאין בתלמוד לידע מהיכן הוציא דבריו טועין להתיר האסור ולאסור את המותר, כי לא עשה כשאר המחברים שהביאו ראיות לדבריהם והראו על המקומות דבריהם בתלמודא ··· אבל הוא כתב ספרו כמתנבא מפי הגבורה בלא טעם ובלא ראיה ··· לכן לא יסמוך אדם על קריאתו בספרו ··· אם לא שימצא ראיה בתלמוד. Quoted also by Karo, introduction to *Kesef Mishneh*.

4. *Bet ha-Beḥirah* on *Nedarim*, *Nazir*, *Sotah*, introduction: מאין הודעת מחלוקת ומשא ומתן ומאין הודעת הדברים אי זהו מקומן ··· אבל לא ראו חכמי הדורות לעזוב ספרי התלמוד בשום פנים.

5. *Or Adonai*, 32: למה שהשמיט מחלוקת הגאונים ושמותיהן גם כן לא העיר על מקומות שרשי הענינים. הנה לא נמלטנו מהמבוכה והספק בשנמצא בספרי זולתו מהמחברים הגדולים הפך הסכמתו ודעותיו.

6. Hershman, *Rabbi Isaac Perfet*, 69.

7. *Bet Joseph*, introduction to *Ṭur Oraḥ Ḥayyim*.

8. *Ḳobeẓ Teshubot ha-Rambam*, I, 140 (p. 26); *Iggerot ha-Rambam*, ed. D. H. Baneth (Jerusalem, 1946), I, 51. See, in general, the well-documented study by I. Kahana, "Ha-Pulemos mi-Sabib le-Ḳebiʿat ha-Halakah keha-Rambam," *Sinai*, XXXVI (1955), 215–248.

revealing its latent processes of reasoning—also had its origin in Rabad's hassagot. He was the first to emphasize the need for such work and, in part, to undertake its implementation. All the standard commentators —starting with R. Shem Tob ibn Gaon and Vidal of Tolosa through R. David b. Zimra and R. Joseph Karo and continuing until this very day—have been preoccupied with this task; the fulcrum around which their commentaries revolve is the enumeration of sources and their explication in a Maimonidean vein. Karo provides an excellent description of the inherent difficulties of the *Mishneh Torah* and the attempts to resolve them: "The generations that followed him could not understand his works well . . . for the source of every decision is concealed from them . . . One wrote a commentary *Maggid Mishneh* in which he revealed the source of every law . . . But he illuminated only six [of the fourteen] parts . . . So I the youngster arose . . . to write on the source of every decision and explain his statements."[9] To this day, the quest for *Mishneh Torah* sources in unknown midrashim, Geonic responsa, variant readings, and so on, continues unabated as one of the main forms of rabbinic scholarship. Again, what more need be said than to call attention to the fact that Maimonides, fully cognizant that his method would invite criticism, contemplated the composition of a *Sefer ha-Be'ur*, some kind of source book which would serve as a supplement to the *Mishneh Torah*.[10]

Rabad's hassagot, then, initiate this type of literature, the common purpose of which was to scrutinize Maimonidean statements—criticize them, interpret them, modify them, relate them to the underlying sources. However, the hassagot are also differentiated from it by virtue of certain distinctive characteristics: the selectivity of its subject matter and the arresting, penetrating brevity of its annotative form. Rabad's work is not a running commentary or full critique.

This heterogeneity, however, is not haphazard. By singling out recurrent types of annotations which constitute distinct categories, it is possible to identify certain hypothetical principles of selectivity in Rabad's critical approach to the *Mishneh Torah*. Rabad nowhere formulates any a priori principles which led him to seek out specific kinds of Maimonidean statements, but most of his animadversions conveniently subsume themselves under a number of characteristic

9. *Kesef Mishneh*, introduction. See a similar statement by R. David b. Zimra, *Yeḳar Tif'eret* (Notes on the *Mishneh Torah*), ed. S. B. Werner (Jerusalem, 1945), 11.

10. Abraham Maimonides, *Birkat Abraham*, ed. Goldberg (Lyck, 1859), 8; see also note 8.

rubrics. I shall describe these in succession, proceeding from the many positive or constructive groups to the negative ones.

2. *Corroborative or Explanatory Hassagot*

Essential for any appreciation of this critique is an understanding of Rabad's lengthy, partially programmatic observation at the end of Maimonides' introduction to the *Mishneh Torah.* In response to Maimonides' final recapitulation about the nature of his work, explanation of the title (*Repetition of the Law*) and justification of the method—in other words, a work of codification without sources, authorities, or reasons with the result that "a person who first studies the Written Law and afterward studies this compendium obtains from it knowledge of the entire Oral Law, without having to consult any other book"—Rabad comments forcefully:

> He intended to improve but did not improve, for he forsook the way of all authors who preceded him. They always adduced proof for their statements and cited the proper authority for each statement; this was very useful, for sometimes the judge would be inclined to forbid or permit something and his proof was based on some other authority. Had he known that there was a greater authority who interpreted the law differently, he might have retracted. Now, therefore, I do not know why I should reverse my tradition or my corroborative views because of the compendium of this author. If the one who differs with me is greater than I—fine; and, if I am greater than he, why should I annul my opinion in deference to his? Moreover, there are matters concerning which the Geonim disagree and this author has selected the opinion of one and incorporated it in his compendium. Why should I rely upon his choice when it is not acceptable to me and I do not know whether the contending authority is competent to differ or not. It can only be that "an overbearing spirit is in him."[1]

Disapproving of the title *Mishneh Torah,* which probably struck him, as it did later scholars, as somewhat audacious in its presumption to serve as the sole companion to Scripture,[2] Rabad focuses attention

1. Last hassagah on the introduction. I have corrected the printed version by the manuscript (38477) of the Jewish Theological Seminary. For the last phrase, see Dan. 5:12.

2. A. Berliner, *Shemot Sefarim ʿIbriyim,* tr. A. M. Haberman (Berlin, 1934), 17 (reprinted in *Ketabim Nibḥarim* [Jerusalem, 1949], II, 148–161). Scholars, generally refusing to use this title, substituted the name *ha-Yad* (numerically equivalent to "fourteen"—the number of books in the code) for Maimonides' title *Mishneh Torah* (Deut. 17:18) and subsequently added the word *ha-ḥazakah* (Deut. 34-12), thus creating the title *ha-Yad ha-Ḥazakah.* See Solomon Duran, *Milḥemet Mizwah* (no pagination, end).

upon one of the crucial contentions against Maimonides' code, one which underscores his own conception of the proper method of codification over and against that of Maimonides. By failing to cite names and adduce proofs, as was the universal procedure with authors and codifiers, Maimonides totally ignored the role of authority in the process of halakic debate. Awareness that some preeminent scholar contradicted a certain hypothesis currently endorsed by the judge weighing the alternatives in a case would cause the latter to reconsider the more authoritative view. This emphasis on the role of individual names as guides in juridical procedure is in keeping with the traditional view found in Tractate *ᶜEduyot*. The transmission of the Oral Law originally was and would have continued to be anonymous if it had remained harmonious and monolithic, but when it split up into a number of schools and became disparate and controversial, the need for naming the authorities arose. In the introduction to his Mishnah commentary Maimonides expresses a similar view, basing himself upon the Mishnah in *ᶜEduyot* which he explains at great length.[3] Rabad obviously felt this to be true not only for the sages of the Mishnah and Talmud, but for all subsequent authorities as well. Inasmuch as the possibility of dissent or the necessity to conform may be determined by the authority of the tribunal or judge issuing a decision, this factual or historical knowledge may often be indispensable.

As a corollary to this, it is to be expected that Rabad will be preoccupied with the indication of sources, the derivation of halakic norms, and the critical assessment of conflicting views. This will serve both as a supplement to Maimonides' opinion and a check on his arbitrariness.

In the opinion of Rabad, Maimonides is also to be censured for pride: "an overbearing spirit is in him." Otherwise, he would not have set himself as sole arbiter between conflicting views and would not have independently resolved basic Geonic controversies once and for ever. Rabad considered this a serious encroachment on his—or any rabbi's—prerogative as scholar and judge, for he too could assess and select. As a matter of fact, Rabad never shies away from a match of strength when, by an apodictic statement, Maimonides asserts his supreme authority and seems to challenge the dissenting reader. For instance, Maimonides asserts in a given context: "He who does not follow this ruling cannot discern between his right hand and his left hand in laws

3. M. *ᶜEduyot*, I, 5, 6; Maimonides, introduction to Mishnah Commentary ed. M. D. Rabinovitz (Tel Aviv, 1948), 39.

relating to monetary transactions." Rabad, cognizant that the issue is much disputed—a number of different views are cited in the *Halakot* of Alfasi—rejects the obligatory character of Maimonides' selection and presents a dissenting view with the following preface: "There are people who do not concur in this teaching and know these laws as well as he does."[4] Elsewhere, enmeshed in a complicated discussion of laws of impurity, in the course of which he disdainfully rejects a statement of Maimonides together with a parallel explanation of "the Greek Rabbi" (Isaac of Siponto), Rabad observes: "These are strange statements and one's mind is not at ease with them. Inasmuch as they have no tradition [in this matter], I said to myself that I also shall answer my part. I too have an understanding heart as well as they."[5] Sometimes, when Maimonides says with assurance "I forbid this," Rabad retorts with equal assurance "I permit it."[6] Even when Maimonides is not obtrusively assertive, Rabad will occasionally take issue with him and conclude assuredly or vindictively: "and whoever does not acknowledge this [interpretation] errs"; "there is no sage who holds such an opinion [as that of Maimonides]."[7] After rejecting Maimonides' explanation of a passage in the Palestinian Talmud as "simplistic" and failing to reconcile this passage with explicit Mishnaic teachings, Rabad remarks: "In general, the Talmud was transmitted only to people possessed of tradition [i.e., authoritative opinions] or capable of logical deductions and reasoned interpretations."[8] Whatever Rabad had in mind by this veiled statement, he certainly meant that Maimonides had no monopoly over traditional or logical interpretations—and perhaps had no access to them at all. In sum, Maimonides' cut and dry, "arrogant" codification approximated ex cathedra legislation too closely. Rabad resented this overbearing attitude and, in general, believed that codification should involve interpretation, analogy, logical inference, and only then the resultant, normative conclusion.[9]

4. *MT*, *ᶜEdut* VIII, 4; see *Ketubot*, 20a, and Alfasi, *ad. loc.*

5. *MT*, *Ṭume'at Met*, XVII, 3.

6. *MT*, *Sheḥiṭah*, XI, 10.

7. *Ibid.*, *Terumot*, I, 22; *Sheḥiṭah*, VI, 8.

8. *Ibid.*, *Shemiṭah we-Yobel*, IX, 8; see Tchernowitz, *Toledoth ha-Posḳim*, I, 278, n. 80. Note the significant variation in this statement as quoted by ha-Me'iri, *Bet ha-Beḥirah* on *Sanhedrin*, ed. A. Sofer, 55: על דבר כיוצא בזה כתבו גדולי המפרשים· לא נתן התלמוד אלא לבעלי הקבלה המומחית או לבעלי הסברא הנכונה ושקול הדעת הצלול·

9. There is room here for a speculative historical correlation. Maimonides' appraisal of the contemporary twelfth-century scene coincided with his historical reconstruction of the period of R. Judah the Patriarch, redactor of the Mishnah. He believed that R. Judah lived during a time of endless persecutions accompanied by—or resulting in—a

The quest for sources, then—an endless, unflagging quest which requires repeated incursions into the labyrinths of rabbinic literature—is one of the major categories of the hassagot. It is a heterogeneous job, potentially antithetical in nature, and reflects both the constructive and destructive aspects of the hassagot. Despite the general clarity of the *Mishneh Torah* and the grandeur of its architectonic structure, the source and exact meaning of statements is sometimes obscured by recondite allusions, paraphrases, or not immediately identifiable concepts. In such cases, Rabad sometimes merely indicates the source for the benefit of the reader: "The verse is interpreted in this way in the *Sifri*" or "He inferred this from the mishnah in *ᶜArakin*." One two-word annotation says only "Abbaye we-Rabba," meaning that the topic discussed by Maimonides is a subject of repeated controversy between these two *Amoraim*.[10] On occasion he adds a word or two of explanation, which aptly supplements Maimonides' brief statement: "He found this matter in tractate *ᶜArakin* . . . and it is there explained in connection with . . ."[11] This search for sources was extended also to post-Talmudic authorities; and Rabad associates Maimonidean opinions with such predecessors as R. Ḥananel, R. Joseph ibn Migas, "his teacher," or "the Geonim" in general. Indication of

serious deterioration of mental capacities and a decline in learning. These circumstances impelled R. Judah to provide a ready, serviceable summary of the Oral Law and thereby preserve its uninterrupted study. His pioneer attempt at codification, in other words, was simply one of the "uses of adversity." Maimonides' depressing description of his own "difficult times" tallies with his picture of the early third century; witness his moving letter to the sages of Provence, *Oẓar Neḥmad*, II (1857), 3–4 (quoted Chapter I, §2, note 21) and his introduction to the *Mishneh Torah*: תלמידים מתמעטין והולכין והצרות מתחדשות ובאות . . . וישראל מתגלגלין והולכין לקצוות. Like R. Judah, he felt compelled to compose a code which would facilitate study and preserve the continuity of the Oral Law.

Rabad, on the other hand, witnessing and participating in the efflorescence of rabbinic culture in Provence—a fact which is attested to by Maimonides himself—could not share Maimonides' pessimism nor feel the need for authoritative summation with such urgency. As for Rabad's view of the early third century, it presumably coincided with his optimistic appraisal of the contemporary scene. For the theory regnant among French rabbis maintained that this was a period of relative peace and calm and only in such auspicious circumstances was R. Judah able to consummate his great task of codification. The Mishnah did not rise desperately from adversity but emerged deliberately from transient good fortune. See Rashi, *Baba Meẓiᶜa*, 33b (ונחו מצרה ושלח וקבץ כל תלמידי א"י), based on *Iggert R. Sherira Gaon*, ed. B. M. Lewin, 21 (ושקטו רבנן ביומי דרבי מכל שמדא). Also the quotation from *Orḥot Ẓaddiḳim* in Assaf, *Meḳorot le-Toledot ha-Ḥinnuk*, I, 24 which is applicable to conditions in Provence. See M. Zucker, "Ḥomer le-Mabo ha-Talmud be-Perushe Rashi," *Bitzaron*, II (1940), 380–381.

10. *MT*, *Roẓeaḥ*, I, 7; *Naḥalot*, III, 1; *Sanhedrin*, XVIII, 3; also *Terumot*, X, 22; *Nedarim*, IX, 18.

11. *MT*, *Mekirah*, XXVII, 8. (The reference *MT* will be omitted for the rest of this chapter.)

these affinities, however, is more of a matter of setting the historical record straight than of providing the textual basis for Maimonides' statements; nor does it always signify agreement on the part of Rabad as is usually the case with the curt references to primary Talmudic sources.[12]

Rabad could not always discover a satisfactory source. He would then, unequivocally but with stylistic restraint, express his disapproval by some such prosaic formula: "I have not found a source or basis for this, neither in the Mishnah nor in the Tosefta nor in the Palestinian Talmud."[13] Still another manner of disapproval is successfully to associate Maimonides' statement with the underlying Talmudic passage and then differ as to Maimonides' use of it. Thus, Rabad observes: "He gathered these [facts] from the Tosefta, but it is not as he says."[14] The following comment clearly shows how sustained this search for sources was: "I searched for this saying and did not find it either in the Mishnah, Tosefta, or Palestinian Talmud." Still pressing the search, he adds, "perhaps he derived it from what was said in the Mishnah concerning . . . and relied upon this." However, this possibility is immediately ruled out by Rabad as "vanity and a striving after wind."[15] This steady probing after sources often required keen conjecture. For instance, commenting upon Maimonides' statement concerning some aspect of dietary law (the ritual fitness of an animal with a lacerated windpipe), Rabad says tersely: "This is an erroneous explanation which he applied to the problem of 'laceration.'" Rabad presumably discovered this source by a process of elimination. Having observed that the Talmudic problem of a "lacerated windpipe" seemed at first glance to be missing from the *Mishneh Torah*, he must have traced Maimonides' statement here to this context, assuming a very different textual interpretation, an "erroneous" one in fact. Maimonides' implied explanation, although apparently shared by Alfasi, is very odd and can only be read into the text by a tour de force, which

12. *Naḥalot*, IV, 6; IX, 8; *Sanhedrin*, XXIV, 1; *Malweh we-Loweh*, XIV, 3; *Zekiyah u-Matanah*, III, V; *Ma'akalot Asurot*, IX, 16; *Kil'ayim*, IV, 9.

13. *Kil'ayim*, II, 12; also, *Sheḳalim*, III, 4; *Terumot*, XIV, 17.

14. *Taᶜanit*, IV, 7.

15. *Shemiṭah we-Yobel*, IV, 6. For more examples of Rabad's scholarly sleuthing and reconstruction of sources even if the Maimonidean statement per se is intrinsically unsound in his opinion, see *Sekirut*, V, 20; *Sheḳalim*, III, 4; *Abot ha-Ṭume'ot*, III, 7; *Maᶜaser Sheni we-Neṭa Rebaᶜi*, III, 8; *Parah Adumah*, VI, 10 is an interesting example, for the reasoning suggested there is already rejected in *BH* (beginning of *Shaᶜar ha-Mayim*), 62.

Rabad decidedly rejects.[16] It is revelatory of his technique that Rabad often admits or implies having gone back to the Talmud in order to check Maimonides' quotations or find relevant sources.[17] This exposé of flaws in Maimonides' use of sources often merges with a full exposition of Rabad's own views. In other words, the so-called source-annotations, somewhat amplified, may lead to those hassagot predicated upon interpretative differences, since the latter, quite understandably, often begin with a reference to the basic sources.

This category of "source-annotations"[18] was overlooked or not appreciated by those scholars who did not note the comprehensive character of the hassagot and viewed Rabad as a critic only. Consequently, when they encountered an annotation which was purely informative and had no polemical overtones, they were amazed and looked upon this as a deviation or eccentricity. Thus, when Rabad points to "the end of tractate *Bekorot*" as the source of a certain statement, R. Joseph Karo, in keeping with his basic view of the hassagot as negative critique, comments: "I do not know why Rabad saw fit in this case to write the source of the law, more so than in other places." He conjectures that, inasmuch as Maimonides' restatement of the law did not follow the original style of the Talmud, Rabad wanted to affirm this

16. *Sheḥiṭah*, III, 24; see *Ḥullin*, 45a, and Alfasi, *ad. loc.* Another example is *Ishut*, III, 20. Although infuriated by Maimonides' statement—"there is no greater breach than this"— Rabad is eager to find for this statement a plausible source which, incorrectly interpreted, might have led Maimonides astray, and he is not slow in coming up with a hypothesis: "An erroneous explanation which he heard concerning [a phrase in *Giṭṭin* 33a] misled him." Partial corroboration for this hypothetical reconstruction is forthcoming from the fact that there was such a textual interpretation as that implied by Maimonides' controversial view; it is quoted by Rashi, who flatly rejects it, in the name of "his teachers." Whether Rabad was acquainted with this freak interpretation from Rashi or knew from other sources that such a view was current, this sleuthing of his in the *Mishneh Torah* is rather artful. It might be observed that quite a prolonged controversy raged over this problem: the sages of Lunel asked Maimonides about his bizarre view; Naḥmanides discussed it at length in his criticism of Maimonides' *Sefer ha-Miẓwot* and was vociferous in his dissent; Maimonides' son finally maintained that a careless scribe was at fault here—and this was repeated by R. Moses ha-Kohen and by Menaḥem ha-Me'iri—and his father never upheld such a view. See *Ishut*, III, 20, and commentaries, *ad. loc.*; *Teshubot ha-Rambam*, ed. A. Freimann, 162; *Birkat Abraham*, ed. Goldberg, 44; M. ha-Me'iri, *Bet ha-Beḥirah* on *Ḳiddushin* (Jerusalem, 1942), 3; another example is *Malweh we-Loweh*, VIII, 5.

17. See, for example, *Ẓiẓit*, I, 15; *Shabbat*, I, 10; XXV, 15; *Yom Ṭob*, VII, 3; *Nezirut*, V, 15; *Ṭume'at Met*, XX, 5.

18. In addition to those already mentioned in the preceding notes, see *Shabbat*, XVIII, 10; *Sheḳalim*, III, 9; *Bikkurim*, IX, 6; *Shemiṭah we-Yobel*, IV, 6, IX, 6; *Nedarim*, VI, 17, and others.

Talmudic passage as the underlying source.[19] Actually, this note is not a rare phenomenon and the explanation given here by Karo is a sound principle applicable in many similar cases.

Rabad's quest was not flawless; he sometimes overlooked the correct source and unjustly condemned Maimonides. In one case where Rabad submits a conjectural source after failing to find a direct one, there is a distinct passage in the Palestinian Talmud which is the basis of the Maimonidean statement.[20] Or, when Rabad solicitously justifies a certain law by logically deducing it from a baraita in *Ḥullin,* Karo notes that this inferential support is gratuitous inasmuch as the law is found explicitly in the Tosefta.[21]

The critical quest for sources, as beneficial and constructive as this may be, is only one of the many positive, appreciatory elements in Rabad's review. He was as much an amiable commentator as a critic, sufficiently open-minded to appreciate Maimonides' achievements; consequently, it is not surprising that his hassagot, viewed as a commentary, assume many diverse forms. They range from short word explanations to lengthy conceptual supplements, from lexical annotation to halakic clarification. Representative of the former are many annotations in *Sefer Ṭohorot,* particularly *Hilkot Kelim,* for its subject matter abounds in lexicographical and terminological difficulties. Maimonides had taken texts not remarkable for their clarity and in the process of recasting them often removed them from the original. He sometimes omits the key word or *terminus technicus* from his restatement of a law, making it difficult for the reader to identify the underlying Talmudic source. This difficulty is compounded when Maimonides substitutes a lengthy expository paraphrase for the key word. In such cases, Rabad, playing the role of commentator or lexicographer, associates the explanatory description with the original Mishnaic or Talmudic word.[22] Such instances of Maimonidean paraphrase are

19. *Nedarim,* IX, 18, and *Kesef Mishneh, ad. loc.*

20. *Shemiṭah we-Yobel,* IV, 6; see also *Ishut,* XXI, 9; *Gerushin,* I, 18; IV, 15. These were noted by Gross, XXIII (1874), 22.

21. *Bikkurim,* IX, 6. R. David b. Zimra repeated Rabad's reference to this mishnah without even mentioning Rabad.

22. E.g., *Kelim,* XI, 20 where Rabad identifies Maimonides' paraphrase with *ḳaligrafon* and praises this descriptive paraphrase as more precise than that of the ᶜ*Aruk*; see M. *Kelim,* XIII, 2; ᶜ*Aruk ha-Shalem,* ed. A. Kohut (New York, 1955), VII, 97; Maimonides' Mishnah Commentary on *Tohorot,* 3 v., ed. Derenbourg (Berlin, 1887), I, 121. This explanation is closer to that of the ᶜ*Aruk* than to this own paraphrase in the

significant for they reveal that Maimonides fully realized the essential interrelationship of codification and commentary and that he did in fact often commentate while codifying. It is also clear, as a corollary of this, that Rabad's strictures against him when he fails to illuminate obscure passages in the course of his codificatory reformulation are well-taken and not at all gratuitous as some Maimonidean commentators would have it.

Examples of this category of explanatory notes are found in other sections of the *Mishneh Torah* as well, not only in connection with the abstruse, generally inoperative laws of cleanness and uncleanness. Maimonides' statement that "something half-cooked on only one side," Rabad explains, is based on the picturesque Talmudic phrase "*ma'akal ben drosai*." While, at first glance, this identification by Rabad appears somewhat puzzling—for it is an apparently obvious matter—it becomes more meaningful and appropriate when one recalls that there are diverse interpretations of this term, with Rashi, for instance, claiming that it means "one-third cooked." Rabad's Provençal follower in Maimonidean critique, R. Moses ha-Kohen, also took issue with Maimonides' statement. By his sententious source reference, Rabad thus aligns himself with the Maimonidean interpretation.[23] Elsewhere, Rabad provides the source of a Maimonidean statement and its interpretative basis.[24] In sum, by pointing out the Talmudic word or phrase for which Maimonides substituted an explanatory paraphrase, this type of note becomes affiliated to a certain extent with Rabad's general indication of sources. It is both a source reference and an apposite explanatory supplement—two decidedly positive functions.[25] Even when Rabad disagrees with Maimonides' explanation, he still traces it back to the original word and supplies what he believes is a superior explanation—as in the case of *betaḥ*, *asufti*, and others.[26]

Sometimes the procedure of this verbal explanation is reversed. This happens when Maimonides, choosing the path of least resistance, evades the latent interpretative function incumbent upon the codifier—a func-

---

Mishneh Torah. See also *Perush ha-Geonim ʿal Seder Ṭohorot*, ed. J. N. Epstein (Berlin, 1921), 28, and n. 23; *Tarbiẓ*, I (1930), 125; see also *Ṭume'at Met*, X, 4 (*male temaya*); XI, 10 (*ilketiyot*).

23. *Shabbat*, IX, 5, and commentaries; see *Menaḥot*, 57a.

24. *Shabbat*, XVIII, 10 (concerning *ʿiraniyot*); see S. Lieberman, *Hilkot Jerushalmi la-Rambam* (New York, 1947), 9, and references cited there.

25. See also *Bet ha-Beḥirah*, VII, 5; *Nizḳe Mamon*, XIII, 13; *Ṭume'at Met*, XIII, 3.

26. *Ibid.*, XIV, 7; XVII, 3; *Malweh we-Loweh*, V, 5.

tion which he periodically executed—by incorporating essentially equivocal words or problematic phrases into his restatement of the law. In such cases, Rabad offers an explanation of his own which vivifies or actualizes the entire law. Rabad felt that by filling in these interpretative lacunae he was doing Maimonides' spadework, for Maimonides should have consistently adhered to the interpretative principle instead of falling back on verbatim quotation. "This man explains where it is unnecessary [to do so] and neglects the places which require [explanation]; why did he not explain here . . . ?" And Rabad goes on to provide an explanation which is lauded by R. Joseph Karo and adopted by R. Samson of Sens and R. Asher b. Yeḥiel.[27] Otherwise, Rabad maintained, one was echoing meaningless or uncommunicative formulas. This point is underscored when Rabad cites several explanations of the problematic word at issue, thereby indicating that there is no scholarly consensus which Maimonides could tacitly adopt or imply.[28] The standard line followed by Maimonidean protagonists—namely, that this is not really a vulnerable deficiency inasmuch as Maimonides is only a codifier or compiler and does not purport to be a commentator—is weakened by the above-mentioned observation that Maimonides frequently and skillfully interpolates commentary into his code. To say as they do, that whatever explanation read into the original passage should also be read into its counterpart in the *Mishneh Torah* is obviously begging the question. In other words, Rabad's parenthetical strictures against Maimonides for mechanically reproducing certain passages in all their

27. *Ṭume'at Met*, XVI, 5, and *Kesef Mishneh, ad. loc.*; see also *Ṭume'at Ẓaraᶜat*, IV, 5; *Ma'akalot Asurot*, XII, 1; *Maᶜaser Sheni*, III, 20.

28. For instance, in the chapter dealing with the law that "no utensils become susceptible to uncleanness until their manufacture is complete," Maimonides, indicating what stage of production makes various wooden utensils susceptible to uncleanness, states: "An *ᶜarak* becomes susceptible after one twist has been made round its side." Now, Maimonides here simply reproduced the original Mishnaic word (*ᶜarak*) found in *Kelim* 16:3, without any explanation. So that the reader may know what the law actually refers to, Rabad, the commentator, adds: "this is explained in the *ᶜAruk* as a sieve." He also explains why this utensil is considered completed and ready for use at an earlier stage than other utensils mentioned by Maimonides in this passage: "the reason being that a person uses these [sieves] as they are, unlike the other utensils which he [Maimonides] mentioned previously." Rabad thus explains the word—even though Maimonides, as we know from his Mishnah commentary, explained it differently (as a "rush basket")—and motivates the practical-*halakic* difference between it and others. See *Kelim*, V, 1; Derenbourg, I, 138; Epstein, 44. Another good example is *Ṭume'at Oklin*, XIII, 11 where Maimonides retains the difficult "*ḳiswah*." The explanation submitted by Rabad against the *ᶜAruk* is similar to that offered by Maimonides in his commentary on *Ṭohorot*. See Derenbourg, III, 190; Epstein, 129; M. *Makshirin*, V, 8 and Sens Commentary, *ad. loc.*

obscurity are valid, while his generous supplementary explanations are welcomed, even by the defensive commentators.[29]

This practice applies, moreover, not only to isolated words but to entire Talmudic passages which Maimonides often retains in their original form, minus any commentatorial expansion or interpolation. In such cases Rabad plays the role of full-fledged commentator as well as careful lexicographer. In one chapter containing four hassagot, for instance, three are of this interpretative type: Rabad quotes the source and explains it in order to elucidate and substantiate Maimonides' statement. Thus, when Maimonides quotes verbatim a mishnah from *Demai*—not a very popular subject to begin with—Rabad supplies a running commentary on the whole passage, interweaving his explanatory comments into the text.[30] In this respect he is actually a Talmudic commentator. The same explanations that he provides could be transferred, without any editorial revision, to the pertinent Talmudic, usually Mishnaic, text, for they constitute hylic fragments of an unintentional commentary, often transcending their role as explanatory supplements to Maimonides' statements.[31]

Rabad availed himself of such lingering linguistic or textual obscurities—which, he felt, should have been clarified in the course of the rearrangement and rewording that accompany codification—to expound entire passages which were not even directly or totally relevant to the specific Maimonidean statement which served as his cue. The hassagot on the *Mishneh Torah* merely served him as a vehicle of expression into which he did not hesitate to introduce seemingly extraneous material—either new ideas or textual interpretations. Rabad quotes a passage from the Tosefta ("I found the following in the Tosefta . . ."), explains it, and concludes: "So it appears to me, and inasmuch as this Tosefta struck me as novel, I wrote it [here] and explained it."[32] Seizing upon

29. See §2, note 27; also *Ṭume'at Oklin*, V, 15; *Sheluḥin we-Shutafin*, VIII, 7. R. David b. Zimra, *Bikkurim*, VIII, 2 writes: לא ידעתי למה לא יפרש הראבד דברי רבנו כמו שמפרש דברי המשנה והירושלמי . . . ואם מפני שהיה לו להאריך ולפרש כבר קדם לו שרבינו מעתיק הלשונות כדי לקצר . . . . Rabad sometimes uses an identical argument in defense of Alfasi; e.g. *Hassagot*, *Beẓah*, 8a: באמת כך אנו נוהגין . . . והרב לא כתב אלא הגמרא כמות שהיא.

30. *Terumot*, III, 24; also, IV, 13, 14, 19.

31. See the remark of Z. Frankel, *Darke ha-Mishnah*, 333.

32. *Miḳwa'ot*, VII, 11. The fact that he added his own novellae to the *Mishneh Torah* speaks volumes about his genuine esteem of the work and his belief in its durable influence. He must have been swayed by its greatness as he made his way through it. Had he considered the work to be of ephemeral value, he would not have "buried" his theories along with it. Rather, Maimonides was in his eyes a "mighty oak" from which it was good to be suspended.

the Maimonidean text, which mentions the principle discussed in the Tosefta, as a pretext, Rabad incorporated this note into the hassagot only because it contained a new idea which he had not yet expressed elsewhere. Similarly, aroused by a parenthetic remark, Rabad quotes a passage from a Tosefta which apparently contradicts a Mishnaic teaching. He then suggests a possible solution of the irksome discrepancy and a resultant harmonization of the texts—all this, it should be clear, having no bearing upon Maimonides' statement, which Rabad accepts in full. It was just that Maimonides' statement conjured up this problem which he, Rabad, hastened to explain.[33] In the same vein is Rabad's famed comment on Exodus 22:2, where he dissents from the accepted midrashic exegesis. The hassagah, which is free of all—even veiled or muted—criticism of Maimonides, provided him with a literary forum from which to present his novel view.[34] Innumerable sections of the Talmud—especially troublesome passages from the Mishnah and Tosefta—are thus indirectly illuminated by Rabad in his capacity as commentator on the *Mishneh Torah* and its underlying texts.

Occasionally Rabad, in his role of straightforward Maimonidean commentator, aligned himself with Maimonidean views, proferring an additional explanation, alternate reason, or apposite proof and elucidation. The explanation sometimes takes the form of a supplement to Maimonides, sort of an extension of his actual statement and the trend of thought behind it.[35] It may also bring out the invisible paper work

33. *Mikwa'ot*, VIII, 7. It is also noteworthy that precisely in this area of *Miḳwa'ot*, where Rabad himself had codified extensively, he emerges more as a commentator than as a critic.

34. *Genebah*, IX, 8; also *Matenot ᶜAniyim*, I, 12; V, 11, and note 55.

35. E.g., *Gerushin*, XIII, 29. Maimonides broaches the question why, in cases deciding a woman's marital status, the halakah validates various forms of testimony—that of women, servants, a single witness, second-hand witnesses, and the like—which are usually disqualified as juridical evidence; why, more specifically, a woman presumed to be married may remarry if indirect or otherwise unreliable testimony relates that her husband died. Maimonides combines two unrelated explanations; (1) such second-rate testimony is valid here because the facts are bound to become known (and, therefore, one will be less prone to lie); (2) the regularly rigorous requirements for testimony were relaxed or suspended "in order that Jewish women should not remain as deserted wives" (*ᶜagunot*). At the end of this discussion Rabad interpolates objectively: "Another reason is that the woman investigates scrupulously and [only then] marries, because of the harsh consequences which are imposed afterward [if she acts prematurely]." Now, clearly, Rabad is not assailing the unique legal provisions, which are indisputable, nor Maimonides' reasons, which are talmudically substaniated; he is merely adding a third reason, which also appears in the Talmudic discussions of this problem. Complete analysis of the problem hinges upon a study of the following statements as well: *Roẓeah*, IX, 14; *Soṭah*, I, 14; *Gerushin*, XII, 15.

which went into the *Mishneh Torah* by indicating the implied Maimonidean explanation of texts or the derivation of laws.[36] He may add precision to an halakic summation by interpolating a brief stipulation.[37] There are cases where the Maimonidean conclusion is intelligible only if predicated upon such an explanation of the original text as that suggested by Rabad.[38] Rabad may also expansively reinterpret a seemingly troublesome statement of Maimonides and thus render it more plausible, elaborate a short remark and thus supply it with clarity, or qualify a potentially ambiguous assertion and thus endow it with precision.

Concerning damage by chattels, Maimonides wrote:

> Unless there is clear proof from witnesses eligible to testify, compensation for damage may not be paid a plaintiff, liability for ransom may not be collected, nor may the animal be killed . . . No one may ever be required to pay compensation on the evidence of witnesses unless they are eligible to give evidence in other cases.

Lest the emphatic specifications concerning eligible witnesses be taken too rigorously, Rabad qualifies the statement as follows: "This means to exclude only witnesses ineligible to testify, but a person is certainly obligated to pay compensation for damage and liability for ransom on the basis of his own testimony; the only difference is that a person may not be killed on the basis of his own testimony." This is undoubtedly an accurate qualification, sustained by Talmudic opinion as well as by Maimonidean statements elsewhere.[39]

Or, concerning the obligations of a bailee or watchman at a time when the bailed object is endangered, Maimonides, reproducing the gist of the discussion in *Baba Meẓiʿa*, formulates the following rule:

> If the herdsman with the aid of other herdsmen and clubs could have saved the animal from being torn or captured but did not call the other herdsmen or bring clubs for the rescue, he is liable, whether he was a gratuitous keeper or one for hire . . . The latter is under a duty to hire other herdsmen and clubs and to pay therefor up to the value of the animal—to be later reimbursed by

36. *Nizḳe Mamon*, XIII, 11; *Bi'at Miḳdash*, V, 11; *Ẓiẓit*, III, 1. Even R. Joseph Karo accepted this elaboration as "an additional explanation rather than an animadversion."

37. E.g., with reference to Maimonides' statement that the finder of lost property "need not return it unless he is given unmistakable marks of identification," Rabad notes: "to the exclusions of white and red" (viz., color identification). Inasmuch as the Talmudic classification of identification marks is complex and Maimonides' treatment of the whole question of the reliability of such marks is far from simple, the three-word note by Rabad is especially helpful. *Gezelah wa-Abedah*, XIII, 2; see *Baba Meẓiʿa*, 26b.

38. See, for example, *Terumot*, IV, 13, 14.

39. *Nizḳe Mamon*, VIII, 13, and *Kesef Mishneh*, *ad. loc.*

the owner—and if, having had an opportunity to hire men and clubs, he failed to do so, he is liable.

Elaborating the nature and extent of the liability, which remains undefined in Maimonides' formulation, Rabad observes: "This matter requires explanation. He does not pay the full value of the animals, for the amount of money which he would have needed to hire the herdsmen is subtracted. If this amount is equal to the value of the animals, we assess how much a person is willing to give in order not to bother with the purchase of equally good animals and the herdsman pays the owner this assessed amount." This explanation is implicitly subscribed to by Maimonides.[40]

In one annotation Rabad observes that "there seems to be an error" in Maimonides' statement. He then suggests a way out and deftly interprets Maimonides' statement, concluding that now "this is plausible." This plausible interpretation of the problematic statement is accepted by the commentators as conveying the real intention of Maimonides.[41] There is an accurate interpretative comment by Rabad on a certain statement in *Hilkot Nedarim*. The fact that the entire annotation is gratuitous, having been occasioned by a faulty version of the original Maimonidean text, is not relevant at the moment; it still serves to illustrate the significant commentatorial strain in the hassagot.[42] In all these instances—and these are merely random illustrations of a significant group[43]—Rabad contributes substantially to the lucidity, precision, or general tenability of the Maimonidean view. The comment found in the *Maggid Mishneh* concerning one of the above examples, "this is clearly what our Master means to say," epitomizes Rabad's role as commentator.[44]

40. *Sekirut*, III, 6, and *Maggid Mishneh, ad. loc.* For another neat example of Rabad's interpretative expansion, see *Genebah*, VII, 5.

41. *Gerushin*, IX, 27; see *Eben ha-ᶜEzer*, 120, and *Ḥelḳat Meḥoḳeḳ, ad. loc.*, n. 20.

42. *Nedarim*, VI, 10, and commentary of R. David b. Zimra. See also *Melakim*, VII, 1, where Rabad spotlights a difficulty; Rabbi Ch. Heller in his edition of *Sefer ha-Mizwot*, 83, n. 8 suggests that the first six words belong to the end of ch. VI.

43. See also *Terumot*, VII, 7; *Nedarim*, III, 9; *Gerushin*, III, 11; *Shofar*, I, 3. It is possible by the traditional method of Talmudic study to introduce valid theoretical differences as underlying many hassagot where Rabad seems simply to be elaborating or elucidating the Maimonidean statement. Interesting in this context are those cases where the commentators disagree as to the purpose of a given *hassagah*: explanation or dissent; see, for example, *Kesef Mishneh* and *Leḥem Mishneh* on *Ḥagigah*, I, 1; *Kesef Mishneh* on *Sheḥiṭah*, VI, 13.

44. *Nizḳe Mamon*, VIII, 13. See also, R. David b. Zimra, *Responsa* (Sedilkow, 1836), II (*Leshonot ha-Rambam*), 155: ואפשר שלא בא להשיג אלא לפרש, שלא נטעה בלשון הרב ז״ל, ויש כיוצא בזה בהשגותיו.

Sometimes Rabad's projected interpretations strain the original text of the *Mishneh Torah* or do not dovetail with the general Maimonidean outlook. His attempted rehabilitation of an apparently troublesome statement—"I do not know what this means; perhaps he wants to say that..."—is rejected by most commentators as alien to the overt meaning.[45] Rabad himself realized that Maimonides' "language does not point to this interpretation" but, inasmuch as "reason warrants it," he overlooked the unbearable strain imposed on Maimonides' original wording.[46]

Notwithstanding his announced intention of selecting the most cogent view and then presenting unilateral decisions, Maimonides occasionally felt compelled to cite two or more opinions. In such cases, Rabad may adduce support for one of the views. Although when Rabad chooses to support the second view, this may be considered as an implicit critique of Maimonides' preferred view, in broader perspective such partially corroborative hassagot also represent the commentatorial aspect of Rabad's work. If Maimonides made an exception to his standard monolithic procedure in order to cite two views—and this is rare—both are worthy of explanation and substantiation. In such cases, Rabad might throw his weight behind one of the views and produce corroborative evidence from a related source: "This is the truth and is so specified in the Palestinian Talmud."[47] In another case when Maimonides cites two versions of a law, Rabad unqualifiedly rejects the second and the commentators agree that the first is indeed the most important.[48]

Whereas in the above cases Rabad simply adds explanatory comments of various kinds—the implicit question which he aims to eliminate emerging only indirectly and allusively—on occasion he adopts a more avowedly defensive technique which is typical of later methods of Maimonidean study and research. He may explicitly call attention to a vulnerable aspect of some Maimonidean conclusion or inference, indicate an apparent textual contradiction or inconsistency, and then proceed to resolve all or part of the difficulties.[49] He may differentiate

45. *Sukkah*, VI, 11.

46. For a good example of avowed differences in interpretation, see *Roẓeah*, XII, 5.

47. *Shabbat*, XXIX, 14; see *Ma'akalot Asurot*, VII, 9, where Rabad curtly endorses the second view.

48. *Yom Ṭob*, II, 12; see also *Sheḳalim*, III, 9; *Nedarim*, II, 4; and the remarks of Z. H. Chajes, *Tiferet le-Mosheh* (Zolkiew, 1840), 8a.

49. E.g., ᶜ*Akum*, III, 9. It should be noted that these questions are directed against the underlying Talmudic source as much as against Maimonides' paraphrase. This

between aspects of the problem and then harmonize texts in keeping with "the approach which the author must have followed."[50] Often his answer is only conjectural—"perhaps" this is what Maimonides had in mind.[51] Sometimes he dissents from a statement, then suggests a possible, harmonistic solution with the caveat, "this is possible but he should have been explicit" or "he should have been careful in his formulation."[52]

An interesting example in a light vein, dealing as it does with an aggadic motif rather than an halakic norm, is Rabad's query on Maimonides' statement that Abraham was the first "to proclaim to the whole world and inform them that there is one God for the whole universe." Rabad is "amazed" that Maimonides depicts Abraham as the first active apostle of monotheism, the first real iconoclast relentlessly crusading against the rampant idolatry; it is inconceivable that Shem and ᶜEber—credited, by rabbinic tradition, with establishment of a school for the study of the Torah and a court for the promulgation of laws—should have refrained from actively protesting against these damnable religious perversions. Having thus raised a naive question, Rabad submits an equally naive answer: "I am amazed, for there were there Shem and ᶜEber and how is it that they did not protest? It is possible, however, that they did protest but never had the occasion to break any icons, for they were concealed from them—until Abraham came and shattered his father's images."[53]

As final evidence for this category, mention should be made of an annotation which not only shows Rabad raising questions and felling them with a few deft strokes of his pen, but articulates his desire to ward off criticism from the *Mishneh Torah*: "These statements are cumbersome and we have nothing on which to base ourselves. If only we could find one thread on which to depend [in explanation of his statement], we would latch on to it." Following a brief enumeration of difficulties Rabad adds that he "did find a thread, as thin as a thread of the warp,

---

hassagah then, like those described earlier, affords Rabad a means of expression, transcending the immediate needs of *MT* critique.

50. *Mekirah*, XV, 13.

51. E.g., *Ṭume'at Met*, XI, 9 (*Kesef Mishneh*, *ad. loc.*, intensifies the question). Many annotations on Maimonides' preliminary enumeration of commandments are of this type: they raise a question or uncover a contradiction and then suggest a way out for Maimonides; see, for example, commandments 7, 60, 146, 149.

52. *Ṭoᶜen we-Niṭᶜan*, I, 8; IV, 8.

53. *ᶜAkum*, I, 3. Rabad seems to be de-individualizing history, viewing all scholars or saints—especially Scriptural personalities—as identical. There is no sense of historical uniqueness, as implied by Maimonides.

on which I can depend." In an ingenious interpretation of uncommon texts he proposes answers to some of the enumerated difficulties. "Behold, this is what I have found; perhaps these statements [of Maimonides] follow this approach." He concludes, however, that "we still have questions about this chapter."[54] Raising questions even though some will remain unanswered is not an act of hostility designed to reveal the vulnerable spots of a certain system; it is an objective, challenging type of annotation which is still typical of Maimonidean commentators today.

Besides resolving hypothetical questions, thereby anticipating and eliminating possible criticism, Rabad sometimes takes issue with questions that were actually directed against the *Mishneh Torah*. "I have noticed that someone questions Maimonides and the Baraita [which underlies his statement] . . . on the basis of Rabba's statement." Announcing that "there is no question here," Rabad reconciles the text used for the question with the corresponding passage of the Baraita which Maimonides incorporated into his formulation of the law.[55] Similarly, concerning Maimonides' statement that "no witnesses are required for the acquisition of title to a note," Rabad remarks that "there is someone who questioned this." Discussing the entire problem cursorily, Rabad also refutes the question directed against the Maimonidean decision.[56] Elsewhere Maimonides concludes that "on this there is universal agreement among the authorities." As a matter of fact there was sustained dissent from this view—already articulated in a responsum of Alfasi. Contemporaries of Rabad—R. Isaac b. Abba Mari of Marseilles, for example—also reviewed this opinion critically. Rabad's pithy, four-word answer to the standard question seems to belong to this group of annotations which purport to refute actual questions already broached rather than to the previous group of hypothetical difficulties merely anticipated by Rabad; although he does not mention the question, his projected solution shows unmistakably that he is grappling with it.[57]

54. *Ṭume'at Met*, XIX, 2; see also *Abot ha-Ṭume'ot*, VIII, 1; *ᶜArakin wa-Ḥaramin*, I, 6; *ᶜAbodat Yom ha-Kippurim*, VI, 5; *Sheluḥin we-Shutafin*, I, 3; III, 11.

55. *Ẓiẓit*, II, 8; In light of what has been said previously concerning Rabad's inclusion of partially extraneous material into these annotations, it is interesting to note that the author of *Migdal ᶜOz* (*ad. loc.*) dismisses the entire question as one concerning the general harmonization of Talmudic texts rather than the specific Maimonidean statement.

56. *Mekirah*, VI, 11.

57. *Malweh we-Loweh*, XXII, 15; see commentaries, especially *Maggid Mishneh*.

Rabad reveals himself as a commentator in yet another, more prosaic but equally significant, way. There are a handful of hassagot where Rabad plays the part of a conscientious proofreader and simply corrects his text of the *Mishneh Torah*, emending, paraphrasing, or interpolating so as to obviate rather basic questions. In practically all these cases he scores a perfect hit, his correction unmistakably recreating the true Maimonidean statement. Here are some typical remarks culled at random from various sections of the work: "It seems to me that there is a mistake here and this is how it should read"; "It seems to me that this is a scribal error and it should be"; "This should be emended as follows"; "All this has neither root nor branch and is the copyist's error"; "There are errors in this reading and I have emended them according to my judgment."[58] Sometimes Rabad is more explicit, clearly indicating his sustained efforts at textual emendation of the *Mishneh Torah*: "There is here a scribal error and I was unable to understand it; it seems to me that this is the way he meant it . . ."[59] Note also the following comment: "I did not know the meaning of this, for it is derived neither from the Talmud or Tosefta and makes no sense. Perhaps it is the copyist's error and should read as follows . . ."[60] Occasionally it is not clear whether Rabad intends to blame the scribe —the standard, helpless whipping boy—or Maimonides himself for textual corruptions. Interesting in this respect are certain minor variants between the printed hassagot and the fragmentary manuscripts available. For example, where the printed hassagah has "this is a great scribal error," the manuscript says only "this is a great error"—implying obviously that the error might be Maimonidean rather than scribal.[61]

Whether Rabad was in possession of more than one copy of the *Mishneh Torah* and was therefore able to cross-check readings which puzzled him at first glance—as he did with such texts as the Tosefta— or whether he sensed intuitively, without textual promptings, that certain crude errors could not but stem from scribal inadvertencies cannot be known. The fact that so many of his proposed emendations coincide almost verbatim with the original readings had by later

58. *Gezelah*, II, 10; *Melakim*, IX, 11; *Sanhedrin*, I, 5; *Genebah*, V, 3; *Zekiyah u-Matanah*, X, 2; see also *Melakim*, IX, 1 (where there are, to be sure, two possible opinions but the text lends itself to this reading); *Mekirah*, XVI, 12; *Sheluḥin we-Shutafin*, VI, 3; *Ṭume'at Met*, VI, 9; *Issure Bi'ah*, XI, 9.

59. *Sheluḥin we-Shutafin*, VI, 5.

60. *Ṭume'at Oklin*, XI, 1.

61. *Issure Bi'ah*, XI, 9. This becomes a standard type of annotation; see, for example, Abraham b. ᶜAzriel, *ᶜArugat ha-Bosem*, ed. Urbach, II, 269.

scholars, such as the authors of *Migdal ᶜOz* and *Kesef Mishneh* who claimed to have access to autograph or otherwise trustworthy copies, might be taken as inferential support for the former possibility. It is, however, minimized by the following consideration. Despite the fact that the text of the *Mishneh Torah* which Rabad worked with remained deficient in many places, he did not for the most part attribute such textual divergencies, deviations, or omissions to a lax scribe but accepted them as reflecting authentic, yet erroneous, Maimonidean opinion. The result was that he put forth a whole array of—from his point of view—bona fide animadversions which are purely gratuitous in the eyes of the later reader supplied with more accurate copies of the *Mishneh Torah.* Rabad criticizes Maimonides for nonexistent statements or censures him for apparent omissions which are actually found in our texts. Maimonides' commentators are unflaggingly vigilant to point out that Rabad was, regrettably, misled by his faulty manuscript.[62]

Such hassagot, emerging from Rabad's faulty manuscripts, cannot be construed to demonstrate that Rabad was a reckless critic out to spike Maimonides as often as possible. They testify instead to the fidelity and perceptivity with which he scrutinized the *Mishneh Torah*, inasmuch as he was able to detect these apparent flaws which Maimonides himself—exonerated from all blame—would not have allowed to pass unheeded. Indeed, Maimonides explicitly commended such painstaking textual study, welcomed beneficial comments in this direction, and was never reluctant to acknowledge scribal inaccuracies. The sages of Provence were repeatedly counseled by Maimonides to emend the text when sane criticism dictated it. In one place he observes that "your complaints are neither against me nor against yourselves but against the scribe and the proofreader—correct the text."[63]

Nor was Rabad the only one who fell victim to erroneous readings. Defective manuscripts of Maimonides' code were distressingly common and holographs or even reliable transcripts made directly from them were highly cherished desiderata among rabbinic students. Shortly after Maimonides' death, his famous antagonist R. Meïr ha-Levi Abulafia of Toledo asked Samuel ibn Tibbon for an autograph copy of

62. See, for example, *ᶜAkum*, III, 6; *Yesode ha-Torah*, VI, 4; *Maᶜaser Sheni*, VIII, 14; *Gezelah wa-Abedah*, XVII, 5; *Ṭume'at Oklin*, II, 21; *Roẓeaḥ*, VII, 6. A good statement is in *Migdal ᶜOz, Malweh we-Loweh*, IX, 1; see also *Sefer ha-Menuḥah*, 9b (on Ḥameẓ u-Maẓah, II, 6).

63. *Teshubot ha-Rambam*, ed. Freimann, 165, also 90; see the references collated by Assaf, *Kiryath Sefer*, XVIII (1941), 150.

the *Mishneh Torah.* R. Aaron ha-Kohen of Lunel rejoiced to have access to such a copy. The authors of the *Migdal ʿOz* and *Kesef Mishneh* frequently mention that they successfully sought autographs or direct transcripts.[64] Maimonides' son Abraham and even his grandson David occasionally claim on the basis of their own copies that a widespread version is actually in need of revision.[65] What is more, in Maimonides' own lifetime, corrupt texts were in circulation; in answering some of the criticism of his strident Oriental critic, Samuel b. Ali, Maimonides stops to correct Samuel's text in keeping with his "original version." Also some responsa postdating the *Mishneh Torah* refer now and then to scribal errors which he wants corrected.[66] Had Rabad been in a position to verify doubtful or erroneous readings by such an "original version," a number of hassagot would surely have been deleted or would never have been written. As it is, these gratuitous annotations attest further to the corruption which crept into Provençal copies of the *Mishneh Torah* at such an early stage.

A more serious cause of misunderstanding and needless criticism for which Maimonides was an exposed, unprotected target and which Rabad had no reason to spare, was the fact that they did not use uniform texts. In the absence of a Masoretic-like text of the Talmud—such as that contemplated by R. Gershom of Mayence at the beginning of the eleventh century—there were basic textual divergences in their "books" which inevitably resulted in divergences of interpretation. Just as a number of disparate Amoraic explanations found in the Palestinian and Babylonian Talmuds stem from the fact that the Mishnah used in Palestinian schools was not identical in all respects with that current in the Babylonian academies, so divergencies of text continued throughout the Middle Ages to give rise to interpretative discrepancies. Medieval rabbis were cognizant of this fact and repeatedly attributed seemingly irreconcilable differences to their origin in heterogeneous texts. Questions might often resolve themselves into a matter of discretion and insight in selecting the best text—and much ingenuity

64. A. Marx, "Maimonides and the Scholars of southern France," 52, n. 8; S. Atlas, *A Section from the* Yad ha-Ḥazaḳah *of Maimonides from a Holograph Manuscript* (London, 1940); and the very important review of this by Assaf, *Kiryath Sefer*, XVIII, 150.

65. See §2, note 16.

66. A. Freimann, *Sefer Yobel le B. M. Lewin* (Jerusalem, 1940), 32. *Teshubot ha-Rambam*, ed. Freimann, 69, 152, 340.

was expended on textual variants—but the prevalence of disparate readings was a reality necessarily taken into consideration by all critics.

Rabad also knew that many statements in the *Mishneh Torah* with which he took issue were based upon divergent texts. In most of these cases he acknowledges, objectively and without rancor or criticism, the underlying divergences without even arbitrating between them. There was no reason for one to condemn another for facts beyond his immediate control; as a result, Rabad merely notes these facts: "our books have a different version"; "we have a different reading here"; "in our books [it reads]"; "this version is not found in our books nor in the *Halakot* of the Master"; "his version is unlike our version."[67] On occasion Rabad even provides Maimonides a way out of criticism by suggesting that "perhaps he found [such a reading] in his version."[68] In one case where Rabad rejects a Maimonidean view he is fair enough to stipulate: "if he found his version of the text like this, fine [for we cannot dispute it]; if, however, this view is his own inference, we do not listen to what he says."[69] Elsewhere, after expressing his amazement at a statement which seems to run counter to the basic opinion of the Mishnah, Rabad concludes candidly: "I subsequently investigated the versions of this text and found that they vary and I found one version which coincides with his statement."[70] Finally, the admissibility of two variant readings—implicit in such hassagot—is sometimes openly defended by Rabad. When Maimonides rejects one of two versions as completely erroneous while bolstering the other by the authority of ancient manuscripts, Rabad notes: "It is true that there are various versions in this matter, but I was able to affirm both of them."[71]

Occasionally Rabad desires to stress that he believes the version adopted by Maimonides to be erratic or indefensible. His language implies that the Maimonidean reading should have been disqualified: "we have not found such a version in the books"; "we have never heard such a version"; "I found this [Maimonidean] reading reversed in some books . . . and this [alternate] is the essential one; I do not know how to explain the other one"; "his text misled him—our texts

67. *Issure Mizbeaḥ*, IV, 4; *Ma'akalot Asurot*, IX, 25; *Issure Mizbeaḥ*, V, 1; *Ma'akalot Asurot*, XI, 18; *ᶜEdut*, VI, 3.
68. *Temurah*, III, 3.
69. *Ṭume'at Ẓaraᶜat*, XII, 8.
70. *ᶜArakin wa-Ḥaramin*, IV, 20.
71. *Malweh we-Loweh*, XV, 1; see *Sifra*, 114b.

read . . . and this is the essential reading."[72] When he feels especially strong about a textual conflict Rabad asserts: "our books do not agree with this reading—it is certainly corrupt"; "the version which he wrote does not agree with the Tosefta nor is it smooth in itself . . . here is the exact version."[73] In the process of selecting one specific reading Rabad occasionally defers to the Maimonidean version: "it seems that he reads this matter as follows . . . and this reading is smoother than our reading"; "I found a version which is the exact opposite of this one, but this is smoothest in my eyes."[74]

It is arbitrary to maintain that Maimonides exerted great efforts in ascertaining the most reliable and logical version of a text while Rabad was generally aloof to such scholarly minutiae. Even a hurried glance at Rabad's writings in general or the hassagot in particular reveals his sustained interest and sane insight in textual problems. As for explicit references to this type of study, Maimonides' impressive, oft-quoted assertions can be balanced by equally significant but less famous statements of Rabad.[75] Nor is it correct to assert that Maimonides' readings are inherently superior because he followed the more trustworthy Spanish texts while Rabad usually adhered to less venerable French manuscripts. Rabad lauds "Spanish books" and constantly relies upon them. When he incorporates French versions, it is not because of a principled commitment but because they impress him as more plausible.[76]

Just as the admissibility of two parallel, equally valid and defensible readings was a widespread methodological canon which contributed a measure of tolerance and restraint to halakic controversy[77] and which occasioned a distinct category of hassagot, mostly neutral and non-combative, similarly, the admissibility of two or more equally tenable interpretations of a uniform text explains the presence of another significant category of neutral, objective hassagot. Over forty annotations

72. *ᶜErubin*, II, 11; *Yom Ṭob*, II, 12; *Kelim*, XVIII, 15; *Maᶜaser*, II, 5; also *Sheḳalim*, III, 4.

73. *Maᶜaseh ha-Ḳorbanot*, XIX, 9; *Ṭume'at Met*, VIII, 5.

74. *Nizḳe Mamon*, III, 4; *Terumot*, X, 16; see also *Parah Adumah*, V, 5.

75. See, for example, *Malweh we-Loweh*, XV, 2; *Ishut*, XI, 13. For Rabad, in addition to the above references see *TD*, 61, 62; Israel Levi, *REJ*, (1899), 108, 119; Freimann, *Kiryath Sefer*, XX (1943), 21.

76. *Hassagot* on Alfasi, *Berakot*, 6b; *KS*, I, 56.

77. A good example is *Berakot*, 12b, and the discussion in Alfasi, 6b and all commentators, *ad. loc.*

are introduced by the noncommittal phrase, "there is one who says," or some variation such as "some explain," "not all agree," "it is possible to say," "some differ concerning," "some commentators submit."[78] The opinions or explanations reproduced in such hassagot are not necessarily binding for Rabad, nor do they peremptorily dismiss Maimonides' view—although his preference in some is unequivocal.

The author of the *Kenesset ha-Gedolah* has already pointed out that, "when Rabad writes 'there is someone who maintains' it cannot be inferred conclusively from this phrase that he adopts the view expressed there."[79] The truth of this assertion is inferentially sustained by the vague, detached introductory formula, by the indefinite, anonymous style. Actual analysis of certain of these hassagot, furthermore, reveals with greater clarity that Rabad was not unalterably committed to these views.[80] They present possible alternatives, often reflecting centuries-old interpretative divergences which had already become formalized or standardized as conflicting schools of thought. Their purpose seems to

78. *Ḳeri'at Shema*, II, 9; *Tefillah*, X, 13; *ᶜAkum*, I, 3; *Sefer Torah*, X, 4; *Ẓiẓit*, III, 9; *Shabbat*, II, 20; VI, 5, 16; XVII, 11; XXVII, 12; *ᶜErubin*, V, 5; *Yom Ṭob*, I, 17; II, 14; *Ḥameẓ u-Maẓah*, II, 11; V, 2; *Shofar*, II, 2; *Sukkah*, VI, 13; *Lulab*, VIII, 9; *Ishut*, V, 15; *Gerushin*, X, 11; *Ma'akalot Asurot*, XI, 21; XII, 10; XV, 18; *Sheḥiṭah*, VII, 4, 8; XI, 13; XIV, 8; *Nedarim*, VI, 7; *ᶜArakin wa-Ḥaramin*, VIII, 11; *Matenot ᶜAniyim*, III, 12; *Ṭume'at Met*, XXII, 3; *Gezelah wa-Abedah*, II, 2; XIII, 20; XV, 4; *Ḥobel u-Maziḳ*, IV, 11; VII, 7; *Mekirah*, V, 10; VI, 11; XI, 4; *Naḥalot*, VII, 3; XI, 8 (and perhaps III, 5—see *Maggid Mishneh*); *ᶜEdut*, VIII, 7; XXII, 2; *Mamrim*, IV, 3.

79. *Kenesset ha-Gedolah*, printed at the beginning of most editions of the *Mishneh Torah*; *Bet Joseph* on *Ṭur Oraḥ Ḥayyim*, 582, beginning.

80. Thus, to give only one example, concerning Maimonides' statement that a slaughtered animal is presumed to be ritually fit even if vital organs such as the lung, brain, or spine were lost before they could be examined for ritually disqualifying physiological defects, Rabad notes tersely: "there are those who differ with respect to the lung," meaning that if this is lost before inspection the presumption is no longer valid. Thanks to a responsum in *Temin Deᶜim* where Rabad discusses this problem at length, it is possible to identify the anonymous reference to "those who differ." This was the view maintained by Rabad's grandfather in opposition to the more lenient view defended by R. Judah b. Barzilai. Even more significant than the identification of the source of the view cited anonymously in Rabad's annotation is the fact that Rabad concurred with Judah b. Barzilai over and against his grandfather. Its citation in the hassagot is therefore to be explained as an aid to the student; inasmuch as this was a serious, frequently debated, question, Rabad saw fit to cite the alternate view. Perhaps he also wished to imply that it was best to follow the more rigid standard, for in the responsum he says that his grandfather's view is a "preventive against inadvertent transgression." Interesting is the fact, overlooked by Rabad or simply not mentioned by him, that the view of his grandfather, which contravenes the explicit opinion of the Palestinian Talmud, is upheld by the *Halakot Gedolot*. Viewed in the context of continued halakic discussion and controversy, it is clear that Rabad's annotation is not just for the sake of critique—his dissensions, for the most part, having both antecedents and sequels. *Sheḥiṭah*, XI, 13, and *Kesef Mishneh ad. loc.*; *TD*, 12; see *Yoreh Deᶜah*, 39:2, where Rabad's opinion is cited by Isserles.

be to deflate Maimonides' sense of certitude and authoritativeness, when this is very pronounced or, more generally, to stimulate further research and analysis by reminding the student of cogent conflicting views. They make for scholarly completeness by encompassing all aspects of a problem as exhaustively as possible in the given framework of discussion. Sometimes, especially when there is a recurrent clash of interpretations, these annotations reflect Rabad's own uncertainty about the correct theory or the proper practice and with the caution or conservatism characteristic of most debates concerning halakic norms, he wished to imply that it is wisest to adhere to the rigid view.[81] Sometimes Rabad uses an introductory formula—"the teachers do not agree with this"—which explicitly indicates the practical consequences at issue.[82] On many occasions these phrases introduce general Provençal views.[83] They are yet another indication of the protean, all-inclusive nature of the hassagot.

One may insist that these "some-say hassagot" are to be construed as latently, yet intentionally hostile, introduced by Rabad under a cloak of anonymous detachedness. This seems particularly plausible when Rabad, in his other writings, fails to espouse the views cited in the hassagot—the implication being that they are cited for the sole purpose of undermining the massive Maimonidean structure. The example concerning liturgy, where Rabad anonymously reproduces a view identical with that of Razah which he had openly repudiated previously, might lend weight to such an interpretation of this category of hassagot. While this motive cannot be ruled out, I am inclined to view these hassagot as intentionally provocative and to view their author as a gadfly in the realm of halakic discussion. The fact that in his earlier writings Rabad disagreed with a few of the views tentatively presented in the hassagot is accounted for by the consideration that for the most part

81. See, for example, *Sheḥiṭah*, VII, 8; *TD*, 12; *Ḥullin* 48a, and commentaries; *Torat ha-Bayit, Hilkot Bediḳah*, 71. This "minority view" seems to have been widespread in Provence—see the opinion of Razah in *Sefer ha-Ma'or* on Alfasi, *ad. loc.* Razah and Rashbah both report that R. Tam sent a responsum to the "sages of Marseille" supporting this view. Can there be any relationship between this "intervention" from northern France and the fact that Rabad subsequently deserted the minority view? Another example is *Ḥameẓ u-Maẓah*, V, 2; *Pesaḥim*, 36a and Rashi, Razah, and Rabad, *ad. loc.*

82. *Ma'akalot Asurot*, XII, 10.

83. E.g., *Ḥobel u-Maziḳ*, VII, 7; *Mekirah*, V, 10, and commentary of ha-Me'ir and *Shiṭṭah Meḳubeẓẓet* on the underlying Talmudic texts; *Tefillah*, X, 13 and *Hagahot Maimuniyot*; see *Berakot*, 12b, and commentaries (especially *Tosafot* and *Talmide R. Jonah*), *ad. loc.* On the use of "France" (*Ẓarefat*) for Provence, see *Sefer ha-Riḳmah*, ed. M. Wilensky, introduction, 4, n.1.

these revolve around practical issues—and there always is in such cases a marked tendency to caution, conformity with majority opinion, and rigidity. Also this view tallies with the unmistakable theoretical objective of many hassagot.[84]

This practice of citing alternate opinions, usually without final commitment, may appear more reasonable or even conventional if we remember that Maimonides, who sought finality and conclusiveness in his code, sometimes did the same, presenting one view and immediately introducing a conflicting opinion with the words "there is one who said." Whether or not the order of presentation is decisive and implies commitment to the first view cannot be fully ascertained—it probably does, as is also the case with R. Joseph Karo who frequently cites more than one view in the *Shulḥan ᶜAruk*—but the very fact that he stopped to cite an alternate view undoubtedly renders it significant. This is particularly so since elsewhere Maimonides cites a second view merely in an attempt to obliterate it completely, to deliver a *coup de grâce*. Both Rabad and Maimonides prefer the anonymous introduction of these alternate views, even when the source is presumably known.[85]

For the sake of further characterization of this group of hassagot by means of comparison and contrast, mention should be made of the annotations (*hagahot*) of R. Moses Isserles on the *Shulḥan ᶜAruk*. Professor Louis Ginzberg, comparing the influence of the *Mishneh Torah* and the *Shulḥan ᶜAruk* as affected by the criticism of Rabad and Isserles respectively,[86] has maintained that Rabad's blunt criticism destroyed confidence in Maimonides, while Isserles' annotations actually supplemented Karo's code extensively, with the result that it was accepted in its corrected form. While Rabad's critique is undoubtedly more personal than that of Isserles and stylistically harsher, it is perfectly clear that Rabad did not aim solely at sabotaging the *Mishneh Torah*. He did much to bolster it. As a matter of fact, together with such works as the *Hagahot Maimuniyot* of Franco-German provenance—which are an accurate counterpart of Isserles' *Hagahot*—

84. The *Mishneh Torah* commentators often acknowledged that these annotations of Rabad merely presented the other side of a standard controversy and then proceeded to catalogue the development of both views—as a rule, without any partisan praise or condemnation. Especially the author of the *Migdal ᶜOz* is accustomed to preface his discussion of these laws by declaring that "this is an old controversy."

85. E.g., *Gerushin*, III, 8. The source of this "some-say" view is explicitly mentioned in Alfasi as "the Gaon." See also *Tefillah*, I, 12; III, 11; *Sheḳalim*, III, 9; *Ma'akalot Asurot*, VII, 9 (which is a standard controversy); and §2, note 48.

86. L. Ginzberg, *JE*, III, 586.

Rabad's annotations may even be said to have helped supplement the *Mishneh Torah*, give it some local color, and bring it up-to-date. With regard to the "some-say" category of annotations in particular, there seems to be a basic difference between Rabad and Isserles; although the latter's criticism may at first glance seem less obtrusive and more constructive, its effect was actually more damaging. For, while Isserles usually employs the "some-say" device to indicate the proper practice, prevalent custom, or most tenable theory over and against the view of Karo, Rabad uses it to present theoretical alternatives to Maimonides' statements, to recall the other side of a standard controversy without deciding between them. Sometimes, to be sure, such an annotation intimates the proper course of action, but for the most part these hassagot are neutral. Consequently, Rabad's strictures could often remain as companions to Maimonides' statements, while Isserles' annotations were designed to supersede Karo's conclusions. They usually conclude reticently "and this is the custom" or "such is the common practice" —and custom played a key role in Isserles' concepts of law—meaning in effect that Karo's formulations, "holding fast to original authorities and material reasons," were worthless. It is true that Isserles' annotations merged formally with Karo's text, but often only to repudiate it; Rabad's "some-say" comments, on the other hand, are neither as exclusive nor as conclusive.

Still another type of annotation which is essentially neutral or even positive and supplementary in many respects is that where Rabad adds to or qualifies Maimonides' statement in order to encompass a given problem in its entirety in one spot. Because of his exacting schemes of classification and in deference to accurate analysis in a logical context rather than well-rounded synthesis replete with parenthetic observations, Maimonides often separated constituent elements of a law. Sometimes he provided the necessary cross references himself but other times he did not, without even bothering to repeat the relevant conclusions of the allied discussions. In such cases Rabad occasionally jotted down a note which anticipates a subsequent Maimonidean statement or else repeats the essence of a statement which Maimonides already formulated but is also pertinent at this juncture.[87] In connection with these notes the commentators, defensively yet accurately, observe

87. E.g., *Gerushin*, XII, 9, and *Maggid Mishneh*; *Yom Ṭob*, VI, 22 (and *Abel*, XI); ʿ*Abadim*, VII, 6 (and *Issure Bi'ah*, III, 13).

that "this is no criticism, for in this chapter our Master is concerned only with" one aspect of a problem while the general laws are discussed elsewhere.[88] Sometimes the commentators state that Rabad's annotation—localized supplement or qualification—is gratuitous inasmuch as its contents are repeated elsewhere by Maimonides.[89]

For instance, Maimonides lists "twenty-four offenses for which a person, man or woman, may be excommunicated." One of these relates to "a scholar of universally objectionable reputation." Rabad adds to this that "there are many others" and, after citing two additional examples at random, reiterates: "and there are more." Now, the two examples adduced by Rabad concerning damnable deeds of recognized scholars are mentioned by Maimonides in their logical, topical context—one in *Hilkot Gerushin* and the other in *Hilkot Nezirut*. Rabad, however, desired to point out that the descriptive category of "a scholar of universally objectionable reputation" did not exhaust the cases of scholars subject to the ban. His emphasis that "there are many others" besides the two he mentioned demonstrates that the purpose of the annotation was merely to expand Maimonides' statement—even with material that Maimonides uses elsewhere.[90]

It is possible to conjecture that Rabad recorded a certain gloss of this type before even reading Maimonides' own elaboration or qualification and then did not bother to delete it. Or perhaps he thought it advisable to leave the note intact, for it facilitated study and obviated the need for cross reference and comparison. It gave all the aspects of a question immediately, even though they could also be collated from scattered references in Maimonides' own work.[91]

There is one more type of annotation which provides a transition from the constructive aspects of Rabad's critique to the destructive. This note, customarily introduced by the phrase "I do not know that this is"—used in the Talmud as a stylistic prelude to the clarification or definition of a given problem or statement[92]—is designed to explore various possible meanings of an ambiguous Maimonidean formulation. It presents the alternatives objectively and may deal either with words or

88. E.g., *Tefillah*, III, 7, and *Kesef Mishneh, ad. loc.*

89. *Bikkurim*, V, 6, and *Kesef Mishneh, ad. loc.* The hassagah is missing in manuscript.

90. *Talmud Torah*, VI, 14.

91. The *Sefer ha-Menuḥah*, for example, instead of rounding out Maimonidean statements, supplies cross-references.

92. E.g., *Ḥullin*, 46a.

concepts. For instance, describing the emotional and intellectual prerequisites for man's cultivation of an all-consuming love of God, Maimonides uses the vivid but difficult word *shigayon*. Whereupon Rabad observes: "We do not know exactly what he meant by this 'shigayon.' It has two possible explanations: (1) in the sense of 'singing,' such as in the verse 'shigayon le-David' (Ps. 7:1); (2) the other meaning is in the sense of 'because of its love you will err' in all your preoccupations, for you will pay no attention to them." Both explanations, conveying basic meanings of the word, are applicable to Maimonides' statement.[93] The same is true for Maimonides' statement concerning the imitation of idolatrous practices: "A Jew should not build public edifices of the same construction as the temples built for idolatry in order to attract a crowd as they do." Rabad detachedly observes: "I do not know what this means. Does he mean to say that one should not make in them figures as they do or should not set up in them sun-images as a sign to gather the public as they do."[94]

Sometimes, this objective clarification is followed by critical gibes which tend to undermine the most plausible meaning or the stated reason of Maimonides' statement. After clarifying the possible meaning of a law concerning the twig-covering of the *sukkah*, Rabad concludes: "nevertheless, the reason he gives cannot be applied if we interpret it this way."[95] On occasion, the clarification may be relegated to implication and allusion while the emphasis is on the resultant question directed against Maimonides.[96] In such cases the formula "I do not know what this means" is polemical in intent.

3. *Critical Glosses and Animadversions*

These corroborative or explanatory aspects of the hassagot deserve to be emphasized, especially since they have for the most part been underrated or neglected. Yet, it would be tendentious to underplay or bemuddle the multifaceted negative critique, often couched in immoderately vitriolic terms, which constitutes quantitatively and

93. *Teshubah*, X, 6; see Prov. 5:19, and commentaries of Rashi and ibn Ezra, *ad. loc.*; also D. Kimḥi, *Sefer ha-Shorashim*, "shagoh." Rabad's clarification is frequently quoted by successors: e.g., E. Azkari, *Sefer Ḥaredim* (Lublin, 1922), 23.

94. *ʿAkum*, XI, 1.

95. *Sukkah*, V, 16.

96. *Ishut*, *II*, 4; *Kele ha-Miḳdash*, VI, 5.

qualitatively the most important part of the hassagot. Just as the favorable or neutral comments have been divided into distinct categories, these destructive animadversions may also be atomized and anatomized for the sake of description and analysis. Errors, real or apparent, serious or trivial, of various sorts—textual, stylistic, interpretative, theoretical, methodological, codificatory, classificatory—evoked various critical reactions from Rabad. Both major types, the approbatory and the dissenting, are perfectly compatible components of this searching review and one need not be obscured in order to illumine the other. Only a balanced analysis of both delineates the true nature of the hassagot.

In his quest for sources Rabad often reached the conclusion that a certain statement of Maimonides' was unfounded. In such cases he usually rejects the Maimonidean view with a simple comment: "I have not found a source for this, neither in the Mishnah nor in the Tosefta nor in the Palestinian Talmud"[1]—without any critical gibes or embellishments. Occasionally the formula is altered in order to make it more colorful or personal: "I do not know whence he derived this, it can only be from his own inference" or "I have not found any source for this, but it must be his own theory."[2] Characteristic of Rabad's method in the hassagot and their general comprehensiveness are the annotations in which Rabad declares that "this statement has no foundation" and suggests, as an inspired afterthought or informed conjecture, hypothetical sources which Maimonides may have had in mind but which are of dubious relevance.[3]

Such comments, conveying the notion that these are Maimonides' fallacious deductions from misconstrued texts, lead to the next category of annotations. In these Rabad either asserts curtly and sharply that the obvious meaning of the Talmud runs counter to the Maimonidean construction or else cites the underlying passages and shows in detail where Maimonides allegedly erred—with a spectrum of short and long variations in between. These interpretative animadversions constitute the largest single category of hassagot. They reveal the keenness as well as, sometimes, the overzealousness or cocksureness of Rabad. Some of them are self-contained discussions of the underlying Talmudic text or texts—interpretations, inferences, and conclusions. By presenting all

1. See §2, note 13; also *Kil'ayim*, VI, 3; *Terumot*, XI, 22; XIV, 17; *Maᶜaser*, XII, 5.
2. *Gerushin*, VIII, 21; *Ḳorban Pesaḥ*, VI, 2.
3. *Meᶜilah*, VI, 5; see §2, note 16.

the relevant material and enabling the reader to follow his reasoning and exegesis step by step, Rabad felt that he would thus reveal to everyone's satisfaction the vulnerability of Maimonides' paraphrase or summation. For instance, Rabad asserts: "This author cited the statements in their simple literal form and when I looked into the Talmud in the proper place in *Keritot*, I did not find that they can be substantiated in accord with this interpretation." He then reproduces the entire Talmudic debate, explains the logical sequence of the argumentation, and, returning to Maimonides' verbatim but misleading statement, adds: "I am amazed how could he think such a thing . . . this is an astonishment of heart."[4] The parenthetic phrase in this full-length criticism, "when I looked into the Talmud," presents Rabad as a serious reviewer, tracing Maimonides' statement to the source, scrutinizing his interpretation, and issuing a verdict of misleading superficiality against him.

The introductory phrases of this category of annotations most clearly indicate their tenor and purpose. "I do not know what this is, for this reason is not appropriate here; the context of the Talmud is as follows . . ." He then quotes and explains it with such precision that the *Maggid Mishneh* observes: "the contents of the hassagot here are perfectly clear."[5] "I do not agree with this . . . and what was said [in the Talmud] is to be interpreted as follows . . ."[6] Sometimes, without any parenthetic gibes, Rabad directly quotes the underlying source—"the language of the Mishnah is"—and explains it, thereby juxtaposing his own interpretation with the different one of Maimonides.[7] *Hilkot Issure Bi'ah* contains a superb example of this lengthy, on-the-spot refutation expressed with vigor and certitude, abetted by copious text citations and explanations, concluding derisively: "whatever he wrote about this matter is only 'much study [which] is a weariness of the flesh.'"[8] Elsewhere Rabad prefaces a fully documented criticism as follows: "I do not understand his words, but I think the explanation to be . . ."[9] Also: "I do not know why he saw fit to explain . . . one can derive no pleasure from this explanation of his . . . and it is in this way that I explain the mishnah; this way is sweet to me and is the correct one, as

4. *Shabbat*, I, 10; see Deut. 28:28 for the ending. The complete text is in the *Kesef Mishneh* and various manuscripts.
5. *Shabbat*, XXV, 24.
6. *Lulab*, VIII, 1.
7. *Shemiṭah we-Yobel*, VI, 3.
8. *Issure Bi'ah*, IX, 15; see Eccles. 12:12.
9. *ᶜArakin*, VII, 16.

every intelligent student will see."[10] These examples, which can be readily multiplied,[11] portray Rabad as a well-stocked commentator taking Maimonides to task for what he considered to be interpretative vagaries and inconsistencies.

Many of Rabad's interpretative strictures appear to be both apposite and convincing. His detailed explanations of texts alongside of the invisible explanations latent in Maimonides' codificatory summations impress the student as most straightforward, literal, or harmonious. There are cases where the Maimonidean paraphrase is startlingly at odds with its sources and no amount of ingenuity—even the cumulative ingenuity of successive generations of scholarly commentators—has been able to account for them. Even when scholars have been able to blunt the edge of Rabad's criticism and reconcile Maimonides' statements with the sources by those methods of critico-comparative study of texts and concepts which Rabad helped to develop, the immediate cogency of Rabad's hassagot still prevails over the "possible" explanation or theory conjecturally read into Maimonides' conclusions. In all such cases, Rabad's animadversions triumphantly speak for themselves. Other times, his dissenting views gain weight and stature when seen in historical perspective, when it is realized that they are supported by the majority of commentators and codifiers, both predecessors and successors. Maimonides' statements, although more or less justifiable, remain eccentric—what Rabad himself sometimes labels as "individual views"—while Rabad's views are in the mainstream of halakic tradition.[12]

Furthermore, many interpretative differences between Rabad and Maimonides are standard issues of controversy among the Geonim as well as the medieval rabbis. Debate on such subjects as certain kinds of labor on the Sabbath, kneading of dough on holidays, ritual blowing of

10. *Ṭume'at Met*, XVIII, 17.

11. See, for example, *Pesule ha-Mukdashin*, II, 14; *Ṭume'at Met*, VII, 7; *Sukkah* VIII, 1; *Shekalim*, IV, 10; *Issure Bi'ah*, IX, 5; *Ma'akalot Asurot*, XII, 1; *Nezirut*, II, 5; *Maᶜaser*, XI, 4; and many others.

12. E.g., *Berakot*, VIII, 11; *Shabbat*, XXV, 24; *ᶜErubin*, V, 15; *Shofar, II*, 8; *Lulab*, VII, 7; *Gerushin*, IV, 15; *Sheḥiṭah*, VI, 8; *Temidin u-Musafin*, VIII, 2; VIII, 15; *Gezelah wa-Abedah*, VI, 1; XV, 1; *Ḥobel u-Mazik*, VI, 7. See, for example, David b. Judah Meser Leon, *Kebod Ḥakamim*, ed. S. Bernfeld (Berlin, 1899), 114: וזאת אם נדקדק בהשגת הראב״ד הקצרה כמו שראוי לדקדק, כי צריכים עיון גדול. Rabad's hassagot, of course, also contain interpretative vagaries and opinions which had absolutely no repercussions in halakic literature. For example, *Sheḥiṭah*, VIII, 13 (see the caustic remarks of R. Asher b. Yeḥiel, *Ḥullin*, IV, 7 and *Maggid Mishneh ad. loc.*: הראבד חשב העולם כולו כטועים); *Sheḥiṭah*, X, 3; *Berakot*, II, 12 (found also in *KS*, II, 1); *Bet ha-Beḥirah*, VI, 14.

the ram's horn on Rosh ha-Shanah, rights of a widow in court—concerning which Rabad impugns or rejects Maimonides' view—is not peculiar to these two twelfth-century Talmudists.[13] Their respective opinions should be considered from the historical perspective of the development of certain juridical views, a development in which Maimonides and Rabad often found themselves defending opposing theories. In these cases, unlike the "some-say" annotations discussed earlier in which Rabad merely cites an alternate view without conclusive commitment to it, Rabad dismisses Maimonides' interpretation completely or at least considered his own so far superior that it was not really worth recognizing an alternate possibility. In this comparative study the traditional commentators are extremely helpful and eminently fair. They provide a history of the dispute, enumerating the issues and the authorities on either side, just as they do sometimes in their treatment of the "some-say" hassagot. Their comments are often introduced by the neutralizing phrase: "this is an old controversy." Often, in deference to the validity of Rabad's view or the persuasiveness of his presentation, they do not arbitrate between the two views; they allow both to stand, implying that both are legitimate, tenable explanations, even though their sympathies are with Maimonides. What is more, they sometimes even express a decided preference for Rabad's opinion, conceding parenthetically that Maimonides' view is "also possible" or defensible.[14]

In addition to such standard controversial opinions where historians of halakah may view Rabad's position as one significant link in a continuous evolution, Rabad also incorporated into the hassagot cherished views of his own which he developed in earlier writings and to which he was committed. He naturally opposed these to divergent Maimonidean views when he had a chance.[15] There is a measure of instinctiveness and immediacy in the way Rabad presents some of these views in the hassagot. The recurrent formulae—"I say," "I always teach," "I do

13. *Shabbat*, I, 7; *Yom Ṭob*, III, 8; *Shofar*, III, 4; *Ishut*, XVIII, 19; also *Ḥameẓ u-Maẓah*, VIII, 8; *Nizḳe Mamon*, XII, 8, and others. It is noteworthy that one of the most creative of modern Maimonidean commentators aimed not to "defend" Maimonides against Rabad's strictures but to define and elucidate their respective theories; see S. Zevin, *Ishim we-Shiṭot* (Tel Aviv, 1952), 47 (about R. Ḥayyim of Brisk).

14. E.g., *Shabbat*, XXVIII, 5; *ᶜAkum*, VIII, 3; *Tefillah*, X, 5, 6; *Yom Ṭob*, IV, 1; *Gerushin*, V, 7; *Shemiṭah we-Yobel*, VI, 3; *Ṭume'at Met*, V, 3; *Roẓeaḥ*, XII, 5.

15. E.g., *Yibbum wa-Ḥaliẓah*, V, 24, and *Sefer ha-Zekut*, Alfasi, *Yebamot*, 38a; *Genebah*, IV, 2; and Rabad, *BK*, 292, and n. 145; *Ṭume'at Oklin*, X, 17, and *Sifra Commentary*, 12a.

not agree," "as for me, I have a different view concerning this"—are striking by their simplicity and directness and the animadversions so introduced are almost invariably traceable to previously expressed views. They appear almost as reflex reactions stimulated by the encounter with the alien or at least different views of Maimonides. When, for instance, Rabad notes: "He was not exact [in his explanation], for the Talmud does not say . . . but rather . . . Nor did he bother to explain [the following phrase] . . . And this is the way we explain . . .," a passage in *Temim Deᶜim* reveals that this interpretation—a unique one which left its mark on subsequent codification—was a vested view of Rabad.[16] Whenever the hassagot can be collated with Rabad's earlier writings, a pattern of consistency and continuity is discernible in which these hassagot necessarily emerge from the rich mine of Rabad's accumulated interpretations, decisions, and customs; in Talmudic texts which are so malleable, it was only natural for Rabad to have had a reservoir of stock explanations which he would not easily suppress in deference to different ones found in the *Mishneh Torah.* Those few *hassagot* where Rabad himself refers to his own writings—for confirmation or for the actual presentation of his view—obviously conform to this pattern.[17]

Even when one is not in a position to ascertain the concordance between the hassagot and previous writings, the style or manner of some hassagot would indicate that Rabad is countering Maimonides' interpretative summation with his own ready, fully formulated views. When Rabad says "we are accustomed to explain . . ."[18] or "I am amazed if . . . and we do not explain this in any other way than . . .,"[19] it would seem that these represent well-rooted views. On the other hand, when Rabad prefaces his animadversions with "I did not find it to be so" or "when I looked into the Talmud I did not find his statements to be tenable,"[20] the impression is that these might be new insights suggested by some problematic aspect of Maimonides' formulation. Maimonides' summation of a difficult law might have focused Rabad's

16. *Ma'akalot Asurot*, IX, 18; *TD*, 5; *Yoreh Deᶜah*, 91:5 and 105:9. See also *ᶜArakin*, V, 8, and *Sifra Commentary*, 7b; *Malweh we-Loweh*, XV, 7 and *Hassagot* on Alfasi, *Giṭṭin*, 24b; *Ṭoᶜen we-Niṭᶜan*, I, 7 and *Hassagot* on Alfasi, *Giṭṭin*, 26a; *Ṭoᶜen we-Niṭᶜan*, III, 14, and *Dibre ha-Ribot*.

17. *Berakot*, VI, 2; *Lulab*, VIII, 5; *Ishut*, XVI, 26; *Gerushin*, XV, 7; *Kil'ayim*, VIII, 7; *Kelim*, II, 5; *Ḥobel u-Maziḳ*, VIII, 4; *Malweh we-Loweh*, VI, 7; XVI, 7.

18. *Nedarim*, I, 11.

19. *Berakot*, VII, 14; see also *Ma'akalot Asurot*, X, 14; *Nedarim*, IX, 8.

20. *Yom Ṭob*, VII, 3; *Milah*, I, 10.

attention on the problem and goaded him to work out an alternative explanation, when Maimonides' view dissatisfied him.

This comparative study of the hassagot and Rabad's other writings sheds light on some of the elliptical hassagot which we shall presently discuss. Rabad's cursory comment that "this does not tally with the Talmud in chapter nine [of tractate *Baba Ḳamma*]," becomes meaningful and clear when studied together with the allied explanations in his *Baba Ḳamma* and *Sifra* commentaries. For some reason—haste or the belief that his stricture would convince anyone checking the source—not only did he not elaborate the view in the hassagah but did not even intimate that the view is presented elsewhere.[21]

In addition to this large category of full-length annotations where Rabad's criticism is amply elaborated and documented, there are many shorter notes which take exception to Maimonides' interpretation but fail to reinforce the criticism with details. Some mention explicitly the relevant texts or sources but indicate only sketchily the outlines of the correct interpretation and conclusion, leaving it for the student to fill in the intermediate steps; "look into that passage,"[22] for "whoever has a heart will understand this."[23] Other notes are still shorter, comprising a bare reference to the text and absolutely no hints as to his own interpretation: "this is not in accord with the halakah as found in the mishnah"; judging by the Talmud I see here only great confusion and the understanding student will look into it"; "these matters are found in the Tosefta of *Oholot* and the understanding student will see them and understand."[24] There are in addition those celebrated hassagot—proverbial ellipses—where an irate, ironical, or impatient Rabad brusquely dismisses Maimonides in a pithy, barbed phrase—without debate, references to sources, or any other amenities of argumentation. Three or four—sometimes even two—disparaging words seem in Rabad's opinion to dispose of Maimonides. It is worth enumerating a number of the most recurrent and characteristic of these, some of which are gems of compressed disdain: "this never was and never came into being"; "there is no gratification in this"; "this is close but not exact"; "this is completely erroneous"; "this is vanity"; "everything which he wrote here is vanity and a striving after wind"; "this formulation is

21. *Meᶜilah*, I, 5; see Rabad, *BK*, 351–352.
22. *Maᶜaser*, I, 10.
23. *Pesule ha-Muḳdashin*, XIX, 3; see also *Issure Bi'ah*, XV, 27.
24. *Ma'akalot Asurot*, XVI, 28; *Shabbat*, V, 16; *Ṭume'at Met*, VII, 7.

darkness and not light"; "confusions reign supreme in this place"; "this is a falsification explicitly evidenced by Scripture"; "this is not smooth"; "there is neither spice nor salt in this"; "this is doubtful"; "this is not clear"; "this explanation has neither flavor nor fragrance and there is here great foolishness"; "these are astonishing statements."[25] There is another type of animadversion, equally brief and not directly informative, but free from personal animus or abuse. In these Rabad merely records the fact of his dissent: "I do not agree with him on this"; "we have a different method of interpretation in this entire matter."[26]

The reasons for the brevity of these hassagot are by no means clear. Some may have been intended as private glosses which Rabad jotted down in order to stimulate students and challenge them to resolve problems on their own once he indicated to them that the problems existed. Certain pointed comments, detachedly indicating the existence of controversy or explicitly urging the reader to follow up a trend of thought, would apparently bear out this conjecture. Note such hassagot: "there is much controversy about this in the Tosefta and Palestinian Talmud"; "this is not so . . . check it carefully and you will find it"; "I found this version in the Tosefta and Palestinian Talmud, but it is not in our Talmud and it is very confused"; "if you will look into the derash of the *Torat Kohanim* together with the mishnah of *Negaᶜim*, you will find"; "these matters are found in the Tosefta of *Oholot* and the understanding student will see them and understand"; "this requires prolonged study"; "this is not according to the Talmud"; "we have a different method of interpretation in this entire matter."[27] They seem to be reminders for discussion, topics for exercises in Talmudic exegesis and codification. Others were perhaps appended to statements so flagrantly erroneous in his opinion that they did not

25. Introduction to *MT*; *Tefillah*, X, 6; *Shabbat*, VIII, 5; XVII, 35; *Ḥameẓ u-Maẓah*, VIII, 8; *Ishut*, XXIII, 2; *Issure Bi'ah*, VIII, 5, 10; *Ma'akalot Asurot*, I, 2; *Sheḥiṭah*, VI, 8, 12; IX, 17; *ᶜArakin*, IV, 17; *Ṭume'at Met*, XIX, 1; *Gezelah wa-Abedah*, VI, 2; also *Matenot ᶜAniyim*, V, 22; *Temidim u-Musafim*, VIII, 1; *Pesule ha-Muḳdashin*, XVII, 6; *Genebah*, IV, 9; *Malweh we-Loweh*, XIII, 3; XIV, 13; XVIII, 4; *Ṭoᶜen we-Niṭᶜan*, IX, 12; *ᶜEdut*, XX, 2.

26. *Kil'ayim*, VIII, 9; *Naḥalot*, III, 6.

27. *Sheḳalim*, III, 7; *Ma'akalot Asurot*, XV, 14; *Nezirut*, III, 11; *Ṭume'at Ẓaraᶜat*, XII, 4; *Ṭume'at Met*, VII, 7; *Sheluḥim we-Shutafin*, III, 11; *Ṭoᶜen we-Niṭᶜan*, VI, 7; *Naḥalot*, III, 6. (There are here two well-known views, both already discussed by R. Joseph ibn Migas, and Rabad's note clearly means to direct the student to the alternate view—see *Maggid Mishneh*); *Nezirut*, IX, 18; *Kil'ayim*, VIII, 9; *Sanhedrin*, XI, 6, and others.

warrant anything more than a curt or even supercilious dismissal. In one place Rabad motivates his brevity: "I see that the opinion of this author is . . . but this is not so [as is clear] from many proofs explicitly stated in the Talmud, but there is no time to write them all [here] . . . and whoever has a heart will understand and will not go astray because of his compilations."[28] Yet one cannot escape the impression that a great number of these elliptical animadversions, practically bordering on intentional obscurity, were temporary, unedited marginalia on Rabad's private copy, not intended for any use—let alone publication—in their present form.[29] They signify his critical reactions, instinctive queries which he did not work out in full; some of them may be taken as verbal equivalents of question marks, exclamation points, crosses, or other symbols with which one might mark up a book on the first reading. It can be demonstrated that Rabad did not annotate the fourteen books of the *Mishneh Torah* systematically and in order, but skipped around from book to book.[30] Some of these, therefore, may have been merely tentative markers, with "notebook status" only, subject to future expansion which was never forthcoming.

This conjecture may be partially substantiated by the following observations. The phrases quoted above, which sometimes comprise complete hassagot in themselves, serve elsewhere merely as prefatory phrases or peripheral gibes. For instance, in chapter seventeen of *Hilkot Shabbat* Rabad comments that "this is completely erroneous"—one of his favorite expressions—while in the preceding chapter he begins an annotation with the same comment but endows it with substance and extension by elaborating the criticism. Similarly, such an accusation as "he made a gross error in this matter" may often stand alone, while sometimes it appears embedded in a more substantive critique as a polemical flavoring or rhetorical embellishment.[31] Although such disparity or unevenness may be intentional on Rabad's part—some anti-Maimonidean strictures warranted elaboration while others did not—it may equally be fortuitous, the result of temporary, incomplete notes left in abeyance.

Secondly, we find that what is obviously a personal memo or mere note awaiting elaboration, in one place, is elaborated in another. There

28. *Ishut*, XIX, 13.
29. Steinschneider communicated this view to Gross (XXIII), 19, n. 2 in writing; see also S. Bernfeld, *Bene ᶜAliyah* (Tel Aviv, 1931), I, 63.
30. See §3, note 66.
31. *Shabbat*, XV, 1, 14; XVII, 35.

are two illustrations of this in an early section of the book. Concerning Maimonides' statement on the problem of the "alien resident" (*ger toshab*), Rabad comments: "I do not agree with him concerning the question of residing in the land of Israel." However, Maimonides later reverts to this problem and there Rabad works out his own, sociologically oriented theory in detail.[32] A slightly different case is Rabad's comment on Maimonides' statement that no wooden structures were permissible in the Temple. Rabad notes several exceptions. It seems as if he were thinking aloud and jotting down undeniable facts which impugned the Maimonidean—and also the Talmudic—rule, facts which had yet to be accounted for somehow. This "accounting" is subsequently done by Rabad when Maimonides repeats the rule and Rabad repeats the troublesome exceptions. Here, however, he has already worked out a subtle answer. The only editorial touch that might be expected in these cases is some sort of cross reference between the related notes, such as that found in many other cases.[33]

Despite their brevity, some of these elliptical animadversions are instructive remarks, totally devoid of invective. Their conciseness and authoritativeness are usually made possible by the fact that they are meant to be read together with Maimonides' statements. They are critical comments woven into the texture of the *Mishneh Torah*. In a few words they make their point, introduce a qualification, or develop an entirely different conception.[34]

Criticism predicated upon what was the consuetudinary law in Provence or, more particularly, in Rabad's own locale may be taken to constitute a further subdivision of the clearly negative hassagot. Custom generally wielded great influence and Rabad was constantly underscoring its value even in halakic debate.[35] It was natural, therefore, that an whole array of dissenting opinions, reflecting local practices and traditions, should have been registered by Rabad against the *Mishneh Torah*. Some of these hassagot include textual interpretation and halakic reasoning, in common with the massive category of inter-

32. *ʿAkum*, X, 6; *Issure Bi'ah*, XIV, 8.
33. *ʿAkum*, VI, 10; *Bet ha-Beḥirah*, I, 9. The same explanation is found in the pseudo-Rabad commentary on *Tamid*.
34. E.g., *Tefillah*, I, 9; *Shabbat*, XXVI, 7; *Megillah*, IV, 9; *Sheḳalim*, III, 9; *Ma'akalot Asurot*, XII, 12; *Sheḥiṭah*, VI, 13; *Nedarim*, IX, 8; *Pesule ha-Muḳdashin*; XIX, 9, 13; *Malweh we-Loweh*, XXIV, 7.
35. See Chapter V.

pretative annotations just described—for theory and practice could never become too divergent in *halakic* development—but their center of gravity seems to be just the actual custom. Instead of starting with interpretation as is usually the case in questions of civil law, here the point of departure is the existing tradition.

Maimonides' codification of facets of ceremonial or ritual law would be most susceptible to such criticism. Customs of prayer, liturgy, benedictions, reading of the Torah, phylacteries and prayer shawl, holiday observance, marriage, ritual slaughtering of animals—there is no completely uniform practice for them throughout the dispersed Jewish communities and Rabad could not be expected to adhere completely to the Maimonidean formulation. Like Rambi before him and ha-Me'iri after him, both of whom expounded Provençal traditions, Rabad was alert to record and elucidate his customs on the margin of the *Mishneh Torah*.[36] This aspect of the hassagot has great affinity with the *Hagahot Maimuniyot* which purported to give Franco-German customs and theories a fair hearing alongside of the predominantly Spanish-African views formulated by Maimonides and also with many hagahot of Isserles who counterbalanced Karo's Spanish-Palestinian views by citing the prevalent views of central and eastern Europe. These hassagot incidentally give us a picture of the state of halakah in Rabad's time and place.

For the most part, this group of hassagot is not marred by the harshness or outraged impetuosity found elsewhere. Rabad's own custom is maintained objectively and uncompromisingly. "I never heard such a thing," "I never saw," "our custom is," "we know no other way than"—such sturdy phrases are used to introduce the statement of fact, but there seems to be no attempt to impose this on the *Mishneh Torah* as is done with many theoretical controversies.[37] Lurking in the style and manner of these hassagot is the awareness that customs may be disparate, just as textual readings or even interpretations of some uniform texts may differ. As his pupil Abraham b. Nathan ha-Yarḥi, a keen student of "comparative customs," put it: "I saw that their religious

36. E.g., *Tefillah*, XII, 15; XIII, 6; *Berakot*, VIII, 14; XI, 16; *Ẓiẓit*, I, 7; *Milah*, III, 1; *ᶜErubin*, I, 16; *Sukkah*, VI, 12; *Issure Bi'ah*, XI, 18; *Sheḥiṭah*, VIII, 14; *Ishut*, III, 23; and others. It has been suggested that non-Jewish local custom also accounts for differences. For instance, Rabad's amazement at Maimonides' requirement of washing one's feet (as well as hands) before prayer (*Tefillah*, IV, 3) is to be seen against the differences between Christian and Islamic practice. See N. Wieder, *Hashpaᶜot Islamiyot ᶜal ha-Pulḥan ha-Yehudi* (Oxford, 1957), 10–22.

37. *Sukkah*, VI, 12; *Ma'akalot Asurot*, VI, 10; IX, 10; XII, 10; *Sheḥiṭah*, VIII, 14.

laws are diverse and divided into seventy languages. . . . Indeed all the religious laws of the people of our God, their customs and doctrines, are all constructed upon the foundation of truth and are all the words of the living God." [38] Only rarely does his presentation of a custom imply that this is absolutely right and all other variations are faulty—and this happens when Talmudic interpretation and halakic reasoning are the underlying issue. Whereas in more common matters, traditional practice often provides its own sanction, regardless of the exactitude of its theoretical derivation, in these cases the abstract halakah is all-important.[39]

We may at this point broach a certain question, raised by others in connection with the *Mishneh Torah*, concerning the aim of the hassagot. Scholars have debated whether the aim of the *Mishneh Torah* was purely theoretical or also practical, whether it was intended to be an academic summary of the law or also a normative guide to observance. Tchernowitz has espoused the view that the *Mishneh Torah* is not at all a code of law but rather a manual of study, "a Talmudic encyclopedia," and should not be classified with the practical codes. In an avowed rebuttal of this, J. L. Maimon has demonstrated that the structure and contents of the *Mishneh Torah* are incomprehensible unless allowance is made for their practical, functional objectives. The aim of the *Mishneh Torah* was jointly theoretical and practical; some sections were meant for study and reflection while others were for practice.[40]

The same must be said for the hassagot. There is in Rabad something of the intellectual gadfly. He valued the ability to see all possible sides of a question, and devoted many annotations to this objective. However, there is also in him something of the practical guardian of halakah. He could not bypass in silence conclusions of Maimonides which he thought were contrary to the standards of correct observance. Just as Maimonides undoubtedly had a theoretical aim in mind and yet produced a book of practical value, so Rabad combined theoretical and practical animadversions. The group of hassagot explicitly dealing with

38. *Sefer ha-Manhig* (Berlin, 1865), 1.

39. E.g., *Gerushin*, I, 25 and commentaries, *ad. loc.* The phrase אני הוא המזכה ומזכה אני במקומי (*Sanhedrin*, 34a) is used by Rabi in a similar context; see his responsum published by Assaf, *Sinai*, XI (1947), 163.

40. Maimon, introduction to photostat of 1480 Rome edition of *MT*, 6; also Tchernowitz, *Toledot ha-Posḳim*, 235 ff.

actual customs reveals in part the concern with practical matters. Analysis of a few others further illustrates the interplay of both these themes, their harmonious coexistence in the same framework of criticism.

Concerning Maimonides' statement that a consuetudinary or equitable oath is administered with the Divine Name or one of its substitutes, Rabad remarks reservedly: "I have heard that the Geonim ordained that the Divine Name or its substitutes are no longer to be used in oaths." This hassagah does not assail the correctness of Maimonides' interpretation of the text in *Sanhedrin* or the accuracy of his formulation of the law. However, inasmuch as the Talmudic opinion had been modified and some elements suspended by subsequent Geonic enactments—very early ones, presumably, for Rashi already speaks of them as ancient—Rabad felt that it should be presented in its altered, currently operative formula. The consensual reaction of the commentators is to defend Maimonides by claiming that his task—and actual habit—was to record the authoritative Talmudic law, regardless of subsequent developments.[41] Whether this view is completely tenable and actually validated by Maimonides' method is not my concern at the present; there are several instances where Maimonides himself records the original Talmudic law but proceeds also to trace post-Talmudic developments.[42] What does interest us is that this implied contrast between Rabad and Maimonides underscores the former's desire to relate the *Mishneh Torah* to contemporary performance. The same tendency is also noticeable in an adjacent annotation which is actually the logical corollary of this one.[43] Many of the "some-say" annotations, especially those which contain a view unlike that maintained by Rabad himself elsewhere, a view usually more rigid than his own, may be taken as directives for the preferred mode of action. There are many hassagot which stress the fact that Maimonides' statement "is not in accord with the practical halakah."[44] This practical strain is in keeping with the character of many of his other works and their general concern with normative guidance.

Rabad's concern with theoretical completeness, is manifest in those hassagot dedicated to text discussion, analysis of alternative

41. *Shebuᶜot,* XI, 13, and commentaries. See *TD,* 63, where Rabad agrees with Maimonides.

42. See, for example, *Sheluḥin we-Shutafin,* III, 7; *Issure Bi'ah,* XI, 6.

43. *Shebuᶜot,* XI, 20.

44. E.g., *Issure Bi'ah,* V, 12, 13, 24.

interpretations, and the like. When Rabad says "this is a true judgment but the proof he brings is not pertinent" or "the halakah is as he says, but not for his reason," he is stressing the importance of correct theory even though practice is unchanged.[45] Sometimes when Maimonides quotes a Talmudic saying and adds an explanation, Rabad suggests a different explanation.[46] Much of Talmudic study, however, bore such a character—detached study for "its own sake." Therefore, more significant and illustrative in this case are those animadversions where Rabad apparently presents what is to him the correct theoretical interpretation even though it is admittedly at odds with the accepted practice. He included in the hassagot theoretical matters even though extraneous considerations may have given rise to a different practice, to which he himself also conformed.[47]

Rabad occasionally facilitates classification of the hassagot by explicitly indicating his specific grievance. One that he refers to frequently is Maimonides' stylistic innovations or aberrations, his translation of Aramaic phrases into Hebrew equivalents: "I saw that this author took upon himself to translate the language of the Talmud into Hebrew and in a different metaphor"; "he speaks to the people in a

45. *Mekirah,* XVI, 3; *Kelim,* XIII, 5.

46. E.g., *Ṭume'at Ẓaraʿat,* X, 12.

47. A telling example is the hassagah dealing with the question of what to do with leavened bread when Passover starts on Sunday. As is known, all leavened bread must be disposed of—usually by burning—before noon on the day preceding Passover. Does this hold true even on the Sabbath, or in such an event should one destroy the leaven on Friday, leaving only enough bread for the remaining means before the holiday? The answer hinged on the interpretation of a passage in tractate *Pesaḥim.* Maimonides codified the view that the leaven should be disposed of on Friday. Rabad here, as well as in the hassagot on Alfasi, maintains that the ceremony of destroying leaven is not pushed ahead to Friday, inasmuch as it properly belongs to the day immediately preceding the holiday. However, in a brief gloss or responsum in *Temim Deʿim,* Rabad concurs with the Maimonidean view. The discrepancy is not too startling if, reviewing the entire history of this problem, we observe that it is characteristic of almost all authorities: theoretically they maintained the view of the hassagot, but in practice they adopted the opposite view. This is true of the Geonim, Rashi, Razah, and even Maimonides himself who expressed the view of Rabad in his Mishnah commentary. The Geonim explicitly motivated the discrepancy: they intentionally altered the theoretical ruling in order to eliminate widespread desecration of the Sabbath. Rabad implies the same in *Temim Deʿim* when he bases his decision upon the fact that "the law was established in this manner"—meaning that this became the established normative precedent even though the theoretical interpretation might be different. The hassagah, therefore, represents the originally widespread theoretical view—introduced presumably for the sake of completeness. *Ḥameẓ u-Maẓah,* III, 3; *Pesaḥim,* 13b, 49a, and commentaries; Alfasi, *Pesaḥim,* 5a, Razah and Rabad *TD,* 28 (כבר הוקבעה הלכה); *Teshubot Rashi,* ed. I. Elfenbein (New York, 1947, 51 (p. 44); *Oẓar ha-Geonim*: *Pesaḥim, ibid.*

different tongue and changes the language of our sages"; "he has . . . confused the language of the Mishnah."[48] Historians such as Weiss, Eppenstein, Lauterbach, and Tchernowitz have therefore deduced that Rabad objected to Maimonides' Hebraist purism, which became one of the targets of his attack.[49]

It is true that Maimonides, emancipating himself from the hybrid Talmudic style, perfected a pure Hebrew idiom, modeled primarily on the concise language of the Mishnah, while Rabad, in common with most medieval rabbis, adhered to the traditional mosaic style—an admixture of Hebrew and Aramaic. As Bacher has shown, Maimonides preserved only an insignificant number of Aramaic words in his *Mishneh Torah*, and these are mostly formal halakic terms which would probably be cumbersome or ambiguous in translation.[50] However, it is too superficial to maintain that Rabad took issue solely with Maimonides' admirable Hebrew style. One would have to assume by the same token that the relatively pure Hebrew of the *Halakot Pesuḳot* or the introduction to the *Halakot Gedolot* would also be distasteful to Rabad. What he really objected to was the confusion and distortion which he believed was generated by this stylistic change, as is clear from the conclusion of the following statement: "I saw this person changing the metaphors and turning them to other matters and as a result of this he falls into error."[51] In every case the introductory phrase condemning Maimonides' abandonment of the standard Aramaic jargon is followed by corroborative text analysis. There is no instance of an isolated comment on style; stylistic oddities are always related to allegedly erroneous interpretative consequences.

Rabad levels still other specific complaints against Maimonides. He

48. *Shebuᶜot*, VI 9; *Bet ha-Beḥirah*, II, 8; *Shemiṭah we-Yobel*, II, 4.

49. E.g., Weiss, *Dor Dor we-Doreshaw*, IV, 300; Tchernowitz, *Toledoth ha-Posḳim*, 235; Lauterbach, *JE*, IX, 85: "They reproached him because he wrote in Hebrew instead of in the customary Talmudic idiom"; S. Eppenstein, "Moses b. Maimon, Ein Lebens- und Charakterbild," *Moses ben Maimon*, ed. I. Guttmann (Leipzig, 1914), II, 72; also S. Rawidowicz, *Sefer ha-Madda* (Berlin, 1922), 17.

50. W. Bacher, *ᶜErke Midrash*, tr. A. Z. Rabinowitz (Tel Aviv, 1923), 326; see also, for an interesting illustration, A. N. Roth, "Ḳeṭaᶜim mi-Mishneh Torah," *Ginze Kaufmann* (Budapest, 1948), 62–71. On the emergence of this style, see E. M. Lifschutz, "Ẓarfatim u-Sefardim," *ha-Shiloaḥ*, XV (1905), 435–442 (reprinted in *Ketabim* [Jerusalem, 1947], v. II); Z. Har- Zahab, *Diḳduḳ ha-Lashon ha-ᶜIbrit* (Tel Aviv, 1951), I, 119–128. On Aramaic as the accepted language of scholars, see the statement of Sherira Gaon quoted by J. Mann, *JQR*, XI (1921), 463: ולפום דשאלתון מן קדמנא בלשון ארמית כמנהגא דרבנן. Also, *idem.*, *Texts and Studies in Jewish History and Literature*, (Cincinnati, 1931), I, 447.

51. *Ṭume'at Met*, XXII, 7.

accuses Maimonides of inconsistency. He suggests that Maimonides sometimes codified the wrong view or classified a law incorrectly.[52] These, however, do not constitute categories of critique as much as they indicate certain recurrent foibles which Rabad stopped to label.

In classifying the hassagot an attempt has been made to discern certain functional categories, both positive and negative, but I have refrained from formulating broad a priori principles about which Maimonides and Rabad allegedly differed and which are in turn reflected in individual controversies. Such theoretical abstraction is a hazardous task, usually failing to survive the test of empirical verification. It has been asserted that Rabad, the arch-conservative Talmudist, regularly inclined to the more rigid view, while Maimonides, the liberal philosopher, chose the lenient alternative whenever possible. Maimonides' use of the Tosefta and Palestinian Talmud and his hypercritical attitude to Geonic writings have been contrasted with Rabad's distrust of the former and his uncritical defense of the Geonim. It has been suggested that their reliance upon the authoritative Alfasi is dialectical: when Maimonides follows Alfasi, Rabad purposely disagrees, and vice versa. Preference for literal or nonliteral interpretation in halakah, classification of laws as Scriptural or rabbinic, desire for or indifference to harmonization of different views or passages, inclusion of philosophic discussions—these architectonic principles have been submitted to explain actual halakic differences between Maimonides and Rabad.[53]

I have tried to demonstrate the calculated arbitrariness of a number of these contentions. The untenable contrast between Maimonides and Rabad concerning their use of and attitude to the Tosefta, Palestinian Talmud, and Geonic writings is discarded in chapter four. The question of different philosophic temperaments in this controversy has been treated separately and, it is hoped, placed in perspective. It has been shown how on a number of occasions Rabad harmonized different views or reconciled allied but apparently discrepant passages—sometimes censuring Maimonides for failing to do so. Examples have also been cited of Maimonidean dissent from Alfasi which met with Rabad's

52. *Terumot*, I, 26; II, 8; *Sheḥiṭah*, XI, 7; *Nedarim*, I, 20; *Terumot*, IV, 9; *Shabbat*, XXVI, 71.

53. See, for example, Gross, XXIII (1874), *passim*; Tchernowitz, *Toledot ha-Posḳim*, *passim*; Lauterbach, *JE*, IX, 86.

approval. Even when Maimonides agrees with Alfasi and Rabad dissents, study of Rabad's earlier writings reveals that this was his consistent view and was not motivated by the fact of Maimonides' alignment with Alfasi.[54] It remains only to test some of the other principles and to conclude whether it is at all possible to abstract such theoretical supercategories.

Rigidity and leniency as absolute characteristics of Rabad and Maimonides respectively are clearly figments of a predisposed imagination. While it is undeniable that Rabad often adopts the harsher of two possible views, one can easily adduce many illustrations to the contrary. Maimonides, for example, is very strict concerning cleanness of the hands as a requisite for prayer, while Rabad believes the requirements to be less exacting.[55] The Maimonidean view on many far-reaching particulars of the whole complex of laws relating to marital and menstrual problems—the laws of purity and uncleanness—is most austere, while Rabad was inclined to liberalize many of these laws.[56] In defense of his more lenient theory in one case Rabad stalwartly proclaims against Maimonides: "The burden of proof is upon him who demands more rigidity."[57] It is then impossible to separate them on these grounds; too many other considerations—especially their varying interpretation of underlying texts and its bearing on related problems—enter into the picture to allow any airtight patterns of rigidity or leniency. Their status is almost equilibrated. Moreover, also in comparison with other medieval Talmudists besides Maimonides, Rabad was by no means always on the extreme right. Louis Ginzberg even reminds us with approval that the nineteenth-century Hebrew writer Pereẓ Smolenskin considered Rabad to be generally more tolerant and lenient than Maimonides.[58]

It has also been said that Maimonides, with the critical acumen of a scientific mind, regularly turned to the literal meaning, while Rabad, having "only" Talmudic training, was more susceptible to nonliteral, homiletical explanations. There are some examples which substantiate

54. E.g., *Ḥobel u-Mazik*, VII, 7, 11; Rabad, *BK*, 60, 68; *Ṭoᶜen we-Niṭᶜan*, I, 7; *Hassagot* on Alfasi, *Giṭṭin*, 26a; see §3, note 16.

55. *Tefillah*, IV, 3.

56. E.g., *Issure Bi'ah*, IV, 15; VI, 6 (*BH*, 27); IX, 6 (*BH*, 39); also *Ḳeri'at Shema* III, 3; *Tefillah*, IV, 3.

57. *Ma'akalot Asurot*, VI, 10.

58. *JE*, I, 105; P. Smolenskin, *ᶜAm ᶜOlam* (Vilna, 1904), 235. See, however, the view of R. Joseph Kolon: בכל מדינות הלועזים נוהגים מנהגים על פי הרמב״ם אשר הוא מן המקילים.

this contention, but many of those usually adduced revolve around equally valid interpretative differences and do not fit into this category at all. For instance, concerning the last eight verses in Deuteronomy describing the death of Moses, the Talmud says that "one person (*yaḥid*) reads them," the word "yaḥid" being somewhat equivocal. Maimonides takes it to mean that, unlike the rest of the Pentateuch, this portion "may be read in the synagogue even when there are less than ten (male adults) present; an individual (yaḥid) may read them without a quorum." Rabad finds this interpretation "strange," and he asks ironically: "what happened to the quorum that was present at the reading of the preceding verses?" He assumes that "yaḥid" means one person and not more; unlike the rest of the Pentateuch which may be divided into small units of as few as three verses per person, these eight verses cannot be separated and must be read in their entirety by one person. Both interpretations seems to be equally literal, explaining "yaḥid" as "one." It should be remembered that there are still other interpretations, such as that of the *Tosafot* which takes "yaḥid" to mean "one uniquely prominent" (*eḥad meyuḥad*)—only such a distinguished person may read these concluding verses of the Pentateuch. If any of the interpretations can qualify as aliteral, this presumably has the best claim.[59]

It is possible to go beyond discrediting such alleged proofs and actually adduce examples to the contrary. Their views on the definition of "concubinage" —an interesting example in its own right—may be cited. Maimonides, adopting a more rigorous view in keeping with "a higher moral ideal," freely interpreted the Biblical "concubine" (*pilegesh*) out of existence and was then free to conclude that any "unmarried contact between a man and a woman . . . is punishable by flagellation." Rabad, basing his argument upon the halakah and the literal interpretation of Scripture, revived the distinction between a harlot (*ḳedeshah*) and a pilegesh: "A ḳedeshah is one who gives herself freely to any man; but one who is permanently at the disposal of one man belongs neither to the category of flagellation nor of biblical prostitution. She is the pilegesh of Scripture." This position was also maintained by Naḥmanides. All undoubtedly endorsed the moralistic principle enunciated by Maimonides, questioning only its interpretative-legal basis. This is merely one example where Maimonides leaves the

59. *Tefillah*, XIII, 6; see I. Karo, *Toledot Yitzhak*, end, who lists all four explanations. Also, *Sefer ha-Miktam* on *Megillah*, 18.

beaten path of literalism and Rabad treads it faithfully.[60] This broadly divisive generalization seems as worthless as its predecessors and the entire endeavor is somewhat futile.

While the hassagot are remarkably broad, as our categorization has shown, they certainly could not pass as the consummate review of the *Mishneh Torah*. Discounting inaccuracies and weaknesses, there are numerous lacunae in them. It is possible to go through the *Mishneh Torah* and select in almost every section a number of standard controversies or very complex issues about which Rabad has nothing to say. There are many obscure Maimonidean formulations which taxed the ingenuity of subsequent students but seemed to have escaped Rabad's notice.[61] Even if Rabad had aligned himself with the Maimonidean view on all the disputed matters—which is most unlikely, even on the basis of statistical probability—one would expect him to illumine the underlying issues or point out the alternate view, as he frequently does. In keeping with his commentatorial role, the puzzling Maimonidean statements should have merited some elucidation, as is frequently the case. A certain measure of unevenness and apparent incompleteness is inherent in Rabad's work.

In light of this, the validity of the argument ex silentio as applied to Rabad's tacit agreement with Maimonides should be re-examined. Later rabbinic scholars, compiling methodological rules for the study of the *Mishneh Torah* and its critiques usually maintained that silence by Rabad was tantamount to support. The author of the *Kenesset ha-Gedolah* says: "We may infer from this that wherever the critics do not attack Maimonides they agree with him."[62] It appears, however, that a necessary amount of incompleteness in the hassagot must be posited. Secondly, there are cases where Rabad is silent but it is known from other writings that he was committed to conflicting views. A study of the *Ba^cale ha-Nefesh* and the corresponding sections of the *Mishneh*

60. *Ishut*, I, 4; *Issure Bi'ah*, XII, 13; *Na^carah Betulah*, II, 17; see Louis Epstein, *Marriage Laws in the Bible and the Talmud* (Cambridge, Mass., 1942), 71.

61. E.g., *Tefillin*, IV, 5; *Shabbat*, X, 1; *Gerushin*, II, 20; V, 13–15; *Sheḥiṭah*, IV, 14; VIII, 23; *Shebu^cot*, V, 4; *Sanhedrin*, IV, 11; *^cEdut*, XIII, 1; *Abel*, VII, 6.

62. Printed at the beginning of most *MT* editions. See also ^cAzariah dei Rossi, *Me'or ^cEnayim: Imre Binah*, 242: שתיקתם נראית כהודאה מקיימת; *Maẓref ha-Kesef* 13. R. Solomon Luria apparently also maintained that silence equaled agreement; see, for example, *Yam Shel Shelomoh*, *Ḥullin*, I, 42: ואף שהרמב"ם גדול בתורה היה וגם הסמ"ג הביא ראיה לדבריו והראב"ד ג"כ לא השיג עליו, מכל מקום לא אשא פנים בתורה . . . For an interesting discussion of this as reflected in Talmudic practice, see R. Margaliyot, "Shetikah la-Ḥakamim," *Azkarah*, ed. J. L. Fishman (Jerusalem, 1937), III, 211–220.

Torah, to mention one fruitful possibility, supplies examples of this.[63] One might, of course, claim that on some occasions Rabad merely changed his mind and the silence really means concurrence. This is not a very universal or convincing principle, for in most of these cases Rabad would be expected to note the development of his thoughts or the reasons for his present and previous views—as he often does.[64] It can only be that he overlooked some of these statements and the argument ex silentio should be invoked with great caution. Inferential reasons or circumstantial evidence must be forthcoming to validate its use.[65]

This leads one to consider and reconstruct the actual composition of the hassagot. The only internal evidence to guide the student in this reconstruction are the cross references. These indicate that the hassagot underwent a certain amount of editorial coordination. However, not only does Rabad often refer back to preceding statements—"this is an error as I have written previously"—but he refers ahead to explanations and views which he already propounded: in *Hilkot Ishut* he says that "we have already written the reason . . . in the book of acquisition."[66] Unless thorough editorial revision is assumed, including deletion of hassagot in one place and their transference to a more central spot, these would indicate that Rabad did not annotate the various books of the code in their present order. He worked on some later parts first, just as Maimonides himself did in the composition of the *Mishneh Torah*.[67] This might account for some of the unevenness.

The printed text of the hassagot seems to be far removed from the original version which left the author's desk. There are traces of interpolations and changes introduced by the printer. For instance, while in the printed text some hassagot are introduced by "thus wrote Rabad of blessed memory" and some merely by "said Abraham," in the various fragmentary manuscripts they invariably begin with "said Abraham."[68] This is undoubtedly the original annotative formula used by Rabad and

63. *Issure Bi'ah*, IV, 13; VI, 3; VIII, 1. The *Sifra* and ᶜ*Abodah Zarah* commentaries also abound with examples.

64. See the pertinent remarks of Benedict, *Sinai*, XX (1957), 236.

65. See, for example, Chapter VI, §1, note 24. For traces of the development of his thought, see Rabad, *BK*, 60, and *Ḥobel u-Maẓiḳ*, VII, 7; also *Shabbat*, XXV, 13.

66. *Ishut*, VI, 14; see *Shabbat*, X, 21; XIX, 24; *Yom Ṭob*, III, 10; V, 14; *Ḥannukah*, III, 7; *Sheḥiṭah*, XI, 10; *Nedarim*, I, 27; *Kil'ayim*, III, 6; *Terumot*, III, 7; X, 26; *Bikkurim*, V, 10; XI, 30, and many others.

67. S. Gandz, "Date of the Composition of Maimonides' Code," *PAAJR*, XVII (1948), 1–9.

68. In *Sefer ha-Madda*, for instance, all start with "said Abraham," except the one on *Yesode ha-Torah*, I, 10, which is quoted in the *Kesef Mishneh*. In *Sefer Ahabah*, all

is the common medieval usage as seen, for example, in the "said Baruch" formula of Baruch b. Samuel of Greece and "said Moses" of the Provençal philosophic commentator Moses Narboni.[69] The more respectful quotation is clearly the result of editorial refinement; it often represents the form in which the hassagot were cited in such early works as the *Migdal ᶜOz* and *Maggid Mishneh* and from which they were lifted into their present position in the text. Another example of posthumous editorial tampering with the text are those hassagot which contain a string of terse comments on various parts of a long Maimonidean statement. In order to give these notes some literary form and cohesion, they were placed in such a framework: "Rabad wrote something on every clause of this passage; on the first clause he wrote . . . on the second he wrote . . . and on the third he wrote . . ."[70] In addition to this tampering the text suffered from the natural process of manuscript corruption. Scores of hassagot, quoted by the *Mishneh Torah* commentators, are not printed in the usual fashion alongside of the text.[71] Some are known only by oblique reference or actual quotation in the works of other writers. Zunz has noted such a missing hassagah in the responsa of R. Moses Alshakar.[72] An interesting hassagah—of dubious authenticity—on mystical speculations is found in the *Nobelot Ḥokmah* of Joseph Solomon del Medigo.[73] The manuscripts contain hassagot which are neither printed nor even mentioned by commentators.[74]. In short,

---

except three (*Tefillah*, V, 7, 14; X, 5) start with the longer formula. For the manuscripts, see §3, note 74. See the interesting observations of J. Avida, "Le-Toledot ha-Hoẓa'ot ha-Rishonot shel Mishneh Torah," *Sinai*, XV (1951), 138–143 and supplement, 247–248; also M. Luzki, *Ha-Hoẓa'ot ha-Shelemot shel Sefer Mishneh Torah*, at end of the new edition of *Mishneh Torah* (New York, 1947).

69. Chapter IV, §2, note 82; M. Narboni, *Be'ur le-Sefer Moreh Nebukim*, ed. J. Goldenthal (New York, 1946), 4a, 5a.

70. *Nizḳe Mamon*, VI, 10; *Gezelah wa-Abedah*, III, 10; *Gerushin*, VI, 7.

71. See, for example, the following hassagot on *Hilkot Shabbat*, omitted or incomplete in the text and quoted in the commentaries: I, 8, 9; II, 14; III, 10, 11; VI, 5, 9; VIII, 8; IX, 14; X, 3, 18; XII, 1, 6; XIV, 6, 18; XX, 7, 11, 14. In addition to hassagot entirely missing in the text, the commentators have many significant variations even in printed hassagot. R. David b. Zimra, for instance, noted many variant readings which he drew from a manuscript of the hassagot; see *Yeḳar Tif'eret* (Notes on the *Mishneh Torah*), ed. S. B. Werner (Jerusalem, 1945), 15. Sometimes only the position of the hassagah is changed, thereby giving it an entirely different meaning; see Avida, *Sinai*, XV, 140.

72. Zunz, *Rashi*, tr. into Hebrew S. Bloch (Warsaw, 1862), 40.

73. *Nobelot Ḥokmah*, p. 5 of unnumbered introduction; see Scholem, *Reshit ha-Kabbalah*, 76, n. 2.

74. The Jewish Theological Seminary has a manuscript (38477) containing most of the hassagot on the first seven books; also Adler Manuscript 1179, containing hassagot on *Issure Bi'ah* and *Ma'akalot Asurot*. See H. Hirschfeld, *Descriptive Catalogue of*

a scientific edition of the text based on all manuscript copies and printed sources, would undoubtedly shed much light on the meaning as well as the spirit of many hassagot.

4. *Rabad's Motives in Composing the Hassagot*

A prominent feature of the hassagot—one that probably attracted the greatest attention—is its recurrent stridency. Although criticism is a commonplace of medieval rabbinic writing and polemicizing is one of its standard features, the chronic harshness of Rabad's style seems markedly different. From a literary point of view, such phrases as "everything which he wrote here is vanity and a striving after wind," "this explanation has neither flavor nor fragrance and there is here great foolishness," "this formulation is darkness and not light," "there is neither spice nor salt in this," may have an importance of their own;[1] they left their mark on polemical writing and have become standard examples of the disdainful repartee. From a commentatorial or theoretical point of view, they demand more explanation. One instinctively asks if there was sufficient provocation for these outbursts or was Rabad sometimes just carried away.

This question arose in the minds of practically all scholars, medieval or modern, concerned with Rabad's writings or with such cognate topics as the *Mishneh Torah*, its reception and influence, or the history of rabbinic literature in general. Most sought to answer this question of harshness by relating it to the more crucial question of motivation: what spurred Rabad on to the composition of the hassagot? In presenting a digest of opinions on this matter, it may be helpful to list chronologically some representative views of pre-modern scholars and then group the views of modern students generically. For, as one reviews these various interpretations, certain recurrent themes emerge and it becomes clear that the different writers and their views may be subsumed under a number of synoptic categories which can be designated as the psychological, ideological, and methodological.

Montefiore Library (London, 1904), 20, n. 96; *Ha-Mazkir*, VIII (1865), 46. Hassagot on *Shabbat*, IV, 2, *Ma'akalot Asurot*, VI, 13, and others are found in the manuscript. See also E. Urbach, "Hassagot ha-Rabad . . . Bidefusim ube-kitbe Yad," *Kiryath Sefer*, XXXII (1959), 360.

1. In addition to §3, note 25, see *Berakot*, VIII, 11; *Milah*, I, 2; *Ishut*, XVIII, 6; XXII, 19; *Issure Bi'ah*, II, 12; IX, 15; XV, 2; *Kelim*, VI, 2; VIII, 2; XII, 13.

The commentators intersperse their defense of Maimonides with parenthetic remarks about Rabad. Most are to the effect that Rabad indulged in critique for critique's sake, that "the very essence of Rabad is to attribute error to our Master."[2] Sometimes they acknowledge that Rabad is "not as a critic but as a commentator."[3] If choice of terms reflects the meaning and intention of the writer, one may infer that many Rishonim apparently conceived of Rabad's critique as fairly objective and frequently favorable. Such scholars as R. Samuel ha-Sardi, R. David b. Levi of Narbonne, Naḥmanides, R. Aaron ha-Kohen of Lunel, R. Manoaḥ (author of the *Sefer ha-Menuḥah*), the author of the *Kol Bo*, R. David b. Zimra, R. Jacob Landau (in the *Agur*), Rashbah, and ha-Me'iri do not describe these critical annotations by the usual term "hassagot" which, in the course of time and contrary to its original connotation, acquired the sense of negative, destructive critique, but by the neutral term "hagahot" which is free of combative overtones.[4] As a sort of indirect proof for this usage, it is indicative that R. Joseph Karo, who believes Rabad to be interested basically in criticism for its own sake, consistently uses "hassagot" to describe his notes, whereas he equally consistently uses "hagahot" to describe the critical notes of R. Moses ha-Kohen, a younger Provençal contemporary of Rabad who engaged in halakic critique of the *Mishneh Torah*—thus implying that Moses ha-Kohen was less strident and more sympathetic than Rabad.[5] Rabad uses both "hassagot" and "hagahot" interchangeably, thus intimating his own broad conception of his work.[6] If the vague statement of David of Estella that Rabad "composed many notes on the

2. *Kesef Mishneh, Bet ha-Beḥirah*, IV, 5; *Ḥameẓ u-Maẓah*, VI, 6; R. David b. Zimra, *Maᶜaser Sheni*, I, 14. Note also R. Manoah, *Sefer ha-Menuḥah* on *Shofar*, I, 1 (הראב״ד השיג כחפצו) and II, 8 (טרח עצמו להשיג בזה). Rabad himself sometimes accuses Razah of indulging in critique for critique's sake; see, for example, *Hassagot* on Alfasi, *Beẓah*, 19a.

3. *Maᶜaser Sheni*, VIII, 15; *Bi'at Miḳdash*, V, 11.

4. *Sefer ha-Terumot*, IV, 6, 3 (cited by Gross, XXIV [1874], 20); ha-Me'iri, *Magen Abot*, 64, and *Bet ha-Beḥirah*, *passim*, under גדולי המגיהים: *MT*, *Gerushin*, II, 13, where the *Kesef Mishneh* quotes Rashbah; note, however, *Torat ha-Bayit*, VI, 2, where Rashbah also speaks of השגותיו של הראב״ד and תשובותיו של הראב״ד: *Orḥot Ḥayyim*, I, 32b; *Sefer ha-Menuḥah* (Pressburg, 1879), 6a, 9b, 17b; *Kol Bo* (Lemberg, 1860), 48; *Sefer ha-Miktam* on *Pesaḥim*, 443; Jacob Landau, Agur (Venice, 1546), 8a; *Derashat ha-Ramban* in *ha-Zofeh me-Ereẓ Hagar*, IV (1920), 153; R. David b. Zimra, *MT*, *Shebuᶜot*, I, 4.

5. Introduction to his commentary *Kesef Mishneh*. Konforte also says that R. Moses ha-Kohen wrote "hagahot" on the *Mishneh Torah*, but S. Ḥones (*Toledot ha-Posḳim*, 232) submits that this is erroneous and should be instead "hassagot." The emendation is gratuitous in light of these comments.

6. See, for example, *MT*, *Terumot*, III, 7; *Meḥusre Kapparah*, IV, 2; *Ṭume'at Met*, VI, 9; *Sanhedrin*, I, 5.

statements of the commentators and Geonim, to explain and refine their sayings"[7] is taken as referring to Rabad's critical writings in general—for he does not mention the hassagot separately—then he too obviously belongs in this group. It seems significant that most of the aforementioned writers who usually employ the more comprehensive term "hagahot" were to some degree in the orbit of Rabad's influence; they benefited from his methods and conclusions, were closer students of his work, and perhaps had more penetrating insights into the nature of his writings.

Among the later Talmudists, R. Solomon Luria underscored the disdainful attitude of the hassagot. His purpose was not to indict Rabad, whom he praises liberally, but to deflate Maimonides, whom he criticizes freely. He finds the harshness of Rabad, "a pure and pious person," very significant.[8]

Among the chroniclers, Gedalyah ibn Yaḥya says that "Rabad did not criticize as a friend seeking knowledge but rather as an enemy revealing Maimonides' shortcomings."[9] At about the same time that he was penning his chronicle in Italy, a poet in Yemen was composing a work of rhymed prose (*maqama*) in which Rabad was maligned for his fierce, unwarranted criticism of the *Mishneh Torah*.[10] That the Yemenite poet expressed this view is self-explanatory in light of the traditional Yemenite reverence for Maimonides.[11]

The sixteenth-century Talmudist and mystic, Menaḥem Azariah Fano, asserts that Rabad threw down the gauntlet at Maimonides the Talmudist in order to discredit Maimonides the philosopher. Rabad criticized the *Mishneh Torah* as thoroughly as he did "in order that everybody should not be drawn after him to study and teach religious beliefs from the *Guide*."[12] By assailing Maimonides' authority in the more central, influential realm of halakah, his philosophic stature would also be diminished.

7. David of Estella, *Ḳiryat Sefer* (Neubauer, *Medieval Jewish Chronicles*), II, 231.

8. *Yam shel Shelomoh*: *Ḥullin*, introduction: שקל הרמב״ם למטרפסיה, שעמד אחד מאנשי דורו, והוא החסיד הטהור הראב״ד, אשר השיג עליו בכמה מקומות וחשב אותו לנקלה כאחד מן הטועים המקלקלים בלמודם ומהרסים. See A. Horodeẓky, "Hashpᶜat ha-Rambam ᶜal ha-Rama," *Emet le-Yaᶜakob* (Berlin, 1937), 56.

9. *Shalshelet ha-Kabbalah* (Warsaw, 1877), 57–58.

10. A. Z. Idelsohn, *Shire Teman* (Diwan of the Hebrew and Arabic Poetry of the Yemenite Jews), (Cincinnati, 1931), 318, n. 333. For the beginning of this *maqama*, see W. Fischel, "A Maqama on Maimonides," *Tarbiẓ*, VI (1935), 421–425.

11. See, for example, the article of J. Ratzaby, in *Yeda ha-ᶜam*, II, 191–197, H. Azulai, *Shem ha-Gedolim*, 97.

12. Menaḥem ᶜAzariah Fano, *Sefer Teshubot*, 108 (p. 111).

That one of the effects—or even aims—of Rabad's criticism may have been to detract from Maimonides' over-all popularity and thus to cushion the impact of his philosophizing tendencies is quite possible. Modern scholars have maintained that one of the reasons for the outbreak of the heated and prolonged controversy in the thirteenth century concerning philosophic studies in general and Maimonides' *Sefer ha-Madda* and *Moreh Nebukim* in particular was the anxiety of the Maimonidean antagonists lest the admittedly great halakic authority of Maimonides lend weight to his philosophic views and make rationalist speculation as a whole more fashionable. This unprecedented conjunction of Talmudic scholarship and philosophic ingenuity in Maimonides helps explain why the antiphilosophic forces, hitherto dormant, were so violently aroused precisely at that period, even though philosophy had already for some time before taken root in Judaism.[13] This also helps explain why the early and most truculent critics of Maimonides—for example, Meïr ha-Levi Abulafia of Toledo or Samuel b. Ali, Gaon of Bagdad—combined halakic strictures with theological refutations. They were concentric circles on the same target.

However, it is impossible to maintain that Rabad knew the *Moreh Nebukim* at first hand and aimed to counteract its influence, for Samuel ibn Tibbon did not complete his Hebrew translation of this work until 1204. As a matter of fact, he did not even receive the third part of the *Moreh Nebukim*—one of the most objectionable sections in the eyes of the anti-Maimunist faction—until 1199.[14] The most that can be said is that Rabad had, in the early stages of his critique, received some oral reports about the *Moreh* (completed about 1191), for in their second letter to Maimonides, which contains the famous twenty-four questions on the *Mishneh Torah* (c. 1195), the sages of Provence request a copy

13. See, for example, J. Sarachek, *Faith and Reason: The Conflict over the Rationalism of Maimonides* (Williamsport, 1935), 10; Julius Guttmann, *Ha-Pilosofiah shel ha-Yahadut* (Jerusalem, 1953), 169; also, Aḥad Haᶜam, "Shilṭon ha-Sekel," *Kol Kitbe Ahad Haᶜam* (Tel Aviv, 1950), 366. It seems, however, that regardless of the question of motivation, in actual practice the two realms of halakic criticism and philosophic controversy were separate. The Talmudists confined their attention to halakic problems. See, for example, *Ḳiddush ha-Ḥodesh*, VII, 7; *Kitab al-Rasail*, 131–132, 138 (for R. Samson of Sens).

14. For the chronology of the correspondence between Maimonides and the sages of southern France, with special reference to the *Moreh Nebukim*, see Marx, *HUCA*, III, 311–358; Z. Diesendruck, "On the Date of the Completion of the Moreh Nebukim," *HUCA*, XII–XIII (1937–1938), 461–497, esp. 465; I. Sonne, "Iggeret ha-Rambam," *Tarbiẓ*, X (1939), 135–154, 309–332; S. M. Stern, "Ḥalifat ha-Miktabim ben ha-Rambam we-Ḥakme Provence," *Zion* XVI (1951), 19–28.

of the *Moreh* about which they had heard.[15] Moreover, Maimonides did not send them even the first two parts, in the Arabic original, until much later, after they had repeated their request in yet another letter. Consequently, if the statement of Menaḥem Azariah Fano is to be taken literally, it means that Rabad was led to his searching critique of the *Mishneh Torah* merely because of hearsay concerning a new philosophy book of Maimonides which he had never seen but which some said was dangerous. Fano may have used the title "*Moreh*" loosely, perhaps as a metonymy natural for any post-Maimonidean, to indicate Maimonides' philosophic contributions in general, including those in the *Mishneh Torah*, which Rabad studied carefully and some of which he criticized. It is worth recalling that Naḥmanides would have taken issue with this interpretation. In his conciliatory letter to the rabbis of northern France, he categorically denied that Rabad considered Maimonides' philosophic views—as expounded in the *Sefer ha-Madda*—heretical or that he found them damnable.[16]

The seventeenth-century chronicler David Konforte formulated the view that Rabad's hassagot came as a challenging reaction to the *Mishneh Torah*. Mentioning other motivations (jealousy or arrogance stemming from his wealth) which he does not consider very compelling, Konforte asserted:

> Because of his great wisdom he criticized Maimonides' *Sefer ha-Yad*, commonly known as the *Mishneh Torah*, from beginning to end. Rabad was certainly aware of the greatness of Maimonides' wisdom—that he was a great rabbi, distinguished and especially expert in all branches of learning. Nevertheless, he criticized him and on several occasions he wrote against him words which are as hard [distasteful] as worm-wood. The reason for this was that Rabad was older than Maimonides and very wealthy . . . yet Rabad's intention was not, God forbid, because of hatred or jealousy or heated rivalry. . . . His intention was to criticize for the sake of future generations: that they should not codify the law in accord with his opinion in all matters, thinking that his formulation of these laws is indisputable. They should know in truth that those laws are controversial and are not as he authoritatively decided.[17]

Sometime later the peripatetic bibliographer H. Azulai observed that "the reason Rabad criticized Maimonides most forcefully is in order

15. *Ḳobeẓ Teshubot ha-Rambam* (Leipzig, 1859), I, 6, n. 24; and *Teshubot ha-Rambam*, ed. Freimann, introduction, LII.

16. *Ḳobeẓ Teshubot ha-Rambam*, III, 9b; see Chapter VI, §1, note 51, and the text there.

17. *Ḳore ha-Dorot* (Pietrekov, 1895), 20.

that the [future] generations should not rely [exclusively] upon him and think that one should not deviate from his statements."[18]

The eighteenth-century ethicist Moses Ḥagiz was perturbed by the fact that the chronic bitterness of Rabad's critique apparently contradicted the accepted norms of respect and restraint which should govern rabbinic writing. He quotes his grandfather as saying that Rabad's criticism was just and necessary—to establish proper perspective. The fact that Rabad's critique was often sympathetic and constructive shows that his harshness was not *ad hominem*.[19]

Among the moderns, some scholars who apparently value the psychological approach to historical problems see the genesis of Rabad's hassagot in simple personal motives—mostly base and negative—camouflaged by commanding erudition, linguistic facility, and feigned halakic indignation. In the eyes of Graetz, jealousy is the ignoble instinct responsible for Rabad's critique. In keeping with his character sketch of Rabad as naturally harsh and vindictive, totally lacking politeness or gentility, and so wanting in an enlightened view of Judaism that he was not only ignorant of secular knowledge but even boastful of this fact, Graetz claims that Rabad begrudged Maimonides the honor which the community of Lunel—and Provence in general—bestowed upon him and it was this envy which precipitated the attack on the *Mishneh Torah*. This psychological explanation also accounts for the sporadic abusiveness of Rabad's critique. To be sure, Graetz then enumerates subsidiary reasons for Rabad's critique, such as the omission by Maimonides of sources, the introduction of alien ideas, the failure to grasp the Talmud fully, but the overarching motive which provided the initial stimulus was undoubtedly jealousy.[20] Harkavy,[21] playing upon a ditty of the late medieval chronicler Joseph Sambary, S. P. Rabinowitz,[22] with some vacillating qualification, and a number of other followers[23] subscribe to this view.

18. H. Azulai, *Shem ha-Gedolim*, 4.

19. M. Ḥagiz, *Mishnat Hakamin* (Tchernowitz, 1864), 86, 88. Ḥagiz who was continually embroiling himself in controversies and who has been characterized as a "contentious wrangler," raised this question and subscribed to an essentially pacific view of the hassagot; see A. L. Frumkin, *Toledot Ḥakme Yerushalayim*, 2 v. (Jerusalem, 1928), II, 124–134.

20. Graetz, IV, 267.

21. A. Harkavy, *Ḥadashim gam Yeshanim*, 56 (notes on Graetz, *ibid.*). Joseph Sambari (Neubauer, *Medieval Jewish Chronicles*, I, 124) maintained that Rabad also composed a comprehensive code similar to the *Mishneh Torah*. This was a failure and Rabad consequently begrudged Maimonides' success: הרמב״ם ז״ל שמיה גרים-הר״מ במ״זל שזכה מזלו ונתפשט חבורו· והראב״ד ז״ל שמיה גרים—הר׳ אבד ז״ל: שלא זכה ואבד חבורו·

22. Graetz, IV, 403, n. 2.

23. I. Rabinovitz, *Iggerot ha-Rambam* (Jerusalem, 1951), 239.

Others lay less stress upon jealousy as an isolated personal factor—but insist that Rabad was instinctually pugilistic, that he lacked "the spiritual quiet of objectivity." He had an irritable and inflammable nature—hence "the passionate (*leidenschaftliche*) tone" of his writings.[24] The implication is that alongside of an incurable superiority complex which caused him to berate the skill and knowledge of others,[25] he harbored deep-seated feelings of enmity which he channeled in the direction of Maimonides upon the appearance of the *Mishneh Torah.* Gross, accusing him of superficiality and obscurity, says that Rabad, seeking the truth "not only with reason but with emotion," treated Maimonides in a "schonungsloser geringschätziger Weise."

Together with this motivational analysis, or perhaps as its consequence—as already intimated by the aforementioned views of Gross and Graetz—comes a damning verdict against the hassagot. Rabad is charged with excessive, unprovoked harshness, flagrant discourteousness, "superb disdain";[26] his criticism is described as "sometimes injudicious,"[27] or "over-virulent";[28] his language is taken to be "harsh and disrespectful"[29] or "violent."[30] Already Joel asserts that Rabad was too extreme in censuring Maimonides, especially if the difference of opinion between them was based only on variant readings or equally acceptable divergent theories.[31] Such scholars as I. H. Weiss, Gross, Graetz, and Tchernowitz concur in this verdict of harshness.

A second school of interpretation posits that Rabad's critique was generated by and predicated upon certain ideological convictions. The most widespread ideological objection mentioned is that Rabad suspected Maimonides of heterodox tendencies and was apprehensive about an imminent spread of heresy as a result of this pernicious Maimonidean influence. Thus, L. Ginzberg explicitly rejects the psychological explanation of personal feeling and assumes that "radical differences of view in matters of faith between the two greatest Tal-

24. Gross, 543; see also *GJ*, 450.
25. Geiger, *Wissenschaftliche Zeitschrift für judische Theologie*, V (1839), 558.
26. *GJ*, 450.
27. J. Munz, *Maimonides: The Story of His Life and Genius* (Boston, 1935), 103.
28. D. Yellin and I. Abrahams, *Maimonides* (Philadelphia, 1903), 124.
29. M. Friedlander, *The Guide of the Perplexed of Maimonides* (London, 1886), introduction, XXVII.
30. Yellin and Abrahams, *Maimonides*, 136.
31. In a short review of a book on Jewish sects, *ha-Maggid*, IX (1865), 186.

mudists of the twelfth century" were responsible for the critique.[32] Eppenstein, rather moderately, contends that Rabad objected in principle to the inclusion of philosophic discussions in an halakic opus,[33] while Tchernowitz states that "one of the basic factors which caused Rabad's critique" was Maimonides' rationalistic philosophy.[34] Most articulate on this matter is S. P. Rabinowitz who substitutes the fear of heresy for Graetz's verdict of jealousy.[35] Pointing to certain hassagot in *Hilkot Teshubah* he aligns himself with Weiss who stated pithily that Rabad viewed Maimonides' work as "a cutting down of the shoots in the garden of religion [i.e., an act of heresy and hostility—cf. *Ḥagigah* 14b] and a revolution in the religious world." In an attempt to explain Rabad's unfounded apprehensions, Weiss had suggested that Maimonides—his immense learning and unimpeachable piety—was not well known by Rabad, because of the great distance and lack of communication between Egypt and Provence.[36] However, inasmuch as the people of Lunel undoubtedly knew of Maimonides' greatness and venerated him so sincerely, Rabinowitz concludes that ignorance of Maimonides' reputation is not a plausible excuse for Rabad's disquietude, and jealousy must have entered into the equation after all—if not as the key constant, at least as a minor variable. Implicit in the ideological view—

32. *JE*, I, 104. It should be noted that Ginzberg uses the phrase "matters of faith" somewhat loosely, applying it both to ideological questions of dogma as well as views on codification.

33. S. Eppenstein, "Moses ben Maimon, Ein Lebens-und Charakterbild," *Moses ben Maimon*, II, 72; see also S. Winniger, *Grosse Judische National-Biographie*, I, 22, and I. Zinberg, *Toledot Sifrut Yisra'el* (Tel Aviv, 1955), I, 306.

34. Ch. Tchernowitz, *Toledot ha-Posḳim*, I, 285; see, however, 271 where he would seem to diminish the importance of this factor.

35. See §4, note 22.

36. I. H. Weiss, *Dor Dor we-Doreshaw*, IV, 300; see *Bet Talmud*, I (1881), 257. Weiss contradicts himself in these two places concerning Rabad's knowledge of Maimonides. Rabinowitz should have noted that Konforte (*Ḳore ha-Dorot*, 20) also assumed that Rabad "undoubtedly knew Maimonides' greatness." However, it seems that the only Maimonidean work actually known in Provence was his *Iggeret Teman*. Provençal veneration of Maimonides, consequently, must have been dependent on "rumor of his fame" rather than direct acquaintance with his great works; see A. Marx, "Maimonides and the Scholars of Southern France," *HUCA*, III (1926), 325 (reprinted in *Studies in Jewish History* [New York, 1944], 48). Knowledge might also have reached them via letters of French scholars who had migrated to Egypt. Phineḥas b. Meshullam, the Judge of Alexandria who played such a central role in Maimonides' correspondence with Provence, was such a scholar; for him and others, see Marx, "Maimonides and the Scholars of Southern France," 50, n. 4; also J. Mann, *Texts and Studies in Jewish History and Literature*, I, 412; S. Assaf, "Yehude Miẓrayim bizmano shel ha-Rambam," *Moznayim*, III (1935), 429; J. Starr, *The Jews in the Byzantine Empire* (Athens, 1939), 241; J. Braslawi, "Ḳiṭᶜe Genizah ᶜal Ḥakamim mi-Ẓarefat we-Ashkenaz be-Ereẓ Israel ube-Miẓrayim biteḳufat ha-Rambam," *Ereẓ Israel* (Jerusalem, 1956), IV, 156–160.

and sometimes explicit, as in the case of Tchernowitz—is a far-reaching antithesis between Maimonides the sophisticated philosopher who rationalizes all statements and Rabad the naive believer who accepts everything literally.

Besides the suspicion of heresy and the antipathy to popular philosophic inquiries, which is most heavily endorsed as the ideological cause for the hassagot, another objection is essentially ideological: Rabad was unalterably opposed to any definitive, systematic formulation of law. All pretenses to finality were repulsive to him. He wanted to perpetuate the state of flux in halakic exegesis, to preserve exposition and debate rather than arrive at conclusions. Ginzberg states that "Rabad opposed the codification of halakah as contrary to the free spirit of rabbinical Judaism."[37] Tchernowitz, in keeping with his schematic division between expansive and restrictive writings, between time-consuming commentaries or novellae and time-saving codes or compendias, makes much of the "fact" that Rabad fought codification.[38]

A third quasi-ideological explanation suggests that Rabad opposed Maimonides' codification because he (Rabad) was "against certitude in halakah." In substantiation—and as an added manifestation—of this trait, it is asserted that Rabad was accustomed to changing his mind, juggling halakic views and often substituting one for another. A few examples of discrepancies between Rabad's earlier and later writings are cited—clear proof that Rabad intentionally changed his mind in order to emphasize that there is no certitude in halakah.[39]

There can be no doubt that dynamic open-mindedness which predisposes a scholar to abandon earlier notions in favor of what now impresses him as the truth is not to be equated with a principled aversion to certitude or calculated indeterminateness. Both Rabad and

37. *JE*, I, 104. Ginzberg's position is somewhat ambiguous, for elsewhere in his article he speaks of Rabad's codificatory activity, which would indicate that Rabad did not eschew codification per se but rather the novel Maimonidean method of codification.

38. Ch. Tchernowitz, *Toledot ha-Posḳim*, I, 11. George Sarton writes: "He [Rabad] naturally criticized the *Yad ha-Ḥazaḳah* of Maimonides, not simply because of the latter's philosophizing tendencies but also because any such attempt at codification was necessarily distaseful to him." This verdict, undoubtedly derived from second-hand works rather than from direct analysis of the hassagot, mirrors quite accurately the prevalent negativistic view of Rabad and the unsympathetic evaluation of his work; current academic notions are usually reflected in popular summaries based upon secondary works. G. Sarton, *Introduction to the History of Science* (Washington, 1931), II, 365; see also 375.

39. Atlas, introduction to Rabad, *BK*, 42.

Maimonides[40] had this trait in common, a trait which they might well have inherited from the rabbis of the Talmud themselves;[41] they were so dedicated to the truth that they even unhesitatingly overturned their own views and methods when convinced of their inaccuracy. It is fitting —and, in a sense, symbolic of this halakic dynamism—that in the continuous process of intellectual introspection and refinement, Rabad sometimes came to champion a view which Maimonides had once entertained or about which Maimonides could not make up his mind.[42]

There is yet a third group of explanations, neither personal nor ideological, which may be designated as more purely academic, operational, or methodological. Unlike those who maintain that Rabad was ideologically opposed to codification as such, some scholars find the main reason for Rabad's sustained querulousness in Maimonides' purposeful failure to relate his statements to Talmudic texts, to demonstrate his conclusions or indicate the sources from which he drew. They grant that Rabad was not opposed to Maimonides' general presentation and classification of the subject matter—he even praised it openly[43]—but resented Maimonides' apodictic air, which precluded the citation of sources.

As a corollary to the absence of sources, it is submitted that Rabad wanted to demonstrate that the Maimonidean view was by no means infallible. Precisely because Maimonides mentions no names and adduces no proofs, because the derivation of normative judgments from hylic Talmudic debates is not traced, the student would be unable to examine the cogency of Maimonides' reasoning or the validity of his deduction. The laws of the *Mishneh Torah* would seem incontrovertible and might threaten to supersede the Talmud. Rabad, therefore, wanted

40. See his own statements in *Iggerot ha-Rambam*, ed. D. H. Baneth (Jerusalem, 1946), I, 58; introduction to Mishnah Commentary, ed. M. D. Rabinovitz (Tel Aviv, 1948), 40; also the statement of Abraham Maimonides in his *Responsa*, ed. Freimann, 82. S. Lieberman, in the introduction to *Hilkot Jerushalmi la-Rambam*, gives many examples of discrepancies between Maimonides' Mishnah Commentary and the *Mishneh Torah* or even between the first draft and final revision of the Commentary itself.

41. See, for example, *Shabbat*, 63b.

42. Lieberman, *Hilkot Jerushalmi*, 8, 11, mentions incidentally a few examples where Rabad's hassagah tallies with the view expressed by Maimonides in the first draft of his Mishnah commentary. The Maimonidean commentators are also aware of this; see, for example, *Nedarim*, IX, 2; *Kil'ayim*, V, 16; *Bet ha-Beḥirah*, II, 14; IV, 5.

43. *MT*, *Kil'ayim*, VI, 2. See, for example, *Milḥamot ha-Shem of Abraham Maimonides*, ed. R. Margaliyot (Jerusalem, 1953), 14, n. 5; J. Michael, *Or ha-Ḥayyim* (Frankfurt a.M., 1891), 542; S. Eisenstadt, "Rambam ke-Mishpeṭan," *Orlogin* (Tel Aviv, 1956), XII, 332–336.

to warn the users of the *Mishneh Torah* that this was not the last word in codification, that some statements were erroneous, others were based on not very persuasive reasoning, and still others were merely one possible alternative, arbitrarily selected. He feared that scholastic stagnation and intellectual atrophy would follow in the wake of the passivity of mind engendered by the authoritativeness of the *Mishneh Torah.* His tenacious strictures would revive critical inquiry and would clearly evidence the necessity and genuine possibility of dissent. As Samuel D. Luzzatto, echoing, in part, the similar sentiment of his older contemporary, the historian M. Jost, put it: "Maimonides sought to obliterate all controversy and to bring the entire Jewish people under the yoke of one uniform conclusion. This was not a worthy endeavor on his part and Rabad justly rose up against him."[44] This is clearly a value judgment as well as an existential description; it is analogous to what we have already noted concerning the previous explanations which also combine motivational analysis with evaluation.

Yet another view maintains that Rabad was not only an antagonist of the *Mishneh Torah* but also a protagonist, that the hassagot contain not only hostile rumblings but also friendly murmurings of approval. As documentation for this view, Reifmann[45] and others have been able to point to a score or two of overtly favorable, even laudatory, remarks by Rabad. Munz has said of Rabad: "He is as eager to praise as to blame. When he believed the latter [Maimonides] to be in the right, his pen dripped with honey; when he thought him in the wrong, it was dipped in gall."[46] In short, when the *Mishneh Torah* reached Provence, Rabad, in common with the other "sages of Narbonne and Lunel" turned to its exhaustive study rather than its exclusive criticism, just as had previously been the case with Alfasi's *Halakot.*

Assaf subscribed to this view and offered an additional reason for its correctness. The fact that Rabad undertook this exacting task at such an advanced age—he was an old man, possibly an octogenarian—shows that he was favorably disposed to the *Mishneh Torah* and welcomed its appearance. His critical review of the work evidences the full measure

44. S. D. Luzzatto, *Kerem Ḥemed,* III (1838), 66; see also *Oẓar Neḥmad,* IV (1864), 176. Elsewhere (*Meḥḳere ha-Yahadut,* I, 181), he repeats that "if not for Rabad who rose against him [Maimonides] and breached the gap, the Mishnah and Talmud might already be forgotten and lost." See J. M. Jost, *Geschichte des Judenthums und seiner Sekten,* 3 v. (Leipzig, 1858), II, 447, who is thus almost unique among nineteenth-century rationalist historians.

45. J. Reifmann, "Rabad Baᶜal ha-Hassagot," *Bet Talmud,* IV (1885), 380.

46. Munz, *Maimonides,* 107.

of his sympathy and appreciation, for purely negative considerations of antagonism would not have aroused a man at this age to such an undertaking.[47] This reason is already intimated parenthetically by Z. H. Chajes.[48]

These appear to be the principal views submitted in explanation of Rabad's hassagot. They suggest comparison with Maimonides' own anticipatory classification of the various kinds of critics that would undoubtedly arise to find fault with his *Mishneh Torah*. The occasion for his statement was the plaintive letter of his trusted disciple Joseph ibn Aknin, who was irritated by the vehement anti-Maimonidean criticism generated in the school of Bagdad and who was eager to retaliate in kind in defense of his master. In his very revelatory reply, counseling Joseph to accept the restraint, tolerance, and detachment which age, experience, and wisdom have imparted to himself, Maimonides enumerates the following types of critics:

> I knew and it was perfectly clear to me at the time that I composed it that it would undoubtedly fall into the hands of a wicked and jealous person who would defame its praiseworthy features and pretend that he does not need it or is in a position to ignore it; and [that it would fall] into the hands of a foolish ignoramus who will not recognize the value of this project and will consider it worthless; and [that it would fall] into the hands of a deluded and confused tyro to whom many places in the book would be incomprehensible, inasmuch as he does not know their source or is unable to comprehend in full the inferences which I inferred with great precision; and [that it would fall] into the hands of a reactionary and obtuse man of piety who will assail the explanations of the fundamentals of faith included in it.[49]

This sensitive prediction, with its emphasis on jealousy, confusion engendered by the lack of sources, and unenlightened rejection of his

47. S. Assaf, "Yaḥaso shel ha-Rabad el ha-Rambam," *Kobeẓ Rabbenu Moses b. Maimon*, ed. J. L. Fishman (Jerusalem, 1935), 276; see also the curt references of Weiss, *Bet Talmud*, I, 259; S. Freehof, *The Responsa Literature* (Philadelphia, 1955), 66; R. Margaliyot, "Ha-Rabad weha-Rambam," *Sinai*, XVIII (1955), 387–390; S. K. Mirsky, "R. Jonathan of Lunel," *Sura* (Jerusalem 1956), 251; M. Uryan, *Ha-Moreh le-Dorot* (Jerusalem, 1956), 65; I. J. Dienstag, "Maimonides as viewed by the Cabalists," *Maimonides: His Teachings and Personality*, ed. S. Federbush (New York, 1956), 100–101; also, Ḥones, *Toledot ha-Posḳim*, 116.

48. Z. H. Chajes, *Tiferet le-Mosheh*, 3. Because Chajes' attitude went completely unnoticed, it is proper to remark that his illustrations, although fewer than those of Reifmann, are well chosen. Inasmuch as Chajes was motivated by a desire to exalt Maimonides and whitewash him from recent criticism, it was natural for him to "demonstrate" that even Maimonides' contemporary critics such as Rabad really admired him—much the same as R. Solomon Luria chose to underscore the harshness of Rabad's critique in order to prove the opposite.

49. *Iggerot ha-Rambam*, ed. D. H. Baneth, I, 51.

explanation of theological principles as the three potential reasons for criticism, is noteworthy. It almost seems as if later students sought, collectively, to attribute all these motives to Rabad, thus making him the bugbear of Maimonidean criticism.

My analysis and classification aligns itself with the third view. I have tried to show that the hassagot can only be understood as a comprehensive review of the *Mishneh Torah*. They contain every conceivable type of annotation and the only common denominator forthcoming to give them a semblance of unity is this concept of a scholar's professional, microscopic review. All narrow characterizations of the contents and objectives of the hassagot are emphatically defined by their heterogeneity and complexity, their breadth and diversity. Any realistic, dispassionate study convinces the student that they cannot be forced into a preconceived classification. They are truly protean. One finds, in the first place, many shades of criticism: authoritative, decisively triumphant, and frequently scornful; firm and steadfast but minus all traces of personal invective; courteous dissent; diffident, incomplete, and occasionally conjectural. There are, in addition, many forms of interpretative and commentatorial notes; listing the source—often obscure or unknown—of a statement and explaining it; reconstructing Maimonides' explanation of a difficult text; showing the derivative process followed by Maimonides in the formulation of a law; approving a Maimonidean view and elaborating it; warding off possible criticism; agreeing with but modifying a view. Sometimes an annotation is nothing more than a mental note in writing, a candid, fluid discussion indicating the pro and con arguments for various possible interpretations and conclusions, including the Maimonidean ones. There are scores of cases where, for the sake of academic completeness or stimulus, Rabad cites an alternative view, without necessarily committing himself to this view or automatically discountenancing the view of Maimonides. A note may on occasion provide supplementary details which Maimonides himself mentions elsewhere but which are necessary for a complete on-the-spot picture, thereby obviating the need of collating the other scattered references. The hassagot also serve as a vehicle of expression for Rabad; he incorporated into them extraneous material which was not directly relevant to a specific statement of Maimonides but was suggested by it. Anything a sensitive scholar systematically studying the *Mishneh Torah* or discursively browsing through any of its sections might come up with is to be found in Rabad's hassagot. Just as relatively lengthy or at least adequately clear annotations alternate with brief, sometimes baffling or obscure notes and no general stylistic characterization based on only one kind would be valid, similarly no one of the many aspects of the hassagot, either personal or scholastic, may be singled out as the fundamental, most typical trait. They are all component parts of this protean review, and each must be analyzed in turn. This reveals that their fundamental trait is their incompressible heterogeneity.

The hassagot are not characterized by emotional numbness or detachment. They were not produced by automation in some university chamber, but were written by an "involved" person with likes and dislikes, deep-seated sentiments, and decided propensities, which he did not care to conceal or anesthetize. As a matter of fact, they frequently intruded into and left their imprint on his scholarship. Rabad was a mature scholar with much experience and great learning, with convictions and ideas. His prestige in the last decade of the twelfth century was immense and he was not accustomed to playing the role of a passive recipient or uncritical reader. A persistently critical vein pervaded much of his halakic writing. He was a master of the taut, acidulous repartee, and used it freely. It was natural for him to lapse into an inordinately harsh style, just as he could sometimes be disarmingly neutral. He could combine personal gibes with straightforward textual criticism. The very same hassagah may begin with a detached citation of source material and then pass to severe condemnation. A theological opinion of Maimonides might have irked him no end and evoked a particularly caustic phrase in the course of his attempted refutation. Maimonides' Hebraization—in Rabad's opinion harmful and confusing—of standard Aramaic idioms and halakic catchwords may have been distasteful to him—and he showed it. The lack of sources was a serious deficiency in his opinion, so he unfailingly exposed it. An apparently overt error or misinterpretation which seemed shockingly elementary to Rabad was mercilessly exposed, without any concern for the author's feelings.

This intensely personal approach should be related not only to Rabad's other writings—his animadversions against Razah are much sharper and personally debasing—but to conventional literary usage as a whole. Even such harshness, to the extent of personal derision and character defamation, is quite noticeable. For instance, Judah ibn

Balᶜam, prominent grammarian and exegete, in one place refers to Saadia Gaon as an "everlasting foundation" and refuses to criticize him while elsewhere he very glibly describes Saadia as "one who has no knowledge about the roots of the Hebrew language."[50] Joseph Kara, who borrowed much from Rashi and often digressed in his commentary to relate Rashi's greatness, did not shrink, when provoked, from referring to Rashi as "one who distorts that which is upright, overturns the words of the living God, leads all Israel astray."[51] Rashi's own son-in-law, Judah b. Nathan, criticizes him freely, often in incredibly bold and satiric terms.[52] Rashi's grandson, Samuel b. Meïr, who repeatedly sings the praises of his grandfather, is not content merely to criticize and dissent occasionally but employs some rather caustic language in the process.[53] Solomon ibn Gabirol was accustomed to "disparage great men and write about them in derisive and insulting terms."[54] R. Tam expresses himself: "You are mistaken . . . and what you have said is ignorance and stupidity."[55] The docile Naḥmanides, usually presented as the silent admirer of predecessors, reaches surprising degrees of virulence in his sporadic refutation of people like Rashi, Abraham ibn Ezra, and Maimonides.[56] A view of Ḥasdai Crescas is refuted with the remark that "no doubt . . . can be raised except by a perverse fool who is incapable of understanding."[57] It would be most instructive to compare Maimonides' criticism of predecessors and contemporaries—in the introduction to the *Sefer ha-Miẓwot*, for instance—with Rabad's criticism. By presenting a certain perspective, these illustrations should suffice to shed a softer light on Rabad's stylistic impetuousness.[58]

It is noteworthy that those scholars whose interests impinged upon Rabad only indirectly as a result of their preoccupation with Maimonidean studies display a more balanced perspective on this point. While granting that his language is regrettably harsh, they recognize that such writing was a common medieval trait and that Maimonides

50. Malter, *Saadia Gaon*, 278, n. 584.
51. Commentary on Is. 2:20.
52. J. N. Epstein, "Perushe ha-Riban . . .," *Tarbiẓ*, IV (1933), 11–34, esp. 28.
53. E.g., Commentary on Gen. 33:18, 49:9; Ex. 33:14. R. Asher b. Yeḥiel, *Responsa*, LV, 9 (p. 86) observes: ומי לנו גדול כרש״י שהאיר עיני הגולה בפירושיו ונחלקו עליו בהרבה מקומות יוצאי ירכו . . . וסתרו דבריו. כי תורת אמת היא ואין מחניפין לשום אדם.
54. Moses ibn Ezra, *Shirat Israel*, ed. B. Halper (Leipzig, 1924), 71.
55. *Teshubot Baᶜale ha-Tosafot*, ed. I. Agus (New York, 1954), 57, n. 11.
56. E.g., Commentary on Gen. 5:4 Ex. 28:41; Levit. 19:16.
57. Wolfson, *Crescas*, 33.
58. See my remarks in *Tarbiẓ*, XXVI (1957), 220.

also indulged in it to a great extent. Thus, Friedlander, the sympathetic student of Maimonidean philosophy, states:

> The language used by Rabbi Abraham b. David in his notes on the *Mishneh Torah* appears harsh and disrespectful, if read together with the text of the criticized passage, but it seems tame and mild if compared with expressions used now and then by Maimonides about men who happened to hold opinions differing from his own.[59]

Obviously following, practically paraphrasing, Friedlander, Yellin and Abrahams repeat: "It is regrettable that Rabad indulged in very violent and disrespectful language, but Maimonides himself was not free from this medieval habit of abusing men who happened to hold opinions differing from his own."[60] This broader perspective substantially palliates the impact of Rabad's harshness.

The same effect is created by a parenthetic observation in the *Kesef Mishneh*, from which one infers that sharp rejoinders by Rabad were sometimes expected as natural. While discussing a problematic statement of Maimonides, upon which Rabad commented mildly and pointedly, Karo observes: "I am amazed at Rabad; how is it that he abandoned his wrathfulness [in this place], for this is a weighty question."[61] It would indeed appear that in many cases Rabad must have advisedly chosen a harsh mode of expression in order to emphasize his contention. This is so when Maimonides' view seemed to be at odds with the sources, and in such cases Rabad's harsh criticism is often in good company. The harshness is more understandable when related to the person of the critic, and when it is recalled that Maimonides had not yet earned the veneration which comes with the passage of time.[62] Furthermore, there are hassagot where an expected barbed remark is not forthcoming; either Rabad missed the real flaw or did not consider it as serious as did subsequent critics and commentators.[63] Seemingly unwarranted harshness is thus balanced by unexpected mildness.

Finally, the harshness pales off into a variety of appreciatory statements, from damning with faint praise to genuine admiration. Rabad indirectly extolls Maimonides' compilation: "By the life of my head,

59. Friedlander, *Guide*, *Introduction*, XXVII.
60. Yellin and Abrahams, *Maimonides*, 124.
61. *Issure Mizbeaḥ*, IV, 15; see also *Nedarim*, I, 14, which was already noticed by Chajes, *Tiferet le-Mosheh*, 3.
62. See, for example, *Berakot*, VIII, 11; *ᶜErubin*, V, 15; *Ishut*, III, 20.
63. E.g., *Ḥameẓ u-Maẓah*, VIII, 14; *Terumot*, IV, 9.

if not that he performed a great and laborious task in gathering the contents of the [Babylonian] Talmud and the Palestinian Talmud and the Tosefta." The significance of this parenthetical praise is heightened when one recalls that it was precisely this fact of "gathering material" which Maimonides singled out in his letter to the Provençal sages: "How I have toiled day and night in compiling this compendium. Certainly, great people such as you will realize what I have done, for I have united subjects which are remote, scattered, and dispersed between hills and mountains." Rabad was undoubtedly one of these "great people" who realized the magnitude of the task and the skill of its execution.[64] The plan and arrangement of the *Mishneh Torah* as a whole is never sweepingly challenged. Rabad may take issue with the classification of a specific law, but he implicitly concurs with the underlying scheme.[65] Many Maimonidean statements are enthusiastically greeted by such laudatory phrases as "this is a fine theory," "he did well to adopt this view," "this is a true statement," "this is true, for he found this view in the Tosefta," "his formulation is sweeter [than that of the Tosefta]," "he did well to codify the view of Samuel," "this is his own theoretical inference, but I like it."[66] Twice Rabad deviates from his rather derogatory, at best, chillingly neutral mode of referring to Maimonides as "this man," "this author," "this collector," and the like, to designate him as "the sage."[67] In a brief responsum criticizing a Maimonidean view on the laws of mourning, Rabad notes qualifyingly that "we have not come to disagree with Maimonides, but we have completed that which he left and perhaps he left it [unresolved] because he was in doubt about it."[68] There are times when Rabad disagrees but still admits that Maimonides expressed a wise insight or an opinion worth considering.[69] Rabad often sought painstakingly to defend Maimonidean statements against criticism. Still a further sign of

64. *Kil'ayim*, VI, 2; *Teshubot ha-Rambam*, ed. Freimann, LII. See perhaps *Nedarim* 49b.

65. See, for example, *Shabbat*, XXVI, 7; XXVII, 14; *Shofar*, II, 8; *Ṭume'at Met*, XXII, 7; *Parah Adumah*, X, 8. These hassagot clearly concern individual statements and not the arrangement of the book as a whole—as maintained, for instance, in *JE*, IX, 85 (by Lauterbach).

66. *Shekenim*, IX, 9; *Sukkah*, V, 10; *Shabbat*, XXIX, 14; *Terumot*, III, 3; *Gezelah wa-Abedah*, III, 15; *Parah Adumah*, VIII, 8; *Sukkah*, V, 24; *Ma'akalot Asurot*, X, 20.

67. *Mekirah*, XXII, 15; *Gezelah wa-Abedah*, II, 14; see also *Maʿaser ʿAni*, I, 12.

68. S. Assaf, "Yaḥaso shel ha-Rabad," *Ḳobeẓ ha-Rambam*, 277; see, however, Tchernowitz, *Toledot ha-Posḳim*, I, 279, n. 82, who doubts Rabad's authorship of this responsum.

69. *Issure Bi'ah*, XVIII, 9.

objectivity is the fact that he occasionally supported the Maimonidean view even when it contradicted that of Alfasi. One finds such comments: "This is well said, even though he did not concur with the opinion of the Master [Alfasi]"; "The Master wrote differently in his *Halakot* and we were amazed at him"; "The explanation written here is better and more adequate than that adduced by the Master."[70] Moreover, how telling is the fact that Rabad passively acquiesces in most of Maimonides' original views and novel deductions, unmistakably heralded by the formula "it seems to me," while some are even patently praised![71] Conventional preconceptions concerning the nature of the hassagot would lead us to expect that these would be the main target of Rabad's shafts, inasmuch as they are the few, uniquely Maimonidean opinions in a generally anonymous collection.

In conclusion, it would be helpful if we could ascertain whether or not Maimonides was acquainted with Rabad's hassagot and how he reacted to them. According to various tales of legendary character, the hassagot reached him in Cairo; some report that he was displeased and even cursed Rabad because of his concentrated attack.[72] According to an earlier, more plausible story quoted by Simeon b. Ẓemaḥ Duran, Maimonides supposedly exclaimed: "In my whole life I have never been vanquished except by a man of one preoccupation." This quotation at least rings true because in a letter written to Jonathan ha-Kohen of Lunel at approximately the same time Maimonides complains about having had to dissipate his energies in a plurality of fields rather than concentrating upon the study of Torah. He claims that all other studies were ancillary to this—the various branches of philosophy are to him only "strange women" as compared with the Torah which is "the wife of my youth"—but the original plaintiveness remains to lend credence to Duran's quotation.[73] Gross's assumption that Maimonides did not

70. *Yom Ṭob*, I, 14; *Ishut*, XVIII, 28; *Zekiyah u-Matanah*, X, 2; see also *Ishut*, XVII, 8; XXIV, 2; *Yibbum wa-Ḥaliẓah*, VI, 27.

71. Maimon, in the introduction to the photostat of the 1480 Rome edition of the *MT* (Jerusalem, 1955), 6, n. 19, has listed these passages.

72. *Seder ha-Dorot* (Warsaw, 1876), 155.

73. Duran, *Sefer ha-Tashbeẓ* (Amsterdam, 1738), 72; *Teshubot ha-Rambam*, ed. Freimann, LII; on the significance of this comparison, see Wolfson, *Philo*, I, 151. The exclamation—מעולם לא נצחני אלא בעל מלאכה אחת—attributed to Maimonides by Duran is also mentioned in the later chronicle of Abraham b. Solomon of Torrutiel (Neubauer, *Chronicles*, I, 102) but is omitted in the chronicle of his predecessor Joseph b. Zaddiḳ of Arevala (*ibid.*, 94). This is striking for, excluding this single discrepancy, both chroniclers have an identical, brief notice on Rabad.

know the hassagot, for he would surely have replied had he known them, is not very convincing.[74] Maimonides did not generally indulge in mutual recriminations. He was reluctant to compose the *Ma'amar Teḥiyat ha-Metim* in defense of his controversial statements concerning resurrection.[75] Despite occasional intemperate outbursts, he was essentially of mild character and could view criticism with philosophic detachment. I have already mentioned the epistle to his favorite pupil Joseph ibn Aknin, urging restraint in the face of criticism. In a letter to Phineḥas b. Meshullam of Alexandria, Maimonides writes: "Even if I myself heard somebody elevating himself at the expense of my degradation, I would not be angry."[76] The fact that he answered the twenty-four halakic criticisms of the Provençal scholars is no reason to assume that he would take time to refute all criticism. These were addressed to him cordially and respectfully in a personal letter; they might even be said to form part of a continuous correspondence between the "sage of Fostat" and the "sages of Lunel."

However, relying on genuine Maimonidean observations about the value of criticism in general, one might be in a position to infer how Maimonides would have evaluated the hassagot. He repeatedly applauded criticism of his code and, when necessary, yielded to it. He felt that as long as criticism was documented it was constructive, regardless of its accuracy: if it was correct, it benefited the author; if erroneous, the critic would learn from his mistakes. The only type of criticism which he resented was the undocumented, ex cathedra animadversion. He confessed that he was terribly irritated by a critic who did not elaborate the reasons for his criticism but merely pontificated that "the author of this compendium erred in his explanation." Such criticism was carping, of dubious sincerity, and benefited no one.[77]

Rabad's oversimplified epigrammatic animadversions would presumably have displeased Maimonides. They would have led him to relegate Rabad to this reproachable category of purposely inarticulate

74. Gross, XXIII (1874), 20. He is actually echoing the view found in *Seder ha-Dorot*, 155.

75. *Ma'amar Teḥiyat ha-Metim*, ed. J. Finkel, *PAAJR*, IX (1939), 1–3; see Elbogen, "Moses ben Maimons Personlichkeit," *MGWJ*, LXXIX (1935), 76–79.

76. *Ḳobeẓ Teshubot ha-Rambam*, I, 26.

77. Freimann, *Sefer Yobel Lewin*, 37. See also Abraham Maimonides, *Milḥamot ha-Shem*, ed. R. Margaliyot, 52: החבורים הגיעו ליד החכמים הגדולים הנכבדים האדירים מרביצי תורה בעלי חכמה ובינה חכמי לוניל הי״ב מימי אבא מרי ז״ל והגיעו אליו בחייו כתביהם הנעימים ושאלותיהם הנפלאות, ומתוך דבריהם ניכר לו ז״ל שהבינו ספריו ושמחו בהם ושמח גם הוא שהגיעו דבריו ליודע אותם, . . . וכתב להם תשובות שאלותם והשיב על ספריהם לכבדם ולפארם כראוי להם.

critics. However, this type of unsubstantiated attack does not preponderate in the hassagot as a whole. The great variety of positive commentatorial annotations as well as the important mass of interpretative animadversions have been noted. Even those where Rabad may have erred—perhaps Maimonides himself might have shown some statements to be erroneous or strained—would not be roundly condemned by Maimonides, in keeping with his expressed opinion. Those where Rabad succeeded in penetrating to the heart of the matter would have been lauded by Maimonides. As a matter of fact, Maimonides' praise of the incisiveness and high quality of the Lunel inquiries is an indirect approbation of Rabad's hassagot, for they were identical in many respects.[78] If he were writing to Rabad he might presumably have said on occasion what he said to the "sages of Lunel": "this is certainly as you say."

78. *Teshubot ha-Rambam,* XLIV.

IV. SOURCES

A descriptive catalogue of the sources utilized by Rabad—beginning with the twenty-four books of Scripture and extending to twelfth-century legal and ethical writings—would read almost like a history of Jewish literature. This wide bibliographical knowledge is all the more noteworthy since books in Provence were not abundant and their lack often impeded or delayed research. Rabi repeatedly had to suspend judgment or withhold comment because the texts required for the complete analysis of a given problem were not available.[1] A clear statement as to the scarcity of books in Provence is found in the will of Judah ibn Tibbon. Among the many examples of his self-sacrificing devotion to his son Samuel, whose affection and allegiance he sought to gain, Judah ibn Tibbon proudly mentions the rare collection of books that he left him. "I have honored thee by providing an extensive library for thy use, and have thus relieved thee of the necessity to borrow books. Most students must bustle about to seek books, often without finding them."[2]

The prevailing dearth of texts notwithstanding, Rabad must have had easy access to most books through his library at Posquières. Unlike his father-in-law and other contemporaries, he never complains in his writings about the inability to peruse a necessary text, while he frequently speaks of checking several copies of the same work. The bulk of his library consisted of halakic literature of all periods and of all forms. Bible commentaries and translations, midrashic collections,

1. *Sifran*, 31: ואין בכאן משניות של סדר זרעים שאעיין בהם; 50: ואין בכאן סדר נשים של הרב ר׳ יהודה ברצלוני.

2. I. Abrahams, ed., *Hebrew Ethical Wills* (Philadelphia, 1948), I, 57. See, in general, S. Assaf, "ᶜAm-ha-Sefer weha-Sefer," *Be-Ohole Yaᶜakob* (Jerusalem, 1943), 1–26; A. Haberman, "*Toledot ha-Sefer ha-ᶜIbri*" (Jerusalem, 1945), 10 ff.; A. Yaᶜari, "Hash'alat Sefarim," *Sinai*, XVII (1953), 122–136, esp. 126.

liturgical writings, chronicles, and philosophic-ethical literature were also well represented. A bibliographical survey of his sources is fairly representative of the Hebrew literature available in twelfth-century Provence and the manner in which this literature was cited, interpreted, or criticized.

Scripture, of course, underlies all Hebrew writing; its use by Rabad or other medieval rabbis can always be assumed and requires no special emphasis. One may, however, call attention to the curt reference in Benjamin of Tudela's description of Rabad which some scholars take as alluding to his mastery of Scripture while others connect it with his codificatory prowess.[3] Whatever the case may be, the fact of his mastery of Scripture is indisputable. He had a wide range of associations and was prepared to utilize them for a variety of purposes.[4] One marvels, for instance, how in the middle of an halakic debate concerning the number of wives a high priest may have, after examining the texts and pitting various hypotheses against each other, Rabad recalls a pertinent, hitherto unnoticed verse from a dry genealogical chapter in Chronicles.[5]

3. Benjamin of Tudela says Rabad is חכם גדול בתלמוד ובפסוק. Unconsciously following the Latin translation of the *Itinerary* which renders *pasuḳ* by "Scriptura," Gross (453) takes this to mean Biblical knowledge. Atlas (Rabad, *BK*, 20) prefers to connect the word with the root "decide" or "adjudge" and takes it to mean that Rabad was a trained judge and codifier. The term *pasuḳ*, it is true, is used in Talmudic literature with reference to Scripture. *Pasuḳ* and *miḳra* are, as a matter of fact, interchangeable; see L. Blau, "Massoretic Studies," *JQR* (Old Series), IX (1897), 125, 127; also, W. Bacher's note in *REJ*, XVI (1888), 277–278. Rabad himself uses the word in this sense; see *MT*, *Ishut*, I, 4. The following statement of R. Judah b. Barzilai concerning Saadia and R. Samuel b. Ḥofni also uses the word with reference to Scripture: שמענו כ׳ ר׳ סעדיה ז״ל והגאון ר׳ שמואל בן חפני שעשו ספרים הרבה לפסוק. Quoted by Bacher, "Le Commentaire de Samuel ibn Hofni," *REJ*, XV (1887), 277, n. 1. So does Judah b. Asher when he says in his will: גם תקבעו עתים ללמוד הפסוק בדקדוק ופירוש. Abrahams, *Hebrew Ethical Wills*, II, 174. See also ha-Me'iri, *Perush le-Sefer Tehillim*, ed. J. Cohen (Jerusalem, 1936), 9: קדושת ספרי הפסוק חלוקה למדרגות. R. Abraham b. Nathan ha-Yarḥi, *ha-Manhig* (Berlin, 1855), 20: אם אינו תלמיד חכם והוא בעל פסוק יעסוק במקראות הקדושה. Joseph Ezobi, *Ḳaᶜarat Kesef*, in Assaf, *Meḳorot* II, 49: עסוק פעם בדקדוק גם בפסוק. Yet, the fact that the word is here used after "Talmud" seems to support Atlas' interpretation. It might even be a corruption of "בפסק."

4. For linguistic (e.g., *MT*, *Shemiṭah we-Yobel*, IV, 21), philosophic (*ibid.*, *Teshubah*, VI, 5) or halakic (*ibid.*, *ᶜAkum*, X, 6) purposes. Interesting as an example of the second type—to bolster a philosophical or ethical view—is *BH*, 3 where Rabad suggests a novel interpretation of Prov. 13:19. D. Kimḥi, *Sefer ha-Shorashim*, sub היה mentions this as a possible explanation. Joseph ibn Kaspi quotes this explanation in the name of Rabad, rather than Kimḥi; this would indicate presumably that it was Rabad's innovation. See *ᶜAsarah Kle Kesef*, ed. I. Last (Pressburg, 1903), 47. While this explanation is reproduced also by R. Jonah Gerondi in his ethical tract *Shaᶜare Teshubah* (I, 31)—in a context similar to that of Rabad—it is not mentioned in his commentary on Proverbs (ed. A. Löwenthal [Berlin, 1910]).

5. *MT*, *Issure Bi'ah*, XVII, 13; see *Kle ha-Miḳdash*, V, 10; *Yebamot*, 59a; *Yomah*, 13a. The juxtaposition of this verse and the halakic question under consideration is not a case of literal exegesis versus free midrashic exposition; see Chapter II, §11, note 3.

A list of verses cited and expounded by Rabad in the course of his writings would be impressive by virtue of its bulk, variety, and originality.[6] Rabad's significance as an exegete—his method, scope, ability, and success in exegesis, even though he never wrote a purely exegetical work—is a subject for independent evaluation.[7]

My bibliographical survey will deal only with the post-Biblical sources used by Rabad. I shall single out for discussion certain general issues and points of significance concerning the history and transmission of this literature, terminology, the status of certain fundamental texts in medieval halakic study, the problem of authority and criticism. The relations between the major centers of learning—France, Spain, Italy, and Provence—as well as the emergence of an indigenous Provençal "type" or "school" comparable to the distinctive northern French and Spanish schools will be considered.

Rabad's sources may be divided into two main groups: Talmudic and post-Talmudic. Under the rubric of Talmudic sources, I shall deal with Mishnah, Tosefta, Babylonian Talmud, Palestinian Talmud, halakic and aggadic Midrashim, minor Talmudic treatises, and the Aramaic versions of the Bible.

1. Talmudic Sources

Rabad speaks in one place of "R. Judah the Patriarch who arranged (sidder) the Mishnah."[8] We know that Rashi uses the term "sidder" to imply that the Mishnah was arranged and systematized by R. Judah but was not reduced by him to definitive written form as maintained by the Spanish school.[9] One may, therefore, speculate whether Rabad's incidental use of the term has the same connotation and whether he thus aligned himself with the French school.[10]

6. The term "kabbalah," used in the Talmud to introduce quotations from the Prophets and Writings, is found only once—*MT*, *Ḥanukkah*, III, 6; see Zunz *ha-Derashot be-Yisra'el*, ed. Albeck (Jerusalem, 1947), 238, n. 23.

7. Gross, 164, already observed: "Er besass allenfalls auch exegetische Kenntnisse, die er sich in Verkehre mit der Jüngern von Joseph b. Isaac Kimchi und wahrscheinlich mit den Letztern selbst angeeignet hatte, aber schriftstellerisch trat er in der Bibelenegese nicht auf." See E. Urbach's conjecture in *Kiryath Sefer*, XXXIV (1959), 108. I have collected much material illustrating the wide range of Rabad's interests and creative attainments in exegesis.

8. Rabad, *BK*, 22.

9. Rashi, *Beẓah*, 2b; see *Iggeret R. Sherira Gaon*, ed. B. M. Lewin (Haifa, 1921), 21; also W. Bacher, *Terminologie*, I, 204; II, 133.

10. For the entire problem, see J. N. Epstein, *Mabo le-Nusaḥ ha-Mishnah* (Jerusalem, 1948), 692 ff.; S. Lieberman, "The Publication of the Mishnah," *Hellenism in Jewish Palestine* (New York, 1950), 83–100.

Among the several manuscripts and different versions of the Mishnah consulted by Rabad there was a rescension of the Mishnah as contained in the Palestinian Talmud.[11] The Palestinian rescension was used by the Geonim and by a small number of Jewish scholars of French and Spanish origin. It contained many variants from the Babylonian text of the Mishnah—and in this lay its importance.[12] Whether divergences, of which there are many, between Rabad's text and our printed text of the Mishnah can be attributed to this Palestinian version or merely to variant Babylonian texts is an open question.[13]

One small detail underscores the great exactitude of the copy of the Mishnah used by Rabad. Originally, unrelated Baraitot were often appended to various tractates of the Mishnah or Talmud because they provided an appropriate aggadic ending or constituted a necessary supplement to the halakic contents of this particular tractate.[14] Such a Baraita is found at the end of *Ḳinnim*. Now, Rabad's commentary on *Ḳinnim* introduces this last passage by the caption "Baraita," while every other section is invariably introduced by the caption *Matnita* (i.e. Mishnah). Either the copyist of the manuscript possessed by Rabad already discerned the nature of this addition, which is quoted in *Shabbat*, and marked it accordingly, or Rabad himself noted that it was a Baraita and added the appropriate superscription.[15]

Rabad uses the Hebrew term *ḥiẓonah* (outside or external) to designate the Baraita.[16] This term, already found in the Midrash, was used loosely by the Geonim and Tosafists not only for the Baraita (those Tannaitic traditions not contained in the Mishnah) but also for the various minor Talmudic treatises.[17] They obviously meant it as a general term of reference for all "external," extra-Talmudic works, which bore the same relation to the authoritative Mishnah and Talmud as the apocryphal writings (*ha-ḥiẓonim*) bore to the canonical books of Scripture. Rabad, as far as I was able to notice, used it in the narrower, more literal sense of Baraita. In one place, he defines the relation

11. *MT*, *Nedarim*, X, 6 (see M. Nedarim, VIII, 5).
12. Epstein, *Mabo*, 1269 ff., esp. 1272.
13. *MT*, *Bet ha-Beḥirah*, II, 14; M. *Middot*, II, 3. This was not noticed by Epstein.
14. Epstein, *Mabo*, 974 ff.
15. *Shabbat*, 152a; Epstein, *Mabo*, 979, n. 10.
16. *BH*, 82; *Hassagot* on Alfasi, *Ketubot*, 56b.
17. *Numbers Rabbah*, XVIII; see M. Higger, ed. *Masseket Semaḥot* (New York, 1931), 9; also, Judah b. Barzilai, *Perush Sefer Yeẓirah*, ed. Halberstam (Berlin, 1885), XII; Marmorstein, *Midrash Ḥaserot Witerot* (London, 1917), 3, n. 10.

of the Baraita to the Mishnah as one of explanation and interpretation.[18]

In addition to the conventional Aramaic form Tosefta, Rabad also used the Hebrew form Tosafot. The latter was a generic term designating all extra-Mishnaic writings[19] and it is therefore not surprising to find Rabad using Tosafot also as synonymous with Baraita.[20]

Rabad was cognizant of the methodological principle that related passages in these parallel extra-Mishnaic writings are not to be emended from one text to the other. He remarks that "many versions vary from the Sifra to other Tosafot and from Tosefta to Tosefta."[21] A similar warning against cross emendation was sounded by Rabad's great contemporary R. Tam: "I announce to the public and proclaim not to emend texts [of the Mishnah] on the basis of the Tosefta and the Baraitot."[22]

In common with most other medieval rabbis,[23] Rabad used the Tosefta extensively. The *Mishneh Torah* hassagot alone contain almost one hundred and fifty references to the Tosefta.[24] On the basis of the Tosefta he explains various statements and adduces proof for specific views. He traces statements back to the Tosefta and examines the meaning of the relevant passages.[25] Frequently, he presents an original interpretation of the Tosefta. He concludes an exposition with the anticipatory explanation of a pertinent Tosefta which might at first glance impugn the consistency of his thesis.[26] In the treatment of those matters for which there is no Talmudic text (e.g., *Zera^cim* and *Ṭohorot*), we find an increased reliance upon the Tosefta.[27] It is also an important

18. *Hassagot*, *Pesaḥim*, 1a: כי כן דרך הברייתות לפרש המשניות.

19. Higger, *Masseket Semaḥot*, 9, 11; Albeck, *Meḥkarim ba-Baraita uba-Tosefta* (Jerusalem, 1944), 60–65. Also, M. Higger, "Sifre ha-Tanna'im bi-Teḳufat ha-Geonim," *Oẓar ha-Ḥayyim*, XIV (1938), 168; L. Ginzberg, *Ginze Shechter* (New York, 1929), II, 556, n. 28; S. Lieberman, *Tosefet Rishonim* (Jerusalem, 1938), II, 7.

20. *Sifra* Commentary, 71b; see *Hassagot*, *Megillah*, 3a where he substitutes "Tosefta" for the term "Baraita" used by Razah.

21. *Sifra Commentary*, 71b: כי הרבה גירסאות מתחלפות מספרא לשאר תוספות ומתוספתא לתוספתא. See *MT*, *Ṭume'at Ẓara^cat*, VIII, 1.

22. *Sefer ha-Yashar*, ed. Rosenthal (Berlin, 1898), introduction: שלא להגיה ספרים מתוך תוספתא ומתוך הברייתות.

23. S. Lieberman, *Tosefet Rishonim*, II, 6–15, esp. 15.

24. I have listed them in my Ph.D. thesis at Harvard (HU 90.7077), ch. IV, n. 121.

25. For examples of these statements, see *MT*, *^cAkum*, IX, 9; *Shabbat*, XVII, 4; *Sheḥiṭah*, XII, 15; *Shabbat*, XXII, 21.

26. *Ibid.*, *Ḥameẓ u-Maẓah*, I, 2.

27. There are about twenty-five references in *Terumot* and *Ma^caser*. *Kelim* alone has eighteen references.

source for comparison, deduction, and interpretation in his Mishnah and Sifra commentaries. In short, precise textual study and a desire to arrive at the original source or primordial form of a Tannaitic statement —two deeply ingrained study habits among serious medieval scholars —necessitated recurrent reference to the Tosefta, as to allied literature.[28] One cannot say, consequently, that Rabad's methodology is characterized by neglect of the Tosefta as distinct from Maimonides' frequent use of it—and that this was a principal cause of friction and source of dissension between them.[29]

This widespread use notwithstanding, the Tosefta was subordinate to the Mishnah, and its authoritativeness was generally curtailed. All medieval scholars—including Maimonides, who explicitly speaks of the primacy of the Mishnah and the inferiority of the Tosefta and Baraita both in style and content[30]—subjected the halakic usefulness of the Tosefta to certain qualifications. It was a flexible auxiliary to be used selectively and discriminatingly.

The reasons for this pervasive attitude are clearly illustrated in Rabad's writings. He posits, first of all, that when a Tosefta passage is irreconcilably opposed to the Mishnah, it cannot be considered authoritative or conclusive.[31] Or, even if it differs from the Amoraic interpretation and conclusion with regard to a Mishnah, it need not be regarded as valid.[32] This principle is self-explanatory: the Tosefta was only supplementary to the main core of the Mishnah, while the tradition of the Babylonian Talmud was the most normative for halakic purposes. Deviationist ideas found in literature parallel to the Mishnah or Babylonian Talmud were usually considered subservient and had either to be harmonized with the authoritative tradition or dismissed. As the Geonim put it, "the Tosefta is not accepted, settled, or definitive."[33]

28. For the Tosafists, see Urbach, *Baᶜale ha-Tosafot*, 540.

29. E.g., Gross, XXIII, 28; Weiss, *Dor Dor we-Doreshaw*, IV, 300.

30. Maimonides, introduction to Mishnah Commentary; see Higger, "Sifre ha-Tanna'im," 170.

31. *MT*, *Meᶜilah*, VI, 4.

32. *KS*, I, 54: והתוספתא עצמה אינה מתוקנת· אבל אין לנן לטרוח ולדחוק בעבור שבוש התוספתא שאינן שניות בתלמוד. *MT*, *Ṭume'at Oklin*, III, 5.

33. See responsum of R. Amram Gaon in L. Ginzberg, *Geonica* (New York, 1909), II, 328, ll. 9–13, 329, ll. 5–6: וששאל׳ תוספתא מהוא לסמוך עליהן: תוספתא לא דבר קצוב הוא ולא דבר מסויים הוא · · · יש מהן שהן הלכה ויש מהן שאין הלכה· כאיוצד׳ כל בראיתא שאין חלוקין עליה בתלמוד רבנן אמורי הלכה כמותה · · · וכל בראיתא דפליגין עלה בתלמוד לית הילכתא כותה. See Ginzberg's comments, *ibid.*, 305; Lieberman, *Tosefet Rishonim*, II, 11. R. Isaiah of Trani (*Or Zaruᶜa*, I, 754) says: אמנם טוב הוא להביא אדם סעד מן הברייתות ומן הירושלמי לבאר דבר שהוא סתום ונעלם בתלמוד· אבל לסתור דברי התלמוד אין סומכין לא על הברייתות לא על הירושלמי· Quoted by Higger, *Halakot wa-Aggadot*, 19.

Rabad emphatically underscores the Tosefta's secondary importance.[34]

A second contributing factor was the corrupt state of the Tosefta text. Rabad describes this condition very succinctly:

> I am surprised at this author [Maimonides] who thought to decide halakic questions on the basis of the Tosefta and Palestinian Talmud and he was unsuccessful, for the texts of the Tosefta and Palestinian Talmud which we have are not sufficiently accurate and are generally inadequate.[35]

He repeatedly refers to the errors and inaccuracies of the text.[36] This unsatisfactory condition of the text, furthermore, often resulted in distortion and confusion. Many Tosefta passages were deemed worthless because they appeared obscure, unintelligible, and contradictory.[37]

This non-normative status of the Tosefta, resulting partially from its corrupt state, undoubtedly accounts in turn for the fact that its text was emended to a greater extent than that of the Mishnah. Rabad did not acquiesce in the status quo of "inaccurate and inadequate" readings. He possessed two copies of the Tosefta and was always checking them, collating their readings, harmonizing variants when possible, or selecting the most plausible one.[38] He realized the affinity between the Palestinian Talmud and the Tosefta and is found pitting his version taken from the Talmud against a version found in the Tosefta, for the former is logically superior.[39] Most of his readings coincide with the standard printed texts.[40]

Despite the awareness of this basic theoretical principle and the practical shortcomings which consigned the Tosefta to a subordinate position notwithstanding, it was occasionally favored over the Mishnah or Talmud, or at least used to qualify the latter. Inasmuch, however, as there was no general rule and no consistency on this point, Rabad sometimes criticizes Maimonides, Razah, or others for following the Tosefta and sometimes for failing to do so. He demolishes opinions by claiming that they are derived solely from the Tosefta and run counter to pre-

34. For a parallel view of the Tosafists, see Urbach, *Baᶜale ha-Tosafot*, 520.

35. *MT*, *Maᶜaser Sheni*, I, 10. See the statement of R. Isaac ibn Ghayyat ומשובשת היא התוספתא בוודאי ... הילכך אין לנו לסמוך עליה. Quoted by Albeck, "Le-Ḥeḳer ha-Talmud," *Tarbiẓ*, IX (1938), 174, n. 15.

36. *MT*, *Temurah*, III, 6; *Ṭume'at Met*, XXII, 10.

37. Zunz, *Rashi*, trans. into Hebrew by Bloch (Warsaw, 1862), 37.

38. *MT*, *Parah Adumah*, VII, 11; *Kelim*, X, 15; XV, 5.

39. *MT*, *ᶜArakin wa-Ḥaramin*, II, 12.

40. Lieberman, *Tosefet Rishonim*, IV, 16 ff.

valent Talmudic views[41] and also rejects explanations because they do not tally with the Tosefta.[42] "I found this matter in the Talmud, Tractate *Nazir*, but the Tosefta is more accurate than the Talmud."[43] He focuses attention on a Tosefta passage which is apparently at odds with a Talmudic view; while most commentators dismiss the Tosefta as not being normative, Rabad tries to reconcile it with the authoritative view.[44] He uses the Tosefta to correct the text of the Mishnah: "this [Mishnah] is erroneous and is recorded in the Tosefta as follows . . ."[45] Original explanations with significant halakic implications are substantiated retrospectively by a Tosefta or are initially stimulated by one.[46] By letting the Tosefta emerge sporadically as the principal element he is, thus, committing those same "offenses" for which he occasionally takes others to task.

The major Halakic Midrashim on Scripture are the (1) *Mekilta*, (2) *Sifra*, (3) *Sifre debe Rab*, and (4) *Sifre Zuṭa*, to which modern research has called attention. Rabad uses them all, some sparsely, some extensively, employing the following nomenclature for them: (1) *Mekilta* or *Mekilta de R. Ishmael*;[47] (2) *Sifra*, *Midrash Sifra*, *Torat Kohanim*, and *Midrash Torat Kohanim*;[48] (3) *Sifre debe Rab*, *Sifre*, or *Midrash Sifre*;[49] (4) *Sifre le-Panim Sheni*.[50] He cites them in corroboration

41. *MT*, *Meᶜilah*, VI, 4; *KS*, I, 54.

42. *Ibid.*, *Kelim*, X, 3; *Ṭume'at Met.* XXI, 3; XXII, 2.

43. *MT*, *Pesule ha-Muḳdashin*, V, 13.

44. *Ibid.*, *ᶜAkum*, III, 9, and commentaries, *ad. loc.*

45. *Ibid.*, *Ṭume'at Oklin*, XII, 6.

46. Rabad, *BK*, 201, 285.

47. *Ibid.*, 2a; *MT*, *Genebah*, IX, 11; Commentary on *ᶜAbodah Zarah*, 16b. See Lauterbach, "The Name of the Mekilta," *JQR*, XI (1920), 169–195 and "The Arrangement and the Divisions of the Mekilta," *HUCA*, I (1924), 427 ff. J. N. Epstein, *Mebo'ot le-Sifrut ha-Tannaim* (Jerusalem, 1957), 547. The name *Mekilta de R. Ishmael* was first used by R. Nissim of Kairwan.

48. Rabad, *BK*, 300; *MT*, *Ṭume'at Oklin*, II, 14, 21; *Ṭume'at Ẓaraᶜat*, VIII, 1. See Epstein, *Mebo'ot*, 645 ff.

49. *MT*, *Ẓiẓit*, I, 10; *Parah*, III, 2; Commentary on *ᶜAbodah Zarah*, 17a.

50. *Sifra Commentary*, 23a; see *Sifre Zuṭa*, ed. Z. Joskowitz (with commentary *Ambuha de-Sifre*), XVI; Epstein, *Mebo'ot*, 741 ff. In one place, when Maimonides quotes a law which is found in the *Sifre Zuṭa* but explains it differently, Rabad remarks: "I do not know whence he derived this." Rabad's confession of ignorance quite evidently refers not to the Tannaitic source of the law but rather to Maimonides' original derivation of the law, arrived at by means of a logical extension of Talmudic exegesis elsewhere. See *MT*, *ᶜAkum*, IV, 4, and commentaries, *ad. loc.*; *Baba Ḳamma*, 82b; *Sifre Zuṭa*, ed. Horovitz (Breslau, 1910), 181. The *MT* commentaries of *ᶜAbodat ha-Melek* and *Ben Aryeh* say that Rabad did not know this source. Even if one emends the *MT* text and omits the phrase "concerning one of thy cities," as suggested by *ᶜAbodat ha-Melek*, there is still no indication that Maimonides meant to base his statement on the *Sifre Zuṭa*.

or elucidation of the Mishnah and Talmud.[51] However, he acknowledges differences in style between these works and will not emend one on the basis of the other.[52] Sometimes discrepancies are so glaring that the divergent readings must be harmonized to some extent.[53] The exegesis of these Midrashim is often subjected to critical analysis.[54]

The Babylonian Talmud is called by Rabad—as by other medieval writers—"our Talmud" (*gemara dilan*). He nowhere refers to an editor or compiler, as he does to R. Judah the Patriarch, redactor of the Mishnah, but speaks rather in terms of "*ba^cale ha-Gemara*"—the masters of the Talmud.[55] Concerning the nomenclature used by Rabad for designating the various tractates, only the term *Masseket Yom-Ṭob* as a parallel title for Tractate *Beẓah* need be noted. Both names are derived from the first sentence of the first Mishnah and already appear in the epistle of Sherira Gaon.[56]

Rabad's attitude to and use of the Palestinian Talmud—*Jerushalmi* or *Gemara dibne ma^caraba*—must be viewed in light of what we know concerning its status and significance in Geonic literature and subsequent halakic study.[57] The generally accepted view, following Louis Ginzberg's recapitulation, runs as follows. The Palestinian Talmud, like the Tosefta, was of secondary value for rabbinic study. The emergent supremacy of the Babylonian Talmud was the direct antecedent of the rapid decline of the Palestinian one. "The view of the Geonim on the relation of the two Talmuds to one another resulted in

51. *MT*, *Ẓiẓit*, I, 10; *Ṭume'at Ẓara^cat*, VIII, 1; *Ṭume'at Oklin*, II, 14. Note his citation (Commentary on *^cAbodah Zarah*, 16b) from *Mekilta*, II, 23b to bolster his explanation of the puzzling loan-word "dimos." Unlike Rashi, and Tosafot *ad. loc.* he explains "dimos" as free.

52. *Sifra Commentary*, 71b; *MT*, *Ṭume'at Ẓara^cat*, VIII, 11; Rabad, *BK*, 300; *Sifra Commentary*, 37a.

53. *Ibid.*, 78b (where he dismisses one reading as erroneous); *ibid.*, 2a. In this case, the temptation to emend a passage—"for it seems to me that there is a linguistic error here"—is controlled because he found the identical reading in *Bekorot*; see also *ibid.*, 23a.

54. *MT*, *Genebah*, IX, 8 (for a criticism of *Mekilta* on Ex. 22); *Parah Adumah*, III, 2 (for *Sifre* on Num. 19).

55. Rabad, *BK*, 74; *MT*, *Nizḳe Mamon*, XII, 5; *Sifra Commentary*, 87b; see *Cuzari*, III, 67; *Naḥmanides*, *Milḥamot*, *Berakot*, 35b.

56. *MT*, *Kil'ayim*, X, 17; *Hassagot*, *Beẓah*, 10b; see Epstein, *Mebo'ot le-Sifrut ha-Tannaim*, 991.

57. S. Poznanski, "ha-Geonim weha-Jerushalmi," *^cInyanim Shonim* (Warsaw, 1909), 3–44; there is here a discriminating review of all theories until his time. L. Ginzberg, *Perushim we-Ḥiddushim Birushalmi* (New York, 1941), 1 ff.; this is a good introduction to the text and history of the Palestinian Talmud. Aptowitzer, *Mabo*, 91 ff.

the complete neglect of the study of the Palestinian Talmud for many centuries." It was subject to gross apathy, did not receive serious consideration, and for almost fourteen hundred years remained a "sealed book." Its incipient rehabilitation in the Middle Ages was inaugurated by R. Nissim ibn Shahin and R. Ḥananel, two of the sages of Kairwan. Under their tutelage and inspiration, the North African Alfasi leaned heavily on the Palestinian Talmud and he, in turn, molded the Spanish attitude toward this Talmud. This trend of recovery reached its crest with Maimonides, for "of all the medieval authors none was more devoted to the study of the Palestinian Talmud and none more influenced by it than he."[58] The use of the Palestinian Talmud by French and German Tosafists was in direct proportion to their acquaintance with the Kairwan commentaries of R. Nissim and especially of R. Ḥananel. From almost complete neglect at the hands of Rashi, R. Tam, and the early scholars—so the conventional description has it—the Palestinian Talmud swung, pendulum-like, to lavish attention from R. Isaac b. Samuel of Dampierre (Ri ha-Zaḳen), R. Eliezer b. Joel (Rabiah), and R. Isaac of Vienna, author of the Or Zaruᶜa. With regard to Provence in particular, it was recognized that the "Palestinian Talmud enjoyed great popularity" there.[59] This was attributed to Provençal dependence on Spanish cultural tendencies and the posthumous infiltration of Alfasi into Provence.

Actually, the base lines of this picture have to be extended somewhat, for the popularity of the Palestinian Talmud seems to have been even greater and its use more uniform. Its use by the Spanish school is admitted by all, its popularity in Provence generally recognized, its importance for later Tosafists definitely acknowledged. Furthermore, Urbach has convincingly shown that the early Tosafists were just as intimate with the Palestinian Talmud as later ones, that R. Tam and R. Isaac b. Abraham (Riba) used it no less than R. Isaac of Dampierre and R. Eliezer b. Nathan (Raban) of Mayence.[60] Benedict has rightly stressed that the role of the Palestinian Talmud in Provençal halakic study was even more profound than generally acknowledged.[61] The Kairwan scholars never abandoned the Palestinian Talmud. Many scholars frequently assert that the Palestinian Talmud is one of their basic sources. The phrase "Mishnah, Tosefta, two Talmuds (Babylonian and Palestinian)" is common. Medieval chroniclers and literary

58. The quotations are from Ginzberg, *Perushim we-Ḥiddushim*, 45, 62, 47, 48.
59. *Ibid.*, Hebrew introduction, 110.
60. Urbach, *Baᶜale ha-Tosafot*, 543 ff.
61. Benedict, 93.

historians similarly praise earlier and contemporary Talmudists for proficiency in "both Talmuds." For example, Abraham ibn Daud says concerning three Narbonne scholars: "They illumined [the meaning of] the Torah . . . by means of the Mishnah, Talmud, and Palestinian Talmud."[62] Aside, then, from a brief part of the Geonic period during which the Palestinian Talmud was mentioned only several dozen times,[63] at what time in the Middle Ages did the Palestinian Talmud fall into neglect and disuse? The point is that the Palestinian Talmud was recognized and used by all—with quantitative differences between them—as an indispensable companion volume to the Babylonian Talmud.

Yet, although more or less popular, it assumed a clearly subordinate position in all matters of legal decisions. Hai Gaon summarized the regnant Geonic attitude in the following formula: "We do not rely upon the Palestinian Talmud in connection with any matter which is definitively decided in our Talmud."[64] This principle of the practical supremacy of the Babylonian Talmud and its corollary concerning the subservience of the Palestinian one was adopted as a rule of thumb and repeated just as pointedly by such figures as Alfasi,[65] Joseph ibn Megas,[66] Jonathan ha-Kohen of Lunel,[67] Razah,[68] R. Meshullam b. Moses,[69] R. Tam,[70] Ri ha-Zaḳen,[71] R. Moses ha-Kohen,[72] R. Asher b.

62. *Sefer ha-Kabbalah*, ed. Neubauer, *Chronicles*, I, 78; see also, ha-Me'iri, *Bet ha-Beḥirah* on *Abot*, 67; David of Estella, *Kiryat Sefer*, ed. Neubauer, *Chronicles*, II, 231; Asher b. Saul of Lunel, *Sefer ha-Minhagot*, *Sifran*, 129; Solomon Luria, quoted by Urbach, *Baᶜale ha-Tosafot*, 213; Epstein, "Tashlum Perush ha-Geonim," *Tarbiẓ*, XVI (1945), 71.

63. Poznanski, "ha-Geonim weha-Jerushalmi," 3–44, for a discussion of this matter. It should be noted that Geonic literature in general was practical and more restricted and there was therefore less occasion to use the Palestinian Talmud. See, moreover, the statement of Sherira Gaon, cited in §1, note 80.

64. Assaf, *Teshubot ha-Geonim* (Jerusalem, 1929), 125–126: ומלתא דפסיקא בתלמוד דילנא לא סמכינן בה על תלמודא דבני ארץ ישר׳ הואיל ושנים רבות איפסיקא הוראה מתמן בשמאדא, והכא הוא דאיתברירי מסקניי. See *ha-Eshkol*, ed. Auerbach, II, 49, 53.

65. Alfasi, *ᶜErubin*, end: דעל גמרא דילן סמכינן.

66. Joseph ibn Megas, *Responsa* (Warsaw, 1870), 81: שאין לנו לדחות מהירושלמי אלא דבר שבא הפכו בבלי, אבל דבר שלא בא הפכו בבבליי אין לנו לדחותו, אבל נסמוך עליו ונדון בו.

67. *Shiṭṭah Meḳubbeẓet*, *Baba Meẓiᶜa*, 12b: כתב ה״ר יהונתן ... ואין אנו חוששים לגמרא דירושלמי, דאותן רבנן בתראי שסדדו לנו התלמוד הבבלי הביאו בו אותן הסברות שהן כהלכה ... ומה שראו שהוא שלא כהלכה הניחו אותו בתלמוד ירושלמי.

68. *Ha-Ma'or ha-Gadol*, *Yebamot*, 22a: שאין אנו סומכין אלא על תלמוד ערוך שבידינו. Also, *ibid.*, *Ketubot*, 21a: כי מפני שתלמודנו תלמודא דבבל, דין הוא שיהא מנהגנו לכתחלה מנהג בבל.

69. *Sefer ha-Miktam* on *Beẓah*, ed. A. Sofer, 185: אך בעל השלמה ז״ל פקפק בזה. איך נגיח תלמוד ערוך שלנו מפני הירושלמי.

70. *Sefer ha-Yashar*, ed. Rosenthal, 25: ראיה מירושלמי במקום שאין מכחיש תלמוד שלנו.

71. Quoted in Urbach, *Baᶜale ha-Tosafot*, 548: שלא קיימא לן כאותו ירושלמי, הואיל וגמרא שלנו לא אמרן.

72. *Hassagot on MT*, *Talmud Torah*, VII, 1, ed. Atlas, *HUCA*, XXVII, 9: ואע״פ שהירושלמי מפרש כדבריו, אינו עיקר כי כחולק עם הגמרא שלנו.

Yeḥiel,[73] and R. Isaiah of Trani[74]—to mention some representative names of the twelfth and thirteenth centuries. Although Maimonides made no explicit statement to this effect, it is clear from his works that he too underwrote Hai Gaon's view. In the *Hilkot Jerushalmi* all those laws which contradict the conclusions of the Babylonian Talmud are, in most cases, omitted.[75] Sporadic exceptions to this rule, far from disrupting it, were almost a fixed corollary of the rule itself.

Rabad fits into this framework. He endorses Hai Gaon's view of the supremacy of the Babylonian Talmud: "Even though the Palestinian Talmud does not tally with what we have said, we are guided solely by our Talmud"; "The passage in the Palestinian Talmud which he [Razah] adduced is unreliable, for our Talmud does not follow that reasoning at all."[76] In a long obiter dictum on the need for a guarded use of the Palestinian Talmud because of its inadequacy, he cavils Maimonides, "who thought to decide halakic questions on the basis of the Tosefta and Palestinian Talmud, but was unsuccessful."[77] This passage, which contains several references to the Palestinian Talmud, introduces another contributory factor making for its secondary role. Its text is corrupt, inadequate, misleading, confused.[78] As was the case with the Tosefta, its inferior status from a practical halakic point of view only contributed further textual corruption to a work that initially lacked the benefits of editorial systematization and improvement.

Its relation to the Babylonian Talmud was, in many respects, similar to that of the Tosefta and Halakic Midrashim to the Mishnah. Although apparently not a special subject of school curriculum and, consequently,

73. Hilkot ha-Rosh, *Giṭṭin*, II, 4: וגם מן הירושלמי אין ראיה, כי הוא פליג אגמרא דידן.

74. R. Isaiah of Trani, *Sefer ha-Makriᶜa* (Munkez, 1900), 47: כיון דפליגי תלמודא דידן עם תלמוד ירושלמי, היאך נוכל להניח תלמוד שלנו ולסמוך על הירושלמי. See also *Shibbale ha-Leḳeṭ ha-Shalem*, 89: ובעל היראים זצ״ל כתד בלא סמכינן על תלמוד ירושלמי שהרי נראה כחולק על תלמוד שלנו, ועל תלמוד שלנו אנו סומכין.

75. Lieberman, *Hilkot Jerushalmi*, 5; see also the indirect statement in one of his responsa: יראה לי שראוי לסמוך על זה ירושלמי, שהרי לא חלק על דברי הבבלי. *Teshubot ha-Rambam*, ed. Freimann, 54. Maimonides used the Palestinian Talmud extensively; already Rabad (*MT*, *Ḳeri'at Shema*, III, 6) notes this. See H. Ehrenreich, "Bet Ab" (Maimonides' attitude to Palestinian Talmud), *Oẓar ha-Ḥayyim*, XI (1935), 153–164. A. Marmorstein attributes an analogous statement, taken from the *Eleventh Century Introduction to the Holy Bible* published by Elkan Adler (Oxford, 1897), to R. Maimon, *Tarbiẓ*, VI (1935), 182–184; see, however, J. N. Epstein's reservations, *ibid.*, 187. The statement reads: וההיא גירסא דירושלמי לא סמכינן עליה, דכל היכא דאיכא פלוגתא בין תרי אולפאני, על גמרא דידן סמכינן, ועל מה שפירשו בעלי תלמודינו כי הוא נכון ומסויים יותר מגמרא דבני מערבא.

76. *MT*, *Nedarim*, VII, 5; *KS*, II, 2.

77. *MT*, *Maᶜaser Sheni*, I, 10.

78. *Ibid.*: וכמה אני תמה על זה המחבר שסבר להורות מתוך התוספתא ומן הירושלמי ולא עלתה בידו כי אין התוספתא והירושלמי אצלינו מתוקנים כל צרכן ולא מספיקים כל הצורך . . . הירושלמי שהעתיק ממנו משובש ודבריו איך יהיו מתוקנים . . . *KS*, I, 32.

having no commentaries of its own—Rabad's pupil, R. Isaac ha-Kohen, being the first known medieval commentator of the Palestinian Talmud—it was adopted by the medieval rabbis as a necessary supplement to and helpful commentary on the Babylonian Talmud. Those same scholars who subscribed to Hai Gaon's view concerning the greater authority of the Babylonian Talmud were among the most assiduous students of the Palestinian Talmud, for the latter, in the words of Hai Gaon himself, "was no worse than the commentaries of the early masters," or, in the words of R. Isaac b. Abba Mari, "you have no Gaon or Yeshivah that is greater than the Palestinian Talmud."[79] That is undoubtedly why Sherira Gaon comments: "It happens every day that we avail ourselves of the Palestinian Talmud, which is a help and a support";[80] and R. Ḥananel remarks "that inasmuch as we found this explicit in the Palestinian Talmud, we abide by its decision."[81] It was certainly not inferior to such nonhalakic works as *Piyyuṭ* (liturgical compositions), *Aggadah*, and *Zohar*, which medieval Talmudists utilized, deriving or corroborating halakot from them wherever relevant, provided they did not run counter to the authoritative views expounded in the Babylonian Talmud.[82] The Palestinian Talmud was a much more pertinent body of literature and of greater halakic value.

The main difference between the use of these other works and the Palestinian Talmud is that occasionally medieval Talmudists accepted and codified the opinion of the Palestinian Talmud against that of the Babylonian. This is a pervasive trait sporadically revealing itself among various writers from the Geonim themselves—there are isolated cases in the *She'eltot* and *Halakot Gedolot*—onwards.[83] This practice in itself

79. *Ha-Eshkol*, II, 49: כל מה שמצינו בתלמוד א״י ואין חולק עליו בתלמודנו או שנותן טעם יפה לדבריו נאחזנו ונסמוך עליו דלא גרע מפרושי הראשונים. Assaf, *Teshubot ha-Geonim*, 126: אבל מילתא דלית עלה פלוגתא בתלמוד דילנא חזיננא מה דאיתמר התם· אינמי לגלויי טעמ׳ דמילתא ··· *Me'ah She*ʿ*arim* on Alfasi, *Ketubot*, n. 19: כיון ··· בירושלמי חזינן דפסק ··· אירושלמי סמכינן ··· ואין לן גאון וישיבה גדולה ממנו. See also Rabi, *Sifran*, 33: דסומכין על הירוש׳ בזמן שאינו חולק על הבבלי·

80. *Teshubot ha-Geonim*, ed. Harkavy (Berlin, 1887), 434: וכי הא מילתא דאיתה בידנא מעשים בכל יום דמיסתייעא מן תלמוד דא׳ יש׳ דסמכא הוא·

81. R. Ḥananel on *Shabbat*, 74b; see R. Nissim, ושמא ענין לא הוא מבואר בתלמודנו אבל הוא מבואר בתלמוד א״י. Ginzberg, *Ginze Schechter*, II, 287.

82. Boaz Cohen, *Ḳuntres ha-Teshubot*, 22–23, and literature cited there. Also, A. Karlin, "Ha-Halakah ba-Piyyuṭim," *Dibre Sefer* (Tel Aviv, 1942), 86–96. On the halakic aspects of Yannai's poetry, see S. Lieberman, *Sinai*, IV (1939), 221 and *Maḥzor Yannai*, ed. I. Davidson (New York, 1919), XX–XXI. Sometimes they even outweighed the Babylonian Talmud; see, for example, *Tosafot*, *Berakot*, 18a.

83. Poznanski, "*ha-Geonim weha-Jerushalmi*," 12, n. 1; ha-Me'iri, *Ḥibbur ha-Teshubah*, 42. For Maimonides, see R. Joseph Kolon, *Teshubot* (Lemberg, 1798), 100: דבר ידוע שרבי׳ משה רגיל לפסוק על פי הירושלמי יותר מכל הפוסקים הידועים אצלינו·

is a revealing indication of the widespread use of the Palestinian Talmud. Theoretically committed to Hai Gaon's principle but pragmatically accustomed to use the Palestinian Talmud for comparative and interpretative purposes, many medieval rabbis, when abetted by concomitant factors, occasionally favored it in the final analysis. That they did this furtively, as it were, is attested by the fact that the outlines of a cycle of mutual recrimination can be traced: one is constantly accusing the other of violating Hai Gaon's precept concerning the superior authority of the Babylonian Talmud. Thus, Razah accuses Rabad and Alfasi, Rabad accuses Razah and Maimonides, the latter's commentators and defenders accuse Rabad; and so the cycle rotates.[84] All granted its use as an auxiliary to the Babylonian Talmud, but they endeavored to keep it hemmed in and never to let it contradict the Babylonian Talmud in matters of actual performance. Yet by virtue of its inherent value and the widespread use it received at their hands, they all were guilty at one time or another of this "offense."

Rabad's use of the Palestinian Talmud conforms to this pattern. In the hassagot on Razah, he is constantly bolstering his explanations and vindicating his opinions with passages from it. He regularly disputes Razah's use and explanation of the Palestinian Talmud.[85] His hassagot on the *Mishneh Torah* alone contain over 110 references to or quotations from it.[86] The *Hilkot Lulab*—to mention only one of the smaller codificatory treatises—is replete with passages from the Palestinian Talmud, some of his famous theories therein having been inspired by it.[87] He repeatedly asserts that it was one of his major halakic sources.[88] It is notable that ha-Me'iri refers to a "Palestinian Talmud from the school of Rabad" which was valued for its great exactitude.[89]

The uses of the Palestinian Talmud were many. It could shed additional light on the Babylonian Talmud and its codification by serving as an arbiter between two possible explanations of a disputed passage. Corroborative proof from the Palestinian Talmud was always a weighty consideration in choosing one view over another.[90] Sometimes

84. *Ha-Ma'or ha-Gadol, Yebamot,* 22a; *ha-Ma'or ha-Ḳaṭan,* *ᶜErubin,* 5a; *KS,* II, 21; *MT, Nedarim,* VII, 5; *Maᶜaser Sheni,* I, 10; *Sefer ha-Hashlamah, Berakot,* 13; *Sefer ha-Zekut, Yebamot,* 24a; *Ketubot,* 42a; *Giṭṭin,* 26a, *Maggid Mishneh, MT, Ishut,* XVIII, 4; *Bet ha-Beḥirah* on *Ḥagigah* (Jerusalem, 1955), 56.

85. E.g., *Hassagot, Pesaḥim,* 4a, 26b, *passim.*

86. I have listed them in my thesis, Harvard HU 90.7077, ch. IV, n. 173.

87. *Hassagot, Sukkah,* 15b.

88. *TD,* 7, 113, 114; Rabad, *BK,* 400.

89. *Bet ha-Beḥirah* on *Beẓah* (New York, 1945), 46: ומכל מקום נזדמנה לי גמרא ירושלמית מישיבתם של גדולי מפרשם ...]

90. *MT, Shabbat,* XXIX, 14, and others.

the very character of a complicated legal discussion might be determined by adducing parallels from it. An obscure passage in the Babylonian Talmud might be explicated by a revealing passage in the Palestinian. In one place Rabad admits that "if not for the Palestinian Talmud everything we have said [in explanation of] our Talmud would be of no avail."[91] He quotes passages from the Palestinian Talmud as modifications and restrictions of Maimonides' statements, as supplying supplementary reasons for certain laws, or as being the source of specific halakot.[92] In the course of these discussions, Rabad often pauses to explain words, phrases, or entire passages.[93] Zechariah Frankel summarized the significance of Rabad's scattered comments on the Palestinian Talmud as an important contribution toward its study: "Rabad occasionally explains the Palestinian Talmud in his hassagot on Maimonides, in his commentary on Tractate ᶜ*Eduyot*, and in many halakot that were cited in the writings of the Rishonim. His explanatory comments are all very acute."[94]

Although entitled to reject any passage in the Palestinian Talmud which appears to contradict the Babylonian, Rabad tried whenever possible to salvage the former by reconciling it with the latter. For instance, Razah summarily rejected a certain passage in the Palestinian Talmud "for its contents do not agree with the Babylonian Talmud." Therefore, he concluded, "we pay no attention to them, for we rely only upon the explicit teaching which we possess [in the Babylonian Talmud]." Rabad counters that the passage in question is not at all contradictory and he refers to his harmonizing explanation of both passages. He triumphantly concludes that "both our Talmud and the Palestinian Talmud in this matter are valid and tenable."[95] In another context, Rabad skillfully weaves the explanation of a passage from the Palestinian Talmud into the texture of his defense of Alfasi and announces: "it is worth relying upon him in order not to reject the Palestinian Talmud."[96] He is found interpreting an obscure text and then identifying it with the Mishnah. Rabad was thus continuing a Provençal trend, which was especially pronounced in his family: to reconcile whenever possible the Palestinian and Babylonian Talmuds.

91. *TD*, 113.
92. *MT*, *Ḳeri'at Shema*, III, 11; *Shofar*, I, 3; *Sheḳalim*, III, 9.
93. *MT*, *Sheḳalim*, II, 10, and many others.
94. Z. Frankel, *Mebo ha-Jerushalmi* (Berlin, 1923), 134b.
95. *KS*, II, 29.
96. *KS*, II, 61.

His father-in-law was very adept at this, as was his relative R. Isaac b. Abba Mari.[97]

The final step was to be swayed by the cogency of a text of the Palestinian Talmud and, momentarily oblivious to Hai Gaon's formula, to base one's conclusion on it. After incorporating an opinion from the Palestinian Talmud into his view, Rabad disarmingly adds: "although one may take issue with this passage on the basis of our Talmud, it is proper and acceptable."[98] In their zealous vigilance to defend and vindicate Maimonides, the *Kesef Mishneh* and *Maggid Mishneh* point out that Rabad often went astray under the influence of the Palestinian Talmud.[99] Not only professed Maimonidean partisans impute this halakic deviation to Rabad, but R. Meshullam b. Moses also rejects Rabad occasionally because Rabad placed a premium on Palestinian interpretations, independent of the Babylonian tradition.[100] Similarly, Naḥmanides scores Rabad for forgetting that "the greatest Geonim were not accustomed to rely on the Palestinian Talmud."[101]

Of the many smaller treatises which were not incorporated into the Talmud or were not compiled until after the redaction of the Talmud, Rabad cited *Abot de R. Nathan*,[102] *Masseket Semaḥot*,[103] *Mishnat R. Eliezer*,[104] *Pirḳe de R. Eliezer*,[105] *Seder ᶜOlam*,[106] *Kallah*,[107] and

97. Assaf, in *Sifran*, 28, n. 8; see *Hassagot* on Alfasi, *Ketubot*, 63a.

98. *MT*, *Yom Ṭob*, VIII, 16.

99. *MT*, *ibid.*, I, 8; *Sheḳalim*, III, 5.

100. *Sefer ha-Hashlamah*, *Berakot*, 13, 25.

101. *Sefer ha-Zekut*, *Yebamot*, 24a.

102. *BH*, 5 (introduced by the term "tanya"); see *Abot de R. Nathan*, ed. S. Schecheter (Vienna, 1887), 8.

103. *MT*, *Ṭume'at Met*, VIII, 5. Although he comments here on its inexactitude, he uses it in the Commentary on ᶜ*Abodah Zarah*, 11a to support his reading of the text. See *Masseket Semaḥot*, ed. M. Higger (New York, 1938), 49, 206. Rabad is not listed among those who used this treatise.

104. *Sifra Commentary*, 3a: ברייתא ר׳ אליעזר בנו של ר׳ יוסי הגלילי שלשים ושתים מדות שהתורה נדרשת בהם. See *The Mishnah of R. Eliezer* (or The Midrash of Thirty-two Hermeneutic Rules), ed. H. G. Enelow (New York, 1933), 24.

105. *KS*, II, 39; ed. Bergman, 65. He refers to it as *Baraita de R. Eliezer*, the same title used in the ᶜ*Aruk* and by R. Tam; see Zunz, *ha-Derashot be-Yisra'el*, ed. Albeck, 134, 417. Rabad is not mentioned here either. For another possible reference, see *Derashah le-Rosh ha-Shanah*, 18.

106. *Sifra Commentary*, 71a; ᶜ*Eduyot*, II, 10; *Commentary on* ᶜ*Abodah Zarah*, 44a. Whereas Rabad uses the traditional title *Seder* ᶜ*Olam*, his pupil R. Abraham b. Nathan ha-Yarḥi, *ha-Manhig*, 2a seems to be the first to designate the work as *Seder* ᶜ*Olam Rabbah* in contradistinction to the less important *Seder* ᶜ*Olam Zuṭa*; see H. Strack, *Introduction to the Talmud and Midrash* (Philadelphia, 1945), 225.

107. *BH*, 82, 83, 86; see *Massektot Kallah*, ed. M. Higger (New York, 1936).

Kallah Rabbati.[108] *Abot de R. Nathan* and *Semaḥot* are treated as "additions" to the Mishnah, in the same class as the Baraita and Tosefta respectively. They are all used infrequently. If not for the general inaccessibility of *Kallah Rabbati*, a seventh- or eighth-century amplification of *Kallah*,[109] one would have expected Rabad to refer to it more often in the *Baᶜale ha-Nefesh*. However, only one or two chapters of this work were known in the Middle Ages and even these did not circulate widely. *Masseket Soferim* underlies Rabad's rejection of a liturgical formula quoted by Maimonides. Since he does not mention it by name, however, it is not possible to ascertain whether he knew this source directly or cited the reading on the basis of actual practice.[110]

Rabad, of course, used the aggadic midrashim on the Pentateuch and Five Scrolls extensively, citing them either by name, by the generic term "haggadah," or anonymously. There are references to *Genesis Rabbah*,[111] *Leviticus Rabbah*,[112] *Lamentations Rabbah*,[113] *Haggadah Midrash Ruth*,[114] *Koheleth Rabbah*,[115] and *Midrash Tanḥuma*.[116] The major shortcoming of the generic "haggadah"—a common term of

108. *BH*, 5. He mentions only *Masseket Kallah* but the quotation is from *Kallah Rabbati*, I. Toledano, *Perush Masseket Kallah Rabbati leha-Yarḥi* (Tiberias, 1906), 18 calls attention to another quotation.

109. Higger, *Kallah*, 36, 106 ff.; see Aptowitzer, "Le Traité de Kalla," *REJ*, LVII (1909), 244. Toledano, *Perush Kallah*, 18, contends that Rashi already used it. Aptowitzer rightfully disputes it. This means that Provençal sages—Rabad and R. Isaac b. Abba Mari—were the first to use *Kallah Rabbati*.

110. *MT*, *Tefillah*, XII, 15; see *Masseket Soferim*, ed. M. Higger (New York, 1937), ch. XIII.

111. *Sifra Commentary*, 14a, 47a; *ᶜEduyot*, II, 5; *MT*, *Teshubah*, III, 7 (=*Genesis Rabbah*, I, 9, the "materials" being listed in different order).

112. *Sifra*, 47a; *BH*, 75; *MT*, *Miḳwa'ot*, III, 12; *Derashah le Rosh ha-Shanah*, see index, 45. Isaac Hirsh Weiss (*Sifra*, VIII) was so startled to find a quotation from this midrash in the *Sifra Commentary* that he singled this out as "proof" that Rabad already had access to *Leviticus Rabbah*!

113. *Sifra*, 88b. He refers to it as *Megillat Ekah*, stemming apparently from the *ᶜAruk*, which is the first to mention this midrash in any form; see Zunz, *ha-Derashot*, 78; Aptowitzer, *Mabo*, 273 for a similar use by Rabiah.

114. Commentary on *ᶜAbodah Zarah*, 3b. Our texts do not have this quotation.

115. *Ibid.*, 16b. Rabad says: ודגמתו בהגדה במכילתא Inasmuch as he adduces two proofs for his explanation, one from *Mekilta* (II, 236) and one from *Koheleth Rabbah* (XI,1), perhaps the manuscript should read בהגדה ובמכילתא In this case, the term "haggadah" would refer only to *Koheleth Rabbah* and not to the *Mekilta*. In any event designation of an halakic midrash by "haggadah" is already found in Judah b. Barzilai; see *Perush Sefer Yezirah*, XI.

116. Commentary on *ᶜAbodah Zarah*, 14a. See *Midrash Tanḥuma*, *Ki Tisa*, 2 (ed. Buber, II, 105). Rabad should thus be included in Buber's list of medieval writers who used the *Tanḥuma*.

anonymous references[117]—is that it obscures the source of midrashic citations.[118] The most famous case is the hassagah where Rabad says vaguely: "and similarly have they said in the haggadah."[119] The exact source is yet to be identified.[120] This is another illustration of the fact that many midrashim known in Provence are no longer extant.

The two standard Aramaic versions of the Bible, *Targum Onkelos* and *Targum Jerushalmi*, are cited by Rabad.[121] When he refers simply to "translation" or "as it is translated," he means *Targum Onkelos.* Their main use is to corroborate linguistic explanations or demonstrate etymological affinities. There is a striking instance of Rabad's questioning the midrashic exegesis of the Targum.[122]

2. *Post-Talmudic Sources*

The post-Talmudic sources used by Rabad may be divided into Geonic writings, Palestinian writings, writings of scholars in Italy and Byzantium, North Africa and Spain, northern France, and Provence.

117. Rabi, for instance, following Geonic precedent, uses it exclusively in order to introduce midrashic quotations; see *Ha-Eshkol*, ed. Albeck, 77; Judah b. Barzilai, *Perush Sefer Yeẓirah*, XI.

118. Nor does it distinguish between midrash and other sources. For example, since the maxim "the eye and the heart are the two agents of sin" is introduced by "they said in the haggadah" (*BH*, 88), one would be inclined to trace it to *Numbers Rabbah*, X, 6, rather than the parallel passage in *Yerushalmi Berakot*, I, 8 (P. 3c), if not for the fact that *Numbers Rabbah* is a late text. See Ginzberg, *Perushim we-Ḥiddushim Birushalmi*, I, 163–164, Lieberman, *Hilkot Jerushalmi*, 21.

119. *MT*, *Ishut*, XIV, 16.

120. Zunz, *ha-Derashot*, 142, 434, n. 56. Rabad combined the Tosefta, *Sotah*, V, 12, with *Abot de R. Natan*, II, 97. See Lieberman, *Tosefet Rishonim*, II, 60. Most later authorities quote Rabad anonymously; see *Ḥiddushe ha-Ramban*, *Yebamot*, 112b, and *Sefer ha-Zekut* on *Yebamot*, 65a; ha-Me'iri, *Bet ha-Beḥirah* on Yebamot, 243–244; R. Nissim, *Nedarim*, 90b, and *Shiṭṭah Mekubbeẓet*, *ad. loc.* Naḥmanides is apparently responsible for the introductory phrase "some Geonim say."

Another example is *BH*, 86: וכן אמרו בהגדה על ענין היצר· אברהם השלים עמו ועליו נאמר ברצות ה׳ דרכי איש · · · See Jerushalmi, *Berakot*, IX, 7 (p. 14b); *Genesis Rabbah*, LIV; *Baba Batra*, 17a; *Pesikta de-R. Kahana*, I. Joseph ibn Naḥmias, *Perush Pirke Abot* (Berlin, 1907), V, 22, has a similar reference; see L. Ginzberg's notes in *ha-Ẓofeh*, II, 128.

121. *MT*, *Ṭume'at Met*, XIV, 7; *Genebah*, IX, 11; Rabad, *BK*, 3a; *Sifra*, 76b; 88a. (This explanation is quoted in the *Tosefot ha-Rosh*, *Moᶜed Ḳaṭan* [Fischel Institute Publications, III, Jerusalem, 1937], 7.)

122. *MT*, *Genebah*, IX, 11; see P. Ḥurgin, "Ha-Halakah be-Targum Onkelos," *Ḥoreb*, IX (1946), 87, n. 15. Also, Epstein, *Mebo'ot le-Sifrut ha-Tannaim*, 518; N. Torczyner, "Ha-Targum ha-Arami la-Torah," *Sefer Magnes* (Jerusalem, 1938), 143–151. Elsewhere (*Sifra*, 95b), though, Rabad says: ואני תמה על המתרגם · · · שאינו שוה למדרש חכמים·

The attitude of medieval writers toward the Geonim is complex. Theoretically, Geonic teachings were sacrosanct and their interpretations were indisputable. Chronologically the immediate successors and direct continuators of the Amoraim, the Geonim of Babylon became also their intellectual heirs. They amplified Talmudic teachings, enacted special ordinances, extended the scope of certain laws in keeping with their spirit, systematized the liturgy, and generally entrenched the halakic way of life among the people. As Louis Ginzberg put it: "the Babylonian Amoraim created a Talmud; the Geonim made of it—the Talmud."[1] It is small wonder that all later Talmudic authorities looked back reverently at the Geonim, usually abided by their opinions, and approached them with the humility and self-effacement expressed in the dictum: "If those before us were sons of angels, we are sons of men, and if those before us were sons of men, we are like asses."[2] Already Sherira Gaon is reported to have said: "Whoever dissents from any of their (Geonic) statements is like one who dissents from God and His Torah."[3] There was here a full measure of the deep-rooted veneration traditionally displayed by later scholars to early masters—by the Amoraim to the Tannaim or by the modern Aḥaronim to the medieval Rishonim.[4]

In actual practice, however, the medieval rabbis found themselves substantially modifying this theoretical commitment. Just as all accepted in principle the authoritativeness of the Geonim and the normativeness of their views, so, in practice, all dissented from or qualified certain views on one occasion or another. The exigencies of study demanded that the authority of the Geonim be tempered by independence of mind. Without wishing to subsume all medieval rabbis under any all-inclusive categories and thus blur their individuality, it is necessary to recognize certain general tendencies within which are to be noted differences of degree rather than of kind. The question of authority—as symbolized by the attitude toward the Geonim—should be treated accordingly. One cannot, for instance, set up straw barriers between rabbinic writers in Spain who allegedly followed the Geonim unquestioningly, and those in France who reviewed the Geonic writings

1. L. Ginzberg, *Geonica*, I, 73.
2. *Shabbat*, 112b; *Yoma*, 9b.
3. *Ḥemdah Genuzah* (Jerusalem, 1863), 1a, see, however, Harkavy, *Teshubot ha-Geonim* (Berlin, 1887), introduction. See M. Alashkar, *Responsa* (Sabioneta, 1544), 54 (p. 115), who quotes Sherira Gaon and Rabad.
4. B. Cohen, *Ḳuntres ha-Teshubot* (Budapest, 1930), 11; *JE*, "Aḥaronim," I, 283.

critically.[5] It is similarly untenable to extol one Talmudist—Maimonides, for instance—as a critical scholar who emancipated himself from authoritarian shackles and thus anticipated later enlightened ideas, while branding another—Rabad or Naḥmanides, for instance—as a reactionary writer who lowered his head before authority and thus stifled free thought.[6] Maimonides may have been freer and more critical in his attitude toward predecessors,[7] while Naḥmanides may have restrained his critique to a greater extent, but not one of them can be said either to have acquiesced in all cases or dissented in all cases. There seems to be a quantitative variety in the frequency of dissent rather than a qualitative difference in the actual fact or nature of dissent.

This can be illustrated not only by actual examples of rejection, modification, or reinterpretation found in medieval writings, but even by explicit statements concerning this question of authority. The attitude of Naḥmanides—both in theory and practice—is very instructive. Naḥmanides is conventionally described as hopelessly conservative, having "unbounded respect for the earlier authorities."[8] Indeed, he himself declares: "We bow before them [the ancients], and even when the reason for their words is not quite evident to us, we submit to them."[9] A number of his works are specifically devoted to the defense of the early masters: the *Milḥamot* and *Sefer ha-Zekut* in defense of Alfasi against the strictures of Razah and Rabad respectively; a critique of Maimonides' *Sefer ha-Mizwot* in defense of the *Halakot Gedolot* against Maimonides' criticism. Yet, how meaningful is the following statement, found in the introduction to the last-mentioned work, which was announced as a purely defensive tract:

> Notwithstanding my ardent desire to be a disciple of the earlier authorities, to establish and maintain their views, to [adorn myself] by making their [views] a gold chain about my neck and a bracelet upon my hand, I shall not serve them as a "donkey carrying books." I shall explain their methods and

5. B. M. Lewin, ed., *Iggeret R. Sherira Gaon*, 26.

6. Reifmann, *Toledot R. Zeraḥyah ha-Levi*, 50, n. 31; Schorr, *He-Ḥaluẓ*, V (1860), 40; see also *Bet Talmud*, IV (1885), 302, where Reifmann recklessly characterizes Maimonides' attitude to the Geonim in terms of Ben ʿAzzai's famous statement: "All the sages of Israel appear to me as paltry as the husk of garlic" (*Bekorot*, 58a).

7. A. Schwarz, "Das Verhältnis Maimun's zu den Gaonen," *Moses ben Maimon*, ed. J. Guttman, I, 409; *Teshubot ha-Rambam*, ed. Freimann, 240; *Iggerot ha-Rambam*, ed. Banet, 57–58; *Teshubot R. Abraham ben ha-Rambam*, ed. Freimann, 81.

8. *JE*, "Moses b. Naḥman," IX, 87; Graetz, V, 46.

9. Quoted in *JE*, IX, 87; see also *Milḥamot*, *Rosh ha-Shanah*, end: ולמדת שכל הפורש מדברי הראשונים כפורש מחייו ה׳ יכפיל שכר טרחנו אשר טרחנו לדונם לזכות וידון אותנו לזכות.

appreciate their value, but when their views can not be comprehended by me, I shall debate before them in all modesty, I shall judge according to what appears best in my eyes . . . for God gives wisdom in all times and in all ages.[10]

This devotion to truth, as they arrived at and saw the truth, is characteristic of all the great medieval rabbis.[11] Opinions of the early masters carried great weight with all of the medieval rabbis, but before these opinions became normative decisions they were carefully scrutinized. It is probably accurate to say that medieval rabbis used Geonic interpretations to support their views but their views were not rigidly conditioned by available Geonic interpretations. This is most clearly seen in the carefully selective, almost eclectic use of some Geonic statements and the periodic dismissal of others. There appears to be an ex post facto reliance upon the weight of Geonic precedent.[12]

A priori declarations of all shades, either of subservience or independence, were substantially modified as they hammered themselves out on the anvil of actual study and analysis. Initial independence was qualified by the inescapable authority of tradition while initial subservience was qualified by the pervasive impulse of creative innovation. A classic statement, similar in spirit to that of Naḥmanides but even more pointed, is that written by his Italian contemporary, R. Isaiah

10. Introduction to his *Hassagot* on Maimonides' *Sefer ha-Miẓwot*; F. Rosenthal, "Die Kritik des Maimonidischen 'Buches der Gesetze' durch Nachmanides," *Moses ben Maimon*, I, 475–495; see also introduction to his Bible Commentary: הא־ל אשר ממנו לבדו אירא, יצילני מיום עברה, and to the *Milḥamot*: ולא לירא אדם בהוראותיה ומשפטיה . . . והא־להים ממנו לבדו אירא. See also, *Milḥamot*, *Shabbat*, 55a: אלא שבעל הלכות כתבה בענין אחר ויש שבוש בהלכותיו בזה. *Sefer ha-Zekut*, *Yebamot*, 9a: ואולי המעיין יפה ממנו ימצא בהן מה שנעלם מעינינו, ואולי אין דברי ההלכות בזה נכונים כי אין השלמות בלתי לה׳ לבדו . . . On the history of the picturesque phrase חמור נושא ספרים see S. Abramson, "Imre Ḥokmah," *Minḥah li-Yehudah*, ed. S. Assaf (Jerusalem, 1950), 27. S. Duran is probably echoing Naḥmanides' declaration in part when he says: ולפי שהאחרונים עם היותם מודים כי לבם אינו אלא כפתחו של היכל לעומת הראשונים שהיה לבם כפתחו של אולם, עם כל זה לא יבושו כי ידברו בסתירת דבריהם, כי כן הוא הראוי לכל חכם או תלמידי שלא ישא פנים לגדול ממנו במה שתראה לו סתירה מבוארת בדבריו . . . See Simeon Duran, *Zohar ha-Raḳiʿa* (Vilna, 1879), 11.

11. J. Mann, *Texts and Studies in Jewish History and Literature*, I, 631: ולא אהדר פני רם . . . ואדע כי . . . יגדילו ויניעו בראשם מתי חמד ומלותם נעורות ויאמרו מי ידבר כי שגגה בפי גאון ודברי איש שררות. This declaration of R. Samuel ha-Nagid with regard to Hai Gaon, although typical, is not representative, because Hai Gaon was his contemporary and the problem of authority had not yet crystallized.

12. See, for example, Razah, Rabad, and Naḥmanides on Alfasi, *Berakot*, 35a–36. Also, the following statements of Razah: *ha-Ma'or ha-Ḳaṭan*, *Shabbat*, 6a, 38a; *Rosh ha-Shanah*, 12a. Rabad, *Hassagot*, *Berakot*, 2a. In one place where Razah had impressively lined up a host of early authorities to support his view, Naḥmanides pointedly counters that one can find support for any view: רבותא למחשב גברי, והא . . . כולם אמרו . . . וקבלה בידיהם מראשונים. What really counts is the cogency and inner consistency of the view. See *Milḥamot*, *Pesaḥim*, 7b.

of Trani, the foremost Talmudic authority of his time in Italy. "My method is," he writes frankly, "that anything which is not perfectly clear to me on the basis of the text, even if Joshua the son of Nun said it, I will not obey. I cannot restrain myself from writing what appears to me."[13] Yet he is by no means reckless in his criticism; this declaration notwithstanding, he abides by Geonic precedent and interpretation as consistently as any other, less outspoken, medieval rabbi.[14] The same balance between critical inclinations and veneration of authority can be seen, from an opposite vantage point, in the writings of R. Joseph Karo. Unlike R. Isaiah of Trani who chose—in prefatory remarks or occasional digressions—to vaunt his independence while conforming to accepted standards in practice, Karo preferred to underscore his subservience in principle while actually writing with independence and self-confidence. His contemporary, R. Ḥayyim b. Beẓalel already observed in the *Wikkuaḥ Mayyim Ḥayyim* that Karo did not really follow the standards he outlined theoretically.[15] His authoritative temper was neutralized by his practical independence.

Rabad's stand on this matter should be determined from this perspective, with an eye to correlating a priori declaration of intention with actual performance. Like most other medieval Talmudists, he refers to the Geonim extensively and with great reverence. When he vindicates their views or is able to bolster his own by relating them to Geonic opinions, he is content and convinced. The Geonim are in his eyes the direct continuators of the Amoraim, and he speaks of both in the same breath: "All the Amoraim and the Geonim following them have concurred on this matter."[16] The Amoraim and Geonim are here considered practically as peers, as successive expounders of the Oral Law. He designates the Geonim as "pillars of the world."[17] Yet, instances of dissent and rejection are not wanting. R. Aḥa, author of the influential *She'eltot* and one of the earliest writers of the Geonic period, although himself not a Gaon,[18] is sometimes criticized or qualified. When

13. *JQR* (Old Series), IV (1892), 93: מכיר אני בעצמי שצפורנן של אותם הרבני׳ הראשונים הקדושים יפה מכרסינו . . . אך דרכי הוא כי כל דבר שאינו נראה לי מתוך הספר אי אמרה יהושע בן נון לא צייתנא ואיני נמנע לכתוב מה שנראה לי . . .

14. See now the suggestive remarks of Benedict, *Sinai*, XX (1957), 231, n. 31, and before him M. Higger, *Halakot wa-Aggadot* (New York, 1933), 9–33, esp. 12–18.

15. *Wikkuaḥ Mayyim Ḥayyim* (Amsterdam, 1711). See L. Ginzberg, *JE*, III, 585.

16. *KS*, I, 14.

17. *Ibid.*, 41. See Razah, *ha-Ma'or ha-Ḳaṭan*, *Shabbat*, 36b: זהו פי׳ . . . על הדרך שדרכו בה איתני עולם כגון רבינו שרירא ורבינו האי . . .

18. Naḥmanides, *Milḥamot*, *Shabbat*, 16a: דרב מובהק הוא אצל הגאונים.

Maimonides asserts that it is best—and he actually does—to rely on the Geonic calculation of Sabbatical Years, Rabad takes issue both with the Geonic view and Maimonidean interpretation of it: "Anyway, I do not agree with their opinion nor with his opinion."[19] On one occasion, when Maimonides refers to "what the Gaon said," Rabad calmly retorts: "I have an entirely different opinion in all these matters."[20] While Razah simply cites a Geonic tradition in his analysis of a problem, Rabad discusses the view at length, asking "whence did the Geonim deduce this matter."[21] He wants to understand the logic behind their statements and is not content merely with the authoritative source. Even Hai Gaon was not always accepted.

One statement of Rabad which concerns the exalted prestige of the Geonim and the binding character of their *halakic* writings deserves special discussion, for it has been taken superficially to imply servile adherence to Geonic precedent. Pursuant to the Talmudic discussion of the liability of a judge who errs concerning a ruling explicitly formulated in the Mishnah, in contradistinction to an erroneous judgment resulting from poor reasoning, medieval scholars posit the question whether an error based on ignorance of Geonic writings is just as serious. Razah quotes a predecessor that if a rabbi errs in passing judgment because he was ignorant of a Geonic decision with which—had he known it—he would have concurred and hence altered his judgment, it is as if he erred concerning a teaching of the Mishnah. Rabad not only consents—"this wise man has spoken the truth"—but adds that if one, knowing the Geonic decision, would have disagreed with it because of his own interpretation or reasoning and hence judged erroneously, it would still be as if he erred concerning a teaching of the Mishnah.

> For, at the present time, we may not differ from the statements of the Geonim because of what appears right in our opinion; we may not explain a Talmud passage in any other way than that of the Geonim with the result that the law as formulated by them would be changed, unless we have irrefutable evidence against their conception of it—which is never the case.[22]

19. *MT*, *Shemiṭah we-Yobel*, X, 6.
20. *Ibid.*, *Tefillah*, I, 10.
21. *Hassagot*, *Pesaḥim*, 24b.
22. *KS*, I, 64. All the views are quoted in the *Hilkot ha-Rosh*, *Sanhedrin*, IV, 6. See also, B. Cohen, *Kuntres ha-Teshubot*, 11; Ginzberg, *Geonica*, I, 205, and Poznanski's review of this, *JQR*, III (1912–1913), 398. It is interesting—as an indication of his understanding of the statement—to note the context in which Ginzberg quotes it. He is looking for an apt summation and appreciation of the Geonic contributions to rabbinic literature.

On the basis of the facts quoted above, it is clear that much of what Rabad says about the necessity for rigid acceptance of Geonic views is metaphorical, for he himself puts forth different interpretations and independent decisions. This statement expresses the widespread admiration for Geonic achievements and stresses that one should not rashly dissent from their views on the basis of superficial disagreement —a universally accepted axiom. The general temper of Rabad's writings does not admit the portrayal of an attitude of unquestioning obedience. It is interesting to note that while R. Isaac b. Sheshet Perfet, like Rabad, approves the thesis that an erroneous decision due to ignorance of a Geonic ruling is as invalid as though the error had arisen from ignorance of a mishnaic ruling, he too, like Rabad, is neither uncritical nor indiscriminate. He allows himself to speak of "unwarranted rigors" or "baseless opinions" in his dissent from or modification of Geonic opinions.[23] Ha-Me'iri who repeats this view, obviously paraphrasing Rabad, adds: "unless one differs from the statements of the Geonim on the basis of a certain proof or a logical reason or the concurrent views of other Geonim and rabbis."[24] Simeon Duran also stresses that when "irrefutable evidence" is forthcoming, one need not hesitate to criticize even "a greater person."[25]

Rabad emphasizes the need for caution in explaining Talmudic passages differently lest this affect the actual practice, the normative law. This deference to custom and its concomitant distrust of practical change are common traits among halakic authorities. While considerable latitude was allowed for theoretical discussion, when it came to practice the established precedent prevailed—even if based on a different interpretation. Statements to this effect can be found, for instance, in the writings of Rashi,[26] Razah,[27] Sages of Lunel,[28] Maimonides,[29]

23. A. Hershmann, *Rabbi Isaac Perfet*, 75.

24. *Bet ha-Beḥirah* on *ᶜAbodah Zarah* (Jerusalem, 1944), 11; see *Bet ha-Beḥirah* on *Sanhedrin* (Frankfurt a. M., 1930), 152.

25. *Zohar ha-Raḳiᶜa*, 11.

26. *Siddur Rashi*, 592 (p. 286); see I. Repha'el, "Rashi bi-Teshubotaw," *Sefer Rashi*, ed. J. Maimon (Jerusalem, 1956), 575.

27. *Ha-Ma'or ha-Ḳaṭan, Shabbat*, 12a: ומנהג קדמנינו הבאים אחרי הרי״ף לסמוך עליו כאשר ישאל איש בדבר הא־להים וממנו פשט המנהג בינינו כמו שהוא נהוג היום ונחנו מה לחלוק ולשנות, ועל כן אנחנו יוצאים בעקבי הראשונים. Also, *ha-Ma'or ha-Gadol, Giṭṭin*, 3b; see Reifmann, *Toledot R. Zeraḥyah*, 51, n. 32.

28. See Razah's statement: וראיתי בפירוש נוטה אחר דברי, ומודה על האמת וכן מקצת חכמי ישיבתו אלא קצתם תופשים בידם דרך החומרא, ... וכ״ש שלא לשנות המנהג ... Quoted by Marx, 222, n. 3.

29. *MT, Shemiṭah we-Yobel*, X, 6; see his letter to the Judge of Alexandria, *Teshubot ha-Rambam*, 141.

R. Eliezer b. Nathan (Raban),[30] the compiler of the *Hagahot Maimuniyot*,[31] R. Isaac b. Moses of Vienna,[32] Naḥmanides,[33] ha-Me'iri,[34] and R. Ẓidkiyah b. Abraham (*Shibbale ha-Leḳeṭ*)[35]—not to mention numerous Aḥaronim.[36] Already Hai Gaon in the eleventh century writes, in a style reminiscent of Rabad, concerning the binding character of traditional interpretations and their practical implications "even if they contain elements which do not tally with what we are inclined to think."[37] Rabad's writings offer many examples of theoretical innovation which is disregarded when it affects questions of practice.[38] Such is probably the main import of this statement.

Rabad's knowledge of Geonic literature was rather extensive.[39] Besides repeated anonymous references to the Geonim collectively,[40] which is the most common term of reference in medieval writings, he mentions a number of individual Geonim by name: R. Amram (and at least once the *Seder Mar Rab Amram*),[41] R. Paltoi,[42] R. Natronai,[43]

30. *Eben ha-ᶜEzer*, 209: אין מורין כן ואין מפרסמין הדבר ... לעשות סייג בדבר. See I. Repha'el, "Rashi bi-Teshubotaw," 575, nn. 35–36. See also *Or Zaruᶜa*, I, 453: מה שכתבתי ... למשא ומתן בעלמא כתבתי, אבל לענין הלכה למעשה, כשבא לידי אני מורה בו לאיסורא כדבריך.

31. *MT*, *Gerushin*, XI, 1. See R. Meïr of Rothenburg, *Responsa* (*Cremona*), 144.

32. Urbach, *Baᶜale ha-Tosafot*, 369: אין אדם רשאי לחדש דבר מעתה, אלא הכל כמו שפסקו האחרונים נעשה.

33. Naḥmanides, *Ḥiddushim* on *Megillah*, 21b; see *Milḥamot*, *Yebamot*, 8a.

34. *Bet ha-Beḥirah*, *Beẓah*, 5.

35. *Shibbale ha-Leḳeṭ ha-Shalem*, ed. Buber (Vilna, 1886), 355: ומכל מקום כתבתי הנראה לי, ולא להורות לעשות מעשה כי איני כדאי, אלא ליישב משמעות ההלכה כפי מה שהראוני מן השמים. ואשר שגיתי ישאני עושני כי כוונתי לשמים.

36. E.g., R. Yom Ṭob Heller, Commentary, *ᶜEduyot*, V, 1.

37. *TD*, 119: ואח"כ אנו מביטים בכל הדברים שנאמרו במשנה או בגמרא בענין הזה ומא שיעלה מהם ויתרץ כאשר את נפשיתינו, מוטב. ואם יש בה כלום שלא יתכוין כאשר בלבבנו ולא יתברר בראיה, אינו עוקר את העיקר. Also the statement of his son R. Sherira Gaon, in *Ḥemdah Genuzah* (Jerusalem, 1863), 1a. See however, A. Marmorstein, "Hai Gaon et les usages des deux écoles," *REJ*, LXXIII (1921), 97–100.

38. *TD*, 63; also 11, 13: אין בנו כח להתיר; *Hassagot* on Alfasi, *Berakot*, 34a. See Commentary on *ᶜAbodah Zarah*, 36a: במקומות הרבה תלמיד חולק על רבו במדרש התורה והלכה כתלמיד, אבל בדבר המותר והגדול אוסר ... אין קטן ממנו רשאי להתירה.

39. Geonic literature was generally widespread in Provence. See, for example, S. Assaf, "Mafteaḥ li-Teshubot ha-Geonim ha-Muba'ot be-Sefer ha-ᶜIṭṭur," *Ha-Ẓofeh*, VI (1922), 289–309. Many collections of Geonic responsa were compiled in Provence; see, for example, *Teshubot ha-Geonim*, ed. J. Musafia (Lyck, 1864).

40. We sometimes find theories in Rabad's writings which contemporaries or successors attribute to the Geonim. E.g., *TD*, 29, and *Kol Bo*, 48; *MT*, *Talmud Torah*, VII, 7, and R. Jonathan ha-Kohen, *Perush Massektot Megillah u-Moᶜed Ḳaṭan*, ed. S. K. Mirsky, 162.

41. *Hassagot*, *Pesaḥim*, 24b; *Megillah*, 14b; see *Berakot*, 35b, and *ha-Ma'or ha-Ḳaṭan*, *ad. loc.*; also *ha-Ma'or ha-Ḳaṭan*, *Yoma*, 4b.

42. M. ha-Me'iri, *Magen Abot*, 105. This is Rabad's quotation from R. Isaac ibn Ghayyat.

43. *TD*, 39; *MT*, *Ẓiẓit*, I, 7. This shows that "the Gaon" unqualified does not always mean Hai Gaon.

R. Saadia, R. Hai. An anonymous reference to "some of the Geonim" can be identified as R. Sar Shalom Gaon.[44]

There is little consistency in the way medieval writers in general and Provençal writers in particular refer to the earliest Geonic work, the *Halakot Gedolot*. Some ascribe it to R. Jehudai Gaon, others to R. Simeon Ḳayyara.[45] Rabad once explicitly names R. Simeon Ḳayyara as the author, but he also speaks vaguely of "R. Jehudai of blessed memory" or "the Gaon R. Jehudai."[46] As a rule, he does not mention any name and merely cites "the author of the *Halakot*."[47]

R. Aḥa of Shabḥa and his halakic compendium *She'eltot* are cited frequently by Rabad.[48] In one place Rabad remarks: "Now, upon whom shall we rely? Let us rely upon the statements of R. Aḥa who was an illustrious rabbi and whose statements are everywhere very exact and detailed."[49] On other occasions, he questions R. Aḥa's statements, analyzes his reasoning, or disagrees with certain conclusions.[50] At least once the vague term "rabbis," used loosely by Rabad, as by other medieval writers, for important predecessors, refers to R. Aḥa.[51] Rabad's text of the *She'eltot* differed considerably from our standard printed text and the quotations or references in his writings are valuable for establishing an exact text of the *She'eltot*.[52] The order in which Rabad quotes authorities cannot, apparently, carry any weight for purposes of determining the chronology of the *Halakot Gedolot* and the *She'eltot*—still a moot question[53]—for sometimes he cites "the author of the *Halakot* and R. Aḥa"[54] and sometimes reverses the sequence.[55]

44. *MT*, *Sheḥiṭah*, VII, 4; *Tosafot*, *Ḥullin*, 48a.

45. Louis Ginzberg himself, who maintained that Franco-German authors usually name R. Jehudai while the Spanish-Provençal ones usually name Simeon Ḳayyara, cited many exceptions to the latter half of his generalization; see *Geonica*, I, 100. Hildesheimer, editor of the *Halakot Gedolot* (Berlin, 1892), lists in his introduction a number of rabbis from various lands who refer to both names alternately.

46. *KS*, II, 29; Marx, 207; *TD*, 62; see also *Hassagot*, *Beẓah*, 8a and Razah, *ad. loc.*; *Shibbale ha-Leḳeṭ ha-Shalem*, 5.

47. *BH*, 10, 57, and others; *MT*, *Nezirut*, V, 6; *Hassagot*, *Pesaḥim*, 26b, *Beẓah* 16b.

48. E.g., *Hassagot*, *Berakot*, 36a, *Shabbat*, 50a, *Pesaḥim*, 6a, 8a; *KS* on *Rosh ha-Hashanah*, ed. Bergmann, 74; *BH*, 5, 6, 65. Sometimes he uses "gaon" for R. Aḥa and sometimes omits it. See §2, note 18.

49. *BH*, 65.

50. *Ibid.*, 6; *Hassagot*, *Berakot*, 36a.

51. *BH*, 5; *MT*, *Issure Bi'ah*, XI, 18.

52. See, for example, *Hassagot*, *Pesaḥim*, 24a, and *She'eltot*, I, 42. Rabbi N. Z. Berlin, the modern editor and commentator of the *She'eltot* (Jerusalem, 1949) used the *BH* extensively for this purpose.

53. Ginzberg, *Geonica*, 98.

54. *BH*, 10.

55. *Hassagot*, *Beẓah*, 1a, 3b. This is the order usually found in Naḥmanides; see, for example, *Milḥamot*, *Yebamot*, 20a.

The reference to R. Saadia Gaon is of interest. In connection with the Talmudic injunction that man is not to add in the liturgy any prayer of praise beyond the prescribed praises already incorporated in the daily service, Rabad asks how it is permissible for people to recite the long laudatory hymn of "R. Saadia, may the memory of the righteous be for a blessing, which contains so many praises."[56] Rabad probably singled out this hymn, which Saadia composed for the prayer book that he compiled, as the best example of this kind of liturgic production and not as an exhaustive illustration, for there must have been others that he knew. It is just that this particular poem of Saadia achieved great popularity, as attested by Ibn Ezra's unstinted praise of it[57] or by the question concerning it directed to Maimonides.[58] It may be noted that the prayer book of Saadia, which Rabad here refers to, was cited abundantly both by his father-in-law Rabi and his pupil Abraham b. Nathan ha-Yarḥi,[59] while it seems to underlie Maimonides' version of the prayer book, which Rabad did not criticize at all. Rabad's acquaintance with Saadia's *Emunot we-Deᶜot* will be discussed in Chapter VI.

R. Hai Gaon, "the Gaon" par excellence in practically all medieval rabbinic writings, is for the most part quoted anonymously by Rabad. Rabad mentions "the commentary of the Gaon" which can be shown to refer to the pseudo-Hai Geonic commentary on *Ṭohorot.*[60] From the fact that some lexicographical explanations which Rabad cites in the name of the *ᶜAruk* are already to be found in this Geonic commentary[61] one might infer that Rabad did not consult the commentary directly or that it was not always accessible. He also cites the *Mekaḥ u-Mimkar*, which was available in the Hebrew translation of R. Isaac b. Reuben Albargeloni.[62] A quotation from his commentary on *Berakot* is quite valuable, for it is only recently that fragments of Hai Gaon's commentaries on the Talmud have been recovered.[63] R. Hai's responsa, for

56. *Shibbale ha-Leḳeṭ ha-Shalem*, 18; *Siddur R. Saadia Gaon*, ed. Assaf, Davidson, Joel (Jerusalem, 1941), 36–37. See also *ha-Ma'or ha-Ḳaṭan, Yoma*, 4b.

57. Commentary on Eccles, 5:1.

58. *Ḳobeẓ Teshubot ha-Rambam*, 128. See A. Haberman, "Gam Elah Bakashot le R. Saadia Gaon," *Tarbiẓ*, XIII (1941), 52–59.

59. *Siddur R. Saadia*, 36–37.

60. *MT, Kelim*, XVIII, 6; *Perush ha-Geonim ᶜal Seder Toharot*, ed. J. N. Epstein (Berlin, 1921), 12, n. 6.

61. E.g., *MT, Kelim*, V, 1; *Ṭume'at Oklin*, XIII, 11.

62. *KS*, II, 2, 11; Commentary on *ᶜAbodah Zarah*, 21a. See Assaf, *Misifrut ha-Geonim*, 17 n. 1.

63. Ginzberg, *Geonica*, 171. See now J. Mann, *Texts and Studies*, I, 538 ff., and *Ginze Ḳedem, ed. B. M. Lewin, passim.*

which he is chiefly known and which established his reputation as the greatest Geonic Talmudist, are used by Rabad a number of times.[64] He makes an interesting observation on the necessity for carefully checking the authenticity and accuracy of responsa, for many have been corrupted by scribal interpolations or inexact transcription.[65] Although Rabad often cites Hai for support, and scrupulously explains and respects his views—in one case he says that if not for the support that Razah drew from an opinion of Hai, he would have raised a wondrous, insoluble question against Razah[66]—he also dissents from his explanations when necessary: "the honor of the Gaon will remain untouched, but the meaning of the passage does not appear to be as he supposed."[67]

Rabad cites a certain view as stemming from the *Shimushe Geonim Ḳadmonim.*[68] Gross takes this novel designation to refer to a specific Geonic book.[69] Albeck assumes that *shimush* means something that is recorded in order that it will be available and useful later.[70] It should be observed that in a parallel discussion of this subject in *Temim De^cim* Rabad cites this same view and says that he found it in "the codified decisions of the early [masters]."[71] Hence, "shimush" may be taken to mean some kind of collection of decisions for practical purposes expounded by successive Geonim.

The *Shimusha Rabbah*, not mentioned by name, apparently underlies Rabad's theory on the order and arrangement of the parchment scrolls within the phylacteries.[72] A responsum of Rabi discusses a similar theory and relates it to the *Shimusha Rabbah.*[73] All later authorities identify Rabad's view with this Geonic compilation.[74] One can infer from this that Rabad did not share R. Judah b. Barzilai's view

64. *TD*, 61, 52; *BH*, 14.
65. *TD*, 62; see *Hassagot*, *Pesaḥim*, 15a.
66. *KS*, I, 12.
67. *Ibid.*, 51; see also, *Hassagot*, *Berakot*, 12a, 24a.
68. *MT*, *Berakot*, VI, 2.
69. Gross, 539.
70. Albeck, *ha-Eshkol*, 93.
71. *TD*, 1; see *Orḥot Ḥayyim*, I, 2b quotes it as ונמצא בתשובות קדמוניות. For discussions of the term "shimush," see L. Ginzberg, *Geonica*, I, 182, n. 1; M. Margaliyot in his edition of *Halakot Ḳeẓubot* (Jerusalem, 1942), 110; Scholem, "Kabbalat R. Jacob," *Mada^ce ha-Yahadut* (Jerusalem, 1927), II, 189; Assaf, *Teḳufat ha-Geonim we-Sifrutah*, 207, 209; S. Kook, "Ḥomer le-Hora'at 'Shimush,'" *Sinai*, XIII (1950), 382–384, who fails to mention Rabad; J. Mann, *The Jews in Egypt and in Palestine* (Oxford, 1920–1922), II, 231.
72. *MT*, Tefillin, III, 5.
73. *TD*, 79.
74. E.g., Menaḥem Azariah Fano, *Sefer Teshubot*, 108.

about the unascertained origin of this work and its proneness to error.[75]

One of the important developments which originated in Palestine during the early medieval period—when Palestine ceased to be a leading center of halakic creativity[76]—was the composition of liturgical poetry, the pioneers in this field being Jose b. Jose, Jannai, and Eleazar Kalir. Rabad may have been acquainted with the *Maḥzor* of Jannai.[77] Of Kalir's poetry, which became a standard part of Jewish liturgy everywhere, Rabad quotes a passage from a hymn which is still recited in the synagogue.[78] It might be observed in connection with Kalir that in the halakic dispute concerning the question of whether or not extraneous liturgical poetry may be included in the service, Rabad defended their inclusion and sanctioned their recitation.[79] Rabad reports that he derived some information from a "R. Amram b. Hillel of Palestine."[80] His knowledge of early mystical tracts concerning *Sheᶜur Ḳomah* will be mentioned in Chapter VI.

In discussing Rabad's commentary on the *Sifra*, mention was made of the general influence of rabbinic writings of Italian and Byzantine scholars[81] in Provence and especially the possible use by Rabad of the *Sifra* commentary of R. Hillel b. Eliakim of Greece. There are a number of stylistic similarities between Rabad and R. Baruch b.

75. Quoted by R. Asher b. Yeḥiel, *Hilkot Tefillin.* See also, R. Isaiah of Trani, *Hilkot Mezuzah* (on *Menaḥot*, 31b), quoted by Higger, *Halakot wa-Aggadot*, 20. See M. A. Fano, *Teshubot*, 107, who describes the contents of this tract as דברי קבלה.

76. S. Eppenstein, "Die geistige Tätigkeit in Palästina bis zum Beginn des 10 Jahrhunderts," *Beiträge zur Geschichte und Literatur im geonäischen zeitalter* (Berlin, 1913), 24–65; Assaf, *Teḳufat ha-Geonim*, 172–180.

77. See his use of Eccles. 3:5 in *BH*, 5. This implication, intimated by the *Targum*, is extended by Jannai; see *Maḥzor Yannai*, ed. I. Davidson (New York, 1919), 20.

78. *KS*, III, 38. Unlike Abraham ibn Ezra, who denounced Kalir for his unintelligible poetry, Rashi and R. Tam lauded Kalir; see *Sefer ha-Pardes*, 174; *Shibbale ha-Leḳeṭ ha-Shalem*, 11.

79. Ha-Me'iri, *Ḥibbur ha-Teshubah*, 266. However, the responsum quoted in *Shibbale ha-Leḳeṭ*, 18, limits their use to private supplications.

80. *Sifra Commentary*, 114a; see *Daᶜat Zekenim: Baᶜale ha-Tosafot ᶜal ha-Torah* (Livorno, 1783), 67a: מצאתי קונדריס מר׳ עמרם בר׳ הלל שהיה מא״י. Epstein, *Ketabim* I, 280.

81. In rabbinic literature Italy and Byzantium are not purely geographical or political designations, for "Italy" included all parts of the peninsula while "Byzantium" or "Greece" (*Yawan*) included Sicily as well as Byzantine regions, properly speaking. See J. N. Epstein, "R. Baruch Me-Ḥalab," *Tarbiẓ*, I (1929), 27, and literature cited there; B. M. Lewin, *Ginze Ḳedem*, V (1934), 129; also, J. Starr, *The Jews in the Byzantine Empire*, 234; *Teshubot R. Abraham b. ha-Rambam*, ed. Freimann, 15, n. 7; 17, n. 3; Eppenstein, *Beiträge*, 194.

Samuel of Greece, who was the first critical reviewer of R. Ḥananel's commentary on the Talmud. Both introduce their critical annotations by the formula "said Abraham" and "said Baruch" respectively. Both are fond of attributing novel interpretations to special divine inspiration: "we have written whatever they have shown us from heaven." The writings of Baruch b. Samuel had reached Provence and Rabad's pupil, R. Meïr b. Isaac of Trinquetaille, used them.[82]

Rabad uses the ᶜ*Aruk*—the foremost medieval Talmudic lexicon—of Nathan b. Yeḥiel of Rome copiously, as do practically all medieval rabbinic scholars. Kohut has compiled a list of quotations from or references to the ᶜ*Aruk* found in Rabad's writings.[83] Besides the many places where Rabad mentions the ᶜ*Aruk* by name, there are cases where he presents in his own name explanations which can be traced back to it. This shows, as Gross observed, that Rabad did not always consult the ᶜ*Aruk* directly.[84] Many explanations of the ᶜ*Aruk* are rejected by Rabad.

Of special interest is Rabad's frequent reference to the Mishnah commentaries of R. Isaac b. Melchizedek of Siponto whom he dubs "the Greek rabbi." Rabad subjects him to very harsh critique. Such statements as "the Greek rabbi's explanation of this is 'a vanity and a striving after wind,'" or "the Greek rabbi offered an explanation which is darkness and obscurity" are typical.[85] Rabad constantly associates Isaac with Maimonides and rejects their conclusions summarily. He intimates that the former must have exerted great influence on Maimonides, who follows very many of his explanations.[86] The quotations from his commentaries found in Rabad's hassagot are an important source for reconstructing the complete text of these commentaries.[87]

Rabad refers once to the *Josippon*[88] as the "book of Joseph b. Gorion."

82. J. N. Epstein, *Tarbiz*, I, 27.

83. A. Kohut, ed., *Aruch Completum* (New York, 1955), I, XXVII.

84. Gross, 449, n. 2.

85. *MT*, *Ṭume'at Met*, I, 11; XXV, 3.

86. *Ibid.*; also, XIV, 7; XVII, 3; XXI, 9, and others. Note that a certain R. Joseph, contemporary of Maimonides in Fostat, singles out Isaac b. Melchizedek's commentary on *Seraᶜim* and *Ṭohorot* as one of the three best, practically indispensable, commentaries on the Mishnah. This would indicate that its use was widespread even in Egypt and that Maimonides had ready access to it. See Assaf, *Kiryath Sefer*, XVIII (1941), 65.

87. Lieberman, *Tosefet Rishonim*, IV, 18–19; see, in general, H. Gross, "Isaak b. Malki-Zedek aus Siponto und seine süditahschen Zeitgenossen," *Magazin für die Wissenschaft des Judentums*, II (1875), 21-22, 25–26, 29–30, 33–34, 37–38, 42–44.

88. It was generally believed that this book was of Italian origin; see, however, I. Baer, "Sefer Josippon," *Sefer Dinaburg* (Jerusalem, 1949), 178–205, who associates it with the German court of Otto the Great and D. Flusser, "Meḥaber Sefer Josippon," *Tarbiz*, XVIII (1953), 109–126, who presents a case for Byzantine origin.

After discussing a knotty chronological problem concerning the Second Commonwealth—a problem which has constantly occupied historians and in connection with which ᶜAzariah dei Rossi, who analyzes the issues at length, quotes Rabad's view[89]—Rabad observes that the interpretation offered by Razah, which is the traditional one, is not in keeping with the "book of Joseph b. Gorion." He therefore carries the discussion further.[90] The probability of Rabad's acquaintance with the writings of Shabbetai Donnolo will be discussed in Chapter VI.

As Talmudic scholarship moved from its old eastern centers in Babylon to its new western centers in Spain, it witnessed in the transition the flowering of an active community in North Africa, whose intellectual center was Kairwan, a city near Tunis. Two of the "sages of Kairwan" are mentioned frequently by Rabad: R. Ḥananel and R. Nissim.

Rabad knew the Biblical as well as Talmudic commentaries of R. Ḥananel. His interpretation of the verses in Exodus concerning theft is adumbrated by R. Ḥananel's explanation.[91] Similarly, his explanation of the verse "thou shalt surely tithe all the increase of thy seed" in Deuteronomy, which differs from all other explanations, is basically the same as that of R. Ḥananel.[92] Rabad often quotes R. Ḥananel together with Alfasi, recognizing that the latter used the former extensively and that their views, for the most part, stand or fall together.[93] R. Ḥananel often appears as an intermediary of Geonic views and versions.[94] Maimonides' indebtedness to R. Ḥananel is also recognized.[95] Rabad sometimes delves into the sources and exact meaning of R. Ḥananel's statements, even though he does not agree with them.[96] One explanation which Rabad quotes—and rejects—in the name of "gaon" is attributed by Razah—who accepts it—to R. Ḥananel. This would imply either that Rabad loosely applied the title "gaon" to R. Ḥananel, which was rather common, or that he had a different source for this view.[97]

89. ᶜAzariah dei Rossi, *Me'or ᶜEnayim*, III, 7.

90. *KS*, III, 34.

91. *MT*, *Genebah*, IX, 8; see S. Rapoport, *Toledot* (Warsaw, 1913), II, 65.

92. R. Baḥya b. Asher, *Commentary*, Deuteronomy 21:5. See Lieberman, *Hilkot Jerushalmi*, 21.

93. E.g., *Hassagot*, *Beẓah*, 21b; *Sukkah*, 3b; *Taᶜanit*, 3a; see a similar evaluation by Naḥmanides, *Sefer ha-Zekut*, *Yebamot*, 36a.

94. E.g., *Hassagot*, *Berakot*, 6b, 9a, 44a.

95. E.g., *MT*, *Sanhedrin*, XXIV, 1: ... דבר זה הוציא ממה שפירש רבינו חננאל. See Bromberg, "R. Ḥananel and Maimonides," *Sinai*, XI (1948–1949), 4–13.

96. *Sifra Commentary*, 23a.

97. *Hassagot*, *Giṭṭin*, 24b.

A view introduced as "a different commentator explained" stems from R. Ḥananel,[98] while other, apparently independent, explanations of Rabad coincide with those of R. Ḥananel.[99] Two favorite phrases of Rabad—"understand this well" and "what they have shown us from heaven"—are also favorites of R. Ḥananel.[100]

It must have been during his sojourn in Barcelona that Rabad became acquainted with the *Sefer ha-Mafteaḥ* of R. Nissim, which was widespread in Spain.[101] Rabad seems to have known at least one of R. Nissim's Talmud commentaries—that on *ᶜErubin*.[102] Even though the authority of R. Nissim was very great, Rabad was not always bound by him. An interesting illustration—interesting both for his attitude to R. Nissim and to Rashi—is the case where Rabad rejects an interpretation of R. Nissim, upon which Razah based his argument, in favor of an interpretation found in Rashi, whom Rabad is supposed to have disdained. Even the textual variants of R. Nissim, which were presumably old and reliable, were not always accepted by Rabad.[103]

While R. Ḥananel and R. Nissim were focusing attention on North Africa, Spain began to emerge as a first-rate cultural center. Although Jewish scholarship in general began to flourish in Spain under the aegis of Ḥasdai ibn Shaprut in the middle of the tenth century, Talmudic learning in particular did not achieve prominence until the time of Samuel ha-Nagid at the beginning of the eleventh century. Reaching exceptional heights in the writings of Alfasi and Maimonides at the end of the eleventh and twelfth centuries respectively, rabbinic study in Spain moved for the most part on an elevated and influential level. Since it was commonly believed that Spanish texts of the Talmud were copied from Babylonian ones and that Spanish authors were meticulous in preserving the correct traditions,[104] their methods were followed and emulated, their texts investigated and checked, their conclusions pondered and discussed.

Provence, in particular, was subject to these influences as a result of

98. *MT*, *Shabbat*, X, 18.

99. The explanation of Rabad, *BK*, 20 is like that of R. Ḥananel; see *Sefer ha-Miktam* on *Sukkah*, 76; *Orḥot Ḥayyim*, I, 113a.

100. A. Berliner, *Migdal Chananel* (Leipzig, 1876), VIII.

101. Benedict, 109. See, in general, S. Assaf, *Tarbiẓ*, XI (1940), 229–259, XII (1940), 28–50, and S. Abramson, *Tarbiẓ*, XXVI (1956), 29–70.

102. B. M. Lewin, "Perush R. Nissim le-ʻErubin," *Emet le-Yaᶜakov* (Berlin, 1937). 72–80.

103. *KS*, II, 4, 14, 23.

104. Ginzberg, *Geonica*, 18.

geographical proximity, which fostered regular personal contact and favored steady literary communication. Rabad's halakic writings reflect with considerable clarity and exactness the extent of Spanish Jewish influence in Provence. He knew practically all the high-ranking Talmudists of Spain. Even the contemporaries of Alfasi generally eclipsed by him—e.g. Isaac ibn Ghayyat, Isaac ibn al-Balia—were still cited frequently by Rabad. A study of his use of their writings reveal not only their prevalence in Provence but also the fact that they were carefully screened and used discriminately.

Besides general references to "Spanish books" and "Spanish texts," which Rabad cherished,[105] he mentions Samuel ha-Nagid (simply as "ha-Nagid")[106] and Isaac b. Reuben Albargeloni.[107] R. Isaac ibn Ghayyat is alternately praised and criticized by him. Rabad invokes his support frequently—"all his [Razah's] statements are shattered like a potsherd, for we rely solely upon what we have decided and R. Isaac ibn Ghayyat also wrote accordingly"[108]—but is equally quick to reject his views completely: "R. ibn Ghayyat's statements in this matter are confused"; "He did not clarify his words."[109] One gets the impression that Rabad implicitly classifies ibn Ghayyat as a regular adversary of Alfasi; indeed, according to Abraham ibn Daud, ibn Ghayyat was one of the few who dared criticize Alfasi during his lifetime.[110] It is for this reason that ibn Ghayyat's refutation of Alfasi—especially, when invoked by Razah—is not deemed striking or weighty while his concurrence is always prominently underscored.[111] In spite of his knowledge of philosophy, Isaac never let secular learning impinge on tradition or get the better of it in case of contradiction.[112] Rabad probably appreciated this characteristic.

With regard to Alfasi, it need only be added here that Rabad stresses the seminal influence of Alfasi's teaching and depicts him as a pivotal personality—a theme which permeates the elegies written by Judah ha-Levi and Moses ibn Ezra on the death of Alfasi,[113] as it does Razah's

105. *KS*, I, 56, II, 20, and others; *Hassagot*, *Pesaḥim*, 13a.
106. *Hassagot* on Alfasi, *Ketubot*, 20b, 38b.
107. *KS*, I, 58.
108. *Hassagot*, *Pesaḥim*, 5a.
109. Marx, 208, n. 5; also *Hassagot*, *Pesaḥim*, 5b; *Sukkah*, 3b.
110. See Weiss, *Dor Dor we-Doreshaw*, IV, 284.
111. E.g., *Hassagot*, *Pesaḥim*, 13a, 16b, 26b.
112. Weiss, *Dor Dor*, 280.
113. *Hassagot* on Alfasi, *Ketubot*, 14a; *Diwan* of Judah ha-Levi, ed. Brody, II, 100: לא עצרו כח נבונים לעמוד, לולא תבונות ממך דרשו. Moses ibn Ezra, *Shirat Israel*, tr. B. Halper, 73: ראש הראשים, אלוף הקדושים, מחכים הישישים. See also Razah's introduction to *Sefer ha-Ma'or*.

introduction to the *Sefer ha-Ma'or*. Such emphasis allowed for a constructive mixture of appreciation and independence.

Rabad treats R. Joseph ibn Migas, about whom his contemporary Abraham ibn Daud says that "even in the time of Moses there was none like him,"[114] with considerable deference. He is referred to as "our master ibn Migas." Rabad knows that ibn Migas was the foremost disciple of Alfasi and in a question concerning the exact meaning of a disputed passage in Alfasi he relies upon the interpretation of ibn Migas, who should certainly know what Alfasi had in mind. He also traces a solution offered by Maimonides back to ibn Migas, but then dismisses the entire matter—"we need not resort to this [answer], for the question needs no answer."[115] It is relevant to observe that ibn Migas, spiritual heir of Alfasi, also criticized his master on occasion.[116] This further illustrates that the conventional dichotomous classifications of critics versus supporters require modification.

A second pupil of Alfasi, author of the first extensive supplement and critique of his master entitled *Sefer ha-Tashlum*, was a popular figure in Provençal circles, as attested by the frequency with which Razah and Isaac b. Abba Mari cite him.[117] Rabad knew him well: he refers to him often and is able even to identify anonymous views as stemming from him.[118] When compelled to dissent, Rabad says frankly: "what R. Ephraim wrote is a mistake."[119] He designates him on occasion

114. *Sefer ha-Kabbalah*, ed. Neubauer, I, 77; see *Seder ha-Dorot*, 153.

115. *MT*, *Ma'akalot Asurot*, IX, 16; *KS*, I, 46; see *MT*, *Kil'ayim*, IV, 9, 15; *Ma^caser*, I, 15; *Shekenim*, VII, 1; *Hassagot* on Alfasi, *Ketubot*, 38b. Note the same approach in *Sefer ha-Zekut*, *Ketubot*, 22a: ה״ר יוסף הלוי בן מיגש, תלמדו של הרב ז״ל

116. *Teshubot ha-Rambam*, ed. Freimann, 353; see Benedict, *Kiryath Sefer*, XXXI (1956), 264.

117. Benedict, *Kiryath Sefer*, XXV (1948–1949), 165; XXVI (1949–1950), 322–338. His fame was so widespread in Provence that he has been described as a Provençal scholar; see Weiss, *Dor Dor*, IV, 285, n. 14.

118. E.g., *Hassagot*, *Pesaḥim*, 14b, and *Milḥamot*, *ad. loc.* In an annotation on the Mishneh Torah (*Ma'akalot Asurot*, VII, 3) where Maimonides formulates his conclusion about a problem in *Ḥullin*, Rabad observes that "this is not like the view of the Master [Alfasi] but like R. Ephraim." Maimonides' view, however, is not the same as that of R. Ephraim, as we know it from a reproduction by Rashbah (*Torat ha-Bayit*). The only thing that can be said for Rabad's identification of Maimonides' view with that of R. Ephraim is that in one respect the practical result of both views is identical, although the reasoning is entirely dissimilar. It might also be that Rabad's text of R. Ephraim's glosses on Alfasi was not perfectly accurate. This possibility is strengthened by the fact that Naḥmanides once claims that Rabad operated with an erroneous version of Alfasi, stemming from the fact that he treated a gloss of R. Ephraim as part of the original text of Alfasi. See *Sefer ha-Zekut*, *Giṭṭin*, 10b. Other glosses of R. Ephraim were incorporated into the text of Alfasi; see Benedict, *Kiryath Sefer*, XXXI (1956), 264.

119. Rabad, *BK*, 96.

by the metaphoric name "Ephrati," which is a term of endearment.[120]

Rabad's wide acquaintance with R. Judah b. Barzilai's writings is illustrated by the fact that he identifies Razah's reference to "one of the wise men of the generation" as Judah b. Barzilai.[121]

Spanish Jewish authors of secular or philosophic works, such as Solomon ibn Gabirol, Judah ha-Levi, Baḥya ibn Pakuda, Abraham bar Ḥiyya, and Abraham ibn Ezra, will be discussed in the chapter dealing with Rabad's acquaintance with extra-Talmudic learning. We shall also see Rabad praising R. Isaac b. Baruch al-Baliya for creating a happy alliance between thorough Talmudic learning and expert astronomical knowledge.

While no personal contact between Rabad and the scholars of northern France is ascertainable, there was definite literary intercourse between them. Rabad was acquainted with the commentaries of Rashi and the discursive annotations of the early Tosafists, and perhaps also with fragmentary writings of some pre-Gershomites.[122] Similarly, his writings and teachings were not slow in spreading throughout France. There were many intellectual affinities and methodological similarities between Rabad and the Tosafists. Their approach to Talmudic study had much in common and there was bound to be mutual influence between them. R. Tam, about whom a late chronicle fancifully related that Rabad came to visit him incognito, was very conscious of sustained intellectual relations between the two parts of France; he cites many examples of French students who went south in quest of learning as well as of Provençal scholars who disseminated Talmudic knowledge in the north.[123] A number of the classics of French Rabbinic literature—such as *Sefer ha-Pardes*, *Sefer ha-Oreh*, and *Maḥzor Vitry*—betray considerable Provençal influence and show signs of cultural cross-fertilization.[124] Perhaps the most telling fact concerning early contact and influence is that Rashi already knew of Provençal responsa and even used Provençal terms for his vernacular paraphrases.[125]

120. *KS*, II, 22; see Aptowitzer, *Mabo*, 321.

121. *Hassagot*, *Beẓah*, 11a.

122. See, for example, *TD*, 31; *Tosafot*, *Pesaḥim*, 115a, the view of R. Joseph Tob ʿElem, who came to Anjou from Narbonne.

123. Kaufman, "Liste de Rabbins," *REJ*, IV (1882), 212, 223; *Sefer ha-Yashar*, ed. Rosenthal, 87, 90; see Assaf, "Sefer Pesaḳim le . . . Baʿale ha-Tosafot," *A. Marx Jubilee Volume*, 13: תשובת ר״ת אשר השיב אל דרום.

124. See, for example, Epstein, "Joseph ibn Platt," *MGWJ*, VII (1900), 289 ff.

125. Benedict, 91. Also *Sefer ha-Yashar* (Vienna, 1811), 579.

More complicated than the fact of his acquaintance with French writings is the question of his attitude toward the leading French scholars, toward the school of the Tosafists. He was very critical of them and did not attach to them the preeminence and authoritativeness with which successors were to invest their writings. Rashi, whom he habitually refers to as "the French rabbi"—reminiscent of the title "the Greek rabbi" which he used for Isaac b. Melchizedek of Siponto and not at all laudatory—is treated like just another commentator.[126] As is his custom, Rabad traces many views back to Rashi, but then he rejects them. Here are some typical expressions: "This is from the Frenchman and it is incorrect"; "This reason is better and more appropriate than the reason of the Frenchman"; "The Frenchman explained . . . and this too is insipid." "He who will examine the matter will find many mistakes in his statements."[127] One may conjecture whether there is any correlation—a dialectical one, perhaps—between Razah's general acceptance and Rabad's general rejection of Rashi. As early in their careers as the *Dibre ha-Ribot*, Razah, in eloquent terms, extolls Rashi at the expense of Rabad and implies that Rashi deserves absolute priority. "Now, kindly listen," Razah writes to Rabad, "even if you repeat all day long [by way of oath] 'crown of the King' and 'Lord of Abraham,' we shall not listen, for Rabbi Solomon [Rashi] wrote in his commentary . . ."[128] In subsequent writings Rabad repeatedly chides Razah for following "the explanations of the Frenchmen that are in need of endless corrections." There are many such instances where Rabad depicts Razah as following "the Frenchmen" while he, by implication, remains an independent Provençal author.[129]

Yet, it would not be accurate to assert that the general Provençal attitude toward their French colleagues, and that of Rabad in particular, was consistently antagonistic or disdainful. There are cases in which Rabad prefers a "French explanation" or textual variant over all others. What could be more meaningful than the fact that Rabad sometimes pits Rashi against Alfasi or even the Geonim and then

126. See §2, notes 127–128. Marx (*Rashi Anniversary Volume*, 11) takes the phrase "ha-Rab ha-Zarefati" to mean "the" great French rabbi and says, in praise of Rashi, that Rabad "treats him with more respect than he does most other scholars." This is obviously not the connotation of Rabad's phrase.

127. Marx, 207, n. 6; 208, n. 1; *KS*, III, 47.

128. *Dibre ha-Ribot*, 40.

129. Marx, 207; *KS*, I, 25; II, 5: זה אין לו אלא מה שמנו אחרים ונעשה זנב הרב הצרפתי ז״ל. See also Naḥmanides, *Milḥamot*, *Shabbat*, 64b: הריני כמשיב על דברי בעל המאור, אע״פ שהם דברי רש״י.

throws his weight behind Rashi: "I also wrote differently from the Master's [Alfasi's] statements . . . and the reason submitted by the French rabbi is a good one." "The explanation of this passage . . . proceeds well in accord with the interpretation of the French rabbi . . . But the Geonim did not explain it in this way."[130] It was noted earlier that Rabad sometimes aligns himself with Rashi against R. Nissim.[131]

Rabad may not always have consulted Rashi's commentary directly. He presumably did not always check the *ᶜAruk* at first hand. As for Rashi, there are many places where Rabad uses such introductory phrases as "some say," "some erase this version," and similarly vague terms when the view cited is that of Rashi.[132] To attribute this vagueness to the literary habit of calculated anonymity is not very convincing, for Rabad's references to Rashi are usually precise. This is especially noticeable in the commentary on *ᶜAbodah Zarah* where "the Frenchman" or slight variants thereof constantly recur; his views are never cited anonymously. This precision is further attested to by the fact that Rabad not only mentions the name—Rashi or more often the "French rabbi"—but even specifies the literary source; he is accustomed to saying "Rashi explained in his Bible commentary" or "the French rabbi explained in the first chapter of Tractate Yoma."[133] Furthermore, besides the conventional introductory phrases, there are some peculiar ones which more definitely sustain this possibility. Such an excessively harsh phrase, reminiscent somewhat of Abraham ibn Ezra's more caustic epithets, as "whoever says this . . . has no brain in his skull" would have to be taken as aimed at Rashi if it is assumed that Rabad always knew Rashi's commentaries at first hand.[134] A witty comment of Naḥmanides, who usually treats Rabad reverently, is also pertinent to this question. In answer to a thesis that Rabad expounded as his own—"it seems that nobody preceded me in this matter"—Naḥmanides observes: "These are the words of Rashi and he [Rabad] merely added the self-praise."[135] Now, it is one thing to lapse into the anonymous style of writing, even when the writer knows the sources explicitly—

130. *TD*, 14; *KS*, I, 54; see Benedict, 96, n. 103, who quotes Guedemann's extreme view also.
131. See §2, note 103; also *KS*, II, 1.
132. Rabad, *BK*, 305; *Sifra*, 14a.
133. *Sifra*, 4a; 6a.
134. Rabad, *BK*, 44.
135. *Ḥiddushim*, *Berakot*, 50a: דבריו כדברי רשי, ולא הוסיף בהם אלא השבח הזה שהוא משבחו.

this is prevalent in the Middle Ages and found also in Rabad.[136] Appropriating other people's views as original insights, however, transcends the habit of anonymity. Rabad was rigidly firm in this respect and was constantly carrying opinions back to their first source. Unless Rabad completely forgot Rashi in this case, one must conclude that he did not always have his works or did not always consult them.

Among the Tosafists, the only two known by name in Provence at this time seem to be R. Samuel b. Meïr (Rashbam) and his younger brother R. Jacob b. Meïr, commonly designated as R. Tam. Rabad's father-in-law already leaned heavily on these two, while Isaac b. Abba Mari corresponded with R. Tam, as is evident from the *ᶜIṭṭur*.[137] Razah not only mentions R. Tam and Rashbam by name, but also refers to the former's *Sefer ha-Yashar* as well as to some early Tosafot "that I found from the school of R. Solomon."[138] There is a responsum of Rabad quoted in the *Shibbale ha-Leḳeṭ* where Rabad most likely refers to Rashbam.[139] It is possible that Rabad mentions R. Tam by name in his commentary on *Baba Ḳamma*.[140] Elsewhere, Rabad cites an opinion of "one who differs [from Maimonides' views] and says . . .," this "one" being R. Tam.[141] Also, Rabad summarizes his lenient view on a question of dietary law and concludes "there is no proof for the one who forbids this." Now, besides an anonymous tradition preserved in Rashi, as far as I know, the only one who maintained a view similar to that refuted by Rabad is R. Tam.[142] Guedemann, who upholds the view that Provençal rabbis looked with disdain upon their French brethren, traces a sharp reference of Rabad—"this is a subtlety of the last Frenchman, let the wind carry it all away"—to R. Tam's *Sefer ha-Yashar*.[143] There are a number of cases where Rabad and R. Tam expound the same unique theories, which are completely outside the mainstream of halakic discussion on these subjects.[144] Similarly, any

136. E.g., *MT*, *Ishut*, I, 4; V, 14; XXII, 10; *Ma'akalot Asurot*, XII, 10; *Yom Ṭob*, VI, 4; *Ẓiẓit*, III, 9; Rabad, *BK*, 31; *Shibbale ha-Leḳeṭ*, 93.

137. Auerbach, *ha-Eshkol*, 110; *TD*, 140; *ᶜIṭṭur*, I, 52a; II, 17d.

138. *Ha-Ma'or ha-Gadol*, *Ḥullin*, 21a; *ha-Ma'or ha-Ḳaṭan*, *Shabbat*, 36b; *KS*, I, 47.

139. *Shibbale ha-Leḳeṭ*, 47.

140 Rabad, *BK*, 139; see Chapter II, §2, note 11.

141. *MT*, *Ẓiẓit*, III, 9; see Hilbitz, *Lileshonot ha-Rambam*, 183–184.

142. *TD*, 12; *Tosafot*, *Ḥullin*, 47a.

143. Guedemann, *ha-Torah weha-Ḥayyim*, I, 6, n. 1.

144. On the question of eating in the *sukkah*, for example, see Tosafot, *Berakot*, 11a and *MT*, *Sukkah*, VI, 12; on a question of ritual law, see Tosafot, *Ḥullin*, 46b, and *MT*, *Sheḥiṭah*, VII, 16; on the form of a writ of divorce, see Tosafot, *Giṭṭin*, 34b; *Pesaḥim*, 6a; *Ḥiddushe ha-Ramban*, *ad. loc.*

number of parallels may be drawn between Rabad and the Tosafot in general. If there is no influence here, there is at least a noteworthy coincidental meeting of great minds. Rabad and R. Tam were similar not only in intellectual greatness but in many character traits—both were impulsive, dynamic, independent, and self-confident, and both were wealthy.[145]

The scholarly career of Rabad's teacher Rambi was significant for its contributions to the evolution of a distinct Provençal tradition and native halakic literature. Exposed to the cross currents of influence from northern French and Spanish Judaism, the Jewish community of southern France also developed its own corpus of literature and accumulated its own body of practices. As early as the twelfth century the "sages of Narbonne" are referred to collectively and their teachings or precedents, which will be very influential for later medieval Talmudists, already carry great weight with contemporary twelfth-century rabbis.[146] Razah, who, despite all his affinities with Rashi, is in many respects outside the mainstream of halakic tradition, lends himself to characterization as the emergent type of native Provençal scholar. He followed closely in the footsteps of his master Rambi. An interesting observation relevant not only to the obvious question of anonymity and plagiarism but also to the genesis of a "Provençal school" in halakah may be found in R. Meshullam b. Moses' introduction to the *Sefer ha-Hashlamah*. He prudently "informs all readers of this book of mine that in many matters I follow in the path" of Razah. This is due, however, not to plagiarism but to the fact that there were many common Provençal traditions which he happened to receive independently from his father, just as Razah received them from his teachers.[147] In light of this, it is worth broaching the question as to how much of this common Provençal tradition Rabad absorbed and what evidence of this is discernible in his writings.

In addition to what he received from his teachers, Rambi of Narbonne and Meshullam of Lunel, as well as his father-in-law, Rabad knew the teachings of R. Isaac b. Merwan ha-Levi, the teacher of many scholars of the previous generation, including Rabi.[148] The legacy he received

145. For R. Tam, see Urbach, *Baᶜale ha-Tosafot*, 55 ff.

146. E.g., *Sefer ha-Ma'or*, *Pesaḥim*, 8a.

147. *Sefer ha-Hashlamah* on *Neziḳin*, ed. I. Lubozky (Paris, 1885), introduction: והנני אודיע לכל קוראי ספרי זה, כי בדברים רבים אני הולך בדרך הרב המאור ז״ל אבל לא כגונב את דבריו, רק כן קבלתים מאבא מרי ז״ל. כי גם המה בחייהם ז״ל פעמים נחלקו במגדל לוניל מרבץ התורה ופעמים הושוו . . .

148. *Shibbale ha-Leḳeṭ*, 51; *KS*, I, 25; *Sefer ha-Terumot*, LI, 6: ראב״ד בשם ר׳ יצחק בן מרן לוי; see *GJ*, 412–413.

from them undoubtedly had a far-reaching influence on his thought. When he wishes to counter Maimonides' reliance upon his teachers, Rabad states confidently: "but my teachers said." [149] He mentions also R. Asher b. Saul (presumably the author of the *Sefer ha-Minhagot*) and R. Abraham b. Joseph, both of whom planned to emigrate to Palestine. Among the "seminaturalized" Provençal writers, he mentions Joseph ibn Plat frequently and knew Judah ibn Tibbon and most likely also Joseph Kimḥi.[150] He composed the *Hilkot Lulab* at the home of Menaḥem b. Isaac of Carcassonne, in whose name he quotes a certain view.[151] He cites the custom of Narbonne in a matter of civil law and opposes it to that of Barcelona.[152] In one case where Razah cites the custom of Narbonne as decisive, Rabad counters that "this law is operative only in Narbonne, whereas we judge according to the opinion of the Master [Alfasi]." [153] There is, finally, an anonymous reference which can be traced back to R. Moses ha-Darshan, the father of Provençal learning.[154]

More significant, however, is the fact that a number of opinions presented by Rabad seem to be common Provençal theses. These may be described as the joint property of "the Provençal sages," just as students of halakah are accustomed to refer to the common theories of "the Spanish sages" or "the French sages." Here are some illustrations:

1. Concerning the question of the ritual propriety of water drawn in vessels (*mayim she'ubim*), Rabad expounds a certain view based on the interpretation of a passage in the *She'eltot*. The Tosafot on *Temurah* contains the record of a written debate on this subject between a northern French tosafist (R. Isaac of Dampierre) and R. Samuel of Lunel. The view presented by the latter "in the name of his teachers"

149. *MT*, *Shekenim*, VII, 6; *Sekirut*, II, 7; *She'elah u-Fiḳadon*, V, 6, and others.

150. See pages 260–261.

151. Ha-Me'iri, *Magen Abot*, 103; see Chapter II.

152. *TD*, 50.

153. *KS*, III, 11.

154. The verse in Ecclesiastes: "Who knoweth the spirit of man whether it goeth upward (*ha-'olah*) and the spirit of the beast whether it goeth downward to the earth" troubled nearly all medieval commentators and thinkers—for instance, Saadia, Rashi, and Abraham ibn Ezra. They differed on the interpretation of the article (*he*) prefixed to the word "goeth upward"; some took it as interrogative, some as definite. In the course of his brief discussion of this verse, Rabad cites and takes issue with "one who says that this is not interrogative." This "one" seems to be R. Moses ha-Darshan who says explicitly "and that *he* in the word *haᶜolah* is not interrogative but the definite article." Moreover, the structure and sequence of both passages—that of Rabad in the *Baᶜale ha-Nefesh* and that of R. Moses ha-Darshan in his commentary—are similar. See *BH*, 80; A. Epstein, *R. Moses ha-Darshan* (Vienna, 1891), 46; for the problem in general, see Malter, *Saadia Gaon*, 224, n. 502.

is identical with that given by Rabad in the *Ba*ᶜ*ale ha-Nefesh*. Now, the identity of this R. Samuel cannot be definitely established. Benedict has noted the identifications conjectured by Zunz and Albeck—that this is Samuel b. Moses, a scholar of the middle of the twelfth century—and added his own, which maintains that this is Samuel b. David, a somewhat younger contemporary of Rabad. If Benedict's view is correct and Samuel's use of the term "teachers" is precise, then Samuel b. David, known for his derashot, should be added to the list of Rabad's disciples. Benedict has, as a matter of fact, pointed out some similarities between Rabad and Samuel, but there is no other evidence of a student-teacher relation. If the view of Zunz and Albeck is correct, Rabad included in the *Ba*ᶜ*ale ha-Nefesh* an interpretation which was widespread in Lunel.[155]

2. Rabad was very fond of his *Hilkot Lulab*; he referred to it in later writings and attacked Razah for quoting it anonymously. It is interesting that in his *Sifra* commentary, Rabad himself introduces the central thesis of this treatise as "there is one who says." If this means that it was a common view—and this is supported by the fact that the ᶜ*Iṭṭur* presents the same view and that subsequent authorities quote Rabad and the ᶜ*Iṭṭur* together—then Razah should not be condemned for quoting it as "some explain."[156]

3. Rabad presents what is virtually an original definition of a pattern of regularity in menstrual cycles (*weset*). Although he is the first to express this in writing—and, in general, the first to elucidate this subject in detail—he explicitly states that "we have received this tradition from the statements of our teachers."[157]

4. Rabad bolsters his critique in one place by saying "all our sages previously agreed . . ." Razah, in the *Sefer ha-Ma'or* on *Ḥullin*, expresses the same view. Now, a view agreed upon by Rabad and Razah is usually the common Provençal view. "Our sages" in Rabad's annotation must refer to the Provençal sages.[158]

5. A rule expounded by Rabad in *Temim De*ᶜ*im*, which is adopted in

155. *BH*, 61; *Tosafot, Temurah*, 12a; *Sefer Miẓwot Gadol, Miẓwot* ᶜ*Aseh*, 248; Benedict, *Kiryath Sefer*, XXVII (1950–1951), 244–245, 246, n. 93. See *Sifran*, 148. The Samuel b. David quoted there by Asher b. Saul of Lunel is presumably this same Provençal writer. See I. Sonne, *Kiryath Sefer*, XXVIII (1953), 416, who demonstrates that Samuel was a teacher of Asher—thus confirming Benedict's conjecture, *Kiryath Sefer*, XXVII, 242.

156. Benedict, *ibid.*, 247, n. 97, collated all the sources.

157. *BH*, 30.

158. *MT, Sheḥiṭah*, I, 24; *Sefer ha-Ma'or, Ḥullin.*

the *Shulḥan* ᶜ*Aruk*, is there quoted in the name of the ᶜ*Iṭṭur*. Since the latter was a code and Rabad had expressed the view only in a fragment, it is only natural to refer back to the ᶜ*Iṭṭur*. It appears, however, to be a Provençal tradition.[159]

6. Razah in the *Sefer ha-Ma'or* and Rabad in the *Temim De*ᶜ*im* submit the same reason for the omission of a certain benediction upon the performance of a commandment.[160]

7. Rabad's dissent from a view of Maimonides is expressed in the brief formula "not all admit [this law] in the case of acquisition." Aside from the inherent halakic interest of this view, it need be observed only that "not all admit" means primarily Provençal scholars.[161]

8. A certain exegetical comment cited by Rabad in his *Derashah* coincides with that expounded by R. Meshullam of Melun and mentioned in the *Eshkol* in the name of "one of our group."[162] A similar coincidence exists concerning a liturgical custom.[163]

9. A view cited anonymously by Rabad in criticism of Maimonides is explicitly attributed in the hassagot of R. Moses ha-Kohen to R. Isaac b. Merwan ha-Levi.[164]

10. Many views cited by R. Moses ha-Kohen in the name of "his teachers" tally with views expounded elsewhere by Rabad.[165] Since we have no evidence indicating a teacher-pupil relation between Rabad and R. Moses ha-Kohen, they most probably are using common Provençal traditions.

These illustrations, which can surely be multiplied, show neither dependence or plagiaristic tendencies on the part of Rabad. They indicate that a core of Provençal traditions was being formed with which Rabad was naturally acquainted and to which he substantially contributed. Anonymity was prevalent in rabbinic—as in all medieval—writing and would certainly take hold of local theories prevalent in any one region such as Provence. A "Provençal school" in halakah was crystallizing.

159. *TD*, 12; *Yoreh De*ᶜ*ah*, 39.

160. *TD*, 29; *Sefer ha-Ma'or*, *Pesaḥim*, end.

161. *MT*, *Mekirah*, V, 9; see *Maggid Mishneh*, *ad. loc.*, and *Shiṭṭah Meḳubbeẓet* on *Baba Batra*, 40a.

162. *Derashah le-Rosh ha-Shanah*, 18; *Tosafot*, *Rosh ha-Shanah*, 8b; see my remarks in *Kiryath Sefer*, XXXII (1958), 443. Ha-Me'iri, *Ḥibbur ha-Teshubah*, 380.

163. *MT*, *Tefillah*, XIII, 6; *Tosafot*, *Baba Batra*, 15a; see *Sefer ha-Miktam* on *Megillah*, 18.

164. *MT*, *Shabbat*, VI, 5, quoted by *Kesef Mishneh*; *Hassagot* of R. Moses ha-Kohen, ed. Atlas, *HUCA*, XXVII (1956), 60.

165. *Ibid.*, 14, 24, 25, 27, 35, *passim*.

V. DISCIPLES AND FOLLOWERS

A person who spent the best years of his life teaching and writing would naturally exert great personal and literary influence. "Oral Law" and "written Law" are the two perennial media of instruction by which a scholar raises up disciples and perpetuates his influence, and Rabad pursued both with avidity and dedication. Rabad imparted to his students and to all who entered his sphere of influence a contagious enthusiasm for Torah, a sense of independence, and a feeling for critical research. If students flocked to his school at Posquières from all regions of Europe, as Benjamin of Tudela informs us, then his influence must have been proportionately far-flung and pervasive, even if sometimes intangible. Distinct traces of his influence are discernible in a select number of direct disciples; innumerable others may be described as his followers.

1. *Disciples*

One of his students was R. Abraham b. Nathan ha-Yarḥi (of Lunel). Like his teacher Rabad, whom he refers to as "our master R. Abraham b. David,"[1] he absorbs various currents of Jewish learning and followed the major trends of Jewish life. Whereas Rabad was strategically situated in an area where French and Spanish Jewish traditions and learning were being cross-fertilized, R. Abraham b. Nathan traveled all over France, Languedoc, and Spain in order to become acquainted with the various modes of Jewish life. He directly observed and absorbed heterogeneous elements of contemporary Judaism.[2] Starting his educa-

1. *Sefer ha-Manhig* (Berlin, 1855), 73, 34.

2. J. Reifmann, "Abraham b. Jarchi," *Magazin für die Wissenschaft des Judentums*, V (1878), 61; D. Cassel, "Ueber Abraham b. Natan aus Lunel, Verfasser des Manhig,"

tion under Rabad, he continued it at Dampierre in northern France under R. Isaac b. Samuel the Elder (Ri ha-Zaḳen), who at this time incarnated the Tosafistic school of Franco-German scholarship.[3] In addition, he visited great Spanish centers of Jewish learning such as Toledo.[4] In this manner, he carried one step further the merger of northern and southern schools initiated by Rabi, Rabad, and other contemporaries. He did it with the immediacy and vitality of personal contact.

His most famous work is *ha-Manhig*, a very readable collection and exposition of religious customs and ceremonies. Customs played a central role in Jewish life. Already the Talmud—both *Masseket Soferim* and the Palestinian Talmud—contains the famous, far-reaching dictum: "Custom causes the law to be suspended."[5] Echoes of this declaration are heard in these representative statements from the *Sefer ha-Pardes*, which emanates from Rashi's sphere of influence, and the *Sefer ha-Yashar* of R. Tam respectively: "They act in accord with the proper and fitting custom and one should not deviate from this custom"; "We rely upon custom and whoever changes is at a disadvantage."[6] Rabad concurred with these sentiments and often expressed himself thus: "The only guiding principle we have is the custom of the people"; "One should rely upon this reason and not mock customs."[7] He constantly referred to the example and precedence of customs and stressed their significance even in halakic controversies. They were an important ingredient of the normative law and often channeled the course of halakic development. Since custom, unless flagrantly at odds with an indisputable halakic norm,[8] was practically sacrosanct, it is understandable

---

Jubelschrift . . . *Leopold Zunz* (Berlin, 1884), 122–137; see the bibliography listed by Higger, "Yarḥi's Commentary," *JQR*, XXIV (1933–1934), n. 1.

3. *Ha-Manhig*, 9, 73, 89. On the importance of the school at Dampierre, where a galaxy of future leaders and teachers was concentrated, see Gross, "Etude sur Simson b. Abraham de Sens," *REJ*, VI (1883), 184–185; E. Urbach, *Baʿale ha-Tosafot* (Jerusalem, 1955), 195–218.

4. *Ha-Manhig*, 1.

5. *Soferim*, XIV, 17 (ed. Higger [New York, 1937], 270 and see the excellent bibliography in n. 103); Jerushalmi, *Baba Meẓi'a* VII, 1. See also M. Margaliyot, *Ha-Ḥillukim sheben Anshe Mizraḥ u-bene Ereẓ Israel* (Jerusalem, 1938), 14–23.

6. *Sefer ha-Pardes ha-Gadol*, 1: ואלו נוהגין המנהג הנאה וההגון ואין לשנות מן המנהג. *Sefer ha-Yashar* אמנהג סמכינן, וכל המשנה ידו על התחתונה.

7. *TD*, 113; *KS* on *Rosh ha-Shanah*, ed. Bergmann, 72; *Hassagot*, *Pesaḥim*, 26b; see *Hassagot*, *Berakot*, 34a: ולולי שהמנהג מעכב עלי הייתי אומר . . . אבל הפסק שנפסקה הלכה למקום שפסק והעם נהגו—הוא מונע ממני זה הפירוש . . .

8. E.g., *Hassagot*, *Pesaḥim* 17a: עוד אני אומר שהמנהג שהוא בטעות אין חוששין לו; *TD*, 29 where Rabad dismisses a venerable custom already endorsed by Rashi, *Responsa*, ed. J. Elfenbein (New York, 1943), 50, as a folkloristic accretion; see *Oraḥ Ḥayyim*, 432, 2.

that anthologies of customs were common in the Middle Ages and often accompanied or were part of actual codifications. R. Abraham b. Nathan's *ha-Manhig* is one of the important works in the genre of "customs literature" which was then making great strides. We shall presently encounter yet another disciple of Rabad, or at least a younger contemporary greatly influenced by him, who also composed a valuable "Book of Customs."[9] By virtue of his wide travels and extensive observation, R. Abraham was able to cite a variety of customs, especially on ritual and liturgic matters. He was in a position to declare authoritatively that "it is the custom in Provence, Burgundy, France, Champagne, Lorraine, Germany."[10] Not only does he engage in an intensive study of "comparative customs" but he also analyzes them critically and sometimes pronounces upon their irrationality. Such and such a custom, he injects parenthetically, "is inconceivable"; thus indirectly he advocates the adoption of one over and against another.[11]

Several more points broadly representative of Provençal culture are suggested by his writings. Elaborate use of Midrash—a trait distinctive of Provençal scholarship from the time of its first prominent figure R. Moses ha-Darshan who actually derived his literary surname from his proficiency in Midrash—is found also in *ha-Manhig*. Its value in this respect is enhanced because it contains citations from nonextant works.[12] The prevalence and influence of the Palestinian Talmud in Provence is again attested to by R. Abraham b. Nathan's frequent quotations. Many of these citations are not found in the printed edition of the Palestinian Talmud. A number of them undoubtedly stem from nonextant Midrashim, a fact which further substantiates and specifically illustrates the general assertion that it was a common literary phenomenon for Mid-

Note the statement of Rabi *TD*, 174: ...לא נכון הדבר, אבל יש אנשים בעולם שכיון שנזרק דבר אחר מפיהם ואפי׳ בטעות מחזיקים בו; and ha-Me'iri, *Magen Abot*, ed. I. Last, 6–11, 102, where he quotes Rabad. Also, Naḥmanides, *Ḥiddushim* on *Megillah*, 21b. Isaiah of Trani, *Sefer ha-Makri*ʿ*a*, 31 (p. 20b): וכל מה שנשא ונתן רבינו תם לא עשה אלא לקיים המנהג שמצא שנהגו העולם שלא יעקור את ההלכה. אבל נראה בעיני שהמנהג הזה הוא שלא כהלכה ושלא כדת. The underlying source is *Soferim*, XIV, 18.

9. *Sefer ha-Minhagot* of Asher b. Saul of Lunel in *Sifran*, 122–183; see § 2, note 1. On the *Sefer ha-Minhagot* of another Provençal writer, Moses b. Samuel, see *Israelitische Letterbode*, IV, 132.

10. S. A. Wertheimer, *Sefer Ginze Yerushalayim* (Jerusalem: 1896–1899), I, 23: ונהגו בפרובינציא בונגונייא, צרפת, קנפיניא, לוהיר, ואלימניא. His spelling of many of these names is unique; Gross did not know these variants; see *GJ*, sub: בונגונייא, לוהיר, קנפניא.

11. E.g., *ha-Manhig*, 10.

12. L. Ginzberg, "Abraham b. Nathan," *JE*, I, 116; Reifmann, "Abraham b. Jarchi," 64.

rashim to be cited under the misnomer of "Palestinian Talmud."[13] As for knowledge of Geonic literature and quotations from it, the impression is that R. Abraham b. Nathan had an even wider acquaintance with Geonic writings than did his Provençal master—a presumably Spanish influence.[14]

With regard to *Weltanschauung* and ideological tendencies in general, it should be observed that the influence of mystical trends of thought is already manifest in ha-Yarḥi's writings.[15] He makes occasional references to "internal [mystical] books" (*sefarim penimiyim*)—a phrase which he appears to have coined on the basis of contemporary philosophic terminology.[16] He is very much concerned with prayer, liturgical forms, and the proper intentions which insure the efficacy of prayer—a concern which is characteristic of a basic Provençal interest of the time. It has been pointed out that the development of a mystique of prayer is the chief contribution of early twelfth-century Provençal Kabbalah—and this same interest existed in halakic literature.[17] Ha-Yarḥi's master, Rabad, dealt with various problems of prayer from both aspects, halakic and mystical.[18] Ha-Yarḥi is also a devotee of the esoteric approach to the study of certain subjects and counsels circumspection in the dissemination of secret lore. This is in keeping with the inclination of his master who takes Maimonides to task for indiscriminately disclosing esoteric subjects to the masses.[19] It is intriguing to speculate upon the significance of the fact that he was the courier of R. Samson of Sens' response to R. Meïr ha-Levi Abulafia in Toledo concerning the condemnation of Maimonides' philosophic and, even, halakic writings.[20]

13. L. Ginzberg, *Geonica* (New York, 1909), I, 85, and literature cited there; B. M. Lewin, *Oẓar ha-Geonim*, *Rosh ha-Shanah*, 89.

14. See, for example, Ginzberg, *Geonica*, 17, n. 2.

15. *Ha-Manhig*, 15.

16. He is the first to designate esoteric literature by this term *penimi* which was used by ibn Tibbon and al-Ḥarizi as synonymous with "internal" or "hidden" in describing the "internal senses." See Wolfson, "The Internal Senses in Latin, Arabic, and Hebrew Philosophic Texts," *Harvard Theological Review*, XXVIII (1935), 69. The presence of this phrase in *Maḥzor Vitry* (144) is a result of R. Abraham b. Nathan's interpolations into this text; see A. Epstein, "Maḥzor Vitry," *Kitbe Abraham Epstein*, ed. A. M. Haberman (Jerusalem, 1950), I, 287, n. 2; also Aptowitzer, *Mabo*, 280. Note its later use by Moses de Leon, for instance: דרכי החכמות הפנימיות in *Ha-Nefesh Ha-Ḥakamah* (Basel, 1608), introduction; also, Joseph Gikatilia, *Sefer Shaᶜare Ẓedeḳ* (Korez, 1785), introduction: ההשגות הפנימיות; *Orḥot Ḥayyim*, I, 18a.

17. G. Scholem, *Reshit ha-Kabbalah* (Jerusalem, 1948), 103; there is a long responsum of Rabi on prayer in *Shibbale ha-Leḳeṭ ha-Shalem*, ed. S. Buber (Vilna, 1886), 18; see also *ha-Eshkol*, ed. Ch. Albeck, XVIII.

18. E.g., *MT*, *Ḳeri'at Shema*, IV, 7; the responsa quoted in *Shibbale ha-Leḳeṭ ha-Shalem*, 8 (also in *Agur* [Venice, 1546], 95), 48, 51, 79; see ch. V.

19. *Ha-Manhig*, 4, 16.

20. Higger, "Yarḥi's Commentary," *JQR*, XXIV, 335.

Mention should be made of R. Abraham's commentary on *Kallah Rabbati*, the first chapter of which was edited half a century ago by Toledano while the second chapter was identified and published by the late Michael Higger.[21] Besides the eyewitness report which R. Abraham gives here concerning the disputed theological doctrines of the first anti-Maimonidean controversy, this commentary is significant in that it undoubtedly mirrors Rabad's interest in the subject matter of *Kallah Rabbati*: problems of marriage, sanctity of family life, exacting ethical requirements in the whole gamut of man's relation with woman. It contains some of the earliest quotations as well as unacknowledged paraphrases from Rabad's *Ba^cale ha-Nefesh*.[22] *Kallah Rabbati* itself was just beginning to circulate and his commentary is thus a pioneer effort.[23]

The following literary curiosity symbolizes in its own indirect way the close contact between master and disciple. A halakic interpretation which originated with Rabad and was incorporated into the *Shulḥan ^cAruk* was inaccurately attributed to R. Abraham's *ha-Manhig*.[24] While such inaccuracies in tracing statements back to their original source are not at all rare, they do reveal some underlying proximity and influence. R. Abraham b. Nathan was close enough to Rabad, in time and in earning, to be credited by posterity for publicizing this view.

Another of Rabad's disciples was R. Isaac ha-Kohen, whom ha-Me'iri describes as "one of the pupils of the great Rabbi Abraham b. David."[25] R. Isaac ha-Kohen was a prominent teacher and legist in Narbonne at the turn of the century. He was most likely the ancestor of R. Aaron ha-Kohen of Lunel, author of the *Orḥot Ḥayyim*, which abounds in quotations from Rabad's writings.[26] One of R. Isaac's pupils was R. Reuben b. Ḥayyim—an outstanding Talmudist quite knowledgeable in secular subjects—who in turn was the highly revered tutor of

21. *Perush Masseket Kallah Rabbati le-Rabbanan ha-Yarḥi*, ed. B. Toledano (Tiberias, 1906); Higger, "Yarḥi's Commentary," 331–348. See Aptowitzer, *MGWJ*, LII (1908), 304–306.

22. Toledano, *Perush Kallah*, introduction, 32.

23. Toledano, *ibid.*, 18; Aptowitzer, "Le Traité de Kalla," *REJ*, LVII (1909), 244.

24. *Oraḥ Ḥayyim*, 451, 7, and *Be'er ha-Golah*, *ad. loc.*; *TD*, 35. This view is already reproduced anonymously in the *Kol Bo*, 48.

25. Ha-Me'iri, *Bet ha-Beḥirah* on *Abot*, ed. S. Waxman (New York, 1944), 69; see also, Gross, "Aaron ha-Cohen und Sein Ritualwerk Orchot Chayim," *MGWJ*, XVIII (1869), 534; L. Ginzberg, *Perushim we-Ḥiddushim Birushalmi* (New York, 1941), I, 109; S. Lieberman, "Mashehu ^cal Mefarshim Ḳadmonim la-Yerushalmi," *Alexander Marx Jubilee Volume* (New York, 1950), 289 ff.

26. *GJ*, 420. Rabad is one of the most oft-quoted rabbis in the book; see *Orḥot Ḥayyim*, II, ed. Schlesinger (Berlin, 1902), 639.

ha-Me'iri.[27] The latter's historical introduction to his commentary on *Abot* is our main source of information concerning R. Isaac ha-Kohen. R. Isaac composed the first known commentary on the Palestinian Talmud. Ha-Me'iri reports that only fragments of this commentary, which covered the main part of three orders of the Palestinian Talmud, were available in his time. It is small wonder that today the commentary is completely nonextant. Rabad's unremitting attention to the Palestinian Talmud—plus the general Provençal preoccupation with it—was certainly a natural incentive to such a pioneer work by one of his disciples.

A third pupil was R. Meïr b. Isaac, who was brought by his father from Carcassonne to attend Rabad's school.[28] Again, it is ha-Me'iri, a relative of R. Meïr b. Isaac, who imparts to us some very interesting details about this student and his relation to Rabad. After his father had left him at Rabad's school in Posquières, R. Meïr spent the rest of his life in Provence under the influence and tutelage of Rabad, and finally advanced from the status of disciple to become Rabad's colleague and companion in learning. As his full title (R. Meïr b. Isaac of Trinquetaille) indicates, he finally settled in Trinquetaille, a suburb of Arles, which must have been an important intellectual center, for a chronicler referred to "the sages of Trinquetaille."[29] R. Meïr was one of these sages.

It happened once, ha-Me'iri relates at comparatively great length, that R. Meïr and his master did not see eye to eye on a problem concerning a document of divorce made out under compulsion (*geṭ meʿuseh*). In the course of their disagreements, Rabad treated his former pupil very disparagingly. R. Meïr was not presumptuous enough to retaliate in kind, but he did summon enough courage to come to his own defense. He wrote to Rabad as follows: "If he [Rabad] is singled out as unique among the Rabbis, then I, after him, am to be singled out as unique among the students."[30] Sustained by his conviction, R. Meïr pleaded

27. Ha-Me'iri, *Ḥibbur ha-Teshubah*, ed. A. Sofer (New York, 1950), 295; introduction, 13 ff.; *Bet ha-Beḥirah* on *Abot*, 69.

28. *Ibid.*, 67; Isaac de Lattes, *Shaʿare Zion*, ed. S. Buber (Jaroslau, 1885), 72; Carmoly, *La France Israelite* (Francfort s/M, 1858), 88–90—one of the best sketches in this oddly uneven book. H. Gross, "Zur Geschichte der Juden in Arles," *MGWJ*, XXVII (1878), 378–380.

29. David of Estella, *Ḳiryat Sefer*, ed. Neubauer, *Chronicles*, II, 233.

30. Ha-Me'iri, *Bet ha-Behirah* on *Abot*, 69: אם הוא יחיד ברבנים, אני אחריו יחיד בתלמידים.

for an unbiased consideration of the conflicting views which might reveal his opinion as a valid one.

This episode is very enlightening. It underscores Rabad's impregnable confidence and buoyant independence. He would brook no disagreement. It does, however, shed an unfavorable light on Rabad's attitude toward one of his former pupils. The friendship which once reigned is replaced by condescension; the comradeship which pervaded the lecture hall is no more. Somehow, R. Meïr wins sympathy and one feels that his sincere strivings for truth and independent reasoning have been abortively and unfairly rebuffed. Even though Rabad may have been meditating upon the dictum that a pupil may not pronounce on any matter or issue a decision in the presence of his master, he should have recalled that his own teacher welcomed criticism and academic nonconformity.

In common with his master, R. Meïr took up the cudgels for Alfasi against the critique leveled at him by Razah. For this purpose he composed a *Sefer ha-ᶜEzer*—a book of support for Alfasi against his critics. Such literary endeavors constitute an important part of the basically pro-Alfasi orientation of Rabad's school. It is interesting to note that in listing the critics and supporters of Alfasi respectively ha-Me'iri mentions Razah's *Sefer ha-Ma'or*, R. Meïr's *Sefer ha-ᶜEzer*, and Naḥmanides' *Milḥamot* but omits Rabad's hassagot on Razah in defense of Alfasi.[31] Rabad's work apparently did not cover all the ground systematically and presumably ha-Me'iri did not want to classify it with the more comprehensive works of R. Meïr and Naḥmanides. The *Sefer ha-ᶜEzer*, one may therefore conclude, was a systematic and inclusive treatise.

R. Meïr's son R. Nathan, who was also his spiritual heir, considered himself, by heredity or by a vicarious identification with his father's studying, a pupil of Rabad. He did extend Rabad's influence and spread his teachings, for he was the teacher of Naḥmanides and of R. Samuel b. Isaac ha-Sardi, two thirteenth-century Catalonian scholars who were definitely in the orbit of Rabad's influence.[32] Both were important intermediaries in the transmission of Rabad's teachings, for they carried great weight with later codifiers. R. Nathan was also, incidentally, a great-grandfather of Estori Parḥi, who came to study in Trinquetaille, and who cites Nathan frequently in his *Kaftor wa-Feraḥ*.[33]

31. Ha-Me'iri, *Bet ha-Behirah* on Abot, 69.

32. *Ibid.*; Lattes *Shaᶜare Zion*, 72; *GJ*, 247; see also, Assaf in *Sifran*, 53 ff.; *Kiryath Sefer*, XXV (1948–1949), 44.

33. Gross, 401, n. 2. See the latest discussion of this relation in: Estori Parḥi, *Kaftor wa-Feraḥ*, ed. Perlow-Maimon (Jerusalem, 1946), 7.

R. Jonathan b. David ha-Kohen, usually associated with Lunel although he also resided in other cities such as Montpellier, is mentioned by Maimonides' son R. Abraham as a disciple of Rabad.[34] R. Jonathan is one of the pivotal personalities in Provençal life. He was a recognized authority in Talmudic scholarship and very active in communal leadership. In addition to his own contributions to scholarship, he encouraged and stimulated other scholars of note or promise to write and create. Like his predecessor R. Meshullam of Lunel who, in turn, is comparable to Samuel ha-Nagid of Granada, Jonathan was both author and patron, scholar and maecenas.

He was in contact with the Tosafists of northern France and corresponded with R. Isaac b. Abraham of Dampierre, teacher of the abovementioned R. Nathan b. Meïr of Trinquetaille. Before his departure for the Holy Land in 1211, R. Jonathan received from R. Isaac a responsum concerning certain commandments which were operative only in Palestine.[35] He also visited Spain. Whereas Rabad went to Barcelona, R. Jonathan went to Toledo where he studied under R. Meïr, the son of R. Joseph ibn Migas, celebrated scholar about whom Maimonides said, "his penetrating insights in Talmud are awe-inspiring to one who observes his views and his profound intelligence in speculation."[36] R. Meïr was a "great scholar" in his own right, having been the recipient of his father's teachings.[37] In this respect, like R. Abraham b. Nathan ha-Yarḥi, R. Jonathan continues the fusion of French and Spanish Jewish learning in the great Provençal centers. Again, as was the case with ha-Yarḥi, this merger was carried forward not only by means of literary communication but also by direct personal contact.

A sensitive vignette of R. Jonathan from the pen of Jonah b. Solomon ibn Bahalul provides some illuminating data which suggest further analogies between Rabad and R. Jonathan. According to this rhymed

34. *Birkat Abraham*, ed. Goldberg (Lyck, 1859), 60. Mirsky's reservations concerning the teacher-pupil relation, because of the statement in the supplement to the *Sefer ha-Kabbalah*, are not very serious. See S. K. Mirsky, "R. Jonathan mi-Lunel," *Sura* (Jerusalem, 1956), II, 247.

35. Gross, *REJ*, VI, 177; *GJ*, 284; N. Wider, "Sifro ha-Nisraf shel Judah ibn Shabbetai," *Meẓudah*, II (1944), 124 ff., especially bibliographical references, 127; Urbach, *Baᶜale ha-Tosafot*, 221. See also the letter of R. Meïr Abulafia, *Kitab al-Rasail* (Paris, 1871), 15–16.

36. Wider, *Meẓudah*, II, 124. The statement on ibn Migas is from Maimonides' introduction to the Mishnah commentary.

37. Abraham ibn Daud, *Sefer ha-Kabbalah*, ed. Neubauer, *Chronicles*, I, 76, 84. Halpern, *Seder ha-Dorot* (Warsaw, 1876), 149.

description,[38] R. Jonathan led an ascetic life, despising and rejecting luxuries and pleasures. For him bliss was synonymous with scholarly attainments. He was an assiduous student and a dedicated teacher, a persevering writer and stimulating guide. His school was a center of attraction for eager students who came "from the whole earth to hear his wisdom and when they heard they marveled." He was extraordinarily well-versed in Talmud and his familiarity with rabbinic literature was encyclopedic.

In the history of the evolution of Alfasi's influence and the various Spanish-French attitudes toward him, R. Jonathan b. David marks the beginning of a new phase of development.[39] Immediately after its appearance, Alfasi's compendium of law eclipsed all previous works of this sort and was generally acclaimed. He practically dominated the scene in Spain, there being only a few dissonant voices in the harmony of acclaim. Ibn Daud reports that two other Isaacs, R. Isaac ibn Albalia and R. Isaac ibn Ghayyat, were Alfasi's antagonists; but in reality there was not much opposition, especially articulate opposition, to him. It was R. Ephraim, a Spaniard who influenced Provençal learning to such an extent that he is often looked upon as being of Provençal origin, who initiated the sustained criticism in his *Sefer ha-Tashlum*, a succession of supplementary annotations, amplifications, and criticisms of Alfasi.[40] Razah's oft-mentioned *Sefer ha-Ma'or* is the best representative of this stage of unfriendly, even hostile, criticism which evoked, almost dialectically, a reasoned defense of Alfasi—by Rabad, R. Meïr b. Isaac, Naḥmanides. A different phase in the history of Alfasi's book is represented by those works which aimed to bring Alfasi up-to-date and supplement his *Halakot*. This was the objective of R. Judah b. Barzilai's *Sefer ha-ᶜIttim*, Rabi's *ha-Eshkol*, and, later, R. Meshullam b. Moses' *Sefer ha-Hashlamah*. A further step in the defense and dissemination of Alfasi's *Halakot* was taken when scholars began to embellish his text with commentaries, as was being done for the Talmud. This phase was

38. Wider, *Meẓudah*, II, 124. Here are some excerpts: ממרביצי התורה היה תמיד, ותבונתו היתה אמונתו. ובמעדני הזמן בעט, זה שבתו בבית מעט. בתוך מדרשו היה לוחם בדברי חכמים. ומכל הארץ באו לשמועתן, לשמוע חכמתו, ובשמעם נפלאו בעיניהם.

39. The basic facts are found in ibn Daud's *Sefer ha-Kabbalah* and Maimonides' introduction to the *Mishneh Torah*; see Weiss, *Dor Dor we-Doreshaw* (Vilna, 1904), IV, 275 ff.; also Aptowitzer, *Mabo*, 374.

40. There is a basic study of R. Ephraim by Benedict, *Kiryath Sefer*, XXVI (1949–1950), 322–338. Razah, introduction to *Sefer ha-Ma'or*, writes: ומצאתי להרב ר׳ אפרים ז״ל בענין הזה דברים לא מסודרים לא מחוברים כי אם מפורדים ומפוזרים, והמעט הנכון מהם בעינ אספתיו על מקומו.

initiated by R. Jonathan ha-Kohen, whose commentaries on Alfasi's text of *Berakot*, *ᶜErubin*, *Megillah*, *Moᶜed Ḳaṭan*, and *Ḥullin* have been printed while many more are extant in manuscripts.[41] Such endeavors, continued after R. Jonathan ha-Kohen by R. Isaiah of Trani, R. Jonah Gerondi, R. Aaron ha-Levi of Barcelona, R. Nissim b. Reuben Gerondi, and R. Joseph Ḥabib, were a decisive step in transforming "the Alfas," as his work is known, into a "miniature Talmud."[42]

This, however, is not tantamount to total acceptance of Alfasi. Operating within a theoretical framework which was overtly favorable to Alfasi, R. Jonathan nevertheless exercised his critical faculties. In common with his teacher and friend, Rabad, R. Jonathan sometimes modified or dissented from certain views of Alfasi.[43]

Still another significant point of contact between Rabad and R. Jonathan is the latter's conception of the nature of Mishnah commentary and his actual contributions to this literary genre. In his commentary on Alfasi's text of *Ketubot*, R. Jonathan prefaces each chapter with an explanation of all the Mishnah selections. This is a self-contained commentary and does not refer the reader to the Talmudic discussion for the conclusions concerning the interpretation of the Mishnah, as does Rashi. Assaf, who first noted the manuscript of this commentary, conjectures that Jonathan might have intended this to serve a dual purpose; a commentary on the Mishnah as well as on Alfasi. As a matter of fact, Jonathan sometimes refers back to what has been explained "in the commentary on the Mishnah."[44] The legacy of Rabad and his commentatorial activities is discernible here, even though it should be noted that in one respect R. Jonathan employs a technique different from that of Rabad. He actually incorporates the Talmudic discussion into the warp and woof of his commentary.

41. J. H. Michael, *Or ha-Ḥayyim* (Frankfurt a.M., 1891), 472; A. Freimann, "Ḳuntres ha-Mefaresh ha-Shalem," *L. Ginzberg Jubilee Volume*, 324 ff.; *Kiryath Sefer*, I, (1924), 61. S. K. Mirsky edited the commentary on *Megillah* and *Moᶜed Ḳaṭan* (Jerusalem, Sura, 1956); see M. ha-Kohen, "Beshule Perush R. Jonathan," *Sinai*, XX (1957), 408–413. The commentary on *Berakot* is printed in the new Talmud edition (Jerusalem, 1959). Fragments of the *Sukkah* commentary were printed in *ha-Me'assef*, IV (1899), 13b ff.; 155a ff.

42. See Steinschneider, *Jewish Literature* (London, 1857), 62. The phrase "miniature Talmud" is used by R. Menaḥem b. Zeraḥ, *Ẓedah la-Derek* (Warsaw, 1880), 6: וחבר הלכות בקוצר תלתא סדרי, ודומה לגמ׳ זעירא. See also Isaac Israeli, *Yesod ᶜOlam*, II, 34b: ויצא טבעו . . . בהלכות כמו תלמוד קטן שחבר.

43. *Commentary of R. Jonathan, Alfasi, ᶜErubin*, 1b, 2b, 4b, and others; commentary on *Megillah* and *Moᶜed Ḳaṭan*, ed. S. K. Mirsky, 49.

44. S. Assaf, "R. Jonathan ha-Kohen of Lunel," *Tarbiẓ*, III (1932), 27–32. See commentary on *ᶜErubin*, 16b, 19a, where Jonathan says מפורש בפירוש המשנה; also *Berakot*, 20a.

Jonathan's admiration for Maimonides and his defense of Maimonides' philosophic doctrines are commonplaces.[45] He was instrumental in securing a copy of the *Moreh Nebukim* for southern France and in expediting its translation by R. Samuel ibn Tibbon. He represented a group of Provençal scholars in writing to Maimonides about the *Mishneh Torah*. Maimonides reciprocated this fervent attachment by writing to R. Jonathan and praising him unstintedly.[46] Some chronicles report that R. Jonathan answered the criticisms leveled by Rabad against Maimonides, "to explain and corroborate the words of Maimonides."[47] While there is no need to look for the roots of this Maimunist orientation in the attitudes of his teacher Rabad—I have not attempted to trace all salient characteristics of Rabad's disciples back to him, but merely to point out influences and similarities—it is likewise superfluous to view this as antithetical to Rabad, as an implicit protest against Rabad's anti-Maimunism. Rabad's stand on the question of secular culture and extraphilosophic learning, first of all, was not negativistic.[48] Secondly, his halakic critique of the *Mishneh Torah* was intended to stimulate study and revision. He might occasionally have resented criticism and dissent of which he was the butt, but theoretically he was committed to a dynamic, polemical conception of Talmudic study.[49]

The scanty literary remains of yet another pupil of Rabad, R. Meïr b. Baruch, consist of three scholastic communications addressed to Abraham Maimonides, concerning the elucidation of abstruse passages in Tractate *Shabbat*. The answers to these questions are not responsa, properly speaking, but part of a learned correspondence—one of the extensions of the abbreviated form of early responsa. Although the manuscript of these responsa is defective in a crucial place, their editor thought it safe to assume from the context that Meïr is speaking of his

45. It is certainly a case of "misplaced concreteness" to call Jonathan a "French philosopher," as does the *JE*. He was first and foremost a Talmudist.

46. The correspondence was edited by A. Freimann, *Teshubot ha-Rambam* (Jerusalem, 1934), LII–LXI.

47. David of Estella, *Ḳiryat Sefer*, Neubauer, *Chronicles*, II, 232: והשיג על ההשגות שהשיג הראב״ד על דברי הר״ם, לבאר ולהעמיד דברי הר״ם. Note the significant remark of R. David b. Judah Meser Leon, *Kebod Ḥakamin*, ed. S. Bernfeld (Berlin, 1899), 120: כי שאלתיה לכמה חכמים ולא ידעו ולא הבינו, גם אין כאן לא מגיד משנה ולא מגדל עוז, ולא רבינו יהונתן הרגילים להשיג על ההשגות... Also, Jonah ibn Bahalal, who writes: גם הבין עניני ספרי משנה תורה ועקריהם, ובא עד קצי סודותיהם שמאסו בהם אשר אין מוח בראשיהם. והיה מפתח פתוחם כאלו הולידם והצמיחם. Wider, *Meẓudah*, II, 124.

48. See Chapter VI.

49. This is attested by his introductions to the hassagot on Alfasi and Maimonides and the *Dibre ha-Ribot*, ed. B. Drachman (New York, 1907), 30; see Chapter I.

teacher Rabad. Abraham Maimonides praises his correspondent effusively—perhaps he called to mind that this was the same Meïr mentioned laudably by his father in the well-known letter to Samuel ibn Tibbon. In answering Meïr, R. Abraham also mentions Rabad and employs his explanations (presumably from Rabad's commentary on *Shabbat*).[50]

2. *Contemporary Followers and Correspondents*

In addition to these formal disciples who received all or part of their training at the hands of Rabad, there are a number of younger contemporaries who were indebted to him. They learned about his teachings indirectly, had occasional discussions with him, perused his writings, or were his correspondents. One of these is R. Asher b. Saul of Lunel, author of a study in religious customs (*Sefer ha-Minhagot*) similar in character to that of R. Abraham b. Nathan but restricted to Provençal customs.[1] This R. Asher is presumably identical with the one for whom Rabad composed the treatise dealing with those commandments currently valid in Palestine. It is necessary to avoid confusing him with his namesake and fellow-inhabitant of Lunel, R. Asher b. Meshullam, especially since the two had many traits and interests in common.[2] Asher mentions Rabad four times in the *Sefer ha-Minhagot* but not once does he dub him "teacher." He must have been in personal contact with Rabad for he transmits teachings which he heard orally from Rabad. The several quotations from the *Sefer Yeẓirah* are of conspicuous interest and reveal the author as displaying a decided inclination to mysticism. His homilies on certain portions of the liturgy (e.g., *Ḳedushah*) are characterized by "very obvious Kabbalistic terminology." Also, pietistic overtones discernible in his writings bring to mind the pietistic asides of the *Baᶜale ha-Nefesh*. His brother, whom he mentions reverently in his writings, was R. Jacob ha-Nazir, a prominent personality in the development of Provençal mysticism.[3]

One of Rabad's constant correspondents was Aaron, the fourth son of R. Meshullam b. Jacob of Lunel. The allegiance and gratitude which

50. The questions and answers were preserved and printed in the collected responsa of Abraham Maimonides, ed. A. Freiman and S. Goitein (Jerusalem, 1937), 1–12. See 1, n. 2 for bibliography on R. Meïr.

1. *Sifran*, 123–182. See S. Schechter, *JQR* (Old Series), V (1893), 182 ff.

2. Assaf in *Sifran*, 123.

3. Scholem, *Reshit ha-Kabbalah*, 72; on Jacob ha-Nazir, see *Sifran*, 124; Scholem, "Mi-Ḥoker Limeḳubbal," *Tarbiẓ*, VI (1935), 96.

Rabad felt toward his master devolved into a close friendship between him and R. Meshullam's sons. R. Asher b. Meshullam, an ascetic with mystical inclinations who was concerned primarily with problems of ethics, must certainly have been in contact with Rabad, whose piety and learning were known far and wide.[4] Rabad mentions R. Aaron as the "trusty and distinguished scholar" and refers the recipient of one of his responsa to a series of letters that he wrote to R. Aaron.[5] Aaron later excelled in the zealous defense of Maimonides' doctrine of resurrection. He rebuffed R. Meïr ha-Levi Abulafia who had sent an indictment of Maimonides to the scholars of Lunel in the expectation that they would rally to his side. R. Aaron frustrated Abulafia's enthusiastic anticipation. He was an expert on calendrical questions, for Judah ibn Tibbon refers his son Samuel to Aaron on all matters pertaining to the calendar.[6] Rabad made light of Maimonides' calendrical knowledge and astronomical learning displayed in the *Mishneh Torah* in the section on the calendar and the proclamation of the new moon.[7]

Aaron's brother-in-law, R. Moses b. Judah, was a second correspondent of Rabad.[8] He was a pupil of Rabad's father-in-law.[9] His father is probably the "great sage" mentioned by Rabi in one of his responsa,[10] while his son R. Meshullam is the author of the *Sefer ha-Hashlamah*, belonging to the genre of supplements to Alfasi.[11] Reference has already been made to his extremely flattering remarks about Rabad and his school at Nîmes, which was in his eyes like the Chamber of Hewn Stones (*Lishkat ha-Gazit*) where the *Sanhedrin* convened. One might speculate whether his boundless admiration for Rabad was in any way conditioned by his controversy with Razah.[12] Even though R. Meshul-

4. *Itinerary*, 3; *TD*, 120; Scholem, *Reshit ha-Kabbalah*, 88. R. Asher urged R. Judah ibn Tibbon to translate the *Tikkun Middot ha-Nefesh* of Gabirol; see also Assaf, *Misifrut ha-Geonim*, 17–31; Rabad and R. Asher are often mentioned together.

5. *TD*, 9.

6. Judah ibn Tibbon's Will, ed. Israel Abrahams, *Hebrew Ethical Wills* (Philadelphia, 1948), 65, 78.

7. *MT*, *Ḳiddush ha-Ḥodesh*, VII, 7, discussed in Chapter VI.

8. *TD*, 7.

9. *Ha-Eshkol*, ed. Albeck, 10. See also Isaac de Lattes, *Shaʿare Zion*, 40–41.

10. *Sifran*, 32.

11. The *Sefer ha-Hashlamah* on *Berakot* was edited by H. Brody (Berlin, 1893), on *Seder Neziḳin* by I. Lubozky (Paris, 1885), and on *Taʿanit and Megillah* by M. Grossberg (Mainz, 1888). A fragment on *Yebamot* was identified by I. Lubozky, *Bidḳe Batim* (Paris, 1896), 1–5. In theory at least, the *Sefer ha-Hashlamah* was a critical supplement to Alfasi, partly approbatory and partly negative: פעם לחזק דבריו ופעם לתמוה עליהם. This is similar to Razah's alleged purpose: דורש ושואל וחוקר ומאיר ומעורר, פעם סומך ועוזר ופעם כמשיב ושובר.

12. Note his son's introduction, ed. Lubozky, *Sefer ha-Hashlamah, Neziḳin*.

lam shares the widespread admiration for Rabad, undoubtedly inherited from his father, he does not hesitate to reject Rabad's views occasionally and to dismiss them as incomprehensible or remarkably strange.[13] R. Meshullam later gave his blessings to R. Meïr b. Simeon of Narbonne, who was conducting an intensive ideological campaign against the new, and in his opinion unfounded, Kabbalah.[14]

Still another correspondent of Rabad was R. Shelemya, about whom almost nothing is known. He is mentioned in the *Sefer ha-Kabbalah* of Abraham ibn Daud and in the *Itinerary* of Benjamin of Tudela.[15] He was obviously from Lunel (even though Benjamin of Tudela counts him among the scholars of Montpellier) and an intimate member of R. Meshullam's circle, for he saw Rabad's letter to R. Moses b. Judah. Moreover, Rabad assumes that he would be in a position to study the letter which he sent to R. Aaron b. Meshullam. R. Shelemya, apparently, was no mean scholar. His writing displays knowledge of the Talmudic text as well as acquaintance with its foremost commentaries. He quotes Rashi and indicates that R. Abraham (Rabi, undoubtedly) subscribed to the same view. Rabad is most cordial in his rejoinder and attentively follows the comments of his correspondent: "What you said seems good and correct and it requires further study."[16]

The identity of R. Judah b. Abraham, the recipient of several responsa in *Temim Deᶜim*, is enigmatic.[17] Rabad praises him effusively and expresses the wish that "may your like multiply in Israel." Gross believes this Judah to be an uncle of Rabad who resided in Nîmes.[18] If this identification is correct, this passage would provide additional allusions to Rabad's grandfather and his family in general. It would present Rabad as acutely conscious of the greatness and dignity which inheres in his genealogical tree. The tone and language of the letter, however, seem to militate against Gross's identification.

13. *Sefer ha-Hashlamah*, *Berakot*, 16: דבריו אינן נראין כלל ודברי תימה הן. *Kesef Mishneh*, *MT*, *Ḥameẓ u-Maẓah*, IV, 4: וכתב בעל ההשלמה אין טעם להשגה זו ...

14. Neubauer, *JQR* (Old Series), IV (1892), 358; Scholem, "Teᶜudah Ḥadashah le-Toledot Reshit ha-Kabbalah," *Sefer Bialik* (Tel Aviv, 1934), 147.

15. Albeck, *ha-Eshkol*, 12, and literature cited there; *GJ*, 280. The kabbalist Moses of Burgos also mentions a certain Shelemya, whom Scholem conjecturally identifies with our Shelemya. He is also mentioned in the novellae of R. Yom Ṭob b. Abraham. See Scholem, "Kabbalot R. Jacob we-R. Isaac," *Madaᶜe ha-Yahadut* (Jerusalem, 1927), II, 191; see also *Sefer ha-Miktam* on *Sukkah*, 26b, 37b.

16. *TD*, 8.

17. *TD*, 11–13.

18. *GJ*, 398. Gross bases this identification upon a text, printed in *Letterbode* II, 182, which reads: תשובות של הראב״ד שהשיב להרב ר׳ יהודה מנמשי ז״ל דודו. It concludes: שהשיב לר׳ יהודה בר׳ אברהם.

This Judah may have been the son of Abraham b. Meïr, a close friend of Rabad. In a different collection, *Baᶜale Asufot,* these responsa are addressed not to R. Judah b. Abraham, but to R. Abraham b. Meïr.[19] This identification would explain the graceful cordiality and unusual politeness with which Rabad writes. Rabad's optative statement that R. Judah would be able to join his Yeshivah also becomes intelligible. Moreover, the salutation "my friend" and an incidental reference to "my grandfather" in the middle of the letter are somewhat incongruous when addressed to an uncle, but most proper when the recipient is an intimate friend.

3. *Descendants*

Rabad's immediate family, children and grandchildren, constitute a sphere where one would expect Rabad's influence to exceed in pervasiveness not only that exerted upon correspondents, younger colleagues, and casual professional acquaintances but even the weightier, formative influence exerted upon receptive students over a period of many years. On the basis of literary remains and historical references, it can be asserted that Rabad's relation with his two sons was not exclusively paternal. There were strong intellectual bonds and deep spiritual affinities between them. One can assume that Rabad imparted to his children both his devotion to and knowledge of halakic learning and rabbinic literature; all his students were exposed to this influence. In addition, it is reported that he transmitted to his children esoteric kabbalistic teachings which he cherished greatly and which he would not disseminate indiscriminately. They were among the select few—or perhaps even the only ones—in whom he confided and through whom he channeled the flow of mystical lore. It is possible, with greater ease than in the case of his pupils, to discern concrete influences of Rabad on his immediate descendants.

Very little can be said about his older son, R. David. His very existence was unknown for many centuries. Even now that his existence is historically ascertained,[1] knowledge of him is minimal. His memory was perpetuated by his son R. Asher, who speaks of him as a saintly and learned person.[2] R. Asher, a key figure in early mystical literature,

19. *Ha-Maggid,* XII (1868), 397.

1. *Oẓar Neḥmad,* IV (1864), 37; see Steinschneider, *ZfhB,* VII, 68. See the comments of Ḥasidah in *ha-Segullah* I (1934), *ᶜAdi me-Har Ḥoreb,* 1–2.

2. *Oẓar Neḥmad,* IV, 38.

quotes him occasionally in his writings and in this manner preserves rather lengthy excerpts from his works.[3] The only other reference to R. David b. Abraham is where his younger brother R. Isaac speaks of him as "my master, my brother, the sage R. David of blessed memory."[4]

Rabad's second son, R. Isaac the Blind, or as he is sometimes called, R. Isaac of Posquières, is a more distinct and colorful personality. Both uncritical medieval mystics and modern historical investigators agree in designating R. Isaac the Blind as the "father of the Kabbalah."[5] He composed a commentary on the *Sefer Yeẓirah*, in which he helped systematize the intricate kabbalistic symbolism concerning prayer and described with considerable definitiveness the interrelations between the ten divine spheres. Prayer was of fundamental importance to Provençal mystics; R. Isaac was one of the leading expounders and theoreticians of this profound mystique of prayer.[6] More significant historically than his literary contributions to the development of mysticism is the fact that R. Isaac seems to have been the acknowledged leader of the close-knit community of Provençal and Catalonian mystics. He was at the helm while the Kabbalah was going through its formative stages. R. Isaac's unofficial supremacy emerges clearly from a most revealing letter which he sent to no lesser scholars than R. Jonah Gerondi and Naḥmanides, the foremost Talmudic authorities in Spain, who were also devotees of the Kabbalah. They turn to R. Isaac for counsel and instruction; he guides them, even admonishes them, and indicates the proper methods of study and writing.[7] Moreover, the unqualified appellation "the pious" (ḥasid), generally appended to his name, attests to the esteem and veneration of subsequent generations for this dominating personality.[8]

R. Isaac was the main recipient of his father's mystical teachings, to which he unswervingly adhered. His father's precedents and methods were his guides in all matters; his father's memory was revered by him. Thus, when rebuking his correspondents for allowing the uninitiated to come in contact with mystical doctrines and also for not being sufficiently cautious in their use of mystical terminology which, by virtue of its picturesque vividness and disarming simplicity, can easily be

3. *Oẓar Neḥmad*, IV, 38.
4. Scholem, "Teᶜudah Ḥadashah," *Sefer Bialik*, 144.
5. *Ibid., passim; Reshit ha-Kabbalah*, 99–126. *GJ*, 450.
6. Scholem, *Reshit ha-Kabbalah*, 103.
7. Scholem, "Teᶜudah Ḥadashah," 143
8. *Reshit ha-Kabbalah*, 102.

misconstrued, he appeals to family precedent: "My ancestors were aristocrats of the land and disseminators of Torah among the people, and not a word [about mysticism] escaped their mouths. They treated the bulk of the people like those who are not expert in wisdom."[9] When he mentions his father by name, he devoutly appends the encomiastic phrase "may the memory of the holy be for a blessing."[10] Furthermore, he reports many doctrines in the name of his father—a fact which accords with the later kabbalistic tradition that Rabad transmitted his mystical teachings to his son. R. Shem Ṭob ibn Gaon, a pupil of Rashbah, writes that "in his Talmudic commentaries Rabad merely alluded to bits of the Kabbalah when he deemed it necessary and no more, for he was satisfied with his son the Rabbi who is known for [his proficiency in] this wisdom which he received from his father."[11] Here is a possible explanation of the strange fact that Rabad, to whom later mystics attributed so many novel doctrines and seminal insights, left no works on Kabbalah.

One basic contrast between father and son deserves comment. Rabad was essentially a "man of halakah." In spite of all the later references to his preeminence in Kabbalah and his adeptness in deducing and interpreting mystical symbols and teachings, halakah was his primary preoccupation. He devoted no special work to mysticism, although it was apparently close to his heart, while philosophy, of which he was not ignorant, remained on the fringe of his writings.[12] He wrote, taught, and "lived" halakah and visibly influenced the course of rabbinic literature. R. Isaac was a "man of Kabbalah." Evidence of halakic knowledge is indirect and inferential. All his writings are on mystical themes, or else all themes are treated in a mystical vein. Despite the fact that he repeatedly counseled restraint in the dissemination of mysticism, he wrote prolifically. His writings were purposely obscure and puzzling and some of his symbols incomprehensible—this was in keeping with the subject's esoteric nature which he wanted to preserve—but the fact remains that he contributed greatly to the development and systematization of speculative mysticism.[13] As far as is known, R. Isaac had no

9. "Teᶜudah," 143: כי אבותי היו אצילי הארץ ומרביצי תורה ברבים, ולא יצא דבר מפיהם ומתנהגים עמהם כאשר בני אדם שאין בקיאין בחכמה.

10. *Ibid.*, 144.

11. Quoted *ibid.*, 152.

12. See Chapter VI. The commentary on *Sefer Yeẓirah*, as has been pointed out by many, is not by Rabad. See the latest discussion by G. Scholem, "Ha-Meḥaber ha-Amiti shel Perush Sefer Yeẓirah," *Peraḳim le-Toledot Sifrut ha-Kabbalah* (Jerusalem, 1931), 2–17.

13. *Reshit ha-Kabbalah*, 122.

children and perhaps he felt that, whereas his father was able to perpetuate this esoteric corpus of kabbalistic knowledge by transmitting it to him orally, he had no choice but to commit it to writing. He had many important pupils—R. Ezra of Gerona, to note only one of the most famous[14]—but no direct heir who could receive the tradition in its totality. His activity constitutes, thus, a most important nexus in the development of Kabbalah.

If R. David is for the most part a *homo absconditus*, his son R. Asher is somewhat better known. R. Asher undoubtedly was still influenced by his grandfather and he mentions his father's great learning with fitting reverence, but he derived most from his uncle R. Isaac. From a statement of R. Isaac we infer that he and R. Asher were always very close to each other. R. Isaac even says that they grew up together. Asher thus had the opportunity to observe his uncle's ways and learn directly the proper traditions concerning the study and teaching of Kabbalah.[15] He wrote freely and with ability. In addition, he assisted his uncle in guiding the movement. He traveled to Spain—to the great center in Gerona—where he advised the local mystics about various matters. His writings, as Professor Scholem observed, were clear and straightforward, for they were intended to serve a practical purpose: to elucidate concepts which had been misconstrued and distorted. The lucidity of his writings by no means indicates that he favored the popularization of kabbalistic lore; it was instead a reaction to the indiscriminate use of symbols by many upstart mystics. Like his grandfather and uncle, he opposed this popularization and aspired to eliminate misunderstanding by revealing the true meaning of the new controversial theosophic doctrines. He deplored the publicizing of these secrets and censured the mystics responsible. Like his uncle, he appeals to the prestige and example of Rabad. After complaining about the situation and emphasizing the need for caution, he concludes: "Therefore have I spoken at great length . . . to make known publicly the opinion of our ancestors [Rabad] who taught us the ways of life, the paths of God."[16]

14. *Reshit ha-Kabbalah*, 128; see also I. Tishbi, ed., *Perush ha-Aggadot le-R. ᶜAzriel* (Jerusalem, 1945); *idem*, "R. Ezra we-R. ᶜAzriel," *Zion*, IX (1944), 178–185; G. Scholem, "Seridim Ḥadashim Mikitbe R. ᶜAzriel," *Sefer Zikkaron le-Asher Gulak* (Jerusalem, 1942), 201–222.

15. "Teᶜudah," 144.

16. *Ibid.*, 151. See R. Todros b. Joseph Abulafia, *Oẓar ha-Kabod* (Novyvdor, 1808), 35a: . . . כבר חיבר ספר גדול בביאורים ע״ד הקבלה החכם רבינו אשר בן החכם רבינו אברהם בר׳ דוד ז״ל והוא ז״ל הרמוז (הרמיז) בלשונו הקדוש ובחכמתו הגדולה הרמזים דקים עמקים מאד, ובדברים מעטים, ולא יבינם אך המשכילים המקובלים.

VI. RELATION TO PHILOSOPHY AND KABBALAH

During the last decades of Rabad's life, Provence was the scene of great intellectual fermentation. A piecemeal accumulation of secular Hebrew writings—the philosophical, ethical, and scientific works of Abraham bar Ḥiyya and Abraham ibn Ezra; several commentaries on the *Sefer Yeẓirah* by Shabbetai Donnolo, Saadia Gaon, and Judah b. Barzilai; the philosophic poems of Solomon ibn Gabirol and Baḥya ibn Pakuda—was significantly augmented by the systematic translations of Judah ibn Tibbon and Joseph Kimḥi: the *Tiḳḳun Middot ha-Nefesh* and *Mibḥar ha-Peninim* of ibn Gabirol, the *Ḥobot ha-Lebabot* of Baḥya ibn Pakuda, the *Cuzari* of Judah ha-Levi, and the *Emunot we-Deᶜot* of Saadia Gaon. Berechiah ha-Naḳdan, fabulist and popularizer who had epitomized the *Emunot we-Deᶜot* on the basis of earlier translations, paraphrased the *Quaestiones Naturales* of Adelard of Bath;[1] Abraham ben Ḥisdai translated Algazali's ethical treatise *Mozene Ẓedeḳ*;[2] Judah Alḥarizi provided a Hebrew translation of Ḥonein ben Isḥak's *Musre ha-Pilosofim*.[3] Thus, toward the end of the twelfth century, a dedicated Provençal student, although a monolinguist, could amass a definite measure of knowledge concerning philosophy—something which, all its lingering limitations notwithstanding, was novel and previously inconceivable.

An undercurrent of mystical speculation, meandering leisurely,

1. Entitled *Dodi we-Nechdi*, ed. H. Gollancz (London, 1920).

2. Ed. Goldenthal, 1839. Haberman and Gutstein maintain that this translation is one of Abraham ben Ḥisdai's earliest, preceding that of *Ben ha-Melek weha-Nazir*; see M. Gutstein, "Midarke ha-Targum," *Gotthold Weil Jubilee Volume* (Jerusalem, 1952), 75, n. 6.

3. Ed. A. Lowenthal (Frankfurt a.M., 1876); see M. Steinschneider, *Die Hebrae--schen Uebersetzungen des Mittelalters* (Berlin, 1893), 350.

sometimes barely trickling, for several centuries, began to swell its course at about the same time. Some of the oldest known kabbalistic texts (the *Sefer ha-Bahir* and an assortment of pseudepigraphic pieces) were redacted or first circulated and the earliest devotees of the new doctrines organized themselves in Provence at this time. Many of the translated philosophic works were capable of stimulating mystical speculation as well as philosophical thought. Saadia, Gabirol, Baḥya, and Halevi are not only central figures in the history of Jewish philosophy but heroes of mysticism as well.[4] Furthermore, "there was the growing influence of Abraham ibn Ezra and Abraham bar Ḥiyya through which neo-Platonic thought, including some of purely mystical character," was disseminated,[5] while the endemic preoccupation of Provençal scholars with midrashic literature also nourished the roots of mystical speculation.[6]

The centers of rabbinic learning in southern France were thus providing a home for a transplanted philosophic literature and an indigenous mystical literature, both of which came to flourish in these regions. This chapter aims to determine Rabad's relation to these two developments of intellectual history in their incipient stages.

4. See, for example, Malter, *Saadia Gaon*, 286, 362; Scholem, "Iḳbotaw shel Gabirol ba-Kabbalah," *Me'assef Sofre Ereẓ Yisrael*, ed. A. Kabak and A. Steinman (Tel Aviv, 1940), 160–178; *idem.*, *Reshit ha-Kabbalah*, 82; I. Efros, "Some Aspects of Yehudah Halevi's Mysticism," *PAAJR*, XI (1941), 27–42. See also, A. Altmann, "Ba ʿayot be-Meḥḳar ha-Neo Aplatoniyut ha-Yehudit," *Tarbiẓ*, XXVII (1958), 501–507.

5. Scholem says this about the German Ḥasidim but it applies also to the Provençal kabbalists; see *Major Trends in Jewish Mysticism*, 86; *Reshit ha-Kabbalah*, 85; "Reste neuplatonischer Spekulation bei den Deutschen Chassidim," *MGWJ*, LXXV (1931), 172–191.

6. Provençal midrashim had special affinity with kabbalistic speculation. *Midrash Bereshit Rabbati*, ed. Albeck (Jerusalem, 1940), quotes the *Sefer Yeẓirah* and the *Otiyyot de-R. Akiba*; see 21, 28, 46. In common with *Numbers Rabbah* and *Midrash Tadshe*, it contains a number of overtly mystical themes and traits; e.g., speculation on Metatron, angelological themes in general, numerological plays, exaggerated use of *Gematria*, rudiments of a mystical anthropology. *Midrash Tadshe* is most noticeably distinguished by its novel interpretation of miracles as symbolic of creation in general, its treatment of some numbers (especially seven and ten) as "holy," inherently meaningful entities, its three-fold division of the soul into *nefesh*, *ruaḥ*, and *neshamah*, and, above all, its intricate, recurrent symbolism of the universe, the Tabernacle, and man as three parallel worlds. See *Midrash Bereshit Rabbati*, 29, 41, and others; A. Epstein, "Le Livre des Jubilés: Philon et le Midrasch Tadsche," *REJ*, XXI (1890), 80–97; XXII (1891), 1–25 (reprinted in *Miḳadmoniyot ha-Yehudim*); especially, S. Belkin, "Midrash Tadshe . . . Midrash Hellenisti Ḳadmon," *Ḥoreb*, XI (1951), 1–52.

There is, besides, a general affinity—in thought content, in exegetical method, in preoccupation with certain abstruse topics, and repeated use of symbols—between aggadic and kabbalistic literature. This is articulated in the aggadic commentaries of R. Ezra and R. Azriel of Gerona; see I. Tishbi, "Aggadah we-Kabbalah be-Perushe ha-Aggadot . . .," *Minḥah li-Yehudah*, ed. S. Assaf (Jerusalem, 1950), 170–174; also G. Scholem, *Major Trends in Jewish Mysticism*, 31.

1. Attitude Toward Secular Learning

A Talmudist, a "man of one preoccupation" to which everything else was decidedly peripheral, Rabad composed no philosophic opus or even minor philosophic essays. Actually, inasmuch as the new philosophic learning was just beginning to take root in Provence, one would not expect Rabad—or anyone else of his time—to issue an integrated exposition of his beliefs and opinions, nor is there reason to expect any pervasive influence of this new literature on his writings. The *Baᶜale ha-Nefesh*, which is most revelatory—in its own discursive and allusive manner—of his theological and ethical views, was written almost simultaneously with the first Tibbonite translations from the Arabic. In his later commentaries, the one on *Baba Ḳamma*, for instance, which was written after 1171 and especially in the various hassagot, which followed the translations, Rabad had little occasion to express himself philosophically and a sense of literary discipline made him shun digressions from his predetermined subject. In the introduction to his *Sifra* commentary he sidestepped a theoretical digression on the indispensability of tradition in order to devote himself to the immediate task of textual exegesis. Even the aggadic portions of those Talmudic tractates which he commented upon evoked few philosophical homilies or kabbalistic allegories. It is almost as if the sparse theoretical material found in his writings crept in surreptitiously and in moments of "weakness" or submission. Even the *Shaᶜar ha-Ḳedushah* is smuggled in somewhat apologetically as a supplement to the five practical chapters of the *Baᶜale ha-Nefesh*. One gets the impression that he was qualified to sit back and theorize—would have enjoyed it—but compelled himself to devote his energies to other, rigidly circumscribed tasks.

However, Rabad did have at his disposal some Hebrew philosophic works. The atmosphere was generally congenial to this learning, especially in the circle of Meshullam. Rabad's personal associations must also have been conducive to acquaintance with this new learning. He was apparently a respected consultant of Judah ibn Tibbon, and it was his insistent urging which led the latter to complete his translation of the *Ḥobot ha-Lebabot*. R. Menaḥem b. Simeon of Posquières, outstanding disciple of Joseph Kimḥi, was his comrade. R. Aaron b. Meshullam of Lunel, recognized expert on astronomy, was one of his regular correspondents. Such personal contacts would see to it that the new literature was channeled in his direction.[7] If, then, there is no reason to expect that this literature played a decisive role in molding Rabad's thinking and terminology, traces of or veiled allusions to this learning and its technical jargon should presumably be discovered in his writings.

In light of this one must turn to the problem of Rabad's ideological attitude toward philosophy and secular sciences in general. A number of writers—starting with Geiger and Zunz and followed by Gross and Atlas[8]—have drawn an impressionistic portrait of Rabad as completely impervious to the humming activity which then enveloped nonhalakic learning. They depict Rabad not only as choosing to remain ignorant of the entire literature which was then circulating in Provence but also as frowning upon its use and denigrating its value. The pigments for their painting are mixed from the following ingredients: they failed to find any immediately explicit references to such learning in Rabad's writing, while there are certain apparently clear statements by Rabad which bear out their contention. Two passages in particular, in which he speaks of his scholastic inferiority and intellectual backwardness and concedes his remoteness from astronomical knowledge are usually adduced in support of this view. In addition, these scholars conventionally assume that Rabad's criticism of several Maimonidean opinions which reflect philosophic thought is a sign of his opposition to philosophy which was embodied in or symbolized by Maimonides. The following is a representative summary of this common view:

> Although all branches of scholarship flourished in Provence, he confined himself to Talmudic studies only; and herein lies his weakness as well as his strength. Rabad himself was aware of his inadequate training, and deplored his shortcomings in other branches of scholarship.[9]

Against this extreme view, a different school of thought indicated that he was acquainted somewhat with philosophic literature and showed a benevolent attitude toward it. Already Steinschneider, who speaks of Rabad in one place as "the learned but mystic and not very scientific" scholar, comments elsewhere in a terse, elliptical style characteristic of

7. The London manuscript of the *Sefer ha-Miktam* edited by Grosberg (introduction, XIV) indicates that Abraham ibn Ezra turned to Rabad for an halakic decision; cf., however, Marx, *ha-Ẓofeh*, II, 58, and *Sefer ha-Miktam*, ed. Sofer, 350.

8. Zunz, "Abraham b. David," *Wissenschaftliche Zeitschrift für judische Theologie*, V (1839), 309; Geiger, *ibid.*, 558; Gross, 402; Atlas, Rabad, *BK*, 20.

9. *Ibid.*, English introduction, XIII; J. Sarachek, *Faith and Reason* (Williamsport, 1935), 66 ff. concludes that Rabad defied all secular learning; see also *Dibre ha-Ribot*, ed. Drachman (New York, 1907), VIII.

Rabad himself that "his style is short and abrupt, and his views are, after all, not far removed from those whose exclusive authority he condemns."[10] Louis Ginzberg stresses that not only was Rabad not an enemy of secular study but he himself was familiar with the new literature and sometimes quoted it.[11] Displaying considerable insight but lacking documentation is the parenthetical opinion of Benedict:

> Even Rabad, the typical halakist, who sometimes emphasizes the fact that he did not occupy himself with sciences, was not so distant from the speculative literature as some think—and this is not the place to elaborate.[12]

Also Reifmann, who states that Rabad completely ignored secular sciences, observes—again, with a metaphorical brevity reminiscent of Rabad—that "secretly he yearned for their love."[13] In the early fifteenth century, the rabbi of Oran, North Africa, who was especially interested in philosophy and Kabbalah and corresponded with his more important contemporary R. Isaac b. Sheshet (Ribash) concerning such problems, comments on Rabad's relation to secular sciences: "He was not well-known in nor did he boast about and let himself be attracted to secular sciences. Yet, it appears that their views are close."[14] Similarly, the philosopher Joseph Solomon del Medigo alludes to Rabad's familiarity with secular learning.[15]

In analyzing this problem, Rabad's stand cannot be assumed a priori to have been negative and reactionary by virtue of the fact that he dared criticize several philosophical-theological views of Maimonides, the supreme exponent of rationalism and Aristotelianism in the Middle Ages. Rabad's hassagot on Maimonides' *Sefer ha-Madda* must be considered in historical context and compared to similar views maintained by predecessors and successors. The divergent opinions should be treated as legitimate issues of controversy, just as so many of his halakic strictures on Maimonides must be viewed historically, as links in the historical development of certain juridical views. His acute animad-

10. Steinschneider, *Jewish Literature* (London, 1851), 87.

11. *JE*, I, 116; see A. Marx, "Bemerkungen," *Zeitschrift für Hebraeische Bibliographie*, X (1906), 95.

12. Benedict, 101, n. 155.

13. Reifmann, *ha-Maggid*, XII (1862), 382.

14. *Responsa of Isaac b. Sheshet*, 118; see Hershman, *Rabbi Isaac Perfet and His Times* (New York, 1943), 173.

15. *Nobelot Ḥokmah* (Basle, 1635), p. 5 of the unnumbered introduction והאריך שם הרב ... כי איש חמודות היה וכל יקר ראתה עינו בתורה ובקבלה ותכונה ופלוסופיא. See also *Maẓref le-Hoḳmah* (Warsaw, 1890), 42: הרב הגדול הראב"ד ... יראה ויבין שהיה חכם בפלוסופיאה, וכל דבריו ערבים, קרובים מאד לשכל.

versions against Maimonides on such problems as anthropomorphism, determinism, and eschatology should not be taken as signs of arbitrary opposition to a philosophic-rationalistic formulation of opinion on these subjects. They should be analyzed as reasoned convictions, with backgrounds of their own. This analysis might indeed locate Rabad in the conservative camp, which was suspicious of excessive philosophizing or rational investigation of traditional beliefs, but certainly no verdict of a blanket condemnation of philosophy is warranted by such disagreement.

It is necessary, therefore, to reexamine the two vague passages generally taken as indicating a negative attitude on the part of Rabad to philosophy and a reluctance to admit the use of philosophic literature. The first is from an introductory passage to Rabad's hassagot on Alfasi, where he humiliatingly proclaims:

> I know well that I am among the inferior creatures that God created and did not achieve success in any of the simple sciences [*ḥokmot*] that are accessible to wise men because of the dullness of my nature and because the troubles and distressing events of the time which occur to men oppressed me. As a result, I did not grow wise. I put my hand to my mouth because intelligence is lacking and the word is not in me.[16]

Rabad continues that, despite these shortcomings, he swallowed his reluctance and was presumptuous enough to dissent from Alfasi's views and even to record his criticisms, lest one suspect him of being a "silent fool who does not differentiate between good and bad."

Now, if this debasing confession of ignorance with regard to sciences (ḥokmot) is to be taken as referring to secular sciences, as Zunz, Geiger, and others have done, it appears incongruous, and not at all justifiable by the context. Probably what misled these scholars is the plural use of the term "ḥokmot" which ordinarily refers to various branches of secular science but which Rabad is obviously using with regard to knowledge or learning in general. For, of what relevance is a disclaimer of secular knowledge in the introduction to a purely Talmudic undertaking? As a matter of fact, self-indictment on the grounds of Talmudic parochialism—if such were actually the case here—might even be taken to be an asset rather than a liability in the critical annotation of a purely Talmudic composition like that of Alfasi, for it would allow greater specialization and more exhaustive knowledge of this one

16. *Hassagot* on Alfasi, *Ketubot*, 14a: ידעתי בנפשי כי מן הנבראים הקלים אשר ברא הא־להים אני ולא השגתי לאחת מן החכמות הקלות אשר לחכמים מפני כובד טבעי ... כי השכל אין והדבר אין בי.

field. Rabad is not here confessing his ignorance of secular sciences or his inability to pursue them, but is engaging in a customary profession of general humility, unworthiness—even in the field of Talmud, with which he deals—and seemingly insurmountable reluctance in undertaking the task of halakic criticism. The whole structure of the passage—the transition from the self-deprecation to the declaration of his intent and the subsequent encomium of Alfasi followed by the reiteration of his own shortcomings—suggests this.[17]

The superficial impression received from the second passage—an animadversion against Maimonides concerning astronomical knowledge derived from foreign sources—is also modified after some analysis. Prefatory to his actual critique of a factual statement by Maimonides, a critique which "has not lost any of its weight even today,"[18] Rabad says somewhat derisively:

> Because this author raises himself up and boasts about this science and in his opinion he reached the very ultimate [in knowledge of it], while I, on the other hand, am not among those proficient in it, for also my teachers did not attain to it—consequently I have not intruded upon his statements to check up on him, but when I encountered this statement which he wrote, it was remarkably strange in my eyes.[19]

Rabad proceeds to explain the error of Maimonides' calendrical calculation and to correct it.

One may safely infer from this passage only the following. Rabad seems to be disclaiming that expert knowledge of astronomy based on foreign sciences of which Maimonides, as alleged by Rabad, "boasted," but no hostility to it can be detected in his remarks.[20] He felt that the

17. Self-deprecation and altruistic praise are conventions of medieval rabbinic composition and need not be illustrated specifically. It is interesting, however, that the identical phrase used by Rabad to indicate his intellectual inferiority is repeated by R. Meshullam b. Moses of Béziers, who knew Rabad's writings very well; see *Sefer ha-Hashlamah* on *Neziḳin*, ed. Lubozky (Paris, 1885), introduction. Razah also comments on his inferiority prior to a lengthy analysis of astronomical theories; see *ha-Ma'or ha-Ḳaṭan, Rosh ha-Shanah*, 20b: ולא בינת אדם לי ולא למדתי חכמה: also, *Sefer ha-Minhagot* in *Sifran*, 129; and Naḥmanides' Bible Commentary, introduction: כאשר חכמתי קטנה ודעתי קצרה. See also Zunz, "Hebräische Redeweisen für bescheidene Meinugs-Aesserung," *Gesammelte Schriften*, I, 41–49. It is interesting to contrast Rabad's statement with that of Naḥmanides, *Sefer ha-Zekut*, introduction: כאשר ידעתי מעלת האיש ההוא בחכמה.

18. A. Fraenkel, "ᶜAl Nimmuḳeyham shel . . .," *Rabbi Kook Memorial Volume* (Jerusalem, 1945), 180. See also A. Akabya, "Sefer Meyuḥad le-ᶜinyene ha-ᶜIbbur," *Sinai*, XV (1952), 137; already Azariah dei Rossi, *Maẓref la-Kesef* (Vilna, 1863), 62: נראה כדאי להשיק שפתי ראב״ד ז״ל אשר . . . סיים על הר״ם ז״ל שהוא בעיניו כמתעתע.

19. *MT*, *Ḳiddush ha-Ḥodesh*, VII, 7.

20. As for Rabad's allegation of Maimonides' boasting, the tone and style in this section of the *Mishneh Torah* are clearly more confident and authoritative than else-

traditional Jewish astronomy was perfectly sufficient for all calendrical problems and he refers to his great teachers who managed very well and even understood the laws regulating the proclamation of the new month without the specialized astronomical knowledge which Maimonides ostentatiously claimed to possess. There is even a somewhat satirical indication that Maimonides was led astray by his secular knowledge in the interpretation of the subject, for after the preliminary contrast between Maimonides' knowledge and his own ignorance, Rabad unhesitatingly goes on to disprove Maimonides' statement and to conclude triumphantly: "He seems to me as one who is straying."[21]

Furthermore, Rabad's opposition was not to the use of astronomical knowledge derived from secular sources in the exploration and solution of calendrical problems but to the fact that this knowledge was not always in keeping with halakic norms, that it was sometimes erroneous for practical religious purposes. Since Maimonides believed himself to be completely proficient in astronomical science while he admittedly was not, Rabad usually maintained a discreet silence. None of Maimonides' statements in this section of the *Mishneh Torah* were objectionable on halakic grounds. However, Rabad was most articulate when astronomical or mathematical discussion affected practical decisions in halakah. This is evident not only from this lone hassagah on *Ḥilkot Ḳiddush ha-Ḥodesh* where he is quick to expose what appears to him as a blatant error in regard to actual practice, but also in his hassagot on Razah concerning the International Date Line, where he allows nothing to pass unscrutinized.[22] Razah uses there very specialized astronomical

where and Maimonides actually appears in his exposition of astronomical theories as if displaying superior knowledge. For instance, after describing the difficulties inherent in the calculation of the calendar and alluding to the "significant controversies between ancient non-Jewish scholars" who investigated the matter, Maimonides states that "great scholars fell into error concerning these matters, did not possess all the knowledge, and doubts were created in their mind concerning these matters." Since, in the course of time and as a result of much research and investigation "the methods of this calculation became known to a few scholars," and there are some books on this subject that are not generally known, Maimonides "saw fit to explain the methods of this calculation in 'order that it be available for whoever desires daringly to come unto the work to do it'" (*ibid.*, XI, 1–4). It is perhaps significant that, although Maimonides is here quoting a verse in Exod. 36.2, he changes the idiom from "nesa'o libo" to "mela'o libo" (Esth. 9.5), which implies daring and even presumption. Such passages may have been in Rabad's mind when he spoke of Maimonides' boasting. Moreover, Rabad may also have seen Maimonides' letter to the Provençal sages concerning astrology (1194) in which he boasts of having studied this topic assiduously and having read just about every available book on the subject of astronomy and astrology. Rabad may have been alluding to—and poking fun at—this boasting.

21. *Ibid.*: והוא בעיני כמתעתע.

22. *KS*, II, 38.

knowledge, derived primarily from the *Cuzari* and the works of Abraham bar Ḥiyya, in establishing the International Date Line—a fact which is important for such matters as observance of the Sabbath in various parts of the world. Rabad's criticism of Razah for the use of secular astronomical learning is predicated on the fact that it led to error in the interpretation of the law. He focuses attention upon the erroneous interpretation and makes the point that there is absolutely no need to use this foreign knowledge. There is no implication of disdain whatsoever in the remark that we should rely exclusively upon professional Talmudists in the solution of halakic questions. Rabad merely objects strongly to unqualified outsiders, deficient in Talmudic training but possessed of some astronomical learning, encroaching upon the field of halakah, for they usually distort it. That Rabad was not hostile to astronomical science as such is clear from the fact that he welcomes its use by trained Talmudists who know how to harmonize it with the halakah. He was not content simply to reject dogmatically the conclusions reached by Razah on the basis of astronomical computation as being irreconcilable with halakah—as could be done unflinchingly by a rabid traditionalist—but refers to the scientific refutation of this view by Isaac b. Baruch ibn al-Baliya, Spanish Talmudist and mathematician who was equally proficient in both fields of learning.[23] Such a person was, in the opinion of Rabad, capable of grappling with these problems, and his solution would deserve serious consideration. Rabad is pleased here both with the invalidation of an erroneous opinion by kindred theoretical arguments and with the harmonization of a Talmudic view with a related scientific theory.

It is possible to cite more indirect corroborative evidence—mostly in the form of appropriate and persuasive arguments ex silentio—that

23. *KS*, II 38: אין לנו ללמוד מדברי מי שאינו מאנשי התלמוד לפי שהם מסבבים פני ההלכה ודברים אשר לא כן· וכבר שמענו כי הנשיא ר׳ יצחק בר׳ ברוך ז״ל שהיה בקי בזו החכמה והיה בקי בהלכה שיבר את דבריהם· ויישר כוחו ששבר. See, for example, what Isaac de Lattes recorded about Isaac b. Baruch (Neubauer, *Chronicles*, II, 234): היה חכם גדול בחכמת התכונה וחבר ספר גדול דרך פסקי, קראו קופת הרוכלים. Also, Isaac Israeli, *Yesod ᶜOlam*, II, 14a–15b. Rabad's reference to Isaac b. Baruch suggests comparison with the following reference by Razah: וכבר השיב עליו הרב הנשיא ר׳ יצחק בר ר׳ ברוך ז״ל ושבר כל דבריו. *Ha-Ma'or Ha-Ḳaṭan, Shabbat*, 11b. Is it too much to conjecture that Rabad is purposely parodying the same phrase in order to make his criticism of Razah more pointed? It is interesting that Rabad implies that Abraham bar Ḥiyya and Judah ha-Levi, upon whom Razah leans and about whose Talmudic knowledge we have no direct information, were not outstanding Talmudists capable of dealing with halakic problems. Note R. Simeon Duran's statement about Abraham ibn Ezra: אעפ״י שהחכם ז״ל לא היה רב בקי בדינין. *Sefer ha-Tashbeẓ* (Amsterdam, 1738), I, 51. For ha-Levi, see S. Zevin, "Ha-Cuzari be-Halakah," *Sinai*, V (1941), 95–108.

Rabad did not dismiss secular science or discredit its literature. His failure to dissent from a number of Maimonidean statements on the importance of secular knowledge is meaningful. Note the following Maimonidean declaration in praise of

> ... the wise men of Greece who composed many books on astronomy which we now possess. The books which the wise men of Israel, who lived in the time of the prophets, from the tribe of Issacher, composed did not reach us. Inasmuch as all these matters are based on clear proofs that are beyond reproach and it is impossible for one to question them, we should not care about the author, irrespective of whether prophets or [scholars from] other nations composed the books.[24]

Rabad is conspicuously silent. Similarly, when Maimonides enumerates the intellectual prerequisites necessary for election to the Sanhedrin, including in his catalogue an impressive array of secular subjects which must be mastered, Rabad tacitly assents. The significance of this assent, with its implicit awareness of the importance of secular learning, is accentuated all the more by the fact that his Provençal successor in Maimonidean criticism R. Moses ha-Kohen pointedly dissented from this statement, inquiring why the members of the Sanhedrin should be obliged to acquire this knowledge.[25]

It would seem that astronomy had great attraction for rabbinic scholars and they tried to use it as much as possible in their treatment of problems of rabbinic astronomy.[26] While Rabad was not opposed to this and even approved its proper use, he was doubtful about the skill of most people in making the proper use of this supplementary secular knowledge. He felt that its misuse was prevalent and that many scholars who had been attracted to and had acquired some knowledge of secular astronomy believed that rabbinic astronomy was incomplete and imperfect. This led Rabad to call attention to the excellence of rabbinic astronomy vis-à-vis secular astronomy and to stress the superior authority of the former. Concerning those who criticized certain astronomical statements of the Talmudic sage R. Gamaliel, Rabad, quoting a wrathful statement of Isaiah, says in an adjacent hassagah on Razah: "'Woe unto them that are wise in their own eyes and prudent in their own sight.' They have not attained even half of his knowledge

24. MT, *Ḳiddush ha-Ḥodesh*, XVII, 24.

25. *Ibid.*, *Sanhedrin*, II, 1, and commentaries, *ad. loc.* On the seventy languages of the *Sanhedrin*, see Ginzberg, *Legends of the Jews*, V, 194–195, nn. 72–73; Lieberman, *Greek in Jewish Palestine*, 15.

26. See, for example, later, Duran, *Sefer ha-Tashbeẓ*, I, 104: אע״פ שהם חכמתנו באמת וצריכות לתורתנו לדעת ענין קביעות החדשים והמועדים אשר תלויים בהם הרבה מצות חמורות...

and yet they ridicule. What about all those remarkable things taught in the Baraita of R. Eliezer [in his name]?"[27] This is comparable to the statement of R. Ḥananel, uttered in response to a similar situation—an implicit contradiction between the Talmudic opinion and certain astronomical teachings, which led some to question or modify the former. He reaffirms the supremacy of the halakic view: "Although contemporary astronomers maintain contradictory views, we pay no attention to them. We are cautioned [to accept] the statements of our masters as they are and not to worry about the statements of others."[28]

The question of Rabad's interpretation of the aggadah is worthy of special comment for his attitude toward aggadah is sometimes taken as a significant correlative of his intellectual attitude in general. Gross remarks that "Rabad was entirely prejudiced in favor of the aggadah and he opposes its frequently absurd utterances to the profoundest ideas of philosophy expressed by Maimonides."[29] Rabad is usually classified as an uncompromising literalist in aggadah, dedicated to the simple, unsophisticated meaning of all legendary lore, while Maimonides is presented as the apostle of spiritualism and allegorization. The proof-text confirming Rabad's servility to the literalness of the aggadah is in the first chapter of *Hilkot ᶜAkum* where Maimonides reports Abraham as proclaiming monotheism at the ripe age of forty, possessed of mature intellectual faculties and after much independent reflection, while Rabad cites a second view mentioned in the Talmud that Abraham was only three years old when he recognized the unity of God; consequently, it is assumed that this perception must have been a supernatural, supra-rational act.[30] This nourishes the generalization concerning Rabad's literalism and naïveté in the interpretation of aggadah.

No attention is given to contrary examples which are abundantly forthcoming. The very first note in the *Mishneh Torah* is a good instance: Rabad disregards an aggadah—concerning the phenomenal age

27. *KS*, II, 39: הוי חכמים בעיניהם . . . כי לא הגיעו לחצי־צפרנו ומלעיגים.

28. A. Berliner, *Migdal Chananel* (Leipzig, 1876), XVII.

29. Gross, XXIII, 167; see I. Elbogen in *Jüdisches Lexikon*, I, 43; Steinschneider, *Jewish Literature*, 87.

30. *MT*, ᶜAkum, I, 3; see *Nedarim*, 32a; see S. Baron, "The Historical Outlook of Maimonides," *Proceedings of the American Academy for Jewish Research*, VI (1935), 119. For additional variants, see Ginzberg, *Legends*, V, 209; S. Abramson, "Imre Ḥokmah," *Minḥah li-Yehudah*, ed. S. Assaf (Jerusalem, 1950), 23. The same hassagah is repeated by R. Moses ha-Kohen, *Hassagot*, ed. Atlas, *HUCA*, XXVII (1956), 11. For other cases, see *MT*, *Melakim*, XII, 1.

of Aḥiyeh the Shilonite who participated in the exodus from Egypt and was also a high-ranking member of King David's court—in pursuit of the correct historical perspective, while Maimonides accepts the aggadah verbatim, regardless of its implicit anachronism.[31] Maimonides' verbatim reproduction of the Talmudic statement that "a person whose sins outnumber his merits dies immediately because of his wickedness," is another case. Rabad, followed later by Naḥmanides and ha-Me'iri, interprets this statement metaphorically in order to resolve some of its difficulties. Maimonides' judgment, he maintains, is in flagrant contradiction to reality "for there are wicked people who have longevity. [The saying means] only that their verdict announcing that they will not fill the days of their life originally decreed for them is immediately sealed."[32] These examples do not detract much from Maimonides' rationalism any more than they justify the ascription of an advanced historical or critical sense to Rabad.[33] They do, however, caution against the fallacy of reductionism and loose generalization.

Even the conventional demonstration based on the divergent statements concerning Abraham's age at the time he proclaimed the monotheistic principle is far from conclusive. There is no reason to assume that Rabad actually espoused the legend that he cites. He merely calls attention to a conflicting source and thus challenges Maimonides' imaginative description of Abraham's rationalistic powers and speculative prowess in discovering the truth about God. There are a number of conflicting legends and variant readings concerning Abraham's age at the time. Just as the age of forty does not necessarily mean that the act was rational, so the age of three does not tell us that it was mystical or intuitional.[34] Furthermore, Rabad cites this view as "there is a

31. *MT*, introduction; see *Baba Batra*, 121a.

32. *MT*, *Teshubah*, III, 2; Naḥmanides, beginning of *Sha^c^ar ha-Gemul* and *Derashat ha-Ramban*, ed. Z. Schwarz, *Ha-Ẓofeh Me-'Erez Hagar*, I (1911), 147; ha-Me'iri, *Ḥibbur ha-Teshubah*, 247; see also Ibn Shu^c^aib, *Derashot* (Constantinople, 1528), end of derashah for *Rosh ha-Shanah*; M. A. Fano, *Sefer ^c^Asarah Ma'amarot* (Venice, 1597), *Ma'amar Ḥikkur ha-Din*, 4b.

33. The same is true for the second hassagah in the introduction, concerning the disciples of R. Judah ha-Nasi. Rabad deletes certain names which Maimonides included, while he adds others which Maimonides omitted. Although a comparison of Rabad's classification with the information found in a standard chronicle like the *Sefer ha-Yuḥasin* corroborates Rabad, this cannot influence one's appraisal of Maimonides' sense of historicism. The names mentioned in the first part of the hassagah are all borderline cases. As for Rabad's addition, it is clear that Maimonides had no intention of exhausting the roster of Rabbi Judah's disciples (see *Kesef Mishneh, ad. loc.*).

34. Nor can one speak of a typically mystical or rationalistic view on this matter. That mystics did not inevitably have to choose the "three-year-old reading" is illustrated by the statements of R. Judah b. Barzilai and R. Eleazer ha-Rokeah; see

legend," and when he introduces a critical note vacuously as "some say" or "there is another opinion," he does not always commit himself to this explanation; he may just be registering a possible alternative. "When Rabad writes 'there is someone who maintains' it cannot be inferred conclusively from this phrase that he adopts the view expressed there."[35] This rule is certainly applicable with regard to the subject here discussed, for elsewhere Rabad explicitly speaks of an intellectual, cognitive perception of God.[36] To introduce another argument from silence, it is notable that Rabad allowed the following intellectualistic statement to stand unqualifiedly: "No one loves the Holy One, blessed is He, except by means of the knowledge with which he knows Him. The love will be according to the knowledge: if it be small, the love will be small; if it be great, the love will be great." That Rabad studied this passage—thus eliminating the possible contention, undoubtedly valid in other cases, that he may have glossed over this section without observing it too carefully—is demonstrated by the lexicographical annotation on the meaning of "shigayon" which he appended to the beginning of this very passage.[37]

Corroborative evidence that Rabad did not always feel obliged to take the aggadah literally is the obiter dictum in which he refers to some aggadot as "corrupting opinion about religious matters."[38] This echoes the middle-of-the-road opinion, for which he could cite a host of precedents, that certain homilies could not and should not be accepted literally. Hai Gaon's verdict on this matter was certainly known to him from his father-in-law's approbatory reproduction of the former's view in his *ha-Eshkol*.[39] A similar view concerning freedom of interpretation with regard to implausible aggadot was espoused in the *Mebo ha-Talmud* of Samuel ha-Nagid as it was in various contexts by R. Ḥananel.[40] Judah b. Barzilai speaks in his *Perush Sefer Yeẓirah* of aggadot "upon which nobody relies."[41] Also in the *Cuzari* he could have found such an

---

Ginzberg, *Legends*, V, 209. Joseph ibn Kaspi, however, does use this as a proof-text for metaphysical speculation; see *Guide to Knowledge*, ed. I. Abrahams, *Hebrew Ethical Wills*, I, 142–143.

35. *Kenesset ha-Gedolah*, *Kelale ha-Rabad* (printed at the beginning of most editions of the *MT*): כשהראב״ד כותב יש מי שאומר אין בלשון זה הכרע שסובר כן; see Chapter III.

36. *BH*, 88.

37. *MT*, *Teshubah*, X, 6.

38. *MT*, *Teshubah*, III, 7.

39. Albeck, *ha-Eshkol*, II, 47. See also Joel Müller, *Mafteaḥ li-Teshubot ha-Geonim* (Berlin, 1891), 205; B. M. Lewin, *Oẓar ha-Geonim*, *Berakot*, II, 91, n. 10, and *Ḥagigah*, 59–60, where references to Saadia are also included. See, in general, S. Rapaport, *ʿErek Milin* (Warsaw, 1914), 24.

40. S. Rapaport, *Toledot*, *R. Hananel* (Warsaw, 1913), III, 23, n. 14.

41. *Perush Sefer Yeẓirah*, ed. Halberstam (Berlin, 1885), 121.

opinion on the need for modifying certain aggadic views.[42] In the *Mishneh Torah*, Maimonides committed himself to and vindicated the metaphorical construction of certain midrashic passages. In one place he counseled: "No one should ever occupy himself with the legendary themes or spend much time on midrashic statements bearing on this and like subjects. He should not deem them of prime importance."[43] Rabad tacitly consents to this Maimonidean formulation, which is basically his own view. These converging considerations, especially the statement on "corrupting" aggadot, should deliver the *coup de grâce* to the preconception concerning Rabad's servility to the literalness of aggadah.

In summation of the question of his attitude to secular learning, there is no reason to posit that Rabad appears as an antagonist of secular learning. The sources nowhere reveal an attitude of uncompromising hostility. If anything, in Rabad's implicit classification of sciences, secular learning was relegated to a secondary position; it occupied a lower rung in the ladder of knowledge. Rabad was no philosopher and did not share Maimonides' enthusiasm for philosophy. His entire *Weltanschauung* differed from that of Maimonides, and no attempt to unify Rabad and Maimonides or gloss over the differences between them has been made.[44] Although he would unquestionably grant that the "four ells of halakah" might be enlarged to provide space for secular learning, he would surely insist that the latter was clearly not on par with Talmudic learning nor was it indispensable. When secular learning—astronomy, for instance—comes into conflict with Talmudic teaching, his sympathies and convictions are with the latter. He felt that his teachers managed very well with problems of rabbinic astronomy without the benefit of specialized, presumably secular, astronomical knowledge. He was too much the "man of halakah" to have acted differently or thought otherwise. He repeatedly stressed that Talmudic study has clear-cut priority over everything else. In an original bit of exegesis, Rabad expresses the idea that all other commitments of a person, even intellectual commitments, should center around an all-embracing commitment to Torah.[45] The

42. *Cuzari*, III, 73.

43. *MT*, *Melakim*, XII, 1.

44. E.g., the belief in "demons"; see *MT*, *Tefillin*, IV, 19; *Sifra Commentary*, 3a, 91a, 110b. Naḥmanides ironically underscores Rabad's naivete in medical matters and implicitly contrasts this with Maimonides: ולענין מה שאמר הר׳ אברהם ז״ל בבני אדם שלוקין בביצה אחת ומולידין, אנו אומרים צא וחזור על בניהם מאין הם, וה׳ משה בן מיימון ז״ל הספרדי מבקיאי הרופאים פי כמ״ש. See *Sefer ha-Zekut*, *Yebamot*, 24a.

45. *Sifra*, 110b.

concluding lines of his commentary on *Ḳinnim* contain the thought that while all knowledge and coherent, analytic thinking are valuable per se, all wisdom is ultimately futile and evanescent if it is not allied to Torah.[46] There is a curious literary discrepancy between two practically similar statements by Maimonides and Rabad which is very symbolic—even if trivial or perhaps unintentional. Both affirm that man should not castigate himself or weaken himself because of a contemptuous attitude toward things of the body. Physical well-being is a necessity, for "one who suffers hunger, thirst, or pain" cannot engage in spiritual activities. Maimonides identifies these activities with "understanding and speculation in the sciences," while Rabad says that one who is weak will necessarily be idle from prayer and study.[47]

As a final indication of Rabad's attitude toward philosophy and secular learning, mention should be made of a preliminary, methodological criticism leveled by Rabad at Maimonides in connection with the problem of free will. Maimonides had elaborately presented the perplexing antinomy between human freedom and divine foreknowledge and then left it as an insoluble problem. Rabad contends that he should never have introduced such an antinomy in the *Mishneh Torah*, which was destined also for laymen and nonprofessionals. It is preferable, Rabad contends, to leave such matters in the realm of faith from the very beginning rather than to analyze them philosophically, speculate about them, and ultimately reduce them to articles of a religious creed.[48]

This animadversion may be taken as an accusation of Maimonides for a breach in the discipline of esoteric knowledge, of confronting untrained laymen with problems that are beyond their grasp. Maimonides would, of course, defend himself against such an accusation, for he himself counseled esotericism and in a number of passages in his writings

46. *Ḳinnim*, end. There are many parallels between this sentiment and the disputed opinion of Hai Gaon concerning the value and usefulness of secular studies. Hai Gaon is quoted by Naḥmanides in his letter to the French scholars concerning the ban against secular studies; *Ḳobez Teshubot ha-Rambam* (Leipzig, 1859), III, 9a. For a discussion of its exact text, see I. H. Weiss, "Rab Hai weha-Ḥokmot ha-Ḥiẓoniot," *he-Asif*, III (1886), 148–152; also, Hershman, *Rabbi Isaac Perfet*, 90, n. 4. See also A. Geiger, "War Hai Gaon ein feind philosphischer Studien," *Jüdische Zeitschrift für Wissenschaft und Leben*, I (1862), 206–217.

47. *MT*, *Deᶜot*, III, 3: שאי אפשר שיבין ויסתכל בחכמות והוא רעב וחולה או אחד מאבריו כואב. *BH*, 87. ויהיה הפסדו מרובה משכרו כי יבטל מן התורה ומן התפלה, ואם ילמד לא תהיה תורתו מיושבת. See *Sefer ha-Minhagot*, *Sifran*, 136.

48. *MT*, *Teshubah*, V, 5. Note the similar opinion in the unauthenticated hassagah quoted in the name of Rabad by Joseph Solomon del Medigo, *Nobelot Hokmah*, p. 5 of the unnumbered introduction: ... לכן אין רצוני להאריך בספיקות שהייתי נבוך בהן זמן רב ואם לא יקשה עליו מאומה מה טוב ומה נעים. כי מי שלא חלה ולא מרגיש אינו צריך לרופא לרפאותו.

explicitly asserted the value and necessity of an esoteric approach to learning.[49] From another point of view, this criticism may be taken as revealing Rabad's lingering distrust of unbridled philosophic speculation. For, although willing occasionally to quote a philosophic answer to a certain problem that was already on the agenda, he suspected that untrammeled speculation could only breed perplexity or disbelief and, even if this would be only a temporary state, it was not worth it—"perhaps for a short time a thought [of uncertainty] concerning this matter will enter their heart." This clearly underscores Rabad's pervasive concern with the practical religious life. He was not a philosopher and had no desire to write philosophy, just as, generally, he shied away from abstract theorizing in favor of concrete exposition and textual elucidation.[50]

In view of all this, we may affirm that Naḥmanides was undoubtedly justified in invoking the authority of Rabad and the sages of Lunel in support of his conciliatory position during the controversy concerning philosophic works, in general, and the study of Maimonides' *Moreh Nebukim* and *Sefer ha-Madda*, in particular. He cites Rabad's essential acceptance of Maimonides. Even though Rabad criticized and disputed several opinions, Naḥmanides asserted, he never accused Maimonides of heresy or impugned his orthodoxy. He never suggested that the book be suppressed or its reading be prohibited. Naḥmanides believes that Rabad would naturally have aligned himself with his own intermediate view.[51]

2. *Use of Philosophic Literature*

This reservedly benevolent attitude is best attested to and substantially bolstered by Rabad's actual use of philosophic literature. While the facts which enable one to determine this attitude do not suggest any systematic reproduction of philosophic theories, one may expect various terms, phrases, and concepts definitely borrowed from philosophy to have crept into his writings. This is revealed by a study resting upon the usual bases of internal evidence: bits of philosophic terminology discovered in his writings; similarities of structure and

49. *Mishnah Commentary*, introduction; *Ḥagigah*, II, 1; *MT*, *Yesode ha-Torah*, II, 12; IV, 10; *Moreh Nebukim*, I, 71.

50. Introduction to *Sifra Commentary*, 1a.

51. *Ḳobeẓ Teshubot ha-Rambam*, III, 9b: וכבר ראו כל בני לוניל והרב הגדול רבי אברהם בר דוד ז״ל הספר ההוא ולא צוו לגנזו ... והרב ר׳ אברהם ב״ר דוד ז״ל השיב על מקצת דבריו, ולא אמר שיש בו צד מינות וצד כפירה חס וחלילה. Naḥmanides is obviously referring to the hassagot on *Sefer ha-Madda* and not on the entire *Mishneh Torah*. Contrast the view of the sixteenth-century Menaḥem ʿAzariah Fano, like Naḥmanides, a prominent Talmudist and mystic: *Teshubot*, 108.

reasoning between Rabad and representatives of the philosophic learning. Such an investigation discloses that Rabad knew a number of philosophic or scientific works, either originally composed in Hebrew or made available in Hebrew translations from the Arabic. These are the astronomical works (*Sefer Ḥokmat ha-Kokawim* and *Sefer ha-ᶜIbbur*) and *Hegyon ha-Nefesh* of Abraham bar Ḥiyya, the *Tiḳḳun Middot ha-Nefesh* of Gabirol, the *Cuzari* of Judah ha-Levi, the *Ḥobot ha-Lebabot* of Baḥya ibn Pakuda, the *Emunot we-Deᶜot* of Saadia, and possibly the *Musre ha-Pilosofim* of Ḥonein ben Ishak, *Ḥakemoni* of Shabbetai Donnolo and *Yesod Mora* of Abraham ibn Ezra. These borrowings and similarities, although not abundant, are strikingly exact and sufficiently technical to warrant the assumption of direct use of these works. The specific contexts in which they usually appear preclude the possibility of their having been learned indirectly.

In the lengthy discussion concerning the International Date Line two authors are mentioned by name. The first is Abraham bar Ḥiyya whose astronomical treatises—*Sefer Ḥokmat ha-Kokawim* and *Sefer ha-ᶜIbbur*, the latter being, incidentally, the oldest Hebrew work on the calculation of the calendar—are knowingly discussed in comparative detail. Rabad does not repeat the titles of these works, which Razah had already specified;[1] he dismisses them as "the treatises of Abraham bar Ḥiyya the Spaniard," but the manner of his discussion and refutation clearly evidences direct knowledge. This knowledge—boastfulness, perhaps—is even reflected in the flippant remark implying that Razah was a dilettante in these matters and the little information which he garnered from his perusal of bar Ḥiyya's works was inadequate.[2]

Rabad's reference to the "eternal thought" (*maḥashabah ḳadmonit*)[3] in which all later creative acts resided most probably reflects Abraham bar Ḥiyya's intellectualistic conception of divine action, formulated in the *Hegyon ha-Nefesh*, where he uses the phrase "pure thought" (*maḥashabah ṭehorah*) to describe the eternal, primordial divine idea which preceded and planned the entire creation.[4] This intellectualistic conception is also found in the *Bahir*, which uses "thought" (*maḥashabah*) to designate the highest divine sphere (*keter*)—a usage which Scholem traces back to the *Hegyon ha-Nefesh*.[5]

1. *Ha-Ma'or ha-Ḳaṭan*, *Rosh ha-Shanah*, 25a.
2. *KS*, II, 38: הנה הוא כמלקט שבלים מאחרי הקוצרים ולא השיג אפילו כמלא מגל.
3. *BH*, 4.
4. *Hegyon ha-Nefesh* (Leipzig, 1860), 2.
5. Scholem, *Reshit ha-Kabbalah*, 61. The *Hegyon ha-Nefesh* is also used by Rabad's contemporary Berechiah ha-Naḳdan. See Guttmann, *MGWJ*, XLVI (1902), 540.

The main source from which Razah derived his information for establishing the International Date Line was the *Cuzari* of Judah ha-Levi. Razah does not mention ha-Levi explicitly; all he gives is a vague reference to "Spanish sages."[6] The name is supplied by Rabad for, as is his custom in many halakic criticisms, he first clarifies his opponent's source, elaborates his view, and only then does he proceed to refute it. Rabad felt that Razah's reproduction of ha-Levi was too nebulous and wanting in precision, and the reader could never understand this matter only from Razah's account—"the halakah is not clearly formulated on the basis of his statement." Consequently, Rabad presented "the gist" of ha-Levi's statements.[7] What he gives is an accurate paraphrase of ha-Levi's four arguments for the centrality of Palestine. The equivocation existing among scholars concerning the question of Rabad's direct use of the *Cuzari* or second-hand acquaintance with its contents can be eliminated by a parallel reading of the two passages.[8] The perfect correlation of thought-content as well as the stylistic affinities speak for themselves. The fact that he does not quote ha-Levi verbatim is in keeping with common medieval literary usage as well as his professed intention of stating only "the gist of his [ha-Levi's] statements." Rabad even reproduces midrashic passages in loose paraphrase rather than in precise literal form.[9]

Judah ha-Levi	*Rabad*
The beginning of the Sabbath must be calculated from Sinai because that is (a) the place where the Torah was given and (b) where Adam was transferred from the Garden of Eden on the eve of the Sabbath. (c) It is there that the calendar began after the six days of creation, for Adam then began to name the days. (d) When the earth was inhabited and people multiplied, they continued counting in the same way.[10]	One who sees this opinion in the *Cuzari* will understand that the beginning of the Sabbath is there, in Palestine, because (a) that is the source of the Torah and the commandments; (b) it was there that Adam was transferred when he left the Garden of Eden; (c) it was there that he named the days; (d) all succeeding generations accepted [this system] from him. . . . This is the gist (*toref*) of his statements.[11]

6. *Ha-Ma'or ha-Ḳaṭan, Rosh ha-Shanah*, 20b.
7. *KS*, II, 38: אין ההלכה יוצאת לאור מדבריו . . . זהו תורף דבריו.
8. Marx, 208, quotes the different views of Gross and Cassel, without expressing his own opinion.
9. See, for example, §2, note 60. Naḥmanides also has a long excerpt from Maimonides' *Ma'amar Teḥiyat ha-Metim* at the end of his *Shaʿar ha-Gemul*—which is more of a paraphrase than a direct quotation.
10. *Cuzari*, II, 18.
11. *KS*, II, 38.

It may be noted that Rabad's use of the Hebrew word "toref" in the sense of "gist" or general idea is in keeping with that common in the writings of Abraham bar Ḥiyya. The word "toref" may also be used—as it is by Maimonides—to introduce a direct quotation.[12]

There is other proof that Rabad borrowed from the *Cuzari*. In explanation of the verse "Out of heaven He made thee to hear His voice . . . and upon earth He made thee to see His great fire,"[13] adduced in the *Baraita* of R. Ishmael[14] to illustrate, *inter alia*, the midrashic statement that "God lowered the upper heavens of heaven down to the mountain top,"[15] Rabad submits that "God showed the form of the upper fire (*esh ᶜelyonah*) on the mountain top."[16] "Esh ᶜelyonah" is the phrase used in the *Cuzari* as the equivalent of what was known in Greek philosophy as "ethereal fire."[17] This is a good example of Rabad's non-literal philosophic exegesis and confirms what has been said about Rabad's interpretation of midrashic statements.

In addition to the works of these two writers whom Rabad mentions by name, he uses other philosophic works anonymously. As for Baḥya ibn Paḳuda's *Ḥobot ha-Lebabot*, whose mystical overtones, pietistic strains, and popular religious character were undoubtedly of great interest to him, he knew not only the Hebrew text but also Judah ibn Tibbon's introduction to the translation. One version of an hassagah reflects ibn Tibbon's observations on the prerequisites for proper translations. Criticizing Maimonides for translating the original Aramaic of the Talmud into Hebrew and, in the process, changing the meaning or not reproducing it faithfully, Rabad remarks: "I acknowledge the truth to be with them who said that one who translates from one language to another must be proficient in the subject matter and in both languages."[18] In the introduction to his translation of the *Ḥobot ha-Lebabot*, Judah ibn Tibbon enumerates three factors which lead translators to corrupt the original works: "(1) They are not proficient in Arabic from which they translate . . . (2) are not proficient in Hebrew to which they translate. (3) They do not understand the statements of the author."[19]

12. Efros, "Philosophical Terminology of Abraham bar Ḥiyya," *JQR*, XX (1930), 137. See also *KS*, II, 10: זהו תורף חזרתו.
13. Deut. 4:36.
14. *Sifra* (*Baraita de R. Ishmael*), 3a.
15. *Mekilta*, II, 275.
16. *Sifra*, 1a: הראה דמות האש העליונות על ראש ההר.
17. *Cuzari*, V, 14.
18. *MT*, *Shebuᶜot*, VI, 9.
19. Judah ibn Tibbon, introduction to *Ḥobot ha-Lebabot*.

There is a more or less literal allusion to the *Ḥobot ha-Lebabot* in Rabad's writings. Speaking of the relation of the Creator and the created, Rabad describes God as beyond both transcendence and immanence:

> Every created being should know that he is not separated from the Creator and [yet] is not compound with him, for whatever is compound is limited and whatever is limited has been created. The Creator exalted be He has none of these attributes for He is eternal, neither limited or created.[20]

This is obviously a reflection of the similar statement by Baḥya in the first chapter of the *Ḥobot ha-Lebabot:*

> Whatever is separate is limited. Whatever is limited is finite. Whatever is finite is compound. Whatever is compound has been created. Whatever has been created has a Creator. We have therefore demonstrated that the Creator is eternal, cause of all causes.[21]

The recently published derashah also reveals Rabad's acquaintance with the *Ḥobot ha-Lebabot*. In the context of his exhortatory, ethical discourse on repentance, Rabad gives a five-fold classification of penitent people: (1) penitent on his own, not motivated by the rebuke of another; (2) penitent as a result of heeding the rebuke of another; (3) penitent only after witnessing the punishment inflicted upon another sinner; (4) penitent only after he himself is castigated; (5) penitent only at "the gates of death."[22] This is an interesting combination of Baḥya's analogous four-fold classification[23] and Saadia's five-fold classification.[24] Rabad's list is to be seen as a composite one, grafting both sources together, but leaning most heavily on Baḥya.

In further describing God's relation to and presence in the world, Rabad says that the existence of created things does not separate God from the world or restrict His Being.

> The Creator is the place of the world but the world is not His place. The analogy of this is that the world is full of air and everything enters into the air. They feel it but it is invisible to them.[25]

This analogy, which, as Professor Scholem mentions, was adopted and elaborated by later kabbalists, is to be traced back to Saadia.[26] Attention should be called to the similar discussion in the *Emunot*

20. *BH*, 88.
21. *Ḥobot ha-Lebabot*, I, 7. This was noted by Scholem, *Reshit ha-Kabbalah*, 82.
22. *Derashah le-Rosh ha-Shanah*, ed. A. S. ha-Levi (London, 1955), 24.
23. *Ḥobot ha-Lebabot*, VII, 6.
24. *Emunot we-Deᶜot*, V, 1.
25. *BH*, 88. See also *Sefer ha-Minhagot*, in *Sifran*, 144. ברוך כבוד ה׳ ממקומו· הוא מקומו של עולם ואין עולם מקומו· ודגמתו אבן שואבת שמעמידים אותה למעלה ונושאה את הברזל מתחתיה·
26. Scholem, *Reshit ha-Kabbalah*, 83.

we-De^cot: "How is it possible to conceive the thought of God's presence everywhere so that no place would be vacant of His presence.[27] Also, Judah b. Barzilai, in his commentary on *Sefer Yeẓirah*, observes that "all places are in me [God], for I am the place of my world and my world is not my place and I am the place of all my creatures."[28]

Interesting in its own right is the question of Rabad's knowledge and use of a ninth-century Arabic collection of ethical apothegms by Ḥonein b. Ishak translated into Hebrew by Judah al-Ḥarizi as *Musre ha-Pilosofim.*[29] According to Steinschneider, this is one of the first non-Jewish Arabic works to be translated into Hebrew.[30] Marx and Ginzberg contend that Rabad's statement in *Hilkot Teshubah* (that "this author did not conduct himself according to the custom of the sages, for one does not start something if he does not know how to finish it") is actually a quotation from the *Musre ha-Pilosofim* ("do not start something which you will be unable to finish").[31] If Rabad actually used this as his literary model, it follows that it is the oldest known quotation from the *Musre ha-Pilosofim* by a French author.[32]

The question of the place of man in creation and, especially, his relation to the angels—in other words, the subject of anthropocentrism which was a favorite of both midrashic and philosophic speculation[33] —is taken up, among others, by Solomon ibn Gabirol. Speaking of the fact that everything was created for the purpose of serving and benefiting man, Gabirol observes in the introduction to the *Tiḳḳun Middot ha-Nefesh*:

27. *Emunot we-De^cot*, II, 13.

28. Judah b. Barzilai, *Perush Sefer Yeẓirah*, ed. S. J. Halberstam (Berlin, 1885), 17. For additional references, especially in the literature of mysticism, see G. Scholem, *Major Trends in Jewish Mysticism*, 108–109, and for Midrash, see G. F. Moore, *Judaism* (Cambridge, Mass., 1944), I, 370.

29. Ed. A. Loewenthal (Frankfurt a.M., 1896).

30. Steinschneider, *Die Hebraeischen Uebersetzungen des Mittelalters*, 350.

31. *MT*, *Teshubah*, V, 5; *Musre ha-Pilosofim*, ed. Loewenthal, 39; Marx, "Bemerkungen zu Steinschneider's Hebraeischen Uebersetzungen," *Zeitschrift für Hebraische Bibliographie*, X (1906), 95; Ginzberg, *JE*, I, 103.

32. The demonstration of this relation is not entirely convincing. First of all, the thought itself is too much of a commonsense maxim to warrant any assertion of literary dependence. Second, the date of the translation is uncertain (Steinschneider, *Hebraeischen Uebersetzungen*, 351) and, in order to date the work before 1216, let alone before 1194, one would have to assume that the introduction was a belated addition to the completed translation (*ibid.*, n. 671). It is, of course, possible that fragments of the work were in circulation or that there were oral traditions from this work.

33. For the midrashic background, see G. F. Moore, *Judaism*, I, 445–451; for the philosophic background, see Malter, *Saadia Gaon*, 212 ff., esp. n. 485. Saadia (*Emunot we-De^cot*, IV, introduction) is the first to formulate the traditional view in philosophic context.

We see that the angels are used for the purposes of serving the needs of the righteous person. We know this from the Patriarch Abraham when [the angels came] to inform and warn him. . . . There are many illustrations of these matters and I will not expatiate to recall them.[34]

The language, imagery, and ideas of Gabirol are reflected in the following passage of Rabad taken from the context of a similar discussion and not distinguished by any philosophic language:

Even the higher spiritual being [angels] are given over to serve the righteous person. We found this [in the case] of the angel who came to inform Sarah. . . . There is no need to expatiate in this matter, for [it is illustrated] in many places which are known to all.[35]

In Gabirol, as well as in other philosophic literature available to Rabad, it was common to point out analogies between the four elements of nature and the four humors of man. This analogy which, as Wolfson has shown, stems from a passage in Galen,[36] is expressed by Solomon ibn Gabirol in the *Tiḳḳun Middot ha-Nefesh* as follows: "God created man with four natural elements, for he has in him blood which is analogous to air, phlegm which is analogous to water."[37] Already, Shabbetai Donnolo, in the first part of *Ḥakemoni*, works with this parallelism: "So He created man also from the four elements: from air, water, fire, and earth, and they are blood, phlegm, choler and melancholy."[38] In discussing the nature and importance of man, Rabad says that "the four elements of man are based upon the four elements of the world and are nourished by them."[39]

Besides these concepts and phrases already described and correlated with the philosophic literature from which they were taken, there are a number of key philosophic terms scattered throughout Rabad's writings. He uses such phrases as "First Cause" (*ᶜilat ha-ᶜilot*), "existence" (*yeshut*), "eternith" (*ḳadmut*), "creation" (*ḥiddush*), "ex nihilo" (*yesh me-ayin*), "rational being" (*ḥay medaber*), "animal soul" (*nefesh behemit*), "predetermination" (*gezerah*), "higher spiritual beings"

34. *Tiḳḳun Middot ha-Nefesh*, introduction.

35. *BH*, 3.

36. Wolfson, "Arabic and Hebrew Terms for Matter and Element," *JQR*, XXXVIII (1947), 56.

37. *Tiḳḳun Middot ha-Nefesh*, 4. See the translation of S. Wise (New York, 1901), 13, where he claims that Gabirol "copies the words" of Donnolo.

38. Shabbetai Donnolo, *Ḥakemoni* (Warsaw, 1884), 12a. That Rabad was acquainted with Donnolo's text of the *Sefer Yeẓirah*, and presumably with his *Ḥakemoni*, may be ascertained on the basis of a quotation from the *Sefer Yeẓirah*; see A. Epstein, "Studien zum Jezira-Buche und seinen Erklärern," *MGWJ*, XXXVII (1893), 268 (and reprinted in *Miḳadmoniyot ha-Yehudim*, ed. A. M. Haberman [Jerusalem, 1957], 205, 207).

39. *BH*, 3.

(*ruḥanim ᶜelyonim*—in the sense of angels).[40] In connection with his use of the term "creatio ex nihilo," Rabad categorically excludes the admission of any preexistent hyle from which God created the world. "Even though the artisan makes the vessel from the fine earth, yet the preexistent earth preceded the vessel and preceded the creating artisan. But nothing preceded God. . . . He created everything ex nihilo."[41] Besides, other Arabicized Hebrew terms, introduced by the contemporary translators—for instance, *ḥaber* in the sense of "compose," *hassagah* for "criticism," *anshe* for devotees of a certain subject—are also used by Rabad.[42]

In the philosophic literature available to Rabad, the problem of human free will versus divine foreknowledge was customarily solved by maintaining that God's knowledge was not causative or determinative. Saadia repeats this middle-of-the-road solution as follows: "The Creator's foreknowledge of things is [not] the cause of their coming into being" or "Its untenability is made clear by the realization that if God's foreknowledge of anything could be the cause of its coming into being."[43] Ha-Levi also reproduces this answer, which was the stock Kalam view:

> The Mutakallims considered this matter in detail, with the result that the divine knowledge of the potential is but casual, that the knowledge of a thing is not the cause of its coming into existence and God's knowledge does not compel.[44]

Maimonides did not believe this to be a satisfactory answer and did not repeat it.[45] In the *Mishneh Torah* he states that the antinomy is insoluble,

40. *BH*, esp. 3, 4, 80, 87, 88.

41. *Ibid.*, 88; see Wolfson, "The Platonic, Aristotelian and Stoic Theories of Creation in Hallevi and Maimonides," *Essays in Honor of . . . Dr. Hertz* (London, 1942), 427–442. The proposition of creation *ex nihilo*, seems to be emphasized elsewhere also, but in midrashic form, actually as a midrashic quotation. Maimonides (*MT Teshubah*, III, 7) describes one of the five categories of heretics as "he who denies that God alone is the First Cause and Rock [*ẓur*] of the Universe." The term *ẓur* used by Maimonides might be interpreted ambiguously either as creator (*yoẓer*) or as artist (*ẓayyar*). Since the second meaning of an artist working with a preexistent eternal and uncreated matter is completely objectionable, Rabad neatly qualifies Maimonides' definition of this type of heretic by referring anonymously to the famous midrashic dialogue (*Genesis Rabbah*, I, 9) in which the heathen philosopher says to the rabbi "Your God was a great artist (*ẓayyar*) but surely He found good materials which assisted Him."

42. For these terms, see Zunz, *Gesammelte Schriften* (Berlin, 1875), I, 51; M. Wilensky, ed., *ha-Riḳma*, 2, n. 8; 19, n. 7.

43. *Emunot we-Deᶜot*, IV, 4.

44. *Cuzari*, V, 20.

45. See also Albo, *ᶜIḳḳarim*, IV, 1, who quotes Saadia and Halevi but remains dissatisfied.

inasmuch as any analysis of the problem necessarily operates in two separate dimensions. The omniscience and prescience of God, on one hand, and the freedom of the will, on the other, are two incommensurate concepts. Divine knowledge, which obliterates the customary subject-object division, is incomprehensible to us and therefore we cannot eliminate or logically circumvent this inherent contradiction between the freedom of man and the knowledge of God. Both, Maimonides concludes, must remain articles of faith.[46]

This exposition—which Husik has termed "agnostic"[47]—displeased Rabad and led him to submit hesitantly a solution of his own:

> Although there is no decisive answer to this [dilemma] it is desirable to provide some answer. I say that if the righteousness or wickedness of man were dependent on the decree of the Creator Blessed be He, we would conclude that His knowledge is His decree and then the question would be very difficult for us. Now that the Creator removed this power from His hand and put it in man's own hand, His prescience is not a decree but may be compared to the foreknowledge of the astrologers who conclude the character of a man from the stars. It is known that whatever happens to man, great or small, God turned over to the power of the stars. He bestowed upon man, however, a mind which gives him the strength to avert the influence of the stars. That is the possibility given to man to be good or bad. The Creator knows the power of the stars and can judge whether the mind has the strength to overcome it. This knowledge is not a decree. But all this is not worth much [as an answer].[48]

The problematic aspect of God's prescience in relation to man's freedom is thus disposed of by Rabad just as it was by Saadia and ha-Levi—prescience is not a decree. When he says that "it is desirable to provide some answer" to this dilemma, he is merely falling back upon the conventional theory which Maimonides had rejected.

Borrowing from astrological works which were current in southern France and reflecting especially Abraham ibn Ezra's writings, Rabad illustrates or vivifies this reproduction of the prevalent Kalam theory by comparing God's foreknowledge to an astrologer's augury, which is able to forecast but does not determine the future. The influence of the stars,

46. *MT*, *Teshubah*, V, 5. See on this R. Isaac b. Sheshet, *Responsa*, 118 (see §1, note 14); R. Shem Tob ibn Shem Tob, *Derashot ha-Torah* (Padua, 1567), 10a; R. Simeon Duran, *Oheb Mishpaṭ*, VI, 116.

47. I. Husik, *A History of Medieval Jewish Philosophy* (New York, 1916), XLVIII, 287.

48. *MT*, *Teshubah* V, 5. Part of this hassagah was translated by Marx, *Studies in Jewish History and Booklore*, 74. See A. Ibn Ezra, *Yesod Mora*, VII, 28b: יש כח במשכיל לבחור הטוב והרע כי אין הגזירות רק כפי המקבל. And Abraham bar Ḥiyya, *Megillat ha-Megaleh*, V, 112: ויהיה מוחזק בידינו שהקב״ה מסיר ממשלת הככבים ומבטל את כחם בכל עת שירצה.

belief in which was a fashionable, widespread doctrine, is not determinative, for God endowed man with adequate intellectual resources with which to avert this influence and liberate his destiny from blind power. Man remains, therefore, in the face of both divine foreknowledge and stellar influence, a free, volitional creature capable of self-determination.[49]

A famous hassagah on the *Mishneh Torah* indirectly involves both the problem of Rabad's attitude toward philosophy as well as his use of philosophic terminology. The issue was the well-known question of divine Incorporeality, which had been discussed at great length and on many occasions by the rabbis and by all Jewish philosophers from Philo to Maimonides. The metaphoric interpretation of all Scriptural anthropomorphisms, in keeping with the explicit Scriptural doctrine of the absolute unlikeness of God, was the accepted view.[50] Maimonides, in his code, makes a five-fold classification of heretics, the third of which is "he who says there is one ruler, but that He is a body and has form."[51] He thus elevated a common belief to the status of rigid dogma. In his animadversion directed against this part of Maimonides' statement, Rabad comments trenchantly:

Why has he called such a person an heretic? There are many people greater than and superior to him who adhere to such a belief on the basis of what they have seen in verses of Scripture and even more in the words of those *aggadot* which corrupt right opinion about religious matters.[52]

This polemical statement, which alludes to the Scriptural sanction of the use of anthropomorphisms and the intensified use of anthropomorphic descriptions by the rabbis, has received varying interpretations

49. For a good summary of astrology among the Jews, see Marx, *Studies*, 63–76 (reprinted from *HUCA*, III [1926], 311–325). Abraham ibn Ezra, Ex. 7:3. On the use of ibn Ezra's commentary in Provence, see also Efros, *JQR*, XVII, 130, n. 14. For another parallel between Rabad and Abraham ibn Ezra, see *Sifra Commentary*, 1a, and *Yesod Mora*, VI, 25b.

50. Wolfson, *Philo*, I, 55 ff., 135; II, 127. A. Geiger, "Die Anthropomorphismen in der Haggadah und die Rabbinen der arabischen Schule," *Niṭᶜe Naᶜamanim* (Sammlung), ed. S. Heilberg (Breslau, 1847), 44–49. See the text of R. Nissim Gaon, *Niṭᶜe Naᶜamanim*, 15a–17a.

51. *MT*, *Teshubah*, III, 7.

52. *Ibid.*: ולמה קרא לזה מין וכמה גדולים וטובים ממנו הלכו בזו המחשבה לפי מה שראו במקראות ויותר ממה שראו בדברי האגדות המשבשות את הדעות. The manuscript of the hassagot in the Jewish Theological Seminary omits the word *mimenu* and thus takes the sting out of this note. For variations of the passage, see D. Kaufmann, *Geschichte der Attributenlehre*, 487–488; M. Kasher, *Torah Shleimah* (New York, 1955), XVI, 288 ff. The version of R. Solomon Luria is identical with our printed one, including the word *mimenu*; see *Yam Shel Shelomoh*, *Ḥullin*, introduction. The underlying phrase is probably I *Kings*, 2:32 (צדיקים וטובים ממנו).

from students who have dealt with Rabad's opinion either directly or parenthetically. Some scholars like Eppenstein, Gross, David Kaufmann, Ezekiel Kaufmann, Rawidowicz, with slight shades of opinion between them,[53] disregarding the very meaningful conclusion of Rabad's animadversion which brands the anthropomorphic legends as corrupting, place him in the camp of anthropomorphists or attributists. Eppenstein states that, although Rabad had a "somewhat more enlightened anschauung," he was subject to an "inner conflict" and did not want to break with the old view. E. Kaufmann, in keeping with his simplified view that anthropomorphism was no problem for the Jews until they were exposed to philosophy, asserts that "the accepted opinion was that the Torah obligates [sic] one to believe that God had form," and he quotes Rabad as corroborative evidence. Against this harsh judgment, other scholars—like Steinschneider, Guedemann, Ginzberg, and Kadushin[54]—maintain that the last phrase clearly indicates that Rabad himself did not subscribe to the principle of corporeality but intended only to defend its adherents against the charge of heresy. Atlas expresses this view as follows:

> It is obvious that Rabad's intention was only to criticize the condemnation of those who under the influence of passages in the Bible and the Talmud erroneously held such notions. Rabad, himself, however writes of those views as being conceived erroneously.[55]

Deserving special mention is Scholem's interpretation which submits that Rabad's hassagah reflects the mystical belief in a logos—"which is like a body to the soul." Although Rabad and the mystics agreed that God as the first Cause was absolutely spiritual, they were willing to sanction all corporeal allusions with reference to the Demiurge.[56]

There is not a shadow of doubt that Rabad was personally committed to the traditional Jewish view which maintained the unlikeness and incorporeality of God as an indispensable corollary of the existence and

53. S. Eppenstein, in *Moses ben Maimon (sein Leben, seine Werke und sein Einfluss)*, ed. J. Guttmann (Leipzig, 1914), II, 73, n. 2. Gross, XXIII, 166; D. Kaufmann, *Attributenlehre*, 487; E. Kaufmann, *Toledot ha-Emunah ha-Yisre'elit* (Tel Aviv, 1937), I, bk. II, 240–241; S. Rawidowicz, "ᶜIyyune Rambam," *Meẓudah*, II (1944), 143, n. 39; and "Saadya's Purification of the Idea of God," *Saadya Studies*, ed. E. Rosenthal (Manchester, 1943), 163, n. 1. See also I. Heinemann, "Ha-he'abḳut ᶜal Hagshamat ha-El . . .," *Iyyun*, I (1946), 157.

54. Steinschneider, *Jewish Literature*, 87; Guedemann, *Ha-Torah weha-Ḥayyim* (Warsaw, 1896), I, 56; Ginzberg, *JE*, I, 103; Kadushin, *The Rabbinic Mind* (New York, 1943), 283, n. 40.

55. Atlas, in Rabad, *BK*, 26.

56. Scholem, *Reshit ha-Kabbalah*, 75.

unity of God. Those Talmudic legends and homilies which nurture the corporeal misconception of God are in his opinion "corrupting right opinion" about religious matters. Albo, neutralizing the acidity of Rabad's hassagah, quotes him as saying: "Certainly the essential principle of belief is that God is incorporeal."[57] Elsewhere in his writings, Rabad is emphatic and unequivocal concerning the elimination of all anthropomorphic attributes with regard to God: "it is not correct to speak in this manner about the Creator."[58] In this statement he implicitly concurs with the Talmudic maxim "the Torah speaks according to the language of men," which is explicitly invoked by Maimonides in the *Mishneh Torah* in connection with the allegorical interpretation of certain grossly anthropomorphic expressions of Scripture—and there also Rabad tacitly assents.[59] As a matter of fact, Rabad quotes the famous rabbinic statement from the *Mekilta*—"We describe God by terms borrowed from His creations in order to cause them to sink into the ear"[60]—with a few minor variations. He says concerning the description of God:

> If Scripture compared the Creator [in His act of creation] to clay in the hands of the potter, it is only that the ear might get it in accordance with its capacity for hearing [understanding]. Any simile applied to God is as remote from the literal sense of the metaphor as east is from west.[61]

Moreover, he was very fond of the *Ḥobot ha-Lebabot*, which is decidedly antianthropomorphistic.[62] He passes over Maimonides' lengthy metaphysical formulation of the absolute incorporeality of God in the very first chapter of *Hilkot Yesode ha-Torah* without comment or qualification. This is another case where an argument ex silentio may convincingly be mustered as corroborative evidence.

Why, then, did Rabad dissent so vociferously when Maimonides, in his enumeration of the "five classes [that] are termed heretics," included those who impute body or form to God together with those who actually deny His existence or posit a plurality of deities? Why did he employ

57. J. Albo, *ᶜIḳḳarim*, I, 2.
58. *BH*, 4.
59. *MT*, *Yesode ha-Torah*, I, 12; see *Berakot*, 31b.
60. *Mekilta*, II, 221.
61. *BH*, 88.
62. Louis Ginzberg (*JE*, I, 103) asserts that Rabad's encouragement of the translation of Baḥya's work is a sign of his allegiance to the antianthropomorphistic view. While the point is a good one, it should be observed that Baḥya's refutation of anthropomorphism occurs in the first chapter (section ten) which was translated at the request of Meshullam. Rabad only urged Judah ibn Tibbon to complete the translation.

such caustic and apparently abusive language, which has puzzled commentators and analysts? Why should he take issue with Maimonides on a matter concerning which they are in theoretical agreement?

The answer is that Rabad objected to the apodictic style in which Maimonides stressed the importance of this dogma. He was not against the belief in incorporeality, but he was against Maimonides' doctrinaire statement that one who affirms the corporeality of God is a heretic. Rabad contended that people to whom philosophic terminology was alien and who, conversely, used traditional terminology in the description of God, were not culpable. Certainly, individuals distinguished by impeccable piety and Talmudic erudition ought not to be stigmatized as heretics and, by implication, be denied a place in the hereafter as a result of their literal reading of Scripture. Literalism of this sort was evidently widespread. Maimonides himself was acquainted with Jews of unshakeable literalist persuasion, whom he condemned unqualifiedly. He reports that he encountered many prominent Talmudists some of whom were uncertain whether God possessed eyes, hands, and feet while others concluded categorically that God had a body with organs and senses.[63] This explains the inner motivation and psychological compulsion which led Maimonides to prefix a philosophical-theological prolegomenon to a code of law, for it was impossible for him to compose a treatise on the details of practical precepts while ignoring the fundamentals of essential beliefs.[64] Younger contemporaries and immediate successors such as Naḥmanides, David Kimḥi, and Maimonides' son Abraham also inform us of the prevalence of these beliefs.[65] Rabad presumably knew such people, whom he held in high esteem, and he was not prepared to dismiss them as second-rate Jews, even though he himself did not favor literalism.

Professor Wolfson calls my attention to a fact which he has often underscored: that the expression implied by Maimonides—Incorporeality—is a purely philosophic term and is not found in Scripture at all. Scripture speaks only of the "unlikeness" of God, which Philo for the first time equated with the doctrine of philosophic incorporeality. In his footsteps, all philosophers identified this philosophic view with

63. *Ma'amar Teḥiyat ha-Metim* in *Iggerot ha-Rambam*, ed. M. D. Rabinovitz (Tel Aviv, 1951), 345.

64. *Ibid.*, 345–346; see, for example, Rawidowicz, *Meẓudah*, VII (1954), 128.

65. Naḥmanides, *Ḳobeẓ Teshubot ha-Rambam*, III, 9b; D. Kimḥi, *ibid.*, 3b; Abraham Maimonides, *Milḥamot ha-Shem*, ed. R. Margaliyot (Jerusalem, 1953), 52; for a later period, see the interesting account in ʿ*Eser Orot* (Pietrekov, 1907), 82.

this Scriptural teaching but recognized that divine Incorporeality is nowhere explicitly taught in Scripture.[66] In his hassagah Rabad does not repeat the term for incorporeality. He must have been thinking only in terms of "unlikeness." An erroneous notion concerning the philosophic conception of the Incorporeality of God did not necessarily imply religious imperfection and need not be condemned. Philosophic interpretations were not, in Rabad's opinion, binding for all Jews.

Such, in essence, is the view, popular and tolerant, expressed also by Baḥya ibn Pakuda in the first section of his philosophic work, the contents of which Rabad had undoubtedly absorbed:

> The foolish and simple person will conceive the Creator in accordance with the literal sense of the Scriptural phrase. And if he assumes the obligation of serving his God and strives to labor for His glory, he has in his simplicity and lack of understanding a great excuse for his erroneous conception. For man is accountable for his thoughts and deeds only according to his powers of apprehension and comprehension, physical strength, and material means.[67]

It is in the spirit of this view of Baḥya that the concurrent opinion of Rabad is reformulated in the fifteenth century by Joseph Albo, the last of the great medieval Jewish philosophers. Albo was well-acquainted with Rabad's theory, which he quotes—with a very meaningful variation—and explains as part of an interesting justification of both philosophic inquiry and speculative nonconformity. His argument runs as follows, the similarities to Rabad being self-evident:

> We say, therefore, that a person whose speculative ability is not sufficient to enable him to reach the true meaning of Scriptural texts, with the result that he believes in the literal meaning and entertains absurd ideas because he thinks they represent the view of the Torah, is not thereby excluded from the community of those who believe in the Torah, Heaven forbid. Nor is it permitted to speak disrespectfully of him and accuse him of perverting the teaching of the Torah and class him among heretics.[68]

3. *Rabad and Kabbalah*

Later kabbalistic writers such as R. Isaac of Acre, R. Shem Tob b. Gaon, and R. Menaḥem Recanati insistently claimed Rabad as one of

66. Wolfson, *Philo*, II, 96 ff.; *idem*, "Spinoza and Religion," *Menorah Journal* (1950), 146–167.
67. *Ḥobot ha-Lebabot*, I, 10.
68. *ʿIkkarim*, I, 2.

their own and placed him in the front ranks of their spiritual progenitors. They depicted him as a mystic who was worthy of receiving—and actually did receive—special revelation.[1] Most of these reports emanate from the school of Naḥmanides and Rashbah and there is no reason to question them. There are also older, more immediately reliable references in the writings of Rabad's son R. Isaac the Blind, who was included by later mystics in the group of three or four founders who were guided by special acts of revelation. R. Isaac speaks of his father's knowledge of mysticism; both he and his nephew R. Asher mention esoteric doctrines which they learned from Rabad.[2] Although these early reports from the pen of his immediate descendants refer with ostensible pride to Rabad's expert knowledge of secret teachings, they nowhere even allude to the acquisition of this knowledge through the medium of revelation. This seems to be a later accretion. In any event, while subsequent kabbalistic opinion is unanimous about Rabad's role, the historian seeks to collect the empirical evidence that is forthcoming to substantiate these reports.

To the historian's despair, nothing from the pen of Rabad is devoted especially to mysticism. Joseph Solomon del Medigo allegedly possessed a book of "the kabbalah of Rabad," but nothing whatsoever is known about such a work.[3] The pseudepigraphic character of the commentary on *Sefer Yeẓirah*—already suspected by such a venerable kabbalist as R. Ḥayyim Vital[4]—has been definitely established. It has even been dated around 1300 and Joseph b. Shalom Ashkenazi has been named as its author.[5] The tract listed by de Rossi as *Roshe Pirḳe Sodot* is also of no help. This listing is known to be erroneous—one of the many misinterpretations which mar de Rossi's catalogue.[6] However, although the

1. See Scholem, *Reshit ha-Kabbalah*, 16, n. 1; A. Heschel, "ᶜ*Al Ruaḥ ha-Ḳodesh* . . .," *Alexander Marx Jubilee Volume* (New York, 1950), 190–192.

2. See Chapter V.

3. *Nobelot Ḥokmah*, 195b; see Michael, *Or ha-Ḥayyim*, 29. Scholem, *Reshit ha-Kabbalah*, 76, n. 2, suggests that this may be the source from which del Medigo (*Nobelot Ḥokmah*, 5a of unnumbered introduction) quoted a long passage in the name of Rabad.

4. R. Ḥayyim Vital, *Eẓ Ḥayyim*, introduction: וביאור ס׳ יצירה להראב״ד איננו להראב״ד ז״ל . . .

5. G. Scholem, "Ha-Meḥaber ha-Amiti shel Perush Sefer Yeẓirah," *Peraḳim* (Jerusalem, 1931), 2–17. For other writings of this author, see also J. Vajda, "Un chapitre de l'histoire du conflit entre la Kabbale et la philosophie. La polémique anti-intellectualiste de Joseph b. Shalom Ashkenazi," *Archives d'histoire doctrinale et littéraire du moyen âge*, XXIII (1956), 45–144, and *idem*, *Tarbiẓ*, XXVII (1958), 290–300.

6. De Rossi, cod. 1220; Gross, XXIII, 175, n. 1; see Scholem, "Mafteaḥ le-Perushim ᶜal ᶜEser Sefirot," *Kiryath Sefer*, X (1934), 499, 505.

ending—"as the sages received from the great Rabbi, the light of Israel's eyes, Rabad"—does not indicate Rabad's authorship, it is nevertheless significant. If it does not provide us with a genuine work by Rabad, it can serve, together with other pseudepigraphic attributions, as an added indication of Rabad's connection with Kabbalah in the eyes of subsequent generations.

Not only is there no extant kabbalistic treatise of Rabad but one even looks despairingly for kabbalistic motifs in his other writings. An allusion to his kabbalistic inclinations can perhaps be discerned in his parenthetical use of the phrase "crown of the king" (*taga de-malka*), and Razah's caustic rebuttal of his opinion which contains the following gibe: "Now, kindly listen, even if you repeat all day long [by way of oath] crown of the king and Lord of Abraham, we shall not listen."[7] He concludes his *Ba^cale ha-Nefesh* by quoting and explaining the famous string of pietistic aphorisms attributed to R. Pineḥas b. Yaïr. What is more, he produces in the course of his explanation a definition of ḥasid which adumbrates that usually associated with German Ḥasidism. The *Sefer Ḥasidim* states: "The essence of ḥasiduth is to act in all things not on but within the line of strict justice, that is to say, not to insist in one's own interest on the letter of the Torah."[8] Rabad says succinctly: "One who acts in all cases within the line of strict justice—that is, beyond the requirements of the law—is called ḥasid."[9] This is certainly noteworthy, but it is not distinctively kabbalistic or even esoteric. It appears that even the kabbalistic "allusions" mentioned by Shem Tob ibn Gaon are hard to verify. Neither his explication of aggadic passages nor his original homilies evoked kabbalistic comments from him. The extant commentaries on *Baba Ḳamma* and *^cAbodah Zarah* have nothing along these lines; the same is true for the

7. *Dibre ha-Ribot*, 33, 40; for *taga* as the "crown of the ineffable name," see now Scholem, *Jewish Gnosticism, Merkabah Mysticism, and Talmudic Tradition* (New York, 1960), 54–55.

8. Scholem, *Major Trends in Jewish Mysticism*, 93. Maimonides also stresses the radicalism and extremism involved in *ḥasiduth*: *Mishnah Commentary, Abot*, V, 7; *MT, De^cot*, I, 5; see Scholem, *Major Trends*, 97, and references there.

9. *BH*, 89. It might be noted here that there was considerable contact between Provence and Germany. R. Samuel he-Ḥasid (b. 1115) visited Provence; see A. Epstein, *Ketabim*, ed. A. Haberman (Jerusalem, 1950), 247; and Scholem, *Major Trends*, 114. It is also reported that the *Sefer ha-Bahir* reached Provence via Germany; see J. Mann, *Texts and Studies in Jewish History*, II, 75, 80; and Scholem, *Reshit ha-Kabbalah*, 18. By 1250, a disciple of R. Eleazar of Worms figures prominently among Provençal mystics; see Scholem, *Reshit ha-Kabbalah*, 49. One version of the *Sefer Ḥasidim* contains an interpolation from *BH*; see Reifmann, *Arba^cah Ḥarashim* (Prague, 1860), 8.

nonhalakic portions of the *Sifra*. Nothing is forthcoming even in those places in his animadversionary writings where one would expect the statements of other authors to have aroused him, or at least to have given him a pretext, to reveal his kabbalistic inclinations.[10] Aside from the hassagah on *Hilkot Yesode ha-Torah*—and even this is a guarded, reticent reaction stimulated by Maimonides' sweeping statement[11]—I venture to state that one will search his numerous writings in vain for mystical doctrines and kabbalistic terminology. They are simply not there.[12]

Consequently, in the absence of statements in Rabad's own works which could be directly identified as kabbalistic, the fact of his actual acquaintance with the doctrines and symbolism of kabbalah rests upon a number of passages, quoted by others in the name of Rabad, which contain kabbalistic concepts and terms.[13] These passages deal with mystical meditations during prayer (*kawwanah*) and, especially, with the doctrine of the ten *sefirot* or emanations, and establish beyond doubt that this doctrine—most distinctive of medieval kabbalah—was already used by Rabad. In these passages attributed to Rabad there is revealed an acquaintance with early *Hekalot* terminology—as in the technical use of *yoẓer bereshit*[14]—and, incidentally, its fusion with contemporary

10. See, for example, *MT*, *Tefillin*, V, 4; *Hagahot Maimuniyot*, *ad. loc. Maḥzo Vitry*, 648, makes the inscription of names of angels on the *mezuzah* obligatory.

11. *MT*, *Yesode ha-Torah*, I, 10. Not only was this abstruse note elicited, as it were, by Maimonides' erroneous interpretation of a perplexing passage, but, in the final analysis, it reveals nothing. It merely alludes to the "great secret of 'front' and 'back,'" which becomes a favorite of kabbalistic exegesis; see, for example, *Sefer ha-Bahir*, section 58; R. Azriel, *Perush Aggadot*, ed. I. Tishbi, 10; Naḥmanides, commentary, Ex. 33:14; also *Oẓar ha-Geonim*, *Berakot*, 15.

12. There are a number of coincidences outside the realm of theosophy between certain opinions of Rabad and the general trend of kabbalistic thought. For example, the rigid view concerning the prohibition of work on the intermediate days of the three major festivals—see *TD*, 40; *Oraḥ Ḥayyim*, 31, 2, and *Be'er ha-Golah*, *ad. loc.*; the custom of fasting on the day before *Rosh ha-Shanah*—see *Derashah le-Rosh ha-Shanah*, 31; *Ṭur Oraḥ Ḥayyim*, 582, and *Bet Joseph*, *ad. loc.*; and my remarks in *Kiryath Sefer*, XXXII (1957), 442; belief in the corporeal composition of angels—see Scholem, "Iḳbotaw shel Gabirol . . .," *Me'assef Ereẓ Israel*, 176, who refers to *MT*, *Teshubah*, VIII, 2. Rabad writes (*Derashah*, 32) that, as a result of Adam's weeping, supplication and repentance, God forgave him and "lengthened his days." Rabbi A. S. ha-Levi, editor of the *Derashah*, kindly informed me that, while there is no overt midrashic source for this, there is an explicit parallel in the *Zohar Ḥadash*, 19a.

13. Scholem, *Reshit ha-Kabbalah*, 66–99. Scholem published and interpreted much manuscript material which is indispensable for any study of the problem. This volume will soon be available in English translation.

14. For example, commenting on the Talmudic homily—"how do we know that the Holy One, blessed be He, puts on phylacteries" (*Berakot*, 6a; *Megillah*, 24b)—R. Asher b. David quotes his grandfather Rabad as follows (*Oẓar Neḥmad*, IV [1864], 37):

philosophic vocabulary—as *ᶜilat ha-ᶜilot.*[15] Both the teachings and the idiom in which they are expressed are axial in kabbalistic literature.

In light of these attributions, the absence of kabbalistic motifs in Rabad's own writings[16] can only be explained on the basis of his unqualified esotericism. This was, of course, by no means peculiar to Kabbalah, for the Talmudic admonition—"one must not discourse on the work of creation before two students, nor on the work of the chariot before one student, unless that student be wise and able to speculate by himself"[17]—was equally applicable to philosophers and mystics in keeping with their individual understanding of "the work of creation" and "the work of the chariot." The specific application of Rabad's esotericism is, however, definitely kabbalistic. His son says that "not a word [about mysticism] escaped" his father's mouth,[18] while Rabad himself observes with regard to one special doctrine: "The subject of 'front' and 'back' is a great secret and it is not proper to reveal it to every man."[19] Even topics which are treated elsewhere in unmistakably

"This is said in reference to the Angel of the Divine Presence, that is Metatron, 'whose name is similar to that of His master' (*Sanhedrin*, 38b; Ex. 23:21 and commentaries, *ad. loc.*). Or perhaps there is yet a being higher than this, emanated from the first cause, and possessing greater power. It was this being that appeared to Moses and that appeared to Ezekiel in the 'appearance of man from above' (Ezek. 1:26) and that appeared to the prophets, but the first cause (*ᶜilat ha-ᶜilot*) never appeared to any person, neither from the aspect [or in the manifestation] of 'right' or 'left,' 'front' or 'back.' This is the secret underlying the 'work of creation': 'Whoever knows—the measurement of the Creator of the World (*yoẓer bereshit*) . . . is certain of his share of the world to come.' In this connection was it said: 'Let us make man in our image.'"

The reference to *yoẓer bereshit* is from *Sheᶜur Ḳomah*, ed. S. Mussajoff in *Sefer Merkabah Shleimah* (Jerusalem, 1922), 38b; see Scholem, *Major Trends*, 66, and, now, *idem, Jewish Gnosticism, Merkabah, Mysticism . . .*, 28, n. 18. On *Metatron* in midrashic and mystical literature, see R. Margaliyot, *Mal'ake ᶜElyon* (Jerusalem, 1945), 73 ff. Scholem, *Reshit ha-Kabbalah*, 76–77, explores the possible meanings of Metatron in this context and shows how the notion of the demiurge merged with the concept of emanations. Rabad also quotes the *Sefer Yeẓirah*; see Gross, XXIII (1874), 176; A. Epstein, "Studien zum Jezira-Buche und seinen Erklärern," *MGWJ*, XXXVII (1893), 268 (reprinted in *Miḳadmoniyot ha-Yehudim*, ed. A. M. Haberman, 204).

15. See also the passage quoted by Scholem, *Reshit ha-Kabbalah*, 73, n. 2. According to the manuscript reading accepted by Scholem, "Der Begriff der Kawwana in der alten Kabbala," *MGWJ*, LXXVIII (1934), 502, it is Rabad who makes a direct reference to the *sefirot Tif'eret* and *Binah*.

16. It would appear that even the kabbalistic statements attributed to Rabad in later writings are oral reports rather than direct literary quotations. Most of them are cited בשם הראב״ד, a few as פי׳ הראב״ד or לשון הרב. The one textual quotation—the hassagah on *MT*, *Yesode ha-Torah*, I, 3, cited in the *Nobelot Ḥokmah*—is, as was noted, of doubtful authenticity.

17. M., *Ḥagigah* II, 1.

18. See Chapter V.

19. *MT*, *Yesode ha-Torah*, I, 10. Prof. Scholem kindly informed me that the statement (quoted by Sassoon, *Ohel David*, II, 1014—אמר אברהם בר דוד בסוד האלף, לא אליכם כל עוברי דרך ענין החכמה הנוראה הזאת כי ליושבים לפני ה׳ יהיה סחרה is pseudepigraphic.

mystical terminology are alluded to in his rabbinic writings in conventional idiom.[20] It should be remembered that such secrecy, to some extent inherent in the mystical lore itself, was also conditioned historically. The major kabbalists were insistent upon reserve and reticence, and their opponents were irritated when a few overzealous kabbalists indulged in indiscreet propagandizing.[21] It took almost a hundred years for Kabbalah to break its narrow bonds and emerge even partially from its shell.

There remains for consideration a vague and elusive problem in semantics, which revolves around Rabad's occasional use of some quasi-mystical phraseology. In the introduction to his commentary on *ᶜEduyot*, which he considered a paragon of scholarship, he places all the blame for errors on his own shoulders while attributing "the good and the upright" to the "secret, as is written 'the secret counsel of the Lord is with them that fear Him; and His covenant, to make them know it.'"[22] It is not rare to find him referring to teachings which "they have shown him from heaven"[23] or asserting that "so has it been revealed to me from 'the secret counsel of the Lord [which] is with them that fear him.'"[24] After expounding an important view concerning a question of purity and uncleanness, he blesses "God who revealed His secrets to those who fear Him."[25] Elsewhere, he claims that "the Holy Spirit formerly appeared in our house of study" and imparted to him certain doctrines which he incorporated in a special treatise.[26] In criticism of a Maimonidean view he remarks that "this is not part of the wonderful secret which is stored away for the upright."[27] Such metaphors, predicated on the basic notion of special revelation, are a standard ingredient of Rabad's style and the question is: did he employ them literally or figuratively? Did he consciously mean to attribute some of

20. E.g., the duality of transcendence and immanence is also stressed by Rabad, *BH*, 88, in semiphilosophical but definitely nonmystical language, with no allusion to the *sefirot*. Concerning the explanation for the joint creation of Adam and Eve, which serves as a prelude to the exposition of a basic mystical theory (Scholem, 79), see the conventional presentation in *BH*, 4.

21. Scholem, "Teᶜudah Ḥadashah . . .," *Sefer Bialik* (Tel Aviv, 1934), 146.

22. Introduction to *ᶜEduyot*: ואולי יקרה בהם שגגה משגגת היד או משגגת הלב ידע הקורא בו, כי העון ולא ברבותי· והנמצא בו מן הטוב והישר ידע כי הוא מן הסוד כענין שנאמר סוד ה׳ ליראיו ובריתו להודיעם·

23. E.g., *TD*, 50, 114; *KS*, III, 37, 38.

24. *MT*, *Bet ha-Beḥirah*, VI, 14.

25. *Ibid.*, *Mishkab U-Moshab*, VII, 7.

26. *Ibid.*, *Lulab*, VIII, 5.

27. *Ibid.*, *Ṭume'at Oklin*, XV, 1.

his critical insights to a form of divine illumination or were these expressions intended to signify the result of concentrated study for which he thanked the omniscient God? Did he intend to transfer a supernatural source of knowledge to the sober, rationally defined realm of halakah?

Divergent interpretations have been offered for the use of this phraseology. Some scholars, unwilling a priori to allow the possibility of Rabad's association with the Kabbalah, insist upon a purely metaphorical interpretation, as if this usage by itself, literally construed, would be sufficient to indicate Rabad's mysticism.[28] Others, convinced of the centrality of Rabad's role in the Kabbalah, accept these phrases literally, endowing them with profound mystical connotations; they serve as an added proof of his mysticism.[29] The correctness of these interpretations is totally divorced from the concomitant motivation: Rabad may have been an early Kabbalist and still used these phrases as conventional rabbinic figures of speech, or vice versa. His reputation as a Kabbalist does not stand or fall on this matter. Even if these phrases were accepted literally, as manifestations of a mystical belief, this fact by itself would not warrant making him a Kabbalist while, on the contrary, other evidence indicative of his incipient knowledge of mystical lore speaks independently of this equivocal corroboration.

Before this terminological issue will yield any tenable conclusions, it should be analyzed from an historical and literary perspective: the extent and nature of the precedents there are for this usage; and the context in which Rabad himself uses the phrases. To state my conclusion in advance, it would seem that there is no internal, stylistic or contextual, proof to warrant the assertion that this assortment of phrases is consciously tinted with mystical beliefs about divine illumination or that the one who employs them ipso facto becomes a mystic. This does not mean that people may not have used these phrases with decidedly mystical connotations nor does it have any bearing on whether people believed that they attained such an exalted state. It suggests only that all such recondite meanings are not immediately and unequivocally manifest to the student who judges by what his eyes can observe: historical precedent and literary context.

28. Gross, XXIII, 169; Atlas in Rabad, *BK*, 30; see also Graetz, V, 358.

29. Scholem, *Reshit ha-Kabbalah*, 71; Heschel, "ᶜAl Ruaḥ ha-Ḳodesh," 193; see also Azulai, *Shem ha-Gedolim*, 11; I. H. Weiss, introduction to *Sifra Commentary*, VIII; S. Spiegel, "On Medieval Hebrew Poetry," *The Jews*, ed. L. Finkelstein, I, 530.

The phrase, "so they have shown me from heaven," with its variations, is not a kabbalistic innovation. It has a venerable pedigree, reaching back to Talmudic texts and Scriptural allusions.[30] The entire concept of special revelation of vital knowledge—"God's secrets"—germinated from a natural fusion of Scriptural verses and homiletical inferences: "In the beginning God revealed His secret to the prophets . . . then he gave it to the upright . . . then he gave it to the God-fearing, as is said: 'The secret counsel of the Lord is with them that fear Him.'"[31] The following benediction serves as the standard refrain in cases where new learning is attributed to this divine source: "Blessed is God who revealed his secret to them, in order to fulfill the verse 'The secret counsel of the Lord, etc.'"[32] Saints and sages, throughout the ages, were thus designated as the special couriers of these secrets and mysteries.[33] Inasmuch as this phrase has an independent, continuous history of its own, its use cannot be meaningfully correlated with any particular phenomenon, such as the swelling of the tides of mysticism in a given period. It has been shown—especially by Higger and Aptowitzer, and their lists are not yet exhaustive[34]—that this phrase crops up in Talmudic works (halakic and aggadic midrashim, of early and late composition), Geonic literature, medieval rabbinic writings, and mystical treatises including the *Zohar*. Geonim such as Sar Shalom, Natronai, Amram, Naḥshon, Sherira, and Hai, rabbis such as Gershom, Rashi, the sages of Lorraine, [en masse], R. Meïr of Rothenburg, Rashbah, and even Maimonides occasionally fall back upon it as a standard literary device. Not only does this rather lengthy list of representative persons, of disparate character and temperament, militate against any uniform literalist interpretation, but so does the wide range of subjects

30. Note the apposite comments of M. Higger, *Massektot Kallah* (New York, 1936), 25 ff.

31. *Midrash ha-Gadol*, Genesis, ed. S. Schechter (Cambridge, 1902), 754. Key verses are Ps. 25:14; Amos 3:7; Prov. 3:32.

32. E.g., J. N. Epstein, "Toratah shel Ereẓ Israel," *Tarbiẓ*, II (1931), 318; see M. *Yadayim*, IV, 2.

33. For the notion of special revelation in Philo, see Wolfson, *Philo*, II, 54; *idem*, "The Philonic God of Revelation and His Latter-Day Deniers," *Harvard Theological Review*, LIII (1960), 104–105. This type of revelation remained possible even after the cessation of prophecy.

34. Higger, *Massektot Kallah*, 25; A. Aptowitzer, *Tarbiẓ*, I (1930), 82, n. 8 (contains a long list of sources), and his *Meḥḳarim be-Sifrut ha-Geonim* (Jerusalem, 1941), 43, n. 70; Heschel, "Ruaḥ ha-Ḳodesh," 193; L. Ginzberg, *Genizah Studies*, II, 273; Assaf, "Ḥamesh Teshubot," *Ẓiyyunim* (Berlin, 1929), 119; B. M. Lewin, "Esa Meshali," *Tarbiẓ*, III (1932), 147; Urbach, "Halakah-u-Nebu'ah," *Tarbiẓ*, XVIII (1946), 22; R. Margaliyot, *She'elot u-Teshubot Min ha-Shamayim* (Jerusalem, 1957); H. Gordon, *The Maggid of Caro*, 132–176.

in connection with which this phrase was invoked or the numerous contexts in which it was applied. It was not reserved for a select number of esoteric doctrines, as might be expected, but was used quite exoterically. Already in Talmudic literature, views on such heterogeneous topics as the Written Law, Oral Law, Circumcision, Intercalation of Years, the Laws of Tithes were subsumed under this lofty designation. The same is true for its use by most Geonim and Rishonim. It is applied loosely in various contexts and is almost always coupled with an accompanying statement such as "this is my opinion" or "my reason dictates this view"—thereby indicating its metaphorical sense. One need only examine the dozens of instances found in medieval literature and note the air of casualness and conventionality with which these phrases are used. Sherira Gaon opens his famous *Epistle* with the following: "and we wrote their answers as they have shown us from heaven."[35] One hardly suspects that questions of chronology and literary criticism would be the subject of special revelation. R. Gershom writes: "I, the undersigned, shall reply to my correspondent as I am inclined to think in this matter and as they have shown me from heaven."[36] Certainly when the poet Moses ibn Ezra says that "God revealed to them the secrets of the Hebrew language and its grammar,"[37] or when the grammarian Jonah ibn Ganaḥ accounts for his achievements by "perseverence in study and investigation, constant preoccupation day and night . . . as if I were prophesying about it,"[38] they use these phrases as figurative equivalents of intuition or inspiration. Suffice it to insert one full-length quotation from the *Shibbale ha-Leḳeṭ*, which illustrates the medieval use of this central phrase: "Therefore it is proper for a person . . . to direct his heart to heaven and if God has endowed him with understanding and wisdom he will understand the statements of those who

35. Lewin, *Iggeret R. Sherira Gaon* (Haifa, 1921), 4: ופקידנא וכתבו תשובות דילהון כי היכי דאחוו לנא מן שמיא.

36. J. Mueller, *Teshubot Ḥakme Ẓarfat we-Loter* (Vienna, 1881), 85: אני החתום למטה אשיב לשואלי דבר לפי שדעתי נוטה, שהראוני מן השמים. Compare to this the later statement of R. Meïr of Rothenburg, quoted by Agus, *R. Meir*, I, 47: תוספ׳ גיטין אין בידי ולא ספרי פסקים בארץ הנגב סבבתי כל אלא כאשר הראוני מן השמים; ואם ימצא שהתוספ׳ וספרי הפוסקים חולקים עלי בשום דבר דעתי מבוטלת. Note also the twelfth-century responsum edited by I. Abrahams, "A Formula and a Responsum," *Jews College Jubilee Volume* (London, 1906), 108; and the responsum of the court of Narbonne to Avignon edited by Assaf, *Sinai*, XI (1947), 157–158.

37. *Shirat Yisrael*, ed. B. Halper (Leipzig, 1924), 63: גלה להם ה׳ את סודות הלשון העברית ודקדוקה . . . ענינים רבים שהיו סתומים קודם לכן נתחוורו כל צרכם.

38. *Sefer ha-Riḳma*, ed. Wilensky, 24: . . . בהתמדת החקירה והעיון ובטורח תמיד לילי ויומי וכאילו הייתי מתנבא בה בנבואה.

forbid as well as those who permit, and will act in accord with that which they have shown him from heaven, for a man can rely only upon what his eyes see and his ears hear and his mind leads him to understand."[39] Taken in context, this can only mean natural perspicacity and the poignant conclusions of rational study.

The Maimonidean expression—"I shall reply in accord with what they have shown me from heaven"[40]—is taken metaphorically even by those who are inclined to a literal interpretation in general, although there is no contextual difference whatsoever.[41] This is probably the best proof that the phrase per se, minus preconceptions about the specific intention of the author, is a neutral literary mannerism. Judging by historical precedent, therefore, there is no reason to expect Rabad's usage to harbor special esoteric beliefs or mystical notions. These phrases, rooted in traditional Scriptural idiom, were quite conventional.

It should also be observed that the term *sod* (secret) by itself was a standard designation for an original, hitherto "concealed" interpretation, entirely devoid of kabbalistic overtones. In Rabad's immediate circle, the translators ibn Tibbon and al-Ḥarizi use it in this sense in their translations from the *Cuzari* and the *Moreh Nebukim*.[42] It appears frequently in the writings of Abraham ibn Ezra.[43] Razah unmistakably has this meaning of conceptual innovation in mind when he writes: "I see fit to transmit to you a great secret and sage insight that is found in the teachings of our masters."[44] Philosophic literature as a whole uses this term to designate true opinion rationally deduced by means of correct allegorical interpretation. It means simply the inner, hidden meaning of a statement or event vis-à-vis the more obvious explanation. Such is the sense in which Maimonides himself uses it in his exoteric *Mishneh Torah*.[45] But even twelfth- and thirteenth-century kabbalists use the term to designate not the supernatural source but the esoteric

39. *Shibbale ha-Leḳeṭ*, II, 1, ed. M. Z. Ḥasidah, *ha-Segullah*, I (1934): יכוין לבו לשמים ואם חננו השם דעת וחכמה יבין בדברי האוסרין ובדברי המתירין, ויעשה כמו שהראוהו מן השמים; כי אין לו לאדם אלא מה שעיניו רואות, ואזניו שומעות, ומבין מדעתו. See also *Shibbale ha-Leḳeṭ ha-Shalem*, ed. Buber (Vilna, 1887), 157: ואין אנו צריכים לחלומו של רבינו יעקב ... ואין משגיחין בדברי חלומות דקיימא לן לא בשמים היא.

40. *Teshubot ha-Rambam*, ed. Freimann, 371: ולפי מה שהראוני מן השמים אשיב.

41. Urbach, *Tarbiẓ*, XVIII, 22, n. 183.

42. *Cuzari*, II, 7; *Moreh Nebukim*, II, 26; see I. Heinemann, "Ha-Pilosof ha-Meshorer," *Ḳobeẓ R. Judah ha-Levi*, ed. I. Zemorah (Tel Aviv, 1950), 174.

43. E.g., *Yesod Mora*, 27b, 31b; Bible Commentary, introduction: ואם הדעת לא תסבול דבר או ישחית אשר בהרגשות יחבר, אז נבקש לו סוד.

44. *Sefer ha-Ẓabah* in *TD*, 115.

45. *Issure Bi'ah*, XIII, 14; *Sanhedrin*, XXII, 7; see also introduction to Mishnah Commentary, ed. Rabinovitz, 64.

content of traditional teachings which are transmitted from the elite of one generation to that of the next.[46] Actually, this entire literary usage, with its minor variations, may be said to stem from the Midrash where the phrase "the secret of the Law" (*sodah shel Torah*) is used to designate that meaning which was to be discovered in Scripture by the non-literal midrashic method of exegesis.[47]

An objective examination of Rabad's usage reveals nothing new or startling. Similar to the indiscriminate usage of these phrases in midrashic, Geonic, and rabbinic texts for a variety of subjects, Rabad himself applies these terms to the discussion of markedly heterogeneous topics: ritual slaughtering, future status of the Temple and Jerusalem, purity and uncleanness, laws of *etrog* and *lulab*, and the International Date Line.[48] There is nothing esoteric here. Furthermore, the context in which these are used or the auxiliary phraseology again indicate the routine, metaphorical connotation. At the conclusion of the sixth chapter of the *Baᶜale ha-Nefesh*, for example, Rabad appends a usual ditty: "So they have shown me from heaven; the 'chapter on water' is completed."[49] There is nothing in this chapter—the weakest in the book—to warrant such an ascription to celestial instruction. The rhymed couplet seems to be only a stylistic ersatz for "with the help of God, I have concluded the chapter on water." The example from the *Sifra* commentary which I. H. Weiss believed to provide conclusive proof for the literal understanding of these phrases seems, upon second analysis, to vindicate the metaphorical understanding. Rabad writes: "I thought about the main version [of this text] and an explanation from heaven happened to come to me and this is the explanation . . . This appears to me to be the true and correct explanation."[50] The juxtaposition of these references to his cognitive faculty and to an "explanation from heaven" is a vivid indication of their mutual interdependence. Moreover, Rabad's hearty endorsement of a direct "explanation from heaven" appears rather gratuitous if not incongruous.[51]

46. Scholem, *Reshit ha-Kabbalah*, 151; P. Sandler, "Pardes," *Sefer Urbach* (Jerusalem, 1955), 224; also, W. Bacher, *Die jüdische Bibelexegese vom Anfang des* 10. *bis zum Ende des* 15 *Jh.* (1892), 12.

47. *Canticles Rabbah*, I, 1, 8; see H. A. Wolfson, *The Philosophy of the Church Fathers* (Cambridge, Mass., 1956), 24.

48. See §3, notes 22–27.

49. *BH*, 78: כך הראוני מן השמים, נשלם שער המים.

50. *Sifra Commentary*, 80a; see Weiss, introduction, VIII.

51. For an analogous example, *KS* on *Rosh ha-Shanah*, ed. Bergmann, 62: עד כאן הראונו מן השמים והוא ראוי לסמוך עליו; n. 116.

As for the use of "sod" in particular, Rabad undoubtedly echoes the standard, nonmystical meaning as reflected in the passages quoted and as originally established by the midrash. He says, in connection with a law concerning ritual slaughter: "The secret that has been revealed to us, without any unevenness or difficulty, is as follows . . ." [52] What follows is an unprecedented interpretation which Rabad arrived at on the basis of reflection and, especially, empirical study. On one occasion he even elaborates and specifies what he means by "sod": "Now I shall reveal to you the secret concealed from people." This had been concealed hitherto only because "the former scholars did not explain it." [53] With Rabad's explanation it ceases to be a secret. It is true that Rabad may use "sod" to designate teachings of kabbalistic content—as in the cryptic hassaqah concerning Maimonides' understanding of Ex. 33:23 [54]—but even in such cases there is no reference to a special source of information.

On one occasion Rabad refers explicitly to the "appearance of the holy spirit" in the house of study. This would seem at first sight to be a conscious, meaningful variation of the standard reference to heaven and, consequently, most troublesome for a nonliteral interpretation. Yet, my contention about the metaphorical value of this entire family of phrases applies in great measure to this as well. The "appearance of the holy spirit" was not rare stylistically.[55] Moreover, inasmuch as there are explicit Talmudic sayings that the holy spirit ceased to appear, this usage is at least partly, if not totally, figurative.[56] Rabad's immediate successors—and fellow kabbalists—did not take this, or other phrases, literally. For instance, Rabad attributed the essence of his treatise on "Lulab" to the "appearance of the holy spirit." This impressive pronouncement notwithstanding, Naḥmanides, Rabad's peer in halakah and one of the pillars of the already articulate Kabbalah, refuted Rabad's view and reinstated the Geonic opinion challenged by him.[57]

52. *TD*, 3.

53. *Hassagot* on Alfasi, *Beẓah*, 10a.

54. *MT*, *Yesode ha-Torah*, I, 10.

55. *Makkot*, 23b; *Sanhedrin*, 11a; Judah ibn Tibbon, introduction to *Ḥobot ha-Lebabot*; Heschel, "Ruaḥ ha-Ḳodesh," 175, n. 1. R. Menaḥem b. Zeraḥ, *Ẓedah la-Derek*, 6, says concerning Alfasi: ואמר עליו ר״י בעל התוספות שילאה בן אדם לחבר חבור כמוהו זולתי ששכינה היתה שורה עליו. And concerning Rashi: ושרתה רוח הקדש על רבינו שלמה וגברה ידו בגמ׳ וחבר פירושים . . . בלשון צח וקצר.

56. *Yoma*. 9b; *Sotah*, 13b, and parallels; see, for example, its figurative use by Alḥarizi, *Taḥkemoni*, 46: כאלו מכוכבי רום גלולה, או מרוח הקודש אצולה. Also, R. Solomon Duran who says that Maimonides wrote בלשון מבוארת וצחה, כאלו רוח הקדש שרתה עליו. Cited by Zlotnick, *Sinai*, VIII (1945), 117, n. 7.

57. *MT*, *Lulab*, VIII, 5, and commentaries, *ad. loc.*; see M. ibn Ḥabib, *Kapot Temarim*, 12 (on *Sukkah*, 32b); Joseph Solomon del Medigo, *Maẓref le-Ḥokmah*, 90.

He certainly would have been more deferential and submissive toward a literal communication from the holy spirit. What is more, Rabad himself cites this view elsewhere as "there is one who says," and Razah cites it anonymously as "some explain."[58] Similarly, Rashbah quotes a view on a controversial issue which Rabad had expounded in his *Baba Ḳamma* commentary under the rubric of a pet, mystical-sounding phrase from Proverbs: "He layeth up sound wisdom [tushiyah] for the upright." Nevertheless, Rashbah dissents and rejects Rabad's view, even though, or perhaps because, he himself also occasionally punctuates his style with analogous phrases.[59]

Another example is Rabad's treatment of a basic problem in ritual slaughter which completely controverted the traditional view prevailing until then and which he introduced as "the secret revealed to him." This view was heatedly discussed by many subsequent scholars including R. Asher b. Yeḥiel, Rashbah, R. Nissim, Ibn Ḥabib, and Joseph Karo. They all debated the theory unreservedly and were not at all fettered by the rhetorical introduction which derived the view from a "revelation." R. Asher b. Yeḥiel is even a trifle satiric and parodies Rabad's proud reliance on "the sight of his eyes and the feel of his hands." He adds that had Rabad introduced this view as a tradition received from his teachers, one could not argue. Inasmuch, however, as he explicitly founded the theory on his own "reasoning," and his demonstrations prove to be worthless, it may be disregarded. It is clear that for Asher b. Yeḥiel the "revealed secret" was synonymous with Rabad's processes of reasoning.[60]

These phrases in question, therefore, while not ruling out mystical tendencies or aspirations, seem to be expressions of a bold, confident approach to halakah. Rabad's frequent use of them underlines the certitude and clarity he felt to be inherent in his theoretical writings and

58. *Sifra Commentary*, 102b; (see Chapter IV, §2, note 156); see also *TD*, 227 (*Hassagot* on Alfasi) which I take to be the stylistic counterpart of "ruaḥ ha-ḳodesh": מפני שראיתי בהלכות לולב דברים סתומים שלא הושבו בגמר׳, גם הרב ר׳ יצחק לא פירש אותם בהלכותיו . . . ואני ברחמי שמים נתבררו אצלנו הדברים מן התוספתא ומן הירושלמי ומקצתו מן הגמרא ובראש השכל הברור האמתי . . . וראש על הראשים הוא הא־ל הבורא יתעלה המלמד אדם דעת . . .

59. Rabad, *BK*, 142. The noun here translated as wisdom—*tushiyah*—came to imply various sorts of special, even esoteric knowledge; see, for example, the use of *anshe tushiyah* by Abraham ibn Ezra, *Shene ha-Me'orot*, ed. M. Steinschneider (Berlin, 1847), 3.

60. *TD*, 3; Rosh on *Ḥullin*, IV, 7, and *Leḥem Ḥamudot, ad. loc.*; *MT*, *Sheḥitah*, VIII, 13, and *Maggid Mishneh, ad. loc.* For the controversy surrounding this halakic issue just among Provençal scholars, see Benedict, *Sinai*, XVI (1953), 66 ff. Note the use of לגלות כל סתום by Aaron b. Meshullam, *ibid.*, 68.

practical decisions. Independent examination of problems from beginning to end assured him of the correctness of his conclusions, even if these were unprecedented. When Rabad concludes chapter two of the commentary on *Ḳinnim* by saying quite conventionally that, prior to his exposition the subject matter had been "like a sealed epistle," this is roughly tantamount to saying more figuratively that what was hitherto a "secret" has now been revealed. There is no literary evidence to warrant any other conclusion.[61]

The separation of halakic and kabbalistic learning by great Talmudists, who were simultaneously devotees of Kabbalah, became almost an inviolable principle.[62] If they were careful to isolate the extraordinary contents of their mystical learning from the ordinary concepts of halakic learning, it seems that they would certainly isolate the "method."[63] In light of Rabad's stature as a "man of halakah," and his unqualified esotericism, there is every reason to assume that he would keep the two disciplines apart.[64] For an immediate precedent, he could look to R. Judah b. Barzilai whose commentary on the *Sefer Yeẓirah* and his *Sefer ha*ᶜ*Ittim* preserved the distinctiveness of both domains.

In sum, the teachings attributed to Rabad, as fragmentary and disjoined as they may be, are representative, adumbrating the nuclear motifs of its two major aspects: the devotional-practical aspect, that is, mysticism of prayer; and the speculative-theoretical aspect, that is, God and the sefirot. In the perspective of later relations between

61. It is possible that Rabad's mystical inclinations led him to endow these essentially neutral phrases with esoteric meaning. As a matter of fact, Ps. 25:14 seems to have become especially common among mystics: see Asher b. David, "Perush shem ha-Meforash," *Ha-Segullah*, I (1934), 1; G. Scholem, *Le-Ḥeḳer Kabbalat R. Isaac b. Jacob ha-Kohen* (Jerusalem, 1934), 7. What must be stressed, however, is their long history of prosaic usage; see also Naḥmanides, *Milhamot*, *Ketubot*, 50a: האל יצילנו משפת יתר וירים מכשול מדרכנו כי בעקבות מלאכו אשר שלח לפנינו, להודות יצאנו, סמוכים על מה שחלק לנו מן השכל, ובטוחים על מקרא שכתוב סוד ה׳ ליראיו ובריתו להודיעם.

62. See, for example, Joseph Solomon del Medigo, *Maẓref le-Ḥokmah*, 90 ff.; R. Solomon Luria, *Responsa*, 98 (see Horodezky, *Yahadut ha-Sekel we-Yahadut ha-Regesh* [Tel Aviv, 1947], 30); Scholem, "Teshubot ha-Meyuḥasot le-R. Joseph Ghikatilia," *J. Freimann Jubilee Volume* (Berlin, 1937), 1 ff.

63. Moreover, even the "method" was two-fold. The first kabbalists who discussed the origins and sources of their tradition traced it back not only to special acts of revelation but also to deep, fruitful speculation and interpretation; such talk was not frequent, for reticence about these transcendental phenomena was the rule. See Scholem, *Major Trends*, 120; *Reshit ha-Kabbalah*, 116; H. Gordon, *The Maggid of Caro*, 133–134.

64. A good illustration of mixing kabbalistic symbolism with halakic analysis is the comment of R. David b. Zimra on *MT*, *Bikkurim*, XII, 1. He is amazed why Rabad failed to associate them: עוד תמהתי על הרב שהוא בקי בחדרי סודות תורתנו הקדושה איך קרי לעריפת פטר חמור מזיק, והלא מתקן הוא למי שיודע סוף המצוה.

kabbalah and philosophy, Rabad's general benevolence toward and knowledge of philosophic literature coupled with his reservations concerning the wisdom of unbridled philosophic speculation seem to be significant. This complex dialectical attitude of partial rapprochement and withdrawal, if not hostility, is quite typical.[65] In the eyes of subsequent generations of kabbalists, Rabad must have been an important link in the transmission of this learning. Just as Provençal students visiting Spain and, later, Spanish émigrés transplanted Spanish learning, both rabbinics and philosophy, to Provence during the twelfth century, so Spanish students visiting Provence or Provençal emissaries transferred kabbalistic traditions to Spain during the first half of the thirteenth century. The Posquières school of Rabad and his son was practically an international center, from which kabbalistic teachings secretly emanated. What del Medigo says about Naḥmanides is equally true for Rabad: they invested this movement with respectability.[66] The route from Posquières to Gerona and Guadalajara is well charted.

65. E.g., *Zohar*, II, 236: אשר אין בה מום, דא מלכות יון, דאינון קרבין לארחא מהימנותא. R. Azriel, quoted by Tishbi, "Aggadah we-Kabbalah," 172: דברי חכמת התורה ודברי בעל המחקר דרך אחד להם ואין הפרש ביניהם. See Horodezky, "ha-Rambam ba-Kabbalah," *Moźnayim*, III (1935), 441 ff.; Scholem, *Major Trends*, 149, 203. Graetz's view that Kabbalah was an avowed enemy of philosophy and constituted the vanguard in the onslaught on philosophic studies can no longer be repeated unqualifiedly.

66. Joseph Solomon del Medigo, *Miktab Aḥuz*, ed. A. Geiger, *Melo Ḥofnayim* (Berlin, 1840), 21.

LIST OF ABBREVIATIONS

NOTE ON REFERENCES

BIBLIOGRAPHY

BIBLIOGRAPHICAL SUPPLEMENT

ADDENDA

INDEX

LIST OF ABBREVIATIONS

b.	*ben* (son of).
Benedict	B. Z. Benedict, "le-Toledotaw shel Merkaz ha-Torah be-Provence," *Tarbiẓ*, XXII (1951), 85–109.
BH	Rabad, *Ba^{c}ale ha-Nefesh.*
GJ	H. Gross, *Gallia Judaica* (Dictionnaire geographique de la France d'après les sources rabbiniques) (Paris, 1897).
Graetz	H. Graetz, *Toledot ^{c}Am Yisrael,* Hebrew trans. S. P. Rabinowitz (Warsaw, 1894).
Gross	H. Gross, "R. Abraham b. David aus Posquières," *Monatsschrift für Geschichte und Wissenschaft des Judenthums,* XXII (1873), 337–344, 398–407, 446–459; XXIII, 19–23, 76–85, 164–182, 275–276.
Hassagot	Rabad's printed hassagot on the *Sefer ha-Ma'or* of Razah. (The page references are according to the standard text of Alfasi's *Halakot.*)
HUCA	*Hebrew Union College Annual.*
Itinerary	*The Itinerary of Rabbi Benjamin of Tudela,* trans. and ed. A. Asher (2 v., London and Berlin, 1840–1841).
JE	*Jewish Encyclopedia.*
JQR	*Jewish Quarterly Review,* New Series.
KS	*Sefer Katub Sham* (*Hassagot ha-Rabad ^{c}al Ba^{c}al ha-Ma'or*), ed., in small installments, M. Z. Ḥasidah, *ha-Segullah* (Jerusalem, 1934).
M.	Mishnah.
Marx	Alexander Marx, "R. Abraham b. David et R. Zeraḥya ha-Levi," *REJ*, LIX (1910), 200–224.
MGWJ	*Monatsschrift für Geschichte und Wissenschaft des Judenthums.*
MT	Maimonides, *Mishneh Torah.* (References to Rabad's hassagot are according to the sections of this work.)
PAAJR	*Proceedings of the American Academy for Jewish Research.*
R.	Rabbi (teacher, "master," or scholar).
Rabad, *BK*	*Novellae of Abraham b. David on Tractate Baba Kamma,* ed. Samuel H. Atlas (London, 1940).
REJ	*Revue des Etudes Juives.*
Rishonim	Collective designation of medieval Talmudic authorities.
Sifran	*Sifran shel Rishonim.* ed. S. Assaf (Jerusalem, 1935). (Contains *Issur Mashehu* of Rabad, *Sefer ha-Minhagot* of Asher b. Saul of Lunel, *Responsa* of Rabi and Joseph ibn Plat, and other sources.)
TD	*Temim De^{c}im,* Warsaw, 1897. (Primarily responsa of Rabad.)
ZfhB	*Zeitschrift für hebräische Bibliographie.*

Proper Names

Rabad	R. Abraham b. David of Posquières.
Rabi	R. Abraham b. Isaac of Narbonne (Rabad's father-in-law).
Rambi	R. Moses b. Joseph of Narbonne (Rabad's teacher).
Rashbah	R. Solomon b. Abraham Adret (prominent Spanish Talmudist, 1235–1310).
Rashi	R. Solomon b. Isaac (outstanding French commentator, 1040–1105).
Razah	R. Zeraḥyah ha-Levi (Rabad's contemporary and antagonist).

NOTE ON REFERENCES

References to the *Katub Sham* (*Ks*) are by the volume and page number of Ḥasidah's edition in *ha-Segullah* starting in 1934: e.g., *KS*, I, 50.

References to the *Mishneh Torah* (*MT*) are by titles of topics, chapter, and section, omitting the name of the books (*Sefarim*) and the introductory word *Hilkot*: e.g., *Mishneh Torah* (*Sefer ha-Madda*), *Hilkot Teshubah*, ch. III, section 7, is cited as *MT*, *Teshubah*, III, 7. The same is true for the hassagot of Rabad on the *Mishneh Torah* and the standard commentaries such as *Kesef Mishneh* and *Maggid Mishneh*.

References to responsa collections and code books are by section rather than page numbers: e.g., *TD*, 5. References to the *Shulḥan ᶜAruk* are by section (and when necessary, paragraph) of each of its four parts: e.g., *Oraḥ Ḥayyim*, 122; *Ḥoshen ha-Mishpaṭ*, 85, 3.

References to the Talmud are by folio and page of the standard editions: e.g., *Berakot*, 2a.

References to the Mishnah are by chapter and section of the specific tractate, preceded by the letter "M.": e.g., M., *Berakot*, I, 2.

Bible quotations are from the English translation of the Jewish Publication Society (*The Holy Scriptures*, 1916).

Translations of Hebrew texts were made by me, but conform as much as possible to the standard translations, which are: *The Mishnah*, by H. Danby (Oxford, 1933); *The Babylonian Talmud*, under the editorship of I. Epstein (London, 1935); *Midrash Rabbah*, under the editorship of H. Freedman and M. Simon (London, 1939). The *Mishneh Torah* of Maimonides is being translated as "The Code of Maimonides" in the Yale Judaica Series. The first two books of the *Mishneh Torah* were previously translated by M. H. Hyamson (New York, 1937). Translations of terms conform for the most part to Marcus Jastrow, *A Dictionary of the Targumim, the Talmud, and the Midrashic Literature* (2 v., New York, 1943).

Transliteration of Hebrew words follows the system used by the *Jewish Encyclopedia*.

BIBLIOGRAPHY

Primary Sources

Aaron ha-Levi of Barcelona, *Sefer ha-Ḥinnuk*. Jerusalem, 1952.

——— *Peḳudat ha-Lewiyim* (on Alfasi's *Halakot*). Mainz, 1874.

Aaron ha-Kohen of Lunel, *Orḥot Ḥayyim*. I, Florence, 1750; II, ed. M. Schlesinger, Berlin, 1902.

Abba Mari b. Moses Yarḥi, *Minḥat Ḳena'ot*. Pressburg, 1838.

Abot de R. Nathan, ed. Solomon Schechter, with introduction, notes, and appendices. New York, 1945.

Abraham b. David (Rabad), *Ba*ᶜ*ale ha-Nefesh* (with the hassagot of Razah). New York (photostat of 1812 edition).

——— Commentary on ᶜ*Eduyot and Ḳinnim*. Standard editions of the Talmud.

——— Commentary on ᶜ*Abodah Zarah*, ed. A. Sofer. To be published.

——— *Derashah le-Rosh ha-Shanah*, ed. A. S. ha-Levi. London, 1955.

——— *Dibre ha-Ribot*. (A Rabbinical Disputation between Zeraḥyah ha-Levi and Abraham b. David), ed. B. Drachman. New York, 1907.

——— *Glosses on the Mishneh Torah*. Manuscript 38477 of Jewish Theological Seminary. (It contains the text of most of the hassagot on the first seven books of Mishneh Torah. A number of interesting variants are to be found there.)

——— *Glosses on the Mishneh Torah*. Manuscript 1179 of Adler collection at the Jewish Theological Seminary. (It contains hassagot on *Hilkot Issure Bi'ah* and *Ma'akalot Asurot*.)

——— *Ḥassagot on Mishneh Torah*. Standard editions of the *Mishneh Torah*.

——— *Issur Mashehu*, ed. S. Assaf. *Sifran shel Rishonim*, 185–198.

——— *Novellae on Tractate Baba Ḳamma*, ed. Samuel H. Atlas. London, 1940.

——— *Sefer Katub Sham* (*Hassagot ha-Rabad* ᶜ*al Ba*ᶜ*al ha-Ma'or*). Ed. in small installments by M. Z. Ḥasidah, *ha-Segullah*. Jerusalem, 1934.

——— *Katuv Sham: Hassagot ha-Rabad* ᶜ*al Ba*ᶜ*al ha-Ma'or* (on *Sukkah* and *Rosh ha-Shanah*), ed. B. Bergmann. Jerusalem, 1957.

——— *Sefer Katub Sham*. Bodleian ms. 2357 (on *Giṭṭin*, *Yebamot*, *Ketubot*, *Baba Ḳamma*, *Baba Meẓi*ᶜ*a*, *Baba Batra*, *Sanhedrin*, *Makkot*).

——— *Sifra Commentary*, ed. I. H. Weiss. New York, 1947 (photostat of Vienna, 1862 edition).

Abraham b. Isaac (Rabi) of Narbonne, *Sefer ha-Eshkol*, ed. B. H. Auerbach. Halberstadt, 1868; a different edition by Ch. Albeck, Jerusalem, 1935.

——— *Responsa*, ed. S. Assaf. *Sifran shel Rishonim*, 1–50.

Abraham b. Nathan ha-Yarḥi, *Commentary on Kallah Rabbati*, ed. M. Higger. *Jewish Quarterly Review*, XXIV (1934), 331–348.
——— *Perush Masseket Kallah Rabbati*, ed. B. Toledano. Tiberias, 1906.
——— *Responsa*, ed. S. Werthelmer. *Ginze Jerusalem*. Jerusalem, 1896.
——— *Sefer ha-Manhig*. Berlin, 1855.
Abraham b. Solomon of Torrutiel, *Supplement to Sefer ha-Kabbalah*. See Neubauer.
Abraham bar Ḥiyya, *Hegyon ha-Nefesh*, ed. Freimann. Leipzig, 1860.
——— *Ḥibbur ha-Meshiḥah weha-Tishboret*, ed. J. Guttmann. Berlin, 1913.
——— *Megillat ha-Megalleh*, ed. Poznanski-Guttmann. Berlin, 1924.
——— *Sefer ha-ᶜIbbur*, ed. Filipowski. London, 1851.
——— *Ẓurat ha-Areẓ*. Offenbach, 1720.
Abraham ibn Daud, *Sefer ha-Kabbalah*, ed. A. Neubauer. *Medieval Jewish Chronicles*, I. Oxford, 1887.
Abraham ibn Ezra, *Perush ha-Torah*. Standard editions of the Hebrew Bible.
——— *Sefer ha-Shem*. Fiorda, 1834.
——— *Sefer ha-Ṭeᶜamim*, ed. J. L. Fleisher. Jerusalem, 1951.
——— *Yesod Mora*. Prague, 1833.
Abrahams, Israel, ed., *Hebrew Ethical Wills*. 2 v. Philadelphia, 1948.
Abudarham, David b. Joseph, *Sefer Abudarham*. Warsaw, 1877.
Abulafia, Meïr ha-Levi, *Kitab al-Rasail*, ed. J. Brill. Paris, 1871.
——— *Or Ẓaddiḳim*. Salonica, 1799.
——— *Yad Ramah* (on Sanhedrin). Salonica, 1798.
Abulafia, Todros ha-Levi, *Oẓar ha-Kabod*. Novydvor, 1808.
Adret, Solomon b. Abraham (Rashbah), *Ḥiddushe ha-Rashbah ᶜal Masseket Niddah*. Jerusalem, 1938.
——— *Torat ha-Bayit*. New York, 1952. *Bet ha-Mayim*, ed. S. Löwinger, *ha-Ẓofeh le-Ḥokmat Yisrael*, XIV (1930), 363–374; *ha-Soker*, I (1933), 7–37.
——— *Responsa*. Vienna, 1812.
——— *Ḥiddushim*. 2 v. New York, 1952.
Ahai, Rab, *She'eltot*. 3 v. Jerusalem, 1949. With comprehensive commentary by Rabbi N. Z. Y. Berlin.
Aḥimaᶜaz b. Paltiel, *Megillat Aḥimaᶜaẓ*, ed. B. Klar. Jerusalem, 1945.
Alashkar, Moses, *Responsa*. Sabbionetta, 1554.
Albo, Joseph, *Sefer ha-ᶜIḳḳarim*. Trans. and notes by I. Husik. 4 v. Philadelphia, 1929–1930.
Alfasi, Isaac, *Sefer ha-Halakot*. Standard editions of the Talmud.
Amram Gaon, *Siddur Rab ᶜAmram*, ed. A. L. Frumkin, Jerusalem, 1912.
Asher b. Saul of Lunel, *Sefer ha-Minhagot*. S. Assaf, ed. *Sifran shel Rishonim*, 121–174.
Asher b. Yeḥiel, *Halakot*. Standard editions of the Talmud.
——— *Responsa*. Venice, 1552.
Ashkenazi, Beẓalel, *Shiṭṭah Meḳubbeẓet* (anthology of commentaries on select tractates of the Talmud), various editions.
——— *Responsa*. Venice, 1595.

Askari, Eleazar, *Sefer Ḥaredim*. Lublin, 1924.
Azariah dei Rossi, *Maẓref la-Kesef*. Vilna, 1865.
——— *Me'or ᶜEnayim*. Vilna, 1863.
Bachrach, Ḥayyim Ya'ir, *Ḥawwot Ya'ir*. Frankfort a/M., 1699.
Baḥya b. Asher, *Perushᶜal ha-Torah*. Pisaro, 1507.
Baḥya ibn Paḳuda, *Sefer Ḥobot ha-Lebabot*, trans. into Hebrew by Judah ibn Tibbon; ed. A. Zifroni. Jerusalem, 1928. English trans.: *Duties of the Heart*, M. Hyamson. New York, 1925.
Benjamin of Tudela, *The Itinerary of Rabbi Benjamin of Tudela*. 2 v. Trans. and ed. A. Asher. London and Berlin, 1840-1841. Also, *Die Reisebeschreibungen des Benjamin von Tudela*, ed. M. Adler and L. Grünhut. Frankfurt a.M., 1904.
Berechiah ha-Naḳdan, *Dodi we-Nechdi*, ed. H. Gollancz. London, 1922.
——— *Ethical Treatises*, ed. with English trans. by Hermann Gollancz. London, 1902.
Birkat Abraham, ed. Goldberg. Lyck, 1859.
Crescas, Hasdai, *Sefer Or Adonai*. Vienna, 1860.
David b. Judah Meser Leon, *Kebod Ḥakamim*, ed. S. Bernfeld. Berlin, 1899.
David b. Levi, *Sefer ha-Miktam* on *Megillah*, ed. M. Grossberg. Lemberg, 1904.
——— *Sefer ha-Miktam* on *Sukkah*, *Beẓah*, *Moᶜed Ḳaṭan*, and *Pesaḥim*, ed. A. Sofer. New York, 1959.
David b. Zimra (Radbaz), *Responsa*.
——— *Yeḳar Tiferet*, ed. S. B. Werner. Jerusalem, 1945.
David of Estella, *Kiryath Sefer*. See Neubauer.
Del Medigo, Joseph Solomon, *Maẓref le-Ḥokmah*. Warsaw, 1890.
——— *Miktab Aḥuz*, ed. A. Geiger. *Melo Ḥofnayim*, Berlin, 1840.
——— *Nobelot Ḥokmah*. Basle, 1635.
Donnolo, Shabbetai, *Ḥakemoni* (printed with other commentaries on the *Sefer Yeẓirah*). Warsaw, 1884.
Dunash b. Labrat, *Shirim*, ed. N. Aloni. Jerusalem, 1947.
Duran, Simeon b. Ẓemaḥ, *Sefer ha-Tashbeẓ*. Amsterdam, 1738.
——— *Sefer Magen Abot*. Leipzig, 1855.
——— *Sefer Oheb Mishpaṭ*. Venice, n.d.
——— *Zohar ha-Raḳiᶜa*. Vilna, 1879.
Duran, Solomon b. Simeon, *Milḥemet Miẓwah*. (n.p.) 1869.
Elijah de Vidas, *Reshit Ḥokmah*. Vilna, 1900.
Estori Parḥi, *Kaftor wa-Feraḥ*, ed. Perlow-Maimon. Jerusalem, 1946.
Fano, Menaḥem ᶜAzariah, *Responsa*. (n.p., n.d.).
——— *Sefer ᶜAsarah Ma'amarot*. Venice, 1597.
Ganz, David, *Ẓemaḥ David*. Warsaw, 1871.
Gedalyah ibn Yaḥyah, *Shalshelet ha-Kabbalah*. Warsaw, 1877.
Gikatilia, J., *Sefer Shaᶜare Ẓedek*. Korez, 1785.
Halakot Gedolot, ed. Azriel Hildesheimer. Berlin, 1892.
Halakot Keẓubot, ed. M. Margaliyot. Jerusalem, 1942.

Ha-Me'iri, Menaḥem, *Bet ha-Beḥirah on Abot*, ed. S. Waxman. New York, 1944.

——— *Bet Yad* (*dine neṭilat yadayim*), printed at end of *Bet ha-Beḥirah* on *Berakot*. Warsaw, 1911.

——— *Bet ha-Beḥirah* on various tractates of Talmud. *Bet ha-Beḥirah* on *Nedarim*, *Nazir*, *Sotah* (Halberstadt, 1860) contains the very important introduction.

——— *Ḥibbur ha-Teshubah*, ed. A. Sofer, with introduction by S. Mirsky. New York, 1950.

——— *Kiryat Sefer*. Smyrna, 1863.

——— *Magen Abot*, ed. I. Last. London, 1909.

——— *Perush le-Sefer Tehillim*, ed. J. Cohen. Jerusalem, 1936.

Ḥagiz, M., *Mishnat Ḥakamim*. Tchnervotz, 1864.

Ḥananel, R., *Perush ᶜal Masseket Pesaḥim*, ed. J. Stern. Paris, 1868.

Ḥayyim b. Beẓalel, *Wikkuaḥ Mayyim Ḥayyim*. Amsterdam, 1711.

Ḥemdah Genuzah. Jerusalem, 1863.

Hillel b. Eliakim of Greece, *Perush la-Sifre*, ed. S. Koleditzky. Jerusalem, 1948.

Iggeret Baᶜale Ḥayyim, trans. Kalonymus b. Kalonymus; ed. M. Habermann. Jerusalem, 1949.

Isaac b. Abba Mari of Marseilles, *Sefer ha-ᶜIṭṭur*. Lemberg, 1860 (New edition, New York, 1955).

Isaac b. Melchizedek of Siponto, *Mishnah Commentary*. Standard editions of Talmud.

Isaac b. Moses of Vienna, *Or Zaruᶜa*. Zhitomir, 1862.

Isaac de Lattes, *Shaᶜare Zion*, ed. S. Buber. Jaroslau, 1885.

Isaiah of Trani, *Sefer ha-Makriᶜa*. Munkez, 1900.

Israel ibn al-Nakawa, *Menorat ha-Ma'or*, ed. H. G. Enelow. 4 v. New York, 1929–1932.

Israeli, Isaac b. Joseph, *Sefer Yesod ᶜOlam*, ed. B. Goldberg. 2 v. Berlin, 1848–1851.

Isserlein, Israel, *Terumat ha-Deshen*. Venice, 1519.

Jacob b. Asher, *Turim*. Various editions.

Jacob b. Judah Landau, *Sefer Agur*. Venice, 1546.

Jacob b. Meïr Tam, R., *Sefer ha-Yashar*. Vienna, 1811. Second part, ed. F. Rosenthal. Berlin, 1898.

Jeruḥam b. Meshullam, *Sefer Toledot Adam we-Ḥawah*. Kapust, 1806.

Jonah b. Abraham Gerondi, *Shaᶜare Teshubah*. Jerusalem, n.d.

——— *Perush Sefer Mishle*, ed. A. Lowenthal. Berlin, 1910.

Jonah ibn Ganaḥ, *Sefer ha-Riḳma*, ed. M. Wilensky. Berlin, 1929.

Jonathan ha-Kohen of Lunel, *Commentary on Berakot and ᶜErubin of Alfasi's Halakot*. El ha-Mekorot edition of Talmud. Jerusalem, 1959.

——— *Commentary* on *Megillah* and *Moᶜed Ḳaṭan*, ed. S. Mirsky. Jerusalem, 1956.

——— *Commentary* on *Ḥullin* (*ᶜAbodat ha-Lewiyim*), ed. S. Bamberger. Frankfurt a.M., 1871.

Jonathan ha-Kohen of Lunel, *Commentary* on *Sukkah* (Fragments), A. Kaminka, *Ha-Me'assef*, IV (1899), 13b ff., 155a ff.
Joseph b. Ẓaddik, *Zeker Ẓaddik*. See Neubauer.
Joseph ibn Kaspi, *Guide to Knowledge*, *Hebrew Ethical Wills*, ed. I. Abrahams. Philadelphia, 1948.
——— *ᶜAsarah Kle Kesef*, ed. I. Last. Pressburg, 1903.
Joseph ibn Megas, *Responsa*. Warsaw, 1870.
Joseph ibn Naḥmias, *Perush Pirke Abot*, ed. M. Bamberger. Berlin, 1907.
Judah al-Ḥarizi, *Taḥkemoni*, ed. I. Topołovsky. Jerusalem, 1952.
Judah b. Barzilai, *Perush Sefer Yeẓirah*, ed. S. J. Halberstam. Berlin, 1885.
——— *Sefer ha-ᶜIttim*, ed. J. Shore. Berlin, 1903.
Judah ha-Levi, *Cuzari*, Heb. trans. by Judah ibn Tibbon; ed. A. Zifroni. Tel-Aviv, 1948. Eng. trans. by H. Hirschfeld. New York, 1946.
Judah ibn Tibbon, "Will," *Hebrew Ethical Wills*, ed. I. Abrahams. Philadelphia, 1948.
Karo, Joseph, *Bet Joseph*. Standard editions of *Turim*.
——— *Kesef Mishneh*. Standard editions of *Mishneh Torah*.
——— *Shulhan ᶜAruk*.
Kimḥi, David, *Perush*. Various editions of the Hebrew Bible.
Kimḥi, Joseph, *Milḥemet Ḥobah*. Constantinople, 1700. Reprinted in J. Eisenstein, *Oẓar ha-Wikkuḥim*. New York, 1928.
——— *Sefer ha-Galuy*, ed. H. J. Mathews. Berlin, 1887.
——— *Sefer ha-Zikkaron*, ed. W. Bacher. Berlin, 1888.
Kol Bo. Venice, 1567.
Kolon, Joseph, *Responsa*. Lemberg, 1798.
Konforte, D., *Ḳore ha-Dorot*. Pietrekov, 1895.
Luria, Solomon, *Yam shel Shelomoh*. Various editions.
Maḥzor Vitry (by Simḥa of Vitry, one of Rashi's disciples), ed. S. Hurwitz. Berlin, 1893.
Maḥzor Yannai (a liturgical work of the seventh century), ed. Israel Davidson. New York, 1919. (Texts and Studies of the Jewish Theological Seminary of America, VI.)
Maimonides, Abraham, *Birkat Abraham*, ed. Goldberg. Lyck, 1859.
——— *Milḥamot ha-Shem*, ed. R. Margaliyot. Jerusalem, 1953.
——— *Teshubot* (Responsa), ed. A. Freimann and S. Goitein. Jerusalem, 1937.
Maimonides, Moses b. Maimon (Rambam), *Hilkot Jerushalmi la-Rambam*, ed. S. Lieberman. New York, 1947. (Texts and Studies of the Jewish Theological Seminary, XIII.)
——— *Iggerot ha-Rambam*, ed. D. H. Baneth. Jerusalem, 1946.
——— *Iggeret Teman* (Arabic original and the Hebrew versions), ed. Abraham S. Halkin; English trans. Boaz Cohen. New York, 1952.
——— *Ḳobeẓ Teshubot ha-Rambam we-Iggerotaw*, ed. A. L. Lichtenberg. Leipzig, 1859.
——— *Mishnah Commentary*. Standard editions of Talmud.
——— *Mishneh Torah*. Standard editions with hassagot of Rabad.

Maimonides, Moses b. Maimon (Rambam), *Sefer ha-Miẓwot*, ed. Ch. Heller.
——— *Teshubot ha-Rambam*, ed. A. Freimann. Jerusalem, 1934.
Manoaḥ b. Simeon of Narbonne, *Sefer ha-Menuḥah*. Pressburg, 1879.
Masseket Kallah and Kallah Rabbati, ed. M. Higger. New York, 1936.
Masseket Semaḥot, ed. M. Higger. New York, 1931.
Masseket Soferim, ed. M. Higger. New York, 1937.
Meïr b. Baruch of Rothenburg, *Hilkot Semaḥot*. Livorno, 1789.
——— *Responsa*. Prague, 1608; Cremona, 1557; Lemberg, 1860.
Meïr ibn Sahula, *Be'ur le-Perush ha-Ramban*. Warsaw, 1875.
Mekilta de-Rabbi Ishmael, ed. Jacob Lauterbach. 3 v. Philadelphia, 1933.
Menaḥem b. Zeraḥ, *Ẓedah la-Derek*. Warsaw, 1880.
Meshullam b. Moses of Béziers, *Sefer ha-Hashlamah* (on *Berakot*), ed. H. Brody. Berlin, 1893.
——— *Sefer ha-Hashlamah* (on *Seder Neziḳin*), ed. I. Lubozky. Paris, 1885.
——— *Sefer ha-Hashlamah* (on *Taᶜanit* and *Megillah*), ed. M. Grossberg. Mainz, 1888.
——— *Tosafot ḥad Miḳamai* (on Yebamot). Standard editions of Talmud.
Midrash Rabbah. 2 v. Vilna ed. 1878.
Misifrut ha-Geonim, ed. S. Assaf. Jerusalem, 1933.
Mishnat R. Eliezer (or *The Midrash of Thirty-two Hermeneutic Rules*), ed. H. G. Enelow. New York, 1933.
Moses b. Jacob of Coucy, *Sefer Miẓwot Gadol*. Venice, 1522.
Moses de Leon, *Ha-Nefesh ha-Ḥakamah*. Basel, 1608.
Moses ha-Darshan, *Midrash Bereshit Rabbati*, ed. Ch. Albeck. Jerusalem, 1940.
Moses ha-Kohen (Ramak), *Hassagot*, ed. S. Atlas. *Hebrew Union College Annual*, XXVII (1956), 1–98.
Moses ibn Ezra, *Shirat Yisra'el*, trans. and notes B. Halper. Leipzig, 1924.
Naḥmanides, Moses b. Naḥman (Ramban), *Derashah le-Rosh ha-Shanah*, ed. Z. Schwarz. *ha-Ẓofeh*, I (1911–1912), 135–157; II (1912), 46–60.
——— *Ḥiddushim*. Various editions.
——— *Hilkot Niddah*. Many editions of the *Baᶜale ha-Nefesh*.
——— *Milḥamot ha-Shem*. Standard editions of the Talmud.
——— *Perush ha-Torah*, ed. C. B. Chavel. 2 v. Jerusalem, 1959–1960.
——— *Sefer ha-Zekut*. Standard editions of the Talmud.
——— *Sefer Torat ha-Adam*. Venice, 1617.
——— *Shaᶜar ha-Gemul*. Naples, 1490.
Nathan b. Yeḥiel of Rome, *ᶜAruk*, ed. and enlarged by A. Kohut. *Aruch ha-Shalem*. 8 v. Vienna, 1926.
Neubauer, Adolf, ed., *Medieval Jewish Chronicles and Chronological Notes*. 2 v. Oxford, 1887–1895.
Orḥot Ẓaddikim. Frankfurt, 1687.
Oẓar ha-Geonim (Thesaurus of Geonic Responsa and Commentaries), ed. M. Lewin, 1928.
Perush ha-Aggadot le-R. ᶜAzriel, ed. I. Tishbi. Jerusalem, 1945.

Perush Talmid ha-Ramban le-Masseket Ta^c^anit, ed. J. Hoffman. New York, 1941.

Perush ha-Geonim ^c^al Seder Tohorot, ed. J. N. Epstein. Berlin, 1921. German title: *Der gaonäische Kommentar zur Mischnaordnung Teharoth.*

Pirḳe de Rabbi Eliezer (Midrashic commentary on parts of the Pentateuch, ascribed to R. Eliezer b. Hyrcanus). Wilna, 1838.

Recanati, Menaḥem, *Sefer Rekanati: Pisḳe Halakot.* Sedilkow, 1836.

Reuben b. Ḥayyim, *Sefer ha-Tamid*, ed. B. Toledano. *Oẓar ha-Ḥayyim*, VII (1931), supplement.

Saadia Gaon, *Emunot we-De'ot* (with commentary *Shebil ha-Emunah*). Yosefov, 1885.

——— *Siddur*, ed. I. Davidson, S. Assaf, B. I. Joel. Jerusalem, 1941.

——— *The Book of Beliefs and Opinions*, trans. Samuel Rosenblatt (Yale Judaica Series, I). New Haven, 1948.

——— *Oeuvres Complets de Saadia*, ed. J. Müller. Paris, 1884.

Sambary, Joseph, *Liḳḳuṭim Midibre Yosef.* See Neubauer.

Samson b. Abraham (Rash) of Sens, *Sifra Commentary.* Warsaw, 1826.

Samuel b. Isaac ha-Sardi, *Sefer ha-Terumot.* Salonica, 1596.

Samuel b. Meïr (Rashbam), *Perush ha-Torah*, ed. D. Rosen. Breslau, 1881.

Seder ^c^Olam Rabbah, ed. B. Ratner. Wilna, 1897.

Sefer ha-Baḥir. Vilna, 1883. Annotated German translation by G. Scholem, Leipzig, 1923.

Sefer ha-Oreh, ed. S. Buber. Lemberg, 1902.

Sefer Ḥasidim, ed. R. Margaliyot. Jerusalem, 1957.

Sefer Josippon. Various editions.

Sefer ha-Pardes ha-Gadol. Warsaw, 1870.

Sefer Yeẓirah. Mantua, 1650.

Sha^c^are Teshubah, ed. M. Meyuhas. Salonica, 1802.

Sha^c^are Ẓedeḳ, ed. N. Modai. Salonica, 1792.

Sherira Gaon, *Iggeret*, ed. B. M. Lewin. Haifa, 1921.

Shibe^c^ah ^c^Enayim. Livorno, 1745. (Contains the *Sefer ha-Zekut* of Naḥmanides.)

She^c^ur Ḳomah in *Sefer Merkabah*, ed. S. Mussajoff. Jerusalem, 1922.

Sifra (or *Torat Kohanim*), ed. I. H. Weiss. New York, 1947 (photostat of Vienna, 1862 edition).

Sifran shel Rishonim, ed. S. Assaf. Jerusalem, 1935. (Contains *Issur Mashehu* of Rabad, Responsa of Rabi and Joseph ibn Plat, and other primary texts.)

Sifre debe Rab, ed. M. Friedmann. Vienna, 1864.

Sifre Zuṭa, ed. Jacob Z. Joskowitz, with commentary *Ambuha de Sifre.* Lodz, 1929.

Solomon b. Isaac (Rashi), *Perush.* Standard editions of Hebrew Bible. Critical edition by A. Berliner. Frankfurt a.M., 1905.

——— *Commentary on Ezechiel*, ed. A. J. Levy. Philadelphia, 1931.

——— *Responsa*, ed. J. Elfenbein. New York, 1943.

Solomon ibn Gabirol, *Mibḥar ha-Peninim*, trans. into Hebrew by Judah ibn Tibbon; Eng. trans. B. H. Ascher. London, 1859.

——— *Selected Religious Poems*, trans. by Israel Zangwill; ed. Israel Davidson. Philadelphia, 1923.

——— *Tiḳḳun Middot ha-Nefesh*. Lyck, 1859. (Translation and an essay on "The Place of Gabirol in the History of the Development of Jewish Ethics," S. S. Wise. New York, 1901.)

Solomon ibn Virga, *Shebet Yehudah*, ed. A. Shohet; introduction Y. Baer. Jerusalem, 1947.

Taku, Moses b. Ḥasdai, "Ketab Tamim," ed. R. Kirchheim. *Oẓar Neḥmad*, III (1860), 54–99.

Temim Deᶜim (Responsa of Rabad for the most part). Warsaw, 1897 (and many previous editions).

Teshubot Baᶜale ha-Tosafot, ed. I. Agus. New York, 1954.

Teshubot Geonim Ḳadmonim, ed. S. L. Rapoport. Berlin, 1848.

Teshubot ha-Geonim, ed. A. Harkavy. Berlin, 1887.

Teshubot ha-Geonim, ed. S. Assaf. Jerusalem, 1929.

Tosefta, ed. M. S. Zuckermandel. Pasewalk, 1880–1882.

Tosefta ki-Feshuta, ed. S. Lieberman, 3 v. New York, 1959.

Tumat Yesharim. Venice, 1662. (Contains *Temim Deᶜim* and Rabad's *hassagot* on Alfasi and Razah.)

Vidal of Tolosa, *Maggid Mishneh*. Standard editions of *Mishneh Torah*.

Yom Ṭob b. Abraham of Seville (Ritba), *Ḥiddushim ᶜal Moᶜed Ḳaṭan*, ed. Ch. Bloch. New York, 1935.

Zabara, Joseph ibn, *Sepher Shaashuim*, ed. Israel Davidson. New York, 1914. (Texts and Studies of the Jewish Theological Seminary of America, IV.)

Zacuto, A., *Yuḥasin ha-Shalem*, ed. H. Filipowski. London, 1857.

Zedekiah ben Abraham 'Anaw, *Shibbale ha-Leḳeṭ ha-Shalem*, ed. S. Buber. Vilna, 1886.

Zeraḥyah ha-Levi (Razah), *Sefer ha-Ma'or*. Standard editions of the Talmud.

——— *Sefer ha-Zabah*, in *Temim De'im*.

Secondary Works

Abrahams, Israel, *Jewish Life in the Middle Ages*. 2nd ed. London, 1932.

Abramson, S., "R. Joseph Rosh ha-Seder," *Kiryath Sefer*, XXVI (1950), 72–96.

Aescoly, A. Z., "Ḥalifat ha-Miktabim ben Yehude Sefarad u-Provence," *Zion*, X (1945), 102–139.

Agus, Irving A., *Rabbi Meir of Rothenburg* (His Life and His Works as Sources for the Religious, Legal, and Social History of the Jews of Germany in the Thirteenth Century). Philadelphia, 1947.

Albeck, Ch., "Le-Ḥeḳer ha-Talmud," *Tarbiẓ*, IX (1938), 163–178.

——— *Mabo la-Mishnah*. Jerusalem, 1959.

——— *Meḥkarim ba-Baraita uba-Tosefta*. Jerusalem, 1944.

——— *Untersuchungen ueber die halakischen Midrashim*. Berlin, 1927.

Albeck, S., "Meḥoḳeḳe Judah," *Festschrift zur Israel Lewy*, ed. M. Brann and J. Elbogen. Breslau, 1911, 104–131.

Altmann, A., "Baᶜyot be-Meḥkar ha-Neo-Aplatoniyut ha-Yehudit," *Tarbiẓ*, XXVII (1938), 501–509.

Anchel, R., *Les Juifs de France*, n.p. 1946.

Ankori, Z., *Karaites in Byzantium*. New York, 1959.

Aptowitzer, A., "Deux Problèmes d'Histoire Littéraire," *Revue des Etudes Juives*, LV (1908), 84–92.

——— "Le Traité de Kalla," *Revue des Etudes Juives*, LVII (1909), 239–245.

——— *Mabo le-Sefer Rabiah*. Jerusalem, 1932.

——— *Meḥḳarim be-Sifrut ha-Geonim*. Jerusalem, 1941.

——— "Teshubot Meyuḥasot le-Rab Hai . . .," *Tarbiẓ*, I (1930), 63–105.

Ashkenazi, E., *Sefer Taᶜam Zekenim*. Frankfurt a.M., 1854.

Ashtor-Strauss, E., "Saladin and the Jews," *Hebrew Union College Annual*, XXVII (1956), 305–327.

Assaf, S., *Be-Ohole Yaᶜakob* (Peraḳim mi-Ḥayye ha-Tarbut shel ha-Yehudim bime ha-Benayim). Jerusalem, 1943.

——— "Darke ha-Talmud u-Kelale ha-Hora'ah," *Sefer ha-Yobel le-Rabi Yehudah Leb ha-Kohen Fishman*. Jerusalem, 1924, 46–68.

——— "Ḥalifat She'elot u-Teshubot ben Sefarad u-ben Ẓarfat we-Ashkenaz," *Tarbiẓ*, VIII (1937), 162–170.

——— "Ḥamesh Teshubot le R. Gershom," *Ẓiyyunim*. Berlin, 1929, 116–121.

——— "Ḳeta miperusho shel Rabi lemasseket Baba Batra," *Oẓar ha-Ḥayyim*, XII (1936), 52–64.

——— "Kinot," *Minḥah le-Yehudah*. Jerusalem, 1950, 162–169.

——— "Ḳobeẓ shel Iggerot R. Samuel b. ᶜEli u-bene doro," *Tarbiẓ*, I (1929), 102–130, 43–84, 15–80.

——— "Liẓemiḥat ha-Merkazim ha-Yisre'eliyim Biteḳufat ha-Geonim," *ha-Shiloaḥ*, XXXV (1918), 8–18, 275–287.

——— "Mafteaḥ li-Teshubot ha-Geonim ha-Muba'ot be-Sefer ha-'Iṭṭur," *Ha-Ẓofeh*, VI (1922), 209–309.

——— *Meḳorot le-Toledot ha-Ḥinnuk be-Yisrael*. 3 v. Tel Aviv, 1925–1936.

——— *Mekorot u-Meḥḳarim be-Toledot Yisra'el*. Jerusalem, 1946.

——— "Miktabim mi-Geone Babel," *Tarbiẓ*, XI (1940), 146–159.

——— "Miperusho shel ha-Rambam le-Masseket Shabbat," *Sinai* II (1940), 103–134.

——— "R. Jonathan ha-Kohen mi-Lunel," *Tarbiẓ*, III (1932), 27–32.

——— "Sefer ha-Ner le R. Isaac ibn Giat," *Tarbiẓ*, III (1932), 213–214.

——— "Sefer Megillat Setarim le-R. Nissim b. Jacob," *Tarbiẓ*, XI (1940), 229–259; XII (1940), 28–50.

——— "Sifre Rab Hai u-Teshubotaw ke-Makor leha-Rambam," *Sinai* II (1938), 522–526.

——— *Teḳufat ha-Geonim we-Sifrutah*. Jerusalem, 1955.

——— "Teshubot min . . . baᶜal ha-Eshkol," *Sinai*, XI (1947), 157–165.

Assaf, S., "Yaḥaso shel ha-Rabad el-Rambam," *Ḳobeẓ Rabbenu Moses b. Maimon*, ed. J. L. Fishman. Jerusalem, 1935, 276–278.

——— "Yehude Miẓrayim bizmano shel ha-Rambam," *Moznayim*, III (1935), 414–432.

Atlas, E., "Ha-Ribash u-bene doro," *ha-Kerem*, I (1887), 1–26.

Azemard, E., *Étude sur les Israelites de Montpellier au moyen-âge*. Nîmes, 1924.

Azulai, H., *Shem ha-Gedolim*. Warsaw, 1878.

Bacher, W., *Die Bibelexegese der jüdischen Religionsphilosophen des Mittelalters von Maimuni*. Strassburg, 1892.

——— *Ha-Rambam Parsham ha-Miḳra*. Tel Aviv, 1932.

Baer, F., *Toledot ha-Yehudim Bisefarad ha-Noẓrit*. Tel Aviv, 1945.

Baron, Salo W., "The Historical Outlook of Maimonides," *Proceedings of the American Academy for Jewish Research*, VI (1935), 5–113.

——— *The Jewish Community*. 3 v. Philadelphia, 1948.

——— *A Social and Religious History of the Jews*. 3 v. New York, 1937. 2nd ed. Philadelphia, V. I–VIII, 1952–1960.

Barul, M., *Menachem ben Simon aus Posquières und sein Kommentar zu Jeremia und Ezechiel*. Berlin, 1907.

Bédaridde, I., *Les Juifs en France, en Italie, et en Espagne*. Paris, 1861.

Belkin, S., "Midrash Tadshe . . . Midrash Hellenisti Ḳadmon," *Ḥoreb*, XI (1951), 1–52.

Ben-Sasson, H., "Rishone ha-Ḳara'im," *Zion*, XV (1950), 42–55.

Benedict, B. Z., "Le-Miklol le-Ḥakme Provence" (R. Samuel b. David), *Kiryath Sefer*, XXVII (1951), 237–249.

——— "Le-Toledotaw shel Merkaz ha-Torah be-Provence," *Tarbiẓ*, XXII (1951), 85–109.

——— "Mabo le-Sefer Baᶜale Asufot," *Sinai*, XIV (1950), 322–329.

——— "Mi-Toratam shel Ḥakme Provence," *Sinai*, XX (1957), 228–241.

——— "Mi-Torato shel R. Aaron b. Meshullam," *Sinai*, XVI (1953), 62–74.

——— "Perush Talmid ha-Ramban le-Masseket Taᶜanit," *Kiryath Sefer*, XXIX (1954), 391–429.

——— "R. Moses b. Joseph of Narbonne," *Tarbiẓ*, XIX (1948), 19–34.

——— Review of Tchernovitz: *Toledot ha-Poskim*, *Kiryath Sefer*, XXV (1949), 164–176.

——— "Sefarim we-Ḳitᶜe sefarim ᶜal Hilkot ha-Rif," *Kiryath Sefer*, XXVIII (1952), 210–233.

——— "Sefer ha-Tashlum shel R. Ephraim," *Kiryath Sefer*, XXVI (1949-1950), 322–338.

——— "Seridim mi-Perushim . . . ᶜal Hilkot ha-Rif," *Tarbiẓ*, XXI (1950), 165–184.

Bergmann, J., *Ha-Ẓedaḳah be-Yisra'el*. Jerusalem, 1944.

Berliner, A., *Geschichte der Juden in Rom*. Frankfurt a.M., 1893.

——— *Ketabim Nibḥarim*, ed. A. M. Haberman. Jerusalem, 1949.

——— and D. Hoffman, *Migdal Chananel* (Ueber Leben und Schriften R. Chananel's in Kairwan, nebst hebraischen Beilagen). Leipzig, 1876.

Bernfeld, S., *Bene ᶜAliyah*, I. Tel-Aviv, 1931.

Bloch, P., "Die zweite Uebersetzung des Saadiahnischen Buches 'Emunoth wedeoth,'" *Monatsschrift für Geschichte und Wissenschaft des Judenthums*, XIX (1870), 401–414, 449–456.

Braslawi, J., "Ḳiṭᶜe Genizah ᶜal Ḥakamim mi-Ẓarfat we-Ashkenaz be-Ereẓ Israel ube-Miẓrayim biteḳufat ha-Rambam," *Ereẓ Israel*, IV (1956), 156–160.

Brody, H., "Kinat Ramah ᶜal ha-Rambam," *Tarbiẓ*, VI (1935), 1–9.

Bromberg, A., *Mekorot le-Fiske ha-Rambam*. Jerusalem, 1947.

——— "R. Ḥananel weha-Rambam," *Sinai*, XI (1948–1949), 4–13, 43–55.

Büchler, A., *Types of Jewish-Palestinian Piety*. London, 1922.

Cabaniss, A., *Agobard of Lyons: A Ninth-Century Ecclesiastic and Critic*. Chicago, 1941.

Carmoly, E., *La France Israelite*. Francfort s/M, 1858.

Catalogue of Hebrew Manuscripts in the Collection of Elkan N. Adler. Cambridge, 1921.

Catalogue of Hebrew Manuscripts in the Jewish National and University Library, ed., B. I. Joel. Jerusalem, 1934.

Chajes, Zvi H., *Tiferet le-Mosheh*. Zolkiew, 1840.

Chertoff, Paul, "ᶜAsarah Baṭlanim," *Jewish Quarterly Review*, XXXIV (1943), 87–99.

Cohen, Boaz, "Classification of Law in the Mishneh Torah," *Jewish Quarterly Review*, XXV (1935), 519–540.

——— *Kuntres ha-Teshubot*. Budapest, 1930. Reprinted from *ha-Ẓofeh*, XIV.

——— "Three Arabic Halakic Discussions of Alfasi," *Jewish Quarterly Review*, XIX (1929), 355–410.

Devic, Cl., and Dom Vaissette, *Histoire Générale de Languedoc*. Toulouse, 1872.

Dienstag, I. J., "Ha-Rambam we-Ḥakme ha-Kabbalah," *Maimonides: His Teachings and Personality*, ed. S. Federbush. New York, 1956, 99–135.

Diesendruck, Z., "On the Date of the Completion of the Moreh Nebukim," *Hebrew Union College Annual*, XII–XIII (1937–1938), 461–497.

Dinaburg, R., *Yisra'el ba-Golah*. 2 v. Tel Aviv, 1946.

Dupont, A., *Les Cités de la Narbonnaise Première*. Nîmes, 1942.

Efros, Israel, *Philosophical Terms in the Moreh Nebukim*. New York, 1924.

——— "Some Aspects of Yehudah Halevi's Mysticism," *Proceedings of the American Academy for Jewish Research*, XI (1941), 27–42.

——— "Studies in pre-Tibbonian Philosophical Terminology," *Jewish Quarterly Review*, XVII (1926), 129–164, 323–368; XX (1929), 113–138.

Eisenstadt, S., "Rambam ke-Mishpeṭan," *Orlogin*, XII (1956), 332–336.

Eisenstein, J., *Oẓar ha-Wikkuḥim*. New York, 1928.

Elbogen, Ismar, *Der jüdische Gottesdienst in seiner geschichtlicher Entwicklung*. Frankfurt a.M., 1931.

——— "Moses ben Maimons Personlichkeit," *Monatsschrift für Geschichte und Wissenschaft des Judenthums*, LXXIX (1935), 76–79.

Emery, Richard, *Heresy and Inquisition in Narbonne*. New York, 1941.

——— *The Jews of Perpignan in the Thirteenth Century*. New York, 1959.

Eppenstein, S., *Beiträge zur Geschichte und Literatur im geonäischen zeitalter.* Berlin, 1913.

Epstein, A., *Glossen zu Gross' Gallia Judaica.* Berlin, 1897.

——— "Joseph ibn Plat und der Pardes," *Monatsschrift für Geschichte und Wissenschaft des Judenthums,* XLIV (1900), 289–296.

——— *Ḳadmoniyot ha-Yehudim,* I. Vienna, 1887.

——— *Ketabim,* ed. A. M. Haberman. 2 v. Jerusalem, 1950.

——— "Le Livre des Jubilés: Philon et le Midrasch Tadsche," *Revue des Etudes Juives,* XXI (1890), 80–97; XXII (1891), 1–25.

——— *R. Moses ha-Darshan.* Vienna, 1891.

——— "Studien zum Jezira-Buche und seinen Erklärern," *Monatsschrift fur Geschichte und Wissenschaft des Judenthums,* XXXVII (1893), 266–269, 458–462.

Epstein, J. N., *Mabo le-Nusaḥ ha-Mishnah.* 2 v. Jerusalem, 1948.

——— *Mebo'ot Le-Sifrut ha-Tannaim.* Jerusalem, 1957.

——— "Mekilta we-Sifre be-Sifre ha-Rambam," *Tarbiẓ,* VI (1935), 99–138.

——— "Perushe ha-Riban . . .," *Tarbiẓ,* IV (1934), 11–34, 153–192.

——— "Rabbenu Baruch me-Ḥalab," *Tarbiẓ,* I (1929), 27–67.

——— "Tashlum Perush ha-Geonim le-Seder Ṭohorot," *Tarbiẓ,* XVI (1944), 71–134.

Epstein, L. M., *Marriage Laws in the Bible and the Talmud.* Cambridge, Mass., 1940.

Feliks, J., "Sefer ha-Yashar le R. Tam," *Sinai,* XXXIX (1956), 52–61, 106–115, 172–182, 224–239, 284–297, 363–373.

Finkelscherer, I., *Moses Maimunis Stellung zum Aberglauben.* Breslau, 1894.

Finkelstein, L., *Mabo le-Massektot Abot we-Abot d'Rabbi Natan.* New York, 1950.

——— "Maimonides and the Tannaitic Midrashim," *Jewish Quarterly Review,* XXV (1935), 469–517.

Fleisher, J. L., "R. Abraham ibn Ezra be-Ẓarefat," *Mizraḥ u-Maᶜarab,* IV (1929–1930), 352–360; V (1930), 38–47, 217–224, 289–300.

Frankel, Zechariah, *Darke ha-Mishnah.* Warsaw, 1923.

——— *Entwurf einer Geschichte der Literatur der nachtalmudischen Responsen.* Breslau, 1865.

——— *Mebo ha-Yerushalmi* (Einleitung in den Jerusalemischer Talmud). Berlin, 1923.

Freehof, Solomon, *The Responsa Literature.* Philadelphia, 1955.

Freimann, A., "Die hebraischen Kommentare zu den 13 Middot des Rabbi Ismael," *Festschrift Adolf Schwarz* (Berlin, 1917), 109–118.

——— "Ḳuntres ha-Mefaresh ha-Shalem," *L. Ginzberg Jubilee Volume.* New York, 1945.

——— "Meschullam b. Kalonymas' Polemik gegen die Karäer," *Judaica: Festschrift zu Hermann Cohen.* Berlin, 1912.

——— "Perush R. Hillel ᶜal Baraita de-R. Ishmael," *Sefer Zikkaron Likbod S. A. Poznanski.* Warsaw, 1927, 170–180.

Freimann, A., Review of "Ḥiddushe ha-Rabad," ed. Atlas. *Kiryath Sefer*, XX (1943), 25–28.

——— "Tashlum ha-ᶜIṭṭur weha-Manhig," *Emet le-Yaᶜakob*. Berlin, 1937, 105–116.

——— "Teshubat ha-Rambam le R. Joseph ha-Maᶜarabi," *Sefer Yobel le-B. M. Lewin*. Jerusalem, 1940, 27–41.

——— "Teshubot R. Maimon ha-Dayyan abi ha-Rambam," *Tarbiẓ*, VI (1935), 164–176.

Gandz, S., "Date of the Composition of Maimonides' Code," *Proceedings of the American Academy for Jewish Research*, XVII (1948), 1–9.

——— "Studies in Hebrew Mathematics and Astronomy," *Proceedings of the American Academy for Jewish Research*, IX (1939), 5–55.

Geiger, A., "Mechilta und Sifre," *Judische Zeitschrift für Wissenschaft und Leben*, IX (1871), 8–30.

——— *Melo Chofnajim*. Berlin, 1840.

——— *Nachgelassene Schriften*. Berlin, 1876–1877.

Germain, A., *L'Ecole de Médicine de Montpellier*. Montpellier, 1880.

Ginzberg, Louis, *Geonica* (The Geonim and their Halakic Writings). 2 v. New York, 1909.

——— *Ginze Schechter. Genizah Studies in Memory of Doctor Solomon Schechter*. 2 v. New York, 1928–1929.

——— *Legends of the Jews*. 7 v. Philadelphia, 1909–1928.

——— *On Jewish Law and Lore*. Philadelphia, 1955.

——— *Perushim we-Ḥiddushim Birushalmi*. 3 v. New York, 1941. (Texts and Studies of the Jewish Theological Seminary, X.)

Gordon, Hersch Loeb, *The Maggid of Caro* (The Mystic Life of the Eminent Codifier Joseph Caro as Revealed in His Secret Diary). New York, 1949.

Gouron, A., *La Reglementation des Métiers en Languedoc au Moyen Age*. Paris, 1958.

Graetz, H., "Die mystiche Literatur in der gaonäischen Epoche," *Monatsschrift für Geschichte und Wissenschaft des Judenthums*, VIII (1859), 67–78, 103–118, 140–153.

——— *Toledot ᶜAm Yisra'el*, Hebrew trans. S. P. Rabinowitz. 9 v. Warsaw, 1894.

Granget, A., *Histoire du Diocese d'Avignon*, I. Avignon, 1862.

Grayzel, Solomon, *The Church and the Jews in the Thirteenth Century*. Philadelphia, 1933.

Gross, H., "Aaron ha-Kohen und Sein Ritualwerk Orchot Chajim," *Monatsschrift für Geschichte und Wissenschaft des Judenthums*, XVIII (1869), 433–450, 531–541.

——— "Etude sur Simson b. Abraham de Sens," *Revue des Etudes Juives*, VI (1883), 167–186; VII, 40–77.

——— *Gallia Judaica: Dictionnaire geographique de la France d'après les sources rabbiniques*. Paris, 1897.

Gross, H., "R. Abraham b. David aus Posquières," *Monatsschrift für Geschichte und Wissenschaft des Judenthums*, XXII (1873), 337–344; 398–407, 446–459, 536–546; XXIII, 19–23, 76–85, 164–182, 275–276.

——— "R. Abraham b. Isaak, ab-bet din aus Narbonne," *Monatsschrift für Geschichte und Wissenschaft des Judenthums*, XVII (1868), 241–255, 281–294.

——— "Meïr b. Simon und seine Schrift Milchemeth Mizwa," *Monatsschrift für Geschichte und Wissenschaft des Judenthums*, XXX (1881), 295–305, 444–452, 554–569.

——— "Zur Geschichte der Juden in Arles," *Monatsschrift für Geschichte und Wissenschaft des Judenthums*, XXVII (1878), 61–71, 130–137, 145–160, 193–201, 248–256, 377–382, 470–477.

——— "Zwei kabbalistische Traditionsketten des R. Eleasar aus Worms," *Monatsschrift für Geschichte und Wissenschaft des Judenthums*, IL (1905), 692–700.

Grünspan, M., "Le-Korot Miẓwat Tefillin we-Haznaḥatah," *Oẓar ha-Ḥayyim*, IV (1928), 159–164.

Guedemann, Moritz, *Geschichte des Erziehungswesens und der Cultur der abendländischen Juden während des Mittelalters und der neueren Zeit.* 3 v. Vienna, 1880–1888. Hebrew trans.: *ha-Torah weha-Ḥayyim*, with additions by A. Friedberg. Warsaw, 1896.

Guiraud, J., *Histoire de l'Inquisition au Moyen Age*. Paris, 1935.

Guttmann, J., *Ha-Pilosofia shel ha-Yahadut*. Jerusalem, 1951.

——— "Zwei Jungst edirte Schriften des Berachya ha-Naḳdan," *Monatsschrift für Geschichte und Wissenschaft des Judenthums*, XLVI (1902), 536–547.

——— ed., *Moses ben Maimon* (Sein Leben, seine Werke und sein Einfluss). 2 v. Leipzig, 1914.

Haberman, A., *Toledot ha-Sefer ha-ᶜIbri*. Jerusalem, 1945.

Halevy, Isaak, *Dorot ha-Rischonim* (Die Geschichte und Literatur Israels). 3 v. Berlin, 1922.

Haskins, C. H., *The Rise of Universities*. New York, 1923.

Heilprin, J., *Seder ha-Dorot*. Warsaw, 1876.

Heinemann, I., "Ha-he'abḳut ᶜal Hagshamat ha-El . . .," *ᶜIyyun*, I (1946), 147–166.

Hershman, Abraham M., *Rabbi Isaac b. Sheshet Perfet and His Times*. New York, 1943.

Heschel, A., *Maimonides: Eine Biographie*. Berlin, 1935.

——— "ᶜAl Ruaḥ ha-Ḳodesh bime ha-Benayim," *Alexander Marx Jubilee Volume*. New York, 1950, 175–208.

Higger, M., *Halakot wa-Agadot*. New York, 1933.

——— Review of "Ḥiddushe ha-Rabad," ed. Atlas. *Jewish Social Studies*, V (1943), 398–400.

——— "Sifre ha-Tannaim bi-Teḳufat ha-Geonim," *Oẓar ha-Ḥayyim*, XIV (1938), 95–120, 143–164, 167–175.

Higger, M., "Yarḥi's Commentary on Kallah Rabbati," *Jewish Quarterly Review*, XXIV (1934), 331–348.

Hilbiz, A., *Lileshonot ha-Rambam*. Jerusalem, 1950.

Hildesheimer, E., "Mystik und Agada im Urteile der Gaonen R. Scherira und Hai," *Jakob Rosenheim Festschrift*. Frankfurt a.M., 1931, 259–273.

Hirschfeld, H., *Descriptive Catalogue of Montefiore Library*. London, 1904.

Hoffman, D., *Zur Einleitung in die halakischen Midrashim*. Berlin, 1887.

Ḥones, S., *Toledot ha-Posḳim*. Warsaw, 1922.

Horodeẓky, S. A., "Ha-Rambam ba-Ḳabbalah u-ba-Ḥasidut," *Moznayim*, III (1935), 441–455.

——— "Hashpaᶜat ha-Rambam ᶜal ha-Rama," *Emet le-Yaᶜakob*. Berlin, 1937, 42–58.

——— *Yahadut ha-Sekel we-Yahadut ha-Regesh*. Tel-Aviv, 1947.

Ḥurgin, P., "Ha-Halakah be-Targum Onkelos," *Ḥoreb*, IX (1946), 79–94.

Hurwitz, Simon, *Responsa of Solomon Luria*. New York, 1938.

Husik, Isaac, *A History of Medieval Jewish Philosophy*. Philadelphia, 1916.

Idelsohn, A. Z., *Shire Teman* (Diwan of Hebrew and Arabic Poetry of the Yemenite Jews). Cincinnati, 1931.

Jeiteles, I., "Die Bedeutung der Pijutim als halachische Quellen," *Jahrbuch der jüdisch-literarischen Gesellschaft*, XIX (1928), 293–306.

Jellinek, A., *Auswahl kabbalistischer Mystik* (*Ginze Ḥokmat ha-Kabbalah*). Leipzig, 1853.

——— *Beiträge zur Geschichte der Kabbala*. Leipzig, 1852.

——— *Ḳuntres ha-Rambam*. Vienna, 1878.

Jost, J. M., *Geschichte des Judenthums und seiner Sekten*. 3 v. Leipzig, 1858.

Juster, J., *Les Juifs dans l'Empire Romain*. 2 v. Paris, 1914.

Kahana, I., "Ha-Pulemos mi-Sabib le-Ḳebiᶜat ha-Halakah keha-Rambam," *Sinai*, XXXVI (1955), 391–411, 530–537.

Kahn, S., "Documents inédits sur les Juifs de Montpellier au Moyen Age," *Revue des Etudes Juives*, XIX (1889), 259–281.

——— *Les Juifs de la Senechausee de Beaucaire*. Paris, 1913.

——— "Les Juifs de Posquières . . . au moyen-âge," *Memoires de l'Académie de Nîmes*, 7th Ser., XXXV (1912), part 3, 1–21.

——— *Notice sur les Israelites de Nîmes* (672–1808). Nîmes, 1901.

Karl, Z., "Ha-Rambam ke-Farshan ha-Miḳra," *Tarbiẓ*, VI (1935), 152–163.

Kasher, M., *Ha-Rambam u-Mekilta de-Rashbi*. New York, 1954.

——— *Torah Shleimah*. New York, 1935– .

Katz, J., *Massoret u-Mashber*. Jerusalem, 1958.

——— Review of Urbach: *Baᶜale ha-Tosafot*, *Kiryath Sefer*, XXXI (1956), 9–16.

——— "Sublanut Datit be-Shitato shel R. Menaḥem ha-Me'iri," *Zion*, XVIII (1953), 15–30.

Katz, S., *The Jews in the Visigothic and Frankish Kingdoms of Spain and Gaul*. Cambridge, Mass., 1937.

Kaufmann, David, *Geschichte der Attributenlehre in der Judischen Religionsphilosophie des Mittelalters*. Gothe, 1877.

Kaufmann, David, "Lettres de Scheschet b. Isaac de Saragosse aux Princes... de Narbonne," *Revue des Etudes Juives*, XXXIX (1899), 62–75.

——— "Liste de Rabbins Dressée par Azriel Trabotto," *Revue des Etudes Juives*, IV (1882), 208–225.

——— "The Etz Chayim of Jacob b. Jehudah of London," *Jewish Quarterly Review* (Old Series), V (1893), 353–375.

Klar, B., *Meḥḳarim we-ᶜIyyunim*. Tel Aviv, 1954.

Kohn, Samuel, *Mardochai ben Hillel: Sein Leben und seine Schriften*. Breslau, 1878.

Kook, S. H., "Ḥomer le-Hora'at 'Shimush'," *Sinai*, XIII (1950), 382–384.

Krauss, S., "L'Emigration de 300 rabbins en Palestine en l'an 1211," *Revue des Etudes Juives*, LXXXII (1926), 333–352.

Lea, H. C., *A History of the Inquisition of the Middle Ages*. New York, 1922.

Lévi, Israel, "Le Roi juif de Narbonne et le Philomène," *Revue des Etudes Juives*, XLVIII (1904), 197–207.

——— "Un recueil de consultations de rabbins de la France méridionale," *Revue des Etudes Juives*, XXXVIII (1899), 103–122.

Levy, Raphael, *The Astrological Works of Abraham ibn Ezra*. Baltimore, 1929.

Lewin, B. M., "Esa Meshali," *Tarbiẓ*, III (1932), 147–160.

——— ed., *Ginze Ḳedem*. I–V. Haifa and Jerusalem, 1928–1934.

——— "Midreshe Halakah u-Fiske ha-Rambam," *Ḳobeẓ Rabbenu Moses b. Maimon*, ed. Fishman. Jerusalem, 1935, 101–145.

——— "Perush R. Nissim le-ᶜErubin," *Emet le-Yaᶜakob*, Berlin, 1937, 72–80.

Lieberman, S., "Ḥazanut Yannai," *Sinai*, IV (1939), 221–250.

——— *Hellenism in Jewish Palestine*. New York, 1950.

——— "Mashehu ᶜal Mefarshim Ḳadmonim la-Yerushalmi," *Alexander Marx Jubilee Volume*. New York, 1950, 287–319.

——— *Tosefet Rishonim*. 4 v. Jerusalem, 1937–1939.

——— *Tosefta Ki-Feshuṭah*. 2 v. New York, 1955.

Liber, M., *Rashi*. Philadelphia, 1948.

Lifschutz, E. M., *Ketabim*. v. I. Jerusalem, 1947.

Loeb, I., "Les Negotiants juifs à Marseille au milieu du XIIIᵉ siècle," *Revue des Etudes Juives*, XVI (1888), 73–83.

——— Review of M. Guedemann, *Geschichte des Erziehungswesens... Revue des Etudes Juives*, II (1881), 158–164.

Lubozky, J., *Bidḳe Batim*. Paris, 1896.

Luzki, M., *Ha-Hoza'ot ha-Shelemot shel Sefer Mishneh Torah*. New York, 1947.

Luzzato, S. D., *Meḥḳere ha-Yahadut*. Warsaw, 1913.

Mach, R., *Der Zaddik in Talmud und Midrasch*. Leiden, 1957.

Maimon, J. L., "Ha-Minhag be-Sifrut ha-Geonim," *Sefer Yobel le-B, M. Lewin*. Jerusalem, 1940, 132–159.

——— *Ḥayye ha-Rambam*. Jerusalem, 1935.

——— *Deyuḳna'ot shel Maᶜalah*. Jerusalem, 1946.

Malter, H., *Life and Works of Saadia Gaon*. Philadelphia, 1942.

Mann, J., "Ha-Tenuᶜot ha-Meshiḥiyot bime Masᶜe ha-Ẓelab ha-Rishonim," *Ha-Teḳufah*, XXIII (1925), 243–261; XXIV (1926), 335–358.

——— *Texts and Studies in Jewish History and Literature.* 2 v. Cincinnati and Philadelphia, 1931–1935.

——— *The Jews in Egypt and Palestine under the Fatimad Caliphs.* 2 v. Oxford, 1920–1922.

Margaliyot, M., *Ha Ḥilluḳim sheben Anshe Mizraḥ u-bene Ereẓ Israel.* Jerusalem, 1938.

Markon, I., "*Mor Deror* explained by Saadya and His Successors," *Saadya Studies*, ed. E. J. Rosenthal. Manchester, 1943, 97–103.

Marmorstein, A., "Hai Gaon et les usages des deux écoles," *Revue des Etudes Juives*, LXXIII (1921), 97–100.

——— Review of Poznanski: *Babylonische Geonim* . . ., *Revue des Etudes Juives*, LXXII (1920), 97–111.

——— "Sefer Dine Tefillah u-Moᶜadim shel R. Maimon abi ha-Rambam," *Tarbiẓ*, VI (1935), 182–184.

——— "Spuren karäischen Einflusses in der gaonäischen Halachah," *Festschrift Adolph Schwarz*, ed. A. Apotwitzer and S. Krauss. Berlin, 1917, 455–470.

——— "The Place of Maimonides' Mishnah Torah in the History and Development of the Halachah," *Moses Maimonides*, ed. I. Epstein. London, 1935, 159–179.

Marx, Alexander, "A New Collection of Manuscripts," *Proceedings of American Academy for Jewish Research*, IV (1932–1933), 135–167.

——— "Bemerkungen zu Steinschneider's hebraeischen Uebersetzungen," *Zeitschrift für hebräische Bibliographie*, X, 1906.

——— "Gabirol's Authorship of the Choice of Pearls and the Two Versions of Joseph Kimḥi's Sheḳel Haḳodesh," *Hebrew Union College Annual*, IV (1927), 438–448.

——— "Ma'amar ᶜal Shenat ha-Ge'ulah," *Ha-Ẓofeh le-Ḥokmat Yisra'el*, V (1921), 194–202.

——— "R. Abraham b. David et R. Zerahya ha-Levi," *Revue des Etudes Juives*, LIX (1910), 200–224.

——— Review of L. Ginzberg "Geonica," *Zeitschrift für hebräische Bibliographie*, XIII (1909), 170 ff.

——— "Sefer ha-Miktam," *Ha-Ẓofeh* Me-Ereẓ *Hagar*, II (1918), 57–61.

——— *Studies in Jewish History and Booklore.* New York, 1944.

——— "Texts by and about Maimonides," *Jewish Quarterly Review*, XXV (1935), 371–428.

——— "The Correspondence between the Rabbis of Southern France and Maimonides about Astrology," *Hebrew Union College Annual*, III (1926), 311–358.

——— "The Scientific Work of Some Outstanding Mediaeval Jewish Scholars," *Essays and Studies . . . Linda R. Miller.* New York, 1933, 117–171.

Maucomble, Jean François de, *Histoire abregée de la Ville de Nîmes*. Amsterdam, 1767.

Menard, *Histoire de la Ville de Nîmes*, I. Nîmes, 1871.

Michael, Joseph H., *Or ha-Ḥayyim*. Frankfurt a.M., 1891.

Mirsky, S., "R. Jonathan mi-Lunel," *Sura*, II. Jerusalem, 1956, 242–266.

Moore, George Foot, *Judaism*. 3 v. Cambridge, Mass., 1944.

Müller, Ernst, *History of Jewish Mysticism*. Oxford, 1946.

Munk, S., *Mélanges de Philosophie Juive et Arabe*. Paris, 1859.

Münz, J., *Maimonides: The Story of His Life and Genius*, English trans. Henry Schnittkind. Boston, 1935.

Nemoy, L., *Karaite Anthology*. New Haven, 1952. Yale Judaica Series, VII.

Neubauer, A., *Catalogue of the Hebrew Manuscripts in the Bodleian Library*. Oxford, 1886.

——— ed., *Medieval Jewish Chronicles and Chronological Notices*. 2 v. Oxford, 1887–1895.

Neubauer, I., *Ha-Rambam ᶜal Dibre Soferim*. Jerusalem, 1957.

Neuhausen, S., "Ḳawim Litemunato shel ha-Rashbam," *Ha-Ẓofeh le-Ḥokmat Yisra'el*, XV (1931), 194–201.

Neuman, Abraham, *The Jews in Spain*. 2 v. Philadelphia, 1948.

Neumark, *Toledot ha-Pilosofia be-Yisra'el*. 2 v. New York, 1921–1929.

Newman, Louis I., *Jewish Influence on Christian Reform Movements*. New York, 1925.

——— "Joseph b. Isaac Kimchi as a Religious Controversialist," *Jewish Studies in Memory of Israel Abrahams*. New York, 1927, 365–372.

Plessner, M., "Liḳḳutim le-Sefer Musre ha-Pilosofim . . . ule-Targumo ha-ᶜIbri," *Tarbiẓ*, XXIV (1954), 60–72.

Pirenne, H., *Economic and Social History of Medieval Europe*. New York, n.d.

Poznanski, S., *Anshe Kairwan*. Warsaw, 1909.

——— *Babylonische Geonim im Nachgaonäischen Zeitalter*. Berlin, 1914.

——— "Ha-Geonim weha-Jerushalmi," *'Inyanim Shonim*. Warsaw, 1909, 3–44.

——— "Liḳḳuṭim min Sefer Megillat Setarim," *ha-Ẓofeh le-Ḥokmat Yisra'el*, V (1921), 177–193, 294–301; VI (1922), 329–350; VII (1923), 17–46.

Rabinowitz, R. N., *Diḳduḳe Soferim*. Münich, 1873.

Rapoport, S., *Toledot*. Warsaw, 1913.

Rawidowicz, S., "Baᶜayat ha-Hagshamah le-Rasag ule-Rambam," *Kenesset*, III (1938), 322–378.

——— "Saadya's Purification of the Idea of God," *Saadya Studies*, ed. E. I. Rosenthal. Manchester, 1943, 139–166.

Regne, Jean, *Etude sur la condition des Juifs de Narbonne du V° au XIV° siècle*. Narbonne, 1912.

Reifmann, J., "Abraham b. Jarchi," *Magazin für die Wissenschaft des Judentums*, V (1878), 60–67.

——— *Arbaᶜah Ḥarashim*. Prague, 1860.

——— "Rabad Baᶜal ha-Hassagot," *Bet Talmud*, IV (1885), 380–382.

Reifmann, J., "Toledot ha-Rabad Ba^cal ha-Hassagot," *ha-Maggid*, XII (1862), 382, 389–390.
——— "Toledot Rabenu Abraham Ba^cal ha-Manhig we-Ḳorot Sefaraw," *ha-Meliẓ*, I, nos. 4–6.
——— *Toledot R. Zeraḥyah ha-Levi.* Prague, 1853.
Reines, H., "Baṭlanim Bimeḳorot ha-Talmud," *Sinai*, XX (1957), 81–89.
Renan, Ernest, *Les Rabbins Français du Commencement du quatorzième Siècle* (*L'Histoire Litteraire de la France*, XXVIII), Paris, 1877.
Repha'el, I., "Rashi bi-Teshubotaw," *Sefer Rashi*, ed. J. Maimon. Jerusalem, 1956, 570–592.
Rosin, David, *Ein Compendium der jüdischen Gesetzeskunde.* Breslau, 1871.
Roth, A. N., "Ḳeṭa^cim mi-Mishneh Torah," *Ginze Kaufmann.* Budapest, 1948, 62–71.
Roth, C., "The Eastertide Stoning of the Jews," *Jewish Quarterly Review*, XXV (1945), 361–371.
——— *The Intellectual Activities of Medieval English Jewry.* London: British Academy Papers, Vol. VIII, n.d.
Rouet, A., *Notice sur la Ville de Lunel au Moyen-Age.* Paris, 1878.
Runciman, Steven, *The Medieval Manichee: A Study of the Christian Dualist Heresy.* Cambridge, 1947.
Sachs, M. J., "Ḳeṭa ḥadash mi-Perush ha-Rambam," *Sinai*, XIII (1949), 66–68.
Saige, G., *Les Juifs du Languedoc.* Paris, 1881.
Saracheck, Joseph, *Faith and Reason: The Conflict over the Rationalism of Maimonides.* Williamsport, 1935.
Sarton, George, *Introduction to the History of Science.* 2 v. Washington, D.C., 1931.
Sassoon, D., *Ohel David* (Descriptive Catalogue of the Hebrew and Samaritan Manuscripts in the Sassoon Library). London, 1932.
Schechter, S., *Studies in Judaism: Second Series.* Philadelphia, 1908.
Scholem, G., "^cAl Nebi'uto shel R. Ezra," *Tarbiẓ*, II (1931), 244–245.
——— *Bibliographia Kabbalistica.* Leipzig, 1927.
——— *Das Buch Bahir* (ins Deutsche uebersetzt und kommentiert). Leipzig, 1923.
——— "Der Begriff der Kawwana in der alter Kabbala," *Monatsschrift für Geschichte und Wissenschaft des Judenthums*, LXXVIII (1934), 492–518.
——— "Die Lehre vom 'Gerechten' in der jüdischen Mystik," *Eranos Jahrbuch*, XXVII (1958), 237–299.
——— "Ha-Meḥaber ha-Amiti shel Perush Sefer Yeẓirah ha-Meyuḥas la-Rabad," *Peraḳim le-Toledot Sifrut ha-Kabbalah.* Jerusalem, 1931, 2–17.
——— "Ikbotaw shel Gabirol ba-Kabbalah," *Me-Assef Sofre Ereẓ Israel*, ed. A. Kabak and A. Steinman. Tel Aviv, 1940, 160–178.
——— *Jewish Gnosticism, Merkabah Mysticism, and Talmudic Tradition.* New York, 1960.
——— "Kabbalot R. Jacob we-R. Isaac," *Mada^ce ha-Yahadut.* II (1927), 165–293.

Scholem, G., "Mafteaḥ le-Perushim ᶜal ᶜEser Sefirot," *Kiryath Sefer*, X (1934), 446.
——— *Major Trends in Jewish Mysticism*. New York, 1941.
——— "Mi-Ḥoḳer Limeḳubbal," *Tarbiẓ*, VI (1935), 90–98.
——— *Peraḳim le-Toledot Sifrut ha-Kabbalah*. Jerusalem, 1931.
——— *Reshit ha-Kabbalah*. Jerusalem, 1948.
——— "Seridim Ḥadashim Mikitbe R. ᶜAzriel," *Sefer Zikkaron le-Asher Gulak*. Jerusalem, 1942, 201–222.
——— "Sidre de-Shimusha Rabba," *Tarbiẓ*, XVI (1945), 196–209.
——— "Teᶜudah Ḥadashah le-Toledot Reshit ha-Kabbalah," *Sefer Bialik*. Tel-Aviv, 1934, 141–162.
Schonblum, S., ed. *Sheloshah Sefarim Niftaḥim*. Lemberg, 1877.
Schwarzfuchs, S., *Études sur l'origine et le développement du Rabbinat au Moyen Age*. Paris, 1957.
Segal, M. H., *Parshanut ha-Mikra*. Jerusalem, 1944.
Shirman, H., *Ha-Shirah ha-ᶜIbrit Bisefarad ube-Provence*. 2 v. Jerusalem. 1956.
——— "Ḥayye Judah ha-Levi," *Tarbiẓ*, IX (1938), 35–54, 219–240, 284–305.
Shrock, A. T., *Rabbi Jonah b. Abraham of Gerona* (His Life and Ethical Works). London, 1948.
Smith, Cyril E., *The University of Toulouse in the Middle Ages*. Milwaukee, 1958.
Sonne, I., "Iggeret ha-Rambam," *Tarbiẓ*, X (1938–1939), 135–154, 309–332.
——— "Ṭiyyulim be-hisṭoriyah ubibliografiyah," *Alexander Marx Jubilee Volume*. New York, 1950, 209–235.
Spiegel, S., "On Medieval Hebrew Poetry," *The Jews*, ed. L. Finkelstein. New York, 1949, I, 528–567.
Starr, J., *The Jews in the Byzantine Empire*. Athens, 1939.
Stein, Ludwig, *Die Willensfreiheit und ihr verhältniss zur göttlichen präscienz und Providenz bei den jüdischen philosophen des Mittelalters*. Berlin, 1882.
Stein, S., "Me'ir b. Simeon's Milḥemeth Miṣwah," *Journal of Jewish Studies*, X (1960), 45–63.
Steinschneider, Moritz, *Die hebraieschen Uebersetzungen des Mittelalters und die Juden als Dolmetscher*. Berlin, 1893.
——— *Gesammelte Schriften*. Berlin, 1925.
——— *Jewish Literature from the Eighth to the Eighteenth Century with an Introduction on Talmud and Midrash*, trans. from the German. London, 1857.
Stern, S. M., "Ḥalifat ha-Miktabim ben ha-Rambam we-Ḥakme Provence," *Zion*, XVI (1951), 19–28.
Strack, H., *Introduction to the Talmud and Midrash*. Philadelphia, 1945.
Tchernowitz, Ch., "Lu lo Ḳam ke-Mosheh," *Moznayim*, III (1935), 381–401.
——— *Toledot ha-Poskim* (History of Jewish Codes). 3 v. New York, 1946.
Tishbi, I., "Aggadah we-Kabbalah be-Perushe ha-Aggadot," *Minḥah li-Yehudah*, ed. S. Assaf. Jerusalem, 1950, 170–174.

Tishbi, I., "R. Ezra we-R. ᶜAzriel," *Zion*, IX (1944), 178–185.
Toledano, B., "Sefer ha-Manhig ha-Shalem le-Raban ha-Yarḥi," *Sinai*, XX (1957), 75–80.
Toledano, J. M., ed., *Sarid U-Falit*. Tel Aviv, n.d.
Torczyner, N., *Ha-Lashon weha-Sefer*. I, Jerusalem, 1948.
Unna, M., *Ha-Ramban*. Jerusalem, 1942.
Urbach, E. E., *Baᶜale ha-Tosafot*. Jerusalem, 1955.
——— "Halakah u-Nebu'ah," *Tarbiẓ*, XVIII (1947), 1–27.
——— "Hassagot ha-Rabad ᶜal Perush Rashi," *Kiryath Sefer*, XXXIV (1959), 101–108.
——— "Hassagot ha-Rabad ... Bidefusim ube-kitbe Yad," *Kiryath Sefer*, XXXIII (1959), 360–375.
——— "Ḥelkam shel ḥakme Ashkenaz ... ba-pulemos ᶜal ha-Rambam," *Zion*, XII (1947), 149–159.
Uryan, M., *Ha-Moreh le-Dorot*. Jerusalem, 1956.
Vajda, G., "Un chapitre de l'histoire du conflit entre la Kabbale et la philosophie. La polémique anti-intellectualiste de Joseph b. Shalom Ashkenzai," *Archives d'histoire doctrinale et littéraire du moyen âge*, 1956, 45–146.
Vogelstein, H. and P. Rieger, *Geschichte der Juden in Rom*. I, Berlin, 1896.
Waxman, M., *History of Jewish Literature*. 4 v. New York, 1930–1941.
Weis, P. R., "Abraham ibn Ezra weha-Kara'im," *Melilah*, I (1944), 35–53; II (1946), 121–134; III–IV (1950), 188–203.
Weiss, Isaac Hirsch, *Dor Dor we-Doreshaw*. 5 v. Vilna, 1904.
——— "Rab Hai weha-Ḥokmot ha-Ḥiẓoniot," *he-Asif*, III (1886), 148–152.
——— "Toledot ha-Rambam," *Bet Talmud*, I (1881), 161–169, 193–200, 225–233, 257–265, 289–296.
Wellesz, J., "Hagahot Maimuniyot," *ha-Goren*, VII (1908), 35–59.
Wertheimer, S. A., ed., *Bate Midrashot*. 2 v. Jerusalem, 1950.
——— *Sefer Ginze Jerusalem*. Jerusalem, 1896–1899.
Wieder, N., *Hashpaᶜot Islamiyot ᶜal ha-Pulḥan ha-Yehudi*. Oxford, 1947.
——— "Sifro ha-Nisraf shel Judah ibn Shabetai," *Meẓudah*, II (1944), 124–132.
Wolfson, H., *Crescas' Critique of Aristotle*. Cambridge, Mass., 1929.
——— *Philo: Foundations of Religious Philosophy in Judaism, Christianity, and Islam*. 2 v. Cambridge, Mass., 1948.
——— "Spinoza and Religion," *Menorah Journal* (1950), 146–167.
——— "The Philonic God of Revelation and His Latter-Day Deniers," *Harvard Theological Review*, LIII (1960), 101–124.
——— "The Platonic, Aristotelian and Stoic Theories of Creation in Halevi and Maimonides," *Essays in Honor of ... Dr. Hertz*. London, 1942, 427–442.
Yaᶜari, A., "Hash'alat Sefarim," *Sinai*, XVII (1953), 122–136.
——— "Perush ha-Mishnah leha-Rambam Bimeḳoro," *Kiryath Sefer*, IX (1932), 101–109, 228–235.
Yellin, D. and I. Abrahams, *Maimonides*. Philadelphia, 1903.

Zeitlin, S., *Maimonides*. New York, 1955.

Zimmels, H. J., *Ashkenazim and Sephardim* (Their Relations, Differences, and Problems as Reflected in the Rabbinical Responsa). London, 1958.

——— "Erez Israel in der Responsenliteratur des Späteren Mittelalters," *Monatsschrift für Geschichte und Wissenschaft des Judenthums*, LXXIV (1930), 44–64.

——— *Rabbi David ibn abi Simra*. Breslau, 1932.

Zinberg, I., *Toledot Sifrut Yisra'el*. 5 v. Tel Aviv, 1955– .

Ziv, A., *R. Moses Isserles*. Jerusalem, 1957.

Zlotnik (Avida), J. L., "Le-Toledot ha-Hoẓa'ot ha-Rishonot shel Mishneh Torah," *Sinai*, XV (1951), 138–143, 247–248.

——— "Shene Ḳeṭᶜaim le-Hashlamat *Sefer ha-ᶜIttim*," *Sinai*, VIII (1945), 116–138.

Zucker, M., "Ḥomer le-Mabo ha-Talmud be-Perushe Rashi," *Bitzaron*, II (1940), 378–390.

Zucrow, S., *Sifrut ha-Halakah*. New York, 1932.

Zunz, Leopold, "Abraham b. Isaak und Abraham b. David," *Wissenschaftliche Zeitschrift für jüdische Theologie*, II (1839), 309–313.

——— *Gesammelte Schriften*. I, Berlin, 1875.

——— *Ha-Derashot be-Yisra'el*, ed. Ch. Albeck. Jerusalem, 1948. (Hebrew trans. of "Die gottesdienstlichen Vorträge der Juden.")

——— *Rashi*, trans. into Hebrew, S. Bloch. Warsaw, 1862.

——— *Zur Geschichte und Literatur*. Berlin, 1845.

BIBLIOGRAPHICAL SUPPLEMENT

This supplement attempts to list some of the relevant and useful studies that have appeared since publication of my book in 1962. The list is obviously selective rather than exhaustive: first, because of the inevitable limitations and peculiar habits of my reading—I am by nature not a bibliographer and do not collect references in any systematic, disciplined way—and second, because the subject is so central and so repercussive that many areas of learning are genuinely relevant. Given the broad context in which we have tried to view Rabad, almost all rabbinic literature and much in philosophy, mysticism, or exegesis are cognate. As a result of the centrality of the *Mishneh Torah* and the *Hassagot* in subsequent halakic writing, Rabad's statements are cited, clarified or criticized, debated or developed in a great number of works in many different genres. It is neither feasible nor sensible to try to encompass all this bibliographic detail. General—bibliographical or historical—works, such as those of J. Dienstag, M. Elon, M. Kasher, N. Rackover, and G. Vajda, or the supplement to the reprint of *Gallia Judaica,* and others, contain much material that will enable the reader to pursue selected themes further. Collectanea such as *Ginze Rishonim, Ḳobeẓ Rishonim,* and *Oẓar Rishonim* on various tractates of the Talmud should also be checked regularly for relevant sources. In the primary sources I have, therefore, concentrated on Provençal works and a few others that are especially representative or significant. Items listed under secondary works are of three kinds: those that refer directly to Rabad's biography or literary achievement; those refering to his period as a whole; and those that refer to aspects of his abiding influence and importance in Jewish history.

Primary Sources

Abraham Azulai, *Ahabah ba-Ta^canugim: Perush ha-Mishnah,* ed. D. Zlotnick. In *Meḥḳarim u-Meḳorot,* ed. H. Dimitrovsky. New York, 1978.

Abraham b. Azriel, *[c]Arugat ha-Bosem,* ed. E. Urbach. Jerusalem, 1963.

Abraham b. David (Rabad), *Ba[c]ale ha-Nefesh* (with *Sela[c] ha-Maḥloḳet* of Razah), ed. J. Kafiḥ. Jerusalem, 1964.

——— *Hassagot* on Alfasi (*Makkot*) in *Sanhedri Gedolah* (on *Makkot*), ed. I. Ralbag. Jerusalem, 1973.

——— *Hibbur Hilkot Lulab* in C. B. Chavel, *Teshubot ha-Ramban,* Jerusalem, 1975, 183–219.

——— *'Issur Mashehu* in Rashba, *Torat ha-Bayit ha-Shalem,* ed. M. Herschler. Jerusalem, 1963.

——— *Katub Sham,* ed. M. Z. Hasidah. Reprinted in Jerusalem, 1969; also in *Torah 'Or* edition of Talmud.

——— *Perush Shebuot* in *Tosefot ha-Rosh le-Masseket Shebuot,* ed. S. Wilman. Jerusalem, 1975.

——— *Seridim mi-Derashat ha-Rabad le-Pesah,* ed. E. Hurvitz. *Ha-Darom,* XXXV (1972), 34–73.

——— *Teshubot u-Pesaḳim,* ed. J. Kafiḥ. Jerusalem, 1964.

Abraham b. Isaac (Rabi) of Narbonne, *Responsa,* ed. J. Kafiḥ. Jerusalem, 1962.

Abraham b. Isaac of Carpentras (min ha-Har), *Perush, Nedarim, Nazir,* ed. M. Blau. 2 v. New York, 1960.

——— *Perush, Sukkah . . . ,* ed. M. Blau. New York, 1975.

——— *Perush, Yebamot,* ed. M. Blau. New York, 1962.

Abraham b. Nathan ha-Yarḥi, *Sefer ha-Manhig,* ed. I. Refael. 2 v. Jerusalem, 1978.

Abraham ibn Daud, *Sefer ha-Kabbalah,* ed. G. Cohen. Philadelphia, 1967.

Abraham ibn Ezra, *Perush ha-Torah,* ed. A. Weiser. Jerusalem, 1976.

Adret, Solomon b. Abraham, *Torat ha-Bayit ha-Shalem,* ed. M. Herschler. Jerusalem, 1963.

Alfasi, Isaac, *She'elot u-Teshubot,* ed. D. Rotstein. New York, 1975.

Asher b. Yehiel, *Tosafot* (*Berakot*), ed. J. Faur. *PAAJR,* XXXIII (1965), 41–65.

Bahya b. Asher, *Be'ur [c]al ha-Torah,* ed. C. Chavel. Jerusalem, 1967.

——— *Kitbe R. Bahya,* ed. C. Chavel. Jerusalem, 1969.

——— *Shulḥan shel 'Arba.* Warsaw, 1879.

Berechiah ha-Naḳdan, *Fables of a Jewish Aesop,* trans. Moses Hadas. New York, 1967.

Cohen, S., trans., *The Holy Letter: A Study in Medieval Jewish Sexual Morality Ascribed to Naḥmanides.* New York, 1958.

David b. ha-Levi, *Sefer ha-Miktam* (on *Berakot*) in *Ginze Rishonim,* IV, ed. M. Herschler. Jerusalem, 1967, 17–122.

——— *Sefer ha-Miktam* (on *Rosh ha-Shanah, Taᶜanit*) in *Ginze Rishonim,* II, ed. M. Herschler. Jerusalem, 1963.

——— *Sefer ha-Miktam* (on *Megillah*), ed. M. Grossberg. Lemberg, 1904; new edition, Jerusalem, 1968.

——— *Sefer ha-Miktam* (on *Pesaḥim, Sukkah, Moᶜed Ḳaṭan*), ed. M. Y. Blau. New York, 1958.

David b. Samuel of Estella, *Sefer ha-Batim* (*ᶜal Ḳeri'at ha-Torah*), ed. M. Blau. New York, 1974.

——— *Sefer ha-Batim,* ed. J. M. Blau. New York, 1978.

Duran, Simeon b. Ẓemaḥ, *Ḥiddushe u-Fisḳe ha-Rashbaẓ le-Masseket Niddah.* Jerusalem, 1967.

——— *Perush ha-Rashbaẓ: Berakot,* ed. D. Z. Hilman. Bnei Brak, n.d.

Ha-Me'iri, Menaḥem, *Bet ha-Beḥirah* (on *Abot*), ed. B. Z. Prag. Jerusalem, 1968.

——— *Bet ha-Beḥirah* (on *Berakot*), ed. S. Dickman. Jerusalem, 1960.

——— *Commentary on Mishle,* ed. M. M. Meshei-Zahab. Jerusalem, 1969.

——— *Commentary on Mishnah,* ed. M. M. Meshei-Zahab. 6 v. Jerusalem, 1971–1974.

——— *Commentary on Torah,* ed. H. Gad. London, 1957.

——— *Kiryat Sefer* (on *Hilkot Sefer Torah, Tefilin, Mezuzah*), ed. M. Herschler. Jerusalem, 1956.

——— *Sefer ha-Middot,* ed. M. M. Meshei-Zahab. Jerusalem, 1966.

——— *Teshubot* (*Magen Abot*), ed. S. A. Wertheimer and Y. H. Deiḥes. Jerusalem, 1958.

Hilkot Hamez u-Mazah, ed. C. Chavel. *Ha-Darom,* XXXV (1972), 5–34.

Hillel b. Eliakim of Greece, *Perush Sifra,* ed. S. Koleditzky. Jerusalem, 1962.

Isaac b. Abba Mari of Marseilles, *Sefer ha-ᶜIṭṭur.* 2 v. Jerusalem, 1970.

Isaac b. Melkizedek, *Perush Zeraᶜim,* ed. N. Zaks. Jerusalem, 1975.

Isaiah of Trani (the First), *Perush Nebi'im u-Ketubim.* 3 v. Jerusalem, 1959, 1965, 1978.

——— *Sefer ha-Makriᶜa.* New York, 1962, 1976.

——— *Sefer ha-Makriᶜa.* Livorno, 1779; new edition, ed. Y. Z. Reichman, Jerusalem, 1974.

Jacob ben Yehudah Hazan of London, *Eṣ Ḥayyim,* ed. I. Brodie. 3 v. Jerusalem, 1962–1967.

Jacob b. Moses of Banleux, *ᶜEzrat Nashim,* ed. M. Blau. New York, 1970.

Jacob b. Reuben, *Milḥamoṭ ha-Shem,* ed. J. Rosenthal. Jerusalem, 1963.

Jeruḥam b. Meshullam, *Sefer Toledot Adam ve-Ḥawah.* Venice, 1553; new edition, Jerusalem, 1975.

Jonathan ha-Kohen of Lunel, *Commentary* (on *Sanhedrin*) in *Sanhedri Gedolah,* II, ed. Y. Kuperberg. Jerusalem, 1969, 1–168.

Jonathan ha-Kohen of Lunel, *Commentary* (on *Abot*) in *Sanhedri Gedolah* (on *Sanhedrin*), I, ed. I. Ralbag. Jerusalem, 1973.

——— *Commentary* (on *Rosh ha-Shanah, Yumah,* and *Ta*[c]*anit*) in *Ginze Rishonim,* II, ed. M. Herschler. Jerusalem, 1963.

——— *Commentary* (on *Sukkah*) in *Ginze Rishonim,* I, ed. M. Herschler. Jerusalem, 1962.

——— *Commentary* (on *Baba Ḳamma*), ed. S. Y. Friedman. Jerusalem, 1969.

——— *Commentary* (on *Berakot*), ed. M. Y. Blau. New York, 1957.

Joseph b. Nathan, *Sefer Yosef ha-Meḳane',* ed. J. Rosenthal. Jerusalem, 1970.

Judah b. Yakar, *Perush ha-Tefillot.* 2 v. Jerusalem, 1968.

Judah ha-Levi, *Sefer ha-Cuzari,* trans. Y. ibn Shmuel. Tel Aviv, 1972.

Kimḥi, Joseph, *Commentary on Job in Tikwat Enosh,* I. Schwarz. Berlin, 1868, 147–166.

——— [c]*Eit Sofer*. Lyck, 1864. Reprinted in Jerusalem, 1970.

——— *Sefer Ḥukah* (*Commentary* on *Mishle*). Breslau, 1868.

——— *Sefer Miklol,* ed. I. Rittenberg. Lyck, 1842. Reprinted in Jerusalem, 1966.

——— *The Book of the Covenant,* trans. F. Talmage. Toronto, 1972.

Maimonides, Moses b. Maimon (Rambam), *Mishneh Torah,* Book III (*Zemanim*), ed. S. Frankel. Jerusalem, 1975. Book IV, 1977.

——— *Teshubot,* ed. J. Blau. 3 v. Jerusalem, 1958.

Manoaḥ b. Simeon of Narbonne, *Sefer ha-Menuḥah,* ed. Elazar Hurvitz. Jerusalem, 1970.

——— *Sefer ha-Menuḥah* in *Ḳobeẓ Rishonim* [c]*al Mishneh Torah.* Jerusalem, 1967.

——— *Sefer ha-Menuḥah.* Pressburg, 1879.

Meir ha-Kohen (of Narbonne), *Sefer ha-Me'orot,* ed. M. Y. Blau. 4 v. New York, 1964–1966.

Meir b. Simeon of Narbonne, *Milḥemet Miẓvah,* ed. J. Blau, in *Shitat ha-Ḳadmonim* [c]*al Nazir.* New York, 1974.

Meshullam b. Jacob Lunel, *'Issur Mashehu* in J. Kafiḥ, *Teshubot u-Pesakim.* (n.p., n.d.).

Meshullam b. Moses of Béziers, *Sefer ha-Hashlamah* (on *Berakot*) in *Ginze Rishonim,* IV, ed. M. Herschler. Jerusalem, 1967, 197–250.

——— *Sefer ha-Hashlamah,* ed. M. Y. Blau. 4 v. New York, 1964–1966.

——— *Sefer ha-Hashlamah* (on *Rosh ha-Shanah, Yumah, Ta*[c]*anit*) in *Ginze Rishonim,* II, ed. M. Herschler. Jerusalem, 1963, 135–172.

——— *Sefer ha-Hashlamah* (on *Sukkah*) in *Ginze Rishonim,* I, ed. M. Herschler. Jerusalem, 1962, 121–172.

——— *Sefer ha-Hashlamah,* ed. A. Ḥapuṭah. 10 v. Tel Aviv, 1961—.

Moses ha-Kohen (Ramak), *Hassagot ha-Ramak* [c]*al ha-Rambam: Madda*[c]*, 'Ahabah, Zemanim,* ed. S. Atlas. Jerusalem, 1969.

Moses ibn Ezra, *Shirat Yisrael,* ed. and trans. A. Halkin. Jerusalem, 1976.

Naḥmanides, Moses b. Nahman (Ramban), *Kitbe Ramban,* ed. C. Chavel. 2 v. Jerusalem, 1963.
——— *Teshubot,* ed. C. Chavel. Jerusalem, 1975.
Orehot Tzaddikim, ed. and trans. S. J. Cohen. New York, 1969.
Perush Kadmon le-Baba Batra, ed. M. Herschler. Jerusalem, 1971.
Sefer Hayashar, ed. and trans. S. J. Cohen. New York, 1973.
Sefer Hilkot ha-Nagid, ed. M. Margaliyot. Jerusalem, 1962.
Solomon ibn Gabirol, *Shire ha-Ḳodesh,* ed. D. Yarden. Jerusalem, 1971.
Solomon Sirillo, *Perush Shekalim,* ed. A. Grabois. Jerusalem, 1958.
Teshubot Ḥakme Provence, ed. A. Schreiber. Jerusalem, 1967.
Tosefot Ḥakme Anglia, ed. E. D. Pines. 4 v. Jerusalem, 1968–1971.
Tosafot Yeshanim ᶜal Massekhet Yebamot, Perek Shelishi, ed. B. S. Wacholder, in *Texts and Responses: Studies Presented to Nahun Glatzer,* ed. M. Fishbane. Leiden, 1975.
Zeraḥyah ha-Levi (Razah), *Commentary* (on *Ḳinnim*) in *Ḥidushe Ḳiddushin,* ed. M. Ashkenazi. n.p., 1751.
——— *Sefer ha-Ma'or,* ed. with commentary by S. Z. Ehrenreich. Jerusalem, 1967.

Secondary Works

Abramson, S., *Ba-Merkazim uba-Tefuẓot.* Jerusalem, 1965.
——— *Bileshon Ḳodemim.* Jerusalem, 1965.
——— *Ḥamishah Sefarim le-R. Nissim Gaon.* Jerusalem, 1965.
——— "ᶜInyanot be-Sefer ha-Yashar le-R. Tam," *KS,* XXXVII (1962).
——— *ᶜInyanot be-Sifrut ha-Geonim.* Jerusalem, 1974.
——— *Kelale ha-Talmud be-Dibre ha- Ramban.* Jerusalem, 1971.
——— "Piyyut le-R. Isaac ibn Ghayyat," *Tarbiẓ,* XLIII (1973–1974), 159–165.
——— "Sifre Halakot shel ha-Rabad," *Tarbiẓ,* XXXVI (1967), 158–179.
Agus, I. A., *The Heroic Age of Franco-German Jewry.* New York, 1969.
——— "The Oral Traditions of Pre-Crusade Ashkenazic Jewry," *Studies and Essays in Honor of Abraham A. Neuman,* ed. M. Ben-Horin et al. Leiden, 1962, 1–16.
——— *Urban Civilization in Pre-Crusade Europe.* 2 v. Lieden, 1968.
Albeck, H., *Mabo' la-Talmudim.* Tel Aviv, 1969.
Altmann, A., "The Religion of the Thinkers. Free Will and Predestination in Maimonides," *Religion in a Religious Age,* ed. S. D. Goitein. Cambridge, 1974, 25–53.
——— *Studies in Religious Philosophy and Mysticism.* New York, 1969.
Appel, G., *A Philosophy of Mizvot.* New York, 1975.
Ashtour, A., *Ḳoroṭ ha-Yehudim bi-Sefarad ha-Muslemit.* 2 v. Jerusalem, 1966.

Assaf, S., *Toratan shel Geonim ve-Rishonim.* Jerusalem, 1933.

Atlas, S., *Netibim ba-Mishpaṭ ha-ᶜIbri.* New York, 1978.

Bachrach, B. S., "A Reassessment of Visigothic Jewish Policy, 589–711," *American Historical Review,* LXXVIII (1973), 11–34.

Barnett, R. D., ed., *The Sephardi Heritage,* I. New York, 1971.

Baron, S. W., *Ancient and Medieval Jewish History: Essays.* New Brunswick, N.J., 1972.

——— "Azariah de' Rossi's Historical Method," in S. W. Baron, *History and Jewish Historians.* Philadelphia, 1964.

Barzilay, I., *Between Reason and Faith.* The Hague, 1967.

Bazak, J., *Le-Maᶜalah min ha-Ḥushim.* Tel Aviv, 1968.

Benayahu, M., "R. Ḥiyya Rofe we-Sifro Maᶜaseh Ḥiyya," 'Areset, II (1960), 109–129.

Benedikt, B., "Caractères originaux de la science rabbinique en Languedoc," *Juifs et Judaisme de Languedoc,* ed. M. Vicarol and B. Blumenkranz. Toulouse, 1977, 159–173.

——— "ᶜal Hagahah 'aḥat shel Ri ha-Levi ibn Migas be-Hilkot ha-Rif," *Kiryath Sefer,* XXXI (1955), 264–265.

——— " ᶜal Megamato shel R. Zerahyah ha-Levi be-Sefer ha-Ma'or," *Sefer Zikkaron le-Benjamin DeVries.* Jerusalem, 1969, 160–167.

——— in *Torah shebeᶜal Peh,* Jerusalem, IV (1962)–XIX (1977). (An important series of annual essays on aspects of the *Mishneh Torah* and problems in the history of halakic interpretation.)

Ben-Sasson, H. H., *Hagut ve-Hanhagah.* Jerusalem, 1959.

——— "Yiḥud ᶜam Yisrael," *Peraḳim,* II (1971), 145–218.

Ben-Shlomoh, J., *Torat ha-Elohut shel R. Mosheh Kordovero.* Jerusalem, 1965.

Berger, D., "The Attitude of St. Bernard of Clairvaux Toward the Jews," *PAAJR,* XL (1972), 89–108.

Berlin, C., *Index to Festchriften in Jewish Studies.* New York, 1971.

Berman, L., "Greek into Hebrew: Samuel ben Judah of Marseilles, Fourteenth Century Philosopher and Translator," *Jewish Medieval and Renaissance Studies,* ed. A. Altmann. Cambridge, 1967, 289–319.

Birnbaum, P., *Karaite Studies.* New York, 1971.

Blumenkranz, B., *Auteurs juifs en France médiévale.* Toulouse, 1975.

——— "Contributions à la nouvelle Gallia Judaica," *Archives Juives,* IV (1967–1968), 27–29, 35–37.

——— "Deux Compilations Canoniques de Florus de Lyon et l'Action Antijuive d'Agobard," *Revue Historique de Droit Francais,* XXXIII (1955), 227–254, 560–582.

——— *Histoire des Juifs en France.* Toulouse, 1972.

——— *Juifs et Chrétiens dans le Monde Occidental.* Paris, 1960.

——— *Les Auteurs Chrétiens Latins du moyen âge sur les Juifs et le Judaisme.* Paris, 1963.

——— "Les Juifs à Blois au moyen âge," *Melanges E. R. Labande: Etudes de Civilization Médiévale.* Poitiers, 1974.

——— "Pour une nouvelle Gallia Judaica," *L'Arche,* CVI (1965), 42–47.

Blumenkranz, B. and M. Levy, *Bibliographie de Juifs en France.* 2d ed. Paris, 1974.

Breuer, M., "Mine'u Benekem min ha-Higgayon," *Miktam le-David: Sefer Zikkaron le-Nishmat Harav D. Ochs.* Ramat Gan, 1978, 242–261.

Chazan, R., "A Jewish Plaint to St. Louis," *HUCA,* XLV (1974), 287–305.

——— "Anti-Usury Efforts in Thirteenth-Century Narbonne and the Jewish Response," *PAAJR,* XLI–XLII (1973–1974), 45–67.

——— "Confrontation in the Synagogue of Narbonne: A Christian Sermon and a Jewish Reply," *HTR,* LXVII (1974), 437–457.

———, ed., *Medieval Jewish Life.* New York, 1976.

——— *Medieval Jewry in Northern France.* Baltimore, 1973.

Chomsky, W., "Hebrew During the Middle Ages," *JQR Anniversary Volume* (1967), 121–136.

Cohen, G. D., "The Story of the Four Captives," *PAAJR,* XXIX (1960–1961), 55–131.

Cohen, Jeremy, "The Nasi of Narbonne: A Problem in Medieval Historiography," *Association for Jewish Studies Review,* II (1977), 45–76.

Dan, J., "Beginnings of Jewish Mysticism in Europe," *The Dark Ages: Jews in Christian Europe,* ed. C. Roth. New Brunswick, 1966, 282–290.

——— "Haḳdamat ha-Rabad le-Sefer Baᶜale ha-Nefesh," *Sinai,* LXXVII (1975), 143–145.

——— *Sifrut ha-Muscar veha-Derush.* Jerusalem, 1975.

——— *Torat ha-sod shel Ḥaside Ashkenaz.* Jerusalem, 1968.

Davidson, H. A., "The Study of Philosophy as a Religious Obligation," *Religion in a Religious Age,* ed. S. D. Goitein. Cambridge, 1974, 53–69.

Denari, Y., "'Abid 'Inesh Dina' Le-Nafsheh," *Dine Israel,* IV (1973), 91–107.

——— "Ha-Minhag veha-Halakah," *Sefer Zikkaron B. de Vries.* Jerusalem, 1969, 168–198.

Dienstag, J. I., "Mishneh Torah leha-Rambam, bibliography," *Studies in Jewish Bibliography, History and Literature in Honor of I. E. Kiev,* ed. C. Berlin. New York, 1971, 21–108.

——— "Terumatam shel Ḥakme Liṭa le-Sifrut ha-Yad ha Ḥazaḳah," *Ḥesed le-Abraham: Sefer Yobel le-Abraham Golomb.* Los Angeles, 1970, 445–496.

Dishon, I., "'Or Ḥadash ᶜal Judah ibn Shabbetai," *Bitzaron,* XXXIII (1972), 56–65.

——— "Sefer ha-Historyiah he-'Abud shel Judah ibn Shabbetai," *Zion,* XXXVI (1971), 191–199.

Elbaum, J., "Shalosh Derashot Ashkenaziyot Ḳedumot," *KS*, XLVIII (1973), 340–347.

Elbogen, I., *Ha-Tefillah be-Yisrael be Hitpathutah ha-Historit,* trans. Y. Amir et al. Tel Aviv, 1972.

Elon, M., *Ha-Mishpaṭ Ha-^{c}Ibri.* 3 v. Jerusalem, 1973.

———, ed., *The Principles of Jewish Law.* Jerusalem, 1975.

Encyclopedia Judaica. 16 v. Jerusalem and New York, 1972.

Eppenstein, S., "Meḥḳarim ^{c}al R. Joseph Kimḥi," *^{c}Iyyun ve-Ḥeḳer.* Jerusalem, 1978, 134–223.

Feldman, Leon, "'Oẓar ha-Kabod ha-Shalem," *Salo Baron Jubilee Volume.* Jerusalem, 1975. Hebrew section, 297–317.

Fleisher, E., "'Ein Mishpat'—Hibbur le-Yiẓḥak ba^{c}al Ezrat Nashim," *KS,* XLVIII (1973), 329–340.

——— "^{c}Iyyunim be-Shirato shel R. Hai Gaon," *Sefer Habermann,* ed. Z. Malachi. Jerusalem, 1977, 239–274.

——— *Shirat ha-Kodesh ha-^{c}Ibrit.* Jerusalem, 1975.

——— "Unpublished Poems by Rav Hai Gaon," *JQR,* LXV (1974), 1–17.

Francus, I., "Hashmatot ve-Ṭa^{c}uyot Ḳedumot be-Hilkot ha-Rif," *Tarbiẓ,* XLVII (1978), 30–49.

——— "^{c}Iyyunim be-Hilkot ha-Rif," *Sinai,* LXXXIII (1978), 97–107.

Frankel, J., *Darko shel Rashi be-Ferusho le-Talmud Babli.* Jerusalem, 1975.

Freehof, S. B., ed., *A Treasury of Responsa.* Philadephia, 1963.

Friedman, S., "Mitosafot ha-Rashbam la-Rif," *Kobez ^{c}al Yad,* VIII (1976).

Golb, N., "New Light on the Persecution of French Jews at the Time of the First Crusade," *PAAJR,* XXXIV (1966), 1–64.

——— *Toledot he-Yehudim be-^{c}Ir Rouen.* Tel Aviv, 1976.

Goldin, J., "Rabad of Posquières" (Review), *Judaism,* XII (1963), 118–123.

Goldreich, A., "Review of Y. Weinstock," *KS,* XLII (1972), 199–209.

Gottlieb, E., *Meḥḳarim be-Sifrut ha-Kabbalah,* ed. J. Hacker. Tel Aviv, 1976.

Grabois, A., "Demuto ha-'Aggadit shel Karl ha-Gadol ba-Meḳorot ha-^{c}Ibriyim shel Yeme ha-Benayim," *Tarbiẓ,* XXXVI (1967), 22–58.

——— "Ha-Ḥevrah ha Yehudit be-Ẓorfat ha-Deromit ba-Me'ot XI–XII ^{c}al pi ha-Kronikah shel 'Almoni mi-Narbonne," *Proceedings of the Sixth World Congress of Jewish Studies,* II (1976), 75–85.

——— "La Dynastie des 'Rois Juifs' de Narbonne," *Narbonne: Archéologie et Histoire,* II. Montpellier, 1973, 49–54.

——— "The 'Habraica Veritas' and Jewish-Christian Intellectual Relations in the Twelfth Century," *Speculum,* L (1975), 613–634.

——— "Une Principante Juive dans la France du Midi a l'Epoque Carolingienne?," *Annales du Midi,* LXXXV (1973), 191–202.

——— "Yehude Saint-Denis U-Meḳomam be-Toledot ha-Minzar," *Zion,* XXX (1965), 115–119.

Grayzel, S., "The Talmud and the Medieval Papacy," *Essays in Honor of Solomon B. Freehof,* ed. W. Jacob. Pittsburgh, 1964.

Greive, H., *Studien zum jüdischen Neuplatonismus: Die Religionsphilosophie des Abraham ibn Ezra.* Berlin, 1973.

Gross, H., *Gallia Judaica.* Reprinted with bibliography supplement by S. Schwartzfuchs, Amsterdam, 1969.

Grossman, A., "Hagiratah shel Mishpaḥat Kalonymos me-Italiyah le-Germaniyah," *Zion,* XL (1975), 154–85.

——— "R. Judah ha-Kohen ve-Sifro 'Sefer ha-Dinim'," *ᶜAle Sefer,* I (1975), 7–34.

Habermann, A. M., *ᶜIyyunim be-Shirah ube-Piyyut.* Jerusalem, 1970.

Haidu, P., "Repetition: Modern Reflections on Medieval Aesthetics," *Modern Language Notes,* XCII (1977), 875–881.

Hailperin, H., *Rashi and the Christian Scholars.* Pittsburgh, 1963.

Ha-Kohen, M., "Beshule Perush R. Jonathan," *Sinai,* XL (1957), 408–413.

Halkin, A. S., "The Medieval Jewish Attitude toward Hebrew," *Biblical and Other Studies,* ed. A. Altmann. Cambridge, 1963, 232–248.

——— "Why Was Levi ben Hayyim Hounded," *PAAJR,* XXXIV (1966), 65–77.

Havazelet, M., *Ha-Rambam veha-Geonim.* Jerusalem, 1967.

Havlin, Z., "Le-Taledot ha-Defusim ha-Rishonim." Introduction to *Mishneh Torah.* Constantinople, 1509. Jerusalem 1973.

Herschler, M., "Hassagot ha-Rabad ᶜal ha-Rif," *Sinai,* LXV (1969), 1–2.

Herskovics, M., "Yaḥas Ḥazal le-Targum Onḳelos . . . ," *Joshua Finkel Festschift,* ed. S. Hoenig. New York, 1974. Hebrew section, 169–176 (on Tefillin I, 19).

Heschel, A., *Torah min ha-Shamayim.* I. London, 1962.

Hilman, D. Z., "Be'ur 'nod ha-naḥ' shebe-hassagot ha-Rabad," *Sefer ha-Zikkaron le R. Y. Weinberg.* Jerusalem, 1970, 105–119.

Hirschberg, H. Z., "ᶜal R. Zechariah Agmati," *Tarbiẓ,* XLII (1973), 379–389.

Hurvitz, E., "Sĕridim Nosafim mi-Sefer Mishneh Torah . . . ," *ha-Darom,* XXXVIII (1974), 4–44.

Hyams, P., "The Jewish Minority in Medieval England 1066–1290," *Journal of Jewish Studies,* XXV (1974), 270–293.

Idel, M., "Keta ᶜIyyuni le-R. Asher b. Meshullam mi-Lunel," *KS,* L (1975), 149–153.

Iserer, H., "Heᶜarot le-Baᶜale ha-Nefesh," *Sinai,* LXII (1968), 41–50.

Kafiḥ, J., "Megillat Setarim le Ri ibn Migas," *Sinai,* LXXII (1973), 34–38.

Kahana, I., *Meḥḳarim be-Sifrut ha-Teshubot.* Jerusalem, 1973.

Kasher, M., "She'elat Kav ha-Taᶜariḥ," *Noam,* XIV (1971).

——— *Haggadah Shelemah*. Jerusalem, 1961.

Kasher, M. and J. Mandelbaum, *Sarei ha-Elef*. New York, 1959.

Katz, J., *Exclusiveness and Tolerance* (Scripta Judaica, III). Oxford, 1961.

——— "Ma^carib bizemano," *Zion*, XXXV (1970), 35–60.

Kedar, B., Toponymic Surnames as Evidence of Origin: Some Medieval Views," *Viator*, IV (1973), 123–129.

Kirschenbaum, A., "Ha-berit ᶜim bene Noah . . . ," *Dine Israel*, VI (1975), 31–49.

Kook, S. H., *ᶜIyyunim u-Meḥkarim*. 2 v. Jerusalem, 1963.

Kupfer, E., "'Iggeret Rabi 'ab bet din Narbonne," *Tarbiẓ*, XXXIX (1970), 356–359.

——— "Hezyonotav shel R. Asher Lemlein," *Kobez ᶜal Yad*, VIII (1976), 387–423.

——— "Lidemutah ha-Tarbutit shel Yahadut Ashkenaz ba-Me'ot ha-'Arbaᶜ ᶜEsreh-Ḥamesh ᶜEsreh," *Tarbiẓ*, XLII (1973), 113–147.

——— "Teshubot bilti Yeduᶜot shel ha-Rambam," *Tarbiẓ*, XXXIX (1970), 170–183.

Lazaroff, A., "Bahya's Asceticism Against its Rabbinic and Islamic Background," *Journal of Jewish Studies*, XXI (1970), 11–38.

Lehmann, O. H., "The Theology of the Mystical Book Bahir and its Sources," *Studia Patristica*, I, ed. K. Aland and F. L. Cross. Berlin, 1957, 477–483.

Levinger, J., *Darke ha-Maḥashabah ha-Hilkatit shel ha-Rambam*. Tel Aviv, 1965.

Liebeschutz, H., "Relations between Jews and Christians in the Middle Ages," *Journal of Jewish Studies*, XVI (1965), 35–46.

Lipman, U. D., *The Jews of Medieval Norwich*. Appendix with Hebrew poems of Meir of Norwich, ed. A. M. Habermann. London, 1967.

Loewinger, D. S., "Rabbi Shem-Toḅ ben Abraham ben Ga'on," *Sefunot*, VII (1963), 7–39.

Mandelbaum, J., "Kuntres Hashlamah le-Sefer Sarei ha-'Elef," *Sefer Adam-Noah Braun*. Jerusalem, 1969, 213–296.

Marcus, I., "The Recensions and Structure of Sefer Hasidim," *PAAJR*, XLV (1978), 131–155.

Marx, A., *Bibliographical Studies and Notes*, ed. M. Schmelzer. New York, 1977.

Merlan, P., "Zur Zahlenlehre im Platonismus und im Sefer Yezira," *Journal of the History of Philosophy*, III (1965), 167–182.

Mesch, B., *Studies in Joseph ibn Caspi*. Leiden, 1975.

Nahon, G., "Contributions à l'histoire des Juifs en France sous Philippe le Bel," *REJ*, CXXI (1962), 59–80.

——— "Le Crédit et les Juifs dans la France du XIIIᵉ siècle," *Annales*, XXIV (1969), 1121–1148.

——— "Les ordonnances de Saint Louis sur les Juifs," *Les nouveaux cahiers*, VI (1970), 18–35.

——— "Une géographie des Juifs dans la France de Louis IX 1126–1270," *Proceedings, Fifth World Congress of Jewish Studies,* II (Jerusalem, 1972).

O'Brien, J., "Jews and Cathari in Medieval France," *Comparative Studies in Society and History,* X (1968), 215–220.

Packard, S., *Twelfth-Century Europe: An Interpretive Essay.* Amherst, 1973.

Pagis, D., *Hiddush u-Massoret be-Shirat ha-Ḥol.* Jerusalem, 1976.

——— "Kobez Piyyutim mi-Provence," *Sefer Hayim Schirmann,* ed. S. Abramson. Jerusalem, 1970, 257–284.

——— *Shirat ha-Ḥol we-Torat ha-Shir.* Jerusalem, 1970.

Pearl, C., *The Medieval Jewish Mind.* London, 1971.

Rabinovitz, H. R., *Deyuḳna'ot shel Darshanim.* Jerusalem, 1967.

——— "R. Judah b. Barzilai," *Ha-Darom,* XXII (1971), 170–176.

Rackover, N., "Genebat Debarim," *Dine Israel,* VI (1975), 93–121.

——— *Ha-Shelihut veha-Harsha'ah Bamishpaṭ Ha-ᶜIbri.* Jerusalem, 1972.

——— *'Oẓar ha-Mishpaṭ (Mafteah Bibliografi),* Jerusalem, 1975.

Rawidowicz, S., *ᶜIyyunim be-Maḥshevet Yisrael.* Jerusalem, 1969.

——— *Studies in Jewish Thought.* Philadelphia, 1974.

Razhaby, J., "Le-Ḥeker Meḳorotav ha-ᶜArbiᶜim shel 'Ben ha-Melek veha-Nazir," *Sefer Habermann,* ed. Z. Malachi. Jerusalem, 1977, 279–318.

Refael, I., "Hilkot Sheḥitah le-R. Abraham ha-Yarḥi," *Sefer Yobel Halbeck.* Jerusalem, 1963, 443–465.

Rosenthal, E., "Medieval Jewish Exegesis," *Journal of Semitic Studies,* IX (1964), 265–281.

——— *Studa Semitica.* I. Cambridge, 1971.

Rosenthal, J., *Meḥḳarium u-Meḳorot,* 2 v. Jerusalem, 1966.

Roth, C., ed., *The Dark Ages: Jews in Christian Europe 711–1096:* World History of the Jewish People. XI. New Brunswick, 1966.

Rubin, A., "The Concept of Repentance Among the Hassidey Ashkenaz," *Journal of Jewish Studies,* XVI (1965), 161–176.

Scheiber, A., " 'Iggareto shel Meshullam b. Kalonymos," *Sefer Raphael Mahler.* Merhavya, 1974, 19–24.

Schepansky, I., *Rabbenu Ephraim: Talmid Ḥaber shel ha-Rif.* Jerusalem, 1976.

Schlanger, J., *La philosophie de Salomon ibn Gabirol.* Leiden, 1968.

Scholem, G., *Die Erforschung der Kabbala von Reuchlin bis zur Gegenwart.* Pforzheim, 1969.

——— *Jewish Mysticism in the Middle Ages.* New York, 1966.

——— "Juedische Mystik in Westeuropa in 12. und 13. Jahrhundert," *Miscellanea Mediaevalia,* IV (Berlin, 1966), 37–54.

——— *Kabbalah.* New York, 1974.

——— *Les Origines de la Kabbale.* Paris, 1966.

——— *On the Kabbalah and its Symbolism.* New York, 1965.

Scholem, G., *The Messianic Idea in Judaism.* New York, 1971.

Schwartzfuchs, S., "De la condition des Juifs en France aux XIIe et XIIIe siècles," *REJ*, CXXV (1966), 226–229.

——— *Les Juifs de France.* Paris, 1975.

——— "The Expulsion of the Jews from France (1306)," *JQR Seventy-Fifth Anniversary Volume,* ed. A. Neuman. Philadelphia, 1967, 482–490.

Shahar, S., "Ha-Katarizm ve-Reshit ha-Kabbalah be-Languedoc," *Tarbiẓ,* XL (1971), 483–507.

Shatzmiller, J., "An Aspect of Social Life of Provencal Jews in the Middle Ages," *Association for Jewish Studies Review,* II (1977), 227–255.

——— "Haẓa^{c}ot ve-Tosafot le-Gallia Judaica," *KS,* XLV (1970), 607–610.

——— "Iggarto shel R. Asher b. R. Gershom," *Meḥḳarim le-Zeker Zvi Avneri.* Haifa, 1970, 129–140.

——— "Litemunat Ha-Maḥloḳet ha-Rishonah ^{c}al Kitbe ha-Rambam," *Zion,* XXXIV (1969), 126–144.

——— *Recherches sur la Communauté Juive de Manosque.* Paris, 1973.

Shefer, S., *Ha-Rif u-Mishnato.* Jerusalem, 1967.

Shifman, P., "Ha-Safeḳ ba-Halakah ubamishpaṭ," *Shenaton ha-Mishpaṭ ha ^{c}Ibri,* I (1974), 328–352.

Shiloh, S., *Dina de-Malhuta Dina.* Jerusalem, 1974.

——— "Yaḥaso shel R. Joseph ibn Megas la-Geonim," *Sinai,* LXVI (1970), 263–268.

Shirman, H., "^{c}Iyyunim be-Ḳobeẓ ha-Shirim shel Abraham ha-Bedersi," *Sefer Yobel le-Y. Baer,* ed. S. Ettinger. Jerusalem, 1961, 154–173.

Shoḥet, A., "Berurim be-Farashat ha-Pulemos ha-Rishon," *Zion,* XXXVI (1971), 26–60.

Shulvass, M., "Crusades, Martyrdom, and the Marranos of Ashkenaz," in *Between the Rhine and the Bosporus.* Chicago, 1964.

Silver, D. J., *Maimonidean Criticism and the Maimonidean Controversy, 1180–1240.* Leiden, 1965.

——— "Who Denounced the Moreh," *JQR Seventy-Fifth Anniversary Volume,* ed. A. Neuman. Philadelphia, 1967, 498–514.

Simonsohn, S., *Toledot ha-Yehudim be-Dukkasut Mantua.* 2 v. Jerusalem, 1962–1964.

Sirat, C., *Hagut Pilosofit bime ha-Benayim.* Jerusalem, 1975.

——— *Les théories des visions sur-naturelles dans la pensée juive du moyen-âge.* Leiden, 1969.

Solomon, N., "Definition and Classification in the Works of the Lithuanian Halakhists," *Dine Israel,* VI (1975), lxxiii–cv.

Soloveitchik, H., "A Note on the Penetration of Roman Law in Provence," *Tijdschrift voor Rechtsgeschiednis,* XL (1972), 227–229.

——— "^{c}Areb be-Ribit," *Zion,* XXXVII (1972), 1–21.

——— "Can Halakic Texts Talk History," *Association for Jewish Studies Review,* III (1978), 152–197.

——— "Pawnbroking. A Study in Ribbit and of the Halakah in Exile," *PAAJR,* XXXVIII–XXXIX (1970–1971), 203–268.

——— "Sheṭar be-Sefer ha-ᶜIṭṭur," *Tarbiẓ,* XLI (1972), 313–324.

——— "Three Themes in the Sefer Hasidim," *Association for Jewish Studies Review,* I (1976), 311–357.

Spiegel, Y., "Gilgule ha-Hagahot shebidefuse Mishneh Torah," *Tagim,* V–VI (1975), 25–39.

——— "Ma-shehu ᶜal Mishneh Torah la-Rambam," *KS,* XLVIII (1972), 493–501.

——— "Sefer Maggid Mishneh," *KS,* XLVI (1971), 554–580.

Stein, S., *Jewish-Christian Disputations in Thirteenth-Century Narbonne.* London, 1969.

Strayer, J., *The Albigensian Crusades.* New York, 1971.

Ta-Shema, I., "'El Melek Ne'eman," *Tarbiẓ,* XXXIX (1970), 184–194.

——— "Gedarav shel Sefer ha-Ma'or ᶜal Hilkot ha-Rif," *Shenaton ha-Mishpaṭ ha-ᶜIbri,* V (1978), 361–406.

——— *R. Zerahyah ha-Levi* (unpublished dissertation). Ramat Gan, 1975.

——— "Shipuṭ ᶜIbri," *Shenaton ha-Mishpaṭ ha-ᶜIbri.* I. Jerusalem, 1974. 353–372.

——— "Sifre ha-Ribot ben ha-Rabad leven Zerahiah ha-Levi mi-Lunel," *KS,* LII (1977–1978), 557–577.

——— "Yeẓirato ha—Sifrutit shel Rabbenu Yosef ibn Megas," *KS,* XLVI (1970), 136–146; XLVI (1971), 541–553; XLVII (1972), 318–322.

——— "Zemanim u-Meḳomot be-Hayyav shel R. Zerahiah," *Sefer Bar-Ilan,* XII (1974), 118–136.

Ta-Shema, I. and H. Ben-Shammai, "Shemoneh Teshubot Hadashot le-Rabbenu Yosef ibn Megas," *Kobez ᶜal Yad,* VIII (1976), 167–185.

Talmage, F., "A Hebrew Polemical Treatise: Anti-Cather and Anti-Orthodox," *HTR,* LX (1967), 323–348.

——— *David Kimhi.* Cambridge, 1974.

——— "Ha-Pulemos ha-'Anṭi Noẓri," *Michael,* IV (1976), 61–71.

Tishbi, I. and J. Dan, eds., *Mibhar Sifrut ha-Musar.* I. Jerusalem, 1970.

Touati, C., *La pensée théologique et philosophique de Gersonide.* Paris, 1973.

——— "Rabad of Posquieres" (Review), *REJ,* CXXIII (1964), 217–220.

Twersky, I., "ᶜAl Hassagot ha-Rabad le-Mishneh Torah," *Harry Wolfson Jubilee Volume.* Jerusalem, 1965, 169–186.

——— "Ḥamishah Sefarim le-Rab Nissim Gaon," *Tarbiẓ,* XXXVII (1968), 318–327.

——— "Joseph ibn Kaspi," *Juifs et judaisme de Languedoc,* ed. B. Blumenkranz. Toulouse, 1977, 185–204.

Twersky, I., "R. Joseph Ashkenazi ve-Sefer Mishneh Torah le-Rambam," *Salo Baron Jubilee Volume,* ed. S. Lieberman. Jerusalem, 1974, 183–194.

——— "Religion and Law," *Religion in a Religious Age,* ed. S. D. Goitein. Cambridge, 1974, 69–82.

——— "Sefer Mishneh Torah: Megamato u-Matarato," *Proceedings of the Israel Academy of Science and Humanities,* V (1972), 1–22.

——— "Some Non-Halakic Aspects of the Mishneh Torah," *Jewish Medieval and Renaissance Studies,* ed. A. Altmann. Cambridge, 1967, 95–118.

——— "The Beginnings of Mishneh Torah Criticism," *Biblical and Other Studies,* ed. A. Altmann. Cambridge, 1963, 161–182.

——— "The Shulḥan ᶜAruk: Enduring Code of Jewish Law," *Judaism,* XVI (1967), 141–159.

——— "Yedayah ha-Penini u-Ferusho la-'Aggadah," *Alexander Altmann Jubilee Volume,* ed. R. Loewe and S. Stein. Alabama, 1979, 73–93.

Urbach, E., "Miteshubotehem shel Ḥakme Provence," *Mazkeret,* ed. I. Zevin. Jerusalem, 1962, 3–30.

Vajda, G., "Heᶜarot le-Ḥibbur ha-Teshubah," *ᶜIyyun,* XX (1970), 242–244.

——— "La philosophie juive en Espagne," *The Sephardi Heritage.* I, ed. R. D. Barnett. London, 1971, 81–111.

——— "Le 'kalam' dans la pensée religieuse juive du Moyen Âge," *Revue de l'Histoire des Religions,* CLXXXIII (1973), 143–160.

——— "Le Néoplatonisme dans la pensée juive du Moyen Âge," *Atti della Accademia Nazionale dei Lincei:* Rendiconti, Classe di Screnze morale, storiche, e filologiche, XXVI (1971), 309–324.

——— "Les études de philosophie juive du Moyen Âge depuis la synthèse de Julius Guttman," *HUCA,* XLIII (1972), 125–147; XLV (1974), 205–242.

——— *Recherches sur la Philosophie et la Kabbale dans la Pensée Juive du Moyen Âge.* Paris, 1962.

Wachholder, B., "Cases of Proselytizing," *JQR,* LI (1961), 288–315.

——— "Rabad of Posquieres" (Review), *JQR,* LVI (1965), 173–180.

——— "Tosafot," *Sinai,* LV (1965), 323–325.

Wakefield, W., *Heresy, Crusade and Inquisition in Southern France, 1100–1250.* Berkeley, 1974.

Warhaftig, Z., *Ha-Hazaḳah ba-Mishpaṭ ha-ᶜIbri.* Jerusalem, 1964.

Waxman, M., "Ha-Maḥashabah ha-Pilosofit shel Abraham bar Hiyya," *Harry Wolfson Jubilee Volume.* Jerusalem, 1965, 143–168.

Weiner, A., *The Prophet Elijah in the Development of Judaism.* London, 1978.

Weinstock, I., *Be-Maᶜagele ha-Nigleh veha-Nistar.* Jerusalem, 1969.

Werblowsky, R. J. Z., "Faith, Hope and Trust—A Study in the Concept of Bittaḥon," *Annual of Jewish Studies,* I (1964), 95–139.

——— *Joseph Karo: Lawyer and Mystic.* Oxford, 1962.

Wijnhoven, J. H., "The Mysticism of Solomon ibn Gabirol," *Journal of Religion,* XLV (1965), 137–152.

Wolfson, H. A., *The Philosophy of the Kalam.* Cambridge, 1976.

——— *Studies in the History and Philosophy of Religion,* ed. I. Twersky and G. Williams. I, Cambridge, 1973; II, Cambridge, 1976.

Wolff, P., *Documents de l'histoire du Languedoc.* Toulouse, 1969.

Yellin, D. and I. Abrahams, *Maimonides: His Life and Works.* Philadelphia, 1903. Reissued with bibliographical supplement by J. Dienstag, New York, 1972.

Yerushalmi, Y., "The Inquisition and the Jews of France in the Time of Bernard Gui," *Harvard Theological Review,* LXIII (1970), 317–375.

Yisraeli, S., "Be'ur 'sod ha-Shem liyere'aiv' shebidibre ha-Rabad," *Shebilim,* XX (1968), 65–68.

Zimmer, E., "Seder ha-Posekim le R. Azriel Trabot," *Sinai,* LXXVI (1975), 237–252.

Zuckerman, A. J., *A Jewish Princedom in Feudal France.* New York, 1972.

Zussman, J., "Shene Kuntresim e-Halakah me'et R. Moshe Botreil," *Kobez ᶜal Yad,* VI (1966), 271–342.

ADDENDA

1. Page 4, note 14:

See G. Cohen, ed., Abraham ibn Daud, *Sefer ha-Qabbalah* (Philadelphia, 1967), p. xvi and note the general discussion of B. Kedar, "Toponymic Surnames as Evidence of Origin: Some Medieval Views," *Viator,* IV (1973), 123–129. Concerning the birthplace of R. Abraham b. Nathan ha-Yarḥi, cf. I. Refael, introduction to his new edition of *Sefer ha-Manhig* (Jerusalem, 1978), 11.

2. Page 4, note 17:

The text of Trabotto was re-edited and the question of its authorship examined by E. Zimmer, "Seder ha-Poseḳim le-R. Azriel Trabot," *Sinai,* LXXVI (1975), 237–252.

3. Page 6, note 23:

Another case concerns the father of R. Isaiah of Trani, about whom see A. Y. Wertheimer, ed., *Perush Nebi'im,* I (Jerusalem, 1959), 17. See also E. M. Lifshitz, *Rashi,* p. 172. I. Ta-Shema, "Zemanim u-Meḳomot," *Bar Ilan Annual,* XII (1974), 119, n. 4, speculates that Razah insinuates in one place that his father was a scholar of greater stature than Rabad's father.

4. Page 6, note 24:

There are, of course, many references to him in the commentary itself, e.g., *ᶜEduyot* 1:3; *Shebuᶜot* 4:2; *Kelim* 3:4; I reviewed all this in Chapter I of my book *Introduction to the Mishneh Torah of Maimonides* (New Haven, 1980).

5. Page 10:

Ta-Shema's articles are important for questions of chronology, e.g., Rabi's death (1159, not 1179); see especially his "Zemanim u-Meḳomot," and "Sifre ha-Ribot."

6. Page 13, note 73:

Also Yedayah Bedersi in his *'Iggeret ha-Hitnazlut.*

7. Page 15, note 81:

See R. Simeon b. Ẓemaḥ Duran, *Tashbeẓ,* III, 238.

8. Page 19, note 1:

Also, C. Haskins, *The Renaissance of the Twelfth Century* (Cambridge, 1927), 209.

9. Page 19ff.:

See A. Grabois, "Ha-Ḥevrah ha-Yehudit be-Ẓarfat ha-Deromit . . . ," *Proceedings of the Sixth World Congress of Jewish Studies,* II (1976), 75–85.

10. Page 20:

On the sociopolitical status, see my "Aspects of the Social and Cultural History of Provencal Jewry," *Journal of World History,* XI (1968), 188–190. On the relations between the Cathari writings and the early Kabbalah, see S. Shahar, *Tarbiẓ,* XL (1971), 483–507. The thesis of A. J. Zuckerman, *A Jewish Princedom in Feudal France* (New York, 1972), has been reviewed (actually repudiated), carefully and critically, by A. Grabois, "Une Principauté Juive . . . ," *Annales du Midi,* LXXXV (1973), 191–202; *idem,* "La Dynastie des 'Rois Juifs' de Narbonne," *Narbonne: Archéologie et histoire* (Montpellier, 1973), 49–54; J. Cohen, "The Nasi of Narbonne: A Problem in Medieval Historiography," *Association for Jewish Studies Review,* II (1977), 45–76.

11. Page 21, note 8:

For the date of *Milḥemet Miẓwah,* see most recently H. Merhavyah, "Li-Zemano shel ha-Ḥibbur Milḥemet Miẓvah," *Tarbiẓ,* XLV (1976), 296–302.

12. Page 22, note 10:

See D. Berger, "The Attitude of St. Bernard of Clairvaux toward the Jews," *PAAJR,* XL (1972), 89–108.

13. Page 25:

Concerning this important Aggadah commentary, which may actually have been composed a generation before Y. Bedersi, see the appendix to my Hebrew article, "Yedayah ha-Penini u-Ferusho la-Aggadah," *Alexander Altmann Jubilee Volume,* ed. R. Loewe (Alabama, 1979), 42–43. Dr. Marc Saperstein has fully analyzed the textual problems in his doctoral dissertation, "The Works of R. Isaac b. Yedayah" (Harvard, 1977), which we hope to publish in the very near future.

On the *Ḥuḳḳe ha-Torah,* see the synopsis of my lecture at the Third World Congress of Jewish Studies (1961) in *Proceedings of the Third World Congress: Synopses of Lectures* (Jerusalem, 1964). I intend shortly to publish this paper, which analyzes the major motifs of the document and seeks to establish firmly the theory of its Provencal provenance. The text has meanwhile been reprinted by N. Golb, *Toledot ha-Yehudim be-ᶜir Rouen* (Tel Aviv, 1976), 181–184; see also 39–40.

14. Page 27:

For R. Asher b. Meshullam, see M. Idel, "Keṭa ᶜIyyuni le-R. Asher b. Meshullam," *KS,* L (1975), 149–153; B. Z. Benedikt, in *Torah Shebe ᶜal Peh* (Jerusalem, 1977), 225–226; E. Urbach, "Miteshubotehem shel Hakeme Provence," 22ff.

15. Page 30, note 8:

See *Sefer ha-Menuḥah* on *Sukkah,* V, II.

16. Page 35:

Note that the responsum concerning Barcelona is apparently by Rabi, not Rabad; see S. Abramson, *Ḥamishah Sefarim le R. Nissim Gaon* (Jerusalem, 1965), 15. Confusion between the two, particularly in attribution of responsa, is widespread; the most recent discussion I have seen is G. Libson, *Shenaton ha-Mishpaṭ ha-ᶜIbri,* V (1978), 87, n. 13.

17. Page 41:

It is, of course, difficult to pinpoint these subjective states—attitudes, motivations, temperamental predispositions—and rhetorical flourishes per se are not always a reliable guide. Style and substance must be correlated. Note the recent attempt of I. Ta-Shema to depict Razah as dogmatic and inflexible, unwilling to revise or modify his formulations, while Rabad regularly and creatively responded to Razah's criticism.

18. Page 52:

It is possible to extend this list of honorific epithets. See especially the salutation of the sages of Lunel (Urbach, "Miteshubotehem," page 6) where he is called שמש החכמה מוציא לאור תעלומה.

19. Page 53:

The relation of the hassagot of R. Moses ha-Kohen to those to Rabad needs to be studied carefully. See, e.g., Rashba, *Teshubot,* 111, where the hassagah of R. Moses on *Talmud Torah,* v, 2, is cited as a comment of Rabad. Not only are there many parallels between the hassagot of Ramak and Rabad, but sometimes (e.g., end of *Milah*) Ramak actually cites Rabad by name. See also *Ḳeri'at Shema,* I, 12, where *Kesef Mishneh* cites Rabad, *Tefillah,* X, 13 in name of R. Manoah.

20. Page 56, note 73:

See now the complete, annotated edition by M. Herschler in Rashba, *Torat ha-Bayit ha-Shalem* (Jerusalem, 1963).

21. Page 56ff.:

For Naḥmanides' attitude to Rabad, see also *Teshubot ha-Ramban,* ed. C. Chavel, 89 (page 134): ואע"פ שאימתו של הרב הגדול הזה ז"ל מוטלת עלינו ברעיוניו ויראתו על פניו, אין משא פנים בדין כי המשפט לאלהים. This is consistent with the attitudes reflected in *Hilkot Niddah* and *Sefer ha-Ẓekut.* One should also study carefully his strictures against Rabad's *Hilkot Lulab,* paying attention not only to substantive halakic critique, to the cognitive impact of formulations, but to the emotive and evaluative overtones as well.

22. Page 58, note 84:

On the interchangeability of the letters "pe" and "bet," see S. Abramson, *R. Nissim Gaon* (Jerusalem, 1965), 325; *idem,* *ᶜInyanot be-Sifrut ha-Geonim* (Jerusalem, 1974), 274, and note Y. Kutsher, *Tarbiẓ,* XVI (1945), 45, n. 17.

23. Page 59:

This analysis could be extended by examining the use made by Naḥmanides' disciples of Rabad's writings; see, e.g., for one of the most recent publications, *Ḥiddushe R. David Bonfid ᶜal Pesaḥim,* ed. A. Shoshana (Jerusalem, 1978), 15.

24. Page 62:

On the method of dialectic, see H. Soloveitchik, "Three Themes in the Sefer Ḥasidim," *Association for Jewish Studies Review,* I (1976), 339ff.; note also N. Solomon, "Definition and Classification in the Works of the Lithuanian Halakhists," *Dine Israel,* VI (1975), lxxxi. My characterization of Rabad's halakic oeuvre was obviously predicated on method rather than literary form; hence the queries and reservations of B. Wachholder in his review, *JQR,* LVI (1965), 180, are beside the point. Formal-structural affinities with R. Hananel are certainly eclipsed by conceptual-methodological ones with R. Tam. For possible influences of Roman Law, see H. Soloveitchik, *Ẓion,* XXXVII (1972), 13–14. Additional analyses of themes, interpretive cruxes, and pivotal problems will further concretize this methodological characterization and confirm Rabad as one of the great architects of halakic reasoning.

25. Page 63, note 104:

Also ha-Me'iri, *Bet ha-Beḥirah, Baba Ḳamma,* p. 119, ונראין דבריהם יותר מדברנו לענין סברא, אלא ששיטת הסוגיא מוכחת כדברינו; Ritba, *Sefer ha-Ẓikkaron* (Jerusalem, 1955), 44, 52; *Shiṭṭah Meḳubezet, Baba Mezi*ᶜ*a,* 13a; Rabad, *Nezirut* II, 5. See Samuel ibn Tibbon, *Yikkawu ha-Mayyim,* page 17, טוב לדחוק הלשון מלדחוק המציאות ; note Naḥmanides' words of caution about the need for conformity between interpretation and text in *Hiddushe ha-Ramban, Baba Batra,* page 121. Commentators occasionally warn against forced interpretations; e.g., *Shebu*ᶜ*ot* V, 18.

26. Page 64:

Wachholder's contention (*op. cit.,* page 175) that "evidently it is Twersky's thesis that there is such a species as a homo halacaeus . . ." is rebuffed by the description I sketch on this page; see also page 145, note 53, and page 199. I frequently underscore the need to recapture the individuality or uniqueness of leading figures and not to blur their intellectual-spiritual profiles by making them so many "faces in the crowd." I try to extricate the classical halakists—Rabad or Maimonides—from historical anonymity and to delineate their individual contours: methods and achievements, critical attitudes and traditional convictions. While I recognize the usefulness of abstract typologies and securely fastened phenomenological distinctions, I resist their being allowed to spread a blanket of bland homogeneity over the creative figures of the past. Indeed, the individuality of the halakists-critics of this period—Rabad, Razah, or R. Tam—is quite prominent.

27. Pages 66–67:

See the reference to Rabad by J. Selden, *De Jure Naturalis* (London, 1640), 156.

28. Page 69:

The complete *Issur Mashehu* is printed in M. Herschler, *Torat ha-Bayit ha-Shalem.*

29. Page 70, note 14:

See A. Grossman, "R. Judah ha-Kohen ve-Sifro 'Sefer ha-Dinim'," *ᶜAle Sefer,* I (1975), 27, ספר הדינים שכתב לפני רבנו גרשום.

30. Page 76, note 42:

Also, R. Baḥya b. Asher, *Shulḥan shel 'Arba* (Warsaw, 1879), 205.

31. Page 78, note 3:

The complete introduction of R. David b. Samuel of Estella (ha-Kokabi) to the *Sefer ha-Batim,* from which Neubauer excerpted (see above, page 18), has now been edited by J. Blau, *Sefer ha-Batim* (New York, 1978); it was also cited—as if he found it de novo—by M. Herschler, *'Issur Ma-Shehu,* in *Torat ha-Bayit,* page 100. Here is the main passage:

> ובעיר נרבונה וגבוליה ולוניל וגבוליה קמו חכמי חרשים ונבוני לחש שמשו בצרפת וספרד, וחדשו דברים רבים לברר דברי התלמוד ודיניו ולישב המאמרים הנראים כסותרים זה את זה. ומהם אשר בארו באור רחב קצת מסכתות מן התלמוד, כגון רבנו אברהם אב בית דין, והוא חבר ספר האשכול: ובימים ההם הופיע בגבול לוניל אור בהיר, הוא הרב הגדול רבנו אברהם בר דוד מפושקיירש, היה חכם גדול בקי בשני התלמודים ותוספתא וספרא וספרי, ופרש רוב התלמוד, וחבר גם כן פירוש תורת כהנים, וכתב ענינים רבים על דברי המפרשים והגאונים לבאר ולצרף דבריהם: ובעת ההיא זרח אור גדול בלוניל הוא הרב ר' זרחיה הלוי וחבר ספר המאור:
>
> ובימים ההם הגדיל י"י לעשות עמנו שלח אלינו מלאך הברית נר מערבי המאור הגדול הרב רבנו משה בן הרב הגדול רבנו מימון מספרד אשר אזן וחקר בכל דברי התורה ומבאריה ואליו נגלו סודותיה ורזיה והיה חכם גדול בטבעיות והאלהיות ובכל אשר יד שכל האדם משגת.

The following emphases of the author are noteworthy: a) the fact of cultural cross-fertilization and scholarly contact between Provence, France and Spain; b) characterization of the method of study, consisting of conceptual innovation as well as harmonization of conflicting texts; c) focus on the centrality of commentary, which suggests that the hassagot are presumably covered by this elastic rubric. Dr. Haym Soloveitchik contends, in a forthcoming article, that Rabad should be seen primarily as a commentator; ha-Me'iri's reference (see above, page 78) is obviously suggestive in this context and supportive of such an appraisal. It should be noted, however, that the references subsumed under this literary sobriquet include Rabad's codificatory and critical writings along with his commentatorial ones. His multifaceted oeuvre was really indivisible and was so pictured by successors. Rabad himself shared this perception; his later critical glosses on Razah—the *Katub Sham*—contain cross-references to *all* his earlier writings. For cross-references to his other works in the *Hassagot* on the *Mishneh Torah,* see above, page 127; also see above, page 180.

The characterization of Maimonides, calling attention to the combination of legal and metaphysical expertise, is also noteworthy; see below, the concluding addendum.

32. Page 83; see also pages 125–126:

Cf., S. Abramson, "Sifre Halakot shel ha-Rabad," *Tarbiz̦,* XXXVI (1967), 158ff.

33. Page 85:

Hilkot Lulab, which was printed originally in *Temim Deᶜim* (Venice, 1622) and omitted in subsequent editions, was reprinted in *Teshubot u-Pesaḳim,* ed. J. Kafiḥ, and *Teshubot ha-Ramban,* ed. C. Chavel.

34. Page 87:

Concerning the phrase *ḥibbur yafeh,* see S. Abramson, *ᶜInyanot be-Sifrut ha-Geonim,* 314–315. The development of the halakic monograph, as distinct from the partial code (as in the earlier works of R. Saadiah, R. Hai, or R. Samuel b. Hofni Gaon) is noteworthy.

35. Page 93:

For use of *Baᶜale ha-Nefesh,* see R. Simeon b. Ẓemaḥ Duran, *Perush Berakot,* ed. D. Z. Hilman (Bnei Brak, n.d.), 149. Also *Sefer ha-Me'orot, Berakot,* 35–36. For a possible antiphilosophical animus of this work, see J. Dan, "Haḳdamat ha-Rabad le-Sefer Baᶜale ha-Nefesh," *Sinai,* LXXVII (1975), 143–145.

36. Page 94, note 75:

See N. Rackover, "Genebat Debarim," *Dine Israel,* VI (1975), 113. The great role of Ramban's *Torat ha-'Adam,* already attested in the *Ṭur,* should be seen in this context.

37. Page 101, note 25:

See A. Scheiber, "ᶜIggarto shel Meshullam b. Kalonymos," *Sefer Raphael Mahler* (Merhavya, 1974), 19–24. E. Urbach, *Baᶜale ha-Tosafot,* 391, notes that R. Moses of Coucy (*Sefer Mizvot Gadol*) is the only French scholar who cites these texts.

38. Page 106:

Prof. J. Zussman informed me that he has collected a number of quotations on *Sheḳalim,* mostly from the commentary of R. Solomon Sirillo, which suggest that Rabad composed a commentary on this tractate. For the omission or erosion of Mishnah study in northern Europe—just when R. Samson of Sens was planning his commentary on *Zeraᶜim* and *Ṭoharot* —see I. Ta-Shema, *Bar Ilan Annual,* XIV–XV (1977), 110.

39. Page 108:

For use of the *ᶜEduyot* commentary by R. Abraham Azulai, see D. Zlotnick's edition *'Ahabah ba-Taᶜanugim: Perush ha-Mishnah,* in *Meḥḳarim u-Meḳorot,* ed. H. Dimitrovsky (New York, 1978).

40. Page 111:

For the derashot, see E. Hurvitz, *Ha-Darom,* XXXV (1972), 34ff.

41. Page 112, note 8:

Also *Sefer Abudarham,* 218, and see J. Gertner, *Sinai,* LXXXII (1978).

42. Page 113ff.:

See J. Kafiḥ, *Teshubot u-Pesaḳim* (Jerusalem, 1964), an important edition that must be used carefully. Other responsa have yet to be collected. Rabbi Kafiḥ himself published an additional responsum in *Sefer Margaliyot,* ed. I. Refael, page 73. One motif is rather salient: Rabad is an eager respondent, welcoming questions, answering promptly and enthusiastically, adapting the style and tonality to the situation. His writing exudes a sense of authority; he emphatically demands respect, attention, and acceptance of his views. Nevertheless, he does not submit curt, undocumented answers but unfolds the process of his reasoning so that the reader may benefit from this (e.g., Urbach, page 7). He concedes that by taking the reader into his confidence and retaining some dialogic qualities in writing, the learning process will be enhanced.

43. Page 126, note 36:

See the most recent bibliographic comments by Z. Havlin, introduction to the reprint of the 1509 Constantinople edition of the *Mishneh Torah* (Jerusalem, 1973).

44. Page 131, note 1:

See also ha-Me'iri, *Magen Abot,* 24.

45. Page 131, note 2:

I have elaborated and documented the refusal of rabbinic scholars to use the title Mishneh Torah in the following articles: "The Beginnings of Mishneh Torah Criticism," 173, n. 55; "R. Joseph Ashkenazi ve-Sefer Mishneh Torah," 185ff.

46. Page 133, note 8:

For other references to use of reason, see, e.g., *Teshubot u-Pesaḳim,* 1, and *passim.*

47. Pages 134–135, note 9:

Maimonides' correlation of intellectual decline and sociopolitical adversity is treated fully in my "The Mishneh Torah of Maimonides," *Proceedings,* Israel Academy of Sciences, V (1976), 265–296. The Hebrew version of the article appeared in *Proceedings,* 1972. It is a basic thought-pattern of his historiosophical apparatus and not merely a convenient argument or theoretical smokescreen.

48. Page 152:

See my Hebrew article "ᶜAl Hassagot ha-Rabad," 179ff.

49. Page 165; see also page 176:

The unsystematic, fragmentary character of his hassagot explains not only the brevity, and sometimes obscurity, of certain glosses but also the unevenness and incomplete "coverage" of the *Mishneh Torah* by Rabad's hassagot. See also "ᶜAl Hassagot ha-Rabad," 174, nn. 41, 42. Many additional examples are forthcoming; see, e.g., *Maᶜaseh ha-Ḳorbanot,* XVIII, 10, and *Shegagot,* VIII, 2. There is a palpable, qualitative difference between various sections; the hassagot on *Hilkot Kelim,* e.g., are very detailed, intense, persistent and personal. The brief strictures, actually compressed expressions of disdain (e.g., *Sheḥiṭah,* VI, 8), warrant further study. I hope to analyze this again in a separate article.

50. Page 171, note 51:

See also *Bet ha-Beḥirah,* II, 8.

51. Page 173:

See the metaphysical explanation of rigidity and leniency by R. Moses Lifshitz, *Leḥem Mishneh* (Lublin, 1642), 33.

52. Page 175, note 62:

R. Jacob Berab in his *'Iggeret ha-Semikah* also espouses this rule and consequently claims that Rabad agreed with Maimonides concerning the reinstitution of ordination inasmuch as he did not criticize the crucial formulation in *Sanhedrin,* IV, 11.

53. Page 176:

For cross references, see *Mishkab u-Moshab*, X, 11: כבר כתבתי עליו במקום אחר שאין זה כלום. Rabad did not supply the exact reference and indeed (as is pointed out in *Kesef Mishneh*), he deals with the issue in three separate places: *Maᶜaser,* XII, *Shemiṭṭah,* VIII, *and 'Edut,* XII.

54. Page 179:

For "hassagot" versus "hagahot," see "ᶜAl Hassagot ha-Rabad," 172.

55. Page 180:

R. Joseph Ashkenazi, sixteenth-century anti-Maimonidean and generally uncompromising antirationalist, also assumed that Rabad knew and condemned the *Moreh;* see G. Scholem, *Tarbiẓ,* XXVIII (1959), 202.

56. Page 182:

Solomon Maimon, *Autobiography,* Heb. trans., ed. F. Lahover (Tel Aviv, 1942), 264, sees Rabad's criticism as the predictable reaction of an "orthodox theologian against an enlightened theologian." He was a zealot, ignorant of sciences, and penned a harsh critique of the Maimonidean code—this is the image projected by Maimon and it is typical of the Enlightenment posture.

57. Page 189:

For Rabad as protagonist as well as antagonist of the *Mishneh Torah,* see also *Hazon 'Ish, Shebiᶜit,* VII: לא כיוון להשיג אלא להשלים and R. Hayyim Soloveitchik, *Ḥiddushe R. Hayyim, Shemiṭah ve-Yobel,* XII, 16: ודברי הראבד הם הוספת ביאור ולא השגה. See my "ᶜAl Hassagot ha-Rabad," 172, and also H. E. Revel, *'Ozar ha-Soṭah* (New York, 1941), 71. Note such a formulation by R. Samuel, *Debar Shmuel* (Venice, 1710), 38 (page 15): ופליאה דעת ממני על הראבד והרב המגיד ושאר המפרשים ז"ל. See also S. H. Kook, *ᶜIyyunim u-Meḥkarim,* I, 306. Cf. per contra, R. Hiyya ha-Rofe, *Maᶜaseh Hiyya,* 57b: הראב"ד והרמ"ך המחפשים בנרות להשינן אפילו בסדר ובלשון חכמים. Also *Kesef Mishneh, Nedarim,* I, 15, *ᶜIssure Mizbeah,* IV, 15.

58. Page 192:

See the *Teshubot Hawwot Yair,* 152, on the occasional use of harsh language by the Talmudic sages.

59. Page 194, note 64:

See the obviously apologetic use made of *Kilayim,* VI, 2, by Moshe b. Menahem Kuniz, *Sefer Ben Yoḥai* (Vienna, 1815), 2a.

60. Page 199, note 3:

S. Abramson, R. Nissim Gaon, 98, and additional examples in S. Assaf, *Meḳorot,* II, 83, 101 (בפסוק ובתלמוד). Also, Elijah Capsali, "Chronicle," *REJ,* LXXIX (1924), 37; R. Moshe b. Makir, *Seder ha-Yom,* 97.

61. Page 202:

See H. Albeck, *Mabo' la-Talmudim,* 608ff. R. David Pardo in his classic *Ḥasde David* analyzes every instance of use of Tosefta by Rabad and Maimonides.

62. Page 208:

See also Ḥiddushe Rashba, *Megillah,* ed. H. Z. Dimitrovsky, page 29 and notes *ad loc.*

63. Page 211:

See the representative statement of Nahmanides, *Torat ha-'Adam* in *Kitbe Ramban,* ed. C. Chavel, II, 169: וזה תימא גדולה אם עלה על דעתו שהגמרות הללו חלוקות בזה. היאך הניח גמרא ערוכה וסמך על הירושלמי. Ha-Me'iri, *Bet ha-Beḥirah, Berakot,* pages 71–72, has some pointed remarks on the Tosefta: יש בה דברים שאי אפשר לישבם ונראה שאין לסמוך עליה ברוב ענינים שבה; on the Jerushalmi—ומכל מקום ירושלמי במקום בבלי אינה משנה. See also *Bet ha-Beḥirah, Megillah,* page 21: ועיקר הדברים שלא לדחות תלמוד ערוך שבידינו מברייתא, או מדברי תלמוד המערב, וכל שכן מסברא. See also *Kesef Mishneh, Mezuzah,* VI, 12, and *Maggid Mishneh, Ishut,* XVIII, 4.

64. Page 225:

Note the prominence given to the *Shimushah Rabbah* in the *Sefer ha-Batim.*

65. Page 229:

See S. Abramson, *Ḥamishah Sefarim le-R. Nissim Gaon.*

66. Page 230:

See H. Z. Taubes, *Liḳḳuṭe R. Isaac ibn Ghayyat: Berakot* (Zurich, 1952). On the Kohelet commentary, see S. Abramson, *Kiryat Sefer,* LII (1977), 156–172.

67. Page 231:

See the edition of eight new responsa of ibn Migas edited by I. Ta-Shema and H. Ben-Shammai, *Kobez ᶜal Yad,* VIII (1976), 167–185. It is significant that Razah's youthful work *Hilkot Sheḥitah* contained a major criticism of ibn Migas.

68. Page 231:

On R. Ephraim, see I. Schepansky, *R. Ephraim: Talmid-Ḥaber shel ha-Rif* (Jerusalem, 1976).

69. Page 234:

Note the exact correspondence between Rabad, *Sekirut,* XIII, 4, and Rashi, *Baba Meziᶜa,* 89b.

70. Page 235:

On knowledge of R. Tam in Provence, see H. Soloveitchik, *PAAJR,* XXXVIII (1970–1971), 260, n. 106. Systematic study of parallel views of these two powerful, innovative figures (see the few examples given by me in n. 144) should be pursued further. See, e.g., Rabad, *'Ishut,* III, 23, and R. Tam, *Tosafot, Pesahim,* 8a; Rashbah, *Ḳiddushin,* 23b. Note also Rabad's criticism of Razah, Alfasi, *Sukkah,* 19b (concerning "shimur") where reference to "the Frenchman" is most likely R. Tam.

71. Page 237, note 154:

Rabad's philological-philosophical position was attacked by Razah in one of his strictures. The issue was very repercussive. See I. Ta-Shema, "Sifre ha-Ribot," 573.

72. Page 240:

For R. Abraham ha-Yarhi's father, see E. Kupfer, *Tarbiẓ,* XXXIX (1970), 356.

73. Pages 241–242:

On Rabad's very reverential attitude to custom, see *Maᶜaser Sheni,* I, 3, and references in Y. Z. Kahana, *Meḥḳarim,* 115. The study of "Provençal custom" remains a desideratum. See now I. Ta-Shema, *Shenaton ha-Mishpaṭ ha-ᶜIbri,* V (1978), especially 386ff.

74. Page 243, note 16:

Also J. Gikatilia, *Ginat Egoz,* pt. II, 55a (חכמה פנימית); cf. I. Refael, *Sefer ha-Manhig,* 19.

75. Page 248, note 38:

B. Septimus has shown that this description applies to R. Jonathan of Quinque rather than our R. Jonathan of Lunel.

76. Page 249:

See the beautiful edition of his commentary (with an important introduction) on *Baba Ḳamma,* ed. S. Friedman (New York, 1969). On Mishnah study (and see also above, pages 107–110), see Friedman's introduction, 7ff. The technique of incorporating the Talmudic discussion into the texture of the Mishnah commentary may actually be described as Maimonidean. Many of R. Jonathan's commentaries have been published in the *Ginze Rishonim* series; some in the works of M. Blau.

77. Page 249, note 42:

See also R. Aaron b. Joseph ha-Levi, *Peḳudat ha-Leviyim,* 11, and ibn Daud, *Sefer ha-Kabbalah,* ed. G. Cohen, 84.

78. Page 252:

The role of R. Meir ha-Levi Abulafia in the Maimonidean controversy was illumined by Dr. Bernard Septimus in his doctoral dissertation (Harvard, 1975), which will shortly be published in expanded form. Abulafia's hassagot on the *Mishneh Torah* are now available in *Sanhedri Gedolah* (Jerusalem, 1968).

79. Page 261:

A representative view is to be found in Max Wiener, *Ha-Dat ha-Yehudit bi-Tekufat ha-'Emanzipaziyah,* trans. from German by L. Zayi (Jerusalem, 1900), 67, who treats Rabad as a symbol of, and precedent for, legalism and irrationalism. See above (addendum 56) concerning S. Maimon.

80. Page 263:

On Razah's greater acquaintance with secular sciences, see I. Ta-Shema, "Sifre ha-Ribot," 570ff. The statement of al-Ghazali concerning philosophers (see M. Watt, *Deliverance from Error: Faith and Practice of Ghazali,* pages 20–21) is relevant in this context: "To refute a system before understanding it and becoming acquainted with its depths is to act blindly."

81. Page 264:

See the peculiar use of this statement by I. Reggio, *Ha-Torah veha-Pilosofiah,* 45.

82. Page 269:

Professor Z. M. Rabinovitz of Tel Aviv called my attention to *Piyyute Yannai,* ed. M. Zulay, 19, 34, which support *Kesef Mishneh.*

83. Page 270, note 34:

Also, Y. Bedersi, *'Iggeret ha-Hitnazlut.*

84. Page 279:

For use of a line from ibn Gabirol's poetry, see I. Ta-Shema, *Ẓemanim u-Meḳomot,* 121. Of course, one swallow does not yet spring make.

85. Page 281, note 46:

On astrology see G. Vajda, *Recherches,* 320ff., especially 338. Also B. Z. Benedikt in *Torah Shebeᶜal Peh* (1977), 223ff. See the reference by R. Moses Almosnino in his supercommentary on ibn Ezra, ed. N. Ben Menachem (Jerusalem, 1946), 28.

86. Page 282:

Cf. the different approach of H. A. Wolfson, *The Philosophy of the Kalam* (Cambridge, 1976), 108–110. One may note, in addition, the following comments on or references to Rabad's famous and, to some extent, persistently enigmatic hassagah: *Minḥat Ḳenaot,* page 183; Abarbanel, *Rosh 'Amanah,* chapter 12; R. Isaac Arama, *Hazut Ḳashah,* 18a. Meshullam da-Piera, in H. Brody, *Yediᶜot ha-Makon le-Ḥeḳer ha-Shirah.* For R. Moses Cordovero (*Pardes Rimmonim*), see J. Ben-Shlomoh, *Torat ha-'Elokut,* pages 25–26. An interesting comparison with Muslim debates is found in M. Plessner's article ("Minut u-Rationalism") in *Meḥḳarim le-Ẓeker Uriel Hed,* ed. G. Baer (Jerusalem, 1971), 3.

87. Page 286:

On this notion of intellectual tolerance, see R. Simeon b. Ẓemaḥ Duran, *Mishpaṭ 'Oheb,* 13ff.

88. Page 289, note 11:

See G. Vajda, *Recherches,* page 96.

89. Page 292, note 29:

Note the more flexible formulation of G. Scholem, *Ursprung und Anfänge der Kabbala* (Berlin, 1962), 181, n. 10: "Es ist eine Frage des Gefühls, wie man das Gewicht solcher Ausdrücke beim Rabed einschätzen will," compared with his apodictic assertion in *Reshit ha-Kabbalah*. For some additional Geonic use of "כפי שהראוני מן השמים", see M. Havatzelet, *Leshonenu,* XXVII–VIII (1964), 314, n. 2.

90. Page 299, note 64:

See a similar example in *Migdal ᶜOz,* Tefillin, III, 5: אני תמיה על מעלת רבינו זל. שהיה מקובל בנסתרות איש מפי איש איך בא להכריע בסברא דבריהם שהם כבשונו של עולם. The impact—or intrusion—of kabbalah on halakic study and adjudication still needs careful study. The varying attitudes of halakists even concerning such a classic issue as whether or not tefillin should be used during the intermediate days of a holiday—where the kabbalistic position is unequivocal—are enlightening; R. Abraham Bornstein (of Sochochov), *'Abne Nezer, ᶜOraḥ Ḥayyim,* 2, affirms forcefully that the normative decision cannot be derived just from the Zohar but must be explicit in the Talmud. See also *op. cit.,* 445, 446 (concerning Shofar).

The fact that all these figures—Rabad, his contemporaries, disciples, or antagonists—combined metahalakic concerns with their halakic creativity is, of course, significant. The relation—whether one of harmony, strife, or tension—is a pivotal theme of Jewish spiritual-intellectual history; see my "Religion and Law," 69ff. Of course, this does not mean merely the integration of philosophic phrases or themes into halakic writing—as seen in the case of Rabad and, more extensively and emphatically, in the work of Razah—but the insistence that halakah must be accompanied by some metahalakic system of reflection and spirituality.

Indeed, concerning the question of one's attitude to philosophy, we must differentiate between phenomenological acceptance (recognition and selective use of philosophic terms and concepts) and axiological acceptance (acknowledgment of the superior worth of philosophy). I think that this difference has been noted with regard to the eighteenth century.

No new light has been shed on Rabad as a kabbalist nor on the implications of his being one of the founding fathers of kabbalah for his attitude to philosophy.

INDEX